AMÉRICA

AMÉRICA

. . .

THE EPIC STORY OF SPANISH NORTH AMERICA, 1493–1898

ROBERT GOODWIN

BLOOMSBURY PUBLISHING
NEW YORK · LONDON · OXFORD · NEW DELHI · SYDNEY

BLOOMSBURY PUBLISHING
Bloomsbury Publishing Inc.
1385 Broadway, New York, NY 10018, USA

BLOOMSBURY, BLOOMSBURY PUBLISHING, and the Diana logo are trademarks of
Bloomsbury Publishing Plc

First published in the United States 2019
Copyright © Robert Goodwin, 2019
Maps created by Gary Antonetti, Ortelius Design

Library of Congress Cataloging-in-Publication Data
Names: Goodwin, Robert, 1969- author.
Title: América: the Epic Story of Spanish North America, 1493-1898 / Robert Goodwin.
Description: New York, NY: Bloomsbury Publishing Inc., 2019. |
Includes bibliographical references and index.
Identifiers: LCCN 2018047043 | ISBN 9781632867223 (hardcover) |
ISBN 9781632867247 (ebook)
Subjects: LCSH: Spain—Colonies—North America. | Southwest,
New—History—To 1848. | Southern States—History.
Classification: LCC E188 .G63 2019 | DDC 979/.01—dc23
LC record available at https://lccn.loc.gov/2018047043

2 4 6 8 10 9 7 5 3 1

Typeset by Westchester Publishing Services
Printed and bound in the U.S.A. by Berryville Graphics Inc., Berryville, Virginia

To find out more about our authors and books visit www.bloomsbury.com and
sign up for our newsletters.

Bloomsbury books may be purchased for business or promotional use. For information on
bulk purchases please contact Macmillan Corporate and Premium Sales Department at
specialmarkets@macmillan.com.

For Theodora

CONTENTS

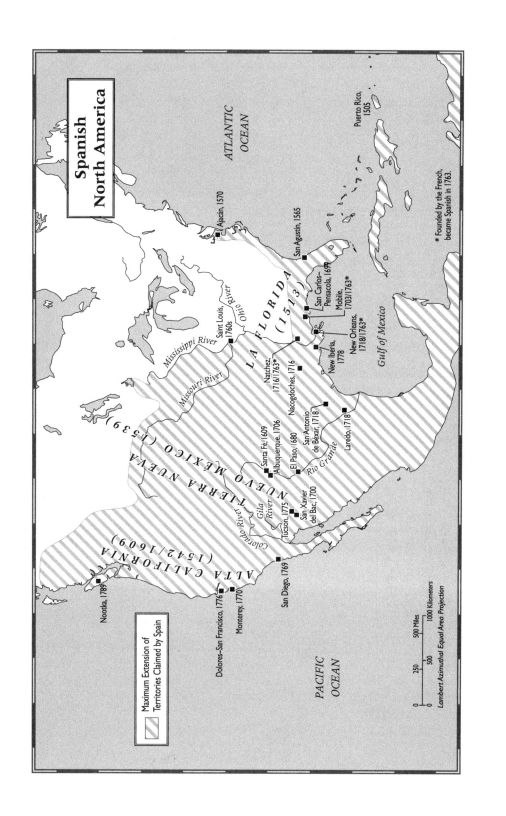

Spanish North America

Maximum Extension of
Territories Claimed by Spain

* Founded by the French,
became Spanish in 1763.

ATLANTIC
OCEAN

PACIFIC
OCEAN

Gulf of Mexico

Puerto Rico,
1505

Ajacán, 1570

San Agustín, 1565

San Carlos–
Pensacola, 1698
Mobile,
1703/1763*

New Orleans,
1718/1763*

New Iberia,
1778

Natchez,
1716/1763*

Nacogdoches, 1716

San Antonio
de Béxar, 1718

Laredo, 1718

Santa Fe, 1609

Albuquerque, 1706

El Paso, 1680

San Xavier
del Bac, 1700

Tucson, 1775

San Diego, 1769

Monterey, 1770

Dolores–San Francisco, 1776

Nootka, 1789

Saint Louis,
1760s

LA FLORIDA
(1513)

TIERRA NUEVA
NUEVO MÉXICO (1539)

ALTA CALIFORNIA
(1542/1609)

Mississippi River

Missouri River

Ohio River

Rio Grande

Colorado River

Gila River

0   250   500 Miles
0   500   1000 Kilometers

Lambert Azimuthal Equal Area Projection

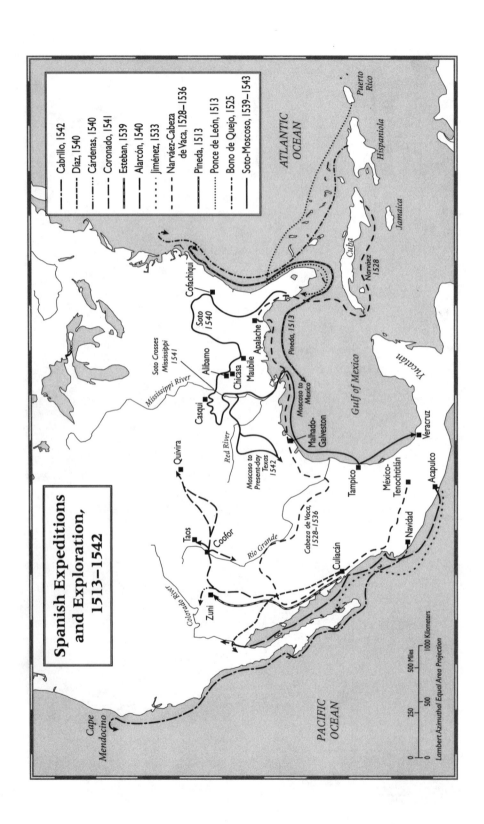

Spanish Expeditions and Exploration, 1513–1542

Cabrillo, 1542
Díaz, 1540
Cárdenas, 1540
Coronado, 1541
Esteban, 1539
Alarcón, 1540
Jiménez, 1533
Narváez-Cabeza de Vaca, 1528–1536
Pineda, 1513
Ponce de León, 1513
Bono de Quejo, 1525
Soto-Moscoso, 1539–1543

PACIFIC OCEAN

ATLANTIC OCEAN

Cape Mendocino

Quivira

Taos

Coofor

Zuni

Colorado River

Rio Grande

Culiacán

Cabeza de Vaca, 1528–1536

Casqui

Red River

Mississippi River

Soto Crosses Mississippi 1541

Alibamo

Chicasa

Maubile

Soto 1540

Cofachiqui

Apalache

Pineda, 1513

Moscoso to Present-day Texas 1542

Malhado-Galveston

Moscoso to Mexico

Gulf of Mexico

Tampico

Veracruz

México-Tenochtitlán

Acapulco

Navidad

Yucatán

Cuba

Narváez 1528

Jamaica

Hispaniola

Puerto Rico

0   250   500 Miles
0   500   1000 Kilometers
Lambert Azimuthal Equal Area Projection

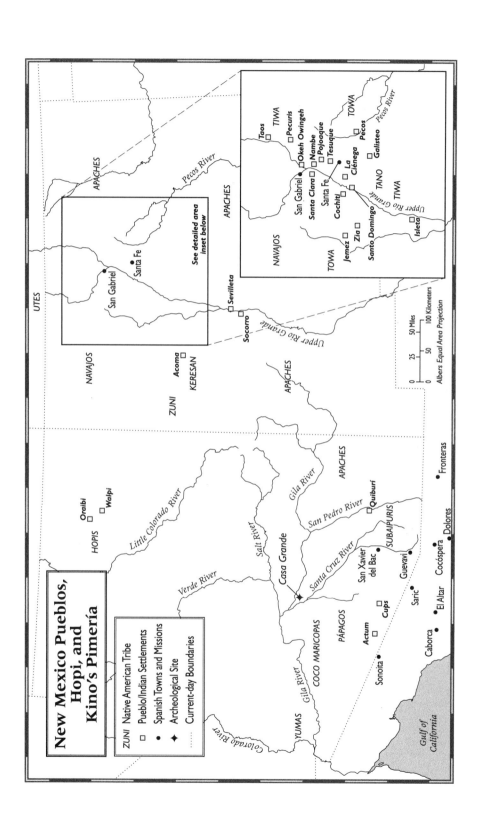

New Mexico Pueblos, Hopi, and Kino's Pimería

ZUNI Native American Tribe
☐ Pueblo/Indian Settlements
● Spanish Towns and Missions
✦ Archeological Site
⋯ Current-day Boundaries

0   25   50 Miles
0   50   100 Kilometers
Albers Equal Area Projection

UTES

NAVAJOS

San Gabriel
Santa Fe

See detailed area
inset below

APACHES

Pecos River

ZUNI

Acoma
KERESAN

Sevilleta
Socorro

Upper Rio Grande

HOPIS
Oraibi
Walpi

Little Colorado River

APACHES

Gila River

Salt River

Verde River

Casa Grande

Santa Cruz River

San Pedro River

Quiburi

SUBAIPURIS

San Xavier
del Bac

Guevavi

Saric

El Altar

Cocóspera

Dolores

Fronteras

PÁPAGOS

Cups

Actum

COCO MARICOPAS

Sonoita

Caborca

YUMAS

Colorado River

Gila River

Gulf of
California

Inset

TIWA
Taos
Picuris

Okeh Owingeh
Nambe
Pojoaque
Tesuque

TOWA
Pecos
Galisteo

San Gabriel
Santa Clara
Santa Fe
La Ciénega
Cochiti
TANO
TIWA

NAVAJOS

TOWA
Jemez
Zia

Santo Domingo

Isleta

Upper Rio Grande

Pecos River

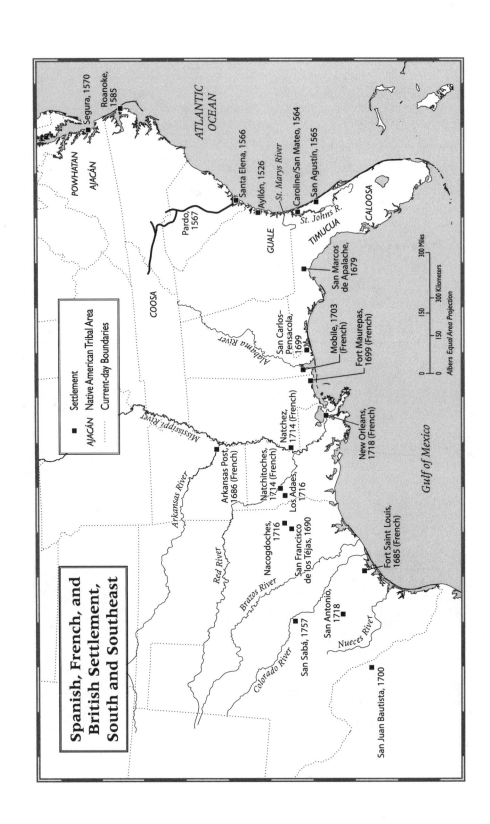

Spanish, French, and British Settlement, South and Southeast

Legend:
- ■ Settlement
- *AJACÁN* Native American Tribal Area
- ‑‑‑ Current-day Boundaries

Scale: 0 — 150 — 300 Miles / 0 — 150 — 300 Kilometers
Albers Equal Area Projection

ATLANTIC OCEAN

POWHATAN
AJACÁN

Segura, 1570
Roanoke, 1585

Santa Elena, 1566
Ayllón, 1526
St. Marys River
Caroline/San Mateo, 1564
San Agustín, 1565

GUALE
Pardo, 1567
St. Johns R.
TIMUCUA
CALOOSA

COOSA
San Marcos de Apalache, 1679

Alabama River

San Carlos–Pensacola, 1699
Mobile, 1703 (French)
Fort Maurepas, 1699 (French)

Mississippi River

Natchez, 1714 (French)
New Orleans, 1718 (French)

Arkansas River
Arkansas Post, 1686 (French)

Natchitoches, 1714 (French)
Los Adaes, 1716

Red River
Nacogdoches, 1716
San Francisco de los Téjas, 1690

Brazos River

Fort Saint Louis, 1685 (French)

Gulf of Mexico

San Antonio, 1718
San Sabá, 1757
Colorado River
Nueces River

San Juan Bautista, 1700

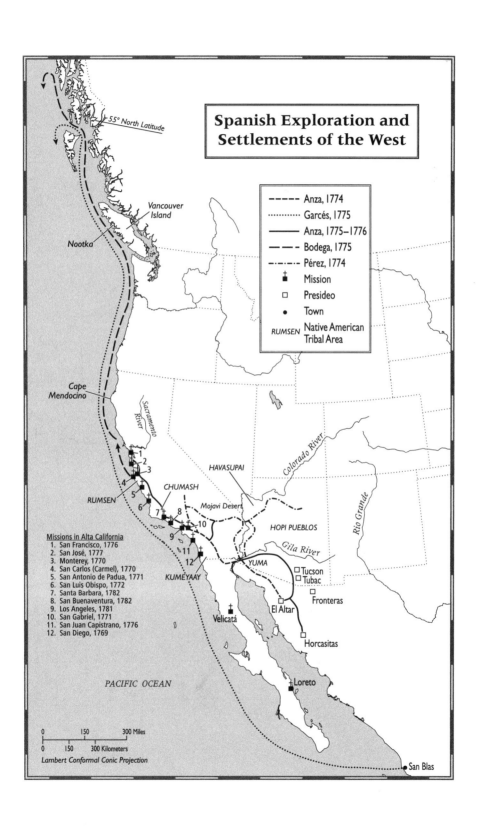

Spanish Exploration and Settlements of the West

55° North Latitude

Vancouver
Island

Nootka

---- Anza, 1774
········· Garcés, 1775
——— Anza, 1775–1776
– – Bodega, 1775
–·–·– Pérez, 1774
✝ ▪ Mission
☐ Presideo
● Town
RUMSEN Native American
Tribal Area

Cape
Mendocino

Sacramento River

1
2
3
4
5
6
7   8
9   10
11
12

CHUMASH

HAVASUPAI

Colorado River

Mojavi Desert

HOPI PUEBLOS

Gila River

Rio Grande

RUMSEN

YUMA

Tucson
Tubac

KUMÉYAAY

Fronteras

El Altar

Velicatá

Horcasitas

Missions in Alta California
1. San Francisco, 1776
2. San José, 1777
3. Monterey, 1770
4. San Carlos (Carmel), 1770
5. San Antonio de Padua, 1771
6. San Luis Obispo, 1772
7. Santa Barbara, 1782
8. San Buenaventura, 1782
9. Los Angeles, 1781
10. San Gabriel, 1771
11. San Juan Capistrano, 1776
12. San Diego, 1769

PACIFIC OCEAN

Loreto

0   150   300 Miles
0   150   300 Kilometers
Lambert Conformal Conic Projection

San Blas

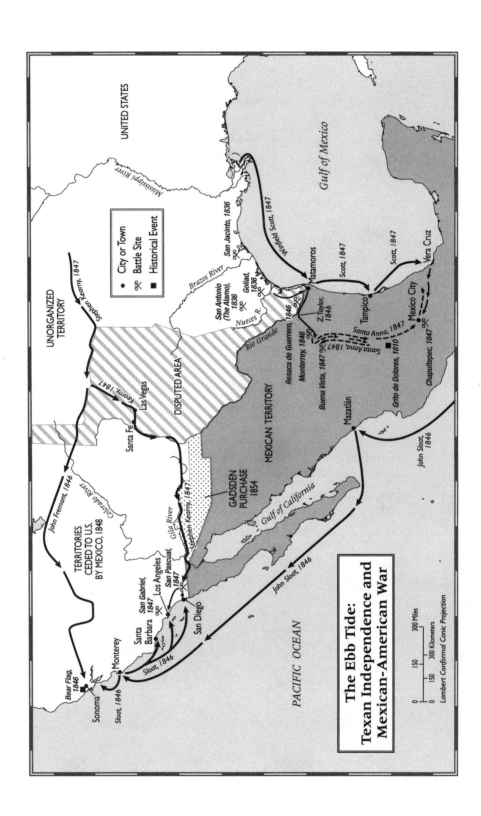

UNITED STATES

Mississippi River

City or Town
Battle Site
Historical Event

San Jacinto, 1836

Brazos River

UNORGANIZED
TERRITORY

Stephen Kearny, 1847

San Antonio
(The Alamo),
1836

Goliad,
1836

Nueces R.

Winfield Scott, 1847

Gulf of Mexico

Matamoros

Scott, 1847

Scott, 1847

Vera Cruz

Kearny, 1847

Las Vegas

DISPUTED AREA

Santa Fe

Rio Grande

Resaca de Guerrero, 1846

Z. Taylor,
1846

Tampico

Monterrey, 1846

Santa Anna, 1847

Buena Vista, 1847

Santa Anna, 1847

Mexico City

Grito de Dolores, 1810

Chapultepec, 1847

John Fremont, 1846

Colorado River

TERRITORIES
CEDED TO U.S.
BY MEXICO, 1848

MEXICAN TERRITORY

Mazatlán

GADSDEN
PURCHASE
1854

Gila River

Stephen Kearny, 1847

Gulf of California

San Gabriel,
1847

Los Angeles

San Pascual,
1847

San Diego

John Sloat,
1846

Santa
Barbara

Bear Flag,
1846

Sonoma

Monterey

Sloat, 1846

Sloat, 1846

John Sloat, 1846

PACIFIC OCEAN

0   150   300 Miles

0   150   300 Kilometers

Lambert Conformal Conic Projection

**The Ebb Tide:
Texan Independence and
Mexican-American War**

PREFACE

The idea for a book about all the parts of the United States that were once claimed by the Spanish Empire originated in the reactions of various readers to a book I wrote about a Spanish expedition to Florida and Texas and the "first African American." I was puzzled that a handful of well-educated friends should express such surprise that Spain had laid claim to so much of the South and the Southwest long before Jamestown or the *Mayflower*. They knew that Spaniards had been there, after all, for names such as Florida, California, New Mexico, Colorado, Nevada, San Antonio, Los Angeles, Santa Fe, and the Rio Grande clearly betray that foundational Spanish presence. But it was almost as though it had happened in some ethereal, mythical past, as easily ignored as Native American lore rather than embraced as European reality, as though it were not of this world, but another. In fact, the subject has rarely been addressed in its entirety by professional historians anywhere, with only a handful of notable exceptions. Perhaps that is because for Spaniards most of those North American territories were but a handful of the many lands lost in the tidal wave of independence that swept across the Spanish Empire at the beginning of the nineteenth century? Perhaps for Mexicans the abject surrender of half their nascent nation at the end of the Mexican-American War is a deep scar best left unscratched? Perhaps for Americans three centuries of Spanish and Mexican sovereignty over most of the country is too quick a challenge to the tradition of brave pioneers progressing westward to forge their private Edens in an unclaimed and virgin wilderness?

However, while the overarching tale of Spanish North America has largely been ignored, a wealth of scholarly material has been published on specific elements and aspects of the story. In the United States, the plethora of academic journals dedicated to the histories of different cities, states, or regions deserve special mention because they have enabled thousands of researchers to share their discoveries, deductions, and conclusions with a global readership. In Spain and Mexico, too, scholars have published extensively, often working from archival sources to produce exhaustive accounts of different historical periods or geographical regions that help to firmly conceive of North America within the context of the Spanish Empire. Some of these researchers have produced translations and, increasingly, transcriptions of myriad original documents uncovered in the archives of Spain, Mexico, Cuba, and elsewhere. They and others have analyzed that material, interpreting the past, allowing us to better comprehend the people and events of a bygone age. To all these scholars and researchers I owe deep gratitude, for without their work this book would not have been possible. But although this book properly belongs alongside so much scholarly research, it is essentially of a different nature, for I have not tried to make use of or "synthesize" all their research. Instead, I have attended to the storytelling, to the creation of a collage whose pieces come together as a vast landscape of this history.

For *América: The Epic Story of Spanish North America*, first among those "dons," in both senses of the word, it might be said, is Barry Ife, Cervantes Professor Emeritus at King's College London, who supervised my PhD thesis many years ago. I first crossed the Ocean Sea with Barry at the helm when he handed me a copy of Bartolomé de las Casas's transcription of Columbus's famous *Diario de Abordo*, the log of his first voyage in 1492. Subsequently, Alexander Samson and Stephen Hart have given me great encouragement, and University College London has allowed me the space to research and write. The staff at Senate House and especially don Jesús Bermejo Roldán at UCL have been wonderful, while Mike Townsend, Mette Lund Newlyn, Kate Wilcox, and their colleagues at the Institute of Historical Research have made me feel truly at home.

It would be impossible to find a more enthusiastic and generous scholar than Jerry Craddock, who was supportive far beyond any call of duty. He and his group of "dons" working on the Cibola Project, based at Berkeley, are publishing on their website, at a remarkable rate, painstaking transcriptions of hundreds of original documents relating to the history of Spanish North America. Richard and Shirley Flint, likewise working for the love of the research, have published similarly careful transcriptions of documents relating to Coronado's expedition to New Mexico and a number of works of interpretation. These are extraordinarily valuable resources, and in most cases they offer very considered translations into English, opening the field to writers and researchers who may struggle with old Spanish. The PARES website, operated by the Spanish Ministerio de Cultura y Deporte, is a catalog and map of material in archives across Spain that allows online access to thousands of original documents, most helpfully those in the Archivo General de Indias, in Seville, repository for almost all Spanish government papers relating to the Americas dating back to the fifteenth century. David Weber's *Spanish Frontier in North America* is the only modern academic book published by a university press to address the entire subject across time and geography, so it was an invaluable place to begin thinking about this book and a frequent source of inspiration. So, too, was John Kessell's *Spain in the Southwest* and the many pioneering works of Herbert Bolton, now over a century old.

I owe incalculable thanks to George Gibson for his early encouragement and editorial input, and to Anton Mueller for piloting the manuscript through the reefs and shoals of publication, and to Charlie Viney for weathering slings and arrows as though a Spanish explorer in sixteenth-century Florida. Patti Ratchford and her design team labored long and hard to produce the jacket this tome now wears so proudly. Thank you, too, to Dana Isaacson for loving the book, to Jenna Dutton, Steve Boldt, and Mike O'Connor for all their attention to detail, and to Grace McNamee and Morgan Jones for all their hard work.

Finally, I am most grateful and indebted of all to Clare Adams, for spending too many arduous vacations roaming across parts of the United States that other visitors rarely reach.

Timeline: Spanish Monarchs and Mexican Presidents

	Catholic Monarchs		
1474–1504	Isabella of Castile	Unified Spanish Crowns of Castile and Aragon.	1492: They sponsored Columbus's voyage of discovery.
1479–1516	Ferdinand of Aragon		1513: Discovery of Florida.
1504–55	Juana "la Loca" of Castile	Reigned but did not rule due to mental illness.	
	House of Habsburg		
1516–56	Charles of Ghent (Carlos I of Spain and Charles V, Holy Roman Emperor)	Left his able empress, Isabella of Portugal, as regent in Spain during extended absences as peripatetic ruler of most of Europe.	1519: Cortés occupies Aztec Mexico. 1528–36: First crossing of North America. 1529: Audiencia of Mexico established. 1532: Discovery of Baja California. 1540–42: First expedition to New Mexico. 1542: New Laws of the Indies.
1556–98	Philip II	Able administrator.	1565: Settlement of Florida, foundation of St. Augustine. 1598: Second invasion of New Mexico.

	House of Habsburg		
1598–1621	Philip III	Largely abdicated responsibilities of rule to his corrupt and self-serving favorite, the Duke of Lerma.	1610: Foundation of Santa Fe and settlement of New Mexico.
1621–65	Philip IV	His rule was defined by his ambitious *valido*, the Count-Duke of Olivares.	
1665–1700	Charles II, "the Bewitched"	Severely disabled by Habsburg consanguinity, his reign was dominated by a struggle for power between his mother and brother.	1680: Pueblo Revolt, temporary loss of New Mexico. 1684: French incursion into Texas and Spanish responses. 1689: First missions in Texas. 1691: Missionaries abandon Texas.
	House of Bourbon		
1700–1746	Philip V	Showed signs of mental instability during his reign. He abdicated in 1724, but returned to the throne on death of his son.	1740: British assault on St. Augustine fails. 1742: Spanish assault on Georgia fails.
1724	Luis I	Reigned briefly until his death following the abdication of Philip V.	
1746–59	Ferdinand VI	First minister was the Marquis of Ensenada, who began introducing a raft of reforms.	1758: Comanches destroy the Franciscan mission at San Saba, Texas.

(*continued*)

	House of Bourbon		
1759–88	Charles III	Able first ministers were the Marquis of Esquilache and the Count of Floridablanca. José de Gálvez was Secretary of the Indies.	1762: Disastrous entry into French and Indian (Seven Years') War. 1763: Spain cedes Floridas to Britain. France cedes Louisiana to Spain in compensation. 1765: José de Gálvez introduces reforms in New Spain. 1769: First missions established in Alta California. 1779: Spain supports American Revolutionaries by declaring war on Britain. 1779: Defeat of Comanche leader Cuerno Verde. 1781: Bernardo de Gálvez captures Pensacola.
1788–1808	Charles IV	Reliant on his favorite, Manuel Godoy. Reign dominated by French Revolution. Eventually ousted by Napoleon Bonaparte.	Spanish North America reaches maximum extent. 1789: Occupation of Nootka Sound.
1808, and 1813–33	Ferdinand VII		Most of Spanish America becomes independent. 1821: Mexican independence and loss of Florida to USA.
	House of Bonaparte		
1808–13	Joseph Bonaparte	Imposed by his brother Napoleon.	1807–14: Peninsular War. 1810–21: Grito de Dolores and Mexican War of Independence. 1812: Liberal Constitution of Cadiz.

	Principal Presidents of Mexico	
1821–23	Emperor Agustín de Iturbide	1821: Mexican independence.
1823–24	Nicolás Bravo	
1824–29	Guadalupe Victoria	
1829	Vicente Guerrero	1829: Spanish occupation of Tampico.
1830–32	Anastasio Bustamante	
1832–33	Manuel Gómez Pedraza	
1833	Antonio López de Santa Anna	
1833–34	Valentín Gómez Farías	
1834–35	Antonio López de Santa Anna	
1835–36	Miguel Barragán	1836: Texas declares independence.
1836–37	José Justo Corro	
1839	Antonio López de Santa Anna	1838: Pastry War, French assault on Veracruz.
1839–41	Anastasio Bustamante	
1841–42	Antonio López de Santa Anna	
1842–43	Nicolás Bravo	
1843 & 1844	Antonio López de Santa Anna	
1845–46	Mariano Paredes	
1846–47	Valentín Gómez Farías	1846: Outbreak of Mexican-American War.
1847	Antonio López de Santa Anna	

(*continued*)

	Principal Presidents of Mexico	
1848	Manuel de la Peña y Peña	1848: Mexican capitulation by Treaty of Guadalupe Hidalgo. USA wins "the West" from Mexico.
1853–55	Antonio López de Santa Anna	1854: Gadsden Purchase establishes the current international border.
	Last Imperial Spanish Monarch	
1886–1931	Alfonso XIII	1898: Puerto Rico ceded to USA.

"An Empire upon Which the Sun Never Sets"

In 1776, all the land west of the Mississippi was claimed by Spain. By the end of the Revolutionary War, a great swath of territory north along the Pacific toward Alaska, a broad stretch along the Gulf Coast, and all of the Florida peninsula in the east were also marked on diplomatic maps as Spanish. As a result of the Peace of Paris, of 1783, almost two thirds of the modern United States was recognized as part of the Spanish Empire. The immense arc of imperial history, which had dawned with Columbus's extraordinary first voyage of discovery, in 1492, had finally reached its zenith. The King of Spain held title to most of the Americas, the Philippines, and a handful of possessions in Africa. But within a lifetime, dusk would come to this "empire upon which," many a proud Spaniard had effused, "the sun never sets."

This book recounts that heliometric rise and meteoric fall of the Spanish Empire across lands that today form part of the United States. In telling this vast and varied story, I have always turned first to the reports, letters, diaries, maps, paintings, and even poetry produced by the men (and occasionally women) who were actors in this Spanish imperial adventure. Theirs are mostly vivid narratives, filled with all the drama and action that an eyewitness can bring to storytelling, but some of the bathos and pathos of failure, too. There is history as it was written by a lawyer-turned-soldier-turned-poet (very much the Renaissance man with a markedly baroque twist), as it was recast by a royal Inca novelist who lived in a dusty village in the deep south of Spain, and as it was painted in oil on canvas by a leading Mexican artist for a patron distraught at the massacre in Texas of his dearly beloved brother and fellow friars by a Comanche war party. There is the daily detail of conquest and settlement described in hundreds of documents, their now-yellowed folios printed with the rich dark ink or inscribed in the unfamiliar handwriting of a bygone age. They pullulate with curious admixtures of fact and fiction, astute manipulations of the truth, peculiar perceptions of the world, intriguingly bizarre opinions, and sometimes astoundingly acute and accurate observation. They are filled with the personal desires, social proclivities, and cultural concerns of their subjects. The frequently idiosyncratic character of those texts sometimes bridges the gulf of centuries, making their long-dead human authors feel present, almost tangible, almost alive. But elsewhere that intimacy brings into a keen, clear focus how strange and alien human nature could be in the distant past.

These many individual stories come together into a broad history of the Spanish Empire in North America, stretching across time and space from sunrise to high noon to sundown.

The origins of the Spanish Empire in the Americas are rooted in medieval Europe. In A.D. 711, a Muslim army from North Africa crossed the narrow strait at the entrance to the Mediterranean and landed at Gibraltar, heralding the swift subjection of almost the whole Iberian Peninsula as a collection of caliphates and principalities that has become known as Moorish Spain. In one small area in the north, a handful of Christians held out against the invaders, and for the next eight centuries the peoples and lands of Iberia were dominated by the slow and intermittent crusade known as the *Reconquista*, the "Reconquest." Three major Christian kingdoms emerged during that period of constant conflict and precarious peace: Portugal in the west, Castile in the heartland and the deep south, and Aragon in the east. The marriage of Isabella of Castile and Ferdinand of Aragon, in 1469, established the royal and political union that would become modern Spain. They led their bellicose subjects in one final campaign against Granada, still ruled by Muhammad XII from his glorious palace-fortress of the Alhambra. He finally surrendered on January 2, 1492, and in the aftermath of victory, Pope Innocent VIII gave Isabella and Ferdinand the title Los Reyes Católicos, "the Catholic Monarchs," by which they have ever since been known. Reveling in an atmosphere of religious jingoism, they issued an edict expelling from their kingdoms all Jews who refused to adopt Christianity, and ten years later they began the forced conversion of their Muslim subjects as well. With little or no catechism, thousands of those neophyte Conversos and Moriscos soon became victims of the notorious Inquisition, which punished them for their ignorance of Christianity and presumed them to be heretics still practicing their ancestral faiths.

In April 1492, as Isabella and Ferdinand relished victory at their camp outside Granada, at a place still called Santa Fé, "Holy Faith," they gave an audience to Christopher Columbus. That most audacious of mariners had long tried to convince rulers and magnates throughout Christendom to sponsor his project to sail across the great Ocean Sea in the west. He was lured by the promise of finding a new route to the rich spice and silk markets of Asia, which had been closed to Europeans by the rise of the Ottoman Empire in the Middle East. No one had taken him seriously because his plans depended on his gross miscalculation of the size of the world, which allowed him to believe the voyage to China to be about half its true distance. Scientists and geographers had been well aware of the real circumference of the globe since at least the second century A.D., and they had always advised their rulers that no ship could complete so long a journey.

However, eight hundred years of *Reconquista* had imbued Spaniards with a warlike spirit of adventure, rooted in a profound determination to defend and promulgate their Christian faith. Across the centuries, successful warlords and their warriors had been rewarded by the crown with fine estates in the newly reconquered territories, and they had been granted seignorial rights over the newly subject peoples who were needed to work those lands. In that frontier world, young men burned with a bellicose restlessness kindled by the promise of aristocracy and set ablaze by their ardent faith. They yearned to win nobility and power with a sword in their hand, to earn individual *honra* and *reputación*, that quintessentially Spanish sense of personal and collective self-esteem rooted in the respect and renown experienced by a whole community but so often enjoyed by a celebrated individual. On the battlefields of medieval Iberia, war and reward, religion and kudos, God and glory and wealth, went hand in glove. That ethos of baronial ambition had encouraged the Spanish settlement of the Canary Islands, far out into the Atlantic, the crucial springboard for the early voyages to the Americas. Moreover, the experience of expansion had taught Spaniards how to govern a newly colonized people and bring them into the Christian fold.

In 1492, a combination of that deep-seated urge to constant colonial movement and the euphoria of victory on the battlefield at Granada moved the Catholic Monarchs to draw up a *capitulación*, a contract, with Columbus. They appointed him Admiral of the Ocean Sea, viceroy and governor of any lands he might discover, granting him a lien of 10 percent on all trade carried on there, and providing him with the three ships he sailed to America that following fall. It was the kind of agreement that Medieval monarchs had often made with ambitious soldiers to facilitate the *Reconquista*.

The following year, 1493, Columbus returned from the Americas with his sensational reports that he had reached *Las Indias*, "the Indies," as he described the lands he had visited, populated by people he called *indios*, "Indians." Until his dying day he remained convinced he had found a route to Asia, but others soon realized that he had in fact discovered a whole New World. The Catholic Monarchs and their courtiers moved quickly to formally assert their sovereignty over those territories. Within two months, Pope Alexander VI, a

Spaniard by birth, issued the papal bull *Inter caetera*, granting possession to the rulers of Castile and their "heirs and successors in perpetuity" over "all islands and mainlands already found and yet to be found, already discovered and yet to be discovered" to the west of a meridian running from pole to pole a hundred leagues, or three hundred miles, west of the Azores, in order "that the name of our Savior be carried into those regions."[1] The Portuguese Crown responded by asserting its claim to all territories south of the Cape Verde islands on the basis of earlier papal bulls recognizing its dominion over heathen and pagan lands along the coast of Africa discovered by its subjects. Eventually, in 1494, the dispute was resolved by the Treaty of Tordesillas, which moved the meridian to 370 leagues west of the Azores (for which reason Brazil was colonized by Portugal and not Spain).[2]

These declarations all asserted a foundational idea of European empire that has become known as the Doctrine of Discovery, by which monarchs claimed sovereignty over their colonial possessions on the basis that they had been first discovered by their subjects or other agents acting under their authority. This became the guiding principle of Spanish imperial expansion. On the ground, explorers staked their claims by making marks on trees, raising crosses, and conducting other rituals. But the point of such theater was that it be witnessed by officials and formally notarized so that written documentation could be remitted to the crown as evidence to substantiate the claim to possession. That engendered a remarkable culture among Spaniards of recording and documenting their voyages, expeditions, and other imperial adventures in reports and maps. In so doing, they laid down the wealth of material that makes it possible to write the history of their exploits.

The Catholic Monarchs were succeeded by their daughter, Juana "la Loca," but she was deemed mentally unstable and her reign devolved to her son, Charles of Ghent, the first Habsburg ruler of Spain, who also inherited half the crowns of Europe. Known in Spain as Carlos I, but more widely as Charles V because he was the fifth Holy Roman Emperor of that name, he was probably the most powerful ruler the world has ever known. He was succeeded by his son, Philip II, who brought both his intuitive gift for bureaucracy and his deep faith to the administration of the empire. He was succeeded by his descendants, the ineffectual Philips III and IV, and the congenital if congenial imbecile Charles II, irreparably damaged by generations of the Habsburg proclivity to consanguinity.

The spectacular rise of the Spanish Empire under the Habsburg dynasty was founded on the ambition and entrepreneurial spirit of individual conquistadors, the men and a few women who explored unknown lands and tried to subject their inhabitants, with varying success. The refrain "Gold, God, and Glory" is often invoked as shorthand to explain the principal motives of the conquistadors and colonists. From the outset, most Spaniards sought wealth, and gold or other precious metals, pearls, and gems were seen as the easiest form of satisfaction, but like their forebears during the *Reconquista*, Spaniards sought glory, *honra*, and *reputación* by winning great estates and control over the Indians they needed to labor on their farms and down their mines. Meanwhile, in that deeply religious age the Church played a crucial role in the imperial project, coveting the souls of so many pagan Native Americans, determined to save them for God through their conversion to Christianity.

The crown harnessed the energy of the conquistadors by adapting and developing a series of institutions designed to reward them, to encourage further exploration and settlement, but also intended to limit the scope of any one individual's personal power. In Spain, the Casa de Contratación, the "House of Trade," was founded at Seville, in 1502, to oversee commerce with the New World, and the Council of the Indies was created as a separate department to govern the Americas, in 1524.

During the early years of empire, the office of *adelantado* was the crucial instrument of exploration and conquest. Derived from the verb *adelantar*, "to go on ahead," it dated back to the medieval *Reconquista*, but was adapted for the Americas. It perfectly reflects the individualism that was the foundation of the whole imperial enterprise. It was bestowed on powerful, well-connected men who were willing and able to take on responsibility for financing and leading large expeditions to "conquer, pacify, and settle" new lands, in exchange for extensive military and judicial powers and often generous commercial rights. It had much in common with the original contract the Catholic Monarchs had awarded to Columbus. However, the crown restricted the authority of the *adelantado* by appointing a series of royal officials such as treasurers or factors who were directly answerable to the crown. Further-more, as the initial phase of exploration and military campaigning gave way to a prolonged period of settlement and the formal incorporation of towns, a considerable range of powers would devolve to the host of municipal office-holders directly responsible to the crown, who accompanied such expeditions.

As more of the Americas and their Indian inhabitants were "conquered and pacified," the crown established a formal institutional framework for royal government. By far the most significant feature of that new administra-tive landscape was the law itself, guaranteed by the crown but to which the king and his officials were also subject. Perhaps the most remarkable feature of the Spaniards' variously remarkable society in the sixteenth century was their widespread trust of the legal system across all levels of the social hierarchy. It engendered a level of enthusiasm for lawsuits that, when analyzed statistically, made Habsburg Castile the most litigious jurisdiction in world history.[3] Thus we find explorers and conquistadors attempting to abide by the law or exploit it to their own advantage even when acting at the very limits of the empire. It also made for a lot of lawyers, many of whom turned their hand to conquest or settlement, but who always brought with them their grounding in the law.

Thus, the major institution of government established by the crown across Spanish America was the *audiencia*, essentially an appellate court made up of a group of *oidores*, or "magistrate-judges." The gravitas of these institutions was underlined for officers and litigants alike by strict protocols governing days and times on which the court sat, while the *oidores* were required to "have a clock, its tick-tock audible at all times," as a reminder to them as they conducted their business.[4] By appealing or merely threatening to appeal to an *audiencia*, ordinary individuals or corporate bodies and even Indians could reliably hold to account other institutions of authority, their neighbors, and their business associates. Furthermore, the *audiencia* also had considerable executive power to implement and impose royal edicts, directives, and laws. In time, the proliferation of *audiencias* was complimented by the appointment of a number of viceroys, governors, and captains general who took charge of the political and military aspects of the administration. These centers of power devolved responsibility at a local and regional level to a range of other royal officials, such as the municipal councilor-administrators called *regidores*, who constituted a *cabildo* or *ayuntamiento*, the "city hall" of an incorporated town; *alguaciles*, who sat as judges; and *alcaldes*, with both judicial and administrative roles.

From the early years of settlement in the Caribbean, the crown rewarded conquistadors with grants of *encomiendas*, by which they were contractually "entrusted" with a defined population of Indians based on an already-existing village, town, or other group. The Indians were allowed considerable autonomy under their own *cacique*, but were expected to provide their *encomendero*, or "trustee," with labor or produce as tribute. In exchange, the *encomendero* insured these Indians were instructed in Christianity, and he was responsible for their political relationship with the crown. In theory, a benevolent trustee could bring great benefits to his Indians, but the *encomienda* system largely led to terrible abuses, with Indians frequently treated as serfs or slaves.

The Church acted as a check on the secular authorities and played a leading role in denouncing and attempting to prevent the worst excesses of the conquistadors and *encomenderos*. That conflict between Church and state, between even humble churchmen and their colonial neighbors, was an essential cleavage in the foundation stone of empire that can be characterized as the desire of the churchmen for Indian souls, in contradistinction to the conquistador-settlers who wanted Indian "bodies" for their labor. However, the reality was more nuanced, for most religious missionaries believed that true conversion to the faith could be best achieved by a mixture of preaching and instruction, much reinforced by the practical inculcation of a "civilizing" work ethic through long, hard toil in the fields and the construction of mission buildings. In fact, the Church wanted Indian bodies as well.

The great sixteenth-century polemicist Bartolomé de las Casas, a Dominican friar often remembered as the "Defender of the Indians," denounced the *encomienda* as "a deadly, all-consuming plague upon these people."[5] Before his almost Damascene conversion on Hispaniola to the cause of protecting Native Americans, he had been an *encomendero* himself. But once he had taken holy orders, for the rest of his long life he approached the suppression of that evil institution and the promotion of the kindly proselytization of indigenous peoples with all the zeal of a convert who has experienced moral epiphany. Las Casas gained the ear of the king and helped to stimulate vigorous intellectual argument about the humanity and rights of Native Americans.

As a result, in the 1540s, Charles V attempted to retrospectively restrict the grants of *encomiendas* to two generations, after which the land and its people would revert to the crown. On his one, more pious, hand, that would bring the *encomienda* to an end in time, while on his other, sovereign, hand, it would prevent the emergence in the New World of the kind of overmighty landowning aristocracy so powerful in Europe. That change was only slowly and partially implemented because it led to a major rebellion of *encomenderos* in Peru, widespread protests across Spanish America, and a massive lobbying campaign in Spain. But over the following decades the *encomienda* was widely replaced by a system in which the Indians became directly subject to the crown, which then organized *repartimientos*, or temporary "distributions," of Indian labor to landlords of former *encomenderos*.

In time, the descendants of the original conquistadors and *encomenderos* grew up with the deeply ingrained sense of grievance that they had been robbed of their birthright by a far-off crown. Born and raised in the Indies, these *criollos*, or "Creoles," as they became known, fostered a widespread and growing sense of their American identities. They had a strong, almost nationalistic pride in belonging to a regional culture that was both distinct from that of other parts of the New World and also markedly different to that of Spain. In New Spain, *criollos* celebrated Mexico City as the economic heart of the global network of imperial trade. Ships came and went to Peru, the

Philippines, and China, to the River Plate in modern Argentina, as well as to Spain and elsewhere in Europe. But even as they reveled in the new wealth of colonial Mexico City, they began to embrace the Aztec past and developed a deep affinity for the history of their homeland. Moreover, as that Creole identity brewed, they increasingly lauded the richness of their exceptionally multicultural and multiethnic world.

In law and in theory, New Spain, as with the rest of Spanish America, was dominated by a hierarchical framework of race and ethnicity. At the apex of this demographic pyramid were the *peninsulares*, who had been born in Spain and who almost exclusively held the highest office. The *criollo* "Spaniards" were effectively second-class members of that elite. There were also significant numbers of Africans, both slaves and over time freemen. By far the largest category was made up of the indigenous Indians, many of whom had little contact with the colonial world. But just as leading conquistadors married princesses and noblewomen from the Mexica or Inca dynasties or recognized their children by Indian mistresses and concubines, so many more humble folk enthusiastically embraced their neighbors. Over the generations, this mixed-race population known as *mestizos* swelled to number hundreds of thousands in an infinite combination of European, African, and Indian ancestry, not to mention genetic contributions from Moriscos and Conversos. That made for a highly fluid sense of identity that was increasingly at odds with the firmly established and deeply conservative sense of Catholic Spanish identity that characterized Spain.

This social, cultural, and ethnic gulf between Spain and America could at times seem as wide as the Atlantic itself and would be one of the foundation stones of Mexican Independence and the rapid collapse of the empire. But under the Habsburgs, while the totem of royal authority underpinned the legal, social, and economic structures and brought a degree of coherence to so much diversity, colonial governments imposed royal rule with a relatively light touch. Much of the real power rested with able viceroys and local oligarchs who understood and sympathized with local and regional realities; corruption was rife, taxes were easily evaded, and the colonies were left to their own devices.

When the last Spanish Habsburg, the imbecile Charles II, died without issue, in 1700, he bequeathed his crown to Philip of Anjou, grandson of Louis XIV of France, thereby ushering in the new ruling House of Bourbon. The first half century of Bourbon rule was characterized by the desire to reform the government of Spain and her empire according to the centralizing and authoritarian French model. While some of the changes were introduced, their effects were not much felt for over fifty years. However, in the second half of the eighteenth century, Charles III began to force through major reforms at home and overseas. In New Spain, his government created a permanent standing army and restructured the administration and defense of the remote northern provinces, established and enforced crown monopolies on commodities such as tobacco and playing cards, and drastically increased the amount of taxes raised and other revenues accruing directly to the crown. These measures were productive for the royal treasury and are often cited by historians as evidence of the efficacy of Bourbon government. But they evidently unbalanced the old freewheeling, *laissez-faire* administration that had stood the test of time.

The crown exerted these new pressures on colonial subjects already struggling desperately at the edges of an empire that was already at full stretch. The northern frontier of New Spain was especially troubled, and imperial control still hung in the balance against relentless Apache raiding and ruthless rebellion among the Seri Indians of the northwest. Madrid then exacerbated that essential problem of imperial overextension, in the 1770s, by forcing through the rapid settlement of Alta California, establishing the chain of famous Franciscan missions supported by a small military presence and a few settlers from other parts of New Spain. By comparison with the Thirteen Colonies thriving on the Eastern Seaboard and in the throes of independence, the Spanish presence from San Francisco to San Diego appears meager indeed. The new iron grip exercised by ministers in Madrid created the political and economic conditions that within a generation or so would convince the *criollos* of New Spain, along with many others across South and Central America, to turn away from Spain and secure their independence.

By the beginning of the nineteenth century, Spain and her empire were gravely weakened by the continual global conflicts that resulted from imperial overreach, by Bourbon impositions on trade and the colonies themselves, and by the seed of republican rebellion first sown in the United States and then fertilized by revolution in France. But the immediate cause of the spectacular collapse of the Spanish Empire was the occupation of Spain herself by French Revolutionary troops and the ensuing Peninsular War. The upheaval across the Spanish world was catastrophic. In New Spain, the many tensions that had been kept in check by imperial authority erupted unfettered, and as the different political forces realigned themselves amid the storm, the independent nation of Mexico emerged.

Nascent Mexico inherited the social fractures of the former colony and descended into further instability and repeated civil war. The Spaniards and the Mexicans had long feared the unstoppable rise of the United States, which had annexed East and West Florida even as Mexicans were securing their independence. First Texas declared independence and not long after was admitted into the union, becoming the springboard for an invasion of Mexico that led to the annexation of all the western states north of the current international border. The sun finally set on this story of the rise and fall of the Spanish Empire in North America in 1898, with the tragic pathos of the loss of Puerto Rico to the United States in the Spanish-American War.

This book is divided into four parts, which reflect broad but clear stages in the life of the Spanish Empire in North America. Part One relives the excitement of the earliest period of exploration and conquest and tries to explain the marvelous myths and delusions that drove so many Spaniards to risk everything in that unknown, wholly New World. Part Two recounts the ways in which Protestant incursions and missionary pressures to proselytize led to the expeditions that established the first permanent settlements in Florida and New Mexico, before turning to the crucial and often bitterly fractious relationship between state and Church that lay at the heart of empire. By focusing on a few charismatic individuals, Part Three charts the long period of major administrative reform in the eighteenth century and the increasing importance of foreign powers in North America. It culminates with the rarely told story of the enormously important support that Spain gave to the American Patriots during the Revolutionary War. Part Four presents the cataclysmic collapse of the empire and the audacious appropriation of all the lands that had once been part of Spanish North America by the United States.

AMÉRICA, 1493

We reached such a state of concord that it was as though she had been trained in a school of harlotry.

—MICHELE DA CUNEO, ITALIAN NOBLEMAN

"¡*TIERRA, TIERRA!* LAND AHOY! The reward is mine," hollered the pilot of the flagship, claiming his prize as the first man to sight land by the dawn's early light.

It was November 3, 1493, and Christopher Columbus, perhaps the greatest navigator in history, had crossed the Atlantic for the third time in the service of the Spanish Crown. His first crossing was, of course, his famous voyage of discovery that he had made the year before with three ships. The second was his almost miraculous return to the Old World with only one tiny caravel, bringing the astounding news that he had reached an archipelago of unknown islands and, he insisted, mainland China. He was rewarded by the Catholic Monarchs, Isabella of Castile and Ferdinand of Aragon, with the title Admiral of the Ocean Sea. Now, little more than a year after he first made landfall in the Americas, he had guided a majestic fleet of seventeen ships and fifteen hundred men from the Canary Islands to the Antilles in only twenty-one days.

It was Sunday, the Lord's Day, *dies Dominicus* in Latin, so he named the first island he saw Dominica. He again breathed the sweet scents of tropical flowers and heard the parakeets squawking in the verdant trees.[1] Brother Bernardo Boil said mass, and everyone gave thanks to the Madonna for their safe landfall at the very edge of the known world.

Columbus turned his fleet north into the beautiful arc of an emerald archipelago, his ships strung out, pearly sails billowing in the golden morning breeze. That night, he anchored off an island he called Marigalante after his grand flagship, the *Santa María la Galante*, and went ashore with a handful of officials to take formal possession of the island chain for Spain. He sailed on to the volcanic bulk of a lushly wooded island, all bathed in cloud and mist, which he baptized Santa María de Guadalupe after a statue of the

Madonna to which Spanish sailors had a special devotion. He had made his own pilgrimage to the remote monastery in Extremadura where this famous image is still displayed, to give thanks for her protection from a terrible storm that struck his little caravel the previous spring as he returned to the Old World from the Indies.

As his fleet approached Guadalupe, he could see a crowd of curious islanders gathered on a brilliant white beach overhung by dark green jungle. They fled when he launched a longboat and a party of his men went ashore. They explored a little settlement that had recently been abandoned. The expedition doctor, a royal physician called Diego Álvarez Chanca, later reported to the Town Council of Seville that they found "two large parrots," "plenty of cotton ready for spinning," and "four or five human arms and legs . . . and endless skulls hanging about the houses like storage jars."[2]

Columbus reminded everyone that the year before he had met some fishermen on the coast of Cuba. He had struggled to understand them but believed they had been trying to tell him that to the east was a great land called *bohío*, "populated by people with one eye in their foreheads." Others, called *caníbales*, came from an island called Carib and mated with a tribe of warrior women from nearby Matinino.[3] These awful fiends loved the taste of human flesh and terrorized their neighbors, abducting men, women, and children for their ghastly feasts. Álvarez Chanca reported that when the shore party returned and brought their gruesome souvenirs aboard Columbus's flagship, "we all assumed that these must be the islands of the Caribs." Europeans came to call these waters the Caribbean.

No one aboard can have needed reminding about these stories, for Columbus had reported them in great detail in an official letter to the crown that had then been carefully edited by government officials and printed for distribution across the Old World to stake a Spanish claim to his discovery. He had contracted with the crown to find a route to China, and so he was desperate to prove that he had fulfilled his obligations by demonstrating that the Antilles might be near the Philippines or that the Caribbean was part of the South China Sea. That made such tales of one-eyed Cyclopes, Amazon women, and the man-eating Anthropophagi, all familiar from classical mythology, tremendously exciting because late-medieval mapmakers marked a whole range of such monstrous races as living at the periphery of Asia. Columbus was expecting to hear such fabulous stories, even if he did not truly expect to meet the fantastical creatures themselves. They fitted his sense of geography and seemed to prove he had succeeded in reaching the Orient. To his dying day, he never admitted that he had failed in that mission, even as his contemporaries realized he had made a far more momentous discovery.

While attempting to locate the tangible geography of the Caribbean within his late-medieval conception of the world, Columbus had completely misunderstood what the Cuban fishermen had told him. In their language, Taino, the word *bohío* simply meant "home." They had been telling him they came from the neighboring island of Haytí, the east of which was ruled by a powerful chief called Caonabó. His name is almost certainly the origin of our word "cannibal," which Europeans confused with "Carib." Many scholars question whether any Caribbean peoples ever practiced cannibalism at all, arguing that it is far more likely that Columbus and his men had come across paraphernalia used in the traditional preparation of the dead for some funeral rite.

Such tales of monstrous races excited the Spanish Crown and European merchants with their promise of a westerly route to the Spice Islands and silk markets of the East, but the imaginations of many other Europeans were set afire by the horror of the *caníbales'* gruesome repasts and the sexual frisson of their liaisons with Amazon-like women.

Another passenger aboard Columbus's fleet, an Italian banker called Amerigo Vespucci, wrote a series of sensational accounts of his voyages to the New World. These were widely published throughout Europe and became so influential that the great German mapmaker Martin Waldseemüller gave Amerigo's name to the new continent on his iconic world map, the *Universalis Cosmographia* of 1507. Vespucci shamelessly exaggerated his description of the "cannibals" who "wage war without art or order" and "slaughter those who are captured." Then, "the victors eat the vanquished, for human flesh is an ordinary article of food among them." By way of proof, he lied, "I have seen a man eat his children and wife, and I knew a man who was widely said to have eaten 300 human cadavers."[4]

From the outset, the image of monstrously evil man-eating natives was engraved on the European imagination. It proved a powerful justification for colonization and imperial expansion, for cannibalism was considered so evil that almost any measure to suppress it was thought reasonable. It came to be seen as a Christian duty to wage war on these man-eaters. They might be killed without compunction, but more important, it was deemed legitimate to enslave them, as much for their own good as that of their neighbors. That created a powerful incentive for Spaniards to claim that any group of Native Americans were cannibals, so that their land and labor could legally be appropriated. Many colonists deliberately falsified evidence against their victims, while others were merely all too eager to believe them. The myth of savage cannibalism would be used again and again to sanction the persecution and extermination of Indians.

In November 1493, Columbus and his men became convinced that Guadalupe was home to Carib cannibals. According to his childhood friend Michele
da Cuneo, an Italian nobleman, they found "two youths who had their geni-
tals severed at the root" and "twelve beautifully fat fifteen-year-old girls,"
apparently being held captive by the islanders. They concluded the boys had
been castrated "so they could not mix with the Carib women or perhaps to
fatten them up like steers" or capons for the pot.[5]

Their voyage continued through a constellation of tiny islets stretching
east and west and south and north, as far as their eyes could see. Columbus
named them for Saint Ursula and her eleven thousand virgin handmaidens
who had undertaken a pilgrimage to Rome during the Dark Ages, but were
all put to the sword by Attila the Hun. Keeping south of the Virgin Islands,
they anchored off Saint Croix, called Ayay by the Indians, and Cuneo took
the *María Galante*'s longboat ashore with a party of two dozen men. For the
first time in history, Europeans walked, ran, spoke, ate, drank, and defecated
in a land that is today part of the modern United States of America. It was
November 14, 1493.

Suddenly, a canoe came racing along the shoreline with four men and two
women "rowing at such a strike that it seemed like a well-manned brigantine," according to Cuneo. The Europeans gave chase, and "when the Caribs
saw flight was useless, both men and women alike took up their bows with
great bravery," which much impressed Álvarez Chanca. One of these women
mortally wounded a Basque sailor with a poisoned arrow. He died a week
later, and Brother Boil became the first Christian priest to conduct a funeral
in the Americas. It was also the first time in history that eyewitnesses documented the killing of a European by a Native American, an unnamed woman
from a U.S. Virgin Island.

Cuneo and his party rammed the canoe and captured the Indians. They
were forced aboard the *María Galante*, snarling like "African lions."[6] One
man was so badly wounded the Spaniards assumed he was dead and threw
him in the sea. But, "suddenly, he started swimming," Cuneo remembered,
"so we hauled him over the gunwales with a grappling iron and smashed in
his head with a padlock."[7] One captive was "a very beautiful Cannibal girl,
whom the Admiral handed over to me," Cuneo crowed:

"She was completely naked as is their custom and when I got her back to
my cabin, I was overtaken by the desire to cavort with her. But, when I
tried to put this desire into practice, she wanted none of it and scratched
me so badly with her fingernails that I wished I had never got started. So,
seeing how things were, in order to get it over and done with, I took up a

rope and gave her a thrashing and you would never believe how she screamed. But, by the end, we reached such a state of concord that it was as though she had been trained in a school of harlotry."[8]

So, the first recorded acts in the Spanish history of the modern United States are the abduction of a handful of indigenous islanders, a brutal murder, and a barbaric rape. As foundational events, they could hardly be more emblematic and predictive of the destructive forces of European imperialism.

The idea of a comely continent ripe for violation ran deep in the Old World psyche, most vividly in the Greek myth in which Zeus disguised himself as a bull to abduct and rape Europa herself. Allegorical images of America as a fecund and naked woman epitomized European conceptions of the New World as a virgin Paradise. In Jan van der Straet's classic drawing *The Discovery of America*, made in the 1580s, a voluptuous young "native" maiden rises from her hammock to greet a European nobleman, modeled on Vespucci, who is armed with the trappings of Christian civilization: his ships, his clothes, his sextant, and his cross. By contrast, an early seventeenth-century engraving by Crispijn de Passe depicts America as strong, fit, and far from defenseless. She holds her bow and the severed head of a victim, while a supplicant Carib presents her with more human trophies, seeming to epitomize the spirit of the unnamed Virgin Islander who killed the Basque. Vespucci's own excitement is palpable as he describes how the "libidinous" cannibal women engorged "their husbands' penises" to a grotesque size using venom from "some poisonous critter." Yet their pleasure came at a price, for many of their menfolk "lose their virile organ and remain eunuchs" as a result, he explained.[9]

Columbus's fleet reached the southern coast of Boriquén, "a beautiful and fertile island" that Columbus baptized San Juan Bautista, for Saint John the Baptist, and which we know today as Puerto Rico. A young and impoverished gentleman called Juan González Ponce de León, possibly the bastard son of the Marquis of Cadiz, may have been among the many men who went ashore. Sixteen years later, he would be appointed Governor of San Juan de Puerto Rico, the first European administrator to take charge of any land that today flies the Stars and Stripes. What is more, in 1513, he would lead the first expedition to explore any part of the modern mainland United States, officially claiming Florida for Spain. But for the moment, Ponce de León was simply another adventurer aboard Columbus's ships.

Columbus was anxious to continue the voyage and reach Haytí, which he had renamed Hispaniola, where his flagship had been wrecked on a reef on

Christmas Eve 1492. The friendly local chieftain, or *cacique* in Taino, a man of noble bearing and fine manners called Guacanagarí, had urged his men to work tirelessly to salvage the cargo. The captain of the third ship had already absconded in search of gold, so Columbus was left with only his tiny caravel for the daunting voyage home. Yet, with his indefatigable ability to find triumph in disaster, he suggested that "Our Lord caused the ship to run aground so that I might establish a settlement" among such "friendly and trustworthy people," ruled over by a king whose bearing, behavior, and even table manners "showed him to be of noble lineage." Unable to accommodate all his men aboard the caravel, Columbus had been forced to establish the first European town in the Americas. He called it Villa de la Navidad, "Christmas Town."[10]

Now, Columbus filled with hope as he sighted Hispaniola's coast. When he reached the limits of Guacanagarí's kingdom, he sent men ashore, but they found four putrefying cadavers with the garrotes still strung around their necks, "one of them in such a condition that it was possible to see that he had been heavily whiskered." The Taino were beardless, so Columbus knew the dead must have been Spaniards.[11] His hopes turned to trepidation.

On the evening of November 27, filled with foreboding, Columbus stood off Navidad and fired his small cannon. No corresponding volley came from the shore. That night, a handful of islanders came aboard the flagship with presents of gold.

"How are the Christians?" Columbus asked through his interpreters.

"Well, they are well," replied one of Guacanagarí's kinsmen, "although some have died of illness and others from fighting among themselves." Both the Indian and Spanish settlements, he said, had recently been brutally attacked by Caonabó, the fearsome chieftain who ruled the east of the island. "The king himself has not come because he has an injured leg."

The following morning, a party went ashore and found both Navidad and the native village razed by fire. Most of the Spaniards were "sprawled on the ground without their eyeballs," Cuneo noted, "so we assumed the natives must have butchered them because whenever they do away with someone they immediately gouge out his eyes and eat them."[12]

With a well-armed escort, Columbus went to visit King Guacanagarí. They found the chieftain apparently unable to rise from his hammock, his thigh much bandaged. He presented them with gold and "with tears in his eyes, he began to speak of the death of the Christians," Álvarez Chanca reported, "some from illness," some "killed by Caonabó."

"I was there with one of the navy surgeons," Álvarez Chanca wrote, "and the Admiral told Guacanagarí that we were wise when it came to human ailments."

"Show them your wound," insisted Columbus.

The surgeon unwound the bandage while Guacanagarí explained that he had been struck with a stone. The doctors examined him, and Álvarez Chanca reported, "It was clear, for all that he acted as though in great pain, that there was as much wrong with the one leg as the other." In other words, nothing was wrong with the noble *cacique* at all.[13]

Brother Boil suspended any sense of Christian charity and harangued Columbus to punish Guacanagarí and his people as traitors and murderers. But the Admiral of the Ocean Sea preferred friendship with the island king, who had come to his rescue the year before and who had borne him such exciting gifts of gold. Life was precarious enough at the edge of the world without making an enemy out of an ally.[14]

On Hispaniola, Columbus founded a new town called Isabella, but over the following weeks the Spaniards failed to find significant deposits of gold, while hunger and disease began to destroy morale.[15] Columbus sent twelve ships home with a plea for supplies and reinforcements. He also requested permission to "enslave the cannibals," assuring the Spanish Crown that once they had been taken "abroad, they would abandon their inhuman ways" and soon "make better slaves than any other race."[16]

Then he abandoned the business of command and leadership among the landlubbers and set out with a handful of caravels to explore Cuba and Jamaica, leaving his brother Diego in charge at Isabella. The colony descended into anarchy. Desperate Spaniards roamed across Hispaniola in brutal and fragmented bands, venting their frustrations and succoring their plight at an awful cost to the indigenous people.

Soon after Columbus returned from his cruise of exploration, a band of Indians killed ten Spaniards in the verdant upland valley known as the Vega Real. He seized the opportunity to unite his riotous men in a war of righteous vengeance against the islanders. But he was also aware that many Portuguese adventurers had made fortunes for themselves along the coast of Africa by capturing men and women for sale as slaves in Europe. So, at the end of a brutal campaign, Columbus mercilessly packed over five hundred Indian prisoners belowdecks aboard four caravels and sent them to market in Spain despite the royal prohibition on enslaving Indians. Hispaniola might have yielded little gold, but slavery seemed a promising way to finance further exploration. Columbus was to be disappointed, for few captives survived their ordeal, and Queen Isabella gave orders that those who had must be returned home.

Meanwhile, Columbus turned his attention to pacifying the rest of the island, which meant defeating the implacable Caonabó. Keen to take his enemy alive, he chose Alonso de Hojeda for the task: "small of stature, but perfectly formed," according to a contemporary, "with a handsome face and large eyes," he was an outstanding athlete and had nerves of steel. During Queen Isabella's visit to Seville, Hojeda had walked out onto a wooden beam projecting twenty feet from the top of the cathedral tower and then pirouetted above the gasping crowd below.[17] Full of vigor, live to the moment, people clearly loved him.

With nine cavalrymen, Hojeda rode deep into enemy territory and asked to parley with the ferocious *cacique*, sending word that he came bearing a gift of beautiful lustered bronze jewelry.

Caonabó came down to the river with a few members of his household and bathed at his leisure. When Hojeda offered to take him for a ride on his horse, Caonabó could not resist the novelty of riding the European beast, and with disastrous overconfidence he agreed. Astride Hojeda's horse, riding pillion, he allowed the Spaniards to place some beautifully ornate bracelets of finely worked bronze on his wrists and anklets on his feet. Needless to say, these were no ornaments, but the most "subtle and discrete of manacles."[18] With his unwitting captive sitting behind him, Hojeda slowly rode away, then dug in his spurs and galloped headlong for Isabella, abducting the only war leader on Hispaniola whom the Spaniards truly feared.

Columbus ordered that Caonabó be transported to Spain, but the ship holding the prisoner was wrecked by a tropical storm while still in port. The great *cacique* drowned, unable to swim for the shore because of his chains. So died Caonabó, the powerful and ferocious Haitian *cacique* from the east whose name gave us the word "cannibal," a valiant, violent, and, it seems, vain man who almost certainly never ate human flesh.

Columbus made peace with Caonabó's brother, baptized him Diego, and invited him to Spain. "This don Diego had a gold necklace that weighed six hundred *castellanos* and which the Admiral made him wear whenever they entered any of the cities or towns" of Castile, wrote a leading historian who hosted Diego in his home.[19] Columbus was ensuring that all across Spain his exotic captive *cacique* should glitter with the promise of riches.

PART I

Myths, Dreams, and History

The Chase & the Catch

King Ferdinand only reigned in his own right in the Crown of Aragon, so when Queen Isabella died in 1504, their daughter, Juana "la Loca," succeeded to the more powerful throne of Castile and so became titular ruler of the Spanish possessions in the Indies. But after a prolonged struggle for power, Ferdinand established himself as regent of Castile, ruling on behalf of Juana on the grounds that she was too mentally unstable for government. He soon remarried, to a much younger French bride, but they produced no issue to complicate the unified Spanish inheritance of the Catholic Monarchs. So when Ferdinand himself died, in 1516, he was succeeded by Juana's son, Charles of Ghent, heir to the great House of Habsburg. Already Duke of Burgundy and Lord of the Low Countries, he then inherited Castile, the Indies, Aragon, Sicily, Sardinia, and Naples.

Charles learned to rule his enormous European empire that eventually stretched from Spain to Bohemia and Holland to Italy with enormous energy, constantly traveling across his domains like a medieval monarch, feasting with his noble vassals, holding court, and fighting wars against his rivals and his enemies. But when he first landed in Spain, he cut a deeply unimpressive and youthful figure of seventeen. Raised in Brussels, he spoke no Spanish and even lisped in his native French because of his giant jaw. The Spanish aristocracy hated his entourage of Flemish courtiers, who treated Castile like a colonial conquest to be plundered. But in 1519, the Prince-Electors of the Holy Roman Empire chose him as their emperor. He ruled over half of Europe.

He was also sovereign of Spanish America, and in that same momentous year of 1519, a renegade captain called Hernán Cortés absconded with an armada that had been assembled by the Governor of Cuba and sailed for the unclaimed coast of Mexico. As Charles prepared to travel to Aachen, Aix-la-Chapelle, to be crowned King of the Romans as a prelude to his imperial coronation by the pope, he received an astonishing gift from Cortés, the first treasure sent back to Europe from Aztec Mexico.

The customs officers of the House of Trade, at Seville, documented "a large gold disc with a design of a beast in its center surrounded by foliage motifs, which weighed 3,800 pesos de oro" and "a large silver disc, which weighed forty-eight silver marks . . . , two necklaces of gold and precious stones, one of which has eight woven threads set with 232 red gems and 173 green stones, with 26 gold bells hanging from the border, in the middle of which there are four large carved gemstone figures encrusted with gold," and it went on and on, page after page.[1] Albrecht Dürer, the greatest artist of the northern Renaissance, saw this treasure displayed in Brussels and wrote glowingly, "In all the days of my life, I have seen nothing to make my heart rejoice so much as these things . . . , for I marveled at the subtle ingenuity of men in foreign lands. Indeed, I cannot express all I felt there."[2]

In a stirring speech to the Castilian parliament, one of Charles's leading ministers declared that "the king, our lord, is more of a king than any other," emperor not just in Europe, but of this "other New World of Gold, created" by God for Charles, a world "not yet born before our times."[3] Over the coming centuries, gold, silver, and trading wealth poured into Spain, making Charles and his descendants if not the wealthiest, at least the most financially liquid monarchs in history. That exceptional access to astounding amounts of bullion, to ready money coined in precious metals, led the Spanish Habsburgs to squander their wealth by financing continual wars to keep control of their rebellious subjects in their European possessions. Silver flowed across the old continent, stimulating enormous economic and social change and making Spain the center of a brave new world, the fulcrum between the Old World and the Americas. Already, in 1519, few doubted that Charles V was the most powerful prince in history.

Cortés had not only remitted his huge "bribe" to his sovereign, but as evidence of the civilization of the world he had stumbled upon, he had also sent to Spain a handful of Totonac noblemen from the coastal region around modern Veracruz as ambassadors from this Land of Gold. They were the first Indians that Charles had met, and he received them graciously, personally requesting that they be properly clothed against the harsh Castilian winter.

In 1519, Charles also encountered for the first time the great Dominican friar Bartolomé de las Casas, who was already engaged in a long and arduous campaign to convince the new Holy Roman Emperor of his Christian duty to protect his new American Indian subjects from rapacious Spanish conquistadors. Over the coming decades, Las Casas would aggressively assert their humanity in the face of powerful opponents who damned the Indians as subhuman monkeys, cannibal sodomites best enslaved to correct their abominable traditions.

The refrain "Gold, God, and Glory" offers a succinct explanation of why hundreds of thousands of Spaniards went to seek a future in the Americas, but its brevity and simplicity mask the many other strange and alien motives that drove imperial expansion. By contrast with those familiar ambitions, during the first century or more of Spanish exploration, many of the greatest adventurers and conquistadors appear to have been lured by the most fabulous hopes and improbable dreams, tough, pragmatic men who were irresistibly drawn to a powerful mixture of myth and illusion. Appearances can deceive, so it is impossible to fathom with any certainty in what ways those tough characters believed in those delusions and why they did so.

The conviction that the Strait of Anián, the Spanish name for the Northwest Passage, must exist can be more or less rationally explained, although some of the theories surrounding its geography are so far-fetched it is hard to comprehend how competent explorers might have believed them. By contrast, Juan Ponce de León's search for the Fountain of Eternal Youth in the interior of the Florida peninsula seems, at first glance, to be bizarre. Equally, we might ask to what extent the first Europeans to visit California really thought it was inhabited by a tribe of women similar to the Amazons of the Ancient World? Or we might wonder incredulously at the idea that a major expedition was organized by the viceroy in Mexico City to go in search of Seven Cities "of Gold" purported by some to have been founded by seven medieval bishops who had fled Moorish persecution in Portugal.

Columbus, in his misguided determination to find a route to Asia, had established the precedent for going in quest of a delusion, a goal that should have been impossible to achieve. Yet of almost equal importance is that by inadvertently discovering America in the process, he also set a precedent for turning fallacy into tangible success. When, in 1519, Hernán Cortés explored and conquered the Aztec Empire, richer in almost every way than the objects of even the conquistadors' most outlandish dreams, many Spaniards seem to have concluded that almost any fantasy could metamorphose into some golden reality in the Americas.

To some extent these fantasies and fables may simply have been a way of addressing the difficulty of aiming at the unknown, at nothing, as it were; and the even greater difficulty of persuading others to join you in the endeavor. It is far easier to tilt at a windmill than to charge at an empty space, to invoke the great Spanish novel of the period, Miguel de Cervantes's *Don Quixote*.

But it is worth asking whether all the conquistadors were really in search of wealth or *reputación* or God's heavenly reward. It may be that the myths and fancies they professed to be the object of their ambitions were imaginative reformulations of a precipitous escapism, of a deep desire for adventure, for movement, novelty, and the excitement of facing danger, for conquering their fears as much as Indians, for the camaraderie of campaign. Many of the most successful of them, such as Cortés and Hernando de Soto, never stopped searching for the ends of rainbows, even after they had found many a miraculous pot of gold along the way. It may partly be that the journey was more important than the destination, the chase was better than the catch.

The specters of fantasy, fable, dreams, and illusion also haunt modern historians of the Spanish Empire. An uncomfortable reality of the historian's art is that contemporary sources are usually replete with errors, misunderstandings, misrepresentations, and outright lies. The maps, paintings, archaeological artifacts, oral traditions, and most of all written documents from which the past must necessarily be reconstructed are far from reliable bearers of fact, influenced as they are by political and cultural prejudice and sometimes simply the essential incompetence of the men who produced them. Álvar Núñez Cabeza de Vaca's famous account of his travails in Florida and Texas is an excellent test case for the study of propaganda in historical narrative, while the many documents generated by Francisco Vázquez de Coronado's expedition show that with care the historian can sometimes formulate a reasonable picture of the past. However, Garcilaso de la Vega's quintessentially Latin American novel, the *Florida del Inca*, about Hernando de Soto's expedition across the Deep South, which was once treated as a reliable historical source, is a fine example of how history is often most effectively imprinted on the collective imagination when it is filtered through the lens of fiction.

Part One, then, offers an overview of the main events and geography of the early years of Spanish imperial expansion into North America. It also examines the motives of the men and women who were protagonists of that history. But in the process, Part One asks fundamental questions about the writing of history, baring naked the sources from which historians must harvest the content needed to compile their tales.

CHAPTER I

"WAR OF BLOOD AND FIRE"

PUERTO RICO

Each night, I stripped off and painted my body in rusty-ochre hues or blackened myself so I could enter the *caciques'* meetings and I heard from their own lips that three days hence they wanted to murder us all.

—JUAN GONZÁLEZ PONCE DE LEÓN, SPANISH NOBLEMAN

COLUMBUS MADE TWO FURTHER important voyages before he died in 1506. He saw the power of the race where the sweet waters of the Orinoco meet the ocean currents and realized so great a river must drain a massive continent. He followed the coast from Venezuela to Honduras and was marooned on Jamaica for a year. But he never found his longed-for route to Asia. Meanwhile, Hispaniola remained anarchic, a fragile foothold in a New World. Influential men complained loudly about Columbus's failure as a leader, and he was clapped in irons and sent back to Spain. Henceforth, he forever refused to remove his shackles and presented himself at court rattling his chains by way of protest, haunting his sovereigns' conscience until his death.

Ferdinand and Isabella appointed as Governor of Hispaniola a classic Castilian aristocrat called Nicolás de Ovando, a formidable figure forged in the tradition of a medieval frontier ravaged by constant warfare between Christian and Islamic Spain. He sailed to Hispaniola with thirty ships and twenty-five hundred men. With a firm hand and an impeccable pedigree, he secured the respect of the colonists and the subjugation of the Indians.

Juan Ponce de León made his second voyage to the Americas in Ovando's fleet, along with his nephew Juan González de León, a young nobleman from Seville who came with a handful of companions, men deeply loyal to his powerful family.[1] There were Andrés López and Lucas Gallego, who had been raised as page boys in the Ponce de León household, and his childhood playmates Francisco Rodríguez and Gonzalo Juárez, vassals who had grown up next door and went to school with González. There was Juan Garrido, a free black African who found a home among them and went on to become a citizen of Mexico City, remembered by historians as the first person to successfully sow wheat in the Americas.[2] Bound by economic and social ties rooted in kinship and seignorial power, these men saw America as a frontier filled with the tantalizing promise of winning land and vassals. The astonishing success of Spanish imperialism owed as much to such parochial intimacies as it did to the grandiose schemes of the crown. Years later, in comfortable retirement in Mexico City, Rodríguez proudly reported that since their first campaigns in Puerto Rico, "I was always alongside Captain Juan González, I fought in every war he did."[3]

Despite the strength of Ovando's forces, Caonabó's widow exhorted her *cacique* kinsmen to resist the alien invaders. Serious trouble erupted when a foolish Spaniard lost control of his dog of war. The ferocious canine attacked an important chief, "gnawing at his midriff," and as the *cacique* fled one way, the dog ran the other, one end of the man's intestines in his jaws, his internal organs unwinding before the eyes of the horrified onlookers. In revenge, the Indians killed eight sailors who had landed on a small island just offshore. In the face of growing hostility, Ovando declared a *guerra de sangre y fuego*, a "war of blood and fire," which meant that no quarter would be given.[4]

Ponce joined the punitive expedition as captain of the troops from Santo Domingo, the capital of Hispaniola. Following a series of bloody skirmishes, he brought the campaign to a successful conclusion when one of his men, a powerfully built Spanish farmhand, defeated the leading *cacique* in single combat.[5] Ponce was rewarded with a large *encomienda* of Indians and a landed estate, which he called Salvaleón in honor of his grandmother's fiefdom in Spain. For many years historians claimed he was a rare example of the beneficent *encomendero*, and although that sentimental image is now largely discredited, he did bring peace to eastern Hispaniola, partly because he established a successful farm. He started a family, built a solid stone house that still stands on the heights of Salvaleón, and became prosperous selling cassava bread to ships sailing for Spain. As a result of that wealth, a healthy trade developed between the Indians on his *encomienda* and the inhabitants of neighboring Puerto Rico.

Every evening, Ponce could look out across the strait and see the sunset gilding the distant hills of Puerto Rico, and he fell prey to the great contagion of the Spanish colonists: he became convinced that those glittering highlands were rich in gold.[6] But Puerto Rico was disputed territory.

Columbus's son Diego Colón asserted his hereditary right to the island as part of a major lawsuit he brought to enforce his father's original contract with the Spanish Crown, which, by fair means and foul, had attempted to derogate as much of the grant as possible. Following the death of Isabella, Ferdinand granted the governorship of Puerto Rico to a sea captain called Vicente Yáñez Pinzón, who had sailed with Columbus during his first two voyages, on the condition that Pinzón settle the island within a year "with as many married or betrothed citizens and inhabitants as possible."[7] On August 8, 1505, Pinzón's men anchored off the coast of Puerto Rico and loaded two sows, a hog, a few she-goats, and a billy goat onto a longboat and rowed them ashore. A notary formally witnessed the release of these animals before the men returned to Hispaniola. By this quirk of historical happenstance, three pigs and a herd of goats became the first legally notarized European settlers of any land that today belongs to the United States.[8]

Pinzón made this cursory attempt to fulfill his contract because he was well aware that Diego's claim was legally sound, while his own grant depended entirely on Ferdinand, whose grip on power in Castile and the Americas had been tenuous since the death of the titular ruler, Isabella. Pinzón was wise to be skeptical, for the Wiley Old Catalan, as Ferdinand was called by contemporaries, was ready to double-cross him. Even as Pinzón's hogs and goats struggled to settle alongside the merciless caiman and humans who hunted them, Ponce had told Ovando that he believed there must be gold on San Juan. Ovando was brokering a secret contract with Ferdinand to reconnoiter the disputed island.

In the spring of 1506, Ponce embarked on the clandestine exploration of Puerto Rico. With his nephew Juan González beside him on the poop deck and a group of family retainers aboard, Ponce dropped anchor at a harbor on the west coast known to the Spanish as Aguada, where "an infinite number" of Indians armed, painted, and ready for war had gathered on the high dunes.[9] Young and dashing, González asked his uncle to send him ashore to find out whether he and the Indians could understand one another.

Years later, the ever faithful Andrés López remembered how the young master "leapt ashore completely alone and approached a squadron of Indians, hollering out to them." All aboard the ships watched spellbound as "he moved up the beach" and "two Indians, with bows and arrows" cocked and ready, "went towards him." All three "spent a long time together, gesturing at the boats," until, "after more than two hours parley," González convinced the two Indians to come down to the longboat and he brought them to the ships.

"I understand the language of this land as well as that of Hispaniola," González told his uncle. Ponce then explained to the two Indian emissaries that "the king has sent me to protect you and ensure that neither Christians nor Caribs should treat you ill and to punish any who might do so."[10] Soon afterward, González went ashore again, and this time he returned with seven *caciques*, all wearing gold pendants from their ears and noses. For four hours, Ponce fed them well and gave them plenty of wine to drink. He clothed them in caps, shirts, and hose and gave them glass beads, combs, and scissors. Then he sent them ashore with plentiful assurances of peace and protection, accompanied by González.

Over the following days, González established friendly relations with the *caciques* of the region. Ponce established a town close to a good natural harbor, but he sited it on a waterlogged meadow caught between a "hill and swampy waters that glistened blue and gray like copper sulfate." It was reported that newly suckled infants turned the same color and quickly died, and "everyone went about sick and pale." In jest, they called the place Caparrosa, or "Copper Sulfate," according to the first Historian Royal of the Indies, Gonzalo Fernández de Oviedo.[11] Meanwhile, González convinced the seven gold-bedecked *caciques* to show him the creeks and rivers where they found the precious metal. He returned "with a bag of gold" samples worth over "1,000 pesos or more."[12] Ponce's excitement was tempered by his fears about Diego's lawsuit, so he sent a swift caravel to take the haul to Ovando, who sent word to Ferdinand of the tantalizing find.

Finally, in May 1508, Ponce formally petitioned the crown for permission to settle Puerto Rico, and that summer he reoccupied Caparrosa, where he built an adobe blockhouse. Two large areas of land were set aside for cultivating cassava. Meanwhile, a team of men collected 836 pesos of gold.[13] But the Council of Castile had already made an interim ruling in favor of Diego Colón, who had strengthened his position by marrying the niece of the powerful Duke of Alba. In July 1509, Diego disembarked at Santo Domingo, assured of the governorship of Puerto Rico. His family and allies celebrated the return of their triumphant son with a prodigal *fiesta*, but as the party reached its climax, a hurricane screamed across the island, destroying most of the ships in the harbor and ruining all but the stone buildings in the town.[14] It was an ill omen.

Diego appointed an *alcalde mayor* to govern Puerto Rico, and with the indigenous population of Hispaniola ravaged by disease, grotesque exploitation, and a listless, helpless despair, the rapacious colonists readily turned their greedy gazes on the relatively virgin neighbor. Hundreds of men hungry for gold, land, and Indians began streaming onto Puerto Rico.

Nonetheless, Ponce played so skillful a hand in the game of power politics unfolding in Spain that in 1510 the crown restored him as Governor of Puerto Rico. He immediately set about reinvesting his own followers and restoring their *encomiendas* and estates. But his political victory over Diego was a poisoned chalice, for hundreds of brutal colonists had already overrun the island, and the indigenous population was seething with a furious sense of injustice and a steely determination to fight for their lives. Furthermore, Ferdinand had encumbered Ponce with a headstrong young lieutenant called Cristóbal de Sotomayor, who Ponce made *encomendero* of Chief Agueýbana and his people.[15] Sotomayor touched off the inevitable conflict.

In 1511, Sotomayor went to discuss the rising tensions in the region around his *encomienda* with Ponce, who later testified that they "ate and drank together. But when don Cristóbal was ready to return to his estates, I told him he ought not to go and that if he must, then he should take a company of men."[16] Instead, Sotomayor asked Juan González to accompany him.

A day or two later, Andrés López was busying himself about his makeshift house and farmstead near Agueýbana's principal settlement when González staggered across his threshold, his skin half-shredded by arrow wounds, his spear-gashed flank and blade-splayed shoulder dripping blood, his head split open by a club. López gave him food and water, and finally the young master was strong enough to tell his tale.[17]

All day, as he had traveled from his own farm to meet Sotomayor, he had seen many Indians preparing for war. He told Andrés López, "I heard Indians saying openly that the whole place was up in arms and that they intend to kill all the Christians."

But Sotomayor had refused to believe him.

"Each night, I stripped off and painted my body in rusty-ochre hues or blackened myself so I could enter the *caciques'* meetings and I heard from their own lips that three days hence they wanted to murder us all."[18]

It had taken González three days to convince Sotomayor of their peril. When the young *encomendero* finally understood, he insisted on going to Agueýbana to demand that he supply them with Indian porters for the journey to Caparrosa. They had traveled barely three miles along the jungle road when the *cacique* himself led the attack. As his men closed in for the kill, González called out to Agueýbana, "My lord, why do you have me killed when I can serve you as your slave?"

"Leave this scum alone and get after the leader," ordered the *cacique*.

That gave González just enough time to climb into a tree, from where he watched the Indians club to death Sotomayor, his nephew, and his men. Agueýbana had saved González's life.

Ponce was appalled by the incident and declared a "war of blood and fire" against every Indian on Puerto Rico.[19] But as his recruiting party traveled from farm to farm, they found hundreds of slaughtered Christians. They had to watch impotently as a great force of Indians burned the town of Aguada to the ground.[20]

González rose from his sickbed and joined a detachment of men under Captain Diego Salazar called the "company of cripples," a Dad's Army made up of men too sick or too young to join the governor's regiment. But during the first skirmish of the war, González showed such bravery, fighting hand-to-hand for almost an hour with a formidable *cacique*, that Ponce put him in charge of one hundred men-at-arms.[21] By day, González led his company in charge after charge against the Indian lines. By night, "he stripped off and painted his body" and took up "a bow and arrow" and infiltrated enemy camps, "pretending to be the messenger of some other *cacique*." After the fighting was over, López reported that "a few of us who understood their language asked some captive *caciques* if González had spoken and eaten with them and they all said he had and that they had all believed him to be an Indian."[22]

González may have had an extraordinary affinity for Taino culture, but he was utterly ruthless in war. During the campaign against Agüeybana, he rounded up seventy old men, divided them into small groups, then distributed them throughout the cowed indigenous settlements round about. Then he had them variously hanged, drawn, quartered, and burned alive in front of the terrified Indians, *pour décourager les autres*. Ponce's forces took thousands of captives, most of whom were branded across the face with an "S" overlaid by the sign of a nail, or *clavo*, " ⊺ ," making the symbol "$," which spelled out *esclavo*, the Spanish for "slave."[23]

With the legal wrangling in the case of *Columbus v. Crown* continuing in Spain, Ponce successfully petitioned Ferdinand to grant the island the coat of arms that remains her blazon today: a silver Lamb of God, representing Christ, sitting comfortably on a red Bible, for the Word of God, with a crosier, the symbol of John the Baptist, and a flag showing a red cross, all set against a green ground, the oldest heraldic device in the United States. But on June 15, 1511, the crown rescinded Ponce's governorship. His first major contribution to European settlement in America had come to an end. Now he could embark on his most famous discovery: *La Florida*.

Over the following months, Ovando and Ponce sent secret reports to Ferdinand. Although those documents are now lost, they appear to have convinced the aging monarch that some Indians on Hispaniola had talked of a large island to the north that they called Bimini, over which Diego Colón clearly had no claim. According to the Indians, there was a remarkable river or natural spring on Bimini that ran with waters that could rejuvenate old men.[24]

In 1506, Ferdinand had married the eighteen-year-old Germaine de Foix, niece of the French king. She was almost forty years his junior, yet try as he might, he had failed to sire an heir. The promise of a miraculous elixir from across the Ocean Sea must have titillated the ancient monarch to distraction. His court was soon alive with talk of this Fountain of Eternal Youth. The humanist Peter Martyr reported to the Vatican that this evidently fabulous notion "had made such an impression on the entire populace that even people superior by birth and influence accepted it as proven fact."[25]

Whatever Ferdinand and Ponce really believed about miraculous elixirs, clearly their more rational purpose was to steal a march on Columbus's heirs. So when Diego solicited a contract to discover Bimini, in February 1512, Ferdinand wrote Ponce again with real urgency: "You should move on the business of Bimini," for, although "another who is well able and well placed" has sought this license, Ferdinand explained, without naming Diego in person, "in order to reward you . . . for what you have done for me on San Juan, I have decided to put you in sole charge of this business," and the king bestowed upon him the powerful offices of *Adelantado*, Governor, and Captain General of Florida and the lands he might settle.[26]

But Ponce had lost control of his base on Puerto Rico. Throughout the first months of 1512 he was harassed by Diego's men. To deprive Ponce of money, they took over the *encomiendas* that he had granted his own colonists, they accused him of fraud to hamper his movements, and they impounded his ships to prevent him from sailing for Bimini. Finally, in the summer, a royal warrant arrived ordering the release of his ships. Ponce could at last go in search of this mysterious island.

His three ships weighed anchor at the Port of San Germán, Puerto Rico, on March 3, 1513. Sailing the familiar waters of the Bahamas, they paused to make minor repairs, then struck out into the open ocean.[27] Running northwest with their hulls creaking and rolling on the Atlantic swell, the landlubbers and even some of the mariners went pale and were as sick as dogs. Ponce had chosen Antón de Alaminos as his pilot, probably the most knowledgeable navigator in the New World. Juan Garrido sailed, too, the great free black conquistador who had helped settle Puerto Rico and who would, in time, play his part in the conquest of Mexico and the discovery of California.

On Easter Sunday, March 27, 1513, known in Spanish as the *Pascua Florida*, they sighted land to the port side. Over the following days, they ran a long coastline in stormy weather, until, on April 2, as the wind and the sea relented, they took soundings and cautiously set a course for land. That night, they anchored in nine fathoms of water, and the next day Juan Ponce de León went ashore with a handful of senior members of the expedition as witnesses and a notary public to make a careful record of his actions. He walked up the beach and announced that he was taking possession of the land in the names of Ferdinand and Juana. He named it *La Florida* because "it was a very pretty sight, with many shady glades" and "because they discovered it during the Easter Holidays." He drew his sword and cut branches from a handful of trees, ordered a sailor to dig a hole in the ground, and had a small building erected, all formal acts of possession.

Alaminos took a sighting with his sextant and reported their position as 30°8' N. If his reading was accurate, they would have been just north of modern St. Augustine, the oldest European town in North America, but the likelihood his figures were precise is remote.[28] Wherever they were on the Atlantic coast, they were the first Europeans known to have set foot in modern Florida, the first to visit the mainland United States. When these ceremonies and formalities were finished, Ponce and the witnesses signed the notary's work.[29] He did not realize it at the time, but Ponce had staked a Spanish claim to most of the unknown vastness of North America. Much of it would be referred to as *La Florida* for over a century to come.

On April 20, they struggled against the Gulf Stream and moved in closer to the land. A group of Native Americans appeared on a beach, so Ponce went ashore with a handful of men in the ships' boats. After a series of confused exchanges, during which Ponce must have much missed his nephew Juan González and his multilingual diplomacy, the Indians attacked, firing arrows and hurling spears. Two Spaniards were wounded and a sailor was knocked senseless. Ponce ordered a hasty retreat, "so as not to provoke trouble among the natives." In the mayhem, the Indians went off with one of the ships' boats and some weapons. Ponce went ashore again at a nearby river mouth to erect a wooden cross, and he posted a notice asserting his claim to possession. The shore party was attacked again by sixty Indians, but this time the Europeans took one man captive so they could teach him Spanish.

The ships rounded a point that Ponce called the Cabo de Corrientes, the "Cape of the Currents," where the ships struggled to make headway despite raising full sail in a good following wind. They anchored in the lee of a headland, near an Indian settlement they understood to be called Abayoa. In the second week of May, they cleared the Florida Keys, calling the long line of islands and reefs "the Martyrs, because from afar their rocky outcrops looked like men in great suffering."[30]

On May 23, they made the west coast of mainland Florida and anchored in a "good bay," almost certainly Charlotte Harbor. They set about careening the hull of one of the ships, an arduous task that meant unloading the vessel, grounding it on the low tide, and rolling it onto its side by hauling on the masts. One side was carefully scraped to remove barnacles, rotten planks were replaced, and the caulking was shorn up. The process was repeated on the other half of the hull. In the meantime, the rigging and cables were repaired and tarred, and the deck was caulked. Of especial importance, the bilge pumps were inspected, and any leather parts that had perished in the salt water were replaced.[31]

A large party of Indians observed these activities from a distance, but then for some unknown reason tried to prevent the Spaniards from weighing anchor. When the Spaniards confronted them, they at first fled, but later returned with furs and gold jewelry. The excited Spaniards pestered them for information about the source of these enticing valuables, which had almost certainly been imported from Cuba. However, a man appeared who spoke some Taino, and Ponce understood him to say that a powerful *cacique* was gathering a quantity of gold to trade with the Spaniards. The man seemed to say that this chief was called Carlos, evidently a corruption of "Caloosa."

In reality, "Carlos" was not preparing a quantity of gold for trade, but a contingent of warriors for battle. The Spanish explorers watched as twenty canoes approached the ships. Fighting ensued, bringing with it the first fatalities documented in the long history of warfare between Indians and Europeans on mainland North America, the lives of a few Indians and a ship's master called Pedro Bello, the first European known to have died on the shores of the continental United States.[32] Ponce called the place Isla de Matanza, "Slaughter Island."[33] The following morning, eighty well-armed canoes attacked the nearest ship. Until nightfall, the Indians fired volley after volley of arrows while the Spaniards kept them at a safe distance with crossbows and gunfire.

In the morning, Ponce abandoned the illusory promise of Carlos's golden kingdom and set out to explore a handful of islands to the west that he called the Tortugas, because of the large number of turtles living there, the name by which they are still known today. Presumably for sport as well as for food, the men slaughtered 160 turtles, 14 sea lions, and 5,000 seabirds, some of them pelicans, before running back well south of the Keys, headed for the Atlantic seaboard.

As they swung east, Alaminos recognized the coast of Cuba on the horizon and guided them to the Bahamas, where they sighted a battered ship that had taken refuge in a shallow bay. Ponce must have assumed, as many modern historians have done, that her experienced pilot, Diego Miruelo, had been sent to spy on him by Diego Colón. As the ships floated at anchor in the poorly sheltered bay, a violent storm blew in, and Miruelo's ship began to sink. Ponce had no choice but to rescue the interfering pilot and his crew. But Ponce was determined to ensure Miruelo's prying eyes should not learn the secret of *La Florida*, and so Ponce personally escorted him back to Hispaniola.

Ponce sent Alaminos north again with the maneuverable brigantine to undertake the first extensive exploration of the coastal waters of North America. No record of that voyage survives, for the secrets of their discoveries were kept well hidden, but they clearly explored a long way west, for Alaminos later demonstrated an intimate knowledge of the coast from Florida to Texas and could easily find the Gulf Stream from the Mexican coast. It seems logical that they should also have gone north along the Atlantic coast. Wherever they explored, they must have realized that Florida formed part of an enormous mainland.

Ponce returned to Puerto Rico to find Diego Colón fighting a brutal war against indigenous Indians who were relentlessly bellicose in their desperation to rid themselves of the Spaniards. Juan González told Ponce how, within days of Diego's arrival, González learned that the Indian *caciques* were stockpiling huge quantities of poisoned arrows and preparing for war. He hurried into town and sounded the alarm as night was falling. But Diego had refused to believe him. As Diego dallied, the Indians launched an assault by the light of a full moon, storming the town, setting fire to buildings, and slaughtering tens of Spaniards. Caparrosa had been burned to the ground; Colón's house and the new church were destroyed. Ponce thanked God that his own family had survived.

As always, González and his comrades took the fight to the enemy. He grappled with a ferocious *cacique* on the seashore, and after an intense struggle, hacked him to death among the waves. That night, González claimed they took sixteen important *caciques* prisoner, which brought peace to that part of the island. But the ever-sarcastic Oviedo reported that the real hero of the war was a "ruddy-red dog of middling size, but great intelligence, called Becerillo," after a famous dog of war described in the great epic poem of medieval Spanish literature, the *Song of El Cid*.[34]

Juan González de León had served both Ponce and Diego Columbus well, but Oviedo observed that González and his followers were "poorly rewarded for their efforts, for it is usual for certain men to enjoy the fruits of others' sweat and toil." So, when the Governor of Cuba, Diego Velázquez, issued a call to arms, this band of experienced Indian fighters answered him. This time, however, the campaign was to be against fellow Spaniards.

CHAPTER 2

REALMS OF GOLD

MEXICO

We Spaniards suffer from a disease of the heart, a disease that can only be cured with gold.

—HERNÁN CORTÉS, CONQUEROR OF MEXICO

HERNÁN CORTÉS WAS FROM EXTREMADURA, in Spain, a harsh hinterland region known as the "cradle of the conquistadors." He was already a well-established member of the colonial elite when, in 1519, he brazenly appropriated a fleet that had been assembled by Diego Velázquez, the Governor of Cuba, and sailed for Mexico. As he explored the coast from Yucatán north, Cortés and his men were so impressed by the city-states and agricultural polities they came across that he called one place Seville. He learned that he was at the edge of the Aztec Empire, dominated by the aristocratic Mexica and ruled by Emperor Montezuma from the beautiful highland capital of Tenochtitlán. This world was as politically sophisticated and as fabulously wealthy as anywhere Columbus had dreamed of reaching in Asia, and nobody in Europe had any idea it existed. But Cortés soon understood that many of the Aztec client states deeply resented their subjection to the Mexica. With breathtaking arrogance, he decided to seize this empire for himself and Charles V, or die in the attempt.

Legend has it that Cortés burned his boats to steel his men to the daunting task of conquest, but in fact he had them beached and scuttled to prevent dissenters from escaping to report his unauthorized activities to Governor Velázquez on Cuba. Cortés then marched inland, through a landscape populated by Aztec vassals who did nothing to oppose him. But he did have to fight a series of ferocious battles against the Tlaxcalans, the Mexicas' most bitter enemies, who tenaciously maintained their independence. Finally, they sued for peace and became Cortés's staunchest, most brutal allies. As a result, they were held in high esteem by Spaniards. Over the coming centuries, they played an important role in the expansion and consolidation of the Spanish Empire, helping to push colonization deep into North America.

Cortés and his men were dazzled by their first sight of Tenochtitlán, a breathtaking metropolis that seemed to float in the shallow waters of Lake Texcoco like an American Venice. They likened it to the golden cities of Arthurian legend, a place straight out of the pages of the bestselling romance of chivalry *Amadis of Gaul*.[1] On one of the great causeways leading from the lakeshore to the city, they were greeted by Emperor Montezuma, and he hung a gorgeous necklace of red seashells and finely worked golden shrimp around Cortés's neck. Tenochtitlán was a magical place that overflowed with gold and silver and exotic riches. They had reached the end of the rainbow, and Cortés told Montezuma, "We Spaniards suffer from a disease of the heart, a disease that can only be cured with gold."[2] Some Mexica magicians believed that Cortés was the deity Quetzalcoatl, so Montezuma played the perfect host for his alien guests, lavishing them with fine foods, hunting expeditions, noble womenfolk, even princesses from his own imperial family. But it was an uneasy peace, for many Mexica princes and noblemen had few illusions about the real nature of their visitors.

Meanwhile, on Cuba, Velázquez appointed a giant ogre of a man called Pánfilo de Narváez to lead an expedition to arrest the errant Cortés. With his flowing ginger beard and a voice so "deep and gruff it sounded as though it came from the tomb," according to one of Cortés's loyal followers, Narváez had shown himself to be ruthless in suppressing Indian resistance to Spanish rule.[3] Juan González de León and his loyal men enlisted in Narváez's punitive force and sailed for Mexico full of excitement and expectation.

Narváez's expedition landed on the Mexican coast in 1520 and began to prepare for the first major battle to be fought between Europeans in the New World. When word reached Cortés, he left his right-hand man, Pedro de Alvarado, with a hundred men in Tenochtitlán and marched toward the coast to meet Narváez.

Cortés was as cunning as he was violent. He made sure Narváez's spies saw the great quantities of gold he had brought with him and also sent his own men into the enemy camp with hefty bribes and offers of more to come. Finally, in the dead of night, Cortés launched his assault. Narváez found his cannon had been spiked and his gunners suborned. Most of his army disappeared into the dark. Narváez lost an eye and was taken prisoner as he and thirty loyal captains defended their redoubt on top of a ceremonial pyramid. His men surrendered, and with the battle won, Cortés distributed so much gold among the vanquished that his own followers complained bitterly.

The sweetness of this almost bloodless victory was soured by the disastrous news that the Mexica nobility had risen up at Tenochtitlán and were besieging Alvarado and the Spaniards within the compound of the Axayáctl Palace. González and his men were in the vanguard of the army made up of a thousand Europeans and two thousand or more Tlaxcalans, which Cortés now swiftly marched to the relief of his lieutenant. When they entered the city, they found the streets empty and the temples abandoned. Years later, González remembered that, disconcertingly, even an effigy of Saint Christopher remained in place in the Great Temple.[4] There was an eerie calm.

The terrifying storm broke slowly. During one early skirmish, González and his comrades managed to hold a vital bridge, allowing a detachment of Spanish troops to retreat from an ill-advised sortie. Almost all of them returned wounded; four or five had been killed. The Mexica established their headquarters in Montezuma's former palace, where the Spaniards had feasted with the emperor and caroused with princesses. Now, Cortés sent a force of three hundred to assault this stronghold, but as they advanced, they found all the drawbridges across the canal in flames. González brandished his cutlass and slashed his way across one last remaining burning beam, lashing out this way and that "like a fighting-bull in the ring," leaving "sixteen lords dead about him," as López, Rodríguez, and Gallego watched. López remembered his astonishment at the "many sumptuous blazons of gold and silver and very precious stones" worn by these enemy aristocrats who lay slain or dying. This was Indian fighting unlike anything they had seen in the Caribbean, except that, as usual, González was badly injured and had to be evacuated. Characteristically, he rose from his hospital bed to help lead an assault on one of the great pyramids. Cortés recalled, "I scolded González fiercely and told him to go back to his quarters to be treated, but he insisted that this was no moment for anyone to be in bed, but instead a time for death and glory." As Cortés led his men up one staircase toward the summit of the pyramid, González charged headlong up another, into a cascade of bouncing logs hurled down at him by five hundred Mexica. Onward and upward he went, and when López and Rodríguez reached the summit, they found their captain bleeding heavily from many blows to his head. But González was still on his feet, tossing enemy after enemy over the far side of the temple.[5]

Cortés forced the captive Montezuma to address his people, but they hurled missiles at their former emperor. The last undisputed ruler of the Aztec Empire died of his injuries two days later, but by that time Cortés could see he and his men were surrounded and outnumbered. That night, he ordered the Spaniards to abandon the city.

They called it the *Noche Triste*, the "unhappy night." Hundreds of Spaniards were slain, many drowned in Lake Texcoco, weighed down by pockets
filled with bullion. Such was the confusion that almost three hundred of
Cortés's men never heard his order to retreat. The Mexica took them prisoner,
and their priests cut out the Europeans' beating hearts, holding them up as
offerings to their bloodthirsty gods, or so it was said.

Cortés rallied his troops on a hill he named Nuestra Señora de los Reme-
dios, "Our Lady of Divine Assistance," after the Madonna in the cathedral of
Seville. When he saw González's injuries, Cortés ordered that his own tent
be used by the surgeons to stitch and dress the brave captain's wounds. He
asked after the fate of only one other man, a naval carpenter called Martín
López Osorio. When he heard that this "skillful and clever man" had survived,
Cortés exclaimed, "Onward, then! For we have need of nothing else."[6]

Even in the aftermath of defeat, Cortés was planning for victory. He had
learned that he must control the waters of Lake Texcoco, and he needed
López to build the boats that would allow him to do so.

Cortés led his broken army on a slow withdrawal, a "Calvary of the conquistadors," during which they were constantly harassed by Mexica attacks.[7]
After ten long days and nights, they reached the safety of Tlaxcalan territory,
where they were welcomed by their loyal allies. There, Cortés ordered Martín
López to build thirteen flat-bottomed barges in portable sections that could
be carried to Lake Texcoco. A train of porters six miles long followed a route
that González and his men had helped to open up along trails that ran
through enemy territory. Cortés declared proudly that the "brigantines played
a great role in the conquest of the city," but as the Spaniards marched back
into the Aztec heartland, they witnessed with fascinated horror the devastation that smallpox was inflicting on the Indian population.[8] It was the cruelest
of the Old World pathogens to which indigenous Americans had no resistance. For the first time in the history of the New World, a war was about to
be won largely because of germs. Nonetheless, the Mexica who survived the
disease fought to the death. The siege of Tenochtitlán lasted almost three
months. The city was almost completely destroyed before Cortés could claim
to have conquered Mexico.

Cortés rewarded the battle-scarred González with a series of large *encomiendas*, named him *Alcalde Mayor* of Veracruz, and ordered his marriage
to Francisca de Ordaz. They were the first European couple married on the
American mainland and had at least two children, the first legitimate Spanish
siblings born in Mexico.[9] Juan González and Juan Garrido went on to join
Cortés's attempt, in 1532, to explore the Pacific and settle a land in the

northwest of Mexico said to be inhabited by Amazons, which they called California. Such stories gave hope to thousands more adventurers who came to the Americas in search of gold and glory.

The Spaniards rebuilt México-Tenochtitlán, as they called their new metropolis, which soon grew into the most dazzling city in the New World, the seat of the viceroyalty of the vast territory of New Spain and of the Gran Norte, the "Great North," which stretched toward the sometimes tempting new horizons of California, New Mexico, and Texas. Over half of the geographical territory of the modern United States would come to be ruled from the former Mexica capital that over the centuries expanded into the giant metropolis it is today, swallowing up the surrounding Aztec towns and cities and even Lake Texcoco itself, eventually becoming known simply as Mexico or Mexico City, a city to which this story will frequently return.

CHAPTER 3

FOUNTAIN OF
ETERNAL YOUTH

LA FLORIDA

"I knew then that he was deluded," Oviedo said, "and that the Indian must have invented any old story this bureaucrat wanted to hear so that he would take him home."

—GONZALO FERNÁNDEZ DE OVIEDO, HISTORIAN ROYAL

MÉXICO-TENOCHTITLÁN WAS DESTINED for a brilliant future, but at the time of Cortés's conquest, Spanish America was governed from Santo Domingo, the capital of Hispaniola, where the crown had established the first *audiencia* in the New World. A trained lawyer called Lucas Vázquez de Ayllón had been a founding *oidor*, a magistrate-judge of this Audiencia of Santo Domingo, and was one of a handful of oligarchs who dominated the politics of Hispaniola. He had been farming and trading in the Caribbean for a quarter of a century and had made a fortune capturing Indians on the outlying islands and selling them as slaves to *encomenderos* whose own vassals had died of disease and ill treatment.

In the summer of 1521, when two pilots employed by a company in which Ayllón was a partner failed to find any Indians in the Bahamas, they headed toward Florida, sailing a long way north before sighting land near the South Santee River in South Carolina. They called it the Jordan because it was June 24, the date on which the Church celebrated the Feast of Saint John, who had baptized Christ in the waters of the Jordan River. They traded with friendly Indians and explored the coast, probably sighting Charleston Harbor, where they kidnapped a young lad they called Chicorano and began training him as an interpreter.

There are various theories about the origin of the name Chicorano, but it is probably a corruption of Cherokee, whose tribal history he recounted to the Spaniards, telling them about some tall people who had lived farther north in the Land of Dukasai, ruled over by a blond king and queen.[1] As his Spanish improved, he was able to describe a cast of priests called the Anicatixe. Later Cherokee legends remember the Anicatixe as a tyrannical and licentious sect who were finally massacred by heroic members of their own tribe in vengeance for especially heinous sexual crimes.[2]

Ayllón's men traded for pearls before tricking about sixty Indians into coming aboard their ships by offering colorful glass beads and red scarves. Then they set sail for Hispaniola with their valuable human cargo.

Ayllón and his partners were excited by the discovery of new peoples and lands in the north of *La Florida*, as the Spaniards called the vast, unexplored, and undefined landmass that would become the United States. Ayllón sailed to Spain to petition the crown for permission to settle there and made his way to Valladolid, the habitual seat of government in Old Castile. There, Ayllón and Chicorano often dined with Peter Martyr, the Italian humanist who coined the term "New World" and was considered at court to be an expert on the Indies. Martyr paints a vivid picture of dinner-party conversation at his exalted table. Ayllón, he explains, was holding forth about the giant blond King of Dukasai: "In place of horses, the king is carried about on the shoulders of strong young men."

But the Dean of Hispaniola was one of the guests; he interrupted sharply, remarking, "I have never spoken to anybody who has seen these beasts of burden."

"I have heard it said by many," Ayllón retorted.

Martyr turned the matter over to Chicorano, a lad "of no little intelligence and quick to learn, who spoke Spanish pretty well." But, he noted, the boy "was unable to sort out this dispute."[3]

Ayllón sold the idea of the new land to his courtly audience, describing a fertile world of virgin oaks, pines, and cypresses, of wild olives, walnuts, vines, and fruit trees, a healthful place where people lived to a great age and cured their sicknesses with medicinal plants. The most brilliant element in his pitch was the fraudulent claim that it was at the same latitude as the prosperous agricultural lands of the Guadalquivir River valley in southern Spain, once praised by Arab poets as Paradise on earth. Even Martyr allowed himself to be seduced by this geographical artifice and advised the emperor to send Ayllón to settle so promising a place.[4]

Martyr had never left Europe, but Fernández de Oviedo, the future Historian Royal of the Indies, who had already served many years in the Americas, was skeptical when he met Ayllón on the road to Seville. "We were friends and when he told me about his expedition it troubled me to learn where he was going," Oviedo recalled. He showed Ayllón a huge pearl Oviedo had himself brought from the Americas, but Ayllón dismissed it as "very small compared with the huge and excellent pearls" that Chicorano "had promised him." "I knew then that he was deluded," Oviedo said, "and that the Indian must have invented any old story this bureaucrat wanted to hear so that he would take him home."[5] Oviedo clearly thought Ayllón a fool.

Ayllón's contract was based on the fiction that his men had already explored as far north as 37°, the latitude of Seville. In 1525, he sent one of his pilots to reconnoiter the coast north from the Santee River, at 33°. The pilot's ship ran north from Jacksonville, sighting Cape Fear and its dangerous shoals, passing Indians who must have been fishing along the glorious beaches of the Outer Banks. He rounded Hatteras, which he called Trafalgar, sailed past Virginia Beach and into Delaware Bay. On the return journey, the ship entered Chesapeake Bay and they saw the Potomac flowing from the west before sailing home to Hispaniola.[6] Ayllón's men had been a long way and seen a lot of sand.

Las Casas was among the crowd who watched Ayllón's fleet of five ships sail from Hispaniola in the summer of 1526 with six hundred greenhorns aboard, men and women he had enlisted in Spain. Ayllón took along a hundred horses and a thousand bushels of corn, three-quarters of a million pounds of cassava bread, and many head of cattle, sheep, and hogs.[7]

The heavily laden flagship foundered on the sandbar at the entrance to the Jordan River, and the entire cargo of food was lost. The air buzzed miserably with mosquitoes and deerflies, and the undergrowth was crawling with chiggers. There was clearly no suitable site for a settlement.[8] Before long, the wily Chicorano fled with the other Indian interpreters.

Disease was spreading quickly among the settlers and the cold weather was closing in by the time Ayllón decided upon Sapelo Sound as the best place for his colony. He called it San Miguel because it was formally founded on the Feast Day of the Archangel Saint Michael, September 29.[9] Ayllón himself fell sick and died three weeks later, on October 18, the feast day of his very own Saint Luke.

Within days, a young malcontent called Ginés Doncel led a mutiny of frightened settlers demanding a return to Hispaniola. They imprisoned the royal officials, leading the noble members of the expedition to confront them. That discord encouraged the Indians to launch a raid, during which they killed a handful of Spaniards with their fine arrows, which Oviedo noted were made of chestnut. With the colonists consumed by anarchy and terror, for unexplained reasons a contingent of black slaves set fire to the shack where Doncel was sleeping. Amid the confusion, two noblemen faced down the rebel leader and his cronies. They drew their swords and in the midst of a ferocious battle, Doncel fled and tried to hide under a bed. The rebels surrendered, but by now it had become clear to everyone that they must all sail for Hispaniola as soon as possible. The voyage home was horrific as dozens of the erstwhile colonists succumbed to freezing winds, sickness, and a lack of food. Only 150 people survived the whole sad ordeal.

The Indians and geography of *La Florida* had defied attempts at settlement by both Ponce de León and Vázquez de Ayllón. Pánfilo de Narváez, the giant captain from Cuba with his ginger beard who had lost an eye during his failed attempt to arrest Cortés, launched his own disastrous attempt the following year.

In 1526, Pánfilo de Narváez successfully petitioned the crown for a contract to conquer and settle *La Florida*. He was appointed Governor and *Adelantado* of Florida, and to raise funds and recruits for this great expedition, he journeyed to Seville, the great inland port set beside the olive-green waters of the Guadalquivir River in southern Spain.

Ferdinand and Isabella had granted a monopoly on all trade with their new American possessions to Seville, in 1503. They had founded the Casa de Contratación, the "House of Trade," to license ships, their pilots, crews, and passengers, and to keep tallies of cargoes and to collect customs duties. But it also fomented trade, organizing and supplying exploratory expeditions and providing crown investment, as well as running the postal services. It collected and collated navigational information, interviewing captains and rescued castaways, recording in the *Padrón General*, or "General Register," what they knew about the currents, winds, and coasts they had seen.

Seville flourished as the riches of the New World flooded in. A proud *sevillano* called Luis de Pedraza described one of the great doorways in the massive medieval walls that "they now call the Postigo de Oro, the Golden Postern, because of the enormous quantities of the stuff that enters through it every day" from the riverbank where the ships were unloaded. In 1536, he wrote, "So much gold came from the newly discovered province of Peru that the ships came using gold and silver as ballast! Twenty-seven wagons went backward and forward delivering the gold to the House of Trade and every single passenger landed twenty or thirty thousand ducats . . . even those of us who saw it find it difficult to believe it is true." [10]

The city grew in wealth, power, and population, from around 25,000 residents in 1520 to as many as 160,000 in the 1600s. Adventurers from across Europe poured in, chasing the promise of a glittering future. Free Africans and slaves thronged the streets, Native Americans wandered hither and thither, even a contingent of samurai passed through in the 1580s. Dazzled by the glittering bullion they saw being unloaded onto the banks of the

Guadalquivir, the nobility of Seville shed their traditional prejudice against trade. A groundbreaking economist, the appropriately named Dominican friar Tomás de Mercado, explained, "The discovery of America presented such an opportunity to acquire enormous wealth that even a few princes were drawn to commerce." The greatest aristocratic houses associated with Seville, the dukes of Medina-Sidonia, Arcos, and Alcalá, eagerly embraced the Indies trade. The minor "nobility" followed suit, "out of greed or need," Mercado wrote, and their sons and daughters "married into merchant families." So "the number of merchants in this city has grown along with their wealth," and "the whole place is afire with every kind of business deal."[11]

Aristocrats and merchants became fabulously rich, building gorgeous palaces and handsome public buildings such as the Casa Lonja, or "Merchants' Exchange," and turning the city into a vibrant cultural paradise teeming with artists and playwrights, scholars and scientists. Luis de Pedraza was similarly profligate with his glowing prose in praise of his hometown, extolling the clean, fresh drinking water gushing into the city along an Ancient Roman aqueduct, the many species of delicious river fish teeming in the waters of the Guadalquivir, and the mouthwatering and nourishing bread from the bakeries of Alcalá, which also supplied the hardtack biscuit for the ships on the Atlantic crossing. In an age of frequent dearth and hunger, he wondered at the many fertile orchards and market gardens assiduously cultivated beyond the huge bulk of the city walls and the astounding abundance of food for sale in more than eighty plazas. He lists more than 130 different types of produce that were usually for sale, "beef, veal, mutton, lamb, pork, cured ham, wild boar, venison, kid, and all sorts of tripe" and "green vegetables, legumes, and squashes," his pen rushing onward across the page as he lists every size of edible bird from well-fattened "geese" to "nightingales, canaries, and sparrows." If Pedraza's menu is at times unfamiliar, it also includes enticing comfort foods such as "doughnuts, quince jelly, cinnamon plums," and any number of succulent fruits.[12]

Wealthy Sevillians invested heavily in their faith, and Pedraza was profoundly moved by the splendor of the churches and convents being constructed in almost every parish. The cathedral had recently been remodeled in the fashionable late-Gothic style. With its "five well lighted naves, soaring columns" and "vaults that delight the eye," all lit by "very beautiful stained-glass windows" and a stunning new lantern, Pedraza believed it the "greatest building in the world."[13]

But the cathedral and its merchant sponsors had a guilty conscience, for although everyone knew Christ had expelled the merchants from the temple, the businessmen of Seville set up their shops within the cathedral precinct so as to avoid municipal and royal taxes. Andrea Navagiero, one many remark-able scholars in the orbit of Charles V's glittering court and ambassador for the great merchant city of Venice, described with wonder the raised marble pavement that ran all the way around the cathedral where wealthy merchants sold their wares. He called it "the most beautiful place in Seville," "a kind of marketplace" where great crowds throng "the streets and the plaza nearby." [14] Known as the *Gradas*, the "Steps," this was the commercial heart of Spain, the Wall Street of the age. Professional auctioneers oversaw the sale of enor-mous quantities of valuable goods such as "worked gold and silver, rich textiles," "all sorts of arms and armor, and any kind of luxury goods you care to imagine," a proud contemporary explained, "and very many slaves" as well. The Bank of Seville was here, "the most liquid counting house I have ever heard of," he claimed.[15] God and Mammon rubbed shoulders in this extraordinary place, which contemporaries likened to Babylon.

In the 1560s, the ecclesiastical authorities fenced off the whole precinct with heavy iron chains to prevent merchants from riding their horses and mules into the cathedral itself. Finally, a few years later, Philip II ordered the powerful Consulado, the Merchants Guild, to construct their own exchange building, the imposing, handsome Casa Lonja, which was designed by Juan de Herrera, the royal architect charged with constructing the king's great monastery-palace at El Escorial. Since the eighteenth century the Casa Lonja has been the home of the Archive of the Indies, repository of most of the documents generated by the bureaucracy of Spanish imperial government.[16]

Pánfilo de Narváez was described by Cortés's follower and chronicler Bernal Díaz del Castillo as "strong of limb, long of face, with a blond beard and a pleasing manner about him; and a virile voice that boomed as though reso-nating from some cavernous vault." Even Las Casas, who mostly damned Narváez as a butcher of Indians, admitted that he exuded "authority," with his "social standing, intelligence, his way with words, and his good manners." [17]

Amid the heady hurly-burly of Seville, Narváez's charisma attracted inves-tors and six hundred men and women to his ranks, half of them destined to suffer terrible privations on the coast of the Gulf of Mexico. Only four men survived the adventure. Álvar Núñez Cabeza de Vaca, the royal treasurer, was a minor Andalusian aristocrat with august roots, who had served in the illustrious household of the troubled Duke of Medina-Sidonia and fought at the tragic battle of Ravenna in Italy, during which twenty thousand Spanish soldiers lost their lives. Alonso del Castillo Maldonado was the son of a prominent Salamanca lawyer, but, deeply affected by his father's death, he scorned his studies to embrace a riotous life of gambling. So his family sent him to either escape or export his sinful pleasures to the Americas.[18] Andrés Dorantes de Carranza, a nobleman from the Salamanca hinterland, was given the rank of captain. He brought with him a slave, the first African about whom we know anything at all in the history of the American South, who had been baptized Esteban and raised at the Portuguese enclave of Azemmour on the Moroccan coast.[19] They are not only the real heroes of this tale, but also the agents of its telling.

On July 17, 1527, Narváez's fleet of five ships weighed anchor at Sanlúcar de Barrameda, at the mouth of the Guadalquivir. But as they set sail, one of the women aboard told her nervous companions that before she embarked she had consulted a Morisca fortune-teller who had fled terrible race riots that erupted in the remote Muslim enclave of Hornachos the year before. She foretold that almost all the men who disembarked in Florida would die there, and that if a few of them were lucky enough to survive, it would be because God worked great miracles on their behalf.[20]

The expedition was beset with problems long before reaching Florida. About 150 men deserted as soon as they reached Hispaniola, and when Narváez moved the fleet to his personal power base on Cuba, two of his ships were destroyed by a hurricane. Then, as he tried to sail the surviving ships and four hundred terrified passengers around the island to Havana to strengthen the fleet in preparation for the settlement of *La Florida*, they were struck by another violent storm, which blew them across the Bahama Channel and into the Gulf of Mexico. The disoriented pilots finally made landfall somewhere on the Florida coast during Holy Week of 1528.

Narváez and his followers set foot on their new home for the first time on Good Friday. It was an ill omen, for this was the first day of their own extended Passion. He took the whole company of four hundred men and women ashore to witness him take formal possession of the land, an important ceremony that legally established the different institutions governing and administering the expedition.

While Narváez as Adelantado of Florida was the overall leader, governor, and military commander of the expedition, he was also subject to the oversight of a handful of royal officials, especially the treasurer, Álvar Núñez Cabeza de Vaca. Moreover, Narváez had to negotiate with a number of officials appointed to run the civil administration of the town they intended to establish. Brother Juan Suárez, the first Bishop of Florida, represented the authority of the Church. Spanish expeditions of exploration and settlement involved a complex set of competing corporate and individual interests that required such skillful leadership it was beyond the political abilities of most who tried.

Narváez presumably slashed at the waters, the sand, and some trees with his sword and ordered the erection of some structure, as Ponce de León had done in 1513, although these actions are not recorded in the surviving documentary records. Cabeza de Vaca simply noted that the royal standard was raised and Narváez displayed his crown contract to the royal officials, who confirmed their obedience to him, before adding emphatically, "Then we showed him *our* contracts and he recognized *our* authority."[21]

By the terms of his contract, Narváez was obliged to read aloud a document known as the *Requerimiento*, which had been drafted by a leading jurist in 1513 to legitimize the subjection of indigenous peoples to the Spanish Crown. This bizarre text was designed to give Native Americans a brief overview of Catholic catechism, from Adam and Eve, through the evangelization of Saint Peter, and on to the papal grant of the Americas to Spain. Thus, the Natives should be told they must submit to the Spanish Crown, which would "embrace them with love and charity." "But, if you do not," it went on, "I will wage total war against you and subject you to the yoke of the Church and His Highness and I will enslave you, your women, and your children."[22] Bizarrely, in an act that approximates to legally serving notice on the Indians, again and again this document was read out by Spaniards across the Americas, whether or not any Indians were present and often without any attempt at translation. It was finally abandoned in 1556, largely thanks to the tireless campaigning of Bartolomé de las Casas.

Furthermore, Narváez's expedition was the first to be subject to a *provisión real*, or "royal edict," issued by Charles V in light of Las Casas's lobbying, which instructed officials in the New World to report all crimes committed against Indians to the crown and enacted other measures to prevent the worst excesses of the conquistadors. This edict obliged Spaniards to explain through an interpreter that they had come to help the Indians desist from "eating human flesh and to teach them about the Holy Faith." What, one must wonder, did the Indians make of this curious combination of an injunction against cannibalism and an exhortation to embrace a faith that put the consumption of the true flesh and blood of Christ at the heart of its most sacred rituals?[23]

All of Narváez's pilots concurred that they must be near a large harbor that they knew as the Bay of the Holy Spirit. But his chief pilot, Diego Miruelo, was certain it lay to the south, while the others thought it was to the north. We have no idea what real geographic feature along the Gulf Coast corresponds to their Bay of the Holy Spirit. With hindsight, it may seem most likely that it was either Charlotte Harbor or Tampa Bay, the obvious large ports along that stretch of coast, but given the conflicting and rudimentary sailing directions available at the time, it is also entirely plausible that some of the pilots were looking for Matagorda Bay in Texas, which also became known as the Bay of the Holy Spirit.

In an effort to settle the matter, Narváez led an exploratory excursion along the coast. As dusk turned to night, "they reached a very large bay which appeared to stretch a long way inland." Whether or not this was the same port the pilots were arguing over, Narváez was almost certainly looking at Tampa Bay.[24] Most researchers now agree that Narváez and his expedition landed on the shores of suburban St. Petersburg, opposite St. John's Pass. But at the time, the pilots remained perplexed, so Narváez led a second reconnaissance, and some Indians took them back to the large bay and showed him corn on the stalk and bits of cloth and shoe leather, which the Indians must have recovered from a shipwreck. Bishop Suárez ordered the Indians to burn some strange cadavers that had carefully been placed inside old Spanish packing cases because he assumed they must be heathen idols. Then, the Indians showed Narváez gold objects, including a rattle, and the Spaniards were overcome with greed. They did not stop to think that the treasure might also be salvage. Instead, they urged the Indians to tell them where the gold had come from, and by signs the Indians "indicated a faraway province called Apalache, where there was much gold."[25]

From that moment on, Narváez was deaf to all but the siren call of golden Apalache, the Native American community for which Appalachia is named. He called a council of his officers and declared before the notary that it was his will to lead the expedition overland in search of this wealthy province.

Cabeza de Vaca immediately objected, "The pilots are neither sure of where to go, nor can they agree on anything, nor do they have any idea where they are . . . We have no interpreters, yet we will be going into territories about which we know nothing. We should embark again and go in search of a harbor and lands better suited to settlement."[26]

"No!" cried Brother Suárez, sick and terrified of the seas.[27]

One by one, the other officers fell into line, and when Cabeza de Vaca had his objection notarized, Narváez rounded on him angrily: "If you are so against this overland expedition and so frightened, stay here and take charge of the ships!"[28]

"I am quite sure that you will never see the ships again," replied Cabeza de Vaca. "But I would rather risk the dangers you and the others will face than be called a coward and have my good name sullied."[29] Family honor and public *reputación* were more valuable currencies than even gold in the world of the conquistadors.

Narváez resolved the disagreement among the pilots by ordering Miruelo to take a maneuverable brigantine and a hundred men and the few women-folk, scout the coast to the south for the Bay of the Holy Spirit, then return to Cuba for reinforcements and supplies. Miruelo may have known the Gulf Coast better than anyone else, but Narváez preferred to silence his dissent. Narváez sent the other pilots north with the remaining ships and their crews and with instructions to find the bay they believed lay in that direction and wait for him there. Then, the same day, he led three hundred adventurers into the unknown, each man carrying a pound of bread and half a pound of cured ham as his daily ration.

"It seems that Time always settles his account with men who are not satis-fied with an honest lot," moralized Oviedo in his official account of the expe-dition. "If only Narváez had been content to live as a gentleman of reputation with an honest and noble wife, blessed by God with children and sufficient estate, he would never have gone looking for further trouble."[30]

But no great conquistador could be expected to find contentment like a Historian Royal, surrounded by stories and the smell of ink and paper, cosseted by the creature comforts of home.

Narváez never saw his ships again. He sent Cabeza de Vaca and Alonso del Castillo on a reconnaissance of the coast, but all they found were shallows and oyster beds. Narváez's expedition slowly ran out of food during their march across Florida, for the few Indians they encountered were hostile. They were given hope by a *cacique* who at first seemed to be a giant, but was in fact being carried on the shoulders of a man entirely covered by a finely decorated hide. At first, he approached offering an alliance for an attack on Apalache, but when night fell, his men shot arrows at one of the Spaniards, and any idea of a compact was abandoned. A cavalryman and his horse were drowned in a fast-flowing river, and "there were many who feasted on the horse that night," Cabeza de Vaca remembered.[31] As yet, no one was hungry enough to eat the cadaver of its rider.

The Spaniards continued through a frightening, phantasmagoric land-scape of towering pines, many rent apart by lightning bolts, and fallen trees rotting in fetid swamps. They hungered after the geese, ducks, and partridges and glimpsed deer, bears, and pumas through the undergrowth, but strangely, they made no report of seeing alligators.

Finally, on June 25, they reached Apalache, which, Oviedo mocked, "was what they most wanted in the whole world."[32] Instead of a gilded Paradise, they found forty wigwams and a few women and children. They satiated their hunger with the stock of golden corncobs set aside for the winter, but over the following days, they were continually harassed by the Indians, who set fire to some wigwams where the soldiers were sleeping and killed an Aztec aristocrat from Texcoco known as Don Pedro.

Narváez ordered a move to a place called Aute, which some captive Indians told him would have plenty of corn and was eight days' journey away, nestled beside the sea. The promise of food was irresistible. Fearsome Pánfilo de Narváez, the Indian killer with his voice from the tomb, gave the order to retreat. As they waded through a deep lagoon, probably Wakulla Springs, the cavalry fought a pitched battle against Indian archers hidden in the dense forest. Their bows were as thick as a man's arm and six feet long and could propel an arrow clean through a sapling as thick as a man's thigh. The Natives killed one man and a handful of horses. When the Europeans reached Aute, they found that Indians had burned it to the ground.

Sickness struck the starving Spaniards, probably typhoid or amoebic dysentery.[33] Cabeza de Vaca, Dorantes, Castillo, and Esteban scoured the coast in search of a harbor, but found only a shallow sound between the shore and the barrier islands. By then, Narváez felt the illness upon him, too, and gave the order to evacuate the expedition to the coast, his addled brain fixed on escape. A third of his men were so ill that the rest struggled to help them make the short journey to the water's edge, possibly near the mouth of the St. Marks River.[34] Brother Suárez went among them, making the sign of the cross, whispering words of comfort, saying the Lord's Prayer or a Hail Mary.

The cavalry was in a riotous mood. Dorantes, Castillo, and the other noblemen among the officers had to prevent them from deserting. But in the history of the Spanish conquistadors, at their moments of greatest desperation, they often discovered the most audacious and ambitious solutions. Someone suggested building a flotilla of boats and sailing to Pánuco, the most northern outpost on the Gulf Coast of New Spain. No one really believed it might be possible, but the following day one of the men offered to make bellows. They built a furnace to melt their stirrups, spurs, and bridles and made nails, hooks, and saws. Every day they butchered a horse for its meat and turned the hides into huge *botas*, the classic wineskins of Spain, to hold drinking water on the voyage. Even the manes and tails were used as caulking and to make ropes.

Brilliant in his delirium, Narváez reined in his rebellious cavalry and inspired such industry from his men that within a couple of months, they had built five twenty-foot longboats. They barely drew six inches above the tranquil surface of the shallow sound when laden with men and supplies, but for seven days the desperate Spaniards maneuvered these vessels through

St. George's Sound and across Apalachicola Bay in the lee of the sandy barrier islands. Finally, they glimpsed the open waters of the Gulf of Mexico somewhere near St. Vincent Sound. Finding a fishing camp, they stole canoes to stabilize their boats and give them extra berth. Bracing themselves, they went to sea.

The little flotilla followed the coast, desperately short of drinking water. Five men died quenching their thirst at a brackish well they dug on a beach. They traded with Indians, who then attacked them. Cabeza de Vaca was wounded in the face during fierce fighting, and Narváez was bashed over the head with a stone. A few days later, the wonderfully named Dorotheo Theodoro, a Greek shipwright, went with an African slave to collect water, never to return. That evening, the powerful current of the Mississippi River, gleaming and glittering by the light of a golden sunset, carried them far from shore, separating the boats.

By the first light of dawn, Cabeza de Vaca made out Narváez's boat near at hand and another in the distance.

"What should we do?" Narváez asked.

"Catch up with the other boat," replied Cabeza de Vaca.

"It is too far out to sea. I shall head for land. And if you want to come, put your men to work rowing!"

Cabeza de Vaca's crew were too sick to keep up, so he called out, "Throw me a line."

"This is no moment for men to command one another. Each must do what he thinks best, for it is every man for himself!"[35]

With that final order, Narváez's once-cherished governorship of Florida became mere jetsam on the winter waves. One evening, on a beach near Matagorda Bay, Texas, he felt too weak to go ashore and fell asleep in the boat. In the dead of night, a freezing north wind blew the pitiful invalid out to sea, never to be heard of again.

CHAPTER 4

AMAZON WOMEN &
CALIFORNIAN DREAMS

BAJA CALIFORNIA

Ye must know that to the right hand of the Indies there was an island called California, hard by the Garden of Eden, inhabited by women of powerful physique who would not permit any men to come among them.

—*LAS SERGAS DE ESPLANDIÁN*, SIXTEENTH-CENTURY
BESTSELLING NOVEL

FERDINAND MAGELLAN MADE HIS FAMOUS first crossing of the Pacific in 1521. When he was killed by islanders in the Philippines, his pilot, Juan Sebastián Elcano, completed the circumnavigation of the globe, landing at Sanlúcar de Barrameda in southern Spain the following year. Hernán Cortés had just written Charles V that "the South Sea is a matter of such importance" that "I have already sent foremen, ship's carpenters, sawyers, blacksmiths, and sailors" to begin building "two caravels for voyages of discovery" to distant lands "and two small brigantines for exploring the coast." He assured his sovereign that "on the basis of what we have been told so far, wonderful things are bound to be discovered... Your Majesty may be certain this will be the greatest service since the discovery of America itself."[1]

Merchants and explorers were convinced a waterway must connect the Pacific with the Atlantic. Mapmakers depicted this cartographic chimera in various ways. It crystallized in the British imagination as the Northwest Passage, while the Spaniards referred to it as the Strait of Anián, after a region of China described by Marco Polo.[2] Charles V commanded Cortés to search for this "strait between the North and the South Seas."[3] When his men failed to find it, Cortés sweetened his next report with the kind of fantasy that American tradition so often sired from the fertile imagery of Old World mythology.

Aztec legend referred to a land in the west called Cihuatlán, "Lady-Land," and Cortés reported stories of an island rich in pearls and gold, inhabited only by women.[4] Since Columbus, Spanish explorers had been haunted by the Ancient Amazons, who had brazenly seduced the Scythian soldiers man by man, "men slayers" who boasted of "throwing javelins and riding horses."[5] Occasionally, reported Cortés, a handful of lucky fellows visited in mating season, but all the boy babes born of those liaisons were murdered at birth. The parallel between Cihuatlán and the Amazons was so obvious that the scribe made note to that effect in the margin of Cortés's report.[6] Years later, Oviedo asked Cortés's bitter enemy Nuño Beltrán de Guzmán about "these women."

"It was just a great big lie to call them Amazons," Guzmán explained. "They do not live without men, and when I went there, I found them all with their husbands."[7]

Cortés and some learned courtiers had read Herodotus's *Histories*, but his men were inspired by the *Deeds of Esplandián*, the continuation of that first bestseller in publishing history, *Amadis of Gaul*.[8] Its pages were filled with magicians, ogres, and princesses, a daring hero, and the extraordinary women who inhabited the Isle of California: "Ye must know that to the right hand of the Indies there was an island called California, hard by the Garden of Eden, inhabited by women of powerful physique who would not permit any men to come among them."[9] Woe betide the ardent youth who dared, for the women fought with an all-consuming courage and were skillful with their golden weapons. They rode into battle astride wild beasts with elephantine ears, tusks skewed heavenward from a grizzly grin, and a single eye that reflected back all that it saw. Sometimes, they mixed amorously with the terrified men of the surrounding islands. Then they murdered them and fed their flesh to the fledglings of the fearsome griffins that flew in their island skies. Thus, they trained these ghastly birds of prey, half-lion, half-eagle, to do their bidding and taught them a taste for human flesh.

Such were the Californian Amazon girls of the conquistadors' imaginations.

Cortés began building ships on the Pacific coast, while at México-Tenochtitlán rival Spaniards vied for power and seething Mexica aristocrats longed to restore the old Aztec order. When a trusted captain, Cristobál de Olid, asserted his independent rule over Honduras, Cortés took the momentous decision to march an enormous army overland to suppress this rebellion. As he explained, in addition to the hundreds of potential Spanish troublemakers he enlisted, he "also took all the most important natives," to prevent them from rising up in his absence.[10] One Aztec historian claimed that Cortés took twenty thousand Mexica troops.[11] The expedition was, perhaps, as much a traditional Mexica campaign for imperial glory as it was a Spanish mission to punish Cristobál de Olid for his treachery.

Even Cortés, as he wrote his report to crown, was unable to disguise the trauma of trying to lead thousands of soldiers and their camp followers through the tropical swamps, jungles, and mountains of Tabasco, Chiapas, and the Laguna del Tigre, before dropping down to the coast through Columbia Forest in modern Belize.[12] In the heart of the jungle, he relied on the Mexica troops to enforce discipline among riotous Spaniards, who retaliated by accusing the Mexica of sedition. Overwhelmed by paranoia, Cortés summarily hanged the last Mexica ruler of the Aztec world, Cuauhtémoc, then took as a concubine his beautiful young wife Ichcaxóchitl, or "Cottonflower," one of Montezuma's daughters. Many Spaniards were outraged, and one veteran captain claimed, "All of us who went on the expedition thought it an utterly unjust and evil act."[13] Yet, on his return to México-Tenochtitlán, Cortés gave Cottonflower the *encomienda* of Tacuba, the richest estate in the Valley of Mexico. Soon afterward, she bore him a baby girl, who was baptized Leonor Cortés Montezuma.[14] Twenty-two years later, this quintessentially Spanish-Mexican aristocrat married into the tight-knit Basque oligarchy that had grown fabulously rich mining the silver fields of Zacatecas. In 1598, her grandson would be the youngest conquistador to take part in the conquest and settlement of New Mexico under the command of her son-in-law, Juan de Oñate.

The great expedition to Honduras succeeded in suppressing the rebellion, and Olid was reportedly beheaded by his own men.[15] But the cost was enormous, and during Cortés's absence, open hostilities had broken out at México-Tenochtitlán between the men who had arrived with Narváez and Cortés's original conquistadors.[16] As reports of anarchy and chaos reached Spain, Charles V decided to appoint Nuño Beltrán de Guzmán as the president of a new Audiencia of Mexico that would govern New Spain. Guzmán had become rich rounding up Indians and selling them as slaves to landowners across the Caribbean while he was Governor of Pánuco, the northern outpost on the distant reaches of the Gulf Coast, which Álvar Núñez Cabeza de Vaca and the other survivors of Narváez's expedition to *La Florida* were hoping to reach on their makeshift boats. To prevent Cortés from challenging the authority of Guzmán and the new Audiencia, Charles V summoned him to Spain to "discuss in person, the important matters you raised" relating to the South Seas.[17]

Charles had already sent two fleets through the Magellan Strait, but one of the ships had been wrecked and the survivors were thought to be marooned in the Spice Islands.[18] He ordered Cortés to send an expedition to search for them. Three ships set sail, ominously enough on Halloween 1527. A fortnight out of port, according to one of the sailors, they sighted an island in the middle of the ocean and tried to reach it. It has been suggested that this was the first recorded sighting of Hawaii by a European, although according to the commander's log, they merely saw flocks of birds and other signs of land.[19] However, soon after, two of their vessels disappeared into a rainy night.

There is an old Hawaiian tradition that says that about that time a foreign ship was wrecked on South Kona. The two survivors, the captain and his wife, became part of the community, and one of their descendants became the Governor of Kauai.[20] As one Hawaiian historian so aptly put it long ago, "It really is a magnificent field to let one's imagination run loose."[21] It is perhaps almost as incredible that the lone remaining vessel managed to cross the ocean and rescued the castaways from the Spice Islands.

Nuño Beltrán de Guzmán was a "natural gangster" who had flourished in the wilds of Pánuco, but his simplistic policies of violence and favoritism quickly made him powerful enemies in México-Tenochtitlán.[22] His most implacable adversary was the first Bishop of Mexico, Juan de Zumárraga, a tough Franciscan from the mountains of the Basque country, who was perhaps the most influential politician in New Spain. Faced with such formidable opposition, in the final weeks of 1529 Guzmán mustered an army of thugs and cutthroats and fled the capital, determined to establish an independent fiefdom of his own. He tortured to death the Aztec ruler of Michoacán, Calzontzín, because he could not tell Guzmán where to find a cache of treasure that did not exist. Guzmán continued across Jalisco and staked his claim to all lands to the north and along the coast of the Gulf of California, a swath of territory he pretentiously called Greater Spain in his formal petition to the emperor to be appointed its governor.

Crown officials made him governor, but renamed the province New Galicia. He established his capital at Compostela, named for the capital of Old Galicia, where, according to medieval legend, the patron saint of Spain, Santiago, James the Great, was buried. Guzmán granted *encomiendas* of Indians to his followers. Meanwhile, his enemies back in México-Tenochtitlán moved to indict him for his crimes.

Cortés had landed at Seville in the spring of 1528. Orange blossom and jasmine scented the languid afternoons, but the conqueror and his entourage of Aztec and Tlaxcalan aristocrats, Indian jugglers, and acrobats soon took the road to Toledo for their audience with the emperor. Charles feted this potentially overmighty subject, ennobling Cortés as the Marquis of the Valley of Oaxaca, appointing him Captain General of New Spain, and marrying him to one of the most desirable brides in all Europe, Juana de Zúñiga.

But when Cortés and his bride returned to México-Tenochtitlán two years later, unimaginably rich and successful, as his glittering caravan wended its way through a landscape he himself had conquered as much by luck as judgment, Cortés ached with disappointment. For all the glory and wealth, for all that Charles had feted him so royally, he returned as neither governor nor viceroy. The emperor had rewarded Cortés's daring conquest of a distant empire with nothing but pomp and splendor and more hard work, a royal contract to "discover, conquer, and settle any island in the South Sea lying within the jurisdiction of New Spain and all those thou mayst find toward the sunset."[23]

The Sirens were singing again. Once more the great conqueror could move across a foreign land in search of nothing and everything. Cortés had the liberty to dream and, as one cynical observer put it, should his dreams come true, then "all in good time, the crown could worry about how to appropriate them for itself."[24]

In 1532, Cortés sent two ships under the command of his cousin Diego Hurtado de Mendoza to explore the coast north of México-Tenochtitlán, with strict instructions to avoid conflict, both with Indians and with Guzmán. His real goal was to test the widely favored theory that a few hundred miles north, near the entrance to the Strait of Anián, the coast ran due west to China.[25]

The voyage was a disaster. First, Guzmán's gunners fired on the ships, then the crew of one ship mutinied and headed home. When they put into port somewhere near modern Puerto Vallarta, most of the Europeans were massacred by Indians. Two men were rescued by Guzmán, who then filed a complaint against Cortés for infringement of his jurisdiction. Meanwhile, Diego Hurtado de Mendoza continued up the coast with the other ship and "was never heard of again."[26]

The following fall, Cortés again sent two ships to search for Pacific islands. On Halloween, a howling gale separated the two vessels. One sailed west to tiny Socorro, four hundred miles off the Mexican coast, where the crew saw "a merman, which surfaced to look at the ship," "frolicking like an ape," and exchanging glances with the sailors "as though it were intelligent." The official report included two sketches of a creature that looks a lot like a sea lion.[27] The other ship coasted north in search of Hurtado de Mendoza, but within a month the crew mutinied under the leadership of the chief pilot, a Basque called, ironically enough, Fortún Jiménez. With promises of fortunes to be had on islands filled with gold and pearls, the Basque enticed many of his countrymen to rebel.[28] They murdered their sleeping commander in the dead of night, forced the friars and the soldiers ashore near Colima, and continued their voyage with the Fates in their sails and each man brimming with unbridled hope.[29] Within days, the lookouts spied a vast landmass. They were the first Europeans to see Baja California.

Fortún anchored in the sweep of a large bay, and his band of Basque brothers went ashore at modern La Paz. Suddenly, an army of Guaycura or Pericúe Indians attacked, slaughtering them as the horrified sailors who had remained aboard ship helplessly watched from the deck. They weighed anchor and went back across the Gulf of California to seek the protection of Guzmán, telling him they had seen a land rich in gold and pearls the size of hen's eggs. Two other men survived the massacre on the beach and reached New Galicia in the longboat. Guzmán interrogated them under torture and learned the truth: they had seen nothing but a "barren land and a few beastly people."[30] Nonetheless, Guzmán sent an expedition to establish a bridgehead on the newly discovered territory, claiming it as his own discovery.

The Audiencia of Mexico ordered Cortés to stay away, which so infuriated the great conquistador that he pawned his estates and his wife's jewels and announced that he was going in person to pacify and settle the new territory that he believed was rightly his.[31] "As soon as it was known in New Spain that Cortés was going to lead the expedition in person, nobody doubted but that it would turn out well," remembered Bernal Díaz.[32]

Juan Garrido was among the recruits, the free black conquistador of Puerto Rico, probably the first African to set foot in Florida. He had been close to Cortés since the conquest of Mexico and became a citizen of México-Tenochtitlán, serving as the doorkeeper of the Audiencia and caretaker of the aqueduct. Cortés once sent him as an envoy to Calzontzin, the ruler of Michoacán, who was subsequently tortured and murdered by Guzmán.[33] Garrido later returned to Michoacán, possibly with Guzmán, hoping to establish a gold mine, which failed.[34]

Cortés announced that he would march his three or four hundred soldiers, their fifty-odd wives, and an unspecified number of Indian auxiliaries through Guzmán's fiefdom of New Galicia to rendezvous with the ships in Sinaloa. It was an awesome display of arrogance, and on February 24, 1535, Cortés swaggered into the small town of Ixtlán, where Guzmán's agents served notice on him to desist from trespass. Cortés responded by leading his expedition deeper into his rival's territory. The following day he asserted his right as Captain General of New Spain to travel through any land held in the name of the crown.[35] Then he rode roughshod over every inch of Guzmán's putrid pride.[36]

Cortés's triumphant caravan reached Chametla in April and he sailed immediately.[37] A fortnight later, on May 3, the Day of the Holy Cross, he disembarked in the crook of the sweeping harbor where Fortún and his cronies had been killed, taking possession of the land. He called it Santa Cruz Bay, but made no mention of California.[38] The parched land was sandy and overgrown with "thistles" so thorny the horses refused to tread on them. "There was nothing to eat," one vituperative survivor complained acerbically, "except for a kind of a pear we found growing on very prickly bushes and some peas a bit like lentils." There was not even grass for the horses, although they found a few puddles to drink from. The local population were few in number, the men went naked, the women wore grass skirts, and they shamelessly copulated in public whenever moved by the urge to do so. "The men took the women from behind like animals." One of the Tlaxcalans was so horrified when he saw California that he hanged himself there and then. A hardened Spaniard simply called it the "worst place in the world."[39]

Cortés sent two ships to collect more supplies, with a note referring to plenty of fish and an abundance of pearls.[40] In reality, his men became so weak that when Indians attacked, they easily killed countless Mexica and Tlaxcalan allies, some Africans, and seven Spanish soldiers. Many "began to openly curse Cortés and his island."[41] Determined to save his colony, he took the remaining ship and went for help. Instead, he came across one of the ships he had sent for supplies, lost in a maze of reefs and shallows. Later he found the other ship lying on a sandbank, its masts broken, its sails lost. The hull was full of rotten food, and the fetid atmosphere belowdecks was so bad that "the eyes of the men who went inside swelled up and they could not see."[42] When Cortés finally returned to Santa Cruz with supplies, the surviving colonists had been reduced to eating weeds. They fell upon the rations he brought so ravenously that their stomachs swelled up and five of them died. The colony clearly had no future, and when a ship brought news that the new viceroy, Antonio de Mendoza, had arrived in México-Tenochtitlán, Cortés abandoned Santa Cruz. Years later, Bernal Díaz claimed that Cortés had christened his godforsaken land California, but the first use of the name remains a mystery.[43]

Returning to the mainland, Cortés learned that all of New Spain was alive with news of his distant cousin an illiterate swineherd called Francisco Pizarro. He had conquered an empire in the south even greater than Aztec Mexico, one that had been ruled by a powerful dynasty called the Incas. No one was interested in California anymore; everyone wanted to go to Peru.

CHAPTER 5

"NAKED AND BAREFOOT"

THE CONTINENT CROSSED

I cannot describe all the many miracles which they recounted about their journey, for those would need a whole book to themselves.
—MATÍAS DE LA MOTA Y PADILLA, EIGHTEENTH-CENTURY HISTORIAN

NUÑO BELTRÁN DE GUZMÁN treated New Galicia as a limitless wilderness in which to hunt and harvest Indian slaves. His followers quickly stripped the land of people, and thousands more fled into the bush and the hills. These once-prosperous valleys of the western seaboard were deserted, the *encomiendas* became impoverished, and bands of Indians filled with hatred and vengeance harried Spaniards on the farms and roads. One crown official reported that Guzmán's colonists "lived every aspect of their lives like men without reason," as though they were savages or animals.[1]

In March 1536, a posse of his most brutal henchmen rode out of the isolated frontier post at Culiacán, raiding for slaves farther north than they had ever been before. They lost their way on one of the Indian trails that cut through the dense chaparral of northern Sinaloa and led out into the Sonoran Desert, with its stands of saguaro.[2] A ruffian called Cebreros pushed on ahead with three other men.

Suddenly, a dozen Indians emerged from the thorny vegetation that overhung the trail in places to form a forbidding tunnel. The Spaniards drew their swords, but two strange figures stepped toward them. One was burned brilliant black by tropical sunshine. He wore a feather headdress and had bells tied to his arms and his legs, and he carried a beautifully decorated gourd, a sacred rattle from the unknown north. The other, tanned golden brown, his long hair and beard bleached blond, cried out in perfect Spanish, "Thanks be to God, thanks be to God!"

The slavers were struck dumb in astonishment. The blond man introduced himself as Álvar Núñez Cabeza de Vaca, royal treasurer of Pánfilo de Narváez's expedition to Florida. The other man, he explained, was an African slave called Esteban. Their two companions, called Andrés Dorantes and Alonso del Castillo, were waiting farther back along the trail. Cebreros escorted these two miraculous travelers and their Indian companions to his immediate superior, another ruthless chancer called Diego de Alcaraz.[3]

Cabeza de Vaca then began to tell his extraordinary story for the first time. The four survivors would tell this tale again and again over the coming months and years, learning how to develop it, always editing, always refining it. Cebreros and Alcaraz no doubt listened with a growing sense of disbelief, for as one skeptical eighteenth-century historian remarked, "I cannot describe all the many miracles which they recounted about their journey, for those would need a whole book to themselves."[4] But five days later, that cynicism gave way to wonder when Esteban and his companions appeared with a throng of six hundred Indian followers and their families, many of whom had come with them from far away.

An ugly altercation ensued when the four survivors refused to allow Alcaraz and his men to chain up the Indians. According to Cabeza de Vaca, Alcaraz ordered "his interpreter to tell the Indians that we were Spaniards just like them," but while "we were hapless and unimportant," Alcaraz and his men "were lords of the land." But the Indians laughed at him and replied with laconic irony that as far as they could see "we had come from where the sun rises, while" he "came from where it sets. We healed the sick, while they murdered the healthy. We were naked and barefoot, but they wore clothes and rode horses."[5] Alcaraz put the four survivors under armed guard and ordered Cebreros to escort them to Culiacán.

The Alcalde of Culiacán, Melchior Díaz, was a good man by contrast with the hoodlums around him, and he wept as he embraced the four survivors. Over the following days, he watched awestruck as they sent messengers into the hinterland carrying sacred gourds as a sign of peace, persuading thousands of refugees who had fled to the hills to return to their lands and rebuild their villages.

During the fortnight the four men spent at Culiacán, Cabeza de Vaca, as royal treasurer, took the lead in giving a formal account of the failure of Narváez's leadership, the collapse of the expedition, and their extraordinary survival. That first report was written down but mislaid long ago, perhaps still remaining undiscovered in an archive in Guadalajara.[6] But we know they must have told Díaz about Narváez's ill-conceived plan to march inland, how golden Apalache turned out to be a bunch of huts, and how they built boats on the coast of Florida. They also explained their remarkable appearance after an absence of eight years and their extraordinary influence over the Indians, telling Díaz how they had traveled across Texas and the Sierra Madre by becoming shamans and performing incredible miracles, curing the sick and the blind, even raising a man from the dead. Thus, God himself had delivered them home.

Rumors of their seemingly impossible adventures quickly spread across the empire, fascinating and enchanting everyone from the emperor and his courtiers to ordinary sailors and shopkeepers. The sober German who governed Venezuela on behalf of Charles V's notorious bankers, the Welser family, wrote his employers, "*Es ist ein wunderlich Ding*, which, take it from me, you must not think is a Fable."[7]

A sensational narrative of the four men's adventures was ostensibly written by Cabeza de Vaca and published at Zamora, Spain, in 1542, as *The Account Given by Álvar Núñez*. In 1555, he had it republished as the *Shipwrecks and Commentaries*, bound together with a report on his conduct while Governor of the Río de la Plata, "the River Plate," in modern Argentina, and it has been known as *Shipwrecks* ever since. Although based on a version of the official testimony the survivors gave in México-Tenochtitlán to the Audiencia in 1536, Cabeza de Vaca extensively reworked the material to present himself in the best possible light as part of a petition made to Charles V the following year to be appointed Governor of Florida. When, instead, he was sent to Río de la Plata, he left the manuscript with his publishers, who appear to have made further significant editorial changes while he was in South America.

The Historian Royal Gonzalo Fernández de Oviedo also wrote a long, less well-known account of the expedition in his *General History of the Indies*, the first important book written about the Americas. Oviedo clearly had access to a different source that was much closer than *Shipwrecks* to the official testimony the survivors of Narváez's disastrous expedition gave in México-Tenochtitlán. But that source was also reworked to some extent before Oviedo saw it, almost certainly by Andrés Dorantes when he also went to Spain to petition the emperor and was rewarded with an *encomienda* in New Spain.

The stories told in these two published accounts are essentially the same but with very significant variations. As a result, while the story itself is a thrilling tale of tribulation and redemption, of Christian magic and heart-warming humanity, well worth the telling, a careful comparison of *Shipwrecks* and Oviedo reveals how history is manipulated and distorted from the moment it is first reported and written down.

The story of how two versions of the same history came into existence and the political forces and personal motives that molded them began when the four survivors crested the purple pass between the Mexican hills and saw the great lake of Texcoco below them crowded with Indian canoes, smoke rising from the chimneys of the great island city, its causeways alive with traffic. In the dry, thin air they saw the vast volcanoes of Popocatépetl and Iztaccihuatl in the distance. They came into the city along the road through Tlatelolco, where Juan Garrido had his gardens, and passed the Church of San Hipólito, hastily erected to celebrate the Spanish conquest.

They were debriefed in private by the two most powerful men in México-Tenochtitlán, the pious and resolute Bishop Juan de Zumárraga, who had forced Guzmán to flee the capital, and the newly arrived Viceroy Antonio de Mendoza, who was a member of one of the most powerful aristocratic families in Castile. Mendoza had been born at the hilltop castle of Alcalá la Real, on the front line of the last great campaign against the Muslims of Granada. Following the final victory in 1492, his father was appointed Alcalde of the Alhambra, the gorgeous palatine fortress of the Nasrid sultans, where Antonio was raised in the bosom of the tiny Christian elite that had conquered and now governed the vanquished populace of the last Islamic kingdom in Western Europe.[8] It was an excellent education for the future viceroy of colonial New Spain.

Mendoza had struck up a close collaboration, even friendship, with Bishop Zumárraga. Together, they encouraged and cajoled the four witnesses to describe in damning detail the crimes they had seen committed by Guzmán and his men against the Indians of New Galicia. They encouraged them to contrast that brutality with their own story of Christian salvation and peaceful proselytizing among a vast new flock of lambs awaiting the ministry of the Church. Once debriefed, the men were formally deposed by the Audiencia, first Cabeza de Vaca, then Dorantes, Castillo, and apparently Esteban as well, even though he was a slave.

The survivors excited the claustrophobic community of conquistadors in México-Tenochtitlán, eager for tales of adventure and the promise of this Tierra Nueva, the "New Country," populated by compliant Indians. They were also paraded in the cathedral, dressed in furs and holding the accoutrements of their Native American shamanism, during the great Feast of Saint James, patron saint of Spain.

This was not, however, a mere curiosity, a kind of freak show, but a seminal moment in the orchestrated presentation of Cabeza de Vaca and his companions as almost perfect examples of a new kind of conquistador. Bartolomé de las Casas's loud and controversially polemical discourse about the enslavement and inhuman treatment of Indians had stimulated political debate across Europe about the moral and legal obligations of empire.

The following year, 1537, when Cabeza de Vaca landed in Spain with his petition to the emperor for the governorship of Florida, he found the imperial court alive with news that the Vatican had issued the papal bull *Sublimis Deus*, "From God on High." Two months earlier, Pope Paul III declared that the "Devil himself" was responsible for those who "publish abroad that the Indians . . . should be treated as dumb brutes created for our service, pretending that they are incapable of receiving the Catholic Faith." Instead, he stated, "The said Indians and all other people who may later be discovered by Christians, are by no means to be deprived of their liberty or the possession of their property, even though they be outside the Faith of Jesus Christ; and that they may and should, freely and legitimately, enjoy their liberty and the possession of their property; nor should they be in any way enslaved."[9]

One of the most brilliant intellectuals of the age, Francisco de Vitoria, turned his formidable mind to the core questions raised by imperialism and indigenous peoples. In a series of lectures given at the University of Salamanca, *On the Indians* and *On the Laws of War*, he laid out rules to govern colonial engagement and established the enduring principles of international law that later influenced James Brown Scott and the Hague Convention of 1907.[10] Vitoria founded his discussion on the concept of Natural Law, the *ius naturae*, which had originated with Aristotle, but which the great medieval theologian Thomas Aquinas had defined as a universal ethical essence with which God had imbued all humanity at the time of the Creation.

Aristotle, however, had stated that humanity was divided into Natural Masters, characterized by their capacity to reason, and Natural Slaves, a category of amiable simpletons who could only understand reason when it was explained to them. That category included women, children, and almost anyone who was not Greek.

Most commentators took these definitions at face value, and it had long seemed obvious to many Europeans that Native Americans must be Natural Slaves. Therefore, because slaves had no rights of property, it must be legitimate to appropriate their wealth and land, as well as their labor. Vitoria argued that the evident political sophistication of the Aztecs and the Incas showed Native Americans were just like Europeans, with governments, laws, customs concerning marriage, trade, the ownership of property, and wars and compacts between their different states.

Vitoria argued that the Indians were rational and so could not be enslaved, nor could their property be lawfully appropriated. Furthermore, they had occupied their lands before the arrival of the Spaniards, which meant they had *dominium* over them; only where the Spaniards encountered genuine wilderness could they claim possession according to the Doctrine of First Discovery. Vitoria then turned to the charge that the Indians had not been baptized and were therefore pagans living in sin, whereby they forfeited *dominium*. Baptism, he said, was irrelevant because infidels such as Jews and Muslims were considered to have *dominium* over their lands and property, and the same rules must be applied universally across all nations.[11]

Vitoria ended his lecture series with a discussion of the how the Spaniards might legitimately claim title over the Indians. Most obviously, he tried to define a theory of Just War by applying humanitarian principles of intervention to prevent harm; for example, when tyrants imposed evil customs on their subjects, such as human sacrifice or cannibalism. During a Just War, he argued, it was legitimate to recover the reasonable costs of the campaign, to destroy fortifications as a preventive measure, and to enslave enemy prisoners.[12] But he also asserted that sovereigns had an obligation under the Law of Nations "to behave hospitably to strangers," and on that basis, he asserted the Spanish Crown might legitimately enforce the rights of its subjects to travel, trade, reside, and even to preach the gospel in peace across the New World.[13]

Cabeza de Vaca had returned to Europe at the beginning of a pivotal period in the ethical history of the Spanish Empire. In 1542, Charles V would attempt to abolish the *encomienda*, and then, in the 1550s, he would officially suspend all campaigning in the Americas while a committee of experts heard evidence on the legality of his subjects' imperial enterprise in the New World.

The new politics of colonialism idealized empire as God's holy mission to peacefully carry out the Christian conquest of Indian souls through preaching and evangelization. Cabeza de Vaca well understood the importance of making his account of the Narváez expedition fit the new paradigm as closely as possible, and so the story told in *Shipwrecks* is steeped in the moral sensibilities of the moment.

In the fall of 1528, when Pánfilo de Narváez abdicated his command and was then blown out to sea never to be seen again, a violent storm had battered the five little boats as they struggled westward, desperately hoping they might reach Pánuco. Cabeza de Vaca reported to the world how he took the tiller of his craft and gazed in anguish at the unconscious men slumped upon one another, awaiting the Fates. "I would that Death had taken me then, that I might not see so many men in such a state," he wrote, but before first light they heard the sound of breakers rolling, and a great wave picked up the boat and flung it onto a beach at Galveston Island. Dorantes, Castillo, Esteban, and forty other men soon appeared. They, too, had lost almost everything when their boat had been tossed onto the Texas shore. There was no news of the other three boats.

The Karankawa Indians were friendly, but their enormous stature terrified the emaciated Spaniards. "I am not sure if they were really very large people, or if our fear made them seem like giants," Cabeza de Vaca wrote. In fact, they had been among the first migrants to cross the frozen Bering Strait fourteen thousand years ago, an isolated tribe who were described by the nineteenth-century settlers who harassed them to extinction as "very tall" and "magnificently formed," with large heads and "splendid white teeth."[14] The Karankawa built shelters for their guests and gave them food, but then the sickness that had afflicted the Spaniards at the Bay of Horses struck again. The deadly contagion hit the Indians so hard that many favored putting all the Spaniards to death until one man persuaded his companions to spare the strangers, pointing out that they, too, were suffering from the disease.

Shipwrecks reports that the Spaniards called the island Malhado, the "Isle of Misfortune," but Oviedo noted that in the report he had read "they did not call it so." In fact, Cabeza de Vaca or his editors had borrowed the name Malhado from an island described in a successful novel of chivalry, *Palmerín de Oliva*, and Oviedo complained that "nor should they have called it Malhado . . . for those Christians were well treated there."[15] But for Cabeza de Vaca, the Christian suffering of the Spaniards was an essential precursor to his eventual redemption.

Moreover, that minor embellishment heralds more important editorial interventions. Cabeza de Vaca claimed that at Malhado, the Karankawas "tried to turn us into doctors, without making us sit any examinations nor asking for our qualifications." "We laughed," he wrote, "but they stopped feeding us until we did as we were told." This is the first time that the famous faith-healing miracles are referred to in *Shipwrecks*. Cabeza de Vaca emphasized the Christian nature of those cures, describing how they healed the sick by "making the sign of the cross and whispering the Lord's Prayer and a Hail Mary."[16] Many readers would have recognized the parallel with Acts 28:8–10, in which Saint Paul cured the father of Publius of a similar disease on an island called Melita, a name not dissimilar to Malhado.[17]

Oviedo, however, makes no reference to the role of the survivors as physicians while they were on Galveston. Instead, in a passage so similar that it must derive from the same original text, he described how they first became shamans and faith healers six years later in a location much farther west, not far from the Rio Grande.[18] Moreover, *Shipwrecks* makes no further mention of faith healing or miracle cures until that same point in the story, six years later. Clearly, Cabeza de Vaca or his editors moved those events forward in their telling of the tale for rhetorical and literary effect. In reality, during that awful winter, Cabeza de Vaca had become separated from the other Spaniards. "I was elsewhere on the mainland," he explained, "where I was so very ill I thought I would die," until "I became a merchant . . . going far inland to trade sea shells for animal pelts and tallow."[19] He would not see the other Spaniards again for five years.

In April 1529, Andrés Dorantes, his cousins Valdivieso and Diego Dorantes, his slave Esteban, Alonso del Castillo, and eight companions began to make their way on foot along the coast toward Pánuco, living on crayfish and seaweed, struggling across swollen rivers. They were typical of the kind of close-knit group of relatives and acquaintances with parochial regional ties who, like Juan González Ponce de León and his entourage, were the building blocks of empire.

Near Aransas Pass, at Matagorda Bay, they came across a lone survivor from one of the other boats, who told them that Captain Pantoja had been murdered and that the governor had been lost at sea, all of which, the man explained, he had learned from Esquivel, who had survived by eating the dead. Suddenly, a band of aggressive Indians appeared, and while Castillo and two other men managed to flee westward, the Indians captured Dorantes, his cousin Diego, and Esteban. For some reason, three days later they let them go. But over the coming days, the Indians began to pick off the survivors one by one, until only Dorantes, Esteban, and Castillo remained alive.

"The Indians enslaved them," Oviedo wrote, "treating them more cruelly than would a Moor, making them carry loads of wood and water and everything else the Indians needed *from their flesh*."[20] Intriguingly, *Shipwrecks* notes that the Indian women usually carried the water, which suggests the captives were at least in part made to do women's work.[21] Moreover, the Moors had such a reputation as "sodomites" among Europeans during this period that it was widely believed anyone captured as a slave by North African pirates would almost certainly be violated. Although the Spanish phrase *a raiz de las carnes* most obviously means "manual labor," Oviedo seems to have been hinting at an alternative interpretation. Indeed, Cabeza de Vaca's description of the Native American practice of *berdache* may shed further light on the suggestion that the captives were forced to adopt the role of women: "I saw the devil's work of one man being married to another," he told horrified readers, "effeminate, weak men, who go about dressed like women and do women's work, carrying heavy loads." Did the Spanish survivors have to become *berdaches* to survive?[22]

The four survivors were reunited in the spring of 1533. The following year, they abandoned the Karankawa during the annual pecan harvest. They pushed deep into the forest of chaparral and prickly pears, and as the golden October sun began to set in the distant west, according to Oviedo, they came across "the kind of very timid Indians they had longed for."[23] Oviedo's account presents this important decision to leave the Karankawa as a joint enterprise in which Dorantes was the primary protagonist and Esteban proved the most valuable leader on the trail, but in *Shipwrecks*, Cabeza de Vaca comes across as a savior who delivers his companions from their bondage "that dare not speak its name."[24]

The following summer, 1535, only nine months or so before the survivors encountered Cebreros in northern Sinaloa, they moved on. Somewhere near the Nueces River, they came across a large group of Indians living in forty or fifty tepees.

"And that was where the Indians first began to fear and revere these few Christians and hold them in high esteem," explained Oviedo. The Indians "approached and signaled for the Christians to rub them and stroke them and make them better. They brought their sick to be cured and the Christians did so by making the sign of the cross and whispering to them like faith-healers in Castile. Although they were more used to suffering tribulations than performing miracles."[25] Intriguingly, according to *Shipwrecks*, the sick prospective patients approached only Castillo with requests to cure them. From there, according to Oviedo, the survivors traveled west and cured the sick among another group of Indians, who celebrated a night dance in their honor. In the morning, some women led them to a great river, almost certainly the Rio Grande.

Shipwrecks, by contrast, presents this journey across West Texas as a magical world of fantasy and fiction in which Cabeza de Vaca took center stage. He was transformed from heroic royal treasurer to a Christlike American messiah, performing the works of the Lord among innocent Indians when he lost his way in the thickly wooded country around modern San Antonio. Night fell but he was not alone, for God guided him to "a burning tree," so he could spend "the cold night by its fire." For five hungry days and nights, Cabeza de Vaca suffered alone. Each night he dug a pit and lit "four fires in the form of a cross" to save himself from the winter winds. "When I found myself in such straits," he wrote, "I had no other comfort than to think of the Passion of Jesus Christ Our Redeemer and the blood he shed for me and I contemplated how greater torment was the crown of thorns than my own suffering."[26] It was the kind of basic Christian metaphor that men such as Las Casas and Zumárraga knew would resonate with a broad audience in Europe and America.

No sooner was Cabeza de Vaca reunited with his companions than envoys arrived from the warlike Susola tribe and asked Castillo to heal some sick people, including one man at death's door. But Cabeza de Vaca told his readers that Castillo "was a very nervous physician, especially when the cures were dangerous to perform."[27] So the Indians turned to Cabeza de Vaca instead, he explained.

As Cabeza de Vaca was telling his story, someone, perhaps Charles V or some skeptical member of the Audiencia, must have asked him why the Indians suddenly turned to him. He said it was because "they remembered that I had healed the sick" at the Nueces River. Yet neither *Shipwrecks* nor Oviedo mentioned those earlier feats of medicine being performed by anyone other than Castillo. Cabeza de Vaca covered up his lie by moving on with his story: "I had to go with them and Dorantes and Esteban came along."

They reached the camp and found the patient, "who was dead," or so Cabeza de Vaca claimed. His eyes had rolled back in their sockets, he had no pulse; he showed "every sign of being dead." Dorantes supposedly confirmed he was lifeless, but Cabeza de Vaca tried to cure him anyway, making the sign of the cross, whispering prayers, and blowing over the man's body again and again. That night, some Indian messengers reported that a miracle had happened and the dead man was walking, talking, and eating.

In *Shipwrecks*, Cabeza de Vaca's miraculous raising of a man from the dead just as Christ resuscitated Lazarus is presented as the true catalyst to their success as medicine men. Castillo's seminal role is briefly and almost grudgingly acknowledged, only for his character to be ruthlessly assassinated. Cabeza de Vaca tried to leave no doubt who should get the credit: "Dorantes and the black man had not healed anyone up until then," he explained with striking inconsistency. Only thanks to his own brilliance did "so many come from near and far to be cured that we all had to become physicians, although I was always the most respected" among them.[28] Oviedo did not record any of this.

It is plain in *Shipwrecks* that these Native Americans needed a messiah, for the devil was abroad in their land in the form of an apocalyptic apparition called Mala Cosa, "Bad Thing." This demonic creature was said to emerge from time to time from a chasm in the earth and attend Indian dances while brandishing a burning torch. Mala Cosa often slashed at Indians with an enormous flint knife and cut out a short section of their intestines, which he threw in the fire. Then he would lay his hands upon their wounds and heal them. The four survivors explained to the Indians that if they "should believe in Our Lord and become Christians," Mala Cosa "would not dare to come again."[29]

These passages of magical realism in *Shipwrecks* established Cabeza de Vaca as the leader of this band of Christian heralds, the first evangelists in Texas.

In reality, the four survivors crossed the Rio Grande into modern Coahuila, Mexico. Esteban went ahead with the Indian guides, part diplomatic emissary for the survivors, part their leader. As they traveled, one tribal group after another obtained the magic medicine and whatever sacred and spiritual benefits they could from the four strangers, then moved them on. According to *Shipwrecks*, Cabeza de Vaca operated on a warrior with an arrowhead buried deep in his chest, just above his heart. Cabeza de Vaca made an incision with his knife, but the missile was difficult to remove, so he worked the point of the knife under the arrowhead and prized it out. He stitched up the wound with a bone needle, and two days later the man seemed completely cured. This episode of elementary battlefield surgery would be credible except that Oviedo made no mention of it at all.

As the survivors traveled, each group of Indians sent heralds or messengers to arrange for their transfer to their nearest neighbors and extracted handsome payment in trade goods for that exchange. The survivors were worried by the apparent violence with which each group forced the next to pay up, calling them robbers and thieves and trying to make them stop. But the survivors were powerless to do so, for the Indians explained this was the custom: it was what both sides wanted. In effect, the Indians told the outsiders to mind their own business.[30]

In their official testimony, the survivors claimed that they had determined their direction of travel throughout this process of moving from one group to another, but they clearly had only the most limited influence over where they were taken. Pánuco was to the south, yet when they reached the great escarpment of the Sierra Madre, they turned north, away from New Spain, away from European civilization. When, months later, incredulous Spanish officials asked them why, the only reply they could offer was that "they knew only too well what the coastal peoples were all about."[31] They could hardly admit that the Indians had been in charge all along.

As they traveled, they feasted on game and delicious pine nuts. Often they survived on some disgusting vetch called *masarrones*, and as they traversed the high hills, they went hungry. Once they came across an encampment where many inhabitants seemed to be suffering from cataracts. So "they cured all the blind and many other sick people, or at least if the Christians did not cure them all, the Indians believed that they could heal them," Oviedo commented.[32]

They continued north through the pine stands and the barren uplands of the Sierra del Carmen and dropped down to the Rio Grande where it ran through the fine Big Bend country with the cool high hills of the Chisos range and the fiery lowlands with their hot springs and the shaded water in Santa Elena Canyon. Their Coahuilan guides had reached the limits of their world and stubbornly refused to continue north into enemy territory. Cabeza de Vaca claimed that this made him so angry that "I went to spend the night outside our camp, far away from the Indians . . . Strange things began to happen. Many fell ill and eight men died." When more perished, the rest became "certain that we could kill them with our thoughts alone."[33] As a result, the terrified Indians agreed to accompany them farther north. But Oviedo reported that it had been Dorantes who had so effectively manipulated their companions, instilling fear in them by feigning anger.

At Junta de los Rios, the four survivors quarreled seriously for the first time, over whether to follow the Rio Grande north or the Conchos River, which seemed to run west. It is unclear what happened, but Esteban and Castillo abandoned their companions and went with two women to a permanent settlement nearby, where they were well received by the father of one of their guides. After three or four days relaxing and feasting on beans and squash and corn, they went to find Cabeza de Vaca and Dorantes, and all four of them followed the Rio Grande northwest toward El Paso.

They traveled in the company of an ever-changing crowd of curious and reverential followers. They met buffalo hunters who had good hides and pleaded with the Christians to make it rain. Some "weepers" greeted them with a strange welcome ritual of brushing their hair down over their faces and crying. They saw people who boiled water by throwing hot stones from the fire into cooking pots made from dried gourds, and others who seemed to eat nothing but dusty chaff.

Esteban "always spoke to them and asked about the different trails and nations and everything else we needed to know."[34] Somewhere, Esteban was told about large settlements to the north at a place called Cíbola, where people lived in huge permanent buildings, the great settlements that came to be called the Pueblos because they looked like the famous hanging *pueblos*, or "villages," of southern Spain and northern Morocco.

Finally, they swung west through southern New Mexico and Arizona or northern Chihuahua, before heading through the Sonora River valley, which they called the Land of Corn. At Ures they were treated to a feast of six hundred splayed deer hearts. Then they went down to the shores of the Sea of Cortez and their meeting with Cebreros.

Oviedo wrote with disbelieving sarcasm of their long journey across America that it "was such a great miracle, no one could believe it except those who saw it happen."[35] But Zumárraga and Guzmán's other powerful enemies in México-Tenochtitlán were especially interested to know what these four men who had established their credentials as peaceful colonists of Christ had to say about the government of New Galicia. Both *Shipwrecks* and Oviedo's account describe in detail the devastating effects of Nuño de Guzmán's slave raiding. The bush was taking over abandoned fields, and everywhere the survivors saw starving, emaciated figures, refugees in their own lands. "We could see that they had been so terrorized they did not dare settle anywhere," wrote Cabeza de Vaca. "Indeed, they had decided that they preferred to die rather than work the land."[36]

How Bishop Juan de Zumárraga must have smiled as he heard that damning testimony, even as he shed tears for the abused. Guzmán's days as Governor of New Galicia were numbered.

CHAPTER 6

THE SEVEN CITIES
OF CÍBOLA

NEW MEXICO

The chief's representative at Cíbola grew angry and said, "I know what kind of people these are. Tell them not to enter the town or they will all be killed!"

—REPORT OF MARCOS DE NIZA, A FRANCISCAN FRIAR

ACROSS THEIR EMPIRE, Spaniards were intoxicated by the astounding combination of the four Narváez survivors' groundbreaking geographical conquest—the first documented crossing of North America—and the political triumph of their apparently peaceful control over the Indians who lived in Tierra Nueva, the "New Country." By connecting Florida to New Galicia and the Atlantic to the Pacific, they had opened up a plethora of possibilities on the Spaniards' mental map of *La Florida*.

Of particular interest to the more practically minded Spaniards was the news of great oceans of grass, the Great Plains, where the Indians hunted enormous herds of wild cattle. At that very moment, Viceroy Antonio de Mendoza was actively promoting the raising of cattle and sheep across New Spain.[1] But more enticing still in those Spanish minds so susceptible to myths and dreams, the survivors had gilded that glorious landscape with stories about a kingdom in the north called Cíbola, where seven rich cities offered the allure of civilization and mineral wealth. In reality, *cibolo* is a word for "buffalo" in the language of the Zuni people, who, in fact, lived in six thriving settlements along the Zuni River. But the idea of the Seven Cities quickly caught the imagination of the Spaniards because of an ancient legend about seven mythical bishoprics founded on an island in the Atlantic by seven refugee Portuguese churchmen who had fled the Moorish armies as they marauded across the Iberian Peninsula in the Middle Ages.

Viceroy Mendoza saw this glorious Tierra Nueva as an opportunity to simultaneously favor his family and followers, enrich himself, and serve the crown. He began preparing the exploration and settlement of the north. Guzmán was finally arrested and remanded to Spain in 1537, allowing Mendoza to appoint his most trusted lieutenant, Francisco Vázquez de Coronado, as Governor of New Galicia. A family friend and ally from the close-knit Granada nobility, Coronado had cemented his position in México-Tenochtitlán by marrying the daughter of a former royal treasurer who brought as a dowry one of the largest *encomiendas* in New Spain.[2]

Against the backdrop of political and moral pressure opposed to armed incursions into Indian territory, Bishop Zumárraga argued that any expedition to Cíbola should be led by Franciscan friars. He suggested Brother Marcos de Niza, "a fine and zealous man of God, to be trusted for his proven virtue and religious learning," and skilled in the use of navigational instruments. Marcos had befriended Las Casas and denounced Spanish brutality during the conquest of Peru.[3] Zumárraga was also so impressed by the Narváez survivors' peaceful exploits among the Indians that he wanted them to work hand in glove with Marcos.[4]

Mendoza favored a strong military element to any expedition, so he wooed Andrés Dorantes, giving him salaried posts in Puebla and Michoacán, then making him captain of the company of fifty cavalrymen who would blaze a new trail north.[5] "I do not know how the plans for this enterprise fell through," Mendoza lamented in a letter to the king, but Dorantes abandoned the project and instead went to Spain to claim an inheritance and seek favor from the crown.[6] In his stead, he sent his slave Esteban.

Mendoza formally appointed Esteban as Marcos's guide, but in reality put Esteban in command of a small army of Texcocan and Tlaxcalan troops, notionally an armed escort for the friars.[7] So, by a curious turn of the Fates, the first European military incursion into modern Arizona and New Mexico would be led by an African slave in charge of Aztec soldiers.

Thus, Coronado set out to establish control as incoming Governor of New Galicia with his own company of soldiers and the most unlikely crew of conquistadors in the history of Spanish imperialism. At Jalisco, on November 20, 1538, he handed over Mendoza's official royal instructions to Marcos, requiring him to spy out the land; document fauna, flora, and any farming; collect samples of minerals; keep a close eye on how far he was from the coast; and make maps of wherever he went.[8] Marcos was required to write a detailed report on his return to México-Tenochtitlán, two copies of which are preserved in the Archive of the Indies, in Seville.

Coronado presumably watched with a healthy sense of skepticism as Marcos departed Culiacán on March 7, 1539, his heart full of faithful zeal, dressed in his Franciscan "skirts," as the soldiers liked to call the priests' habits. Esteban wore his bells and his feathers and brought his mystic rattles. The Aztec commanders wore their own dramatic military plumage. They were a striking lot, even for that frontier. But Esteban worked his diplomatic magic, sending freed Indian slaves ahead as heralds of peace. One community after another welcomed them with such enthusiasm that it significantly slowed their progress.

A week or so out, Marcos's companion, Brother Honorato, fell sick, and they decided to leave him behind near the Petatlán River in Sinaloa. Marcos was now the only European member of Mendoza's expedition. The Indians called him Sayota, or so he said, "which means a man from heaven." But then he also reported that the Indians had told him of an inland valley where the people wore golden earplugs and ate from golden crockery. "But as my orders were to keep near the coast, I decided to look into it on the way home."[9] Coronado was interested, however, and began making plans to visit this wealthy province called Topira, "where the Indians lined their homes with gold and silver."[10] Presumably these were garbled local accounts of Aztec Tenochtitlán, but among potential settlers and conquistadors they fueled interest in New Galicia and Tierra Nueva.

Marcos decided to spend Easter at a large settlement called Vacapa, which was well stocked with game, while Esteban went on ahead. Inspired by the liturgical season, Marcos devised a simple system by which Esteban could report back to him by sending a small cross if he found anything interesting, a medium-size cross if it was exciting, and a very large cross indeed if he discovered something spectacular. The two men would never see each other again.

Four days later, messengers appeared, Christlike, carrying a huge cross "as tall as a man" and reported to Marcos that Esteban "had been told about the greatest place on earth," and that the Seven Cities of Cíbola were only thirty days' journey hence. Esteban had even recruited a native of this fabulous province, who described at length its vast stone buildings that were four stories tall and decorated with turquoise. The local Indians had confirmed all this, claiming that they often traded with Cíbola and sometimes worked there as seasonal laborers.[11]

Having celebrated Easter Sunday at Vacapa, Marcos hurried onward. Esteban was a long way ahead and attracting a growing entourage. More and more important figures from the communities through which he traveled joined his party. His route is uncertain, but he probably went up the Sonora River valley, with its broad and babbling stream, its cornfields, its abundant game, and its thousand and one stories about the fabulously wealthy north.

He moved on swiftly beyond modern Arizpe, where the valley narrows, and across the desert highlands and down to the San Pedro River, near the modern international border crossing at Douglas, Arizona, and Agua Prieta, Mexico. Esteban was moving much faster than Marcos. By the middle of April, he climbed into the empty hill country where the steep escarpment called the Mogollon Rim looms above San Carlos and Fort Apache and the White River. From there, the trails led him toward Show Low and Zuni.

Marcos, the first ordained Christian to preach in the American Southwest, eventually reached the San Pedro valley, with its farming communities that imported prized turquoise jewelry from Cíbola, and an old man told him the masons there built houses of stone and mortar up to ten stories tall that lined ordered streets and plazas. Marcos also reported news of a place called Toton-teac, well beyond the Seven Cities, where people raised livestock the size of large dogs and hunted cowlike creatures with a single curved horn.

By the beginning of May, he was making his way into the hills, still pursuing his errant African guide. Every night, the party stopped at campsites where they saw the remains of the shelters and fires used by Esteban's advance guard. A fortnight later, one of Esteban's Aztec soldiers staggered into camp "covered in sweat, his body and face badly battered."

"A day's journey from Cíbola," he breathlessly explained, "Esteban sent messengers ahead, just as he always did, carrying his gourd-rattle, with its strings of little bells and its red and white feathers. But when they handed the rattle to the chief's representative at Cíbola, he grew angry and threw it on the ground and said: 'I know what kind of people these are. Tell them not to enter the town or they will all be killed!'

"The messengers went back to Esteban and told him what had happened. 'Oh, that is nothing,' he said, 'everyone who first shows annoyance always gives me the best welcome in the end.'"

"Esteban continued on to Cíbola. But the people there would not allow him into the town. They shut him up in a large house outside the walls and took away all his trade goods, his turquoise, and other gifts he had collected along the way. That night, they gave him and his companions neither food nor water.

"In the morning," the Indian explained, "I was hungry, so I left the house and went to drink from a nearby river. Not long afterward, I saw Esteban fleeing from the townspeople. I saw them kill some of his companions, so I ascended the river, keeping myself out of sight, and made my way to the trail."

Many in Marcos's entourage began to weep at this "ruinous news," and he took himself off to pray and think for a while.

Then two more fugitives turned up, "badly injured and covered in blood." They had escaped a terrible massacre by hiding under the bodies of dead and dying comrades. "We never saw Esteban again," they explained, "although we think that they must have shot him with arrows as they did with everyone else."

Marcos claimed in his report that his Indian companions blamed him for the death of their brethren and refused to continue. So he set out alone, with only two guides from the San Pedro valley. Finally, he climbed a hill and looked across the Promised Land to Cíbola, like Moses viewing Jericho from the heights of Pisgah.[12]

"The town is beautiful to behold," he wrote. "The best I have seen here in the Indies and it has more inhabitants than Mexico City."[13]

According to his report, Marcos took possession of the Seven Cities in the name of the viceroy and called the region San Francisco, built a large cairn, placed a small cross among the stones, and no doubt said a prayer. He then turned around and rushed back to Culiacán as fast as his legs would carry him.

Brother Marcos de Niza's assertion that Cíbola was another Tenochtitlán is evident fantasy. However, while improbable, it is not impossible that Marcos had managed to view from afar one of the six busy pueblos of a few hundred inhabitants that thrived in the Zuni Valley in the sixteenth century.[14]

Not surprisingly, the moment Marcos reached México-Tenochtitlán, Cortés attempted to discredit his claim to have penetrated so far, stating, "What he says he has seen, I told him about myself and everything he refers to is exactly the same as the Indians said to me."[15] Cortés clearly wanted Tierra Nueva for himself, but that does not necessarily mean he was lying.

For all Cortés's public skepticism, Marcos electrified New Spain with his official report that Cíbola was as populous as México-Tenochtitlán and that it had declared war on Esteban and the Franciscans. He also seems to have outdone even those exaggerations at the viceroy's dining table and in the company of other would-be conquistadors. Even his barber was soon spreading stories of walled cities where women wore gold necklaces and men had belts of gold and used official weights and yardsticks in their trade.[16]

Viceroy Mendoza was determined that Coronado should take charge of the assimilation of Tierra Nueva into the empire. First, he sent the veteran frontier raiders Melchior Díaz and Juan de Zaldívar with sixteen cavalrymen to establish an official crown presence in the Promised Land. The small posse rode north into bitter winter weather, reaching an ancient ruin known as Chichilticale, often used as a campsite by Indian traders traveling to Zuni, probably the Kuykendall Ruin in the isolated Sulphur Springs Valley south of Wilcox, Arizona.[17] The cold forced them to retreat into the populated San

Pedro River valley, where their amiable hosts told them about Zuni culture and society. Their report to Mendoza is an embryonic work of ethnography, the first European account of the traditional construction of the pueblos, the adobe walls, the flat roofs supported by wooden beams, and the fortresslike honeycombs of apartments entered by ladders. It describes clothing, diet, and ceremonies at which singers and ensembles of flautists accompanied ritual dancers. They also sent a ceremonial kachina mask as evidence of idolatry and included in their report the terrible but politically charged calumny that "they eat human flesh."[18]

In the meantime, Mendoza ordered Coronado to prepare his great expedition to Tierra Nueva as quickly as possible. Hundreds of hopeful conquistadors answered the call of the recruiting fifes and drums, their minds filled with delusions of wealth and dreams of honor and *reputación*. Could Cíbola, they wondered, be an American Xanadu, a gateway to the Orient, to the silks of China and the spices of the East Indies? Juan de Zaldívar spent thousands of pesos on a private posse of servants and slaves and went on to make the first sketch of a bison drawn by a European. Eventually he became one of the richest men in the world at the silver mines of Zacatecas, but that is another story.

The expedition was not primarily a military undertaking, nor a search for gold. It was "an imperial town seeking a site for itself, governed by a council of leading citizens" who expected to be rewarded for their service with land and Indians.[19] Most of all, the conquistadors aspired to an American sense of aristocracy, to win great *encomiendas* such as those of New Spain. Captain Tristán de Luna signed up and came with eight horses, his arms and armor, and his retainers. He died years later trying to settle the Gulf Coast of Florida.[20] Melchior Pérez spent four thousand pesos and brought over a thousand pigs and sheep. All these men lost almost everything.[21]

As many as two thousand Indian adventurers came, too, wealthy Mexicas, Tlaxcalans, and young men from Michoacán in search of glory, all brought up in their own imperial warrior tradition of capturing and enslaving their foe. The Codex Aubin, a beautiful manuscript produced by Aztec historians in the 1570s, records in traditional hieroglyphs and Nahuatl text how eight hundred Tenocha-Aztecs from around Lake Texcoco marched to *yancuic tlalpan*, "the new land," in the year 8-reed, 1540.[22] Their names are not recorded.

Mendoza watched the long caravan leave Compostela on February 24, 1540. Providing fodder for the many hundreds of horses and the other livestock was as much a problem as feeding the people. Coronado ordered Tristán de Luna to establish the new Spanish town of San Gerónimo in the fertile Sonora River valley to serve as a base for the main body of the expedition. Coronado then set out himself with his *maestre de campo*, his distant cousin

López de Cárdenas, Marcos de Niza, eighty Spanish soldiers, and most of the Aztec allies. Throughout their march over the watershed and down the San Pedro, deep into Arizona, they were constantly harassed by hostile Indians, who tipped their arrows with a deadly toxin.[23] The notorious "Knight of Pueblos and Plains" was at last riding across U.S. soil, but Coronado was far from welcome.[24]

Coronado's expedition to Tierra Nueva is exceptionally well documented, primarily because he and his captains were later charged with a long list of crimes against the indigenous population and subjected to a lengthy trial. But there is also an excellent narrative account by a member of the expedition called Pedro de Castañeda, as well as many other shorter reports and items of related material.[25]

According to Castañeda, morale among the advance guard was already low when they reached Chichilticale and saw it was merely a roofless adobe ruin weathered by the wind. At that moment, most of them understood that Marcos de Niza, for all that he was guiding them, had almost certainly never seen Cíbola.[26] Nonetheless, Coronado led his army across the arid mountain terrain, toiling along a terrible trail, often leading their starving horses, and watched over by the sinister specters of huge goats with enormous horns. Two men were so famished they ate some plants that turned out to be poisonous and died.[27] But, finally, the army descended to the Little Colorado River, flush with pecans and mulberries and grass for the horses.

Four Indian messengers approached from the opposite direction, but the atmosphere was tense. That evening, as Coronado's party prepared their bivouac, they were confronted by a detachment of Zuni warriors, who only retreated when Cárdenas leaped into the saddle and faced them down.

In the morning, the army marched the last ten miles to Zuni along Hemlock Canyon. When they finally sighted Cíbola, the furious Spanish soldiers "hurled a hundred curses at Brother Marcos."[28] Now they knew for sure there would be no golden city, no easy wealth, no precious stones, no great estates, no aristocratic reward.

Coronado ordered Cárdenas to approach the pueblo with two Franciscans.[29] The *Requerimiento* was read to four hundred Zuni warriors massed before the gates and translated by a Sonoran interpreter. A bow chief responded by marking a line in the dirt, and when Coronado ordered the army to approach, the Zuni archers launched a volley of arrows from lightly drawn bows as a formal warning. One struck Brother Luis and became harmlessly entangled in his cassock. For the Spaniards, that was a declaration of war.

Coronado sought permission to attack. The terrified friars readily gave their assent. When the cavalry charged, the Zunis took refuge inside the pueblo.

The terrible "men in metal" had finally arrived.[30] In fact, Coronado was one of only a handful of Spanish soldiers who could afford full battle armor. Most of his men were anyway so weak they could hardly stand or cock their crossbows, let alone wear heavy metal protective clothing. So with a great shout of "Santiago!" Coronado invoked the patron saint and holy warlord of Spain, and he himself charged into the fray. With his armor glittering in the sunshine and the colorful plume in his helmet, he made an obvious target.[31] As he tried to climb a scaling ladder, the Zuni soldiers dropped a huge stone slab, striking him on the head. He collapsed amid a storm of arrows, and Cárdenas had to drag him to safety. Coronado remained sense- less for three hours. It was an ignominious beginning, but when he recov- ered his wits, he ordered the artillery to open fire. A storm of cannonballs battered the pueblo as the broad valley resounded to the sound of the guns. The Zuni commanders began an orderly retreat to the summit of Dowa Yalanne, "Corn Mountain," the sacred red mesa, a natural castle that soars above the Zuni River, the refuge of their people since earliest times.[32] Coronado's army entered the deserted pueblo and feasted on the plentiful supplies of food they found.

It is debated whether the pueblo Coronado occupied was Hawiku or Kiakima, both now easily identified ruins on the Zuni reservation. He reck- oned it consisted of about two hundred dwellings within the walls, with three hundred other homesteads scattered about the surrounding countryside. He wrote Mendoza that the celebrated Seven Cities of Cíbola were just "seven little settlements," all within a few miles of one another. "It is," he said, a "cold and snowy . . . , utterly flat landscape," without "fruit or fruit trees," a lack of firewood, "few birds," a desiccated world in which the people seemed to venerate water above all else. "God knows I should have wished for better news to send Your Lordship."[33]

The Zunis opened a tentative dialogue with the invaders, and after some procrastination, they produced a young Indian lad from the Petatlán River to act as interpreter. Coronado asked about Esteban and claimed in his report to Mendoza that the Zunis had confessed to killing him; when asked why, they explained that "the Indians from Chichilticale had told them he was evil and quite unlike the Christians. For the Christians," they are supposed to have asserted, "kill none of their women, while Esteban had murdered them and beaten them."[34] While the Spaniards' ill treatment of the Indians is well documented, the notion that Esteban was a serial killer is implausible. He had proved himself a brilliant diplomat among hundreds of different Native American groups, and murdering womenfolk was not an obvious way to achieve that. Moreover, he clearly liked Indian women. Castañeda remarked that "those Indians got along much better with the black man" than with the Franciscans, who disapproved of Esteban "because he took along with him all the women" the Indians offered him and "accumulated turquoise and much else."[35]

Later, in 1622, a Spanish traveler in Sonora came across a "very dark and evil looking *mulatto*, of severe countenance," called Abara, the *cacique* of the village of Tesia, on the Mayo River. Abara said he was Esteban's son and recounted how his father had been "so captivated by the beauty of the handsome women" of the region "that he had hidden himself away" from the Spaniards "and took four or five wives according to the local custom."[36] Esteban, it seems, was not killed at Zuni, but returned south to start a family in Sonora. Why, you may well ask, should he have even contemplated doing anything else?

Perhaps the Zunis said they had killed Esteban merely because they wished they had, for he was a harbinger of doom. During the seasonal ceremonies that take place across Pueblo country, powerful spirits known as kachinas become manifest in the human world by taking possession of the physical bodies of dancers wearing masks and costumes associated with a particular kachina. Man and spirit essentially become indistinguishable to all but the initiated.[37] Today, Esteban is associated in Pueblo culture with the "black" kachina Chakwaina, "a horrible ogre who emerged as a tangible symbol of the Spanish conquest."[38]

Meanwhile, Antonio de Mendoza's chamberlain, Hernando de Alarcón, had sailed from Acapulco, on May 9, with three ships laden with supplies for Coronado. Alarcón proved to be so tenacious an explorer and so able a diplomat that he almost achieved his impossible goal of delivering his cargo. His account of his voyage up the Colorado and Gila rivers is compelling reading and was translated in full by the great sixteenth-century English editor Richard Hakluyt.[39]

After weeks at sea, Alarcón's flotilla reached the head of the Gulf of California, where the Colorado, the "Red River," tinged the waters a dark vermilion. Alarcón headed upstream with two longboats and only twenty men. Near the modern border town of Gadsden, they had a tense encounter with the Cocopa inhabitants. Alarcón stood placidly in the prow of his boat and drifted toward the fifty or so men gathered on the bank with their bows cocked, waving feather war flags. As soon as his boat touched the bank, he threw his shield and his sword down into the bottom of the hull and stood on them as a sign of peace. Then he grabbed the royal pennant and lowered it out of sight. A few of the Cocopas approached, and Alarcón gave them trinkets. An old man came forward proffering a staff decorated with shells by way of exchange. Alarcón handed out more glass beads and received mesquite bread and corn in return. The Indians asked for a demonstration of an harquebus, or so Alarcón claimed, but then reacted so angrily when he fired it off, that he took to his boat and left. He had learned that gaudy gifts rather than firepower were the key to friendship.

Alarcón continued up the shallow river with his men wading, towing the boats. The following day they met a group of Yumas near the confluence of the Colorado and Gila rivers, who seemed friendly and there was brisk trade in beads, bells, and caps in exchange for well-tanned hides and tortillas made from roughly ground corn. Then as night fell, prudent Alarcón withdrew to the deep water in the middle of the river. Before dawn, they heard excited shouting from both banks, and crowds of people swam out to the boats with further offerings of corn. Many Yumas tried their hand at praying to little crosses Alarcón gave them and competed with one another to tug on the towropes. But a wise old man harangued them with great energy and then turned to the Spanish chieftain.

"He desired to knowe what nation we were and whence wee came," Alarcón reported to Mendoza. "By signes I came to understand that the thing which they most esteemed and reverenced was the Sunne," so "I answered that we were Christians and that I was sent by the Sunne . . . whereat they marvelled and then they began to beholde me from the toppe to the toe."

The skeptical old Yuma questioned how that might be, for the "Sunne . . . went aloft in the skie and these many yeeres had never sent any other" men like the Spaniards. Artful Alarcón replied that when the sun rose in the morning, it was near the earth, and it "made mee in that land" to bring peace to the Yuma and their neighbors.

The old man asked "wherefore we understood not all other men, seeing we were the children of the Sunne," who "also had begotten him and given him a language," and wanted to know why "he had not sent mee sooner to pacifie the warres."

Alarcón assured him that the sun "knew well that they dwelt there, but . . . had many other buisnesses and because I was but yong hee sent me no sooner."

"Comest thou hither to bee our Lord?" the man asked.

"Not to be their Lord, but rather to be their Brother," Alarcón said he had replied.

"Seeing thou doest us so much good and art the child of the Sunne, wee will all receive thee for our Lord," the man finally shouted, turning to his people and announcing that Alarcón was the son of the sun.

Alarcón asked this able interrogator if he had ever heard reports of white men with beards. The elders talked of such people, the old man admitted, but in a distant land. He had never heard of Cíbola.

The Spaniards erected a large cross, demonstrated to the Yumas how to pray, then moved on, almost certainly following the Gila River east toward Phoenix. Alarcón continued to befriend the inhabitants, but at some point he crossed a major cultural boundary. One night, as Indians and Spaniards warmed themselves by the fire by the river, another influential and friendly Indian discreetly drew Alarcón's attention to an enemy war party lurking in the woods, preparing to attack. The friendly Indians swam to the opposite bank and the Spaniards withdrew to their boats.

This alert ally, the first documented tourist in the history of the Southwest, said he had been to Cíbola, a month's journey hence, "because it was a great thing and had very hie houses of stone." Alarcón invited him to share a meal, and when the plates were laid, he said he had seen four green ones at Cíbola and a dog like the one the Spaniards had in their boat. These, he said, had belonged "to a blacke man which had a beard." He had heard it said that the "king caused him afterward to be killed." Alarcón urged his men to continue their extraordinary voyage up the Gila River to a place called Quicoma; there, the local *cacique* hinted that he, too, had been to Cíbola, where he met a "Negro which ware about his legs and armes certain things which did ring."

"I demanded upon what occasion he was killed."

"The lord of Cíbola inquired of him whether he had other brethren: he answered that he had an infinite number and that they had a great store of weapons . . . Many of the chiefe men consulted together and resolved to kil him that he might not give newes unto these his brethren."

Esteban, the *cacique* said, had been slain and cut up into little pieces, which were distributed to all the lords as a fiat of his death.

Presently, this well-traveled *cacique* recognized an old friend among the crowds lining the riverbank who had heard that men with beards and calling themselves Christians had arrived at Cíbola. They were thieves and rapists, the man said, and he advocated murdering Alarcón and his men. But the cordial *cacique* insisted that his Spaniards were sons of the sun, which seemed to reassure his murderous friend.

Alarcón tried to persuade these men to find him an Indian who would take a message to Coronado, but none were prepared to go because they had heard that "a fierce nation like us and of the same qualities" were at war with

Zunis because they had killed Esteban. Moreover, they explained, they were preparing for war with the neighboring lord of Cumana. The news that the Indians were on a war footing worried Alarcón; he feared they might have changed their minds about the benevolence of the "Sonne of the Sunne" and be readying an attack on the Spaniards. Outnumbered, far from the ships, and faced with the Indians' recalcitrance, Alarcón decided to retreat downstream.

Meanwhile, at Zuni, Coronado was concerned that Marcos de Niza "no longer felt safe, now that . . . his report had turned out to be entirely lies."[40] So he ordered Melchior Díaz to escort Marcos back to Sonora, instruct Tristán de Luna to bring the main body of the expedition to Zuni, and then go in search of Alarcón at the head of the Gulf of California.

Díaz missed the supply ships by a few weeks but found a cross that Alarcón had erected near the mouth of the Colorado, then took his posse over the river and explored far toward the setting sun.[41] They were the first men to ride horses in Alta California, within the boundaries of the modern state, but one ill-fated night during the return to Sonora, Díaz threw his lance at a puppy that was yapping around the sheep. It stuck in the ground, and as his horse galloped onward, the Spaniard was badly gored in the groin by the jagged wood. Twenty days later, kindly Melchior Díaz, who had wept when welcoming the four Narváez survivors to Culiacán, died in agony.[42]

The Zunis told Coronado about their famously self-contained and self-sufficient Hopi neighbors to the northwest, so he sent Cárdenas to make contact. After days in the saddle, his band of horsemen approached the thriving settlement of Awatovi on Antelope Mesa. At first, the inhabitants tried to prevent the unwelcome visitors from entering their pueblo, but then prudently allowed them to stay a short while, during which they spoke glowingly about a thriving, wealthy world located in the direction of the setting sun.

Cárdenas penetrated deep into northern Arizona in search of this ficti-tious prize, but his Hopi guides led him to the rim of an enormous chasm, "two leagues deep," he later claimed, with "such precipitous crags, that we could scarcely see the river, which looked like a little stream, although according to what they said it must have been wider than the river at Seville."[43] He said they spent days searching for a way into this vast abyss, but the foot-path the Hopis showed them looked extremely dangerous, quite possibly a trap. They turned around and went back to Zuni, the first Europeans to set eyes on the Grand Canyon.

At Zuni, about twenty men arrived from Pecos Pueblo, the most easterly of the archipelago of loosely affiliated polities on the Upper Rio Grande.

The delegation was led by a venerable old man the Spaniards called "the *cacique*," but they were most impressed by a tall young captain, an ambitious, adventurous, outward-looking, outward-going character who wore a welcoming mien on his tough countenance and a fine display of whiskers on his upper lip. They called him Bigotes, "the Mustache." Coronado handed over the usual decorative trinkets, but in return the Pecos offered him shields and leather war helmets, defensive weapons imbued with an obvious symbolism. He took an interest in some hides they had given him, and Bigotes explained they came from giant herds of animals that roamed toward the rising sun. He showed Coronado one of his men who sported a tattoo of a bison. Then Bigotes began to solicit Spanish support for a campaign against the Plains Indians who had launched devastating raids on the eastern Pueblos.

Coronado arranged for Bigotes to guide a reconnaissance party under Hernando de Alvarado to the Upper Rio Grande and then out onto the plains, while the rest of the advance guard waited for the main expedition to catch up. This typically heterogeneous party of twenty-three Spaniards, most of the men from Pecos, and an unspecified number of Mexican allies set out at the end of August along the main road east. They drank from the cool spring water in the pool by the cliff they called El Morro, "the Snout," and skirted the edge of the strange Malpais, a jagged triangle of solidified lava almost thirty miles across. They visited the impenetrable fortress town of Acoma, "one of the best defended places ever seen," Alvarado reported, set "on high crag and with such a terrifying ascent that we regretted going up there."[44] At the Rio Grande, representatives of twelve different pueblos formally welcomed them with a procession of fifers.

At Pecos, the harvest was being brought in, and the Spaniards luxuriated in an abundance of food. But they could see the farmland was poor, and there was obviously neither gold nor silver. Alvarado toured a number of pueblos and guessed that a total of twenty thousand households lived in the region. As Castañeda remarked, "there are many *encomiendas* in New Spain with a larger number of people" than that.[45] But with hunger haunting their progress across the barren landscape, the abundant harvest of the Rio Grande pueblos was a welcome discovery. Alvarado sent word to Coronado and prepared to explore the Great Plains.

Bigotes aroused Alvarado's suspicions by announcing he would not accompany them in person, but he provided two Plains Indians as guides. The Spaniards thought one of them looked enough like an Ottoman to call him El Turco, "the Turk." The other they named Ysopete, "Little Aesop," after the Ancient-Greek fabricator of fables. These two led the expedition along either the Canadian or the Pecos River onto the plains. After four days, the inter-lopers saw bison for the first time.

The violent confrontation of man and bovine has been deeply rooted in Spanish culture since prehistoric Iberians battled the aurochs, the ancestor of the modern fighting bull, on the plains of Castile. During the Middle Ages, knights and noblemen fought bulls from horseback for sport, and by the sixteenth century bullfighting was an established form of entertainment in Spain. Alvarado and his men were expert amateurs eager to show off their knowledge and technique. "These bulls," Castañeda observed with his trained eye, "are so impressive of stature that not a single horse failed to shy away from the sight of them when they came face to face for the first time." He noted the fine hair of their hindquarters, like merino wool, and the great mass of hair at the front, which he likened to a lion's mane. "They have a beard like a Billy goat . . . which trails behind them when they retreat." But what really caught the attention of this experienced toreador were the short, fat horns, the huge hump of muscle at the nape of the neck that could effort-lessly toss a horse and rider, the way they charged with their head dropped low, and that their eyes were close set to the sides so that whether fleeing or attacking they could see their enemy.[46] They were a strange taurine treasure, and there were "as many of them as there are fish in the sea," one man remembered.[47] A surfeit of Castilian virility made manifest amid this Ocean of Grass rekindled the pride of these hopelessly lost souls. Despite a few moments of drama, over the coming weeks they feasted on the flesh of these majestic beasts, more succulent than the beef of Spain, these hungry men reported, brimming with nostalgia for home.[48]

With the Spaniards as drunk on the thrill of the chase as they were reinvigo-rated by this plentiful diet, El Turco tried to explain that they should change direction and head for his homeland, Quivira. There, they would find "large towns and gold and silver and linen," or at least that is what Alvarado under-stood.[49] As the excited men allowed their imaginations to run wild, they came to believe that almost within reach was a wonderful world where a vast river flowed, filled with "fish as big as horses and canoes with twenty oarsmen on each side, and sails . . . a great golden eagle at the prow," ruled by lords who ate from silver plates and slept beneath a tree hung with golden bells.[50]

El Turco was probably trying to describe the wealthy Caddo culture of the Arkansas River known to archaeologists as the Fort Coffee phase. The huge river "two leagues wide" was clearly the Mississippi. Mark Twain described fish of an unbelievable size on the river, and modern reports of catfish as big as small cars are common, while a 357-pound alligator was taken out of an oxbow lake in 2011.[51]

Whatever the reality underlying Alvarado's wishful vision, El Turco also convinced him that Bigotes had various gold objects acquired from this fantastic place. Alvarado decided to return to Pecos, where he found the Pueblo on a war footing. The unsuspecting Bigotes pressed Alvarado to join his campaign against a neighboring province. Alvarado appeared to acquiesce, but once they were two days' march from Pecos, he seized Bigotes, the *cacique*, El Turco, and Ysopete, and chained them up like slaves. They were imprisoned at a pueblo called Coofor, which Cárdenas had requisitioned as the winter billet for the rest of the expedition. Although Coronado later denied it at his trial on charges of misconduct and brutality, witnesses testified that he and Alvarado tried to terrify Bigotes into giving up the gold objects by threatening him with their dogs of war. The brave Pecos warrior insisted that El Turco had lied, so they unleashed Pedro de Tovar's savage hound. They only called off the beast after Bigotes had been badly bitten. The outraged Pueblo Indians berated Coronado and Alvarado for such treachery, and Castañeda candidly confessed that "from then on, the Spaniards' word of peace was discredited."[52]

The coldest weather in many winters struck the Upper Rio Grande, and everyone, stranger and Pueblo alike, hunkered down.[53] The Spaniards were warm enough crowded together in the adobe apartments of Coofor, but their Mexican allies began to freeze in their nearby encampment of hastily built wattle-and-daub shacks. Coronado appealed to the Tiwas for help and sent two posses downriver to collect clothing and blankets.

When the Tiwas shut the gates of their towns, the Spaniards forced a delegation of their leaders to hand over the ceremonial robes and furs from their own backs. One minor Spanish nobleman stooped to stealing a few chickens and blankets from an Indian farmer, then took a fancy to his wife as well, so he made the man hold the reins of his mount while he went upstairs and raped her. A delegation of *caciques* whom Cárdenas had forced to vacate Coofor complained in person to Coronado, but he refused to prosecute the crime because the unhappy victim could only recognize the rapist's horse and not the miscreant himself.

The following night, the Tiwas vented their anger, cudgeling to death five unlucky Mexican hostlers and running off sixty horses. Cárdenas went to investigate and found one of the towns closed up and barricaded. The Indians were in "great uproar and dressed for war, running down the horses as though they were bulls in the ring and firing arrows at them."[54] Coronado ordered the *Requerimiento* read. "The Tiwas replied," one witness remembered vividly, "that they did not know His Majesty, nor did they wish to serve him, nor have him as their lord."[55]

Cárdenas led the punitive assault. After a day and a half of fierce fighting, the Tiwas waved a large cross and sued for peace, but the Spaniards put to the sword most of the sixty men who emerged from the burning pueblo. They tied a few survivors to stakes and forced El Turco and Ysopete to watch as they burned them alive.[56] The rest of the Tiwas retreated to a fortified citadel called Moho on top of Santa Ana Mesa, with its forbidding crags of black basalt. There they held out for fifty days, but by the ides of March their water was running out. They surrendered their women and children to the mercy of their foe and prepared to fight to the death. Five Spaniards lost their lives in the battle, many more were wounded, and the Mexican casualties went unrecorded. More than two hundred Tiwas were slaughtered.[57]

When the first gay birdsong of spring reached Coofor on a seasonal breeze, Coronado called a council of his officers and officials. At Easter, the expedition abandoned the Rio Grande to go in search of golden Quivira of El Turco's imagination, far in the east across the Ocean of Grass.

At Pecos Pueblo, Coronado released Bigotes from imprisonment as a futile gesture of goodwill, then led his long caravan up the Canadian River and onto the Great Plains. For ten days, El Turco led them through this strange landscape "so featureless it was like being far out to sea." They saw no living thing other than bison and grass. Tens of thousands of bison had trampled broad dirt trails as hard as asphalt through millions of acres of grasses six to ten feet tall. Here and there, the bison blocked these highways and fouled the watering places. In a letter to his king, Coronado confessed to drinking a liquid "so evil it was more muck than water."[58]

A group of Querecho Indian hunters watched in wonder as the Spanish toreadors performed their dance of death with bison after bison. That night, the two groups spent an uneasy night camped beside each other amid the grass. "They did not live in houses, but carried around bunches of poles," which they turned into "cabins, tying them together at the top and then surrounding them with hides," Coronado and his captains noted in the first detailed description of a tepee in American history. Another Spaniard commented on how the Indians used dogs to drag the poles from place to place.[59]

El Turco steered the Spaniards on a southwesterly course, onto the Llano Estacado of the Texas Panhandle. But Ysopete grumbled they should be farther north. When they came to a major junction in the trails, he dramatically fell to his knees, blocking El Turco's favored southern path, and made the universal gesture of moving a flat hand back and forth across his throat.[60] Coronado and his captains were perplexed, so they sent scouts in each direction. Ysopete could show his party nothing but grass, but El Turco's group soon came across a much-tattooed and numerous nomadic people called the Teyas.

An old Teya told them he had met the Narváez survivors, and Castañeda pointedly noted that the group saw an "Indian woman as white as if she were from Castile."[61] The Indians asked the Spaniards to bless their large haul of hides as Esteban and Cabeza de Vaca had done, but Coronado allowed his Spaniards and Indians to appropriate them as a "gift." That afternoon, as the expedition pitched camp in grassy meadows beside a river between the steep sides of a small canyon, a violent "twister" swept in, "with very high winds and hailstones the size of drinking-bowls that fell as dense as raindrops and piled up two palms deep in no time."[62] The hail rent the tents and smashed the crockery, bruised the men and stampeded the livestock. Remains of this mayhem including chain mail, crossbow bolts, horseshoes, nails, and ceramic shards have been discovered by collectors and archaeologists in Blanco Canyon, about thirty-five miles northeast of Lubbock, Texas.[63]

With much of their supplies destroyed and no means of provisioning so large an expedition in the field, Coronado gathered his officers in council. They agreed they had to return to the Rio Grande, but that Coronado himself should continue onward, leading a posse of thirty men to Quivira.

Ysopete guided Coronado and his riders northeast to the Arkansas River in southern Kansas, where they turned downstream. They lived on bison meat, cooked on campfires of dried bison dung. Finally, seventy-seven days out of the Rio Grande valley, they came to Quivira, which has been identified with archaeological sites near Great Bend, northwest of Wichita. The people cultivated corn on soils that seemed well suited to growing European crops and welcomed the strangers peacefully. But instead of "stone buildings of many stories," they found huts of "straw," Coronado confessed to the king, concluding that "these people are as primitive as all the others."[64] He spent a month at Quivira, searching for some sign of a fine civilization. The Quiviras told him about a chief called Harahey, who ruled in the east. Convinced he must be a shipwrecked Spaniard, Coronado sent him a letter by Quivira messengers.

The messengers returned with two hundred naked Indians.[65] The Spaniards' dreams of a golden land had become a nightmare. Ysopete accused El Turco of deliberately leading the expedition far out into the plains so that they would all starve to death and of urging the Quiviras to kill the Spaniards' horses. Finally, Coronado vented a terrible anger born of disaster and disappointment on this brave Plains Indian and ordered Francisco Martin, a butcher by trade, to garrote El Turco in secret.[66]

The explorers returned to the Rio Grande to spend another freezing winter amid the hostility of the Pueblos.

The Spaniards celebrated the coming of spring by racing their horses, but joy soon turned to despair when Coronado was thrown and kicked in the head by the horse coming up behind him. He never fully recovered. With Coronado convalescent, Cárdenas galloped into Coofor with shocking news. The Indians of Sonora had burned San Géronimo to the ground and slaughtered all the settlers. Coronado was cast into the blackest despair and ranted deliriously about "an alchemist he knew in Salamanca who had predicted he would become a powerful lord in a foreign land, but would suffer a fall so serious he could not get back up."[67] Coronado gave the order to return home. Two Franciscans insisted on remaining to establish missions at Pecos and Zuni with a handful of Mexicans, Africans, a flock of sheep, and a Portuguese lad who turned up a few months later at Pánuco with news that both friars had been murdered.[68]

As Coronado's party retreated south into New Galicia, he realized he was Governor of a world that had suffered Armageddon. Viceroy Mendoza himself had led the huge army of Spanish and Aztec troops that brutally suppressed a massive uprising of Caxcanes and Zacatecos in the conflict known as the Mixton War. Mendoza's soldiers left behind a terrible disease that devastated the vanquished Indians. Across New Galicia, crops went untended, food was scarce, and the *encomiendas* became almost worthless. Spanish settlers started to abandon this godforsaken outpost of empire.[69] The terrified burghers of the administrative capital at Guadalajara wrote to the crown, warning, "The natives of this province are as restless as ever. Indeed, but a few leagues from the city, their braves most foully assault their peaceful brethren who are our friends."[70] Coronado's expedition traveled through that devastated landscape while men and women of every rank deserted him. By the time he reached Culiacán, only fifteen men remained.

That summer of 1542, Antonio de Mendoza also sent Juan Rodríguez Cabrillo with two ships he had appropriated from the estate of Pedro de Alvarado on a reconnaissance of the coast of California. The expedition anchored in San Diego Bay, in September. Cabrillo continued north, and at a place they called *Puerto Sardinas*, "Sardine Harbor," some Native Americans came aboard the flagship and danced to the sounds of a Spanish drum and bagpipes. The expedition sighted Monterey and reached the mouth of the Russian River, but as winter was setting in, he described the *sierra* as "nevada," the mountains were covered in snow. During the return journey, Cabrillo badly injured his leg on some rocks and died of the infection, a sad end to the leader of the first European expedition to explore the California coast.[71]

Meanwhile, the crown prosecutor had been preparing his case against the senior officers of Coronado's expedition for "great cruelties perpetrated" against the Pueblos. Cárdenas was convicted and sentenced to banishment from New Spain and a year of military service in Granada. Coronado lived out his life in México-Tenochtitlán, where he died in 1554. Only the two Franciscans had succeeded in their missions. Both had achieved the joy of Christian martyrdom. Amen.

CHAPTER 7

AN INCA'S TALE, THE *FLORIDA*

THE DEEP SOUTH

As she spoke, the Lady of Cofachiqui slowly unwound a great string of pearls as fat as cobnuts that looped around her neck three times and fell down to her thighs.

—GARCILASO DE LA VEGA, EL INCA

BY THE TIME CABEZA DE VACA returned to Spain in 1537, the royal court was already bewitched by rumors of how he and his companions had survived the Narváez expedition as Indian shamans. But for all his celebrity, he was deeply disappointed that Charles V had already appointed Hernando de Soto as Adelantado of Florida, and also Governor of Cuba "so that you can better manage and supply your expedition."[1]

Cabeza de Vaca had come to claim the prize of *La Florida* as his by right of moral endeavor. But Soto had just returned fresh from the conquest of Peru "with more than a hundred thousand pesos in gold and silver," according to Oviedo. Brimming with swashbuckling swagger, Soto "spent it all, so that when he set out for Florida he was burdened with thousands of pesos of debt."[2] Such was the excitement among the most noble youngsters of the realm that, according to one account, Soto was forced to "leave behind many men of rank because of a lack of shipping."[3] Indeed, at first even Cabeza de Vaca contracted to go with him and only pulled out when he was appointed Governor of the Río de la Plata, but that is a different tale of woe.[4]

On Whitsun, the Feast of the Holy Spirit, in 1539, Soto's lookouts sighted the Florida coast. The following day 513 men, 237 horses, and 1,000 hogs disembarked from nine ships, possibly near Tampa Bay, possibly at Charlotte Harbor.[5]

In the early history of the Spanish failure to tame Florida, the Spaniards' myriad dreams of wealth and glory materialized as a collective nightmare, a terrible story filled with Christian suffering and conquistador cruelty. Soto was "much given to the sport of hunting and killing Indians," Oviedo wrote. "I say hunting, because the conquistadors have always set fearless dogs upon the Indians that rip them to pieces."[6] But half of Soto's arrogant followers lost their lives trespassing across that alien land.

The history of Soto's disaster is familiar in many ways from the story of how Narváez's expedition foundered, for they were similar enterprises pursuing similar goals in the same place. What occurred can be most accurately reconstructed from two reasonably reliable sources. The only eyewitness report is by the royal factor, Luis Fernández de Biedma, a brief account that largely reflects his official task of supplying the expedition as it moved across America.[7] Oviedo gives a more rounded version in his *General History*, which he based on the testimony of Soto's private secretary, Rodrigo Rangel, to the Audiencia of Santo Domingo. But even Oviedo's narrative comes to an abrupt end, leaving modern readers in permanent suspense; the manuscript containing the final chapters went missing long ago.

Historians have often also turned to a much-embellished "chronicle" published in Portuguese in 1554, apparently as a purely commercial project. This is attributed to an anonymous "Gentleman of Elvas" who supposedly survived Soto's expedition. Although in places it reads like a powerful narrative written by an eyewitness to real events, it is encumbered by anecdotes and episodes clearly designed to aggrandize the role of the Portuguese participants and is encrusted with rhetorical flourishes typical of Renaissance history writing, such as the verbatim reporting of great speeches made by Indian chiefs with the grandiloquence of the great Greek and Roman orators from the classics.

However, the most engrossing and fascinating narrative inspired by Soto's misadventures, Garcilaso de la Vega's *Florida del Inca*, is a *tour de force* of fantasy and illusion. The scholars who made the classic translation of this "novel" into English called it "a splendid specimen of sixteenth-century literary art," the "first truly American work," which "has won for Garcilaso the distinction of being the first American to attain pre-eminence in literature."[8] Published in 1605, the same year as the first-ever modern novel, Miguel de Cervantes's *Don Quixote*, the *Florida del Inca* is the first great work of fiction ever written about America, perhaps best described as a historical novel loosely based on true events that teased its readers with its claims to be a faithful rendition of reality.

Indeed, the story of Garcilaso de la Vega's book and the life if its author are both tales that are not only more worthy of telling than a dry historical account of Soto's debacle, but also tales more easily told given the inadequacy of the primary sources. So Garcilaso's biography and the tale he wrote are the stories retold in the following pages, albeit with half an eye on the Elvas text and the "real" history as recounted by Ranjel and Biedma.

In April 1539, a few weeks before Soto first set foot on the beaches of Florida, the infant Garcilaso was baptized Gómez Suárez de Figueroa in Lima, Peru. His father, Sebastián Garcilaso de la Vega, was a prominent conquistador, a minor nobleman who had served alongside Cortés in Mexico and Pizarro and Soto in Peru. Father and son could also boast of being related to the most charismatic aristocrat of the Spanish Renaissance, Garcilaso de la Vega, a gallant soldier and brilliant literary celebrity remembered by contemporaries as the "Prince of Poets." The young Gómez was raised in the household of his Inca mother, the royal princess Chimpu Ocllu, where his uncles and cousins gathered to talk "about the origins and majesty of their regal dynasty, their great empire, their deeds and conquests, their government and their laws," and "wept for their dead royalty and the demise of their republic."[9] "I loved to listen to them," Gómez recalled years later.

His parents never married, and when his father abandoned Chimpu Ocllu for a Spanish spouse, Gómez was both distraught and amazed that a mere hidalgo from the rural gentry of some impoverished corner of distant Spain should reject heavenly Christian union with the royal Inca bloodline.[10] Nonetheless, Gómez's father took an interest in his education so that the young man became proficient in the arts of war and was "taught a bit of grammar by a procession of seven different teachers," even as the violent civil uprising against the crown led by Pizarro's brother Gonzalo raged around them.[11] Sebastián Garcilaso bequeathed his son a comfortable inheritance so that he might go to Spain and continue his studies. As Gómez was preparing to leave Cuzco for the last time, a sympathetic royal official showed him the mummified cadavers of five Inca royals, all of them his own relatives. They "were in tact, with their hair and eyelashes, wearing the clothes they did in life. They had their *llatus*, or "miters," on their heads and they were sitting with their arms across their chests and their eyes lowered toward the ground."[12] It was a fine memory to take to Europe.

In Spain, Gómez was welcomed into the household of his kindly uncle Alonso de Vargas, a battle-weary old soldier who had married too late in life to have children of his own. He had retired to the comfortable life of a rentier in the wine-producing town of Montilla, south of Cordova.[13] He encouraged Gómez to go to Madrid and petition for some reward in recognition of his father's service.[14] But Cortés's great biographer, López de Gómara, had written in his *History of the Indies and Conquest of Mexico* that Gómez's father had favored the Gonzalo Pizarro when he notoriously rebelled against the crown, writing that during one decisive battle "Pizarro would have been in grave danger had Garcilaso not given him a horse."[15] So, when young Gómez finally gained a royal audience, a senior member of the council simply sneered, "What reward do you think His Majesty will give you? After your father handed Pizarro such a major victory?"

"Those reports are all false," Gómez pleaded.

"It has been written down by historians," the councilor replied, "yet *you* still try to deny it?"

"With that," Gómez later explained, "I waved goodbye to my hopes."[16]

But he had learned an important lesson about the power of the written word in sixteenth-century Spain. Almost immediately, in November 1563, he began using his father's surname, Garcilaso de la Vega, loudly proclaiming his connection to the greatest poet of the age. Later, in 1586, he added the epithet El Inca.[17]

As Garcilaso de la Vega, El Inca, he became best known for his monumental history of Peru in two parts, the *Royal Commentaries* and *The General History of Peru*, in which he portrayed the Inca Empire using the most positive and seductive rhetorical gambit imaginable to his Renaissance readers, presenting it as the Andean Rome, a cradle of American civilization and sophistication.

Garcilaso inherited his uncle's estates and established a comfortable life for himself at Montilla with a Moorish slave called Beatriz de Vega and their two or three children.[18] He must have met the great novelist Miguel de Cervantes, who passed through working as a jobbing tax-collector. He also enjoyed the company of his cousin Luis de Góngora, one of the most erudite and sophisticated poets of all time, who lived nearby in Cordova.

One day a battered conquistador, Gonzalo Silvestre, who had served in Peru and then went to Florida with Soto, rattled into town. He was so "old and obese" and "so afflicted by syphilitic buboes" that he had to be carried from Cordova on "a wagon drawn by oxen."[19] But Garcilaso was glad to befriend this specter from his troubled childhood, a man who had served alongside his father in Peru. They struck up a friendship rooted in common nostalgia and a shared sense of injustice at the imperial order. A copy of López de Gómara's *History* that they read together turned up in the 1930s, its margins filled with critical commentary and caustic remarks. The more measured annotations are in Garcilaso's handwriting, but Silvestre's notes are filled with bombastic rancor at a book he said "should be burnt along with whoever wrote it!"[20] When the old man finally died, Garcilaso carried out his friend's final request to be buried wearing his sword and dressed in full armor.[21]

Garcilaso crafted the *Florida del Inca* from the wealth of distorted memories that poured from Silvestre's subconscious, addled by wine, febrile with syphilis. But Garcilaso also brought immense erudition to that storytelling, drawing on Aristotle, Plato, and Plutarch, the great neoclassical authors of Renaissance Italy, and works of history and science in Latin, Spanish, Portuguese, and Italian.[22] "Imprisoned in my little corner of the world," as he put it, Garcilaso had collected a fine private library in which Dante rubbed shoulders with Columbus's *Diario*, and Oviedo and Gómara sat side by side with Herodotus and Thucydides, the Greek fathers of history.[23] There were no novels of chivalry on Garcilaso's shelves by the time he died, but like so many great figures of the age, he admitted he had been an avid devotee of those bestsellers of sixteenth-century Spain.[24] "I owe thanks to Pedro Mexía," one of the great intellectuals of the age, "for killing off my youthful love" of "books of chivalry" and "convincing me to loathe them forever," Garcilaso claimed in the *Florida*.[25]

To erudite contemporaries, that denial of his youthful literary passion was obviously heavily pregnant with tacit irony, for throughout the *Florida*, the Inca brazenly luxuriates in the populist glitter of chivalric literature.[26]

It is almost axiomatic that novels of chivalry should begin with an assertion that the history they contain is a true account obtained from a reliable source, and in his prologue to the *Florida*, Garcilaso assured his readers that "the greatest care has been taken to write about events as they really happened," and that his source had given an "account of everything he saw."

This was a giant wink to readers, intended to put them in mind of an intellectual debate about the principles of history and fiction, which had originated with Aristotle and Plato. Miguel de Cervantes summed up one side of the argument, suggesting, "A poet may sing of deeds not as they really were, but as they should have been, but a historian must write them not as they should have been, but as they really were."[27] But the genre of the modern novel, which Cervantes had sired in all its vainglorious postmodern relativism when he wrote *Don Quixote*, stands astride that imaginary gulf we hope to perceive between truth and fiction. That trait of essential ambiguity was directly inherited from books of chivalry, which so boldly bent the accepted genres of their age by "bridging the gap between these categories of History and Poetry."[28]

Garcilaso, like Cervantes, warned his readers not to believe a word of what was coming, then set them wondering whether those words might not contain a far greater moral and philosophical truth.

From time to time, this retelling of Garcilaso's *Florida* will be seasoned with facts gleaned from other, more conventional historical sources, but what follows is more fiction than fact. While this may be an unfamiliar intrusion of what sixteenth-century Spanish moralists called literary "lies" into historical discourse, the *Florida* is probably best understood as a natural progression from the tendency to apparently mendacious assertion in the reports of Ponce de León or Ayllón and more thoroughly developed and crafted by Cabeza de Vaca and Dorantes. It is a logical next step in the art of storytelling, and it shines a bright and sometimes uncomfortable light on the historian's art and the very notion of historical truth itself.

The main narrative of the *Florida* begins with Soto disembarking full of pride and hope on the shores of North America at a great harbor he calls *Bahía Honda*, or "Deep Bay." Yet, immediately, on that first page, Garcilaso wrote that "the Indians attacked with such force" the Spaniards had "to retreat to the water's edge." The ruling *cacique*, Hirrihigua, was "filled with hatred for the Spaniards" because of "senseless offenses committed" against him by Pánfilo de Narváez, "offenses which are too evil to relate," the narrator tells us. Hirrihigua's bellicose attitude toward Soto is rooted in a righteous desire for vengeance typical of the knights-errant of chivalric literature. From the outset, the Inca author appealed to his readers' sympathy on behalf of his Indian characters.

Soon, four more hostile Indian "noblemen and knights" appear. Garcilaso remarks with subtle irony that "to call them knights may seem inappropriate as they did not have any horses," but it is in fact legitimate "because in Spain the word means 'noble' and there were some very aristocratic Indians indeed."[29] The nobility of the Indians should not be doubted, but what should we make of men who commit unspeakable evils? What evil, Garcilaso invites us to wonder, had Narváez done?

For the moment, the Inca forced his readers to be patient.

We know that soon after landing in Florida, Soto reported to officials in Cuba, "On my arrival here, I received news of a Christian in the possession of a chief."[30] This was Juan Ortiz, one of four men who had gone missing from a search party sent to look for Narváez in 1528. Ortiz would become so valuable over the coming months as an interpreter for the expedition that Soto claimed he "has given us a new lease of life. Without him, I do not know what might become of us!"[31]

Garcilaso takes us back in time to tell Ortiz's tale, a parable of suffering and salvation.

"So as to better illustrate Hirrihigua's fury," the Inca explains, he describes the "cruel and evil treatment of" Ortiz and his companions.[32] They were stripped naked and, one by one, released "like wild animals" into the village plaza, where a handful of archers "shot arrows at them." Hirrihigua "took great pleasure in watching them flee hither and thither" until, like noble fighting bulls in the ring, "they found relief in death." Only the eighteen-year-old Juan Ortiz survived, because the *cacique*'s wife and daughters took pity on his youth. But although Hirrihigua spared Ortiz's life, the embittered chief treated him with such hatred that he "often envied his companions their fate."

Hirrihigua sent Ortiz to guard the village cemetery deep in the forest. But one night, he fell asleep at his post and a lion made off with the cadaver of a small child. When Ortiz woke, he set off in pursuit and soon heard the unmistakable sound of the king of the jungle masticating. Commending himself to God, the young Spaniard let loose an arrow and slew the beast. He put the chewed pieces of child back in the coffin and triumphantly presented the carcass of the lion to Hirrihigua. "The whole tribe held that deed in the highest admiration," the Inca notes, but it brought no respite for Ortiz, for "each and every time that the *cacique* recalled how Narváez had set dogs of war on his mother and let them eat her, and every time he tried to blow his own nose and found it was not there" because the Spaniards had cut it off, "the devil bade him take his revenge on Juan Ortiz," as though he were Narváez himself.[33]

These, then, were the mysterious "offenses too awful to relate."

Hirrihigua's daughter helped Ortiz to escape into the territory of a neighboring *cacique* who sought her hand in marriage, the gallant Mocozo, a name that is inexplicably similar to that of Soto's lieutenant Luis de Moscoso! This gallant *cacique* "gave Ortiz a friendly welcome," promised him protection, and "treated him honorably." The two men became such close friends that Mocozo even refused to surrender Ortiz to Hirrihigua when the angry chieftain called off "the marriage Mocozo so ardently desired." Garcilaso remarked caustically that Mocozo "behaved far better than many a Christian prince . . . as many ancient and modern histories bear witness." Indeed, "the magnanimous behavior of that heathen prince should be a powerful example for true believers to follow."

One day, Mocozo sent for Ortiz. "My brother, a Spanish captain is at the village of your great friend Hirrihigua with a thousand men-at-arms and many horse. You well know all the favors I have done you; now is your chance to thank me. Go to this general and beg him to receive me as a friend and servant, for I offer to put under his protection my person, my household, and my estates."[34]

Ortiz set out with this message dressed in "a loincloth and a fine feather headdress," all covered in tattoos and carrying his bow and arrows. When

Soto's men first saw him, they unsheathed their weapons, ready to attack. His Indian companions fled, but Ortiz stood his ground and cried out: "Xivilla, Xivilla!"

Garcilaso playfully suggested that Ortiz was trying to say he was from Seville but had forgotten how to speak Spanish after so many years among the Indians. But this was a joke intended to poke fun at the impenetrable accent still typical of parts of southern Spain where "S" is pronounced "sth." Far from forgetting his mother tongue, Ortiz had simply never spoken Spanish properly in the first place.

The *Florida* describes formal talks during which Mocozo swore an oath of allegiance to the Spanish Crown, representing the encounter as though it had been conducted by men well versed in the art of Renaissance diplomacy. The Spaniards marveled at Mocozo's poise and polish, "asking about the emperor and his gentle-knights," saying that "one day he would take pleasure in seeing it all." He seemed such "a thoroughly able courtier that it was as though he had been born and raised among the officers and the gentlemen" of the expedition.[35]

In stark contrast to this noble Indian Mocozo, Garcilaso now turns his narrative spotlight on the ignoble figure of Vasco Porcallo, Soto's second-in-command and one of the most venal men to settle Cuba. At the head of a small posse, he recklessly "spurred on his horse headlong into the marshy waters . . . of an evil swamp." Rider and mount "should have drowned right there and then," but "he escaped thanks to Divine Providence," Garcilaso remarks, without telling his readers how. But as Porcallo dragged himself from the terrifying slime, his mind filled with a cowardly longing for "his great estates and rest and relaxation at home" on Cuba. With that, he turned tail and abandoned the expedition.[36]

Leaving nearly a hundred men at Bahía Honda and with Mocozo weeping like a chivalrous knight-errant at his friends' departure, Soto led the main body of his expedition to establish their winter headquarters at a place called Ocale, "where," he wrote his Cuban officials, "we shall want for nothing, if what they say about it turns out to be true."[37] He led an advance party, trying to skirt an impassable swamp, but his Indian captives guided them into a most difficult, boggy terrain, where they were ambushed. The Spaniards fought off their assailants, and Soto then had the guides "thrown to the dogs and killed." That was enough to encourage one terrified captive to show them the right route.[38]

Having finally established a labyrinthine path through the swampy badlands, Soto turned to Gonzalo Silvestre and gave him the most daunting of missions: "You have the best horse in our army, which is the worse for you, for we must all rise to the toughest challenges, and you can best serve our expedition by returning this very night to the main camp and bringing everyone to join us here."[39]

Silvestre clearly loved his "extremely fine horse, a chestnut brown so dark it was almost black, with a white sock on its left hand and a blaze" the length of its face. He set out with a man called Juan López, riding through the terrifying night. By the flickering "light of huge bonfires," they saw "great squadrons of Indians who seemed to be dancing, singing, eating, and drinking." It was an exhausting ride and López eventually faltered. "'Let me sleep awhile,'" he pleaded, "and fell from his horse, dead tired." At that moment, the night sky went black and "so much water fell from the heavens that it seemed like Noah's Flood."

By first light, they were on their way again, but when they reached an all-important ford across the deepest of the swamplands, "so many canoes appeared upon the water from among the reeds and rushes that these two Spaniards were moved to poetic metaphor and said to each other that they looked like leaves that had fallen from the trees." For all that they could see the danger that awaited, these two brave men well knew that it was better to be bold than timid. They spurred their steeds into the water. Arrows rained down on them so that when, "by no small miracle worked by the Good Lord," they reached the other side, they looked back, to see the waters "covered in arrows, like a city street strewn with grass for some solemn feast day."

Ocale was "a little village" where they found enough "corn and vegetables to last a week," according to the factor Luis Fernández de Biedma's eyewitness testimony, whose business was to remember such detail. Starving, constantly harassed by Indian archers, and with no sign of a suitable place to establish a settlement, Soto knew he must keep his expedition moving. Ortiz had repeatedly reported that a populous and fertile province called Apalache lay to the north, which Soto well knew to be "a poor and barren land" from Cabeza de Vaca's account. But Soto also knew it had a good harbor on the Gulf Coast at a place called Aute.[40] He was clearly already thinking about retreat or retrenchment at a port easily accessible to Spanish shipping.

The road to Apalache ran through a vast province ruled by a terrifyingly vengeful leader, Vitachuco, and his pusillanimous brothers. Soto easily intimidated these spineless siblings, who sent messengers to the valiant Vitachuco that the Spaniards came "offering peace and friendship," but advising him that "there was no hope they might be defeated in battle," for "they were children of the Sun and Moon, gods who had come whence the Sunrise."

Vitachuco's response was so "extraordinary" that not even "the bravest of knights" described by "Ariosto and the other great poets could match the proud words of this Indian." Garcilaso explicitly states that much of this speech has been forgotten across the ages, before announcing, "Nonetheless, his very words are recorded in the following chapter." Why let the truth get in the way of a good story?

"Thirty-five years old, tall of stature, brave of heart," Vitachuco admonished his brothers for their perfidy: "Oh, how ye be young and of judgment short to praise such as Spaniards thus. Their prison renders ye weak and cowardly of spirit, their slaves who serve them with women's words. Know ye not but they must like their treacherous predecessors be, who wrought so many countless cruelties upon our lands? Their deeds betray them as the devil's spawn, not children of our Sun God and the Moon. They are not content to settle any lands they find, but their pleasure is to wander vain and idle and live by the sweat and toil of other men. Brigands, adulterers, murderers all, they do but steal and rob and rape our wives and daughters, too. Tell them, then, that should they with their hostile paces tread upon my lands, then they shall never leave, but every one of them shall die roasted on my fires and boiled in my pots!"[41]

Vitachuco decided to "hide his hatred" and sued for peace. He made a great show of friendship and servitude, but all while he was plotting the murderous downfall of the Spaniards. "He imagined the adoration of the neighboring nations, their words of praise and their applause. He fantasized about the women who should dance for him, singing ballads in honor of his deeds."

The plot was betrayed, and during a bloody battle the Spaniards captured Vitachuco and his lieutenants. Soto asked them why they had rebelled, and the older men explained it was their "duty as military officers, chosen by their prince for their spirit, strength, and courage." Then the younger warriors spoke up: " 'We left our homes longing for battle out of ambition for glory, for the greatest honors are earned in war. But now that fate has robbed us of victory, we must be subjected to the tribulations reserved for the vanquished. Do what you will with our lives, for we are now yours." When the Spaniards heard these noble sentiments, "they showed their compassion and pity with tears."

Soto was even magnanimous to vituperative Vitachuco and kept him close. They ate together. But the warrior chief would not be cowed, and one day, after dinner, he attacked the Spaniard and grabbed him by the hair and pummeled him "with a ferocity and determination that can scarce be imagined." Soto collapsed senseless before his knights and soldiers had time to draw their swords and with a dozen thrusts and cuts dispatch that bravest of Indians. Across the camp, his captive followers swelled with brio and rose in revolt, smashing down "cauldrons of food" on the heads of their new masters, "battering them with plates, bowls, jugs, and jars," seizing "benches, stools, and tables," and launching themselves into the fray. Garcilaso called this Battle of the Cooking Pots "a laughing matter," but "bloody and cruel for the poor Indians" who were slaughtered or chained as slaves.

Within days, bloodied but victorious, Soto vacated Vitachuco's land and pressed on to "the famous province of Apalache."[42]

In 1987, an inquisitive archaeologist called Calvin Jones, who specialized in finding seventeenth-century Spanish mission sites in Florida, thought he had identified another on a low ridge in Tallahassee where construction workers were breaking ground for an office complex. The developer allowed him in to "dig around for a day or two," a decision his investors and insurers must have regretted, for Jones soon realized that he had discovered Soto's camp at Apalache. Two teams of professional archaeologists and amateur enthusiasts dug up thousands of artifacts, shards of majolica pots from Spain, simple olive jars, tableware, links of chain mail, coins, a crossbow bolt, iron nails, and hundreds of glass beads. They found lumps of clay imprinted with the shape of the palm branches that had been part of the wattle-and-daub buildings of the Indian settlement. The clay had been baked solid by fire, presumably when Soto finally burned Apalache to the ground.[43]

The expedition spent the winter at Apalache. Soto established a route to Aute, where the Narváez expedition had built their makeshift boats. He sent messengers to Bahía Honda with orders that the rest of the expedition should strike camp and advance to join him by both land and sea, a journey that offered Silvestre further opportunity for uneventful heroism. But throughout the Spaniards' stay in the now-tranquil suburbs of Tallahassee, they were harried by Native American war parties.

In March 1540, Soto's nephew Diego made the mistake of "galloping after a fleeing Indian to show off his skill and daring in the saddle." The fearless fugitive took cover beneath a tree, sprung his bow, and loosed an arrow straight and true that felled Diego's horse beneath him. Another Spanish knight galloped to his rescue, but again the Indian shot his horse from under him with a single arrow. The two Spaniards advanced on foot, swords drawn, but their foe fled into the forest, shouting insults as he went. Suddenly, the Indians seem less noble, more savage, and in the following chapter of the

Florida a band of Indians attacked a Portuguese soldier who strayed too far from the Spanish compound in search of fresh fruit. "No sooner had he fallen to the ground, than they cut off his head, by which I mean the whole crown," Garcilaso explains, "which they took away as evidence of their deed."[44] This is the earliest scalping ever described in print, recorded decades after it supposedly took place in a work that is evident fiction.

While at Apalache, Soto captured two young men who claimed to have traveled widely in the company of merchants. They told him of a distant province called Cofachiqui, rich in gold, silver, and pearls.

Soto's arrival at Cofachiqui is the centerpiece of Garcilaso's *Florida*, the heart and soul of his story, located exactly halfway through the narrative. But the prologue to this episode is dark indeed. Soto fell in with the powerful chief Patofa, who commanded eight thousand men. As the Spanish and the Indian armies entered the province of Cofachiqui, Patofa's men moved ahead and began burning settlements and scalping their victims. But then as mysteriously as these psychopathic legions had appeared, they disappeared into the night, homeward bound. For the next three days, the Spaniards proceeded through deserted country until Soto ordered them to rest "at the most beautiful spot set in the shade of mulberries and other trees laden with ripe fruit." That night, not far off across a broad river, the scouts "saw firelight and heard the sounds of dogs barking, children crying, and men and women chattering away." It is very much the kind of pastoral Paradise where knights-errant rested in the stories of old. Only the bleating sheep and lowing cattle are missing.[45]

The following day, Soto rode to the riverbank with two hundred men. Ortiz shouted across the river, and soon six venerable Indians boarded a canoe and did homage to the Sun and Moon, facing east and west in turn, before facing Soto himself, seated on the heavy folding chair he used as a portable throne.

"My lord," they asked, "do you come in peace or war?"

Soto requested a peaceful passage through their lands. The Indians explained that they were "vassals of a lady, young and ripe for marriage who had recently succeeded" to reign over her people. This maiden princess, who seems to have materialized from some tale of chivalry, then embarked with eight noblewomen in a large and sumptuously bedecked canoe propelled by ranks of oarsmen. "The whole spectacle was reminiscent of Cleopatra sailing up the Cydnus River" to seduce "Mark Antony and rule over him with all the power of his passion for that famously beautiful and intelligent Egyptian woman."

The Lady of Cofachiqui spoke alone with Soto. She offered to feed and house his army and invited him to stay at her own private palace. The

Spaniard thanked her profusely for her generosity. They talked of her lands, and "the Spaniards marveled at such fine words that revealed so much intelligence in a savage woman born and raised so far from civilization."

"As she spoke, the Lady of Cofachiqui slowly unwound a great string of pearls as fat as cobnuts that looped around her neck three times and fell down to her thighs." When she had finished, she told Juan Ortiz to give them to Soto, for modesty forbade she do so herself. But Soto replied, "Tell her I would hold it of much greater esteem to receive such a gift from her own hands. To do so cannot compromise her honesty, for this is the all-important business of peace and friendship between nations."

The Lady of Cofachiqui, "young and ripe for marriage," as we know, "stood up to give him the pearls." Soto also stood to receive them, then he took "a gold ring set with a handsome ruby from his own finger and gave it to the lady." With great deference, she slipped it slowly "onto one of her own fingers."[46]

For Garcilaso, the symbolism of this remarkable moment clearly reflects his private dreams of a real marriage between his Indian-princess mother and his conquistador father, and the romance between these emblematic characters remains a platonic political ideal. The harsh reality reported by Oviedo is that Soto chained up the female ruler of Cofachiqui along with all the other women the Spaniards had taken as slaves.[47]

There was neither gold nor silver at Apalache, but there were pearls aplenty. According to Garcilaso, the Lady of Cofachiqui told Soto that he could help himself to as many as he liked from the vast quantities that she kept in the temples of the dead. Soto and the royal officials set out for the cemetery, riding a "good league" through fertile fields and orchards that seemed to them like an enchanted garden. The splendid funeral palace was set in the heart of a large settlement. A hundred paces long by forty wide, it had high walls and a steeply pitched roof that was richly decorated with luxuriant feathers and long and looping ropes of the fattest pearls and seashells, all arranged in perfect symmetry and glittering gloriously in the Florida sunshine. The entrance was by two vast doors guarded by stunningly lifelike wooden statues of fearsome giants arranged in pairs and armed with clubs, poles, spears, axes, and bows and arrows, all made to perfection. Inside, the sarcophagi rested on wonderfully worked wooden shelves ordered along the walls, surmounted by sculpted likenesses of the dead and a line of richly ornamented shields. Above these, two cycles of life-size figures ran around the top of the walls like a classical frieze, in which groups of men and women posed resplendent in gorgeous strings of pearls. Little towers of ordered chests or caskets divided the vast room into long intersecting passages. The Spaniards were amazed at the unimaginable quantity of pearls they found inside these caskets, so many that all nine hundred men and their horses would have been unable to carry away so much booty, or so Garcilaso wrote.

From Cofachiqui, the expedition turned southwest along the Tennessee River valley, before ascending the Tombigbee into traditional Chickasaw territory south of Tupelo, where they struck out northwestward to reach the Mississippi somewhere downriver from Memphis.[48] Some of the names recorded by Garcilaso and the other chroniclers are delightfully evocative of an American timelessness. "Tascaluza" was a "fearsome chief, almost a giant"; his son was killed in a thrilling set-piece battle at "Maubile"; and the great Battle of "Alibamo," fought against the "Chicasa," ended with a duel between a Spanish crossbowman and an ancestral Chickasaw archer. This was conducted in an exemplarily chivalrous spirit, worthy of the most exaggerated sense of southern aristocracy.

The second half of Garcilaso's *Florida*, from his rousing Renaissance crescendo at Cofachiqui until the end, is a story of slow physical and mental attrition as the expedition weathered one Native American assault after another and failed to find whatever it may have been that they were looking for by then. Oviedo records that the expedition crossed the Mississippi on June 18, 1541, as seven thousand Arkansas archers massed on the opposite bank, firing volley after volley of arrows.[49] From there, they waded through the worst swamps they had yet negotiated toward an important province called Casqui. Archaeologists are pretty certain this must have been centered on the large pyramid-shaped mound and a plaza encompassed by a moat and palisade that have been excavated at Parkin, thirty miles west of Memphis.[50] By then, Soto's men were increasingly unhappy, and he was clearly feeling the strain. Garcilaso then describes the moment of great drama when, one night, Soto sprang furiously from this bed and dressed down one of the royal officials in front of both Spaniards and Indians.[51] But in the morning, they set out west again, "because the Indians said that eleven days away they hunted for cows"—bison, in other words.[52]

That fall, they crossed the great cultural frontier between the Mississippian and Caddoan Indian worlds and visited a place called Tula. "These Indians were quite different," Garcilaso reported, for "the men and women all had ugly faces and incredibly long and pointy heads."[53] They were also implacably hostile. It was the closest that Soto and his expedition came to seeing the Great Plains. That winter, Juan Ortiz died, and in the spring, a "rich and noble knight from Seville" ran away with "an extremely beautiful eighteen-year-old maiden, the daughter of an Indian chief."[54] It was an ill omen for the gentry to be "going native." Biedma noted that Soto had sensed that he was seriously ill and had begun to speak openly of finding a route to the sea so they could get relief from Cuba.[55]

Yet, that very spring, less than four hundred miles away, Francisco Vázquez de Coronado was wandering lost in the Ocean of Grass, searching for the ever-elusive chimera that was Quivira. Weeks earlier, as Coronado was crossing the Llano Estacado in the Texas Panhandle, a Teya or Teja Indian woman from East Texas who had been living among the Pueblos and had accompanied his expedition chose her moment to escape. She fled east, heading for home along the Red River. Soon afterward, she came across some of Soto's men somewhere near the Arkansas River, and to their astonishment she was able to name many of Coronado's captains.[56] The two expeditions had come astonishingly close.

As the all-smothering humidity of summer shrouded the Spanish camp on the banks of the Mississippi, Soto felt feverish humors rising and knew he was going to die. He appointed Luis de Moscoso as his successor and ordered his men to visit him. Two by two and three by three, they came, and Soto bade them each farewell. He called for the priests and confessed his sins. On June 28, 1542, Hernando de Soto, that "most magnanimous and never-once-defeated gentle-knight, died at the age of forty-two."[57]

The new Governor of Florida held a council of his officers, and they decided to strike out in the direction of New Spain. The expedition headed west into Caddo country, and the Spaniards were impressed by the fertile soil and rich agriculture, and the farmsteads and ceremonial centers strung out across the countryside like the *pazos* of Galicia in Spain.[58] Moscoso led them into the hills of East Texas, and they entered a country "where buffalo sometimes roamed." According to Biedma, they were told of "people like ourselves," probably Coronado's men, but they assumed they themselves were the source of these rumors "because we had been going round in so many circles."[59] By the banks of a river that scholars suggest might be either the Colorado or the Brazos, Moscoso and his dispirited men realized they would have to retrace their route and return to the Mississippi River.[60]

That winter, they built seven makeshift boats and set off down the Mississippi, their minds full of hopes and fears. They were attacked by a contingent of fifty Indians in canoes who "killed twelve very noble men that day," recalled Biedma.[61] It was the last fatal skirmish of their long journey, for they were carried far out to sea on the Mississippi flood. Turning toward the setting sun, they slowly sailed toward Pánuco. Three hundred survivors finally reached

México-Tenochtitlán in the summer of 1543, where they were welcomed by Viceroy Mendoza himself, who feasted them all at his own table, keen to hear firsthand what had happened.[62]

Florida had once again defeated an army of would-be conquistadors, but it had furnished the Inca Garcilaso de la Vega with a wonderful literary triumph, the first truly American novel, by a South American, about North America, for all that he wrote in Spain for European readers.

PART II

THE AGE OF SETTLEMENT

HERESY & GODLINESS

THE EXCITEMENT OF THE FIRST HALF CENTURY or so of exploration and experiment gave way to a period of consolidation and settlement. In North America, Sebastián Vizcaíno's voyage of 1602 and 1603 along the coast of Alta California was the only serious attempt at exploration, although in reality it added little to Cabrillo's expedition of 1542. That sparked some enthusiasm for establishing a permanent settlement at a fine harbor he named Monterrey, for the incumbent Viceroy of New Spain who had sponsored his mission. "It is all you could hope for," he reported, "as a comfortable port for the ships trading with the Philippines."[1] However, Monterey and California remained an imperial dream that would not materialize as reality for over a century and a half. Instead, in North America, Spaniards established a permanent colony at St. Augustine on the East Coast; and with the help of Mexica and Tlaxcalan allies, they created the Kingdom of New Mexico, while an Austrian Jesuit began planting missions in southern Arizona. The impulse to establish and maintain these important bridgeheads was definitively religious, albeit in markedly different ways.

In 1517, Martin Luther had challenged the long-entrenched theology and corruption of the Roman Church by pinning his famous *Ninety-Five Theses* to the door of the parish church at Wittenberg. From that moment, Europe had been battered by the violent storms of religious schism. As Holy Roman Emperor, Charles V was the secular leader of Christendom, and he felt the enormous weight of his responsibility to heal the wound. But he struggled to rule his vast and varied possessions in the tradition of a medieval peripatetic monarch, continually traveling, constantly feasting with his vassals and his rivals in the interests of diplomacy, or leading his armies in person on the battlefields of Europe and North Africa. Luther had divided the princes and peoples of the Empire. In Charles's ancestral homeland, the Low Countries, Reformers vandalized churches and harassed priests, while the perfidious English burned Catholics as heretics. In deeply conservative and pious Spain, grown rich and powerful on American treasure, the Inquisition pursued Protestants with a terrifying piety previously reserved for Jews and witches.

Charles invested enormous emotional energy trying to achieve reconciliation through a great Ecumenical Council of the Church, which eventually
met in three long sessions between 1545 and 1563 at the alpine city of Trent
on the southern border of the Empire. But uncompromisingly reactionary
Spanish cardinals dominated the sessions, destroying all hope of reconciliation by their loud and incendiary intransigence. So Charles spent his final
years as the most powerful ruler in Europe at war with his own Protestant
subjects. He was exhausted in body and spirit: physically tormented by gout,
syphilis, arthritis, and the gastric agonies brought on by his enormous appetite, and mentally anguished by the fear his own soul would be damned for
allowing the heresy of Reformation. Sometimes he would weep for days on
end, finding solace in tinkering with his collection of clocks that so rhythmi-
cally marked his passage to the grave. Over the course of 1555 and 1556, while
at Brussels, he astonished his subjects by abdicating his hereditary kingdoms
to his son, who became Philip II of Spain, and by engineering the election of
his brother Ferdinand as Holy Roman Emperor. Having divided an inheritance that was too large to rule between the two great branches of the House
of Habsburg, the most powerful ruler Europe has ever known retired to pray,
eat, and die at a humble monastery in Old Castile.

Philip was a Spaniard by birth and characteristically Spanish in the zealous
orthodoxy of his faith. He had watched his father broken by the relentless
responsibility of direct rule and chose instead to invent a modern form of
government for his new global world. He became a bureaucratic monarch,
establishing a permanent capital at Madrid, rarely leaving Spain and managing
his affairs from a desk, experiencing his realms through the virtual world of
pen and ink, of written reports, maps, and paintings. He made decisions in
conjunction with his councils and ruled vicariously through regents, viceroys, and *audiencias*, and an enormous army of officials.

When news that French Protestant Huguenots were attempting to settle the
Eastern Seaboard of North America, he treated their removal as of the utmost
urgency. He felt keenly his duty as sovereign and custodian of the souls of his
Indian subjects, and he was horrified that the Lutherans might indoctrinate
them with their evil heresies. Thus, St. Augustine, the oldest continually
inhabited European settlement in the United States, was founded as a bulwark
against Protestantism.

By contrast, the momentum to colonize New Mexico built up gradually
over more than half a century following Coronado's great exploration. The
fabulous notion of Cíbola remained, but the secular urge to settlement was a

more practical expansion in search of land, labor, and mineral wealth. While the initial invasion of the Pueblos' world, led by Juan de Oñate, was primarily a military operation, the eventual consolidation of that early occupation was given greatest support by the Franciscan Order. The prominence of the friars in the economy of colonial New Mexico and their role within the Pueblo communities led to continual conflict with the crown authorities and the civil administration of the kingdom. In its isolation, New Mexico was like a crucible in which the archetypal rivalries of the imperial system were reduced to their essences and then combusted together in constant conflagration. In 1680, so much discordant alchemy led to a massive rebellion among the Pueblos.

Philip II died, in 1598, to be succeeded in turn by three generations of ineffectual monarchs, who left the business of leadership and government in the hands of others: Philip III relied almost entirely on his venial favorite, the Duke of Lerma; Philip IV eventually sacked his ambitious *valido*, the Count-Duke of Olivares; while the reign of the congenital imbecile Charles II was characterized by a constant struggle for power and influence at court. The imperial administration and bureaucracy continued to function, but under these three monarchs there was relatively limited direction from the crown and their subjects in the colonies enjoyed considerable autonomy in commerce and government. That economic independence emerged at a time when more and more men and women of Spanish descent were born and raised in the New World. They studied at new universities in the Americas, they traded there, they married one another, and so they experienced a growing sense of their identity as Americans or *criollos*, "Creoles," as they were known. In New Spain, they took an interest in their Aztec past even as they enjoyed the privileges that came with their European roots. However, that sense of Americanness was harnessed to their resentment at the suppression of the *encomiendas* and the way Creoles were largely excluded from the highest offices, with only a handful ever being appointed as viceroys, for example. Those lucrative and powerful positions were reserved for "real" Spaniards, *peninsulares*, or *gachupines*, as they were pejoratively called.

Moreover, few *criollos* could claim a "pure" Spanish bloodline, for most had mixed parentage somewhere in their ancestry in a world where the Indian population was still the vast majority and African slaves were a common sight on the streets of urban centers. While to be mixed race was generally perceived to be a disadvantage, that was not always the case, for some *criollos* could revel in their direct descent from the Mexica nobility and even from the imperial family itself. Moreover, New Spain had some wealthy Indians, an indigenous aristocracy that coexisted with the Creole elite.

Thus, when Juan de Oñate mustered his enormous expedition to New Mexico, he took with him Indian troops and settlers from around México-Tenochtitlán, while he could proudly claim that his own son, Cristóbal, was directly descended from Montezuma through the maternal line.

CHAPTER 8

"HANG ALL THE LUTHERANS"

THE ATLANTIC COAST

Remember, they are Lutherans and this must be a war of blood and fire, so
that they cannot preach their evil and detestable religion in this land!
—PEDRO MENÉNDEZ DE AVILÉS, ADELANTADO OF FLORIDA

FOLLOWING THE NIGHTMARES SUFFERED by Francisco de Coronado
and Hernando de Soto in New Mexico and *La Florida*, Spaniards turned
their American hopes and imperial dreams toward Peru and the allure of the
astonishing silver strike at Potosí, described as a "mountain made of silver."
Then, in 1565, the mariner and explorer Miguel López de Legazpi finally
extended the Spanish Empire onto the Asian continent that had been Columbus's goal when he first sailed, in 1492. He named the Philippines for his new
sovereign and established an entrepot at Manila that would become the center
of a rich trade in luxury goods, in silks, ivories, and spices. That valuable
merchandize was shipped from Asia across the Pacific and on to Europe,
putting Mexico City and New Spain at the heart of imperial commerce.

But Spaniards did not neglect North America entirely. In 1549, a Dominican mission to Tampa Bay was abandoned after Brother Luis Cáncer was
bludgeoned to death by Indians on the beach in full view of his brethren still
aboard ship. But the tragic split in the Christian communion led Philip II to
expend extraordinary resources on securing Florida for Spain and the Catholic faith.

Philip II had been brought up keenly aware of his father's fear that Lutherans
might spread their dreadful heresies among the indigenous peoples of the
Americas. The pope himself had declared those lambs and their meadows
were the preserve of Spain, and so the King of Castile must by rights be their
shepherd. For Philip, that fear became reality almost as soon as he became
king.

Foreign pirates had long troubled Spanish shipping and possessions in the New World, but the religious conflict in Europe had encouraged English, Dutch, and French Protestants to incorporate themselves as "privateers" with influential financial backers and the covert support of their sovereigns. The main return route to Europe through the Bahama Channel and along the Atlantic coast became an area of special concern for Spain. So, in 1557, Philip II instructed Luis de Velasco, Mendoza's successor as Viceroy of New Spain, to establish one naval base on the Gulf Coast and another on the Atlantic coast, to be connected by an overland route. Two years later, the new Governor of Florida, Tristán de Luna, the veteran commander of Coronado's campaign to Cíbola, disembarked fifteen hundred soldiers and colonists at Pensacola, but within days "a wild storm blew in from the north," he reported to the king, "doing irreparable damage to the ships, with the loss of many mariners and passengers." Only one small caravel survived. The expedition lost almost everything: food, equipment, and livestock.[1]

Despair turned fleetingly to hope when a reconnaissance party found plentiful supplies of corn on the Alabama River above Mobile. But by then Luna was running a raging fever and, half-delirious, he lost control of his frightened followers. Three dozen soldiers formally asked that they and their families be returned to New Spain, complaining that "there is no prospect of getting food from anywhere" and "across the whole country the Indians are in revolt."[2] Luna responded by declaring to his assembled officers that any further such requests would be considered traitorous. A week later, the large contingent of Aztec settlers complained they had eaten all the roots, shrubs, and grasses within twelve miles of the camp. There was nothing left.

Luna announced his intention to lead most of the expedition inland in search of food, but one of his officers asked how they could go anywhere on their famished horses. They "are so exhausted" that "if we go hunting, within half a league," we end up "leaving them behind and come back carrying the saddles," he claimed with unbridled sarcasm. In an extraordinary testament to Spanish respect for the law and royal justice, instead of raising arms against their deranged governor, Luna's captains formally initiated legal proceedings against him, the first documented lawsuit on U.S. soil. Luna responded by charging his men with mutiny and sentencing them to death, before referring their cases to the viceroy.[3]

The expedition friars refused Communion to Luna throughout that long, lonely winter of discontent at Pensacola, but Easter brought a spectacular reconciliation. On Palm Sunday 1560, at the rustic altar of the makeshift church, adorned with sparkling silver and a few paintings of the saints, Brother Dominic preached a moving sermon about the Passion of Our Lord. Then, before he took Communion, the "blessed father looked at his God and wept," and "with the gravitas God gives to those who serve him" he "addressed the governor by name."

Luna rose and knelt before the altar to embrace his reacceptance into the Communion.

"Doest thou believe that this be the body of our Lord Jesus Christ?" the padre asked.

"I believe, O Lord!"

"Doest thou believe that this same Lord shall cometh to judge the quick and the dead?"

"I believe, O Lord!"

"As thou art the cause of so much sin for thou wouldst not meet in council with thine captains, if thou hast not as yet heard the words of men, then let thee now listen to the Virgin Mary's Son. In the name of the Lord whom I hold in mine hands, I command and beseech thee that it be done and I promise the Lord shall bringeth aid to everyone."

Luna turned to the people: "My lords, ye have seen what the father hath done and ye have heard these strange words. That fault be mine, it seemeth. So here, before God, I pardon ye all and I beg ye for the love of God to pardon me."[4]

Luna burst into tears, his captains prostrated themselves before him, and two days later a heaven-sent ship arrived from Havana to rescue them. Yet again, Florida had defeated a Spanish attempt at settlement.

In 1563, Philip II learned the dreaded news that French Protestant Huguenots had tried to settle the Eastern Seaboard of North America. A ship sailing in English waters had rescued a few Frenchmen who had abandoned their tiny post of Charlesfort on Parris Island, South Carolina, then crossed the Atlantic in a makeshift boat.[5] Two years later, a Spanish naval vessel policing Caribbean waters arrested a ragged group of French pirates. They claimed to be Catholic refugees from a French outpost called Fort Caroline at Santa Elena, on the St. Johns River, and said they had fled the grievous ill treatment meted out by the Lutheran officers in charge.[6]

Fearful and furious, Philip turned to a brilliant sailor called Pedro Menéndez de Avilés, a swashbuckling counter-corsair famous for the countless pirate vessels he had taken as prizes while policing the coasts of Spain. In that Age of Chivalry, he had gilded his reputation by rescuing a bride and her bridesmaids who had been captured by French buccaneers off the Galician coast while on their way to the wedding. But he had personally gained Philip's trust as commander of the fleet that brought the new king back to Spain following his father's abdications at Brussels. With their ships becalmed off the coast of Asturias, Menéndez had sensed a storm brewing in the waters where he had been raised and urged the king to come ashore in the longboat. Philip, his entourage, and his baggage were safely on land by the time a terrifying gale blew in.[7]

Philip rewarded this charismatic commander by making him captain general of the two great Indies fleets that returned each year from New Spain and Peru laden with treasure and valuable merchandise. That appointment was fraught with the dangers of domestic politics, for by royal warrant the gift of that office belonged to the House of Trade, in Seville. The new king clearly believed Menéndez would help him stand up to the entrenched interests of the Andalusian oligarchs who ran the House of Trade and the notoriously ornery merchants of the Consulado. But that rivalry almost destroyed Menéndez.

The furious officers of the House of Trade began to charge Menéndez's agents and merchant allies with smuggling contraband. In 1563, on his return from the Indies, Menéndez himself ascended the Guadalquivir in the dead of night aboard a light vessel. Witnesses claimed to have watched him and his servants staggering through the streets, weighed down by silver bars and heavy coffers, and he himself was charged with smuggling.[8] But by the time the magistrates issued the warrant for his arrest, he was already on his way to Madrid to seek royal protection. There, he petitioned his king.

Philip responded by instructing Menéndez to carry the new Viceroy of Peru across the Atlantic, but on his return to Seville, the Consulado refused to release funds for the fleet. Instead, the House of Trade imprisoned Menéndez in a luxurious apartment within the Atarazanas, the royal shipyard by the banks of the Guadalquivir. Philip ordered his release, but the oligarchs refused to obey.[9] As the captain general paced his gilded cage, his son Juan took charge of the fleets. But, as he guided the ships through the Bermuda Triangle, they were scattered by a hurricane. The flagship, with Juan aboard, was never again seen. We can only guess at the paternal frustration felt by Menéndez, a master mariner who must have yearned to go in search of his lost son along the coasts of *La Florida*.

Aware that Philip was horrified by the prospect of Protestant outposts on the Florida coast, Menéndez wrote a long memorandum in which he set out a tempting scheme for the colonization of Florida. But, he warned, "It will be most difficult to gain control of those lands once the Lutherans settle there because they and the Indians will readily form an alliance because their religions are almost the same."[10] Menéndez had both invented for himself a divine mission and artfully extricated himself from the poisoned chalice of the captaincy general. He absconded from his gilded cage and fled to Madrid, where the Council of the Indies fined him a thousand ducats for smuggling and banned him from working the Indies fleets for a year.

Philip II appointed Menéndez Adelantado of Florida, with the most generous contractual conditions settled on an individual by the Spanish Crown since Columbus. Menéndez's heirs were granted the title in perpetuity and three and half million acres of land, half as much again as the current largest landowner in the United States and almost exactly the size of Connecticut. He was ceded a raft of commercial privileges, exemptions from taxes and inspections, fishing rights, a lien of 6.6 percent in perpetuity on all royal revenues generated in Florida, and the right to sublicense or even sell his privileges to a third party.

In the summer of 1565, Menéndez sailed with 34 ships and 2,646 soldiers and settlers out of Cadiz, racing to reach the East Coast of North America before the famous French corsair Jean Ribault, who had already sailed from Dieppe with Protestant reinforcements. It was late in the season and the Spanish fleet was scattered by a hurricane. Menéndez pushed on with only five ships, determined to reach *La Florida* ahead of the Frenchmen.

On the Feast of Saint Augustine, August 28, the Spanish lookouts sighted the fine harbor where Menéndez would establish his settlement, today the oldest continuously occupied European city in the United States. The next day, at three o'clock in the afternoon, in the tremendous tenebrism of a summer storm dramatized by the chiaroscuro of baroque clouds and glittering Tridentine lightning, they sighted four French galleons at anchor near the mouth of the St. Johns River. That night, the Spaniards drew alongside and shouted at the Lutheran heretics that they would burn them alive. After a brief chase, they saw by the first light of dawn that the French had evaded them.

Menéndez retreated to St. Augustine. Under the watchful, inquisitive gaze of a number of native Timucuans, he took formal possession of the land for the Spanish Crown, established the municipal government, and invested the officials. The Cabildo of St. Augustine met for the first time since the town had been founded. It was September 8, 1565. As work began on the Spanish fortress, the French sailed south to take the fight to their Catholic foe, and with a hurricane rising, they made the disastrous decision to pursue the massive Spanish galleass the *San Pelayo*.

The Timucuans told Menéndez how to reach Fort Caroline overland, so he gathered his captains in council and proposed his bold plan: "My lords, I believe that seeing as the French armada has come looking for us, it is reasonable to assume it has been reinforced with their best troops. They have a strong contrary wind and cannot return, so it seems to me we should take five hundred men and open a route through the forest. We will attack at dawn and take the fort. Remember, they are Lutherans and this must be a war of blood and fire"—that chilling Spanish phrase that meant no quarter should be given—"so that they cannot preach their evil and detestable religion in this land!"[11]

Leaving three hundred men at St. Augustine, Menéndez took five hundred harquebusiers on a sodden march through storm-drenched lowlands. "The men were tired and exhausted, and there was so much rain that they could save neither powder nor fuses, and even the biscuits in their satchels were dripping wet," he reported.[12] Menéndez made his men pray until, at dawn, they attacked.

He had guessed correctly: the most able fighting men had sailed with the fleet that had pursued the *Pelayo*, so the defenses at Caroline were in great disarray, The French who remained were outnumbered two to one, and most of them were sick and hopelessly ill-prepared to resist the Spanish assault. Almost no preparation had been made against a Spanish attack. As Menéndez led his men into the fray with a great shout of "Santiago!" many of the French sentries fled into the forest. The Spaniards ruthlessly put to the sword the few men who tried to sound the alarm.

When some French soldiers opened the main gate of the fort to see what the commotion was about, the Spaniards forced their way in, and by the time the sun was a lance length above the horizon, they had slaughtered 135 Frenchmen. Once Menéndez was in control of the little fort, he gave the order to spare the women and children. Three French ships were still at anchor in the harbor, and with the summer storm still providing a theatrical backdrop of gale-force winds and driving rain, Menéndez offered them safe conduct should they set sail for France with the women and children. But the French commander was the red-blooded son of Jean Ribault. He replied that he would prefer to fight for the honor of his king. Menéndez ordered one of his gunners to fire, and the able marksman holed one of the ships below the waterline. Those aboard fled to the other ships, and they all sailed for France without the women and children. Menéndez renamed the place Fort San Mateo and left a small garrison on guard.

When Menéndez returned to St. Augustine, he learned the French ships that had pursued the *Pelayo* had been wrecked in a storm and a large number of survivors were making their way up the coast. He set out with a small contingent of soldiers and came across the Frenchmen, stranded on the far side of a large river. They sent a delegation to the Spaniards to plead for a safe passage home for all the survivors. Menéndez told them he had put every man at Caroline to the sword but that he would take care of any Catholics. The rest, he said, could surrender and throw themselves on his Christian mercy if they wished. Supremely well versed in the art of piracy, he knew such a threat would elicit a promise of payment. His victims revealed that they could pay him fifty thousand ducats for their liberty. The Spaniards ferried their prisoners across the river and eight Catholics were boarded onto a ship.

Menéndez told the rest that because he had few men to guard them, he would have to bind their hands for the long march to St. Augustine. He then marched them into the dunes and after a short distance ordered them to stop. That evening, as the sun set bloodred beneath the Mannerist clouds of a Counter-Reformation sky, he ordered his men to slit the throats of all two hundred heretics, although at least one of them, a barber-surgeon, survived by feigning that he was dead and falling to the ground. The river there has been called the Matanzas, "Slaughters," ever since.

The following day, Indians brought news that more Frenchmen had reached the river with their commander, the pirate Jean Ribault. Again, Menéndez encouraged the French to parley. Again, he told them he had slaughtered their comrades at Caroline. He also warned them he had executed two hundred more at that very place only days before. Fifty Frenchmen turned around and fled, but 150 desperate victims offered him all the money they had. Again, he spared the Catholics. Again, the Lutherans were martyred for their faith. No doubt there was a kind of savage pragmatism about so much slaughter, for Menéndez well knew he could never hope to feed so many prisoners. However, he wrote Philip II that "these Frenchmen had made plenty of Indian friends . . . especially two or three who taught their heresies to the *caciques*. It is astonishing to see," he emphasized, "how these Lutherans have bewitched these poor primitive people." [13]

On his return to St. Augustine, Menéndez understood that his enterprise was collapsing. The Spanish expedition was desperately short of food, and his men were murmuring sedition. Fort San Mateo had burned to the ground, probably from deliberate sabotage. When the Indians told him that the Frenchmen who had not surrendered at Matanzas had ensconced themselves on the point at Cape Canaveral, Menéndez left his brother Bartolomé in command and marched south with 250 men.

When the French saw them coming, they abandoned their fort and a half-built ship and fled into the woods. Menéndez then offered them a clear guarantee of safety, and seventy-five men surrendered; this time, he spared them all. He moved on to parley with the rulers of the Ais tribe, fishermen with a reputation for ruthlessness toward the Spanish sailors who were wrecked on their shores. This equally ruthless commander was desperate for news of his lost son, but the Ais could not offer him even a glimmer of hope.

Menéndez took two small boats and sailed for Cuba, leaving two hundred men and fifty French captives among the Ais. Their rations soon ran out and one traumatized survivor admitted, "Such were the hunger and hardships suffered that some of the Frenchmen were killed and eaten" by the Spaniards.[14] The Ais became hostile. A hundred Spaniards mutinied and marched south in search of succor or an alternative perdition.

Over the winter, as Menéndez worked to rebuild his shattered expedition, he heard rumors of a community of marooned Christians who had survived among the Caloosa Indians of the Gulf Coast. He must have wondered whether one of them might be his son Juan. So, in February, he took two fast-moving brigantines to investigate. Exploring the shallow sounds behind the barrier islands at Port Charlotte, a man approached, paddling hard in a canoe. He was tattooed all over and naked but for a sporran made of deer hide. When he was close enough, he shouted his greeting: "Christian brethren, welcome, welcome! For eight days we have awaited you, for God and the Madonna told us you would come."[15] Everyone aboard the ships knew then he must be a Spaniard.

Hernando de Escalante Fontaneda had lived for almost twenty years among the Caloosa, since the ship carrying him to school in Spain was wrecked along their coast. When the Spaniards asked eagerly about the Fountain of Eternal Youth, he replied with undisguised sarcasm, "I bathed in many rivers . . . , but it was my misfortune that I never managed to find it."[16] He was one of a dozen Christians, mostly women and children, who had periodically witnessed the ritual sacrifice of hundreds of their companions.

Half-Caloosa and half-European in culture, Escalante brilliantly brokered an alliance between Spain and the Caloosa, to be cemented by the marriage of Menéndez to the sister of the powerful *cacique*, called King Carlos by the Spaniards.

The Spanish Adelantado of Florida disembarked for his solemn wedding with a splendid troupe of minstrels: two fife players, three trumpeters, a harpist, a viola player, all kept in time by the sonorous rhythm of a great bass drum; they were accompanied by a "little dwarf, a great singer and dancer."[17] Menéndez also brought two hundred harquebusiers, their fuses smoldering just in case. The Spaniards estimated that two thousand Indians were packed inside King Carlos's great house as Menéndez entered with his little entourage of twenty noblemen. The *cacique* sat on a capacious throne, with a great lady beside him on a dais. "She was thirty-five years old, no beauty, and so stern of countenance it seemed as though she had been raised to gravitas."[18]

Carlos took Menéndez by the hands as a choir of young women sang and his closest relatives danced. One by one, the leading Caloosa noblemen greeted their foreign guest, and Menéndez asked to speak. He read slowly but with confidence from a prepared script that the interpreters had spelled out phonetically in the Caloosa language. His hosts were charmed and impressed, but then the *cacique*'s mood darkened and his people must have stifled their tittering.

For a moment, gravitas teetered on the brink of farce, for Menéndez had begun to address the great lady as though she were King Carlos's queen. He turned to the real queen, twenty years old and "the most beautiful of all the Indian women present," with "very good hands and eyes" and "very good eyebrows," the Spaniards thought, wearing a "gorgeous pearl necklace and a choker of gold beads."[19] Menéndez had mistaken her for his bride and serenaded her with such glowing praise she blushed deeply, while Carlos's cheeks glowed with jealousy. The Spaniards had to quickly calm the brewing storm by handing out gifts of chemises and mirrors for the royal women and knives and hatchets to the men. The feasting began.

During a pause in the revels, Carlos turned to Menéndez and invited him to comply with Caloosa conjugal custom and lie with his bride in an adjacent chamber.

"But I cannot lie with a woman who is not Christian," protested the agitated Spaniard.

"My sister and my people are already Christians," Carlos responded.

As the party continued, Menéndez retired to do his duty with his new wife, and "in the morning, she arose happy and the Christian women said that she was very pleased."[20]

We do not know how the elaborate charade of this marriage alliance originated, but the obvious model for the Spaniards was the recent marriage of Philip II to the vivacious young Elizabeth Valois in the hope of securing detente with France. Menéndez sent his new bride to Cuba and turned his attention to the Atlantic coast.

Europeans' sense of American geography developed slowly during the sixteenth century. Mariners often accurately charted the reality of the newly emerging continent, but others perpetuated fantastical notions of what might be discovered. Knowledge of the Atlantic coast of North America was especially thin but was greatly influenced by the Italian navigator Giovanni Verrazano, who in 1524 mistook the Outer Banks of the Carolinas for a narrow isthmus dividing the Atlantic from the Pacific, and is said to have been eaten by Caribs four years later.[21]

From the incrementally skewed conception of the continent, Menéndez came to believe that two great waterways cut across North America. The Río

Salado, "Salt River," was probably based on real knowledge of the St. Lawrence River. He thought it must run southwest from its mouth at about 60° north but could easily be reached by ascending a river that emptied into the Atlantic either at the Chesapeake or Delaware bays. The mouth of the other great waterway was on the Pacific coast at about 50°, which may have been based upon the confused memory of an undocumented visit to Vancouver Bay. At a point 45° north, these two great arms were divided only by a narrow isthmus, an idea that might be based on Indian knowledge of the Great Lakes. Coupling this compelling idea of a landmass crisscrossed by waterways to the reports that the expeditions led by Coronado and Soto had almost met somewhere in Arkansas, Menéndez convinced himself that he should seek a way to traverse North America.[22]

In the summer of 1566, having resupplied St. Augustine and hanged a boatload of mutineers, Menéndez coasted north, establishing cordial relations at Sapelo Sound with the Guale Indians of the area, probably pronounced "Wha-ley" by the Spaniards. At the prominent headland just north of Savannah they called Cape Santa Elena, Menéndez befriended some Orista Indians and began building a town and a fort on Parris Island. He then instructed Captain Juan Pardo to lead the first of two expeditions deep inland to explore the possibility of opening a route toward the silver mines of Zacatecas in northern New Spain.

In 1567 and 1568, Pardo led over a hundred men across the Blue Ridge Mountains through Swannanoa Gap and followed the Tennessee River valley as far as Trascaluza in Alabama, where he was welcomed by various *caciques*, both men and women, many of whom remembered Soto and his men. Over the following winter he explored south through the Appalachians. Pardo left a chain of tiny military outposts along the route, potential stages on the endless road to New Spain, but the Indians of the region soon tired of the indolent, insolent intruders and threw them out.[23] As Pardo's men straggled into Santa Elena two years later, there was little enthusiasm to try again.

Menéndez returned to St. Augustine but was forced to evacuate most of the garrison to Cuba when Indians destroyed their food supplies.[24] There, he learned Philip II had been so pleased to hear that Lutheran heresy had been so brutally uprooted in North America that the king had sent a thousand troops and settlers as reinforcements.[25]

Menéndez eventually turned to the Jesuit Order to provide the spiritual marrow of his colonial enterprise, and in 1570 Father Juan Bautista Segura landed at Chesapeake Bay with eight priests and four young catechists: twelve devout apostles yearning to preach the word of God. Menéndez pleaded with Segura to accept a contingent of troops for their protection, but Segura believed that God had blessed him with a far more potent talisman: an influential ambassador the Spaniards called Don Luis Paquiquineo. This Algonquian Indian from Chesapeake Bay had already spent a long time traveling in the Spaniards' realms of gold.[26]

Much of Paquiquineo's story has been lost in the mists of myth and legend. Some have suggested that he was Pocahontas's uncle, the elder brother of her father, Chief Powhatan, and even entertained the alluring notion he was one and the same as Powhatan's valiant successor, Opechancanough, who led the Great Massacre of the Virginia Colony, in 1622. The English colonists at Jamestown remembered Paquiquineo as "skilled in the art of governing his rude countrymen," and an exceptionally impressive figure, "a man of large stature, noble presence, and extraordinary parts."[27] His first documented appearance in history is in an expenses claim filed in Spain by a ship's captain for clothes so Paquiquineo could be presented at court "superbly and sumptuously dressed." It was reported that "the king and his courtiers were greatly pleased."[28]

Still, Paquiquineo pleaded with Philip to be allowed to return home and embarked on the next fleet headed for New Spain, where he miraculously survived smallpox following his conversion to Christianity. He took the Christian name of the viceroy, Luis de Velasco. Menéndez had personally asked Philip II for permission to take Paquiquineo back "because he is a Lord of that land," he and "the friars who have experience of it will be most fruitful in converting the Indians."[29] But during the passage to Chesapeake, Paquiquineo was alarmed by the brash bravado of the Spanish soldiers and guided them into the wrong harbor, hoping to jump ship. But then a great gale blew the ship so far into the Atlantic that the captain decided to run with the wind back to Spain.

Paquiquineo went to live with the Jesuits in Seville, where he seduced his hosts into believing he would be their spiritual beachhead at Chesapeake. He "assured them that they would want for nothing, for corn, fish, and game were plentiful in his land and that he and his family would defend them from the Indians."[30] But on his return to America, Paquiquineo went back to traditional ways, accumulating the many wives essential to his prestige as a chief, with a household large enough to entertain on the lavish scale required by the mores of regional diplomacy.[31] Father Segura severely admonished him for those sins, leading Paquiquineo to turn on the Jesuits.

Without Paquiquineo's friendship the Jesuits were helpless. Far from providing for them, he seems to have advised the local people to refuse to help them, and they were forced to forage for fruit and nuts. Desperately hungry, Father Quirós visited Paquiquineo and begged for help, but the merciless Indian cudgeled him to death. Tearing the black robes from the warm cadaver to wear as a disguise, he set out for the Jesuit mission with a band of warriors. Segura was celebrating Candlemas and welcomed him with open arms, but Paquiquineo smashed open the priest's head with a huge club.[32] The other Jesuits knelt in prayer, fervently crossing themselves as they were murdered one by one, "beaten, shot with arrows, and beheaded . . . Like timid lambs, they were offered up in sacrifice to Our Lord at the hands of this new Judas." Afterward, the Indians "made cups out of their skulls and toasted one another drunkenly, wearing the robes of these fortunate martyrs, chanting about their deeds and victories," Jesuit historians reported.

Only one little acolyte, a child called Alonso, survived under the protection of Powhatan to tell the tale to Menéndez, who remarked with bitter sarcasm, "These blessed fathers seem to think that his Holiness the Pope only sent them there to be martyred and cut into pieces by these savages."[33] Menéndez could feel fortune and Florida slipping from his grasp.

In 1585, Queen Elizabeth I's favorite pirate, Sir Francis Drake, launched devastating raids on Spanish cities around the Caribbean. Havana braced for the worst, but the English fleet sailed on by, heading for home. On June 6, 1586, Drake's forty-two ships were sighted off St. Augustine, and the following day, at sunrise, he landed an army of twenty-five hundred men, as much for the sport as the spoils.[34] The eighty Spaniards trapped inside the fort stoutly resisted as English guns boomed a relentless rhythm of ball and grapeshot. They held out until midday, but finally, one Englishman remembered, "like fainte harted Cowardes they ranne awaie" into the woods.[35]

The following day, the Spaniards' Indian allies attacked the English "with a verie strawnge crie," but fell back after a brief skirmish.[36] Drake's men set about sacking the town. Although the pickings were paltry compared to their Caribbean plunder, they found a royal coffer containing five thousand ducats and eighteen bronze cannon. They slaughtered 250 horses they could not steal, felled an entire orchard of fruit trees, burned the fort, and sailed away, leaving the Spaniards with the clothes they stood up in and enough food to last little more than a fortnight.[37] The almost three hundred soldiers, women, and children thanked God for their lives.

In Madrid, many influential voices called for Florida to be abandoned, but persistent rumors that the English had established the Roanoke colony in modern North Carolina made Philip II all the more determined to keep a Catholic foothold on that vulnerable coast.[38] He ordered the consolidation of resources at St. Augustine, and a phoenix of sorts rose from the ashes. By the end of the century, the town had a population of about seven hundred soldiers and settlers and a few hundred Indian and African slaves. A few Guale *caciques* provided labor and professed allegiance to the Spanish Crown in return for military support in their quarrels with neighboring tribes. Meanwhile, a handful of tough Franciscan missionaries claimed to have baptized fourteen thousand souls for God, although six friars paid with their lives for that mass salvation during the Juanillo Revolt of 1597.[39]

CHAPTER 9

POETRY & CONQUEST

NEW MEXICO

Arms, and the man I sing, of valor, prudence,
And strength, of a hero whose stalwart patience,
When tossed upon a foaming Sea of Sorrow
Defied his rivals' poisonous envy unbowed,
Of brave Spaniards' distant deeds in America's west,
And their discovery of an undiscovered world, *Plus Ultra*,
Of their toils, their battles, their sufferings and success.

—GASPAR PÉREZ DE VILLAGRÁ

DURING THE VIOLENT EARLY HISTORY of New Galicia, Coronado's deputy Cristóbal de Oñate stood out for his moral rectitude and pragmatic resilience. Described by a venerable eighteenth-century historian as "one of the most chivalrous gentlemen ever to come out of the Basque Country,"[1] even the judicial inquiry that excoriated Coronado's government referred to him as a "noble gentleman who served exceptionally well" and was "utterly without blame."[2] He almost single-handedly saved New Galicia for the crown by encouraging a handful of Basque associates to prospect for gold and silver in the Sierra Madre. One of these men, Juan de Tolosa, known as Longbeard, rode "time and again into the dangerous, war-torn hill country" that was overrun by Zacatecos patriots. In 1546, one of his Indian slaves supposedly said scornfully, "Seeing as you will go to so much effort to find this particular sort of dirt, I will guide you to a place where you can sink your hands into it and satiate your greed."[3] He led Tolosa to one of the richest silver strikes in history.[4]

Tolosa formed a mining company with Oñate and the other Basques and founded the town of Zacatecas. Rugged adventurers flooded in, restless risk-takers, eager Indians and Spaniards, Africans and mixed-race *castas*, escaping their pasts, thirsting for life and wealth, pioneers who dared to dream of shaping their own destinies. But they lived in constant fear of hostile Zacatecos determined to rid their ancestral homeland of this alien swarm. One traumatized Spanish migrant wrote home, "I have not put down my weapons since leaving Mexico City, for the land is boiling with a species of Indian invented by the devil."[5] Remote farms with their settlements of friendly Indians and their priests also offered the ruthless Zacatecos easy pickings. The ranchers complained to the viceroy that the "Indians' daring is such that they come down onto the plains from their craggy mountain redoubts and have killed many, scalping their victims and cutting out their hearts and entrails and even eating the flesh of those they murder."[6] The men who conquered New Mexico were raised in that tough frontier world. The Bishop of Guadalajara declared, "The Spaniards born and raised here are the strongest, most robust, and hardworking people, as sharp of mind and as spirited in character as any Castilian."[7]

The founding fathers of Zacatecas carved out vast landholdings from hostile surroundings. They lived like medieval feudal barons, protecting a host of vassal-like clients, brothers, cousins, retainers, hangers-on, and hirelings.[8] Oñate and his partners were rough-and-ready bachelors who almost overnight had achieved uncommon extremes of wealth and eligibility; they quickly interlaced their families in a complex web of marriage alliances. Oñate married the spirited daughter of one of Nuño de Guzmán's disgraced henchmen, whose claim to be an honest widow was only discredited five centuries later when an eagle-eyed researcher noticed that her first husband had still been alive in Spain in the 1570s.[9] Their consequently posthumously illegitimate son, Juan de Oñate, would lead the settlement of the Upper Rio Grande and become the first Governor of New Mexico. Juan de Tolosa made the most majestic match of all, marrying Leonor Cortés Montezuma, Cortés's natural daughter by his concubine Cottonflower, herself Montezuma's daughter and quite simply a "young woman with the noblest blood lines in the colony of New Spain."[10] Their daughter married Juan de Oñate. Cristóbal de Oñate married his stepdaughter to his nephew Vicente de Zaldívar (brother of Juan), and their sons Vicente and Cristóbal married the daughters of Juan de Oñate and Tolosa, which meant that Vicente was Juan de Oñate's brother-in-law, second cousin once removed, and his half nephew as well. The scholar who has done most to unravel this seemingly impenetrable genetic tangle described it as "complicated . . . almost beyond understanding."[11]

The younger generations pushed the frontier farther north, founding the province of Nueva Vizcaya, "New Biscay," in honor of their Basque roots, in 1562. They established the remote mining camp of Santa Bárbara, barely a dozen households huddled high up the Conchos River system, the most northern outpost of New Spain. The settlers farmed pigs, cattle, sheep, and goats. There were fish in the river and game birds aplenty in nearby marsh-land. It was fertile country with a temperate climate, surrounded by pine stands and oak forests, and Spanish fruit trees and vegetables flourished in the valley.[12] The pull of adventure abated and dreams of Cíbola faded, but they never went away. They saw the ruins of Paquimé, the long-deserted "city" at Casa Grandes, and were "astonished" by "the great size of such solid, six-or-seven-story structures, like fortresses with their towers and ramparts" and "fine courtyards paved with slabs of stone."[13] They avidly read Cabeza de Vaca's *Shipwrecks* and met many "noble, friendly, brave, gallant, and handsome Natives who confirmed that all the stories of miracles and other things contained therein were true," and "by signs they indicated that Cíbola was but three day's journey hence."[14]

By the late 1570s, a posse of ruffians were making a living of sorts at Santa Bárbara by raiding for slaves far up-country. On one of these forays they captured a man who told them that "much farther on there were large towns where the people had cotton and blankets and ate turkeys, beans, squash, and beef."[15] Back at the mining camp, talk turned once more to New Mexico and Cabeza de Vaca's book and memories of Coronado. In 1580, a Franciscan friar called Agustín Rodríguez secured a license to go in search of that half-forgotten country under the protection of a small troop of soldiers led by Captain Francisco Sánchez, known ever since by his nickname Chamuscado, or "Burnt Beard." The soldiers returned after months in the saddle and reported that the friars had stayed behind to proselytize a remarkably civi-lized pagan nation who had "welcomed them peacefully" at large towns of up to "four or five hundred houses." They had ridden thirty leagues in search of the "Cíbola cows" and seen herds of two or three hundred of those "hunch-backed" creatures, "low to the ground," with "small curled horns."[16]

Rumors soon reached Santa Bárbara that the supposedly "civilized pagans" had murdered the Franciscan missionaries. A wealthy rancher called Antonio Espejo from the heartland of New Spain, already a fugitive from a murder charge, offered to lead a small party of soldiers in search of the friars and to prolong his flight from justice. They soon learned that the Franciscans had indeed been killed, but for a year this intrepid band explored almost all the Pueblos country, even meeting Mexican Indians at Zuni who had stayed behind when Coronado evacuated New Mexico. They rode west into Arizona and probably reached somewhere near modern Prescott, returning to Santa Bárbara in 1584 by descending the Pecos River.[17]

Perhaps the most remarkable, if incidental, incursion into New Mexico followed the scandalous discovery by the Inquisition that Luis de Carvajal, the first governor of the newly created province of Nuevo León, south of

Texas, and most of his family and settlers were secretly practicing Jews. His second-in-command, Gaspar Castaño de Sosa, presumably also a Jew, although there is no proof, fled north with over a hundred families and huge herds of livestock before he was arrested and banished to the Philippines. His followers apparently returned south, but folk memories of Jewish ancestry have long been a part of New Mexican lore, possibly ever since.[18]

In 1593, a minor frontier warlord called Leyva explored the northern pueblos and rode northeast across the Great Plains, possibly into modern Kansas. He was murdered there by a soldier called Humaña, who subsequently led eighteen men north to Nebraska, where they were all killed by Apaches, except for an Indian guide who reported the story years later.

Philip II instructed the Viceroy of New Spain to appoint a man with the "requisite credentials and personal qualities" to undertake the settlement of New Mexico as quickly as possible. The viceroy recommended Juan de Oñate because, as another influential contemporary put it, no other man was as well placed to "gather together the men and women" necessary to the success of the enterprise, "for he has so many powerful relatives and friends" and "because he is so highly esteemed by the soldiers of that region."[19] Oñate signed a provisional contract for the "totally peaceful and friendly" settlement of New Mexico and began amassing troops and settlers, including a huge contingent of Tlaxcalans, at Chihuahua.[20]

Oñate appointed as general legal counsel to the expedition a man called Gaspar Pérez de Villagrá, "Small of stature . . . thickset and powerful . . . bald," but with "a full gray beard and two deep wrinkles in his forehead," he was of typical Castilian peasant stock.[21] His immigrant parents had established a successful tanning business and became involved in transatlantic trade, which allowed the fourteen-year-old Gaspar to study law at Salamanca University. He graduated in 1576 and returned to Mexico with a three-year-old boy, described as his cousin, but presumably his bastard. He then disappeared from the historical record until joining Oñate's enterprise. Perhaps the most attractive character in the story of Oñate's settlement of New Mexico, he is remembered today for recounting the story of their exploration and conquest of the Pueblo world in a remarkable and in many ways bizarre epic poem that was published in Spain in 1610, the *History of New Mexico*. Oñate chose his lawyer well, for Villagrá may have been an eccentric and indifferent poet, but he evidently advised his client brilliantly though the extraordinarily difficult launch of the expedition.

Oñate's enemies somehow convinced the Council of the Indies and the by-now decrepit and gout-ridden Philip II to consider replacing him with a geriatric aristocrat called Pedro Ponce de León who had never been to the New

World, but almost certainly a distant cousin, many times removed, of the discoverer of Florida.[22] When the viceroy received the warrant suspending the departure of the expedition, he told his attorney general he was "very worried and perplexed" and consulted the Audiencia of Mexico. Oñate's people would almost certainly desert should they learn of the king's dithering, so the viceroy instructed his courier to serve the royal warrant with the utmost secrecy.

The official audit in preparation for departure was already under way when the messenger arrived and handed over documents in the presence of only a handful of officials, notaries, and confidants, including Villagrá. Oñate formally accepted the warrant, "kissed it, and duly touched it against the top of his head as a sign of his obedience to the crown."[23] Villagrá's verses transport us back to the emotion of the moment and his pride in Oñate's stoicism and presence of mind:

> Calm of countenance and circumspect, don Juan
> With well feigned joy rode hither and thither
> Among his men, 'pon a gaily garland'd steed,
> That they discover not too soon his injury.

But in private, in his tent, Villagrá advised Oñate, who then gave his formal response: "I shall duly abide by my king's command, for all that there are many just reasons to appeal this warrant, and despite the great losses my men and I will suffer by this adjournment of our venture. For the provisions will spoil, many of the horses, oxen, mules, cattle, and sheep now gathered in their herds will soon be scattered, and many men will fast desert as they begin to suspect what is afoot."[24]

Then he formally put his sovereign on notice that although he would bide his time, "I have, to date, spent above 100,000 pesos in this business and my captains and my men above 200,000 more. They have sold homes, estates, and chattels, for they trusted in what had been agreed and contracted with the crown. If His Majesty should order me to abandon the expedition, then, with all due respect, I will plead for justice and sue for all damages, losses, and interest due to us."[25]

Villagrá quietly pointed out that Oñate must ensure the official audit be completed, whether to expedite his departure before the senile monarch and the Fates changed their minds again, or to ensure the value of the enterprise be properly notarized to support his claim for damages against the crown.

Villagrá's inspiration for his History of New Mexico was a stirring and popular epic poem about the conquistadors of Chile known as the Araucana, which mentions his distant cousin Francisco de Villagrá. But although Villagrá has been called the "Homer of New Mexico" because his verses are replete with echoes from the *Iliad* and the *Odyssey,* he most obviously drew on the *Aeneid,* Virgil's great mythmaking hymn to the adventures of the wandering Trojan refugee whose descendants founded Rome.[26] Villagrá even borrowed Virgil's opening words *Arma virumque cano,* translated by the great seventeenth-century English dramatist John Dryden as "Arms and the man I sing..." Thus Villagrá's *History of New Mexico* begins:

> Arms, and the man I sing, of valor, prudence,
> And strength, of a hero whose stalwart patience,
> When tossed upon a foaming Sea of Sorrow
> Defied his rivals' poisonous envy unbowed,
> Of brave Spaniards' distant deeds in America's west,
> And their discovery of an undiscovered world, *Plus Ultra,*
> Of their toils, their battles, their sufferings and success.[27]

But while Aeneas was a mortal forced to "labor long by sea and land" because he suffered the "unrelenting hatred of Juno," Villagrá introduced Oñate as a victim of royal bureaucracy and the political machinations of his rivals. Across line after line of verse, he attempted to enliven the administrative wrangling with a series of increasingly improbable similes referring to storms at sea, shipwrecks, and even a tsunami. He led readers through the first revision of the contract, described the arrival of the chief auditor, until finally—far from breathless after so much epic inaction—he described the moment "a courier arrived in great haste," happy and excited and asking for a tip because he thought he was bringing the long-awaited order for the expedition to depart. But, in a trice, Gaspar tells us:

> Deceit ever wears a cloak of innocence
> And so, when the sealed missive the courier,
> Happy and unwitting brought, was in utmost
> Secret opened, instead of glad tidings there,
> Was the document I copy here verbatim.

Within the poem, Villagrá included the almost unedited texts of both the royal warrant and the viceroy's covering letter. There is something sublimely quixotic about borrowing the august tradition of epic verse to tell a story of bureaucratic skullduggery, government incompetence, and the legal niceties of contractual relationships, without a man being killed, a woman abducted, nor a sword drawn. Nonetheless, that eccentric rhetorical gambit reflected the enormous respect that most sixteenth-century Spaniards had for the institution of the law and their faith in litigation as relatively equitable. The royal censor who approved the text for publication described Villagrá's "many verses" as "free of poetic flourish or artistry, for in reality it is a true narrative history."[28] Almost all critics and historians since have treated the poem as an essentially reliable account of Oñate's expedition.

Whereas Garcilaso el Inca's *Florida* perverted the principle attributed to Aristotle that historians should record "events as they were, adding nothing, nor taking anything away from the truth" (to reuse Cervantes's formulation), Villagrá appears to confound the principle that "a poet can sing of deeds not as they were, but as they should have been." But perhaps we should not be so easily deceived, for although the royal censor also praised Villagrá for "keeping quiet" about his own exploits while "singing the praises" of Oñate, in reality Villagrá is frequently a heroic protagonist of his own tale.[29] The written word is never as truthful as it seems, Cervantes might have advised.

Villagrá vividly describes how the expedition began to disintegrate before Oñate's omniscient but impotent gaze. The governor, he sings,

Surveyed the noble suffering of his camp,
The mangy lodgings of his fatigued friars,
The servants, officials, and other settlers
The babes, children, and their mothers,
Living roofless in the wilderness . . .

The settlers began to desert, pilfering any supplies they could carry. Suddenly, Doña Eufemia, the royal ensign's wife, a woman of "singular courage and enormous strength of character," harangued the disheartened throng. She berated them for shamelessly turning their backs on so honorable a mission, as though they were women. "Could they really be men?" she asked. Could they really be noble Spaniards?

Almost every senior figure in the colonial establishment in Mexico felt a deep sense of anger and frustration at the crown's shoddy treatment of Oñate, rooted in their sense of themselves as *criollos*, American Spaniards born and raised in the New World. They experienced a collective sense of exasperation at the arrogance of interfering institutions in the Old World that knew next to nothing of the *criollos*' homeland. In a remarkably forthright letter to the crown, one influential member of the Audiencia of Mexico fumed that "the

Council of the Indies" was well aware of the lamentable outcome of "every expedition that has been organized in Spain with orders to bring recruits from over there. For they always sign up the poor who are taken in by promises of great piles of gold; and when they get here and discover that they have been lied to, they desert and go off on their own." "How," he asked, was Ponce de León going to provide "four or five mounts for each of the two hundred men-at-arms, not to mention the pack animals, weapons, harquebuses, vehicles, clothing, and everything else, four or five thousand head of livestock, the tents, the twelve hundred oxen . . . ?" "I ask Your Majesty," he went on, "to do yourself a favor and understand the reality of the situation."

The viceroy, for all that he was a proud Spaniard, wrote the king, "Over here those who are experienced and intelligent are very doubtful that anyone who comes from Spain and who has neither wealth nor family here will be able to recruit the people necessary." What is more, he advised, "if the expedition is granted to someone else, don Juan will have a reasonable claim in law" and "Your Majesty will be defeated if such a claim is heard, and he will have to be given satisfaction at great expense and in violation of the warrants ordering that such expeditions should be made without cost to the royal exchequer."[30] In the end, Ponce de León proved to be so old and sick he failed to organize his expedition in Spain. Philip II gave the order for Oñate to proceed.

For Villagrá, that potent sense of *criollo* identity is rooted in geography, which he evokes with great precision by using contemporary scientific language:

> We learned the country's longitude precisely,
> Must be two hundred degrees and seventy,
> As measured by the up-to-date meridian,
> Nearest where the Gulf of Mexico meets land.[31]

He characterizes that distant north as "five thousand leagues of vastness inhabited by pagans wholly ignorant of Christ," before explaining that the Mexica believed their ancestral homeland of Azatlán lay somewhere in that wilderness.

> Fame has broadcast far 'n' wide, how Mexica sages
> Keep quick their histories of long-past ages
> By means of certain very ancient pictures
> Hieroglyphs they decipher and, like scripture,
> They debate among themselves . . .

In which they documented those Ancient Aztecs,
Their ancestors whose reverèd names now echo
In their erstwhile capital of Mexico,
But in times of yore, first ventured forth
From those newly traversed regions in the north.[32]

The Mexican Indians among Oñate's men excitedly discussed that history as the expedition set out:

Those indigenous children of Aztec blood
All of one nature, of one substance bred,
Then spoke all in one voice of their history,
In the farthest reaches of the north, of how
From a dark, unhomely boreal cavern
A pair of most valiant brothers sallied forth
Scions of a noble house, of monarchy,
Children of a truly royal king of kings,
Young princes zealous of their reputations,
Quick to triumph, adventure, and feats of arms
In strands afar remote where they might subject
Foreign kings to their imperial ambitions.

He might be describing the Spaniards.

In great detail, Villagrá described that Ancient Mexica army that marched out of Azatlán to found Tenochtitlán, drawing on the pageantry of European chivalry. He eulogizes their "well-armed soldiery" with their "solid Turkish bows, their pikes and maces," the myriad "flags and standards," "dazzling tents and pavilions," and the inevitable "ladies, damsels, and their chaperones," who were the all-important audience for so much chivalrous braggadocio, with so many "sumptuous costumes and liveries."[33] But according to Aztec history, the devil tried to sow sedition among their ancestral leaders:

As those poor sinners marched onward south,
The malevolent devil in the guise of a crone,
Brazen and frightful, blocked the road ahead,
Long harpy-gray locks tangling down from its scalp,
Skeletal visage leering fleshless and wan,
Ember eyes in smoldering sockets, parched lips,
Four fangs grinning out from a hideous mouth,
Great mangy breasts, starving, flaccid, dry, wrinkly,

And gangling, with nipples stretched dangling over
Wide, sinewy, chest . . .

It goes on, describing how the bones of this horrid creature's "terrifying" limbs "whinnied" or "neighed" as it moved about.[34]

This demonic figure spoke to the Mexica, making references to Greeks, Romans, and Carthage, which would, of course, have bemused the assembled ranks of Mexica migrants, who as yet knew nothing of the Old World. However, Villagrá also intoned the Mexica myth that they chose the site of Tenochtitlán when they saw an eagle standing on a cactus and eating a snake:

> Settle not near Romans nor Carthaginians,
> But where an eagle stands 'pon the spiny pads
> Of a prickly pear fast-rooted on a crag,
> Lapped all around by crystal clear waters,
> Feasting on a great talon-grasped serpent . . .[35]

The ghastly figure of an evil old crone or witch is common to many cultures, but scholars have identified the Mexica goddess Coatlicue or the god Tezauhtéotl as probable influences. Villagrá, however, writing for a European audience, likened this figure to Circe of the *Odyssey*, although he presumably also had in mind Iris's attempt to prevent the foundation of Rome by appearing as Beroe in the *Aeneid*.[36]

Again, Villagrá blurred the distinction between the cultures of the Old and New Worlds, proudly identifying Oñate's expedition as a Mexican endeavor. But this invocation of *criollo* chauvinism reached its zenith when he turned his attention to the leading Spanish members of the expedition.

> The great Marquis of the Valley begat a daughter
> By a princess, one of three girls to Montezuma born,
> Last of those ancient Kings of Mexico to rule his lands.
> The Marquis married this rich prize to Juan de Tolosa,
> Who with two others had found such abundant silver.

Tolosa, Villagrá explains, won New Galicia with Cristóbal de Oñate. Then he turns his attention to the younger generations.

> Father of Don Juan de Oñate, he who wed
> The great-granddaughter of the Aztec King,
> By whom his own son Cristóbal was born,

Descendent of the Marquis and all these kings,
And who, not yet ten years old, sallied with us
To serve in our conquests like young Hannibal.

To clarify, this ten-year-old is Juan de Oñate's son Cristóbal, great-grandson of Cottonflower Montezuma, who was in a sense the expedition mascot and who embodied this noble union of Mexica and Spanish blood.

The very name "New Mexico" heralded a change at the heart of colonial sentiment. Spaniards had named one newly claimed province after another for places in Spain: New Spain, New Galicia, New León, New Biscay, New Granada, and many more. But New Mexico was the first time Spanish settlers gave the indigenous name of a long-established place in the Americas to a wholly new province. It was an obvious choice to colonists who had grown up aware of the founding myths of the Aztecs and who were marching toward the legendary home of Azatlán alongside hundreds of Indian servants and companions-in-arms. It was also an intelligent exercise in public relations, as Mexico was closely associated with gold and glory. Nonetheless, the name New Mexico appeared as a purely American baptism, a baptism asserting a New World dream in the spirit of a legendary Aztec past that predated the arrival of Europeans.

Oñate and his expedition were subjected to the final bureaucratic indignity of the official inspection and audit, carried out with eager thoroughness by an elderly commissioner general. He finally granted his grudging permission to continue but refused to certify his decision in writing and simply abandoned the camp "without a single word of encouragement to the poor, unfortunate soldiers."[37] Finally free of metropolitan authority, Captain Farfán wrote a short farce, acted out by two talented servants of African descent, which ended with Oñate's character giving the commissioner a good thrashing, to the general delight of the spectators.[38]

"Eighty laden wagons," many carts, and Oñate's two personal "carriages" trundled off slowly along the trail, raising clouds of dust. Like the Israelite's Exodus to the Promised Land or Ringling's traveling circus, "great gatherings of oxen" plodded onward, "trips of goats wandered the wayside, herds of fighting bulls followed flocks of sheep, and the colts and gentle mares frolicked while the neighing stallions trotted and the cows and mules all roused themselves and took to the road."[39] They reached the Rio Grande on April 19, a few miles south of El Paso, "The Crossing" of great Indian trail. The usually dry official record of the itinerary reflects their relief at leaving the harsh highlands of the Sierra Madre with an almost lyrical evocation of the "cool shade" of a bucolic resting place beside a river teeming with "catfish, bass, and a white fish almost half a yard long." The banks were green with "dense bushes, willows, and many mesquite trees both great and small," a scene not easily imagined today from the bridge to Juárez.[40] Eleven days later, the Feast of the Ascension, Oñate ordered everybody to dress in their finest clothes for the formal ceremony to take possession of the kingdoms and provinces of New Mexico.[41] Brother Alonso Martínez preached a moving sermon, and afterward Captain Farfán directed "a great play" in which an allegorical figure of New Mexico humbled herself before the Church and begged that Original Sin be washed from her pagan inhabitants by the Holy Sacrament of Baptism. The course of the Rio Grande has shifted time and again over the years, so it is possible this was the first-ever European theater performed within the frontiers of the modern United States.[42]

The expedition crossed the river on May 4, but over the following weeks the vast, unwieldy caravan spread out as it moved north. The ill-disciplined cavalry were impatient with the laborious progress of the wagons and those on foot. Oñate tried to keep them busy by sending out scouting posses, but he was extremely concerned to make a good first impression on the Indian inhabitants, issuing strict orders that no one should enter any settlements. When one errant captain disobeyed him, Oñate made a great show of condemning the man to be garroted, before graciously pardoning him thanks to the pleas of his friends and comrades. Perhaps Captain Farfán wrote that script?

Oñate and Zaldívar themselves began to ride on ahead, drawn by the promise of the Pueblo world. They found the most southerly settlement, Qualacu, abandoned by its terrified inhabitants. But it was an exciting moment nonetheless; finally they could explore the streets of a pueblo, peer inside its houses, and enter the ceremonial kivas, the sacred quasi-subterranean ritual spaces that the Spaniards called *estufas*, or "stoves," because their roofs looked like the kilns in the potteries of Spain. But Oñate was roughly woken from any metaphorical reverie he allowed himself when messengers arrived with news that that in his absence, the undercurrent of discontent among his followers had begun to turn into outright dissent as the main body of the expedition struggled across an eighty-mile stretch of desert, which became known as the *Jornada del Muerto*, "Dead Man's March." Suffering from extreme thirst, many of the settlers had begun clamoring to go home. Villagrá had stemmed the unrest temporarily when he noticed that one of the dogs had muddy paws and realized a watering hole had to be nearby. But Oñate understood that he himself must ride back and use his mercurial powers of persuasion to keep the settlers from turning round.[43]

Two weeks later, Oñate had calmed his stormy followers and was once more leading the vanguard through increasingly friendly and well-populated

Pueblo communities. He was offered a large quantity of corn at a place he called *Socorro*, "Succor," the name it bears to this day. They camped in another pueblo, which he named New Seville, modern Sevilleta, because the way it sat in a crook of the river reminded them of the great capital of southern Spain. On the feast of his own saint, John the Baptist, June 23, Oñate established his headquarters at Caypa (modern Ohkay Owingeh) and christened it San Juan. He organized a fine tournament to celebrate the holiday in which two bands of cavalrymen clashed, wielding weapons with great skill, according to Villagrá, who must have been one of the participants.[44]

They were watched by great crowds of curious Pueblo spectators, who had come to Caypa for the dancing and ceremonies associated with the summer solstice and must have thought the Spaniards' rituals to be strangely exotic. The Spaniards visited two large kivas, where they counted "sixty painted idols," which Villagrá described as "vast numbers of ferocious and arrogant demons," in reality the sacred kachina masks and costumes collected together for the dance ceremonies. As the soldiers relaxed after the sports, three Indians approached Oñate, and one of them began shouting out the days of the week in Spanish, and then explained that two Christians, called Cristóbal and Tomás, were living at Kewa, six miles away, which the Spaniards called Santo Domingo.

Oñate went to investigate. His posse spent a disturbing night at Puaray, where the Indians welcomed them with a great display of hospitality and offered the friars recently whitewashed quarters. But that night, according to Villagrá, as the whitewash slowly dried, the Franciscans watched in horror as graphic images emerged from underneath the paint of the martyrdom of Brothers Agustín and Francisco. The posse all moved on to Kewa.

Tomás and Cristóbal turned out to be Mexican Indians who had arrived with one of the earlier Spanish expeditions. On July 7, they were sworn in as legal translators so that Oñate could receive the formal acceptance of vassalage from a large number of Pueblo leaders then assembled at Santo Domingo. According to the official expedition record, the *caciques* of Tamy, Acotziya, Cachichi, Yatez, Tipoti, Cochiti, and Kewa all rendered homage to Spain, as did the Chiguas, and the Pueblos of the west, Piaque, Axoytze, Piamato, Quioyoco, and Camitze, the Jemez and Yxcaguayo, Qiameca, Zia, Quiusta, Lecca, Potze, Tziaguatzi, Tzyiti, Caatzo, Taos, Comitze, Ayquin, Tziati, Pequen, Cachchi, Chuchin, Baguacatxuti, Ynocohocpi, Acacagua, and Tzijaatica.[45]

Brother Martínez said mass in the main plaza, but then the entire company retired to the great kiva, where Oñate addressed the Pueblo leaders: "I am sent by Philip of Spain, the most powerful king in the world, who desires the salvation of your souls and wishes you to be his vassals so he may provide you with the same protection and justice he has afforded to the other natives of the East and West Indies in order that you shall be able to live in civilized peace and harmony and benefit from trades and skills, and agriculture and animal husbandry."

From time to time, as Oñate was speaking, the chiefs murmured among themselves. When he had finished, after further discussion, the assembled chiefs announced that they "were unanimous in their consent and they showed great joy at becoming vassals of our most Christian king." They began to kneel before Oñate, who then explained the basic tenets of the faith, urging them to accept baptism so that when their bodies died, their souls should go to heaven "and enjoy a life of great joy in God forever." He warned that otherwise "they will go to hell and suffer great torment for all eternity."[46]

Far away in Spain, Philip II lay on his deathbed at his great monastery-palace of El Escorial tormented by gout, covered in festering sores, "consumed by the evil fire that was burning even in his bones."[47] He prayed fervently, terrified that his immortal soul would suffer such agonies for all eternity. On September 13, one of the most able rulers in history died. He was succeeded by his feckless son, Philip III, who soon left the government of Spain and her empire in the hands of his corrupt and petty favorite, the Duke of Lerma.

On the Upper Rio Grande, the last wagons in the train finally rumbled into San Juan on August 18. The settlers had been forced to abandon twenty-two carts and much of their luggage. Their dissent was turning rebellious. Oñate learned that possibly a third of the soldiers were plotting to seize as many Indians as they could, steal what they could carry from the settlers, and then head back to New Spain with their ill-gotten spoils. He threatened to execute the ringleaders, but two days later he forgave them in a moving address to his assembled adventurers, which became known as the "Speech of Tears."[48]

A few days later, four men ran off with a large herd of horses and fled south. Oñate sent Villagrá with a sheriff and sixteen deputies to hunt them down. The lawmen caught up with the thieves near Todos los Santos. There, Villagrá slit the throats of two men he knew had been born in Spain without even allowing them time to confess their sins to God. But he was acquainted with the others, who were from Mexico. Fearful of potential repercussions from their friends, he allowed them to escape.[49]

Epic poems usually recount monumental histories characterized by endless feats of arms, desperate courage in the face of fearful odds, awe-inspiring heroism, and the eventual triumph of a tragic protagonist. But the first deadly event in Villagrá's *History*, the first violent encounter about which the poet sings, is this brutal, ignoble, and essentially minor mission to enforce the law. It is a moment of sublimely grotesque bathos that paints even the poet himself as murderous.

In September, as Oñate tried to settle the expedition at San Juan, an Indian from New Galicia called Jusepe turned up, the only survivor of the party that had traveled onto the Great Plains five years before. Jusepe had fled following the horrific quarrel that led Humaña to hack Leyva to death with a meat cleaver and had then been captured by Apaches. Now, he had finally escaped, and once again among Spaniards, he whetted their appetites with stories of vast herds of bison and great Indian settlements.[50] With another harsh winter looming, a limited supply of food, and his men becoming dangerously restless, Oñate sent Vicente de Zaldívar, with sixty of the most troublesome soldiers, to visit the "land of cows."

The covetous adventurers were overjoyed at the sight of more than a hundred thousand grazing bison and immediately began trying to round them up. Every man imagined himself and his descendants as great ranchers, dreaming of the nobility of owning land and cattle. For three days these men sought to make that aristocratic dream a reality through the sweat and toil of constructing a vast corral from cottonwood logs. When they tried to stampede the herd into the pens, even more powerful and more cunning than Spanish fighting bulls, the animals charged their would-be captors. These experienced Spanish cowboys persisted for days, trying "a thousand different ways" to round up their prey, without success. "They are remarkably wild and ferocious and killed three of our horses," Zaldívar reported. But the Spaniards killed many of these beasts and thought their "fat was better than lard, their bulls better eating than beef, their cows better than veal or mutton." These hard men may have dreamed of gold and silver, but they quickly saw real promise in these novel beasts: strange cattle like their own, yet different and excitingly North American.[51]

The men came across a large Apache trading party returning from the upper Pueblos and bought buffalo meat, hides, fat, and salt with cotton blankets, pottery, corn, and semiprecious stones. Zaldívar's report of his foray onto the Plains contains the first recorded European observation of Apache culture. It describes how the Spaniards were so impressed by the design and great size of their tepees, especially by a tanning process that made the hide covering highly flexible and lightweight, that Zaldívar bought one. He was also intrigued that the Apaches "used a great team of saggy-haired dogs, harnessed like mules," to transport their various accoutrements, including the tepees; "a sight to be seen," he noted, albeit "very comical."[52]

With most of the troublemakers trying to turn themselves into cowboys on the plains, Oñate was in a sufficiently confident mood to lead a large detachment of men in search of a route to the South Sea.[53] Leaving orders that Juan de Zaldívar should follow along when he returned from the Great Plains, Oñate headed west. At Acoma, he surveyed the famously impregnable citadel perched like an eagle's nest upon the crest of a rose-pink rocky mesa, home to notoriously bellicose inhabitants schooled by generations of conflict with their Navajo neighbors. He must have sensed danger, for although the Acomas were friendly and invited him to visit their main kiva, he politely declined. Then, instead of receiving homage within the heart of the pueblo, as he had done everywhere else, he conducted the ceremony in great haste and at the foot of the crag. He hurried on toward Zuni, passing the soaring sandstone crag known as El Morro, or "the Snout," where you can still see the Indian petrographs of armed Spaniards on horseback painted on the smooth sandstone wall known as Inscription Rock, beside the welcome water tank, and read the famous graffito: DON JUAN DE OÑATE PASÓ POR AQUÍ EN 1605, although it is probably a fake.

When Oñate's party reached the Zuni pueblo that Coronado had called Granada, the friars were delighted to find its inhabitants had continued to revere some large crosses, which Coronado had erected, by adorning them with feathered prayer sticks. The party also met the descendants of two Mexica Indians who had stayed behind after Coronado left, no doubt glad to live in a land that had as yet resisted European colonization, a land their Aztec legends associated with ancestral Azatlán.[54] Captain Farfán visited Zuni Salt Lake, twenty-five miles to the south, which he described as "the best such salt flat in all the world, a league across, with the whitest salt, of the finest grain." Oñate also sent three soldiers to round up a handful of horses that had broken loose during a blizzard somewhere near El Morro.[55]

Meanwhile, after Villagrá had dispensed his summary justice, he continued to Santa Bárbara and mailed a long report to the viceroy, "extolling the virtues, wealth, and fecundity of New Mexico." That document is lost, but it is easy to imagine the kind of gold-spangled idyll he must have conjured up from a later letter written by Oñate that extols "the vast mining wealth they were beginning to discover" and the "proximity of the South Sea" to a land filled with an ever "growing number of vassals."[56] Villagrá's mission complete, he returned north, heading for San Juan. But at Puaray, he learned Oñate was heading west. Sending the sheriff and his deputies back to the capital, Villagrá set off alone to catch up with his leader.

Oñate himself described how, on November 8, "the three soldiers who had been rounding up the horses near El Morro returned to Zuni with Villagrá, whom they had found nearly dead and without his mount, his arms, or his armor."[57] Villagrá had a disturbing story to tell. To the great relief of the reader, at last his verse offers us the recognizably epic figure of a lone knight astride his horse, riding through hostile country. Finally, halfway through the *History*, the poet delivers on his opening promise of valor and heroism. Finally, he sings "of arms and the man," albeit that man is himself.

"At the friendly town of Puaray," he recalled in his *History*, "a Spanish lad told me that you, my general, had left only the day before. So I set out in haste, hoping to soon catch up with you. But when I reached the great stronghold of Acoma, I realized that the barbarians were well prepared, waiting for me like crouching greyhounds poised for the chase."

They surrounded Villagrá but kept their distance for fear of his horse. He asked them for food. Their leader, a young war chief called Zutacapán, with casually amiable mien, invited Villagrá to dismount so they could feast together. But when the sensible Spaniard politely declined, Zutacapán was first sullen, then angry. Villagrá rode ahead a little way, then turned to face this menacing "band of barbarian cowards."

Zutacapán spoke: "Are there other Castillas behind you? How many? How many days hence are they?" He indicated that Villagrá should count the numbers on his fingers.

Wily Villagrá flashed up both hands ten times and then a single hand with three digits extended.

"One hundred and three," he told them, "well armed and two days up the trail."

"Get thee gone," shouted Zutacapán, or some such phrase, and Villagrá rode headlong into the deadly winter sunset.

Well after midnight he finally dismounted and allowed his trusty steed to graze, a creature he remembered with great fondness over a decade later:

No more gorgeous animal to fleetest mares
So nimble and so thoroughbred was born.
With strong, stout tether I secured the beast,
But woke in agitation upon the morn
And hastened to prepare him for the road
For troubled weather foretold a violent storm.

The early light of dawn was as yet a glimmer in the east as horse and rider galloped headlong for a narrow pass between two cliffs, but just as

The thunderclap follows on the lightning bolt,
So it was my unhappy fate, that as we passed,
The very ground beneath the valiant stallion
Gave way, a gaping mouth that swallowed us
And daubed her lips with noble equine blood.

Villagrá had, quite literally, fallen into a trap. His precious horse was instantly killed. But "I climbed out of the horrid grave that Zutacapán had dug for me," he explained, and Oñate reported to the king that it was "by the grace of God he did not perish."[58]

The dark night and the heavy snowstorm had given Villagrá a narrow advantage. He hid his armor and other baggage behind a boulder, keeping only a sword and a dagger, that he might die honorably in battle like an Aztec of old rather than be taken captive and ransomed like a European aristocrat. Clearly an attentive reader of Virgil, he seems to have opportunely remembered that in Book Eight of the *Aeneid* one of the characters steals cows from Hercules and then puts his boots on backward so as to confuse those sent to pursue him. Villagrá now used the same subterfuge to throw off the Acoma war party, a ruse so celebrated by his comrades that Oñate even mentioned it months later in the documents appointing Villagrá a captain of cavalry.[59]

Oñate and his men explored northern Arizona, visiting the remote Hopi Pueblos, and found signs of mineral wealth along the Verde River. By early December, the men were anxious to return to their families for Christmas, and Oñate was worried that there was still no news from either Juan or Vicente de Zaldívar. Oñate gave the order to return to San Juan. At the water tank by El Morro, they came across six cavalrymen led by the ensign Bernabé de las Casas, who babbled uncontrollably in his distress until Oñate slowly coaxed out of him a coherent account.

At first, Juan de Zaldívar and his men had been welcomed by the Acomas, Las Casas explained, and "a captain and two soldiers went up to the pueblo for water and firewood. But the captain returned with paltry supplies, complaining that the Indians were being recalcitrant." Zaldívar ordered his party to retreat to a stream a few miles away, then returned with a dozen men and climbed the crag and entered the pueblo. "The Acomas gave us a tour of the kivas and other sights and told us to come back the following day for some corn flour." The Spaniards left some hatchets and other trade goods as a down payment, but when they returned, something went badly wrong. Years later, a number of disaffected Spanish deserters claimed the soldiers behaved violently and that an Acoma woman killed one of them defending her honor. Another disgruntled witness said the trouble started when a soldier stole a couple of turkeys. Whatever the trigger, the Acomas launched a vicious attack.[60]

Bernabé de las Casas stayed below, holding the horses. "I heard shouting in the pueblo and saw sixty Indians who had been watching me from a distance go back up" to the crag. "I fought with some other Indians I thought were coming to steal the horses. Then I heard gunfire." A terrified Indian ally ran up, telling him that many Spaniards had already been killed. Las Casas said he looked up and saw two men jumping from the crag to escape a cascade of rocks and arrows. It was a three- or four-hundred-foot drop, but one of them landed in a sand dune and survived. Others were similarly lucky. So "I gathered up the injured men and some Indian allies who escaped and got them back to our camp." At the final reckoning, the Acomas had killed Juan de Zaldívar and ten of his men.

Villagrá dramatized the deadly skirmish in his *History*, portraying Zaldívar as determined to prevent the fray until the last moment, when he recognized that violence was inevitable. Then,

> As the venomous viper, trod beneath the heel
> Of some rustic peasant farmer, spits and angers
> In the face of its perdition, coils and springs,
> Forked tongue flickering 'bout poisoned fangs,
> So brave Zaldívar ordered his harquebusiers fire . . .

Why, one wonders, did Villagrá liken Zaldíver to so incontrovertible an emblem of evil as a serpent?

Villagrá then served up a graphic description of the fighting. One Castilian died clubbed to death, "his fragmented skull and brains all mixed together on the bloody ground." Another man's "ribs were smashed to pieces and his gallbladder burst." Zaldívar fell in single combat with the impetuous and warmongering Zutacapán and was then set upon by a crowd of Acomas who, "barking and howling like rabid dogs, smashed his bones and body to a bloody pulp."[61] As in a modern western, Villagrá designed his imagery to provoke such self-righteous indignation in his audience as might justify the inevitably hellish retribution.

Oñate heard this sorry history by the water tank at El Morro and knelt down and wept and prayed all night before a tall cross. In the morning, he addressed his frightened men:

My lords and my companions, the Heavens know
My soul felt grief to see you all thus grief struck,
Unhappy, orphaned by these untimely deaths,
Our rock Zaldívar's gone and many others dear
To us, their flesh time-served, their spirits free.
They buried some alive, half cleavèd others,
Flayed, quartered, whipped, and crucified
Our friends, all contented Christian martyrs now.
So lift your souls to God, be not yet faint,
For by His very hand we shall be consoled.

He rallied his men and marched for the relative safety of San Juan.

Oñate's war against the Acomas is the dramatic denouement of Villagrá's *History*, filled with daring deeds and valiant speeches befitting epic form. The campaign was prosecuted by Vicente de Zaldívar, and whatever the facts of this bloody episode, the viceroy and other influential figures in Mexico City came to believe that he committed a terrible atrocity against the Acomas in revenge for his brother's death. Much of Villagrá's purpose in composing his *History* was to deny that version of events, not least because he was the legal counsel accused of failing to prevent the carnage.

So Villagrá painted Zutacapán as the villain of his tale, an impetuous hothead who[62]

Of the most rude, base, and vulgar stock was born,
Of lowly fathers as never once were called
To offer counsel in august cabinet.
Ambitious Zutacapán, proud, arrogant,
Ravenous for power and reputation,
Climbed bold and swift, high 'pon a roof to stand
And addressed the agitated Acomas:

"Hear my entreaty, ladies and gentlemen,
Unhappy people doomed to slavery,
Hear ye not the harsh Castilian trumpets sound?
Nor, the measured tread of their hostile paces
Coming near? Will ye still dream of liberty
If they catch us unprepared? To arms, to arms!
Lest they come as foe! If they come in friendship,
Well then, we might lay our weapons aside!

But I say war, everywhere shall be war,
A merciless war by fire and blood and sword
'Gainst these foreign traitors who would trample us!

"Bold and valiant men, what worse infamy,
What more base affront might we suffer now,
Than submit as vassals to these foreigners,
And be forced to give them our food each day
When we hold liberty so dear, as do they?"

Zutacapán's words had roused a raucous rabble round him, but his own son spoke up and tried to temper his father's angry rhetoric, warning, "You know these invading Spaniards come well prepared like great warriors, always on their guard, always sleeping with their arms to hand. Yet they have left every pueblo they have entered in a happy state of peace. But if they find us up in arms, they will wage war and can we fight this day against so many?"

Just as in Homer's *Iliad* wise old Nestor seconded the peaceful faction among the young Greeks, Villagrá sang of how at Acoma "a noble old man called Chumpo, 120 years old, who in his day was known for his intelligence and good sense," took his turn to speak. This old sage convinced everyone except Zutacapán, who worked up a frenzied wrath and, with fire in his eyes like a furious fighting bull, cursed and gnashed his teeth. Suddenly, he attacked old Chumpo. Until then, Zutacapán's son had "held back as a gunner holds his burning taper by a well-primed harquebus," but now, "like a bolt of lightning from the clouds," he seized his father's club. Then the riotous warriors slunk away.

These scenes of passionate argument over the merits of conflict, set against a powerful sense of foreboding and an increasingly intoxicating sense of excitement at the inevitable mortal combat to come, are a straightforward imitation of the first book of the *Iliad*, in which the Greeks debate the campaign against Troy. At the beginning of the poem, Villagrá co-opted Mexica origin myths and presented them alongside and as almost interchangeable with the Classics of the Ancient World. Now, he likened the "savage and pagan" Acomas to the greatest of Homer's Greek heroes, to Achilles, Agamemnon, Nestor, and the list goes on and on in the poem.

The Spaniards spent a terrifying Christmas at San Juan, certain that the spirit of resistance would be strengthened across the Pueblo world as news spread of the Acomas' victory. Many must have longed to abandon New Mexico altogether, but Oñate knew he could only save his colony with a swift and merciless reprisal. Under Spanish law, any punitive expedition needed to be legally sanctioned. He convened a hearing at which the survivors testified as to the origins of the outbreak of the fighting. He sought counsel from the Franciscans as to whether he might wage Just War against the aggressors. Finally, he ruled that the purpose of any assault on Acoma must be to bring the Indians to trial, appointed Vicente de Zaldívar to lead a company of sixty men to detain the enemy, and sent Villagrá to advise on the legitimacy of any action. Each man confessed and took Communion and sallied forth in a state of grace, ready to look death in the eye.[63]

Meanwhile, the Acomas danced their winter dances with a growing sense of trepidation. War was inevitable. When the Spaniards arrived on January 12, 1599, a detachment of Acoma men was waiting, ready for battle, "armed with their bows and arrows, clubs, rocks, and the swords and chain mail they had stripped from the Spaniards they had murdered."[64] Full of bravado, they shouted, "We have killed your comrades, so if you have come to fight, we shall kill you, too!"[65]

Villagrá sang of how all the while the Spanish Council of War were debating the daunting task before them, atop the rock, war-hungry Zutacapán led his men in a bloodcurdling war dance:

> They bucked and shied, proud arrogant stallions
> Champing at the bit, jumping, prancing fleetly,
> Whooping, chanting their hellish clamor until dawn.

Villagrá reports that there was still dissent upon the rock. Like the great Roman general Scipio Africanus before the walls of the ancient Numantia, in Spain, Zutacapán's wise son chastised his people for their untimely feasting and urged them, "To arms! Strengthen our defenses, set sentries, prepare to face the enemy!" But the frenzied rabble danced on.

Vicente de Zaldívar rode alone to the foot of the crag, and like a chivalrous knight in shining armor, he boldly issued a challenge to the Acomas. Then he slowly went back to his men. Suddenly, the Spanish army charged. It seemed the most foolhardy of attacks, a direct assault on the main stairway that snaked up between vertical walls of rock. But as battle raged, the wily Zaldívar quietly led a dozen of his bravest men around the back of this rocky fortress. They scaled, handhold by foothold, the smooth cliff face. At the top, only a narrow cleavage in the rock separated them from Acoma troops.

> Four hundred barbarians rushed toward them.
> The peerless dozen then soaked their swords in blood

At the narrow pass and held that bridgehead firm.
Up spake brave Zaldívar, leader of his men:
"Christian knights, 'tis my patron, Saint Vincent's Day,
May we triumph with his holy protection!"

As battle raged, Zaldívar espied an Acoma wearing his brother's blood-stained clothes.

Like Jacob when he held Joseph's bloody cloak,
Zaldívar paused, transfixed, and then bestirred,
Attacked with falconlike ferocity,
Cutting through their savage ranks, wounding, killing,
He slew his prey, the prized garments now a shroud.

The even-tempered Acoma general Gicombo, a hero who had always pleaded peace, showed his mettle when badly wounded in the heat of battle. As night fell and the fighting relented, Villagrá described how his beautiful lady, Luzcoija, tended to his shattered sword arm. In his woe-bedraggled fury, Gicombo rounded on Zutacapán:

"Should memorable Gicombo, fierce Bempol,
Noble Zutancalpo, perish in the fight,
And death take Zutacapán and his cronies
For his own, then bury us all together
With our arms, that we may settle our earthly
Quarrels entombed within a common sepulcher."

Like the gods of Olympus or the Spaniards themselves, the Acomas lived amid perpetual difference and debate, an unquestionably civilized nation worthy of the reader's respect and sympathy. Villagrá then described noble Gicombo's last tender moments with Luzcoija as the first rays of the rising sun heralded a new day of battle.

By dawn's early light, a handful of foolhardy Spaniards strayed across the chasm and then pulled up the stout log they had used as a bridge. They were stranded. The Acomas immediately attacked. The fighting was terrible. The harquebusiers fired, felling many, but there was no time to reload:

With sword and dagger, like butcher boys they fought,
Slicing open those barbarian breasts, fountains
Of blood streaming from eye, leg, head, and throat . . .

For all the carnage, these Spanish slaughtermen were outnumbered and took refuge on a sheltered ledge. Our poet-lawyer was swift to act:

Nine paces from the edge I poised myself,
The sergeant held my shield, I slipped his grasp,
Running headlong at that chasm of perdition,
Desperately I leaped long across the breach,
And landing safely upon the other side,
Dragged the log and opened up the bridge.

Zaldívar and the reinforcements filed across. The battle was all but won. Villagrá likened the Spaniards to reapers at harvesttime, wielding their sickles like Death herself, horsemen of the Acoma Apocalypse. Again and again, he insists on the undaunted courage of the enemy:

Yet, though they stumbled on o'er banks of bodies,
Their fresh, red blood never ceased to flow and gush,
Bathing the rock so that all was wet with death,
These furious, fiery barbarians slackened not,
Nor sought surrender, but charged our guns . . .

Zaldívar ordered two small cannon hauled up to the top of the rock. The endgame began. Villagrá's grand finale is bathed in a deeply emotive pathos, macabrely baroque in its representation of the tragic nobility of the Acomas' last stand. Gicombo speaks:

"O harsh fates, how would ye my spirit break!
How the ever-violent storm disturbs my brain,
Troubling me with flowing blood and burning fire,
Confounding us with subjection and defeat.
O unworthy Acomas, your base infamy
Brings upon us this most horrid punishment.
And thou, evil Zutacapán, instrument
Of our misfortunes, the gods shall punish thee."

The noblest warriors died jumping from their cliff,
Preferring death to the ignominy of servitude.
Noble Bempol embraced his little daughter
And holding her he leaped into oblivion.
Many wailing maidens followed where they went.

Gicombo through ash and embers homeward strode,
Lest beautiful Luzcoija, a Spaniard might enjoy.
But as he his belovèd sought amid the flames,
Upon him came Zaldívar and his soldiers.
The cornered savage, raging, a wild boar at bay,
Spied the broad beauty of Luzcoija's forehead,
He raised his powerful club, smashed her lovely skull,
Her peerless eyes popped their sockets. Dead, she fell.
At Zaldívar's order, they shot *him*. Dead. Too, he fell.

In the final scenes of the poem, wise old Chumpo sued for peace and persuaded the surviving Acomas to surrender. The Spaniards asked him to show them where Juan de Zaldívar fell in battle. On that spot, Vicente spoke with great emotion:

"Another Troy we have witnessed, noble knights!
Here in all his valor, strength, and rare renown,
Shall for all eternity, lie gloriously,
Never yet forgotten, Juan de Zaldívar."

As Vicente knelt, weeping and praying, the victorious Spaniards were alarmed by a sudden commotion, which turned out to be the Indian women-folk "chopping up Zutacapán's body, like skillful cooks mincing meat."

Chumpo asked to see the brave "tall Castilian with the long white beard who rode a white horse and wielded a mighty broadsword" and the "fair maiden, more beautiful than the sun himself," whom the Acomas had seen at this venerable warrior's side. The Christians were awestruck, for they realized the patron saint of Spain, Santiago the Moor Slayer, often depicted in the Americas as Santiago the Indian Slayer, had materialized on the battlefield to help them just as he had so often during their ancestors' medieval crusades against Islamic Spain. What was more, the Madonna herself seemed to have interceded in this battle. It was January 24, the feast of Our Lady of Peace, a perfect day for miracles.

Villagrá's story came to an end with the capture of two of the bravest and fiercest leaders of the resistance. The two men were briefly impris-oned, but then, in a final act of defiance, they climbed tall poplars, secured nooses around their necks, and shouted, "Spanish soldiers, we leave you our miserable, dangling bodies in commemoration of your illustrious victory."

The two men leaped together into space,
Now, their sightless eyes show only white,
Their limbs are limp, their powerful muscles slack,
Swollen tongues silent between grimacing teeth.
Acoma fruit hanging from cottonwood trees.

Villagrá promised to continue the poem, but never did. So, his *History of New Mexico* ends with this highly stylized portrayal of the Battle of Acoma. Yet there may be more to his account than mere colorful fiction. The speeches made by the opposing parties during the Acomas' councils of war belong to the tradition of Renaissance history writing that simplified an author's commentary on complex and nuanced political positions by lending them the voices of real protagonists. No reader at the time would have understood these debates to have taken place exactly as described. But readers would have sensed that while the poet was obviously positive about the peaceful faction among the Indians, he also showed sympathy toward Zutacapán's misguided hostility, painting it as understandable and even tragically honorable. Villagrá was briefly appointed Sheriff of Acoma, which must have given him the chance to canvass many survivors about how and why they had started the war. It may be that essential truths are intentionally visible beneath that thick veneer of lyric romanticism. What is more, not all of those truths reflect especially well on the Spaniards in general, nor Juan de Zaldívar in particular.

In 1614, Oñate, Vicente de Zaldívar, Villagrá, and many of their comrades were convicted by a court in New Spain of committing a brutal massacre at Acoma, killing between six hundred and eight hundred Indians either in battle or in the aftermath.[66] By contrast with Villagrá's classical war largely characterized by bravery and nobility on both sides, the charge sheet accused the Spaniards of bloodthirsty subterfuge. A number of witnesses testified that following an initial bloody skirmish, the Acomas sued for peace and took food to the Spanish camp. With a truce agreed, the Spaniards entered the pueblo under a guarantee of peace, but then forced the defenseless Indians inside the large kivas, the *estufas*, or "stoves," where they burned or smoked them to death.[67]

Villagrá published the *History* as a public exhortation to Philip III to exonerate Oñate and his henchmen:

My quill, so rough and ready pleads, Your Majesty,
O Christian Philip, yonder in New Mexico,

Shall rise a phoenix of ardent Faith among
The ruinous, dancing flames and ashes we saw there.
Greatest King, lend me your ears that you shall learn
Calumny's power and see how she afflicts
With unjust struggles your most loyal subjects.

Now, for once, I dare believe my pen might fly,
And that fickle language truth might testify,
Hear my words, Majesty, for I bore witness
To every act and deed reported here in verse.[68]

At San Juan, Oñate and the settlers had waited nervously for news from Acoma. At one stage, such was the paranoia that Doña Eufemia marshaled the women to take up defensive positions. Finally, Vicente de Zaldívar returned to San Juan with a large number of prisoners, and Oñate put them on trial. The Indians' sentences were intended to be exemplary. The children were spared official punishment and were put in the charge of Brother Martínez and Vicente de Zaldívar, while all the men and women over the age of twelve were condemned to twenty years of slavery. In addition, all men over twenty-five were to have one foot amputated.

Oñate had won the war, but could he win the peace? His colony clearly needed reinforcements, so he sent a handful of his most trusted men, including the playwright Farfán, with the poet Villagrá to petition the viceroy for support. In the report Oñate sent with them to the crown, he wrote glowingly of a land so rich that "there is none better among all Your Majesty's possessions in all the Indies."[69] The emissaries also carried with them a letter of fulsome praise for the country and their governor, signed by the leading members of the colony.[70] The emissaries soon learned to embellish their own marvelous stories about the cultural sophistication of the Pueblo peoples, ripe for conversion to the Catholic faith. They traveled armed with samples of buffalo hide and mining ores to tempt new settlers. They also arrived in Mexico City with sixty or more young girls from Acoma, destined to be brought up in the convents of the capital at Oñate's personal expense. In late June, Villagrá presented his fantasies and this flock of future nuns to the delighted viceroy, who immediately sent out for apples and pears and took great pleasure in watching the bashful child captives relish their succulent snack.[71] He expressed his disquiet about the massacre in a letter to the king but took no further action. He did not want to provoke the collapse of the fragile colony. Instead, he gave Villagrá official approval to recruit men to relieve the beleaguered colony.[72]

By August of the following year, 1600, Villagrá was at Santa Bárbara with his company of nineteen "of the most honorable" men, a handful of willing Franciscan missionaries, a large quantity of flour, and six hundred head of cattle.[73] Then, with the audit complete, on the eve of their departure something happened to make this most loyal captain and able adviser seek sanctuary in the Franciscan church and abandon the expedition altogether. Historical documents offer no explanation for this apparently sudden and incomprehensible desertion, an offense punishable by death under martial law, as he himself knew only too well. Yet the officials of the expedition simply referred his case to the viceroy, and no further action was taken. What is more, Villagrá remained on friendly terms with Oñate and Zaldívar, and the following year he was appointed sheriff of a mining settlement south of Santa Bárbara.[74] We know not why.

While Villagrá and Farfán pounded recruiting drums across New Spain, Oñate struggled to preserve his benighted colony. He requisitioned San Gabriel Pueblo as his new headquarters because it was more easily defended and relocated its inhabitants. He sent Zaldívar across Arizona to find a route to the South Sea, a quest that relieved pressure on the scant resources at headquarters. The expedition almost reached the Gulf of California, but retreated when faced with hostile Yuma Indians.

To great rejoicing the relief expedition finally reached San Gabriel on Christmas Eve 1600, but a few new recruits with a meager cargo of supplies could not dispel the discontent for long.

One of the captains, Aguilar, had long proved himself a useful warrior, but an unsettling influence. Now, he repeatedly sought permission to abandon New Mexico and return to his family. Oñate finally pretended to acquiesce, but then one night he secretly handed out knives to a handful of servants and sent for Aguilar on the pretext of completing the paperwork. When the victim arrived, Oñate shouted, "Kill the traitor, stab him now!"

A black slave and an Indian servant attacked but failed to wound Aguilar because he was wearing thick leather armor. So Oñate grabbed a sword, pushed the man down onto a bed, and stabbed him between the legs.

"You have to strike down here," he shouted at the two lackeys.[75]

That, at least, was the story told under oath by Oñate's enemies. Whatever the reality, soon afterward Zaldívar killed another man who had been granted permission to return to New Spain. Under extreme pressure and without Villagrá's steadying voice of reason, Oñate's policy of harsh sentencing and subsequent leniency descended into tyranny. His previously sound judgment failed him. Yet again, a Spanish conquistador responded to desperation with movement and action. As Coronado had done, Oñate went onto the Great Plains in search of a largely imaginary Native American civilization, that strange chimerical pot of gold that the Spaniards knew as Quivira. Zaldívar went with the expedition, leaving the settlers on the Rio Grande without a leader.

The expedition of over seventy men, seven hundred horses, and a train of carts and mules followed the Canadian River through Apache country. The Indians were friendly, the river was replete with fish, and its banks were fecund with fruit. They encountered enormous herds of bison, and all agreed their meat was better than beef and their hair was fine like the fleeces of the merino sheep that dominated the lucrative wool trade of Spain. Somewhere on the Texas-Oklahoma border, they steered due north and came across a huge encampment of five thousand Indians, a "robust" and "dirty" people, all "dark and ugly." They were well armed and said they were at war with another people who lived in a town of twelve hundred houses spread out along the Arkansas River. This was beautiful country, with fields of corn and seemingly friendly Indians. But as Oñate led his men deeper into the continental heartland, more and more of his party became unnerved. He was forced to hold a council of his captains. The majority urged him to begin the return march.

Meanwhile, most of the settlers had abandoned San Gabriel and returned to New Spain. Only a couple of dozen men remained loyal. While Oñate sentenced the deserters to death, they were already at Santa Bárbara accusing him of bloodthirsty butchery and outright lies. Zaldívar made the long journey first to Mexico City and then to Spain to defend his leader and canvass support for New Mexico.

In the meantime, Oñate had managed to reach the mouth of the Colorado River, where he took formal possession of the Gulf of California in January 1605. On his return, he offered his resignation in a letter to the viceroy, who ordered him to remain in charge at San Gabriel until a suitable replacement could be found.

In 1608, the future of Spanish New Mexico hung in the balance. The Council of the Indies favored withdrawal, but struggled to solve the problem of the Indians who had already been baptized. Then, a Franciscan arrived in Mexico City with the glorious and improbably timely report that over seven thousand Pueblo Indians had been converted to Christianity that summer. Whether mass baptisms accompanied by minimal catechism had really taken place or whether this was an untruth designed to serve a higher purpose, the news ensured the crown would assume responsibility for the loss-making province.

The following year, Pedro de Peralta was installed as Governor of New Mexico and immediately undertook the foundation of a new capital at a place he called Santa Fé, today the oldest European state capital in the United States. The Tlaxcalan conquistadors established their own suburb on the opposite bank of the Río de Santa Fé with its chapel of San Miguel. They called the place Analco, which means "on the other side of the stream" in Nahuatl.[76]

Oñate and his nephew returned to their mines and estates in Nueva Vizcaya, which under close management began to produce fabulous profits. Zaldívar was said to have accumulated a fortune of more than three million ducats and became a generous benefactor to the Jesuits of Zacatecas. In 1614, Oñate and Zaldívar and their most loyal men were tried and convicted on many charges relating to the conquest of New Mexico, but in pragmatic terms their sentences were easy to bear. Nonetheless, while Zaldívar settled into the luxurious life of a wealthy frontiersman, Oñate and Villagrá both showed their determination to clear their names and went to Spain to do so. Each man succeeded. Villagrá died aboard ship on the Atlantic in 1620, sailing to take up a post as an *alcalde mayor* in Guatemala, while Oñate was admitted to the Order of Santiago and died in Spain, in 1625, while inspecting a remote mining area with a team of officials appointed to report on how to improve royal revenues.[77] He was seventy-five years old, the first European to have founded a permanent colony in North America.

CHAPTER 10

GOD & GOVERNMENT

NEW MEXICO

The priests [started] to forbid the . . .
Kachina dances and did not let the [people]
concern themselves about the clouds and the rain.

—HOPI ORAL HISTORY

These scoundrel friars say that these [dances] are evil . . .
They are very beneficial, and were I not governor,
I would go out and dance myself.

—BERNARDO LÓPEZ DE MENDIZÁBAL, GOVERNOR OF NEW MEXICO

HOPI ORAL HISTORY RECORDS that at first the Pueblos thought the Spaniards were associated with their traditional savior figure, the "white brother, the Bahana." They were soon disabused and "the people [became] very much afraid . . . so scared they could do nothing but allow themselves to be made slaves." Most of all, Hopis today associate their subjection with the Franciscan priests, whom they called the *Tütáachi*, a word that approximates to "dictator."[1] They still remember the destruction of their own "altars and customs" and the work gangs forced to climb high into the San Francisco mountains to fell pine and spruce to be hewn into huge beams for the new churches. Twenty to thirty men were needed to carry them, and many collapsed by the wayside, where they were abandoned to die on the orders of the friars.[2]

The oldest documented oral account of seventeenth-century Pueblo history was copied down over a century ago by a Mennonite missionary.[3] "A long time ago" at Oraibi Pueblo, it begins, a truce was agreed with the warlike Spaniards, and the Hopi helped build them a mission "house" and large "assembly" room with "a tower in which bells were suspended." "The old people say [it] was built in a spiral or snail-house shaped form," and the archaeological evidence confirms that anyone entering the mission through the church would indeed have had to turn left, left, and left again to reach the friars' lodgings.[4] But this visualization of the mission is deeply rooted, for spirals or labyrinth symbols called *Tápu'át*, meaning "Mother and Child," are emblematic of Mother Earth and the Path of Emergence in the origin stories that underpin Hopi culture.[5]

The Hopi remember that the priests washed their heads and made them gather at the "assembly house on Sundays" to listen to their sermons, then they "asked the Hopi to work for them" and "requested them to get drinking water from . . . far away." Despite these impositions, "for four years, everything went along well and it rained often." But then "the priests [started] to forbid the . . . Kachina dances and did not let the [people] concern themselves about the clouds and the rain." As a result, the fifth year was dry and the Hopi were tired and hungry. "The chiefs called a council."

"We are not getting along well," they agreed. "We are not happy" and "it does not rain."

The Hopi decided to revive their own religion. It rained a little, but not enough.

Some friars also violated the "chastity of the women and maidens" until "finally the Hopi became angry." During a long council meeting in the chief's kiva, they discussed whether they should kill one of their priests. "Finally, the Badger clan volunteered to kill him," mocking the others for their lack of bravery. At dawn, the assassins dragged their sleeping victim out of the mission "and then cut his throat," threw his corpse "into a gulch, and piled stones upon it." In another version of the story, the man's head was severed and his heart cut out.[6] This bloodshed sparked a general uprising against the Spaniards, and "from that time on the Hopi again [have] had their dances."

At Shungopovi Pueblo, a youth was incensed when a friar raped his sister. A neighboring chief put that anger to good use. He knew the lad was a powerful runner, so he sent him as a messenger to the other chiefs. "All the priests will be killed on the fourth day after the full moon" was his simple message. The chief also gave him a "cotton string with knots in it" and told him that "each day" he should "untie one of the knots until they were all out." That would signal the moment to martyr the missionaries.

At Shungopovi, a group of unarmed Indians overpowered the priest as he brandished his sword "and tied his hands behind his back. They made a tripod out of the great pine beams lying outside and "they hung him on the beams, kindled the fire and burned him" alive.[7] That is how Hopi history remembers the Franciscans and the origins of the Great Pueblo Revolt of 1680, when the Spaniards were expelled from New Mexico.

By contrast, a jubilant seventeenth-century Franciscan friar called Juan de Prada celebrated the Spanish missions in New Mexico by describing them as forming "a large cross," with the span from Zuni in the west to Pecos in the east transecting the settlements along the Rio Grande itself.[8] That use of the central image of Christianity as a way of mapping Pueblo geography is enormously symbolic of how the Spaniards tried to understand the indigenous inhabitants, just as the Pueblos used their spiral symbol to characterize the Spaniards' mission. Each saw the other through different lenses.

The newly arrived Franciscans began by negotiating with the Pueblos over the location of their missions. The friars tended to build their churches and dependencies near the apartment complexes where the Indians lived, but were only exceptionally integrated into the fabric of the pueblo. A plan of sorts was drawn, but the Indians did the actual construction work, with women and children building the massive walls, while the men were carpenters, according to their traditional gender roles. As a result, the friars favored construction out of the traditional adobe blocks used by the Pueblos, large bricks molded from clay and dirt and dried in the sun and held together by mud. Much of the distinctive character of these buildings, especially the lack of arches and domes and the consequent absence of side aisles in the churches, are a consequence of using traditional building materials.

The walls of the churches were either laid directly on the ground or within a shallow trench. The walls were tapered to reduce the load as the courses of adobe blocks rose in height, while every few feet a layer of wooden beams was introduced to prevent the mud from cracking. The roof was supported by a washboard of lateral wooden beams, with one or two bell towers rising above the rest of the building. Inside, these simple high halls are dark because adobe allows for few windows, which results in a powerful effect of chiaroscuro where the sunbeams shine in, an effect heightened by the need for candlelight.

A Franciscan friar called Alonso de Benavides did most to attract the attention of the world to New Mexico when he landed in Spain, in 1630, and published a glowing account of the "spiritual and temporal wealth that the Divine Majesty had achieved . . . through the padres." He claimed they had converted as many as eighty-six thousand Pueblo Indians to the True Faith and extolled a land of "great riches in mineral wealth." "So great are the spiritual and temporal treasures we have discovered, so many the marvels and miracles, that the Viceroy of Mexico thought it best that I come in person to report to Your Majesty," he explained.[9]

Benavides's account offered king and counselors such an illusion in narrative that they felt as if they were indeed traveling to the most remote realm in the empire. He began by vividly describing the dangers of getting there, running the gauntlet of "ferocious, savage, and indomitable" tribes for a hundred leagues along the *Camino Real*, the "Royal Road." But as his text approached New Mexico itself, he guided his readers through an Earthly Paradise of well-watered, fertile land and hillsides pregnant with mineral wealth. He introduced the Mansos, or "Timid," people, wild men who enjoy feasting on raw bison, but a friendly lot, fearful of the Spaniards and ripe for Christian conversion. Then he described the pueblos themselves, with their "adobe buildings of one or two stories with ladders into the plazas," built by "people who wear clothes and live under the government and rule of their captains." He enthuses about "their great cultivation of crops from seed, their vast hunting grounds . . . and the many kinds of fish in their rivers. The soil of this province is fertile," and the hills were laden with "silver and gold." [10] He described the myriad mission schools where thousands of newly baptized Indians were being taught the gospels. Benavides praised "how well they adopt Christian ways" and eulogized the "splendid Apache nation," already beginning to follow the Lord, like their Navajo neighbors. He knew what he was doing. [11] Philip IV had inherited a morally and fiscally bankrupt empire from his supine father and his feckless favorite. Under the tutelage of his own ambitious and visionary *valido*, the Count-Duke of Olivares, the king was determined to restore the Habsburg dynasty to the greatness of Charles V and Philip II. New Mexico, it seemed, might soon be alive to the sound of God and Mammon dancing to the tune of Spanish imperialism.

The Franciscans brought to New Mexico both firmly held beliefs about how to inculcate a spirit of Christian community among the Pueblos and the tools and equipment to put those ideas into action. Benavides documented every object he took with him, from the silver chalices and gold-plated patens, candlesticks, incense, liturgical clothing, altar frontals of damask silk and silver brocade, books and breviaries, iron molds for making the sacrament, to the Turkish carpets, paper, knives, scissors, sandals, needles, awls, oil, vinegar, bedsheets, sugar, saffron, cinnamon, almonds, axes, a barber's whetstone, hoes, rosaries, plowshares, twenty-three thousand nails of assorted sizes, four thousand tacks, capers, and an enormous number of assorted boxes and trunks to keep it all in. [12]

Pope Gregory the Great had famously described art as "the Bible of the illiterate," so Benavides transported five large oil paintings with gilded frames and two figures of Christ that had carefully been packed in specially made cases.[13] He also brought a statue of the Madonna that is believed to be the famous image of *La Conquistadora*, or "Our Lady of Conquest," a copy of the Virgin of the Rosary in the cathedral at Toledo in Spain, and the oldest continuously venerated image of the Virgin in the United States, which remains today in the Cathedral Church of San Francisco in Santa Fe. Her "face is indeed beautiful," one devout observer writes, "with small mouth and eyes, a thin nose," and "nothing doll-like" nor "sentimental about it. It is a queenly face, conscious of majesty, yet not at all haughty."[14] The statue is twenty-eight inches high, carved from willow, and covered with gesso, a fine plaster layer that was coated with gold leaf as an undercoat of luster for the highly realistic polychrome painting of hands, face, and clothing, which brought it to life.

Benavides also took a number of choir books and musical instruments. Song and harmony had been used to draw Indians to Church culture since the first decades of Spanish rule in the Americas.[15] By the early seventeenth century Indian choirs in the churches of northern New Spain rivaled the choristers of Mexico City.[16] The New Mexican neophytes, or "newly cultivated" converts, learned to chant psalms, sing plainsong, and rejoice in polyphony and became skillful musicians who could play a range of string and woodwind instruments.[17] Benavides described using music to persuade a Navajo chief to come to peace.[18] One enthusiastic contemporary, Esteban de Perea, wrote of a world alive with the sounds of "counterpoint, plainchant . . . and the organ, bassoon, and cornet."[19] The organs were presumably small and designed to be portable, but nonetheless they must have been heavy, bulky, and delicate instruments to carry by oxcart all the way from New Spain. Mostly, the missionaries organized ensembles of flutes and a type of oboe or shawm known as a *chirimía*, which produces a deep, mellifluous sound.[20]

Benavides wanted his king and counselors to know that the Franciscans' task was Herculean, so he spiced his cheerful picture of a potential Promised Land with latent menace. The friars, he explained, were fighting a constant battle to defeat traditional belief systems at Zuni, while the Hopi "wizards" murmured darkly of murdering their priest. He recounted that as he was preaching to the nomadic Jumanos of West Texas, an angry "witch doctor" screamed at him, "You Christians are crazy. Now you want to teach us to be *locos*, too!"

"In what way are we mad?" Benavides asked.

"You Christians are so crazy that you all get together and then whip yourselves in the streets like madmen, shedding blood. I don't want to be mad."

As Benavides explained, "He must have seen some Holy Week procession" in which penitents across the Spanish Catholic world flagellated themselves as part of intensely moving Easter celebrations.[21] The practice has all but died out, but the Brotherhood of the Penitentes remains a potent part of New Mexican folklore, and their simple meetinghouses can be seen in the high hills. By the early twentieth century, tales of their brutal forms of penitence, including live crucifixions, horrified and titillated the American newcomers, much as the Franciscans had appalled the Jumano wizard three centuries earlier. That excitement reached a hysterical nadir with a heavily fictionalized documentary, *The Lash of the Penitentes*, first shown in 1936.[22]

Spanish rule in New Mexico, Benavides implied, was tenuous. As yet Santa Fe had no main church, and only 250 Spaniards lived there. "Only fifty men could bear arms," and the "lack of weapons" was frightening. If not for the terrifying effects of their harquebuses and "the utmost rigor" with which they had "punished any rebel Pueblo," the Indians "would have often tried to murder the Spaniards." That remark was prescient, indeed.[23]

That "utmost rigor" was not only inflicted on recalcitrant Indians by secular Spanish soldiers. Benavides documents how an *hechicera*, or "sorceress," was vaporized by a bolt of lightning while trying to persuade four Indian companions to abandon the principles of Catholic wedlock, the good Lord moving to perform a wonder in his inimitable way. But the Franciscans generally preferred their miraculous interventions to be more benign. In his account of the Jumanos of West Texas, Benavides elaborated possibly the most scintillating miracle of his age, laying the documentary foundation for one of the most celebrated and contentious events in the evangelization of the New World.

The old New Mexico hand Esteban de Perea had led a group of thirty Franciscan reinforcements into Santa Fe at Whitsun 1629. He had been charged with investigating reports that a Spanish nun, María de Ágreda, had repeatedly materialized in Texas to proselytize the Plains Indians, while simultaneously sleeping in her convent in northern Spain. No one in Santa Fe had heard anything like it, but someone suggested asking some Jumanos who were then at Socorro trading hides. Perea reported that "on July 22, about fifty Jumano Indians . . . came to Isleta Pueblo asking the friars to teach them the gospels." These would-be converts explained that, not far from modern Roswell, "a woman with a habit had insisted that they come." Perea showed them a painting of an elderly Franciscan nun. "They were happy and discussed it among themselves" and claimed that the nun they had met was dressed like the woman in the portrait, "except that she was much younger and more beautiful."[24] Two friars accompanied the Jumanos back onto the plains, and at a large settlement they were welcomed by a "procession of Indians carrying two crosses before them, as though they had been taught in heaven" itself. The friars responded by holding up the crucifixes that hung about their necks, and the Jumanos, "as though Christians by ancient lineage, all came to kiss and venerate them." They explained that a "lady in blue" had shown them what to do.[25]

In the spring of 1631, Benavides hurried to Ágreda to visit María at her simple convent. She described to him in "such detail so many things about the places, houses, roads, and towns of those provinces" that he "realized it must all be true."[26] He even acquired "the very habit Sister María wore when she went to New Mexico. The veil," he effused, "radiates such a fragrance that it is a comfort to the spirit."[27]

María de Ágreda's testimony in Spain was astonishing. She recalled watching over Benavides as he baptized Piros Indians; she described another friar's "long face and high color . . . She knew everybody and knew Chief One-Eye very well indeed." She "had sent the embassy from Quivira" to the friars who ministered to the Jumanos in West Texas.[28] But she also told him about hostile heathens in the East called the Titlas, who had murdered her mysterious alter ego, as well as two mysterious foreign Franciscans no one knew anything about. Benavides insisted her portrait be painted so it could be shown to the Jumanos. Rumor had it that they shouted with joy when they saw it: "That is her, she brought us knowledge of the true God."[29]

Years later, the Inquisition took an interest in many aspects of María's strange mysticism and concluded that Benavides had greatly exaggerated the story. She confessed that during a period of intense personal suffering in the early 1620s, she had prayed desperately for the success of the Franciscan missions in New Mexico. She admitted to intense experiences in which she saw herself among different Indian tribes, but she could not vouch for whether these were visionary or real. She later wrote Philip IV himself to explain, "*I told them the truth*, [and] not before time . . . for I have had many prelates and confessors who obtained all their information from one another and from the nuns, adding and subtracting" from her story as they went along. "My only concern now is that I have given the right answers, for I am alone, without counsel." María de Ágreda had unburdened herself to the Inquisition and had expressed her relief at doing so to her sovereign. Philip replied, "I feel the pain God has sent you, but truth is unbending, and the clear light of your virtue shall shine through so much fog."[30]

The legend of the Little Blue Lady persists today among the Native Americans of New Mexico, but God saw fit that Benavides should be lost at sea in

1635, before he could begin his work as Archbishop of Goa, the Portuguese colony in India.[31]

Benavides portrayed New Mexico as a distant and intensely isolated place, a world of simple but civilized Pueblo farmers, Franciscan missionaries, and Spanish settlers who shared an almost tangible confinement because they were surrounded by aggressive wild men who lived without reason: Apaches, Navajos, and Utes. In the rarefied atmosphere of New Mexico, the rivalry between Church and state at the heart of the Spanish imperial system, between the twin institutions of power, one demanding dominion over souls and the other over bodies, degenerated into an unremitting and rancorous conflict that ended in Armageddon.

The first serious friction between the Franciscans and the secular government in Santa Fe erupted in 1613, when a troublesome father commissary excommunicated Governor Peralta and used forged documents to orchestrate his imprisonment, thus establishing what has been called the Evil Tradition, which festered in New Mexico for most of the seventeenth century.[32] Matters took a major turn for the worse with the arrival of a new governor, Luís de Rosas, in 1637, who refused to listen to the friars' entreaties to punish his predecessor, with whom they had quarreled. The friars turned on Rosas, painting him as obsessively determined to make as much money as possible out of New Mexico, extorting whatever he might from neighboring tribes, and launching slave raids against nomadic groups.[33] Esteban de Perea lampooned him as an eccentric figure who encouraged the Indians "to weave a great many blankets" and "then dye them," but in his eagerness to urge them to work he could often himself be seen "in the midst of the dyers with his face and hands so black with ink that he could only be distinguished from the Indians by his clothing . . . which did great disservice to his office."[34]

Rosas, the Franciscans claimed, had little respect for religion and is supposed to have led a detachment of troops out of a church in the middle of mass shouting, "Father, shut up! Every time you speak you lie!" "Many of the Christian Indians then asked how they were supposed to believe what the father said if the governor stated in public that they were liars," the offended officiant reported later.[35] Rosas had support among members of the town council, which remitted documents to the viceroy detailing a long list of complaints against the clergy in which they clearly identified the root of the problem.

Franciscan authority in New Mexico had three arms, each with its own separate tribunal, each keen to assert its jurisdiction. The *custos*, the leader of the community of friars, had the powers of a bishop and could instigate legal proceedings in the religious courts and sentence the guilty. The Inquisition was a separate institution with its own significant powers, and finally there was the Cruzada, which originated in the Middle Ages to raise revenue for religious wars against Islam, but now collected taxes on behalf of the Church. Although all these bodies were run by the Franciscans, they were extremely jealous of their powers, and all of them displayed a dangerous proclivity to impose their authority on ordinary individuals with threats of excommunication or by withholding the sacraments.

The town council told the viceroy that New Mexico was too small and too isolated to need so many religious tribunals and begged that these diverse authorities be concentrated in a single office. They urged the appointment of a Rosas ally called Juan de Vidania as prelate of New Mexico, so the friars responded by vilifying him as inept in Latin and incompetent in the law.

In a serious and sinister turn of events, a number of Franciscans were implicated in the cold-blooded murder of another Rosas supporter. When Vidania agreed to preside over this victim's burial within the cathedral at Santa Fe, the furious friars locked him in his cell at the convent. So Rosas stormed the building with a handful of armed men and set him free and then forcibly expelled the Franciscans from the capital. The following spring Rosas himself battered two friars until they were "bathed in blood."[36] But Rosas had also made many enemies among the ordinary citizens of Santa Fe, and when his term as governor came to an end, the town council locked him up inside the Palace of the Governors to ensure he could not abscond to New Spain before his replacement arrived to carry out the official *residencia*, or "audit," of his term of office. During that confinement, on January 22, 1642, a jealous husband insisted that the constables search Rosas's comfortable jail, where they found the man's errant wife hiding underneath the ex-governor's bed. For two days, the cuckold tried to force the authorities to take action to restore his honor, but no one seems to have much cared. He finally lost patience with due process, broke into the palace, and murdered Rosas with a dozen thrusts of his sword.[37]

Relations between Church and state in New Mexico temporarily improved with the arrival of a new governor, Juan Manso, the vigorous young nephew of a former Franciscan *custo*. Such was the new amity that the guardian of the monastery in Santa Fe perpetrated the most extraordinary subterfuges to cover for Manso's lasting affair with the wife of an army captain, which produced two children. The guardian conducted a fake funeral for one of the infants so Manso could send the child to his father's household in Mexico

City, then baptized the other one twice, for reasons now obscure. The guardian then hanged himself to avoid confessing whatever sins had been committed, and it was said that Manso was so affected by the whole business that he suffered terrifying hallucinations until he died, falling off a mule.[38]

The father prelate who had the misfortune to clear up the guardian's suicide described New Mexico as a "land where most" of "the one hundred citizens" "are ignorant," including many "*mulattoes, mestizos*, and all who have any Spanish blood, even though it is slight."[39] By most reports, this was a world alive with unorthodox superstitions, where almost no one could read and write and few could sign their name, many took part in Indian rituals, adultery and fornication were usual, and incest not uncommon. This was a world in which a father who had been severely punished for beating his daughter to death tried to get revenge by forcing another daughter to accuse the governor of rape. Law and morality hung in the balance in seventeenth-century New Mexico. And it is hardly surprising that the work of the missionaries was affected by such shocking shenanigans.

In the spring of 1559, a new governor, Bernardo López de Mendizábal, and his half-Irish wife made their way along the Camino Real. A *criollo* born in New Spain, educated at the Jesuit college in Puebla, he had studied canon law at the University of Mexico. A belligerent and outspoken character who rarely attended mass, he quarreled with the new *custos*, Juan Ramírez, before they had even departed Mexico City together.[40] When López arrived at Socorro, he scolded the local friar for failing to arrange a sufficiently pompous reception, declaring, "A Governor should be received like the Holy Sacrament at Corpus Christi," and retaliated by refusing to organize an appropriate civic welcome for Ramírez.[41]

Having ensured the enmity of the Franciscans, López then doubled the rate of pay for Indian day laborers in the middle of the harvest season, infuriating an influential group of citizens. The friars were equally outraged because they needed Indians to work their extensive fields and herd their vast flocks of sheep and other livestock, which they claimed were essential insurance against future famine. López suggested the Indians were perfectly capable of looking after themselves if they spent the time cultivating their own crops instead of working for the friars. He banned the export of livestock from New Mexico just as the Franciscans were rounding up a massive flock intended for market in New Spain.

López repeatedly championed Indians in their complaints against the Franciscans. When one Pueblo woman accused an elderly priest for reneging on his promise to give her a blanket if she gave him sexual relief, López requisitioned a blanket from the convent and gave it her, humiliating the venerable friar. Such cases are legion. He initiated criminal charges against a priest who had murdered a woman in Taos and forced religious authorities to investigate when a man from Tajique alleged his wife had long been having an affair with a senior Franciscan. A troubled young friar called Silvestre Vélez de Escalante bemoaned that the "extremely grave perils we suffer against the chastity we promised God are numerous, especially when we find ourselves alone and beyond the cloister," because of "the guile of the common enemy of mankind," the devil. He quoted the warning given by a senior Franciscan to the Commissary General of New Mexico that he should "exercise very great vigilance lest the friars barter with the infidels for boys or girls, pelts, or any other thing." The reason for that vigilance was clear: to prevent "the very great scandal that results from doing so." The reputation of the missions far outweighed any concern over the welfare of individual Pueblo Indians, for honor was a vital part of collective corporate identity in the seventeenth-century Spanish world.[42] Many believed in a moral obligation to preserve the good name or *reputación* and *honra* of a community or an individual, which were far more important than any allegiance to the truth. According to the ingrained mores of the day, the friars may or may not have erred, but their sins should be dealt with in private if at all; to bring them into the open was deeply shameful to the Franciscans, the Spanish community, the crown, and ultimately God. López's contemporaries would have understood his actions in those terms, and the Franciscans complained that as a direct result of his actions "the ministers suffer great persecution and dishonor" and as a result the Indians "are lost, without faith."[43]

The Pueblos knew well enough that many friars coveted their womenfolk as much as their labor and their souls. Hopi history remembers the degenerate missionary to Shungopovi who insisted that "all the young girls be brought to him when they were about thirteen or fourteen years old," so "they would become better women!" Not content with this adolescent harem, he was also forever "sending some man or other . . . far away," to get "water from different springs or rivers." He always chose "men who had pretty wives," and no sooner was the husband out of the way than "the priest . . . would come to visit his wife."[44] The Hopi debated executing the alien criminal.

"He is not the savior and it is your duty to kill him," the chief of Shungopovi urged the Mishongnovi, who by ancient tradition were the warriors responsible for protecting the tribe.

"If I end his life, my own is ended," the chief of the Mishongnovi responded, terrified of Spanish reprisals.[45]

* * *

López made enemies easily. He maintained a household of Apache captives and assorted slaves and servants from New Spain who spent their time drinking, brawling, and thieving in the streets of Santa Fe. One New Mexican testified that "had a demon come to govern, he would not have done so much harm nor governed so badly . . . for it was as though he was host to a whole kingdom of demons."[46]

López had begun his official audit of Manso's government of New Mexico by trying to extort an enormous bribe out of his predecessor and replacing a number of officials with his own supporters, alienating a host of influential colonists. They arranged for Manso to escape so he could complain directly to the viceroy. Further complaints trickled into Mexico over the following months, including an accusation that López had encouraged dances and idolatry at Isleta Pueblo. This reflected what would become one of the most serious charges leveled against him, for he had scandalized the friars in the most dangerous way imaginable, by issuing a decree allowing the Indians to celebrate their traditional dances. For the Franciscans, these central rituals in the Pueblo belief system were incantations to the devil. López responded by announcing that for all "these scoundrel friars say that these are evil" practices, in fact "they are very beneficial, and were I not governor, I would go out and dance myself."[47]

In the spring of 1661, a new *custos* with long experience among the Hopi, Friar Alonso de Posada, arrived in New Mexico. He had also been appointed commissary of the Inquisition, and he set to work right away, banning all Indian dances and ordering the friars to collect and burn the ceremonial masks that are so important to the kachina culture of the Pueblos. In August, a new governor, Diego de Peñalosa, arrived and began his *residencia*, or "audit" of López's regime. As the charges mounted up, he put López under house arrest as a way of protecting him from the fury of his enemies. Peñalosa then offered to let López write his own *residencia* in exchange for ten thousand pesos. But López insisted the matter be referred to the Audiencia of Mexico, while he remained at Santa Fe. The Audiencia eventually absolved him of half the charges, but upheld the rest, ruling he must be fined three thousand pesos and banning from holding office for eight years. Yet by far their most intriguing ruling to arise from the case was the Audiencia's insistence that the friars prove that the kachina dances were the work of the devil. Meanwhile, an Inquisitorial tribunal ordered the arrest of López and his wife on a long list of charges, including heresy, blasphemy, and spiritual perversion.

The rulings of the Audiencia and the Inquisition reached Santa Fe in August 1662. Peñalosa had already employed highly dubious procedures to secure possession of sizable quantities of López's clothes, leather goods, and tanned hides, and a large quantity of silver bullion. Peñalosa now seized even more property on the pretext it must be sold to cover the costs of the *residencia*. Within a fortnight, he had begun removing herds of cattle, flocks of sheep, mules, and oxen, hides, pine nuts, and silver bullion south along the Camino Real. "I have left them three thousand pesos," he is reported as saying, "let them be satisfied!"[48] Friar Posada collected the rest of López's possessions, including 410 pounds of chocolate, then chained him up in one of his own carts and began escorting him to New Spain.

Posada paused for two weeks at El Paso to write up his report. While there, he was shown a new directive from the Audiencia ordering the release of López and reinstatement of his property pending an appeal. Posada immediately seized on behalf of the Inquisition the goods and livestock that Peñalosa had requisitioned as part of the *residencia* and transported them to Mexico City, where he placed his prisoner in the custody of the Inquisition jail. Days later, the trial began, but López was by then ill and it was immediately suspended. He died in September 1664 and was posthumously exonerated of all charges six years later.

Peñalosa was furious when he learned that Friar Posada had embargoed López's wealth. He lampooned the Inquisitors as "puppets" and "petty clerics."[49] When one of his constables arrested a criminal by violating his claim of sanctuary in the church at Santo Domingo, the long-standing hostility between Church and state once again burst into flames. When Posada ordered the governor to return the prisoner to the church within a day on pain of excommunication, Peñalosa set out with a posse of armed men for the *custos*'s mission at Pecos Pueblo. The two men took a turn in the cloister, and Peñalosa asked angrily, "Father, can the *custos* excommunicate the governor?"

"Sir, that depends on the case, for if it falls within canon law, he can."

"Were the *custos* to excommunicate me, I should hang or garrote him. Even if the pope came to excommunicate me, I would hang him."

"It is better to leave His Holiness on the supreme throne. As for hanging him, he is not here."

Peñalosa threw back the lapel of his cape and flashed the pair of pistols he was carrying and insisted that Posada return with him to Santa Fe. The following morning, Peñalosa imprisoned the friar in the Palace of the Governors.[50] But Peñalosa had overplayed his hand, and in 1668, the Inquisition in Mexico City sentenced him to do penance in an *auto-da-fé* and then banished him from the New World altogether.

Diego de Peñalosa was suddenly poor and faced a hopeless future within the Spanish Empire. So he made his way to Paris, where he found an eager audience for his stories about New Mexico, and his daring proposal for a

French invasion of Spanish North America encouraged the great adventurer René-Robert Cavelier, Sieur de La Salle to launch the first European expedition to descend the Mississippi River. Peñalosa had invited French trespassers into Spanish North America.

By 1669, New Mexico was "almost exhausted by two calamities," according to Brother Juan Bernal: relentless Apache raiding and a terrible famine, heralded with biblical symbolism by a plague of locusts, that lasted until 1672.[51] "Many Indians have perished from hunger, they lie dead along the roads, in the washes, and in their homes." At the worst-hit pueblo, Humanas, "four hundred and fifty died of hunger." People were trying to toast bison hides in their desperation.[52] Indians and Spaniards turned to the missions for succor, with their large stores of grain and extensive herds of cattle and flocks of sheep. Hunger and Apache assaults forced the Franciscans to abandon the Salinas Pueblos to the southeast, and the refugees put such a strain on already-meager resources that the Indians at Senecu murdered their friar.[53] It was a harbinger of doom for Spanish New Mexico and a warning sign of the Great Pueblo Revolt.

CHAPTER 11

PO'PAY'S PUEBLO REVOLT

NEW MEXICO

Within and around the world, within and around the hills and mountains, within and around the valleys, your authority returns to you. Therefore, return to your people and travel the corn pollen trail again . . . *Sengi di ho!*
—PO'PAY, PUEBLO PATRIOT

"EVER SINCE THE SPANIARDS first explored this kingdom," an eighty-year-old Pueblo explained in 1680, "such has been the strength of feeling in every Indian's heart toward the friars and the Spaniards for removing our idols and suppressing our magic, that we old men have passed it down from one generation to the next. I have heard such talk since I was old enough to understand it!" [1]

Throughout the seventeenth century, different Pueblo communities violently resisted the Spanish trespass. But those isolated moments of insurgency all ended in disaster, for the leaders failed to unite enough of the Pueblos to succeed. Even the widely respected Indian governor of the Salinas towns, baptized Esteban Clemente by the friars, failed to garner enough support for his simple plot to hobble the Spanish soldiers by driving their horses into the mountains before launching an all-out assault. He was betrayed, captured, and executed. [2]

Clemente's insurrection bears out the old man's testimony. When Clemente was arrested and his property was seized, it was clear he had maintained his traditional beliefs. "A great quantity of idols" was discovered in his house, along with many "jars full of idolatrous powdered herbs, feathers, and other disgusting things." [3] As a Spanish officeholder, Clemente was an obvious beneficiary in political and material terms of the colonial presence. Yet he rebelled for spiritual reasons, deeply rooted in his sense of identity as a Tompiro.

Before the arrival of the Spaniards, the many different Pueblo tribes had traded with one another, they had political interaction, there were common

Juan Pantoja de la Cruz, *The Emperor Charles V*, 1605. Charles of Ghent was probably the most powerful ruler the world has ever known. He inherited half of Europe; then, with Cortés's conquest of Mexico, he became if not the richest ruler in history, certainly the most solvent as gold and silver poured into Spain. MADRID: MUSEO DEL PRADO

La Salle's ship *La Belle*, 1684. SEVILLE: ARCHIVO GENERAL DE INDIAS, MAPAS Y PLANOS, INGENIOS Y MUESTRAS 9. COURTESY OF THE MINISTERIO DE CULTURA Y DEPORTE

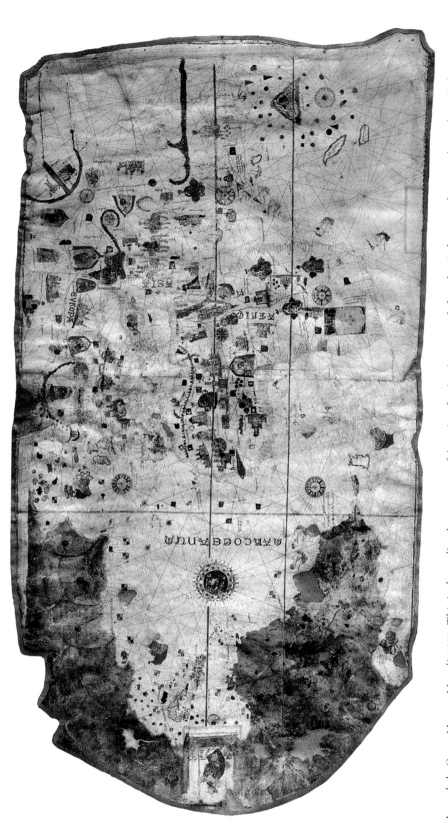

Juan de la Cosa, *Mappa Mundi*, 1500. This is the earliest known map of America, fascinating as much for what it does not show as what it does. Cuba, Hispaniola, and the other islands are clear and the Florida peninsula appears to be represented, as are Venezuela and Northern Brazil. Otherwise, it is largely conjecture. MADRID: MUSEO NAVAL. COURTESY OF THE HISTORY COLLECTION/ALAMY STOCK PHOTO

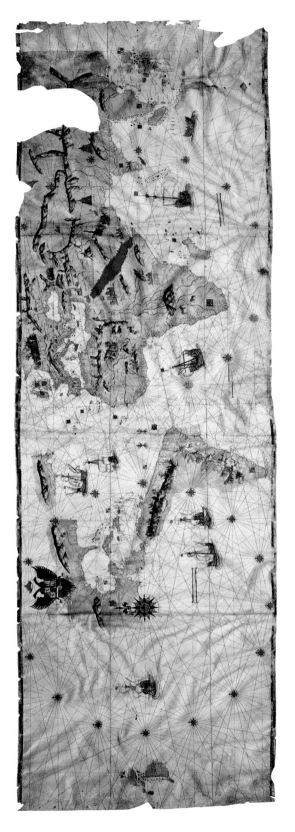

Juan Vespucci, *World Map*, Seville, 1526. The Gulf of Mexico and the east coast of South America are shown in considerable detail, as is the isthmus at Panama. Note how little of North America is represented, with a large gap or gulf between Newfoundland/Nova Scotia and somewhere near St. Augustine.

Jan van der Straet, *Discovery of America: Vespucci Landing in America*, c. 1587. Amerigo Vespucci was a financier who wrote an excitable account of his travels in the New World and lent his name to the new continents, thanks to the cartographer Martin Waldseemüller. NEW YORK: THE METROPOLITAN MUSEUM OF ART

D. FR. BARTHOLOME DE LAS CASAS
Del Orden de Predicadores, Obispo de Chiapa
Varon apostolico, y el mas zeloso de la felicidad
de los Indios.
Nació en Sevilla d año de 1474, y murió en Ma
d de 1566.

Tomás López Enguídanos, *Bartolomé de Las Casas*, 1791. Las Casas was a colonist of Hispaniola who took orders as a Dominican friar and became known as the Defender of the Indians for his advocacy for the rights of indigenous Americans.

MADRID: BIBLIOTECA NACIONAL DE ESPAÑA

HERNANDO DE SOTO.

Anonymous, *Hernando de Soto*, in William Henry Milburn, *The Lance, Cross and Canoe* (New York and St. Louis: 1892). De Soto became rich during the conquest of Inca Peru, but lost everything, including his life, attempting to settle *La Florida*.

COURTESY OF THE LIBRARY OF CONGRESS DUPLICATION SERVICES, LC-USZ62-104329

Spanish Horseman, Native American Pictographs in Canyon del Muerto, Arizona. This remarkable image is the earliest extant representation of Europeans made by Native Americans in North America. COURTESY OF PRISMA BY DUKAS PRESSEAGENTUR GMBH/ALAMY STOCK PHOTO

LEFT: Anonymous Zuni artist, *Chakwaina Kachina*. This is the "black" Kachina, often described as an "ogre" and widely thought to be Esteban, the African slave who led the expedition to visit the Pueblo Indians of New Mexico with Friar Marcos de Niza. COURTESY OF LEGENDS OF AMERICA

ABOVE: Vicente de Zaldívar, *Bison*, 1598. This is the earliest known European image of an American bison. The Spaniards enjoyed practicing their bullfighting skills with these majestic animals. SEVILLE: ARCHIVO GENERAL DE INDIAS: MP-ESTAMPAS, 1; COURTESY OF THE MINISTERIO DE CULTURA Y DEPORTE

P.Ioañes Bapt: de Segura, Gabriel Gomez, Petrus de Linarez, Sqncti Sauelli,
Christoph: Rotund₉ Hisp: S.I. in Florida pro Christi fide trucidati A.1571. 8 Fe
C. Screta del.   Melch. Küsell f.

Melchior Küsell, *Murder of Father Segura*, from Mathias Tanner, *Societas Iesu Militans*
(Prague: 1675). The Adelantado of Florida, Menéndez de Avilés: "These blessed fathers seem to
think that his Holiness the Pope only sent them there to be martyred and cut into pieces by these
savages." COURTESY OF BRIDWELL LIBRARY SPECIAL COLLECTIONS, PERKINS SCHOOL OF THEOLOGY,
SOUTHERN METHODIST UNIVERSITY

cultural currents, they sometimes fought, they intermarried, and very occasionally clans or societies migrated from one settlement to another. In short, they were pretty good neighbors who felt a sense of their kindred spirit in contradistinction to the Apaches, Navajos, Mansos, and Jumanos roundabout. But the Pueblos did not see themselves as belonging to a homogenous ethnic group. They spoke different languages, their spiritual traditions had distinctive characteristics, their social and political structures varied. The Pueblos felt their differences as keenly as the peoples of Europe, for all that they did not constantly express them with quite the same warmongering fanaticism.

By the 1670s, however, after seventy years of Spanish domination, subjected to institutions and encumbered by a taxonomy that treated them all as a single people, the younger generations developed a novel sense of their identity as Pueblos and even Indians, which they shared with many Apaches and Navajos.[4] A Tewa medicine man called Po'pay from San Juan (modern Ohkay Owingeh) harnessed that new sense of a common identity to forge an alliance broad enough to defeat the foreigners.

In 1675, the Spaniards were greatly alarmed by a strange incident in which Pueblo "sorcerers" were rumored to have bewitched a friar. Po'pay was one of forty-seven medicine men rounded up and imprisoned at Santa Fe. They were beaten and whipped in the main plaza, and three men were hanged. But soon, seventy well-armed Pueblo Indians burst into the Palace of the Governors and forced the officials to release the remaining prisoners, including Po'pay. This was a crucial moment in establishing a shared Pueblo identity. The Indians were both infuriated by the mass brutalization of their medicine men and also emboldened by the success of the rescue.[5] When a new governor, Antonio de Otermín, arrived in 1678, he found the colony on the brink of war.

Po'pay had been identified as a serious threat to peace, and the Spaniards harried him into exile at the Tewa town of Taos in the far north. There, he allied himself with another Tewa refugee called Taqu, two local "magicians" known as Saca and Chato, and a man from San Ildefonso known to history by his Christian name, Francisco. Together these Pueblo patriots kept the metaphorical embers of rebellion burning at Taos in the esoteric confines of the main kiva, the underground ceremonial chamber so sacred to Pueblo religion. They "sent two hides painted with symbols signifying a conspiracy" to be shown to war leaders across the Pueblo world "in order to prepare the people for another uprising," a Keres from San Felipe called Pedro Naranjo later testified. Governor Luis Tupatu of Picuris and the Keres war chief Catiti soon joined the conspiracy, along with twenty unnamed Tewa "captains of war."

Pueblo oral historians may know what really went on in the kiva, but their history remains secret and so goes unwritten. Naranjo stated under oath to a

Spanish inquiry that "three figures," called "Caudi, Tilimi, and Tleume," had "appeared to Po'pay" and "shot fire from their fingertips." They said "they had gone underground as far as Lake Copala" and "told him to make a length of cord out of yucca fibers and then tie knots in it as a sign of the number of days until it was time to rise up" against the enemy.[6] Yet Lake Copala is part of Aztec legend, and the names of the three figures look Nahuatl in origin.[7] Moreover, another Indian mentioned a celestial messenger who had remained as the representative of Pose-yemu, after the Aztec emperor Montezuma "had left these parts."[8] Intriguingly, two messengers captured by the Spaniards while spreading word of the revolt testified that "among the Indians it was said that a letter urging them to rise up had been sent from far away in the north by a representative of Pose-yemu who was very tall, black, and had very large yellow eyes,"[9] all characteristic features of Chakwaina, the kachina associated with Esteban, the African who first met the Zunis, in 1539.[10]

Clearly, the references to Copala, the three figures, and Montezuma were influenced by Aztec tradition. But did they originate with Aztec or Tlaxcalan settlers? Or was the close association of Montezuma with Pose-yemu already a part of Pueblo culture, perhaps dating back to Esteban or even before that?[11] Or, was the testimony of these Indians modified by Nahuatl-speaking interpreters involved in their interrogation?

Pose-yemu is a deity of universal significance across the Pueblo world, a son of the Sun who was created out of a piñon nut by World Man in the mythological past, and the Pueblos still laugh heartily at an old joke about the Spaniards' failure to understand that he was given different names in the Tewa, Tano, Towa, and Keresan languages.[12] Such humor highlights the problem that Spanish sources are generally one-sided, though the echo of an indigenous voice is occasionally heard, as in the reported testimony of these Indians.

At Taos, the patriot commanders chose the next full moon, August 11, as the day to begin the bloody final chapter of the Spanish history of New Mexico. Their precise plans will never be known, but the basic message sent out to the allies can be deduced and it was ambitious. The first stage of the war would be a simultaneous assault in every northern pueblo on its Spanish inhabitants. Every priest, every man, woman, and child, were to be overpowered and killed. Then, armed with Spanish weapons, the Pueblos would combine forces, and, supported by Apache allies, they would descend on Santa Fe and trap the main body of settlers and soldiers in their own capital. The slaughter would begin. No quarter would be given. Meanwhile, Manso allies were supposed to lay waste to the Río de Abajo, the stretch south toward El Paso.

The patriots worried that some Indians might have misgivings about the coming revolt, for they had been raised in a world of Spaniards, Tlaxcalans, and Pueblos, and even if they did not like it, they were accustomed to its colonial ways. For example, the patriot leaders thought the Piros in the far south were so integrated into Spanish life that they could not be trusted and excluded them altogether from the plot to rebel. The couriers sent forth with the knotted cords to announce the trysting day were sworn to total secrecy on pain of death. It was made plain to each Pueblo that every man must do his duty or be executed as a traitor. Po'pay even murdered his own brother-in-law in cold blood when he learned he might be spying for the Spaniards.[13]

On August 9, Po'pay learned that a handful of Tano and Keres Indians had betrayed two young messengers sent to alert them to the uprising. Otermín himself interrogated these youths at Santa Fe, but while they confessed to most of what they knew, they were resourceful enough to pretend that the rebellion was scheduled for August 13.[14] As soon as Po'pay and the other leaders learned that news, they sent out emergency orders to begin the war immediately. Their message promised, "Any Indian who should kill a Spaniard will take an Indian woman for his wife, and he who kills four will get four wives."[15]

Taos rose that very night. About seventy Spaniards lived in the surrounding valley, but just two military officers escaped, the flanks of their horses running with blood as they spurred them on, riding for their lives, while their wives and children, servants and neighbors, were all put to death.

Po'pay's order to attack traveled with lightning speed. By dawn of August 10, the men of Tesuque were mustering a mile outside their pueblo, most wearing war paint and armed with bows, arrows, lances, and shields. They watched two Spaniards on horseback approaching along the trail and quickly recognized the familiar faces of Brother Juan Pío and a soldier called Pedro Hidalgo.

"What is all this, my children?" the friar asked. "Have you gone mad?"

The brave Franciscan rode on along the shallow valley, calling to the crowd of Indians to come to town and hear morning mass. Meanwhile, Hidalgo rode up toward the ridge above with the vague intention of heading them off, but the soldier had not climbed far when he turned and saw an Indian called El Obi coming back along the trail carrying the friar's shield. Just behind him was another man Hidalgo knew well: Nicolás the interpreter was caked in white war paint now splattered with bright red blood. Hidalgo turned and rode headlong for Santa Fe with a few Tewa grabbing at his bridle as a torrent of arrows rained down all around them.[16]

At Sandia, the Pueblos assaulted a painting of Our Lady of the Immaculate Conception that had served as the altarpiece of the main church, putting out the Madonna's eyes and mutilating her mouth before stoning the sacred image of her purity from Original Sin. They whipped a crucifix until the varnish and paint fell from Christ's tortured body like real strips of skin. They hacked the arms from a statue of Saint Francis and smeared two sculptures with shit. They pulled down the great bells from the campanile, whose loathsome toll had called them to their daily toil and prayers. Then they burned the church to the ground. At the mission, they converted the friars' cells into a kind of kiva and hung it with kachina masks and magical herbs and feathers.[17]

Increasingly terrifying reports cascaded into Santa Fe. Word came from Nambe Pueblo that the insurgents had slaughtered two friars, three Spaniards and their wives and children, and the rest of their households. A large division of the Pueblo army was said to be mustering at Santa Clara, a day's march from the capital. There, two more friars had been martyred, two soldiers killed, and Captain Anaya's children abducted.

At five o'clock in the afternoon, the two terrified military officers from Taos rode into the capital, bringing word that the northern Pueblos had risen up and telling of their narrow escape. A detachment of Indians had fired guns and arrows at them on the road. The awful news kept coming as other refugees reached Santa Fe with stories of Spaniards, Tlaxcalans, and friendly Pueblos trying to hold out in ranches and churches. Governor Otermín began to lose tally of the massacre. By Monday, August 12, he knew that at least thirty people had been killed in Nambe and Posuaque pueblos alone, mostly children. In the eastern pueblos toward Pecos, four friars, two soldiers, and their families were dead. Then Otermín learned that three Franciscans had been martyred at Santo Domingo. Squads of mounted Indians were rounding up livestock and patrolling the roads.[18] The governor was powerless to save them.

Otermín ordered the population to gather in the Palace of the Governors and even began to arm the older children. He gave instructions to gather every harquebus, blunderbuss, sword, dagger, and any other weapon or piece of ammunition in the royal armory to prevent them from falling into enemy hands. He stationed sentinels and harquebusiers on the roof, then began fortifying the building, digging trenches and opening loopholes in its wooden shutters. He told the Franciscans to collect the plate and sacred objects from the church and to use up the consecrated Holy Sacrament. Ironically, the image of La Conquistadora that had been so carefully transported to New Mexico by Benavides over fifty years before was among the precious objects brought into the makeshift bastion to be saved from the "savages," whose subjection had been celebrated by her name. Otermín was preparing to be besieged. He even ordered people to bring in their livestock.[19] The palace was soon filled with a thousand men and women and hundreds of head of sheep and cattle. The smell must have been worse than a feedlot on a southern summer day.

In the dead of night, a Tano well known to the Spaniards as Juan Tagno led an army of over five hundred warriors drawn from the eastern Pueblos onto the high ground of the Tlaxcalan suburb around the chapel of San Miguel, across the river from Santa Fe. At dawn, he paraded on horseback, draped with a scarlet humeral veil, the liturgical vestment that looks like a sumptuous silk poncho, open at the front. Underneath, Juan Tagno was dressed like a Spanish soldier, with a thick leather jacket, a dagger hanging from his belt, and armed with harquebus and sword. The Spaniards called to him and he rode into town to parley with Otermín. The Spanish general asked this man he had long thought of as a friend, "How can you do such a thing when I had placed great confidence in you?"

"The Indians who come with me and those whom we are waiting for are all coming to destroy the town," Juan Tagno replied. "We are bringing two crosses, one red and the other white, so that Your Lordship may choose: red signifies war, and white that you Spaniards shall abandon the kingdom."

"I desire to avoid war," Otermín replied, "should you quieten down, I would pardon the crimes you have committed."[20]

Even the suggestion he would pardon the wholesale slaughter of Spaniards and their allies is indication enough that Otermín was succumbing to hopelessness. When Juan rode back to his camp and repeated this offer to his men, they ridiculed the arrogance of the Spaniard's reply and filled the air with a cacophony of trumpets and shouts. They rang the bells of San Miguel before burning the chapel to the ground.

Otermín realized that any delay would allow Pueblo and Apache reinforcements from the north to arrive, so he ordered a contingent of men to attack the enemy. The battle raged all day through the streets of Santa Fe, where the Spaniards' military discipline and sense of desperation gave them the upper hand. In the face of the Pueblos' enthusiastic but inaccurate harquebus fire, they doggedly won ground, house by house, street by street. But as the sun began to set and Otermín dared to dream of victory, the very large array of Indians from the north under the leadership of Po'pay attacked, capturing the low hill behind the Palace of the Governors. From there, they fired on anyone who dared show himself above the parapets. Then the Pueblo sappers cut the water supply to the palace.

The Spaniards and their allies held out for nine nights amid the squalor of their refuge. They saw the tower of flames as the church burned and listened to the enemy singing songs of victory in the streets, pillaging the town, shop by shop, home by home. The besiegers taunted them with cries of "The Spanish God and the Madonna are dead and your saints mere lumps of rotten wood!"[21] The livestock began to perish in the fetid courtyard, and with a terrible thirst raging among men, women, and children, Otermín and his captains knew they must again take the fight to the enemy. "His Lordship determined that it were better and nobler to die fighting than of starvation and of thirst."[22]

At dawn, on August 20, the well-armed Spaniards, the stout Tlaxcalans, and their *casta* comrades burst forth from their palace prison and "invoking the name of the blessed Madonna," they fought for their wives and the tender babes who suckled at their breasts, they fought for the effigies of their God. They fought the battle of their lives, and when the day was done, three hundred Pueblo warriors lay dead in the streets of Santa Fe and fifteen hundred more had fled. Four Spaniards had lost their lives, and Otermín was wounded in the face and torso. But the battle had been lost and won. The governor looked sternly into the faces of forty-seven unhappy captive enemy men. They told him they had acted "out of fear" of the terrifying "Indian who lives far to the north, who became lieutenant to Pohe-yemu when Montezuma left."[23] They explained that their orders had been to kill all the priests and the menfolk, even the children, leaving only the women and girls alive. Otermín ordered all forty-seven shot.

The following day, Otermín issued the inevitable order to abandon the Spanish capital of New Mexico. His plan was to regroup at Isleta Pueblo in the well-populated Río de Abajo, with its many Spanish farms and friendly Piros, where he believed his lieutenant Alonso García must be mustering a large force for the fight back. Otermín hastily organized the distribution of clothing to the refugees and rounded up livestock to take south on the hoof. La Conquistadora was ignominiously loaded onto a wagon or a mule, yet another refugee.

That morning, Otermín's sorry caravan rumbled out of Santa Fe, and over the following days they were repeatedly harassed by squadrons of mounted Pueblo and Apache warriors. They narrowly avoided disaster near Santo Domingo when a soldier stumbled upon a large contingent of Indians lying in ambush. They came across an Indian who had deserted the Spaniards during the siege of Santa Fe who told Otermín that he had fled because "I concluded that all you Spaniards had to perish along with you, Governor; and that even should you be not defeated, you would take me to a distant land."[24] Even this former friend thought Spanish New Mexico was already history.

Meanwhile, the Pueblo armies regrouped in the great plaza at Santa Fe. According to Pueblo tradition, a series of speakers addressed the victorious warriors, giving thanks to the Great Spirit and the twin gods of war, Maseway and Oyoyeway. Poquete from Tesuque told the assembled throng, "We have killed as many Spaniards as they have killed of our number. No matter. Let them go, that we shall live as we wish! Now, let us occupy this town and settle wherever we may want!"[25]

After more rousing speeches, Po'pay himself finally launched into a long and powerful oration: "Within and around the world, within and around the hills and mountains, within and around the valleys, your authority returns to you. Therefore, return to your people and travel the corn pollen trail again. A trail with no pebbles, no boulders, and no obstructions. Go home and enjoy your families, the birds, the clouds, the mist, the rain, the lightning, the wind, the rivers, the mountains, the trees, and the sky. Remember the words of our leaders upon arriving home, go to the rivers and cleanse yourselves of the recent past. Lastly, don't forget, each morning before our father, the sun, makes his appearance, to take feathers in one hand and corn pollen in the other hand and offer them to the deities in the mountains, in the clouds, in the valleys, to the north, to the west, to the south, to the east, to Sipofinae and to Saynema. *Sengi di ho!*"

The assembled warriors offered a prayer to the war gods, scattering corn pollen to the winds. One warrior is said to have prayed aloud, "I shall remember with gratitude the great men that I have seen and met here and those no longer with us. Those who have sacrificed so much for the benefit of my people. Let me keep their high cause in my heart."[26]

Over the following days, across the towns and villages of the Pueblo world, the victorious warriors performed the Bow and Arrow Dance, which is done in many pueblos to this day.[27]

Po'pay and his war chiefs progressed across the Pueblo world, quick with the joy and pride of victory. He proclaimed that the kachinas and traditional deities were more powerful than the Christian God and ordered the people to burn the churches and religious imagery, the rosaries and the crucifixes. He commanded them to stop using Christian names and instructed them to cleanse themselves of baptism by washing with soap made from yucca root, with its powerful spiritual properties, and to reject the Christian sacrament of marriage by abandoning their wives. He threatened to have whipped all transgressors, and he put to death the few brave Christian souls who refused to be cowed. He instructed the Pueblo people to plant only traditional Pueblo crops and to burn the Spanish seeds, to heap up piles of stones and make offerings of corn and tobacco. He asked them to teach the children all these things.[28]

But even as Po'pay in his incipient despotism tried to force the total erasure of Spanish culture upon a people who had long both absorbed and rejected that culture, he himself was falling under its spell. When he reached Santa Ana Pueblo with his entourage, he had a sumptuous Spanish banquet prepared from the foodstuffs that the friars and the Spaniards had left behind. He presided from the head of the large table covered with linen in the Spanish fashion. He called for two chalices, and he and Alonso Catiti proclaimed insulting toasts against the Spanish, ridiculing their manners and their speech. As though Catiti were the Father *Custos* of the Franciscans, Po'pay chortled, "To thine health, Very Reverend Father."

"To thine, Thy Lordship," Catiti replied.[29]

Such satire is a dangerous game to play, for the purpose of carnival is to give the humble a taste of might and grandeur and make us prey to the sophisticated proclivities of that merciless goddess irony. Catiti filled his home with Spanish luxuries; Pueblo and Navajo leaders paraded themselves in splendid liturgical clothing. Po'pay tried to establish levels of tribute that each Pueblo owed to him. But the people had not risked all to submit to a caricature of Spanish tyranny, and his influence waned so quickly that within the year this brilliant insurgent leader disappeared from Pueblo and Spanish history alike.[30] His former comrade Luis Tupatu rose to prominence and began a long, slow process of *détente*.

August faded into September, and Otermín continued his retreat down the Camino Real through an apocalyptic landscape. After the destruction at Sandia, the retreating Spaniards and their allies moved from ranch to ranch, seeing more death and devastation and enemy horsemen. The ousted governor questioned a lone Indian, who told him that Alonso García had gathered a large crowd of refugees and led them south toward the mission at the great river crossing called El Paso. The following day, Otermín's advance guard rode into the deserted streets of Isleta. Not a soul remained.

When the fighting had begun, García valiantly led a tiny force of eight men to the rescue of two officers and some friars trapped at Jemez and Zia. He had ridden on to Santo Domingo to confirm that all the friars and four further men were dead and found the cadavers of Agustín de Carvajal and Cristóbal de Anaya, slaughtered on their farms alongside their wives and children. He saw another six bodies by the wayside. "Everywhere the cry was up that the lord governor and everyone from Sandia as far as Taos had been killed."[31] García was forced to take refuge at his own estate, where he and his six sons spent two terrifying days besieged within the farmhouse, surrounded by mounted Pueblo troops baying for blood.

Finally, García and his men had fought their way to Isleta, where terrified survivors were gathering from across the Río de Abajo. There, he repeatedly sought news of what had happened at Santa Fe, but heard nothing other than overwhelming rumors that everyone was dead. He knew that the supply caravan from Mexico City was due to reach Mission Guadalupe at El Paso soon with much needed provisions and fresh soldiers. So, with the Franciscans pestering him to lead the survivors south to safety, he had finally given the order to abandon Isleta and head south.

On September 14, at Socorro, Otermín presided over a meeting of all his captains and officials and the leading Franciscans. With twenty-five hundred hungry and frightened refugees to think of and barely a hundred and fifty men in a condition to fight, they agreed to withdraw, and fifteen days later, they established a temporary camp a few miles north of El Paso. Large numbers began to desert into New Spain, and Otermín was desperately concerned that his colony of New Mexico in exile would dwindle to naught. On October 5, the senior figures of the colony formally petitioned the governor to establish a permanent settlement across the Rio Grande from Mission Guadalupe, where the land "has very good grazing and lumber and where the poor can put up shacks and huts against the rigors of the coming winter that threaten us."[32] Otermín agreed and began making preparations for the move.[33]

Otermín was replaced in 1683, and for almost a decade his successors showed little stomach to undertake a campaign to reconquer New Mexico. Finally, in 1692, Diego de Vargas led a force of three hundred men back into New Mexico and soon reported to the viceroy that he had won a bloodless reconquest of the Pueblo Indians. "It is my desire," he wrote, "that before anything else is done, the soldiers should in person first build the church, setting up in it the patroness of the kingdom, who was saved from the savages, Our Lady of the Conquest, as she is known."[34] The bells of the cathedral in Mexico City peeled the victory, and the call went out for volunteers to repopulate the most northern kingdom in the Spanish American Empire. A motley gathering of impoverished tailors, cobblers, masons, cartwrights, millers, cabinetmakers, musicians, carpenters, assorted metalsmiths, barbers, painters, pavers, chandlers, and a cutler and their families signed up to begin a new chapter in their lives. Seventy families reached Santa Fe in the bitter cold of December, with snow on the ground and frost in the air, to find that the Indian inhabitants had recast the fabric of the Spanish town as a classic pueblo apartment complex. At first, all was peaceful, but within days Vargas learned of a planned assault by an alliance of Tewas, Tanos, and Picuris.

A bloody battle ensued. Seventy Indian prisoners were executed, and four hundred more were enslaved. Over the coming months, Vargas would put down rebellions at Jemez, San Cristobal, Nambe, and finally at Santa Clara, where Lucas Naranjo was shot and beheaded. But as dawn broke on New Year's Eve 1693, the Spaniards were finally ready to celebrate a new start.[35] Vargas personally oversaw the hasty construction of a roof for the ruined chapel of San Miguel and had La Conquistadora placed inside. She had come home.

The success of the Pueblo Revolt was a direct consequence of the strength of Pueblo culture long before the arrival of the colonists and the weakness of the Spanish New Mexico because of its isolation and its internal conflicts. However, the Pueblos' success was short-lived because they had become sufficiently dependent on imperial institutions and even integrated into the colonial culture that they found it impossible to survive without them. As the Pueblos took stock of a world without Spaniards, the political influence of Luis Tupatu grew so significantly that by the summer of 1683 he felt sufficiently confident in his leadership to send an embassy to Otermín, then still ensconced at his new capital at El Paso.

Tupatu briefed his envoys in great secrecy, spelling out to them the unhappy truth that "without the Spaniards they had run out of everything and had no cattle, nor sheep, nor horses, nor knives, nor hoes, nor clothing, nor medicines for the sick." The message was clear: somehow an accommodation would have to be reached with the enemy. The delegates were to convey to Otermín and his officers that "if they cared to return, the Spaniards would be well received."

When the Spaniards threatened to torture one of these ambassadors, he confessed that the Pueblos were in trouble. His picture of the Pueblos' problems went much further than Tupatu's invocation of material and cultural deficiencies. The ambassador was clearly terrified by the Pueblos' inability to defend themselves and the grotesque failings of their revolutionary leaders. He claimed that twenty Taos Indians had been killed by Ute raiders, while Alonso Catiti had appropriated most of the sheep for himself. All the cattle and horses had ended up at Picuris, much livestock had been eaten by hungry Pueblos, and Apache raiders had run off the rest. The ambassador assured the Spaniards that Luis Tupatu had remained a faithful Christian and had buried various liturgical objects beneath the altar of the main church at Picuris to prevent their coming to harm.[36]

The Pueblos were clearly divided over the benefits of a Spanish presence, but this division after so many decades of abuse, and Vargas's ability to reestablish New Mexico, are testimony to the extent to which seventy years of Spanish presence had permanently imprinted itself on the peoples of the Upper Rio Grande. The expulsion of the Spaniards in 1680 may be evidence that the empire had overreached itself, and that colonial authority was limited, but the relative ease of the Spaniards' return is testimony to the power of imperialism.

CHAPTER 12

MANHUNT

TEXAS

Unhappy, gloom-laden resting place,
Where lurk the Melancholy,
Bad luck, and evil Fates
Who sent thy people angry death.

—GIOVANNI BAUTISTA SCHIAPAPRIA

OTERMÍN'S RETREAT FROM SANTA FE LED to the permanent settlement at El Paso and the first mission within the boundaries of modern Texas at Corpus Christi de la Ysleta. But with New Mexico still a frontier and a sense that the Spanish imperial presence was already spread thin in North America, there was little enthusiasm to explore east of the Rio Grande. Only one long expedition was made beyond the Lower Rio Grande before the arrival of French trespassers on territory that Spain still claimed by virtue of first discovery forced the Spanish authorities to take action to secure Texas for the empire.[1]

The story of serious Spanish interest in Texas began in Paris, when the great Canadian adventurer René-Robert Cavelier sought an audience with Louis XIV, the Sun King.[2] Born at Rouen, France, Cavelier had taken orders as a Jesuit before fleeing to Canada, where he was rewarded for his outstanding service with the Lordship of La Salle in Montreal.[3] He had a remarkable story to tell his sovereign, for in 1682 he had led the first European descent of the Mississippi and returned upstream the following year, feeding on alligator meat and founding Fort Saint Louis on the Illinois River.[4] He offered to plant a colony called La Louisianne in the fertile land above the mouth of the river, the perfect entrepôt to connect Canada with the markets of the Caribbean and Mexico, close to the silver mines of Zacatecas, and which would rely on the support of thousands of Indian warriors from around Saint Louis.[5] Louis

XIV rewarded La Salle with command of all lands that he might occupy for France between the Mississippi and Nueva Vizcaya.[6] As he left the glittering dreamland of Versailles into the gray light of a northern French winter, La Salle must have wondered what in the world he had committed himself to do.

While in the Caribbean, after a night of raucous debauchery, a number of sailors from La Salle's flagship deserted to join a band of notorious buccaneers. When the Spanish Windward Fleet hunted down these pirates, they took prisoner a young lad who had formed a close friendship with La Salle's personal servant during the Atlantic crossing. Under interrogation, the boy explained in detail to the Spanish that the French planned to settle near the mouth of the "Micipipi."[7] The authorities in Santo Domingo sent ships to investigate and appointed an army officer called Alonso de León to lead an expedition overland from New Spain to expel the trespassers. León had been born and raised at Cadereyta, a town founded by his father on the frontier where Nuevo León and Coahuila gaze at Texas over the Rio Grande. After his father died, León was appointed captain of the presidio and *alcalde* of the town. He was well qualified to launch a military expedition deep into Texas.[8]

León kept journals of the five major expeditions he led across the Rio Grande, which offer a vivid sense of Texas at the time Europeans made their first tentative steps toward permanent settlement.[9] His first forays failed to find any sign of the interlopers, but a seaborne expedition found the battered remains of a French ship beached high by some winter storm near Matagorda Bay. Yet there was no sign of its passengers and crew.[10] The Spaniards concluded La Salle was no longer a threat and, in 1688, León, now Governor of Nuevo León, turned his attention to suppressing increasing levels of violence between Indians and settlers across his jurisdiction. He sent Agustín de la Cruz, a descendant of the first Tlaxcalan settlers who had been encouraged to settle the Saltillo suburb of San Esteban de Nueva Tlaxcala, in the 1590s, to bolster the region against Chichimeca raiding parties.[11]

Cruz crossed the Rio Grande and discovered an Indian encampment centered on a structure he reported as "a large hall roofed with buffalo hides." Inside, "I met a tall man, so white he looked Spanish, with graying hair, but his face was scarred or tattooed," whom "the Indians held in the highest esteem."[12] The two men struggled to communicate using the Indians' language, but Cruz understood that the man "was French . . . that he had been sent by God to establish some settlements . . . and that he had been trying to gather together various Indian nations from the area to go to war with some Indian enemies."[13] Thus, remarkably, the first parley ever held on Texas soil between representatives of two rival European powers was conducted in a long-lost

Native American language by a Tlaxcalan and a Frenchman who had had more or less become an Indian.

León was deeply concerned that a Frenchman appeared to command so many Native Americans and feared he might be the vanguard of a well-organized operation. León set out with an elite squad of eighteen men to visit this strange neighbor. Three hundred armed Indians lined up to welcome them. León, another officer, and a friar entered the great tepee and saw the Frenchman seated on a sort of divan strewn with hides and cushions. Suddenly, this exotic figure dropped to his knees and kissed the friar's skirts, thumping his chest and saying, "*Yo francés*, me French."

The man introduced himself as Jean Henri, which León transcribed into his journal as "capitan monsiur Yan Jarri," later translated as Juan Henrique.[14] He reluctantly agreed to accompany the Spaniards to Coahuila, but they struggled to understand one another. Henri seemed to be saying that "Philip," the governor of a French town that had been founded fifteen years before beside a large river, had ordered him to create an alliance among the different Indian nations of the region. As the garbled interrogation continued, the Spaniards understood that the town was served by six Capuchin friars and defended by two stone castles, one Dutch and the other French.[15]

León was perplexed by these apparently preposterous claims and sent Henri to Mexico City, where the viceroy found his testimony so fluid and contradictory that he concluded the prisoner "could not be in his right mind."[16] Part of the problem is probably that Henri had told León he was born at Orléans in France, in one of the parishes dedicated to Saint John the Baptist. In Mexico, Henri said he was from a place the Spaniards transcribed as "Xeble," which confused the issue at the time and has bemused modern scholars since. However, just as Garcilaso, the Inca, rendered Juan Ortiz's greeting to Soto's men as "Xivilla," because "S" in the southern-Spanish accent was often pronounced "sth" or "shhh," so "Xelbe" looks like a phonetic rendering of Chevilly, an important seigneurial estate just north of Orléans, and elsewhere Henri is mentioned as coming from "Cheblié."[17] Already inclined to distrust their witness, the interrogators proceeded in such excruciating French that at one point Henri merely gurgled back at them uncomprehendingly, no doubt shrugging his Gallic shoulders, a response they described as "a senseless chuckle." It would seem logical to conclude that the French fort and settlement he had described to León was either Orléans in France or possibly somewhere in Canada, but his Spanish interrogators became convinced it must be on the Mexican Gulf. The viceroy ordered León to prepare a new expedition and sent Henri to help him locate the French settlement.

León set out on March 23, 1689, accompanied by a self-important Franciscan, Damián Massanet, who was determined to "to find some semblance of news about the land that the venerable Mother María de Ágreda had visited so often."[18] As the expedition approached the Rio Grande, Henri was rapturously received by five hundred Indians drawn from five different tribes camped on the right bank, but the Spaniards were grim faced when they saw four tall stakes hung with sixteen fresh scalps. It was a timely reminder of life and death in the land they were about to enter.

They forded the Rio Grande on April 1 and began to travel through a landscape of "pleasant valleys," "low hills," and "creeks," all with plenty of pasture for the livestock. There were stands of mesquite and live oak, and pecan forests, which León called walnuts, good and ripe, "as large as those of Spain, although very difficult to crack."[19] An Indian guide told them that six days hence there were "men like us living in six or seven houses with their women and children."[20] León wondered if these might be La Salle and his people. The Indian mentioned "large white stones with crosses carved into them and other pictures done with great precision and apparently very old," the first known description of a petroglyph in Texas history.[21] On Holy Saturday, they started to see wild vines. León ordered a barrel of wine broken open, and the whole company enjoyed a glass or more. The drunken hostlers allowed the horses to stampede, and most of the men spent Easter Sunday rounding up the strays.

Five days later, they met two large groups of Native Americans, who told them that only four Frenchmen were left alive and they had left four days earlier to join the Tejas, or "Texas," a Caddoan tribe of wealthy farmers whose ancestors had been visited by Soto's men a century and a half before. They said the other Frenchmen who had settled in "six houses" on "the bay" had been struck by smallpox. Some had died of the disease, and the survivors "were killed by the coastal Indians . . . three moons ago."[22] Soon afterward, Henri recognized some Indians who said they knew the route the four French refugees had taken, so León had his ensign write a letter to them in French, the friar added a few words in Latin for effect, and then an Indian messenger set out with it along the trail. As far as we know, this was the first letter written and posted in Texas; appropriately enough, the address of the recipients was care of the Texas Indians.

As they continued, they began to notice an increasing number of Indians who had various everyday objects of European life, including some French books that León bought by barter. The Franciscan Massanet later claimed he had realized Henri was trying to lead the expedition in the wrong direction and convinced León to go the right way. To which León, he said, had responded amiably: "Come on, Father, we will go wherever thou shouldst wish."

They crossed some broad plains where a herd of buffalo grazed and found a fine creek. There, Henri finally admitted, "Sire, me know well there be houses on small river."[23] The following day, April 22, they finally reached their goal. Fort Saint Louis was located "on flat ground, wonderfully situated to repel any assault," León observed admiringly.[24]

But the French colony was a scene of utter devastation. The timber fort, the little chapel, and the six wattle-and-daub huts had been ransacked. Smashed-up packing cases, broken barrels, furniture, and other belongings were strewn about. Cannon lay littered here and there; a hundred harquebuses had been destroyed. In the midst of all this wreckage "we found three dead people lying in a field, one of whom seemed to have been a woman to judge by the dress that was still stuck to the bones."[25]

The friars sang a funeral mass, and León's secretary, an Italian intellectual called Giovanni Bautista Schiapapria, composed a moving eulogy to the dead woman, the first European verses composed in Texas, so far as we know. Even in the rough-and-ready state recorded by León, these three stanzas are a *tour de force* of Renaissance and Baroque imagery, a wholly unexpected moment of sublime poetry frozen in midcomposition on that unhappy riverbank:

Unhappy, gloom-laden resting place,
Where lurk the Melancholy,
Bad luck, and evil Fates
Who sent thy people angry death.
Now I must contemplate alone
Thy miserable misfortune,
O Muse of life's inconstancy!
A wild, murderous, inhuman adversary
With willful hand unleashed
Such unforgiving cruelty
Upon such youthful innocence,
As e'en condemned a newborn babe.

O ye fine beauties of France!
Roses sweet who walked these meadows
And with snow-white hands
Caressed the fleeting lilies
With thy perfect embroidery
And outshone in artifice

The nymphs of Ancient Greece.
And now even the wild woods,
Milled and threshed themselves,
In vain, watch over ye in death,
Their own perdition framed by your mortality.

And thou, cold corpse,
Once so full of eager brio,
Now fodder for the beasts,
As witnessed by thy injury.
Tenderly I frame thee now,
O perfect picture of sad misfortune.
Enjoy thy everlasting glory!
Thou hast departed earthly life
Pierced by too many wounds,
But for a home in heaven's breast!
So beg thou of our eternal God
That he should spare us all the agonies of hell.[26]

Henri led León on a tour of the surrounding area. On the sandy shores of Matagorda Bay they found the remains of a shipwreck, sighted the pass between the barrier islands, and came across the Karankawa band they thought must have killed the Frenchmen. When they returned to Fort Saint Louis, a messenger was waiting with a letter from one of the French fugitives announcing their imminent arrival and their determination to escape their life among the "savages."

With his objective achieved, León ordered the main body of the expedition to return to Coahuila and set out with thirty soldiers in search of the Frenchmen. On May Day, they found two French survivors, "scarred and tattooed like the Indians" and dressed in "skins and hides." They were living under the protection of the "Chief of the Texas ... an Indian of obvious ability."[27]

The Frenchmen told a sorry tale.

La Salle's ships missed the Mississippi delta, and battered by gales and high seas, he convinced himself that Matagorda Bay marked a westerly entrance to the great river.[28] A number of officers advised against trying to take the ships across the sandbar at the entrance to the bay, but La Salle plied the captains and pilots with plenty of wine. Thus emboldened, they brought the *Belle* safely into the haven, but inexplicably, the *Aimable* foundered and began to sink. The naval officers aboard the naval flagship *Joly* were convinced the captain had deliberately wrecked his ship. No one knew why. It spelled disaster, for the *Joly* soon departed, its work complete, leaving only the *Belle* behind, a poor sailing ship that was already slowly rotting.

La Salle seemed impervious to their predicament and poured every pound of his irascible energy into moving the colony to the "unhappy, gloom-laden" site on Garcitas Creek where its ruins would be discovered by Alonso de León. His colonists were a motley crew of work-shy aristocrats and ruffians, ne'er-do-wells, and chancers; La Salle was perhaps the most outrageous chancer of them all. Neither commander nor men had the discipline needed to succeed or even to subsist. One volunteer was bitten by a rattlesnake and died a slow and painful death. Some ate poisonous fruit; others were so stupid as to swallow prickly pears without removing the thornlike hairs. A number deserted. The first to go were an Italian glove maker and Jean Henri.

La Salle soon sought his own escape from this awful reality. At the start of January 1686, he led twenty men in search of the branch of the Mississippi delta he desperately wanted to find. Only eight of them returned from that fruitless sojourn. In La Salle's absence, many colonists had tried to abscond aboard the *Belle*, but her drunken captain lost control of her in winds and currents and she ran aground on Matagorda Island, where her wreck was recovered by archaeologists in the 1990s. La Salle knew the only hope was to reach Saint Louis, on the Illinois River. He acquired five horses from some Indians, then deserted his own colony, setting off with the horses heavily burdened with his own worldly wealth, while seventeen settlers trudged along beside them.

Somewhere near the Trinity River, the resentment of his followers boiled over when La Salle's nephew high-handedly requisitioned meat from a buffalo that one of the men had killed. In the dead of night, some of them smashed in the nephew's head with an ax and then shot La Salle the following day. Meanwhile, the colony was struck by smallpox, and more than a hundred died. The Karankawa finished off the few survivors. This was the story the two Frenchmen told, although they failed to confess to León that they themselves had been involved in the murder of La Salle. Later, they helped Vargas resettle New Mexico, both married at Santa Fe, and in a final twist of fate, one of them was killed during a Pawnee raid that had been encouraged by the French.

Alonso de León rode home and sent his report to the viceroy.

León was a pragmatist and advised that only a strong military presence could hope to control a troubled territory such as Texas in which wealthy Caddoan farmers fought one another for fun at the heart of a world continually swept bare by terrifying posses of mounted Plains Indians who rustled cattle and children. But Father Massanet advised that his missionaries be

allowed to colonize alone, "as María de Ágreda had, when the venerable
Mother walked among these same Texas Indians."[29] This was the age-old
debate of empire between Church and soldiery, and as the Franciscans offered
the cheaper program, Massanet won the argument. The viceroy ordered León
to escort the friars to East Texas, help them build their church and mission,
and then withdraw, casting them onto the winds of Fate.

León and Massanet disliked each other intensely but set out together to
found Mission San Francisco de los Tejas. Together, they crossed the Rio
Grande near modern Laredo and continued to the ruined French settlement
on Garcitas Creek, where two more French survivors appeared and joined the
expedition. The great caravan of Spaniards, Tlaxcalans, Coahuilans, and now
Frenchmen was joyously received by Chief Texas, who rode alongside León,
guiding them to a large settlement sprawling beside a babbling creek in the
bottom of a beautiful valley. They had reached the proposed site of the mission
on San Pedro Creek near modern Augusta, the first Spanish attempt at a
permanent settlement in Texas.[30]

León was entertained by Chief Texas, his mother, his wife, and his daughter.
His people thronged around as they ate a sumptuous lunch of tamales and
atole, a kind of corn porridge. The following day the friars sang the Te Deum,
and another meal was served, of stewed beans, but all this was mere prelude
to the Feast of Corpus Christi. Chief Texas and many leading Indians took
their places in the great procession led by the friars carrying the Holy Sacrament to the chapel they had erected in the heart of the village. A mass was
sung, and afterward the ensigns raised the royal standard: León accepted
homage from Chief Texas in the name of the king and solemnly appointed
him Governor of the Texas and presented him with his official Spanish staff
of office, with its little cross at the top. The chief then formally requested that
a number of missionaries remain among his people, and León gave possession of the mission to Father Massanet. Finally, León boomed out, "Long live
the king!"

"Huzzah!" responded the Spaniards and Tlaxcalans.

"Long live the king!"

"Huzzah!" came the reply, perhaps with the chief and a few Texas
joining in.

"Long live the king!"

"Huzzah!" the whole company bellowed across East Texas.

Father Massanet oversaw the construction of his mission in a pleasant
meadow beside a stream they called the Río de San Miguel, the "River of
Michael Archangel," set amid fields of corn, beans, squash, and watermelon.
When it was finished, León gave orders for the expedition to begin its return

journey to Coahuila and went in search of three French children he had heard were living with a group of Indians to the north. His posse moved quickly across the prairies, passing herds of bison, until they finally came upon Robert and Madelaine Talon living with a tribe called the Cascossi. But as León negotiated their release, something went wrong. With tempers running high on both sides, the Cascossi produced another French boy and tried to exact an exorbitant price while making threatening gestures with their weapons. The Spaniards opened fire. Within seconds, four Cascossi were dead and many more were injured. The Spaniards withdrew with great discipline, taking with them the three Christian children.

León died at home in Coahuila, the now largely forgotten founding father of the Lone Star State. But Texas now existed as an imperial province, and the viceroy appointed a distinguished military officer, Domingo Terán de los Ríos, as its first governor. He set foot on Texas soil for the first time in the spring of 1691 along with fifty soldiers and a baker's dozen of Franciscans, including Brother Francisco Hidalgo, another largely unsung hero of early Texas history. Terán was still full of confidence when he camped not far from the site of the Alamo in fine fertile country by the banks of a full-flowing river, which he named San Antonio, for Saint Anthony of Padua. But his mood changed when a large contingent of Indians brought letters from the missionaries in East Texas describing an awful contagion devastating the newly baptized faithful. The expedition lumbered on to Austin.

In stifling humidity, beneath the summer sun, the whole of Texas seemed blighted by vicious mosquitoes and other evil insects. Everyone itched, sores became infected. The drinking water was brackish, their flocks of sheep and goats dwindled. They reached San Francisco too afflicted by their own woes to offer much solace to the ailing missionaries. The whole sorry lot of them were short of food, desiccated by drought, and ravaged by illness. Worse, the Indians had become so hostile that even Massanet was beginning to admit that a military presence was necessary. By the fall, Terán had decided to abandon Texas. He left nine soldiers and three friars at San Francisco, conferred his command on his lieutenant, and sailed from Matagorda aboard a supply ship to Mexico. The first Governor of Texas fled, damning his luck, concluding "no rational person has ever seen a worse" place.[31] In the dead of night, on October 25, Massanet set fire to his mission and escaped to Coahuila. Only Brother Hidalgo would never forget the Caddo souls they left behind that night.

For the moment, Texas was simply too big for the Spanish Empire to populate with sufficient settlers to create a permanent colony. Even La Salle's incursion had been an opportunistic and speculative venture by the French Crown. But Louis XIV would soon take a more serious interest in the Gulf Coast, turning Texas into a borderland between New Spain and La Louisi-anne. But first, this story would not be complete without turning to Arizona and the great Jesuit missionary Eusebio Kino.

CHAPTER 13

PADRE KINO, THE JESUIT SOUTHWEST

ARIZONA

In his continuous peregrinations . . . he discovered the Casa Grande, the Gila and Colorado rivers, the Coco Maricopa and the Suma nations. Now he rests in the Lord, buried in this chapel of San Francisco Xavier on the Gospel side.

—AGUSTÍN DE CAMPOS, WRITING ABOUT EUSEBIO KINO

EUSEBIO FRANCISCO KINO WAS BORN in a small village near Trent, studied at Freiberg, became a Jesuit, and in 1678, at the age of thirty-four, he set out on the lifelong journey that would lead him to California and Pimería Alta, southern Arizona, where he founded the famous mission at San Xavier del Bac, "the Dove of the Desert." In Mexico City, in 1681, he published what remains the key scientific paper on Kirch's Comet, "for," he explained, "comets portend unhappy times and tragic misfortunes." [1]

Kino was one of the most charismatic missionaries in the empire, combining erudition, intellect, and a strikingly unjudgmental curiosity toward the peoples of Pimería. As much as preaching the Word of God, he brought the promise of protection to the Indians of a troubled borderland, their traditional lands ever-more hemmed in by Apaches and Spanish colonists. He also demonstrated by example the value of agriculture and animal husbandry. He picked his companions and assistants well and had little interest in his own material comforts. Throughout his "life as a missionary" in America, "he used but two sheepskins and a coarse blanket for his mattress and a saddle for his pillow" and "spent most of the night in prayer," with such "bloody self-discipline" as to "shock his Indian followers." [2]

On April 1, 1683, he landed at La Paz, Baja, with the title of Bishop of California, excited to begin the missionary work for which he had so long yearned. He took his final vows as a priest and saw the Pacific for the first time. He worked tirelessly to win the hearts of the Native Americans with offers of food and schooling for their children. It was said that everywhere he went, a troop of youngsters was sure to follow, running beside him or riding on the haunches of his horse. But the violent hostility of many Indians forced the soldiers and the missionaries to temporarily abandon Baja.[3]

Kino petitioned the viceroy to allow the Jesuits to return to Baja, but fearful that rebellion might spread as a result of the Pueblo Revolt, the crown ordered every resource available to be spent on pacifying northern New Spain. Kino was given the task of establishing missions in the area then known as Pimería Alta, northern Sonora and southern Arizona, among the ancestors of the modern O'odham, Yuma, Pima, and Maricopa. Kino founded Mission Dolores, in 1687, fifty miles south of the modern international border crossing at Nogales, as his base for the evangelization of the region. From there, he explored north to the Gila and Colorado rivers, proselytizing and teaching, mapping and documenting the land and its people. Over the next quarter of a century he would make at least fourteen major excursions into Arizona and California, often with an intelligent young army officer called Juan Mateo Manje, founding San Xavier del Bac, in 1700, and Guevavi and Tumacácori in successive years.

The ranchers and miners around Dolores became jealous of his sway over the Indians and tried to convince them that Kino would force them into endless hard work or hang them for rebellion. Instead, he built a *campanile* with a ring of beautifully cast bells, which drew in hundreds of potential converts with their sonorous peal. In late 1690, Father Juan María Salvatierra arrived to inspect Kino's work, and the two men struck up a firm friendship as they rode the trails and visited missions. At Sáric, just south of the remote modern border crossing at Sasabe, they were welcomed by seven hundred Indians and met emissaries from Bac and Tumacácori on the Santa Cruz River, who begged the missionaries to visit their settlements. Filled with joy, Kino and Salvatierra saddled their horses and followed the Guevavi Valley northeast to Tumacácori, where they were greeted with overwhelming enthusiasm by a group of Sobaípuri or O'odham chiefs who had traveled sixty miles or more to meet them.

In 1692, Kino returned to the Santa Cruz and began preaching to a potential flock of eight hundred seemingly meek farmers living at Bac. He showed them on a "map of the world how far we missionaries had traveled to bring them knowledge of Salvation . . . , by sea to Veracruz, to Mexico City, Guadalajara, Sonora, on to Dolores and now their own homeland." What his audience really made of this geography lesson has gone unrecorded, but Kino was convinced that they had "listened with pleasure" and had told him "they wanted to become Christians."[4]

The following year, with Kino as host, a huge crowd of missionaries and Indians gathered at Dolores for the dedication of the mission church. Pima pilgrims from traditionally hostile bands came from the north and west, and Kino decided to devote the rest of that year to brokering peace across all of Pimería.

The twenty-four-year-old Captain Manje met Kino for the first time in 1694 and began one of his first official reports by paraphrasing Seneca's reference to "the natural desire of the human soul to discover secrets."[5] The two men shared an unbridled sense of adventure. On their first trip together, when they finally reached the Gulf of California, exhausted and desperately thirsty, Manje proudly reported that "ever since Sonora was first settled sixty years ago, no one has ever reached it, we were the first!"[6]

Soon afterward, while Kino oversaw the construction of a ship to supply Baja, Manje led a party north up the San Miguel River and spent his first night within the modern United States, at a place called Cups, near the modern O'odham hamlet of Comobabi. The inhabitants fed his appetite for exploration by telling him that five days to the north "beside a large river . . . there were some large and solid buildings that were very tall."[7] Manje returned to Dolores with this intriguing news and headed off to deal with a wave of Apache raids. Kino set out to investigate and was astounded to find "a four-story building as large as a castle or the biggest church in all of Sonora, which it is said was abandoned by Montezuma's ancestors" and which he referred to as the Casa Grande.[8]

Sonora was a tinderbox of Pima rivalries, Apache raiders, Spanish soldiers, and the uneasy presence of the priests and other colonists. In 1695, a dedicated missionary called Javier Saeta was murdered by Indian raiders, leading to brutal Spanish reprisals against groups of completely innocent Pimas. Kino was forced to withdraw to Mexico City, where he wrote a moving biography recounting Saeta's love for his flock, his awful martyrdom, and the tragic retaliation, which had destroyed peaceful communities, turning them against the Spaniards. But all that was simply an emotive prelude to a long manifesto on how best to take the word of God to the Indians, which Kino attributed to Saeta himself.

"Every kind of spiritual harvest must first depend on true Christian Charity" and "Divine Love," for the life of a missionary was tough indeed, praised by many but willingly suffered by few. Not many were cut out for a life among the "rough, anarchic, stupid, and obstinate Indians" much given to "vices." It takes a lot of "stubborn patience, tolerance," and "hard work" to turn them into "friendly and loving charges," Saeta "used to say, for the work is akin to breaking in a troublesome donkey." With generosity, gentle instruction, and by being encouraged to enjoy the fruits of their labors at the missions, Kino argued, these simple people would readily become part of God's flock.[9]

Kino also understood that crown support for the missions could be stimulated by more worldly concerns. A few years later, he urged the viceroy to establish a chain of missions along the coast of Alta California to provide protection for the Manila galleons returning from China and the Philippines laden with luxuries. He also suggested opening an overland trail to Asia through a land he called Yeso, modern Alaska. All this would be paid for by the improvement of Pimería itself, if only the rich farmland were fully exploited, the mineral wealth extracted, and the people put to work as productive Christians.[10]

When the violence finally waned in Pimería, Kino returned to Dolores determined to sow seeds of peace among the Pimas. He sent out invitations to a great *fiesta*, and hundreds of rival Indian leaders descended on the mission. Many begged for baptism, among them the powerful *caciques* of the San Pedro River, chiefs Coro and Humari. Kino celebrated Christmas at Quíburi, just west of Tombstone in Cochise County, then moved on to Bac. "I was received with great affection by the people of this large settlement and many chiefs who had come from roundabout."[11] He taught them how to sow wheat and corn and to husband cattle, sheep, goats, and even horses. They begged him to send them a missionary of their own.

Many Spanish settlers blamed the northern Pimas for recent turmoil, so Kino knew it was imperative to establish their innocence. Manje used his influence to arrange an expedition to Casa Grande. The two men traveled north through fine country with good grazing land that had been abandoned by terrified Spanish settlers, descended the Santa Cruz River as far as the modern border, and then headed east toward the San Pedro. Manje described a landscape of "fertile valleys, leafy cottonwood groves, rich pastures," and "broad prairies" inhabited by peaceful O'odham, who "dressed in cotton and leather," "grew plenty of corn, *frijoles*, and other beans," and who welcomed the travelers, symbolically sweeping the trail clean before them. They traveled through the lowlands of the Coronado National Memorial, skirting the hills on an old Indian trail now asphalted as Arizona State Route 92. At Huachuca City they were eagerly received by happy Indians who set up great bowers of cane for them to pass through, as their ancestors had done for Esteban and Marcos de Niza a century and a half before.

When they reached Quiburí, just above modern Fairbank, they were joined by a contingent of twenty-two soldiers from Fronteras, thirty miles south of Douglas. They found Chief Coro and his people celebrating their recent triumph in a battle with Apache raiders. Manje described the centerpiece of "these festivities, in which they performed an exquisite dance around a tall pole from which nine scalps were suspended along with other spoils of war." Coro welcomed the visitors warmly, fed them handsomely, and invited the soldiers to join the festivities. As the soldiers danced around the hanging scalps and Kino preached to Coro's people, Manje admired the "beautifully cultivated farmland, for the river . . . runs through it and they have built lovely irrigation canals." Both Kino and Manje thought they could now "promise the Spaniards that in future we can rely on these [Indians] to give Sonora a well-needed rest after so many years of violence and robbery."[12]

Chief Coro offered to accompany his Spanish guests as far as Casa Grande with thirty-six of his most able archers, for he wanted Kino to broker a peace with his great rival Humari, chief of the northern Sobaípuri. North of modern Benson, where the San Pedro enters a steep-sided valley, Coro warned Manje to keep the river between their party and the mountainous country to the east. He was worried that Humari might have formed an alliance with the Apaches, and over the next seventy miles they constantly posted lookouts. Instead, they found Humari and his people celebrating their own victory over the Apaches, with six scalps hung high, drying in the sun. Humari gently reprimanded Kino for not bringing a friar to administer to their souls and lavished the whole party with food, giving so much to the soldiers they could not carry it all. Here and there, along the way, Kino baptized a handful of Indians. At major settlements, Manje presented staffs of office to the leading Indians, for "we could see no sign of evil intent or any alliance with the enemy," he explained.[13]

Chiefs Humari and Coro wanted Spanish protection from the increasing threat of raids by the Apaches and their allies from the Great Plains, and they understood Christianity was the price they would have to pay. For these chiefs, the friars were a "human shield," to use the modern terminology, for they believed that Apache raiders would think twice before attacking a community that was notionally Christian for fear of Spanish reprisals.

Farther north, Manje noticed the Indians had "very good quality" ponchos, "blankets that cover them from the shoulders to their feet, some with very colorful designs and others in black and tied at the waist with a very particular kind of strangely platted belt that seems to be made of silk."[14] There was no sign of the enemy. At the confluence of the Gila and San Pedro rivers, Kino rewarded the entire company by handing out sweet cakes that he had brought especially for the occasion. They were nearing the Casa Grande, and the whole company was impatient to see these strange structures. There was speculation that they must have been built by the Aztecs before they left their northern homeland. But Manje was skeptical: "God alone knows the truth of the matter, so while everyone else may believe what he thinks is reasonable, I will suspend judgment," he wrote.[15]

At first sight of Casa Grande, they "wondered why it was about a league from the river and without water." But as they came closer, "they saw a large water channel carried by a great embankment three yards high and six or seven wide . . . which had not only brought water to the Casa Grande, but had also made a great circuit, enclosing and irrigating a stretch of farmland many leagues in length and breadth."[16] Kino said mass at the largest of the ruins, then Manje wrote a detailed description. The largest structure was four stories high, "thirty-six paces long, and twenty-one wide," with the main quarters in the middle surrounded on all four sides by extensions of three smaller rooms. The walls were at least two yards thick and made of mortar and adobe, so smooth on the inside that they looked like lusterware, while "the corners of the window" openings and doorways "were very precisely squared off, but without lintels" or other support. At a distance of an harquebus shot, they saw twelve similar ruins that showed signs of fire damage, except for one ground-floor room, which had thin round beams made of cedar or juniper covered with a high adobe ceiling, which Manje thought "of great interest." They found many further ruins for two leagues roundabout and "lots of broken pottery and cooking pots of fine terra-cotta, painted in many colors like ewers from Guadalajara." From all this, Kino and Manje "deduced that it must have been a very large town or city," built by a well "organized people who had a government." But, they noted, "There was not a patch of grazing land anywhere near these buildings, as though someone had salted the earth there."[17]

They continued to the first settlement of Coco Maricopas, which Kino christened San Andrés. He had baptized their chief at Dolores the year before and now preached to at least four hundred of his people. While there, Kino and Manje turned their attention from archaeology to anthropology. They were intrigued that the northern O'odham seemed to be somewhat redheaded and a good deal paler than those in the south. They wondered if they might be of European origin.[18] But then Manje allowed himself to be distracted by prospecting and metallurgy, for he questioned a man who described "cracking open some red metal" so that "drops the color of lead come out of it, like thick water, which slips through the fingers" and "forms little pools." Manje was convinced quicksilver must be in the nearby Phoenix hills, which there was.[19]

They returned to Dolores, where Kino wrote long letters to military officials and the viceroy confirming that the northern Pimas were unquestionably their friends.

*　*　*

That winter, a huge force of six hundred Apaches struck Cocóspera to the north of Dolores, killing two women, nine men, and carrying off food and horses. Pursued by a detachment of troops, the Indians fell back to Quiburí and attacked the satellite settlement of Gaybanipitea, a few miles south of the main town. According to Kino, many of the assailants were women, who fought with equal ferocity to their menfolk. They scaled the walls of the adobe fort, killed the chief and a couple of his men, and burned the settlement to the ground. Chief Coro led the fight back and sent a full report of the battle to Dolores with the death toll marked in notches on a stick.

Coro had found the Apache raiders feasting on barbecued meat, fried beans, and *pinole*. Their leader, Capotcari, proposed that each side put up ten of their best men to fight, following a carefully choreographed formula by which each warrior confronted one opposite number. Battle commenced with each man unleashing arrows at his opponent, but while the plainsmen were good shots, Coro was proud to relate that his Pimas were far more dexterous in avoiding their opponents' missiles. One by one, the Apaches fell senseless on the ground, until only stout Capotcari stood between his people and their ruin. His opponent slowly gained ground until, with a spring, he threw the Apache down and bashed out his brains with a stone. Capotcari's followers ran for the hills as Coro's archers loosed arrow after arrow tipped with deadly venom, killing thirty-one men and twenty-three women, their cadavers left strewn across the surrounding terrain. Over the following days, three hundred Indian raiders surrendered at Spanish presidios in Chihuahua and New Mexico. Across Sonora, the Spaniards rejoiced at the news.[20]

In October 1698, Kino set out with a military escort led by Captain Diego Carrasco to explore the Gila River from Casa Grande to the sea. Carrasco was delighted by the magnificent welcome at Bac, passing ceremonial crosses and beneath the familiar cane bowers for five or six miles, and the "hardworking natives" who "harvest plenty of food in this very agreeable valley, with its fine cottonwood stands and good farmland and many wells." On a later visit, Kino was met by forty children carrying crosses and three hundred adults. As they proceeded beyond Tucson, Carrasco extolled the "cornfields and abundant beans, melons, and squash" and the "generosity with which the people fed us." They passed a great well, which many speculated must have been built by the Aztecs, the large sinkhole known as Montezuma Well.[21]

Instead of descending the Gila from Casa Grande, they struck out overland, reaching the Gulf of California some way south of the Colorado, then followed the Sonoita River north to the modern border, stopping at the village of Actum, somewhere in the foothills to the southwest of the Tohono O'odham

High School on the road from Why. At every settlement, Kino preached the gospel and baptized a few children, so that by the time he returned to Dolores, by his own count he had saved 439 young souls, while Carrasco had appointed forty new royal officials and given them their staffs of office.[22]

The following year, Kino set out again, this time with Manje. Riding north and west, they admired the great tower of Baboquivari Peak, which they thought had the appearance "of a tall castle," though they called it Noah's Ark.[23] They soon reached a tiny settlement of sixty people whom they knew as the Pápagos, somewhere near the modern Franciscan mission to the Tohono O'odham Nation, and called the place Santa Eulalia.

At Santa Eulalia, they were shown a "large enclosure with stone walls" and a "smoke-blackened cave" and told a local myth: Once upon a time, "a monstrous and audacious giant with the snout of a pig, claws like an eagle, and the appearance of a woman had come from the north and lived in that place." "I don't know how much is fantastical additions," Kino observed. "She rounded up as many Pápagos as she could with her wings so as to satisfy her voracious appetite. But the Pápagos" concocted a cunning plan: They collected a great pile of firewood, then captured "two enemy Indians to use as bait." They invited the monster to come and eat these two unhappy souls at the end of a great ceremony, which they held in the stone corral. So that they could appear to keep up the "dancing for three days" without a break, the Pápagos took turns, "changing over in great secrecy." Finally, at the end of the festivities, the monster went back to its cave and fell into a deep sleep—presumably replete from feasting on the enemy Indians, although Manje does not report this element in the tale. The Pápagos then "blocked up the entrance to the cave with the firewood and set fire to it. The monster groaned in the heat of the flames and died, suffocated by the dense smoke."[24]

Kino and Manje discussed other stories about giants in the Americas and noted that Cortés had sent huge bones to Spain—bones that we now know came from dinosaurs. Interestingly, the O'odham were still telling a version of the story in the early twentieth century, which concluded with the people feasting on the roasted flesh of the fiend.[25]

Kino and Manje pushed on to Sonoita, where they established a small ranch with thirty-six head of cattle. There, the O'odham told them a tale about a white woman who had visited them long ago but was killed by hostile tribes to the north. They briefly wondered if this might be María de Ágreda, but dismissed the idea as another local myth. The two friends struck out almost due west along a trail that came to be known as the Camino del Diablo, the "Devil's Way," "suffering the inevitable tribulations that new discoveries bring with them," as Manje dryly observed.[26] With the whole party already wracked by terrible thirst, they rode by the light of the moon, and at four o'clock in the morning, they clambered up a rocky outcrop to reach a natural pool of rain-water, which they called Aguas de la Luna, "the Waters of the Moon," modern Heart Tank in the parched Sierra Pina.[27]

They carried on and saw veins of minerals in the barren mountains, which they speculated might contain silver. Finally, they reached the verdant banks of the Gila River, where eight hundred Yumas gave them a fine welcome. Manje thought their hosts were "a comely and handsome race, much paler than the other Indian nations. They paint themselves red and black and wear many necklaces of little black and white snail shells . . . and mother-of-pearl pendants" dangled from their ears. He was intrigued that they seemed to tattoo only the fattest of their womenfolk as a mark of respect for their great weight.[28]

Some old Yumas told them that "when they were young, a very beautiful white woman came to their lands, wearing white, brown, and blue, down to her feet, and a head scarf or veil with which she covered her head. She spoke to them, shouted at them, and reprimanded them, in a language they did not understand. The various nations of the Colorado River twice shot arrows at her and left her for dead, but she got up and flew off home," wherever that might be, for "they did not know." This was evidently a new manifestation of the myth of the Lady in Blue, María de Ágreda, but the skeptical Manje noted in his account, "I will simply pause to add that they did not understand her; but should God, who does not do things imperfectly, have worked so great a miracle as to transport her from Spain to these regions, he would have bestowed upon her the ability to speak in a language they did understand."[29] A century and a half before, of course, a wise old Indian had asked the same question of Hernando de Alarcón when he claimed to be a "Sonne of the Sunne."

Manje was keen to find a route to the mouth of the Colorado River so that he could confirm "the old report of General Oñate on his exploration in 1604" that "there was a port where a thousand ships could shelter."[30] But Kino insisted that instead they must return to Pimería by following the Gila upstream, which he decided to rename the River of the Apostles because "all the inhabitants are fishermen and have plenty of nets and other equipment to catch fish all year round."[31]

On April 28, 1700, Eusebio Francisco Kino began laying the foundation for a church dedicated to San Francisco Xavier at the great settlement of Bac. "All the people labored with a great sense of pleasure and devotion, some digging, others hauling good blocks of stone from a little hill a mile away," Kino recorded in his journal. He was especially taken with the excellent water supply and imagined a bucolic future for his well-irrigated mission that, "with its great cloister and nearby vegetable gardens, will have the best farmland in all of Nueva Vizcaya."[32]

Over the following half decade, Kino grew obsessed with discovering an overland route to California. With still considerable doubt as to whether Baja was an island or a peninsula, in 1700 he descended the Gila to Yuma Junction and climbed a hill to survey the land through a telescope. A year later, he saw Baja from the volcanic heights above Puerto Peñasco and noted, "There can be no better place to represent the condition of the world on the Day of Judgment." Two days later, a party of Indians approached across that extraordinary, sulfurous landscape and "sat down according to the custom of California and drank so much water that only a mule could complete with them." Kino was sure they must have come along overland trails from Baja. A week later, he climbed a high peak thirty miles or so to northwest, somewhere near the modern border. It was sunset and the excited missionary "saw the sea stretched out below to the south quite clearly and the arc of the California mountains . . . joining with the hills and peaks of New Spain."[33] Finally, there was no doubt that Baja California was part of the mainland.

In the spring of 1711, Kino was taken gravely ill during mass. He was carried to his quarters, where his hide mattress and his rough blankets were laid out, his saddle as his pillow, as always. Father Campos pleaded with him to lie in a more comfortable bed, but Kino would have none of it. "He died as he had lived, with extreme humility and poverty," one faithful follower documented. "In his continuous peregrinations . . . he discovered the Casa Grande, the Gila and Colorado rivers, the Coco Maricopa and Suma nations. Now he rests in the Lord, buried in this chapel of San Francisco Xavier on the Gospel side."[34]

CHAPTER 14

LOVE & THE
COMANCHE DAWN

TEXAS

As the brave men looked behind them,
The Indians fired their weapons,
Spewing leaden balls a-burning,
Felling father and companion,
Who then breathed their final breaths.

—FATHER MANUEL ARROYO

LOUIS XIV OF FRANCE ONLY SERIOUSLY TURNED his attention to the
southern reaches of the Mississippi when his counselors became concerned
about British expansion in North America. Following King William's War,
fought by the French against the English in New York, New Hampshire, and
especially Maine and Quebec, Pierre Le Moyne d'Iberville in 1699 built and
garrisoned a number of forts around Biloxi. During an exploratory foray on the
Mississippi River, his men met a boat of British settlers coming upstream.
The Frenchmen announced the land was theirs, and the British departed
at the place still known as English Turn. Iberville constructed a fort on the
first solid ground he could find above the mouth of the river to discourage
further foreign incursions. While surveying the site, he was amazed to be
greeted by Henri de Tonti, the man La Salle had long ago left as lieutenant
at Saint Louis.[1] However tentatively, the Mississippi was now a French shipping lane.

The last Habsburg king of Spain, Charles II, was born genetically crippled by
generations of inbreeding among his illustrious ancestors. He had only fourteen great-great-great-grandparents instead of the usual thirty-two. The papal
nuncio described him as "as weak in body as he is in mind . . . , torpid and
indolent . . . lacking his own will."[2] In 1699, a desperate group of courtiers

attempted to exorcise his demons, and he has ever since been known as Carlos the Bewitched. He failed to sire an heir, preferring to play endless games of spillikins with his beautiful French queen, who influenced the only major political decision he ever made. On his deathbed, he named as his successor Philip of Anjou, grandson of the French Bourbon Louis XIV, forging a familial bond between these two Bourbon monarchies that occasionally broke down into conflict, but more often produced a political and military alliance to confront the inexorable rise of Britain as a world power. Charles finally died on All Saints' Day 1700, and Philip of Anjou was at first welcomed by the Spanish grandees and populous. But he turned out to be a depressive seventeen-year-old who rejected Spanish culture and struggled to learn the language. He told his tutor, "I cannot bear Spain!"[3]

The Bourbon axis of France and Spain posed a threat to England and her allies, who favored the succession of the Habsburg Archduke Charles of Austria. In 1701, Britain, the Dutch Provinces, and the Austrian Empire declared war, igniting the first conflict in history with truly global reach, known in Europe as the War of the Spanish Succession and in the English colonies as Queen Anne's War.

As the fighting erupted across Europe, Governor James Moore of Carolina led a major assault on St. Augustine, but the Spanish garrison held out inside the famous fortress of San Marcos. Moore was removed as governor on his return to Charleston. Furious at his disgrace, he gathered a rabble of murderous outlaws, allied himself to a bloodthirsty contingent of a fifteen hundred Creek and Yamasee warriors, and laid waste to the Franciscan missions of Apalache, massacring three thousand Indian subjects of the Spanish Crown and turning five thousand more into refugees. Spanish reports claimed that many Catholics had been skinned alive. "They cut out the tongue and eyes" of one Spaniard, "cut off his ears . . . stuck burning splinters in his wounds and set fire to him while he was tied at the foot of a cross."[4] Spanish Florida was now little more than a fiction, reduced to the beleaguered garrisons at St. Augustine and Pensacola, which one Spanish officer admitted "would have been abandoned were it not for French support" from Biloxi.[5]

In Europe, to the astonishment of those around him, Philip was invigorated by the sights, sounds, and smells of battle and spent long hours in the saddle, encouraging his troops. In 1707, his forces won a seemingly decisive victory in Spain, but Louis XIV lost his nerve in the face of a series of setbacks in northern Europe and negotiated for peace. When the French troops began to withdraw across the Pyrenees, Philip responded with regal ire, "God has placed the crown of Spain on my head. I shall keep it as long as I have blood in my veins. I owe it to my conscience, my honor, and the love of my subjects.

I shall never give up Spain so long as I live, for I would rather die fighting for every inch of her soil!"[6]

The Spaniards rallied. Louis returned to the fray. When Bourbon forces defeated the English army in December 1710, Philip's succession was secured, and the war was all but over. But Philip paid a high price for peace: by the Treaty of Utrecht, in 1713, he gave up his Italian territories to Charles of Austria, now Holy Roman Emperor, and the Duke of Savoy, while Menorca in the Mediterranean, and Gibraltar were ceded to Britain. But Philip had proved himself a loyal Spaniard and firmly established the dynasty that still reigns in Spain today.

As the war drew to a conclusion, French Louisiana began to falter as a functional colony. To keep the settlers and soldiers fed, most had to be billeted on Indian communities. So Louis XIV leased the colony to a private company, which appointed as its new governor an entrepreneurial explorer called Antoine de la Mothe, Sieur de Cadillac, the founder of Detroit. At mission San Juan Bautista, the "Gateway to Texas," beside the Rio Grande a few miles north of modern Laredo, Brother Hidalgo had never forgotten the Texas Indians he had been forced to abandon when San Francisco was evacuated. In his zeal to save their souls, he sent an SOS to Cadillac, begging French priests to enter East Texas. He may have hoped the threat of a French incursion would be enough to goad Spanish officials into action. But Cadillac was intrigued by the possibility of opening up trade with New Spain, so he turned to the remarkable figure of Louis Juchereau de Saint-Denis to reconnoiter a route from Louisiana to New Spain.[7]

"The noble bearing of this tall, well-proportioned, and remarkably handsome person was in keeping with the lofty spirit of his soul," Louisiana's venerable nineteenth-century champion Charles Gayarré told his students of Saint-Denis. "A knight-errant in his feelings and in his doings throughout life, he was imbued with the spirit of romance."[8]

This action hero of the prairies set out from Mobile for Texas, in the autumn of 1713, with a psychotic surgeon called Médard Jallot and Pierre and Robert Talon, the French children rescued from the Caddos by Alonso de León. Saint-Denis built warehouses to store their goods at Natchitoches, then headed west in the company of Chief Bernardino and twenty-five of his men.[9] Gayarré described Saint-Denis's "halloo for joy" when the explorers saw the Sabine River and rested on the "downy couches" of grass, while "enjoying" the occasional "delicious repast" of "bear" or "buffalo." Jallot was even delighted when they were attacked by two hundred Karankawa, for he was "a passionate lover of his art, never in a good humor except when tending a wound," Gayarré remarked.[10] This peculiar party reached San Juan Bautista on July 19, 1714, and

Saint-Denis introduced himself to Captain Diego Ramón, who arrested him as an illegal foreign merchant.

But the Spaniard was as intrigued as Cadillac by the possibility that a new king might free up commerce between the two Bourbon monarchies. He imprisoned Saint-Denis within his own household, where his beautiful seventeen-year-old granddaughter Manuela Sánchez caught the eye of his flamboyant guest. That long, hot summer, Saint-Denis wooed his future wife, but before any wedding could be celebrated, a posse of soldiers arrived to escort him to Mexico City.

While Saint-Denis was away, the independent tribes of the region attacked San Juan Bautista. "On Ash Wednesday, at the stroke of midnight, the gentiles and the mission Indians fell upon the presidio." Saint-Denis's beloved Manuela awoke to the war cries and "amid flames and screams, it seemed like hell" itself, "as though all the infernal furies had been let loose." Captain Ramón and his men held out "all that unhappy night" with only eight serviceable muskets. At dawn, just as they thought the battle lost, the corporal guarding the horses managed to stampede the whole herd into the middle of the fray, scattering the assailants.[11]

Far away, in Mexico, Saint-Denis told the viceroy that the Caddos of East Texas were begging for friars and that he was simply a messenger for the Hasinai chiefs who had responded to Hidalgo's call for help. Saint-Denis's easy charm worked its magic so thoroughly that the following year he returned to San Juan Bautista with a Spanish commission in an expedition to reestablish missions at San Francisco de los Tejas.

On his return, Saint-Denis married Manuela, but the bridegroom was soon in the saddle again, guiding an expedition led by Ramón's eldest son, Domingo, escorting Hidalgo to East Texas. Saint-Denis reestablished San Francisco and founded San José on Shawnee Creek and Our Lady of the Immaculate Conception fifteen miles from modern Nacogdoches. Meanwhile, a contingent of Franciscans from Zacatecas founded Guadalupe in the Indian settlement at Nacogdoches. Further missions were later founded, including San Miguel de los Adaes, near Robeline in Louisiana, which would become the capital of Texas from 1729 to 1770 and is now an important archaeological site.[12]

Saint-Denis set out for Mobile, where he sold a herd of horses and acquired assorted valuable merchandise to bring back into New Spain. When he finally returned to San Juan Bautista, he was delighted to meet his infant daughter, but perplexed to discover that Spanish spies at Mobile had reported his illicit trading to the governor of Pensacola. Diego Ramón must have shown his grandson-in-law his orders to confiscate the smuggled merchandise. The two men talked over the awkward situation and agreed that Saint-Denis should plead their case with the new viceroy.

In Mexico City, another old hand from San Juan Bautista, the eighty-year-old Brother Olivares, was energetically advocating for a new mission at the site that Terán de los Ríos had identified near the headwaters of the San Antonio. It would serve as a bridgehead to the eastern missions and a chance to prose-lytize the "wild" tribes of West Texas. "We have come to know fifty nations," and although "their languages are different . . . they carry out their trade by signs." "They are physically good-looking" and they "welcome the priests and the Spaniards" and "all of them want to be Christians," Olivares assured the viceroy. "We have not seen any formal idolatry among them," he claimed, but admitted that during their dances they consumed peyote, which "unsettled their minds and caused hallucinations." Nonetheless, this "multitude of heathens" was ripe for "the Holy Church." [13]

The viceroy appointed Martín de Alarcón Governor of Texas and issued a general order that Olivares be given every assistance to ensure his mission at San Antonio would take root. The old friar hurried north, but in the shadow of Time's scythe, he became impatient and irascible at the inevitable delays. He hoped to hurry Alarcón into action by accusing Diego Ramón of hiding French smugglers at his presidio, which only further postponed the expedi-tion into Texas while Alarcón investigated such serious and evidently well-founded allegations. Alarcón wrote the viceroy that "all this region is full of contraband merchandise" brought by Saint-Denis. [14]

Saint-Denis was imprisoned, but when the judge appointed to examine the case questioned him about his recent expedition to Mobile, he replied, "I am a married man living among Spaniards, and I now devote my life to the service of the Spanish king. I have forsaken my nation." So, "I went to Mobile to bring back a few personal possessions so as to never have to return nor be again among the French. I brought thirteen bundles of merchandise," he admitted, "Brittany linen, narrow cloth, serge, and red flannel, a small box of lace, a length of woolen cloth, and one or two lengths of brocade for my wife. I have brought all this to buy livestock and in that way support my wife and children." [15]

Saint-Denis asked that his goods be returned so he could get on with being the quintessential Texan, fiercely independent of mind, determined to make a life for himself and his family on an extensive ranch with a large herd of cattle, as much as possible master of his own universe. For all that most of his biographers have doubted this testimony, the judge clearly sympathized with Saint-Denis's claims and ordered his release and the restoration of his property.[16] But it was a bad time for a Frenchman in the Spanish empire, for Spanish forces occupied Sardinia in 1717, sparking a war with Britain, Austria, and France. A warrant was issued for Saint-Denis's arrest, and he rode hell-for-leather to San Juan Bautista, said a passing *adiós* or *adieu* to his family, and fled to Natchitoches. Happily, when peace was restored between the Bourbon Crowns, Manuela was given permission to join him in French Louisiana.

Alarcón finally reached the source of the San Antonio, on April 25, 1718, at the head of seventy-two soldiers and settlers, a massive caravan of mules laden with provisions, and equipment and great herds of livestock, including more than five hundred horses. The springs gushed water that tasted "sweet and fine," and all seemed "very pretty," with the pecans, mulberries, the cottonwoods that the Spaniards call *álamos*, and plenty of grapevines.[17] Brother Olivares founded the mission, and work began on quarters for the Indian neophytes and the monastic cloisters. But the famous chapel at the Alamo was not built until 1744.[18] Alarcón established the Presidio of San Antonio de Béxar, named for the viceroy's father, the Duke of Béjar.

For more than a year, the friars in East Texas had been sending frantic pleas for help as their missions were struck by disease and poor harvests. They subsisted on occasional Caddo handouts and by shooting crows. "Dark and tough, this meat was repulsive, but necessity lent it such flavor as to make for a tasty dish," they observed.[19] Two earlier relief parties had got some provisions through, which had given the friars hope, only for it to be dashed when Alarcón arrived in the early fall with neither settlers nor soldiers to reinforce their isolated outpost of empire.[20]

The great European War of the Quadruple Alliance, which erupted across the Italian states over the Spanish invasion of Sardinia, came to East Texas in 1719, when Philippe Blondel, commander at French Natchitoches, attacked the Spanish mission San Miguel de los Adaes with half a dozen men. A lay brother and an unarmed soldier still in his nightshirt surrendered without a fight, and the Frenchmen searched the pathetically impoverished settlement for any meager spoils. They found a few liturgical objects and the occupants of the chicken coop. Blondel tied up the chickens and strapped them to the haunches of his horse, but the flustered birds flapped their wings and clucked so loudly that his highly strung equine reared up and tossed its rider. The Frenchman unleashed the fury of his wounded pride on the errant fowl. "He did not spare the lives of the chickens according to the civilized rules of war," the lay brother later reported, "since they had so treacherously endangered his."[21]

This farce has become known as the Chicken War, appropriately enough in a part of the world still famous for exporting poultry.[22] Nevertheless, it had serious consequences because Blondel convinced the lay brother he was merely the vanguard of a hundred Frenchmen already on the march for Texas and then allowed his prisoner to escape. When the brother reached Nacogdoches with this report, the friars preached patience to Captain Domingo Ramón—Diego's son and the military commander in eastern Texas—urging him to wait for a report from some friendly Indians who set off to scout out the situation. But Domingo was worried. The Caddos had been showing signs of hostility, they had acquired muskets from the French, and Domingo had no confidence in his ragged garrison of misfits should real fighting break out. So he gave the order to abandon East Texas to her Native Americans and their new French neighbors, who were more interested in trade than religion, more eager for marriage alliances with Indians than the love of God.

In 1719, the Marquis San Miguel de Aguayo, a wealthy aristocrat of Aragonese descent with an enormous holding of over twenty-six thousand square miles in Coahuila, was appointed Governor of Texas.[23] His enormous expedition reached the Rio Grande at Christmas 1720. With five hundred men, twenty-eight hundred horses, forty-eight hundred head of cattle, and sixty-four hundred sheep and goats, he crossed the swollen river, then sent Domingo Ramón with forty men to establish a fortress on the site of La Salle's ruins at Garcitas Creek. Aguayo ordered the construction of a new adobe fortress at San Antonio, then took a northerly route across Texas to the Caddo settlements in the east. He was greeted by Chief Hasinai and eight other *caciques* with tears of joy and shared a peace pipe with the chief of the Neches. Over the following days, the Indians brought the Spanish corn, beans, and watermelons. Aguayo handed out gifts. On August 1, at the Spanish camp on the Neches River, he met Saint-Denis and forced him to accept a truce on the condition that all Frenchmen vacate Texas.[24]

Aguayo ordered the construction of a formidable hexagonal presidio at Los Adaes, to be called Our Lady of Pilar, in honor of the patroness of the Aragonese capital at Saragossa, and gave it a garrison of a hundred men. With the security of friars and the future settlers thus assured, he refounded the six missions of East Texas, then left for Matagorda Bay to inspect Domingo Ramón's progress on the new presidio, which Aguayo named after Our Lady of Loreto. At the end of May, Aguayo arrived home at Monclova, demobilized his troops, resigned his governorship, wrote a long account of his services for the king, and retired into private life.

For the first time, Spaniards had secured their permanent presence in East Texas and could claim dominion over the whole area of the modern state. But subsequent administrations failed to build on these solid foundations. Following an inspection by Colonel Pedro de Rivera, three of the eastern missions were relocated to San Antonio, the Texas Presidio was closed, and troop numbers were allowed to dwindle. The Caddos and the Texas were depleted by disease and their culture undermined as they adopted mission life to survive. The vacuum was filled by large numbers of Apaches, themselves refugees from a new and terrifying presence on the southern plains, the Comanches.

Spanish Texas remained a tenuous reality.

By the Treaty of Utrecht, of 1713, which settled the War of the Spanish Succession, British slave merchants of the South Sea Company were granted, for thirty years, the valuable *asiento de negros,* or official Spanish license, to import almost five thousand Africans into Spanish America along with other trading rights. The burgeoning British presence in the Americas led to greatly increased levels of smuggling, which often went hand in glove with brutal piracy. Rear Admiral Charles Stewart of the English Royal Navy privately told the Duke of Newcastle, "The sloops which sail from [Jamaica] manned and armed for this illicit trade, have more than once bragged to me of having murdered seven or eight Spaniards on their own shores."[25]

But these murderous "peddlers" met their match in Captain Fandiño of the Spanish Coast Guard, who pursued them with brutal efficiency.[26] In the summer of 1731, a ship docked at London and her master, Robert Jenkins, went ashore to complain that months earlier, off Havana, Fandiño had strung him up and cut off one of his ears and told him, "Take this to your king and tell him if he were here, I would do the same to him."[27] Remarkably, Jenkins was allowed an audience with George II—given the ear of the king, as it were—but no further action was taken, probably because the evidence suggests Jenkins's ear was still firmly attached to his head in the natural way. However, he continued to carry an ear around with him, either bottled or preserved in salt and wrapped in a handkerchief—the documentary sources are uncertain—and as Fandiño and his colleagues had more and more success, capturing at least fifty-two British smuggling ships and their cargoes in the following years, the story of Jenkins's supposedly severed ear became the *cause célèbre* for a war party in London that opposed Prime Minister Walpole's determination to remain at peace with Spain. In 1738, in a theatrical performance orchestrated by the war hawk Lord Shelburne, Jenkins gave evidence to Parliament, flamboyantly brandishing his ear and waving it about, although one West Indian sugar planter was sure that "if any members had had the fancy to have lifted up his wig, they would have found his ears as whole as their own."[28] The ruse succeeded, for Parliament voted to declare war on Spain.

The main battles in this conflict, which became known as the War of Jenkins' Ear, were British assaults on Spanish ports in the Caribbean, notably Portobelo. In North America, the outbreak of hostilities led General James Oglethorpe, who had founded Savannah, Georgia, in 1733, to make a badly botched attack on St. Augustine. Manuel de Montiano, the Governor of Florida, was well prepared, and although the British landed about two thousand men on Anastasia Island, they were outgunned by six Spanish galleys that controlled the channel. Meanwhile the Scottish and Indian garrison at Fort Mose was easily defeated by a contingent of Spanish troops, forcing Oglethorpe to lift his siege and flee. Two years later, in 1742, Montiano retaliated, landing two thousand troops on the Georgia coast, but he was repelled by Oglethorpe, bringing the war on the Atlantic Seaboard to an end.

Spanish Texas survived. There was an influx of farming families brought in from the mountainous Canary Island of Tenerife who slowly adapted to a life of ranching. Three missions briefly sprouted on the San Gabriel River in midcentury, although they soon succumbed to a lurid tale of adultery and murder when the lusty young captain of the nearby presidio persuaded an Indian tailor to settle nearby. From the outset the captain was more interested in seducing the man's young wife than his tailoring, and when the cuckold objected, the captain threw him in the stocks. The troops followed their captain's example and took up with the Indian women who came to the mission for spiritual enlightenment. Afterward, the women unburdened their sins in the confessional, leading the scandalized friars to excommunicate the entire garrison. The captain responded by organizing the first documented "drive-by" shooting in Texan history. As two friars and the tailor began eating their supper on a balmy evening in May 1752, the night air reverberated to the sound of a musket shot. The tailor fell dead. One of the friars grabbed the candle and ran to the door, and an Indian arrow killed him outright. As a result of these scandalous events, the captain and five soldiers were reassigned to another presidio in Coahuila, but by then the disaffected Indians and the horrified missionaries had already begun to desert San Gabriel.[29]

The greatest problem facing Texas was the Comanches, first reported near San Antonio in 1743. Even the Apaches were terrorized into tentatively seeking peace with the Spaniards, which encouraged plans to establish missions in the Hill Country north of San Antonio. The idea was given serious impetus when one of the richest men in New Spain, Pedro Romero de Terreros, offered to fund the foundation of the new missions on the condition that his cousin Father Giraldo de Terreros be put in charge of them.[30] Father Terreros arrived in San Antonio in December 1756 with contingents of friars from Zacatecas and Querétero, ready to found two missions. Captain Parrilla brought troops for the presidio. Ten days later, a group of Apaches appeared and swore allegiance to the Spanish Crown. They were feted by the missionaries and stayed for three days, constantly pestering their hosts for sugar and tobacco. Parrilla thought them "unpacified and as savage and treacherous as ever."[31]

The first mission was established just south of the San Saba River, near modern Menard, with the presidio across a good ford two miles to the north. By the beginning of May 1757, the Franciscans were ready to begin their work. They enlisted nine old Tlaxcalan families from San Esteban de Nueva Tlascala who knew the area well as settlers and who, one official believed, "would undoubtedly give rise to one of the most opulent and advantageous settlements of these realms."[32] Apaches began trickling in, and by the middle of June three thousand were camped nearby. But they were on their seasonal migration to hunt bison on the plains and had not come to join the mission. Nevertheless, their chief promised to become a Christian on his return, giving the friars hope. Parrilla wrote the viceroy that he thought the whole project "a difficult undertaking" and suggested that "the favorable reports about the business" were merely the result of "the slipperiness that has always been typical of the missionaries and inhabitants of Texas." A month later, the Apaches reappeared laden with meat and hides, but they could not be persuaded to linger. Instead, they set off to south, "as if propelled by some unseen danger."[33]

Three friars abandoned the mission in the fall, accusing Terreros of incompetence. "We find no reason why we should remain with this enterprise," they wrote, "which we consider ill-conceived and illogical from the outset."[34] As winter approached, groups of Apaches arrived seeking temporary shelter and bringing rumors of a great Comanche army mustering to the north.

On March 16, 1758, Father Terreros had just finished the morning mass when a volley of shots heralded an onslaught by mounted Comanches. When they had finished, two friars, seven soldiers, the mission administrator, his son, and a small child had been killed, burned, or horribly mutilated.[35] The horrific reports of the massacre moved many in Mexico City, especially Romero de Terreros and the Franciscan community. Junípero Serra, the founding father of California, then at Querétaro, reported the violent martyrdom in a letter to his nephew. At the College of San Fernando in Mexico City, Father Manuel Arroyo began composing his *Account of the Sacrileges*, a moving elegy to the sacrifice of the friars that evoked the full horror of the events and which coincided closely with the recorded testimony of the survivors.[36] Pedro Romero de Terreros commissioned a large oil painting, *The Destruction of San Saba*, usually attributed to José de Páez, the rising young star at the workshop of Miguel Cabrera, the leading artist in Mexico City.[37] Painting and poem, viewed and read alongside each other, offer a haunting representation of the tragic events.

The *Destruction* is typical of a style of history painting that is unfamiliar and awkward to the twenty-first-century eye. The main image is made up of a series of vignettes that capture the key moments of the action as it unfolded, like a disordered comic strip. It is framed to left and right by full-length portraits of the murdered Franciscans Giraldo de Terreros and José Santiesteban. They are shown with the classically calm, otherworldly mien used to portray martyrdom, saintly spirits untroubled by the graphically depicted torments that have been inflicted on their earthly bodies. In the foreground, three stone plaques in trompe l'oeil are inscribed with the respective lives of the two martyrs and captions explaining the events depicted in the main image, each flagged with a letter of the alphabet.

Father Manuel's poem begins with what he refers to as a "flight filled with lament," in which he exhorts the "spheres to tremble" and "earth and heavens to be dumbfounded / the stars to stop / the planets to be still / the sun to darken" for the world "should be a chaos of sadness and care." He evokes the way grief suspends the normal passage of time and the eternal tranquillity of martyrdom, which Páez portrayed in the contemplative expressions of the brutalized friars. This may be a hymn of lament for "a most ferocious, evil, horrible, and bloody assault," but it is filled with the joy of celestial celebration, encapsulating the sacrificial ethos of the Franciscan mission, "offering up their blood in imitation of the Holy Lamb of God."

Arroyo contrasts the way the friars, "members of the apostolic guild," "arrived very happy at San Saba," with the foundation of the presidio and its "firearms, muskets, swords, lances," portents of war. Within a few dozen lines, the "infernal Dragon" and "Lucifer" have "united the warlike Indians now marching on this place all troubled by ire and fury." Five nations of "Indian butchers," Arroyo starkly wrote, had gathered for the attack. Other sources indicate the Comanches came with large numbers of Wichita and Caddo allies, including the Texas, swelling their army to three thousand. They were a terrifying sight, faces painted black and red, wearing animal skins and armed to the teeth with guns, sabers, and spears. The attacks began at sunrise, down by the river, where they stripped inhabitants who were washing or collecting water and severely beat them. As Giraldo de Terreros finished mass, the shout of "Indians! Indians!" announced the terrifying day. A volley of musket fire wounded one of the sentries, who fled toward the mission.

The friars had time to close the stockade and the settlers took up defensive positions, while Brother Santiesteban remained in the church, praying.[38]

The Comanches turned to subterfuge, "clothing their fury" in "a cape of friendship," shouting friendly greetings. One of the soldiers peered through the palisade and recognized a Texas chief he had often had cordial dealings with in the past. Páez's *Destruction of San Saba* clearly shows the Comanche commander flying the white flag of peace in the foreground, and it can be seen again above the mounted Indians thronging against the left wall of the palisade, one in a white headdress, while Father Terreros looks up at them, his hands outstretched in an imploring gesture of peace. Caption H reads, "He goes to greet them with great love, and he and Father Molina spend much time with them."

Terreros flung open the gates. The Indians poured in, including an army of small boys, brought along for a lesson in the wiles of warfare, who can be seen behind the horses with their buffalo-hide armor. The friars handed out tobacco and other gifts, and the Texas told them they had no wish to harm their friends. But the massively built Comanche chief remained in the saddle, wearing the long coat of a French uniform, arrogant and aloof in his every move. The most striking features of his representation in the painting are the red coat and the white flag.

That this Comanche was wearing that uniform was hugely symbolic of French perfidy, indicating that they had allied themselves to these notoriously "savage heathen." Spanish officials were disgusted by the way the French regarded "Indians as so civilized that they marry Indian women," while it was "the greatest vanity of the principal Indians to offer their women up to the incontinent appetite of the French."[39] But the Spanish were furious when the French sold weapons to the "savages," simply because they "found their greatest glory in that which is most profitable to them."

Many Indians began looting the mission, removing food, clothing, saddles, bridles, and even horses, as can be seen in the painting in the scene to the left, within the mission compound. After some initial hesitation, "with treachery in their hearts," the Indians "came up with another ruse: to beg Father Terreros to go to the presidio with them."

> Terreros, our blessèd Father
> Knew the dire straits before them,
> But no coward this Franciscan
> His only choice, to go with them,
> So he took a comrade with him,
> The bravest soldier then amongst them,
> They rode forth amidst the rabble

Of the heathen evil warriors
With their muskets all to hand,
Their sabers and their lances
And their arrows and their shields.
But scarcely in the saddle,
As the brave men looked behind them,
The Indians fired their weapons,
Spewing leaden balls a-burning,
Felling father and companion,
Who then breathed their final breaths.
Yet the evil savagery continued:
And further ravenous for cruelty
They stripped the Father of his habits,
And they thrust his sacred crosier
In his heart no longer beating,
And they scalped him of his tonsure,
And then they shot the soldier dead . . .

The scene can be seen in the painting, where caption Y describes how Terreros did indeed leave the mission with a single soldier, but they only managed to ride a short distance before they were shot. The friar was then skewered with his own crosier and scalped. Parrilla reported that the friar's body "was pierced by two bullets and a lance thrust."[40] The full-length image of Terreros on the right-hand side of the painting shows an arrow in his heart, two lead balls in his chest, and the broken crosier hanging like a *banderilla* from a fighting bull. He is shown fully clothed for reasons of decorum, but in the scene immediately to the right of his head, the painter shows him apparently naked, being run through with his crosier.

The story moves to the presidio, the collection of huts in the top left of the painting. Parrilla had sent a posse of men to find out what was happening at the mission, but they were intercepted and a battle ensued in which two Spaniards were killed, which can be seen above and to the right of Torreros's head. Six other men fled, but José Vázquez survived by fighting valiantly, felling Indians to the left and right, eventually taking refuge at the mission. "He stood alone, holding out for a long time, sword in hand, and sent many of them to hell," the poem proudly recalls, and he can be seen beneath the trees just beyond the mission, badly wounded, making his getaway.

In the painting, flames dance on the roofs of the mission buildings, and the poem refers to the "horrendous crackling sound" of the fire. Santiesteban was still in the chapel,

In humble supplication,
Jesus Christ he was embracing,
When the Gentiles smashed the door down,
Hungry lions, they attacked him,
Shot him down with bullets
Then beheaded him and stabbed him.
Then like violent rabid canines
They profaned the sacred pictures . . .

Both the death of Santiesteban and the assault on the sacred image of the Immaculate Conception within the compound can clearly be seen in the painting. To the right of the church is the scene described under caption Q: "The death of the majordomo. They plucked out his eyes and skinned him alive."

The real miracle of this story for the survivors still holed up in the mission was the arrival of Captain Parrilla at the head of a scouting party of only fourteen men. With night falling, the Indians assumed many more soldiers were coming and withdrew, allowing the survivors to slip away unnoticed through a gap in the fence. Brother Molina was so badly injured he had to drag himself through the bush on hands and knees, but at least four men escaped, and the little party can be seen in the distance in the top right of the painting, above the crucifix held by Santiesteban, Christ's arms outstretched in symbolic protection of the survivors.[41] Perhaps some of these figures, the woman carrying a babe in arms, represent a few lucky Tlaxcalans?

The following year, Parrilla led a punitive expedition north to the Brazos River, where he surprised a camp of Tonkawas, slaughtering 55 and taking another 150 prisoners. He continued to a well-fortified Wichita settlement on the Red River at Spanish Fort, where the Comanches and their allies were ensconced. The ensuing battle lasted all day, and both sides took heavy casualties. Fifty Indians were killed, including the commander, but nineteen Spaniards were also killed and another twenty deserted. Unwilling to risk further casualties, Parrilla withdrew. Many criticized that decision, and the battle has often been described as a significant Spanish defeat. In reality, it was a stalemate that marked the extreme limit of Spanish military might in the face of well-organized Plains Indians armed with French firearms.[42]

PART III

THE BOURBON REFORMS

A FEW GOOD MEN

DURING THE EARLY 1750S, French forces began to occupy the Ohio Country west of the Alleghenies and south of Lake Erie, establishing a series of forts as far south as modern Pittsburgh in order to secure the Ohio River and access to the Mississippi for New France. The British government was deeply alarmed by this resurgence of French expansionism in North America and instructed the colonial authorities that where necessary they should use force to defend British interests in the region.

In 1754, the Governor of Virginia promoted the twenty-two-year-old George Washington to the rank of lieutenant-colonel and gave him command of two hundred men with orders to confront the French. It was a wholly inadequate force for the task. Nonetheless, brimming with youthful valor, Washington advanced his men over the mountains and toward the enemy, determined to carry out his orders, hopeful he would soon receive reinforcements. From his camp at Great Meadows, early in the morning of May 28, Washington set out with a detachment of forty-seven men and some Indian allies and attacked a small contingent of French troops that had in fact been sent to parley with him. Contemporary reports differ as to what happened next. It appears that the French, who were still in the middle of breakfast, announced their mission as messengers and ambassadors, but that during the ceasefire, Washington lost control of his Indian allies, who scalped thirteen or fourteen Frenchmen, including their commander. It was a brutal way to be blooded in the ways of war for the young and inexperienced Virginian soldier. Two weeks later, Washington's now reinforced army was hunted down by a large French force led by the brother of the murdered officer. The French trapped the Virginians inside the inadequate defenses of the hastily built Fort Necessity, but Washington urged his men to stout resistance, terrified they would all be slaughtered in revenge for the earlier massacre. After eight hours of fierce fighting, to Washington's astonishment, the French offered him the chance to surrender with honor, allowing him to retreat with his weapons and his colors.[1]

Those were the first skirmishes of the Seven Years' War, known in America as the French and Indian War, a "titanic struggle for imperial domination" between France and Britain that drew in all the great European powers and their colonies around the world. Fighting did not break out in Europe until 1756, when France attacked the Mediterranean island of Menorca (a British possession since the Treaty of Utrecht of 1713) and Prussia invaded Saxony.[2]

By 1759, with war burning across Europe, it was widely reported that the King of Spain, Ferdinand VI, "was," in the words of the British Ambassador at Madrid, "irrecoverably out of his senses and his bodily disorders were daily increasing." That summer, the third Bourbon ruler of Spain died in agony,[3] to be succeeded by his half-brother Charles III, "a giant among Bourbon midgets," according to one distinguished historian.[4] For all that he spent much of every day out shooting and hunting and Goya's famous portrait makes him look more like a gamekeeper than a monarch, he was uniquely well qualified as a statesman because he had already spent a quarter of a century as ruler of Naples. Charles believed in strong government and picked his ministers according to their abilities rather than their birth, preferring men of humble origins who owed everything to his own royal favor.[5] When he landed at Barcelona, on October 17, 1759, to assume the Spanish throne, by far the most important member of his entourage to disembark the appropriately named *Phoenix* was the recently elevated Marquis of Esquilache, a humble customs officer who had risen through the ranks and would become Charles's leading minister in Madrid.

The royal party was rapturously received, and the queen reported that "the whole country has gone crazy with delight."[6] But at Saragossa, Charles learned that British troops had occupied Quebec and now threatened to take control of the Mississippi valley. He sent a strongly worded memorandum to London, but the British Prime Minister, William Pitt, merely professed to be puzzled that the message had been sent before Charles had been able to discuss the matter with his Spanish ministers. Pitt wondered whether "this step may not be the result of the French Ambassador's infusions?"[7] With the British colonies ascendant in the fighting in North America, France lobbied Madrid ever more loudly in an attempt to persuade Charles to enter the war.

Charles III had inherited a kingdom and an empire that while rooted in the congenial chaos that had characterized the Habsburg administration—with its eclectic range of kingdoms, regions, and provinces, and over-mighty special-interest groups such as Church, aristocracy, and military, and a whole range of other organizations—had since been exposed to half a century of Bourbon aspirations to establish the apparatus of a powerful centralizing state subject to the authority of the crown. The new king and his ministers brought vigor and experience to those hitherto largely ineffective attempts to establish strong government, managing to subordinate individuals and corporate bodies to the will of the crown in the interests of what government ministers referred to as "the common good."[8] In Spain, the state took control of planning and development in agriculture, industry, and commerce, formalized the extensive reforms of the military begun by Philip V, and radically modernized the universities, bringing a new emphasis on Roman Law to legal studies, for example.[9] Perhaps no institution better illustrates the Bourbon obsession with the concentration of absolute royal power in the hands of a few top men than the *intendencia*, a form of regional prefecture that had slowly been introduced into Spain since the reign of Philip V. These *intendencias* were administered by two *intendentes*, one to collect taxes and encourage economic growth, the other to oversee defense. Both had almost dictatorial powers and were answerable only to the crown.

The same reforming zeal was imposed on Spanish America, and the key protagonists of the coming chapters perfectly exemplify the way that policy was ruthlessly carried out in the Indies. As Visitador, or "Inspector General," of New Spain, José de Gálvez imposed administrative reform and brutally suppressed the resulting rebellion in the north of the viceroyalty before returning to Madrid. He rose to become Secretary of the Indies and provided the political impetus for Junípero Serra to establish the famous Franciscan missions of California. José's nephew Bernardo de Gálvez was an exemplary soldier and served on the front line against the Apaches in northern New Spain, before becoming Governor of Louisiana. Juan Bautista de Anza the Younger built on the legacy of his father, Juan Anza the Elder, to become an effective and greatly admired frontier soldier and then Governor of New Mexico. These men were all from humble families and owed everything to the crown and its administration. Their stories and experiences and those of their many companions whose interwoven biographies provide the structure of Part Three of this book bring into focus the complications, both personal and general, of that Bourbon imposition of authority, highlighting its successes and its failures. Ultimately, they clearly demonstrate that the state needed the service of brilliant individuals to put its programs into practice. However, the reforms they effected on the ground destabilized the organic tangle of bonds that held together the empire, replacing them with a veneer of ordered, apparently powerful institutions, which ultimately proved weak and divisive. Charles III's newly authoritarian crown probably did more to create conditions of resentment among his subjects across the globe than it did to consolidate control of his kingdoms: the reforms plowed the soil in which within a generation the seeds of independence began to take root and germinate across the Spanish Empire.

Of especial importance were the protectionist practices surrounding trade and taxation that sought to limit all commerce with the Indies to the Port of Cadiz, in Spain, and a limited number of ports and fairs in the Americas. Those restrictions drove much of the Indies trade into a highly developed and widely exploited black market that forced most merchants to engage in smuggling and the evasion of taxes. British traders ruthlessly took control of so much of that illegal trade that one French official claimed the British made more money from the Spanish colonies than Spain did herself, bandying around the implausible suggestion that four hundred British ships plied the ports of the Indies while the Spanish had only ten.[10] The Spanish Ambassador to Versailles advised, "It is very clear that the British intend to reign as despots on the highs seas." Spain and France "can no longer stand by doing nothing about this daring policy that will lose us everything" and is a deep "affront to our honor and our dignity."[11]

Charles's advisers in Madrid and the Americas were more measured in their tone, but their assessment was almost as stark. The Captain General of Cuba warned that "should Spain fail to prevent the advance of the English, our American dominions will soon be subject to the greed of a nation that is at war with France to smooth the path to a much easier and richer conquest." Another report argued that were the British allowed to expand into Louisiana, they would not stop until they had control of New Spain herself.[12]

The stage was set for Spain to enter the French and Indian War at a moment when Britain was already all but certain of total victory in North America. But before returning, in chapter 16, to the fray and the consequences of British success, it is time to introduce the main protagonists of part three more fully and glimpse, in chapter 15, the geographical stage on which their dramas were played out.

José de Gálvez y Gallardo was born on January 2, 1720, at the tiny village of Macharaviaya, above the great port city of Malaga in Andalusia. His family were rural laborers, but belonged to the old *hidalgo* class, poor, but noble, proud to claim their pure Christian bloodlines going back generations. Legend has it that the young José worked as a shepherd boy while attending a tiny village school, where he attracted the attention of a local priest, who recommended him to the Bishop of Malaga.

José de Gálvez was one of a remarkably successful brood who exemplified Charles III's preference for men from humble origins. His eldest brother, Matías, born in 1717, rose to be Viceroy of first Guatemala and then New Spain; his son Bernardo, even more prominent than his father and uncle in this story, was born in 1746 and served as Governor of Louisiana and then Havana during the American Revolutionary War, enabling him to provide crucial support to the Thirteen Colonies. Meanwhile, as Secretary of the Indies, José de Gálvez was a staunch political advocate for supporting American independence, eventually persuading Charles III to declare war on Britain.

In 1784, some wag in Mexico City posted a ditty likening the Gálvez to the Holy Trinity:

Who rules in this world?
Well, first is José,
Matías is second,
And Bernardo third.

Advocate . . . viceroy,
Viceroy . . . minister
And minister . . . king!

Father over here,
Son in Havana,
The Spirit in Spain![13]

A third brother, Miguel, became Ambassador to Catherine the Great's court in St. Petersburg; a fourth, Antonio, had a distinguished military career, becoming Commander General of the Port of Cadiz; his illegitimate daughter grew up to be a successful playwright. Clearly this family was blessed with exceptionally ambitious and able genes, but even they, like other successful administrators, owed everything to their sovereign. They were not simply loyal, but were themselves woven into the fabric of the institution of the crown.[14]

José de Gálvez began to study for the priesthood as an escape from poverty, but eventually graduated in law from Salamanca and began practicing as an attorney in Madrid. According to legend, he greatly impressed the king by suing the crown on behalf of a wealthy foreign client, telling his monarch, "*Señor, antes que el rey está la ley,*" or "Sire, the law is above the king." A contemporary aristocrat reveals the more prosaic grain of truth around which this romantic pearl was cultured: "For years . . . he was undistinguished among the swarm of lawyers," until "he married a Frenchwoman" called Lucía Romet y Pichelín, "after which the [French] ambassador took him up for [his] own business and that of [his] nation."[15]

Following Charles III's entry into Madrid, in 1760, Gálvez boldly submitted a short paper on the commercial state of the Indies in which he criticized the overregulation of commerce, the excessive influence of various merchant groups, and a general acceptance of graft. The "greatest abuse of all is the constant acquisition of real estate by the Church," he suggested, and advised that any solution to so many problems must be based on free trade within the empire and a thorough revision of the administrative structure, beginning with the Laws of the Indies. Moreover, the men charged with running these overseas institutions should be drawn from the army and the professions to ensure their integrity and loyalty, men such as himself and his family, the kind of men Charles III favored anyway.[16]

Charles chose Gálvez himself to go to New Spain and impose the new program of royal authority there as inspector general. He embarked with his nephew Bernardo de Gálvez, both of them headed for an American baptism by fire in the war-torn north, the farthest reaches of El Gran Norte, where Seri and Apache fighters rained constant havoc on the Spanish, *criollo*, and Mexican settlers from the south.

Junípero Serra was baptized on the island of Mallorca as José Miquel in 1713, during a period of famine and disease in the aftermath of the War of the Spanish Succession. Like the Gálvez, his parents were tenant farmers, "humble peasants, honorable, devout, and exemplary," according to his greatest biographer and close friend Francisco Palóu.[17] But he may have had little claim to being an Old Christian, for his maternal grandmother had been called Joanna Serra i Abram, while her mother—Serra's great-grandmother—had been called Joanna Abram y Salom, compelling evidence of his Jewish heritage, for all that they were all unquestionably practicing Catholics. Moreover, it has also been claimed that the Serra family was descended from Muslim converts.[18]

The family lived in the mountain town of Petra, which had an influential Franciscan monastery where the brothers ran a small school. The young José Miquel excelled in his studies and eventually took orders himself, adopting the religious name Junípero at the start of his novitiate in honor of a devoutly religious idiot savant who had been a follower of Saint Francis of Assisi himself in the thirteenth century. The original Juniper is remembered for his criminal eccentricity, for hacking the trotter from a live pig to cook up for a sick Franciscan, or saving time in the kitchen by stewing together everything in the larder, including chickens with their feathers, creating such a feast that "there was not a pig in all of Rome so famished that he would have eaten it." But he won over converts with his good-natured simplicity and great charity.

"Would to God, my brethren," Saint Francis had declaimed, "that I had a forest of such Junipers!" [19]

This curious and unusual choice of name almost seems to presage Serra's conception of Native Americans as childlike savages blessed with simple goodness. He was ordained at twenty-six and began teaching theology. But he was greatly influenced by the story of a Franciscan from Petra who had become a missionary in New Spain, and Serra also read about María de Ágreda. From an early age, Serra experienced a strong calling to bring Christ to those blissful pagans who inhabited the distant wildernesses of his imagination, so he and two students, Francisco Palóu and Juan Crespí, petitioned their order to send them to the New World.

On August 2, 1749, on the eve of sailing for America, Serra was clearly emotional as he wrote from Cadiz to his cousin, asking him to "console my parents who I have no doubt will not lack their own sorrows. Tell them I still feel great sadness that I am not there to comfort them as I once did." Serra reminded them that once, when his father was ill, he had exhorted his son "to be a good Franciscan." "Oh Papa," Serra wrote, "I always remember those words, so be not sad that I should do your bidding, for it is the will of God as well." [20]

The Franciscan missionaries suffered on the Atlantic crossing, for the pilots were "rather worried" by the "very rough seas" at Michaelmas, and the friars experienced terrible thirst when caught in the doldrums, "bringing on such a fever that I think I would have drunk from the filthiest puddle," Serra confessed. [21] When a loquacious Dominican friar admired Serra's stoicism, he supposedly replied, "I have found an excellent way to avoid being thirsty: eat little and talk even less." [22]

When they finally landed at Veracruz, Serra insisted on walking through the winter snows to the Franciscan College of San Fernando in Mexico City with Francisco Palóu at his side. One night, a mysterious Spaniard emerged from the darkness to guide them across a swollen river and offer them shelter. For some inexplicable reason they believed this man must have been a manifestation of Saint Joseph, for all that Saint Christopher seems a more likely candidate for this role. Later, Serra was much bitten by mosquitoes, and overnight he scratched his leg badly. The wound became infected and never healed. He was left with a sore that he wore as a badge of pious honor for the rest of his life. [23]

At San Fernando, Serra soon became popular among his fellow "Fernandinos" and spent long years working tirelessly at the missions in the Sierra Gorda in northern Querétaro, two hundred miles north of Mexico City. He gained a reputation as a strict disciplinarian, imposing "paternalistic rigor," a euphemism for whippings and beatings, on wayward Indians and also served as Inquisitor for the Holy Office alongside Juan Crespí.[24]

But his calling was California.

Juan Bautista de Anza the Younger is an iconic figure in the history of Spanish North America, born, raised, and blooded in the violent frontier regions of the Internal Provinces of Texas, New Mexico, Coahuila, Nuevo León, Chihuahua, Sonora, Nueva Vizcaia, New Galicia, and Baja California. Anza knew the world of ceaseless Apache raiding and Indian fighting in that rough, barren country better than anyone. Through determination and strength of character, he forged an overland route from Sonora to supply the Franciscan missions of California and was later appointed Governor of the Kingdom of New Mexico. He was baptized on July 7, 1736, by a family friend and Jesuit priest, Carlos de Rojas, at Cuquiarachic, thirty-odd miles south of the modern border crossing at Douglas, Arizona. His father, Juan Bautista de Anza the Elder, was the commander of the neighboring Presidio of Fronteras. An able army captain born in the tough mountain regions of the Basque country in northern Spain, Anza the Elder had brought a sufficient sense of stability and security to that troubled borderland to encourage a slow trickle of settlers and mining prospectors to risk their lives there in the hopes of fulfilling their dreams or, perhaps, simply as a way of escaping their nightmares.

The Anzas, father and son, epitomize the opportunities that the Americas held for humble Spaniards prepared to risk their lives and work hard in the interests of the crown at the edge of empire. They were military officers within the Bourbon system, but they were part of the long tradition of Basque settlement in northern New Spain that went back to Cristóbal de Oñate and the great silver strike at Zacatecas. Their story vividly illustrates the harsh reality of life in the Internal Provinces, the same harsh reality that José and Bernardo de Gálvez were soon to experience, but which must have been unimaginable in the comforts of the Madrid court or even the tough upland farms of Andalusia.

CHAPTER 15

LOS ANZA & THE APACHES

EL GRAN NORTE

ON A FINE AUTUMNAL AFTERNOON in the middle of November 1736, Anza the Elder was sitting as magistrate in a remote mining camp when an exhausted rider arrived with a sealed letter from Anza's deputy, signed and dated at a lonely ranch. All year, poor prospectors had been probing the canyon country a few miles west of Nogales, a desolate, barren world where even Apache raiders rarely lingered long. The prospectors were overjoyed when the summer downpours washed out the dry arroyos, tearing up the streambeds to reveal what lay beneath the surface. Anza read the letter with growing amazement, then interrogated the messenger. Surely the news was too astonishing to be true?

Three weeks earlier, a Yaqui Indian and his young children had found two large nuggets of ore rich in silver. News quickly spread, and within days dozens of men, women, children, and their dogs were digging up long stretches of the valley floor. They found plenty more nuggets, but the truly unbelievable strike was a long slab of pure silver that was later weighed at a ton and a quarter, with a value of forty-two thousand pesos, double the total annual wage bill for the garrison at Fronteras.[1] Anza was skeptical. Could this really be a pure, natural seam, like Tolosa's historic strike at Zacatecas, in 1546? One of Anza's Jesuit advisers suggested the metal might have been put there by the devil.[2] Anza himself had thought it must be either ancient buried treasure, in which case half was due to the crown, or, more likely, the remains of an illegal smelting operation, which he should confiscate entirely.

Anza set out before dawn to impose royal authority on that fabulously wealthy wilderness. When he reached the canyon, he counted two hundred miners frantically burrowing into hillsides scarred by ditches, pits, and piles of earth, burned brush, and makeshift shelters. He ordered all work to stop, and his soldiers took control of the valley. Then he began his investigation, interviewing some of the miners, including the Yaqui who first struck lucky, and went to see the marvelous slab of silver, still half-buried, partially hacked into pieces, yet still too heavy to move. Having gathered the evidence, Anza appointed a panel of experts to assess the strike. Within months, they had ruled the ore was natural. The miners would pay no more tax than the royal fifth.

Anza established a base for his operations at his deputy's nearby ranch, known locally as La Arizona, where he began auditing the silver and ore he was able to recover from the prospectors, much of it already removed from the site. In early January, aware that Mexico City would now be rife with rumors, Anza sent his full report to the Viceroy of New Spain. Among the documents he filed was the declaration of a local merchant, made to Anza's deputy "at the post of La Arizona, on November 21, 1736," about the amount of silver the merchant had personally handled since the strike.[3] It is the earliest written record of the name Arizona. The root of the word is uncertain, but given the many influential Basques in the region, it is entirely plausible that it comes from the Basque *hariz*, meaning "oak," and *ona*, meaning "good," although the evidence is perhaps not as conclusive as enthusiasts of the hypothesis would like.[4] In his covering letters to the Bishop of Mexico and the Viceroy, Anza explained, "Toward the end of September, various nuggets and slabs of silver weighing more than one hundred *arrobas* were discovered between the Guevavi Mission and the Arizona Ranch."[5] His report made the name Arizona a shorthand for the promise that dreams might come true.*

The stability that Anza the elder brought to northen Sonora encouraged the Church to extend and reinforce the missions. In 1732, three new missionaries

---

* Over a century later, in 1856, a lawyer called W. Claude Jones helped draw up a proposal to the U.S. Congress for the founding of a new territory between the Mexican border and the Colorado River. He first suggested its name be "Pima Land," a direct translation of the Spanish *Pimería*, but at the last moment he was reminded of the legendary silver strike and instead wrote down *Arizona* (Sacks, "The Creation of the Territory of Arizona"). Jones was once described by a federal judge as "an erratic genius," "quick, fertile, penetrating, poetic and flashing." Jones claimed his mother was from Barcelona, where his father had been U.S. consul, although records show that was pure fantasy. "Too much under the influence of his appetites and passions," he eventually had to resign as a U.S. attorney in New Mexico when he abducted and married a twelve-year-old Mexican girl, whom he soon abandoned. When the Civil War broke out, he supported the rebels in the hopes the Confederacy would create the Territory of Arizona. Then, as the Union gained the upper hand, he tried to turn coat. After the amnesty, he moved to Tucson, married another teenager at the territorial capital in Prescott, fled to San Francisco, took ship for Honolulu, where he was elected a senator and sat as a judge, married a teenage Hawaiian princess, and sired a numerous family (Finch, "William Claude Jones"). His most lasting legacy is the State of Arizona.

arrived to revivify Kino's foundations on the Santa Cruz River at Guevavi, Suamca, and the modern jewel of San Xavier del Bac, with its glorious church rising amid an oasis of fecund greenery just south of Tucson, the oldest European structure in Arizona.[6] But that stability and sense of security were the reward for dangerous work done by brave men. On May 9, 1740, Anza was returning to Fronteras from Bac and Guevavi. At Sumaca, a missionary warned him an Apache band had been scouting the road ahead. He set out with a handful of men in the early morning, riding the trail that followed the headwaters of the Santa Cruz north and east, only a few hundred yards south of the modern border. They traveled close together through the valley, but as they came into open country to the south of the Coronado National Monument, Anza trotted on ahead. The Apaches were hidden in the high chaparral. "They attacked, knocked him to the ground, and in no time they had taken his scalp as a prize."[7]

Anza the Younger was four years old, an orphan of his frontier home. His mother moved with her six children to Arizpe, where the Jesuit Carlos de Rojas was based and must have been a welcome paternal influence. The family was probably also helped by the boy's godfather, a wealthy miner and leading figure in the Royal Basque Society, which had been established by the northern gentry who were so proud of their Basque roots. When Anza turned sixteen, his brother-in-law, another prominent figure in that close-knit network, took him on as a cadet at Presidio of Fronteras. He learned in the field and was commissioned a lieutenant at the age of nineteen. According to one admiring Jesuit, he was "truly his father's son," for as well as his name, "he inherited his father's good character, strength of personality, bravery, and his rapport with his men."[8]

In 1760, Anza was appointed Captain of the Presidio of Tubac, now a small community dedicated to arts and crafts in southern Arizona, then the most northerly garrison in New Spain. During his first sally, hostile Indians harried his posse of cavalrymen, and Anza was wounded by an arrow. His mother died soon afterward, a victim of anxiety as much as old age, perhaps? But the following year was much happier, for Carlos de Rojas married Anza to his sweetheart, Ana María Pérez Serrano, the daughter of a mine owner, and the newlyweds set up home at Tubac.

The happiness of Anza's married life at the presidio was constantly tempered by his responsibilities to defend settlers and missionaries from Indian raids. In 1766, he responded to increasing tensions across the whole region by launching a major expedition to stamp Spanish authority along the frontier. He mustered troops from his own presidio at Tubac, from Fronteras, and the neighboring Terrenate, along with a contingent of thirty Pimas from the San

Pedro River valley, and set out almost due east, more or less twenty miles north of the modern border. He saw smoke rising from a minor mountain range to his left and, he reported, immediately led his troops "straight toward this sure sign of the enemy." "But the enemy saw me" first, and when he reached the smoldering fires, he saw signs "that there had been more than a hundred of them camped there with their families." Suddenly, "twenty braves deliberately showed themselves on the summit of the range." Anza knew he "could not maneuver on the rough ground," so to lure them into a fight, "I ordered that several horses be let loose." The Apaches "attacked with gusto . . . I was lying in ambush, and my musketeers were able to do them real damage." The following day Anza attacked another Apache band that was guarding "a great quantity of agave they had harvested . . . on the summit of a high hill," killing a handful of them and taking some women captive. He reported that he had killed or captured a total of forty Apaches, including fifteen women, many of whom were nursing or pregnant. But when he reached Tubac, he learned that while he had been on campaign, Apache rustlers had run off over three hundred head of cattle from the mission at San Xavier del Bac.[9]

In the spring of 1766, as Anza was taking the fight to the Apaches of the Sierra Madre, the Marquis of Rubí was making his way north, with orders from the Council of the Indies to conduct a thorough inspection of all the presidios and garrisons of the Internal Provinces. He set out to accomplish this mammoth undertaking accompanied by an able captain in the Royal Engineers, Nicolás de Lafora, who kept a detailed record of their extraordinary journey of twenty-three months, during which they rode seventy-six hundred miles, almost all of it through hostile territory. They had a taste of what was to come at Pasaje, where the accounts were in a lamentable state, the troops had not been properly paid and were habitually overcharged for their rations, and all the guns in the armory were of different calibers, the swords were flimsy, the shields and uniforms of many designs, and there was not enough gunpowder. The Captain of the Presidio was unable to give a satisfactory explanation for any of those problems.[10] As Rubí and Lafora moved north into Chihuahua, they began to understand the truly awesome nature of the task ahead. The presidio on the Conchos River had been abandoned, leaving twenty-five "civilized" families of Indian weavers at the nearby Mission San Francisco largely unprotected. Lafora noted in his diary, "There is plenty of silver in these hills, but the seams are not worked out of fear for the barbarians."[11]

From there, they set out for Junta de los Rios, where the Conchos joins the Rio Grande, an essential anchor in any defense of the north because it controlled the main corridor through which Indian raiders could enter or escape the Sierra Madre. But while they were on the road, they learned that the Governor of Nueva Vizcaya had ordered the garrison to abandon the presidio to prevent Rubí from uncovering whatever corrupt practices the Governor hoped to hide. Rubí turned north toward El Paso, picking up the Camino Real near a large ranch called Agua Nueva, where a few terrified farmhands scratched a living. Lafora commented that at every watering hole there was the threat of Apache attack.[12]

Rubí was impressed by El Paso, with its bucolic surroundings and five thousand inhabitants, probably the most populous place in the Internal Provinces. "All this land is well cultivated and almost anything that is planted there will grow. But it has especially good grapes, to rival those of Spain, and a great abundance of many European fruits, which are often left to rot on the trees. They make a very average wine and a better grape spirit, although they do not always harvest enough corn for their needs because so much of the land is planted with vines."[13] Rubí concluded that El Paso should be able to defend itself and advised relocating its presidio and garrison thirty miles back along roads by which they had just come, so as to afford protection to travelers.

Rubí and Lafora set out for New Mexico across the plain beneath the Organ Mountains, where Apache bands were known to camp, according to the nervous Lafora, and then on to La Jornada del Muerto, "Dead Man's March." As they were preparing to make a night crossing of that waterless stretch of road, a sentry noticed a handful of Apache spies and chased them away. Despite that warning, Rubí carelessly allowed some Suma Indian shepherds accompanying his party to drift ahead with a flock of sheep. Suddenly, the Apaches attacked and drove off some of the animals. The soldiers set out in a reckless pursuit. With his party dangerously stretched out, Rubí could only watch as a fearsome contingent of warriors appeared on horseback on the hills above the road and came toward the main body of the expedition. Lafora was clear in his assessment: "If they had all charged us with any serious intent, there were not enough men left behind to put up a defense." But the wary Apaches stayed out of range of the soldiers' guns and retreated onto a ridge along which "all of them followed us on our right hand for the rest of the day."[14]

Rubí and Lafora stopped at Alburquerque—which had not yet dropped its first "R"—a bustling community of five hundred Spaniards and uncounted Indians. They visited Sandia, their first sight of a pueblo, divided into two groups of apartments, one inhabited by Tiwas and the other by Hopis. At Bernalillo they met the lonely friar living among a hundred Keres families. Finally, on August 19, they arrived in Santa Fe, a land of "poor silver mines," good fishing, and "mountain forests of pines, oaks, rowans, giant juniper bushes, and inhabited by all sorts of birds, bears, wolves, coyotes, wild goats, and deer the size of a mule with horns that are two yards long from base to tip." [15]

Lafora's logbook evokes an unsettling sense of New Mexico as a Christian island amid an ocean of hostile heathens. "Indians and Spaniards alike are well prepared for war," he explained. "From a very young age, they learn how to handle weapons and horses in order to defend themselves," for "they are surrounded on every side" by an "infinite number of pagan nations . . . The Spaniards arm themselves as they do everywhere, but are especially dexterous with their lances, which they handle with perfection." But Lafora and Rubí were clearly concerned that "because of a lack of powder they are less skilled with their guns." However, the Pueblo Indians were exceptionally skilled in the "use of bows and arrows, spears and lances, and they even had a few guns and many of them had their leather armor." But at Santa Fe they thought the presidio itself "impossible to defend." [16]

Rubí was back at El Paso by the end of September, then headed southwest, west, and finally north in a long sweeping arc that took him through the valleys of northern Chihuahua and Sonora. Everywhere, Lafora documented abandoned farms and settlements and other consequences of Apache raiding. As they traveled this region, time and again they heard glowing reports of Juan Bautista de Anza, and they pushed on toward Tubac, keen to spend the Christmas season in the company of a man who was so widely liked and admired and who knew the frontier so well and had such long experience of Apache warfare.

They were not disappointed. Rubí in his report described Anza as "a complete officer" worthy of the "king's recognition." "I can scarcely believe it," Rubí exclaimed, for "he governed his garrison with a generosity uncommon in these lands," selling the men supplies at below the regulation price instead of gouging them, as almost every other officer and official seemed to be doing. Tubac was well stocked with Catalan carbines, good swords, lances, shields, and other military equipment. Anza arranged for his troops to demonstrate their martial skills in a thrilling display that left Rubí greatly impressed, reporting the outstanding horsemanship of the lancers and noting that they were mostly superb marksmen. [17]

Rubí also got to see some real action. While he was at Tubac, a band of Mescalero Apaches came down "like Arabs" into the valley from "their inaccessible badlands" high in the mountains above the Gila River "to harvest the agave growing on some nearby plains." It made him realize just how important this most northern presidio was to the defense of Sonora. It was a front line against the many hostile tribes from the Colorado River valley, as well as the Apache, and it was essential that the garrison patrol the territory to east and west. "They cannot make a mistake when it comes to identifying any sign of incursions across our borders and assessing when and how many enemies there were, where they were going, and what their plans might be."[18]

The close ties of an extended family necessary to fomenting the sense of collective social responsibility that made security and stability possible in northern New Spain made for a potentially divisive claustrophobia as well.

For over a decade, in the 1770s, Anza's extended family pursued a bitter vendetta against José Antonio Vildósola, who had just been appointed Captain of the Presidio of Terrenate, not far from Anza's own command at Tubac. It cannot have been a pleasant business for Anza, for he had fought alongside José during the campaigns against the Seri Indians in the Cerro Prieto, and before that Anza had cut his teeth as a young "Indian fighter" serving under José's brother Gabriel Vildósola. But José had married Anza's niece, María Rosa, and María Rosa was the cause of all the trouble.[19] When José came home for Christmas in 1769, after two years of constant service as a cavalry officer fighting the Seri Indians, María Rosa refused to see him. Instead, she took refuge at the nearby mission with their two children. Her father had to explain to the increasingly fraught José that she was seven months pregnant.

Adulterous husbands were such an integral part of normal society in New Spain that, while often reported to judicial and religious authorities, infidelities were also admired by the husbands' peers and were frequently the subject of ribald humor. In most reported cases, wealthy men philandered with slaves, servants, Indian and *mestiza* women, and occasionally a lowly Spanish girl. By stark contrast, little documentary evidence exists of the infidelities of their wives and daughters. Women had fewer opportunities to stray because they were encouraged to remain at home amid their household or to be accompanied when out and about. Moreover, they had good reason to be faithful, for to be caught meant terrible social dishonor for them, their children, their relatives, and not least their husbands.

The Spanish concept of honor in the eighteenth century defies definition. Nonetheless, it was intuitively understood by everyone and utterly central to the way society worked. *Honra* was how a community, family, or person thought of themselves, and *reputación* was how they were thought of by others. Together they represented the collective social worth of the group and all its subsets. It was an extremely emotive subject. The most prolific popular Spanish dramatist of the seventeenth century, Lope de Vega, wrote that "the best plots are about honor because they excite the most powerful emotions in everyone." Any actor who plays the role of a "cuckolder" finds himself so "loathed by one and all" that shopkeepers refuse to sell him their wares and "commoners run away from him" in the street.[20] Even when dishonor was fictional, it seemed so toxic it was thought contagious.

Honra had to be upheld across the scale, from an overarching sense of Spanish nationhood, to social class, a region, town, village, family, and, in the final reckoning, the individual. All individuals owned a share in the *honra* and *reputación* of their community as much as they had custody of their own honor. To dishonor oneself brought shame on the entire community.

María had jeopardized the honor of her husband, her children, her parents, her extended family, even her servants, as well as her own. All of their professional careers might be adversely affected and social standing all but destroyed. She had undermined the reputation of her sex, social class, and her neighbors; she had betrayed every strand of her identity. She had also sinned against the honor of the Catholic faith. As a result, many powerful people were greatly interested in covering up the scandal. Indeed, such drastic consequences go a long way to explain the relative rarity of references to adulterous women in the historical record. It was not that married noble-women were sexually continent, but simply that it was in nobody's interest to document their infidelities. In fact, we know that many large towns in New Spain had *casas de depósito*, where women could seek refuge during pregnancies resulting from premarital sex or adultery or to escape violent husbands and even incestuous relatives.[21]

At first, José Antonio Vildósola acquiesced in the conspiracy of silence. He ordered his household to keep the pregnancy a secret. Close relatives were drafted as nurses and midwives. Vildósola then left town and returned to fighting Seri Indians alongside Juan Bautista de Anza. When that campaign finally came to an end in December 1770, Vildósola was rewarded with the command of the Presidio of Terrenate, on the San Pedro River sixty miles south of his Anza's presidio at Tubac. Anza undoubtedly valued Vildósola as an experienced frontier captain, but Anza also likely hoped the posting might help foment a permanent reconciliation with María Rosa. At about this time, she began writing desperate, pleading letters to her husband, begging his forgiveness, "if only for the sake of the children," and claiming she "would have sooner died that be the cause of their separation."[22] For Vildósola, however, forgiveness was too much to ask.

During 1772, Vildósola suffered a string of military setbacks, and Apache raiders ran off hundreds of horses. His men complained about him and he was reprimanded by the viceroy for abusing his role as paymaster. Later, he was accused of having an affair with his lieutenant's wife, who was also Anza's sister.

María Rosa's powerful relatives appear to have eventually abandoned all attempts at an amicable accommodation and instead embarked on the total destruction of Vildósola's professional reputation, partly out of revenge, but also in the hopes of recovering some or all of her considerable dowry. In March 1773, he was removed from his post, arrested, and imprisoned. But his formidable military reputation and a strong personal relationship with José de Gálvez led the Council of the Indies to question Vildósola's fall from grace. The Viceroy of New Spain described him as of "generous spirit, extreme courage, strength, and great ability in matters of war," although he could also be "avaricious and cruel."[23] He was temporarily reappointed as Captain of Terrenate in 1779, pending further investigations. María Rosa and her family responded by accusing him of deserting his wife and failing to provide for her financially. She asked for the return of her dowry. But then the viceroy asked Vildósola for his testimony, and the proud frontiersman risked his own *reputación* by telling the truth.

The viceroy struck a deal with Vildósola, offering to clear his name and arrange for his promotion, but hinting strongly that the king would look more favorably on his case if he returned to his wife, a condition to which he eventually agreed. In 1783, after further consideration by officials in Madrid, he was promoted to the rank of colonel, for the king viewed Vildósola's ability as a soldier as far more important than his soiled *honra* as a cuckold.

CHAPTER 16

LOS GÁLVEZ

CALIFORNIA & SONORA

The Indian is generally of sound character because of his tough upbringing . . . The skill, ability, and dexterity with which they carry out a raid is quite incredible . . . We Spaniards accuse them of cruelty, [yet] I do not know what they must think of us? [They] wage war against us out of a hatred . . . born of such tyrannies they have suffered as are too shameful to mention.

—BERNARDO DE GÁLVEZ

THE BRITISH AMBASSADOR at Madrid had "long observed the jealousy of Spain at the British conquests" during the early years of the French and Indian, or Seven Years', War. But Charles III steadfastly resisted entering the conflict until the summer of 1761, when "two ships . . . arrived at Cadiz with very rich cargoes from the West Indies," a "circumstance" which "raised the language of the Catholic King's Ministers," and the court brimmed with overconfidence.[1]

Charles III agreed to an alliance with France known as the Third Bourbon Family Compact and declared war at the very moment Britain had gained a decisive upper hand. The Royal Navy humiliated Spain, occupying both Manila and Havana. The peace negotiations led to the Treaty of Fontainebleau and the Treaty of Paris, of 1762 and 1763, by which France gave Louisiana to Spain, while Spain recovered Havana, but had to cede to Britain all of Florida, everything east of the Mississippi, and valuable logging rights in Honduras. That defeat engendered an almost irrational paranoia at Charles's court that foreign powers might at any moment seize the rest of his North American possessions and perhaps New Spain itself. The fear of Protestant British Americans marching across the continent acquired a new resonance when they began selling guns to the Comanches. Then reports reached Spain from St. Petersburg that Empress Catherine the Great was personally encouraging Russian merchants to trade for animal pelts along the Alaska coast.[2]

In 1764, the same year the British Parliament passed the notorious American Duties Act, General Juan de Villalba arrived in New Spain with 1,130 Spanish soldiers and orders to recruit a standing army in New Spain large enough to intimidate Britain, France, and their American colonies. The following year, 1765, as the Stamp Act goaded British America toward rebellion, José de Gálvez landed at Veracruz as Inspector General of New Spain with sweeping powers to "impose the best possible practice in the collection of taxes" so that the viceroyalty could pay for Villalba's army. Gálvez was instructed to crack down on smuggling, make a detailed review of the law courts, probe for corrupt practices among officials and judges, and impose lucrative royal monopolies on the sale of playing cards and tobacco.[3]

The incumbent viceroy, the aristocratic Marquis of Cruillas, felt humiliated that his authority should be so publicly undermined by such plebeian rivals and responded with petty hauteur.[4] But Gálvez had great charm and could soon boast, "I have managed to persuade the viceroy and Villalba to attend four *juntas* in order to deal with all the military matters so long delayed by the enmity between them."[5] Those meetings paid especial attention to defending and expanding the Internal Provinces, and Gálvez became especially focused on occupying the famous Port of Monterey in Alta California, which he saw as the crucial bastion of any defense policy in the Pacific. It had been reputed to be the best haven along the California coast since Sebastián Vizcaíno named it, in 1602, and galleons making the return journey from the Philippines usually made landfall not far to its north. Gálvez realized that Baja California and Sonora must form the foundations of any expansion along the Pacific seaboard and into the west and northwest of the continent. He listened carefully to the experienced Mexican officers, who warned him about the aggressive Apache raiding parties that rampaged across the northern borderlands with increasing frequency as they themselves fled the relentless advance of the Comanches. The Comanches were described in one official report as "an Indian nation as savage as they are warlike, always on the move and at war with all other nations," so "singular a people that I have included this description here as a warning."[6] It is a description many an Indian might well have used of Europeans, and in fact the rise of the warlike Comanches has itself been explained in terms of the pressure placed across the continent by colonial encroachment. Terror, Gálvez's advisers told him, had become a way of life for the settlers, soldiers, and missionaries of northern New Spain. It was his first inkling of the true privations of Juan Bautista de Anza's world.

As friendly tribes such as the Pima, Ópata, and Tarahumara, the historical inhabitants of those borderlands, began to lose faith in the Spaniards' ability to protect them, they started to feel they had little option but to join the Apaches or turn on the Spaniards for themselves. "Now they have elected a captain general," who they call "the Earthquake," the desperate Governor of Sonora reported in March 1766, "who is recognized by our old Pima enemies who are again up in arms." This Indian war chief accepted all comers to his rebel army and beseeched them to "be happy, forget the few belongings you have left behind, make many arrows with good flint heads, for these are the currency with which you will buy cattle, horses, and clothes."[7]

Gálvez was greatly relieved when the Marquis of Croix, a Fleming who had risen through the ranks of the Spanish army, arrived in Mexico City as the new Viceroy of New Spain. The two men quickly became friends and developed a strong working relationship. Moreover, the new viceroy had arrived with his nephew Teodoro de Croix, who would prove to be as able a frontier soldier as Gálvez's own nephew Bernardo. Later, as viceroy himself, Teodoro would form a close friendship with Bernardo when he, as Governor of Louisiana, was giving vital clandestine support to the American Patriots.

Gálvez's instructions as inspector general required him to consider how to establish one or more *intendencias* in New Spain, and in 1767, he and Croix drafted plans to bring California, Sonora, Sinaloa, and Nueva Vizcaya under a single Comandancia General.[8] Once the rebellious Indians were subdued, Arizpe in northern Sonora would become the administrative capital, and a free port would be established on the mainland at San Blas, to connect Baja and Monterey with New Spain. A new settlement was proposed at the confluence of the Gila and Colorado rivers among the Yuma, and a land route would be opened to Alta California. The exchequer would establish banks to secure mining wealth and tax offices to collect the duty.[9]

It was clear to everyone in Mexico City that Gálvez himself should take overall charge of implementing the administrative reforms. Disturbingly, however, he was increasingly convinced that both Baja and Sonora were an American "Ophir," the fabulously wealthy "golden port" of the Old Testament, describing it to the Secretary of the Indies as "a northern treasure-house" filled with "many gold and silver mines." As one old hand sarcastically put it, Gálvez truly "believes those stories about a land of precious metals and mountains made of almost solid silver."[10] To some, he seemed to be losing touch with reality.

Far away, near Waxhaw Creek on the Carolinas border, on March 15, 1767, a babe was born to a newly widowed Irishwoman. She called him Andrew Jackson after his father and went on to raise a boy who was both precociously bright and deeply troubled in equal measure. A lifetime later, in the prelude to a vicious election campaign, when the sixty-year-old Jackson read a news-paper article denouncing his mother as "a common prostitute . . . who married a mulatto," he broke down in tears and had to be comforted by his wife. It is, of course, a cliché that the weak spot of gangsters and political strongmen is their maternal bond, but that Jackson exhibited his distress through tears and not anger was wholly out of character for a man who had supposedly been involved in fourteen duels and gunfights over matters of honor and the like. He would mature to be the nemesis of John Quincy Adams at the ballot box, the Creek Indians in the Southeast, the British at New Orleans, and most important for this story the Spanish in Florida.

On May 30, 1767, Viceroy Croix received royal orders from Madrid that left him dismayed and perplexed. He must expel every Jesuit from New Spain. This astounding and successful program of intellectual and religious "cleansing," enacted across the Spanish world, well illustrates the totalitarian instincts of Charles III's new authoritarian regime. It also starkly demon-strates the extent to which that metropolitan government was at odds with its subjects in the Americas. It is not much of an exaggeration to suggest that the expulsion of the Jesuits might well have lost Charles New Spain were it not for the determined actions of Croix and Gálvez, who saved the colony for the crown.

The Company of Jesus had been outstandingly successful since its founda-tion by Ignatius Loyola in the sixteenth century, and its power and influence had made it many enemies. But the Jesuits were also victims of their outspoken views and intellectualism. Charles III disliked them for their theoretical defense of the legitimacy of regicide and their special status of a direct alle-giance to the pope, while his ministers were suspicious of their aristocratic connections. Their enemies had implicated the Jesuits in orchestrating major riots in Madrid directed against Charles III's favorite and chief minister, the Marquis of Esquilache, who had been blamed for the humiliation of the Treaty of Paris, of 1763. A special commission had concluded that the Jesuits were indeed guilty of "fanaticism and sedition," and on February 27, 1767, Charles had issued a secret royal decree expelling them from Spain and her dominions.[11]

Croix wrote his brother that "seeing as every inhabitant" of New Spain "from the most high and mighty to the lowest of the low, from the richest to the poorest, are all pupils and zealous supporters of the Company, you will readily understand that I took great care not to trust any of them . . . The secret would have played out infamously . . . so I only told Gálvez and your son Teodoro . . . As a result, we three made all the necessary arrangements, writing the orders out by our own hand, which I then dispatched by special messengers so that the king's will should be done everywhere at the same time on the same day," July 8.[12]

Croix's dispatches reached Sonora three days late. The governor of the province broke the seal and read his orders, which explained in detail how to ensure the expulsion be secret, swift, and ruthlessly effective. Even the troops employed should be kept in the dark until the last minute. Deeply troubled, the governor went to work. He picked five trusted men, including Juan Bautista de Anza, and reluctantly sent them instructions, exhorting them to "look after the reverend fathers ... Allow them tablecloths, napkins, cutlery, and plates so they might eat decently" and make sure they have "lard, spices, jam, honey" and everything else they need to "cook and season their food."[13]

Anza was heartbroken. He would have to go to Arizpe and break the tragic news to Carlos de Rojas; he would have to force his friends to leave San Xavier del Bac. He remained stoical, but one of the captains charged with escorting the fathers to the main mustering point at Matute was driven almost mad, according to his prisoners, every night loudly lamenting his misfortune at having to enforce this decree.[14]

Croix and Gálvez appointed as Governor of California a forty-four-year-old career officer called Gaspar de Portolá, who had seen distinguished service in Italy during the Seven Years' War, and charged him with expelling the Jesuits from Baja.[15] He tried to sail across the Sea of Cortez to the capital at Loreto in August 1767, with Junípero Serra's famous biographer Francisco Palóu and an advance party of Franciscans who were to take over as missionaries. Their sloop was battered by a terrible storm, which abated when Palóu threw some "holy" grass into the sea, but nonetheless the captain insisted on returning to port.[16] Portolá tried again in October and landed at Cape San José, the southern tip of Baja, after a truly Old Testament voyage of forty days on rough seas. There, he met the officer in charge of the Santa Cruz garrison, Fernando Rivera y Moncada, with whom Portolá would share many an adventure.

Rivera explained that Portolá now faced leading his fifty dragoons overland to Loreto, a journey that one sarcastic Alsatian Jesuit explained "gave him more of a chance than he might have wanted to assure himself that his fine and noble Kingdom of California was indeed a bucolic, well-watered Promised Land of shady plains and healthy peoples."[17] In reality, it seemed as though God had forsaken the place in anticipation of the Jesuits' expulsion. Portolá's party was constantly short of water, and the tough thornbushes tore the men's uniforms and shredded their flesh as though they were penitents during Holy Week. Later, he suggested with bitter irony that his men should be issued with the famous leather armor used in the Internal Provinces that was so effective against Apache arrows.[18] They finally reached the capital at Loreto on December 17.

Portolá set about expelling the Jesuits, who by then knew their fate. He gently served the decree on the four priests at Loreto and took them into custody. He seized the keys to their buildings and storehouses, secured what little silver the religious order possessed, then returned the keys so they could feed themselves. Meanwhile, Father Ducrue wrote the rest of the missionaries, urging cooperation in order to maintain order among the neophyte Indians. The whole population of Loreto gathered on the beach, where Indians and Spaniards alike wept as the Black Robes, as Jesuits are known, were embarked on February 3, 1768.[19] The Alsatian graciously acknowledged that "under the circumstances, for the sake of the good Governor Gaspar Portolá's reputation, I have to thank all the honorable Spaniards for showing great respect, courtesy, and kindliness toward us." Portolá must have spoken for almost every official in New Spain when he "consistently and solemnly repeated that he was much troubled by this commission."[20]

Governor Portolá's spiritual grief was compounded by the practical problem of how to feed the soldiers and mission Indians. Since Kino's time, Baja had been dependent on an annual consignment of grain sent by the Jesuits in Sonora. Without that succor, Portolá's men would starve, so he sent Croix a long list of everything that was urgently needed.[21]

Portolá then set about trying to establish his administration at Loreto. With no sign of the promised Franciscan replacements for the Jesuits, he had to arrange for ordinary soldiers to run the twenty missions for over a year. He made spirited attempts to sound optimistic about the prospects for winning the hearts of the Indians and relayed promising if improbable reports of rich mines in the north, but Portolá was quickly so disillusioned that his correspondence is peppered with references to "this miserable" or "unhappy peninsula" where there is nothing but "sand" and "thorns."[22]

The widespread anger at the expulsion of the much-loved Jesuits combined with Gálvez's aggressive economic reforms and tightening of government control were a touchstone to widespread rioting and public calls for rebellion. At Potosí, an angry mob refused to allow the soldiers to remove the Black Robes. The Jesuit fathers themselves rang the bells of their college's *campanile* to quiet the crowd, but the people's blood was up and they "were determined to murder the mayor, the sheriff, and the few Spaniards," who had been forced to take refuge inside the college. When a leading churchman tried to calm the situation by displaying the divine presence of the Holy Sacrament, the mob threw stones at him and somebody shot an arrow, although clearly not with murderous intent because it lodged harmlessly in his robes. Finally, the musketeers opened fire and the mob moved on, breaking open the jail-house and freeing the inmates. When a notorious bandit called Pablo Vicente smashed the gallows, the crowd hailed him as their leader. He then broke into the magazine and stole all the gunpowder, before leading his followers on a rampage, looting the town's shops and warehouses. Vicente then sealed his leadership by stealing the fine cape and silver staff of office from the house of a royal official.[23]

As reports of anarchy spreading across the hinterland cascaded into Mexico City, an outraged Gálvez convinced Croix to let him put down the rebellion in person. The inspector general marched on Potosí with seven hundred veteran troops. At seven in the morning of July 24, 1767, Gálvez told Croix, "I stationed my veteran dragoons in the streets and then I rode to the doors of the Jesuit college, where I set a guard of royal grenadiers. I went in, prayed, and then I ordered the church be shut up and I gathered the fathers together." He chas-tised his prisoners, "The supreme authority of his majesty the king and of his viceroy have been grievously insulted by the repeated sedition of the savage plebeian scum of this province. Now I have had to come in person to this college, the only kernel of discord that still needs to be uprooted here."[24]

A formidable force of fifty dragoons and thirty veterans took the Jesuits away.

The rebels, Gálvez reported, an "evil underclass of vagabonds and crimi-nals, were ensconced like Gypsies in the mining camps of the Cerro de San Pedro, the San Pedro Hill. These scum," he raged, "have infected the whole population."[25] With the support of Gálvez's troops, the local sheriff felt emboldened enough to encircle the rebel camp and force them to capitu-late.[26] Gálvez invoked his powers as a military commander and began the summary justice of his brutal court-martial. Despite no evidence of any loss of life during the disturbances, on August 7 Gálvez sentenced eleven men to death by hanging. He forced their wives and children to parade beneath their cadavers as they swung from the scaffold and praised "a local Indian, a born hangman, who" worked so fast he "could have done away with a hundred more" in less than an hour.[27] But Potosí was a mere taste of what was to come. For four months Gálvez traveled the region, conducting 3,000 trials, ordering 85 executions and 73 floggings, banishing 117, and condemning 675 men to a life of hard labor.[28]

"These punishments horrified the entire kingdom, accustomed as it was to see only convicted criminals led to the scaffold, after confession, in conformity with wise laws," one anonymous observer commented. Gálvez even seemed to have shocked himself with the ferocity of his justice and was seen weeping uncontrollably as he "climbed onto the scaffold and lectured the people" about the "need for the most severe punishment." He appeared consumed by guilt and openly confessed that "an infinite number of mistakes will clearly come to light if the many cases in which I have ruled in so short a time are carefully examined."[29] He told Croix that he had suffered a "violent distemper in my brain" because of "my enormous labors" and wrote to an official in Madrid, "It seems I am only here to suffer the greatest trials and tribulations. Woe is me, may God get me out of here!"[30]

Junípero Serra was overjoyed when he learned the Franciscans had been charged with taking over the Jesuit missions, and that he had been chosen to lead fifteen friars to California. But the college authorities at San Fernando were reluctant to take on the isolated peninsula and persuaded the viceroy to send them to Sonora instead. Serra sent Palóu to Mexico City to negotiate, and a combination of Gálvez's support and a new guardian at San Fernando restored the original arrangement. Serra sailed for Loreto in April 1768.[31]

In May, Gálvez was already at Guadalajara on his way to the port at San Blas when he received his official orders from Madrid to send an exploratory expedition to Monterey.[32] He convened a special *junta* to plan the logistics of this ambitious project. They determined that presidios and missions should be established at both San Diego and Monterey and decided to send two large parties overland, to be supported by two ships recently constructed at San Blas: the *San Carlos* and *San Antonio*.[33]

Gálvez spent eight months at Loreto, working to establish Baja as a base for the greatest expansion of the Spanish Empire in North America since Juan de Oñate marched into New Mexico. At Loreto, Gálvez learned firsthand that his Promised Land was no Ophir, for even the famous pearl fisheries of the southern gulf shores had been overfished into near oblivion.[34] The following year, he turned his attention to Sonora, establishing his headquarters at the mining center of Álamos, today a beautiful colonial town set in a verdant valley and famous for its festival of classical music. For three and a half months he worked tirelessly to establish a bank, an office of the treasury, and other administrative institutions.

With an eye to the future, Gálvez wrote Croix, asking him to send Gálvez's nephew Bernardo to the north so he might learn the crafts and arts of frontier warfare. In April, Bernardo reached Chihuahua, where Captain Lope de Cuéllar was preparing a long campaign across the broad arc of *Apachería*, "Apache Land," from the Pecos River in Texas to the Gila in Arizona. Cuéllar tried to appoint Bernardo as captain of fifty volunteers, but Uncle José wrote, "We may expect bravery and loyal service from one so young, but as yet he has neither wisdom nor experience."[35] Instead, Bernardo de Gálvez took charge of the day-to-day command of the troops while serving directly under Cuéllar, and the two men quickly formed a close friendship.

The tranquility of Gálvez's bureaucratic interlude at Álamos was shattered when a handful of Indian villages in the former Jesuit mission fields along the Fuerte River reacted angrily to the imposition of new taxes and an attempt to stop them from carrying their traditional weapons. A group of insurgents attacked some Spanish militiamen, killing three of them. Gálvez responded by executing twenty-one villagers.[36] Again he seems to have been distressed by his own brutal response. "Such evils must be sacrificed on the altar of the law," he told the Governor of Sonora, but continued that for all "it may be important to look after my own health at the moment, there is too much to do, my mind wants to wander everywhere." Eight days later he admitted that he was "really unwell" because "the climate here does not suit me and I am weary of the serious problems of these provinces." He wrote to Croix that he was about to die.[37]

Gálvez began to behave so strangely that he was confessed by a priest in preparation for death. During Indian festivities to celebrate Michaelmas, he danced all night and partook of those "strange stews that are only delicious to Indians" and were presumably made with peyote.[38] He again fell into a deep depression, but a few days later he woke up his sergeant major in the middle of the night to tell him that he had received a dispatch from Saint Francis of Assisi "warning him that his commanders were ignorant of how to wage war against the Indians and that he could defeat the enemy simply by bringing six hundred *monas*, or "monkeys," from Guatemala, dressing them as soldiers, and making them run around the Cerro Prieto," where the Indians were ensconced. Modern critics have always assumed that these *monas* must have been monkeys, but the word had long been slang for "drunkard," in its origin "an unhappy and melancholic drunk."[39] Had Gálvez perhaps turned to the absurdly potent regional tequila known as Bacanora? He woke up ten soldiers and shook them by the hand, asking them for their friendship, before ordering the treasurer to pay each man whatever he asked for out of the government coffers. The officers and officials distracted Gálvez with breakfast, but during the meal he threatened to "cut off the head of anyone who discussed his state of mind and burn it on a bonfire."[40] The surgeon diagnosed "malign fever." Gálvez was "bled five times in three days," but remained out of his mind. His closest confidants warned Croix and sent urgent word to Bernardo.

*   *   *

In late April, a troublesome Chiricahua Apache chief called Frijoles turned up at the presidio at Janos, seemingly suing for peace. Lope de Cuéllar sent word that that this potentially dangerous visitor should be held prisoner. A few days later Chiricahua raiders captured five soldiers as they went about their preparations for the coming campaign against the Apaches.[41] No one was killed, few horses seem to have been taken, but the Chiricahuas now had a handful of hostages of their own. As Cuéllar marched his army toward Janos, two old Chiricahua women approached the camp carrying a letter that offered peace and the return of the hostages in exchange for Frijoles. It was Bernardo's first serious lesson in the ways of frontier diplomacy.

Bernardo wrote the official report of the ensuing campaign, which gives us a remarkable first glimpse into the mind of this insightful and resourceful soldier and servant of the Spanish Crown. Very much his own man as well as a leader of other men, his bravery and honorable nature are evident from this documentary outset.

Cuéllar decided to press on toward Janos with Bernardo and a detachment of thirty cavalrymen, who could move more quickly through the mountains than the main body of troops. When they reached Janos, Cuéllar sent a small party to climb a nearby hill and send smoke signals to let the Chiricahuas know that the commander had arrived. Then Cuéllar set about interrogating Frijoles: "I have found it necessary to detain you . . . for experience has shown how fickle you Indians can be. For no reason, you broke the peace agreement we had at El Paso, last year."

"I came to these parts at the invitation of various war chiefs who asked me to join them on a raid to rustle horses," Frijoles confessed.

"Therefore, by holding you I can secure the peace which you have asked for."

A week later, two women arrived at the presidio. They were given something to eat, allowed to rest, then were interviewed by the officers.

"We have been sent by a war chief who goes by the name El Zurdo, or 'Southpaw,' to ask you to release Frijoles."

Cuéllar pointed out to them that two different emissaries had previously turned up offering to exchange Frijoles for all five of the captives.

"There is no way that they are going to hand over more than a single soldier for Frijoles," one woman explained. "The others will be brought one by one in exchange for horses, food, and other things. We Indians are not so foolish as to hand over all the hostages at once."

Frijoles himself pointed out that El Zurdo was reneging on his earlier offer, but the women were adamant.

"Where are the hostages held?" someone asked.

"They are being held near the presidio," one of the women replied.

Then the women handed over a letter written by one of the Spanish captives, dated June 17, in which he explained that four of them had been moved eighty leagues from Janos, to a large encampment among some cottonwoods, with nearly 250 armed warriors and 400 women, children, and old men.

Cuéllar ordered everyone to be as friendly as possible to the two women. But the next day, Janos came to life, and as night fell, he set out as silently as possible with a column of over 160 cavalrymen, volunteers, and their Indian allies to hunt down El Zurdo and his people. At dawn, they reached a fine campsite, well hidden by trees and bushes, where they rested. As dusk came on, they resumed their march. In the morning, their Ópata scouts found fresh tracks. The Chiricahuas were on the move.

"Have they left because they have got wind of us?" the frustrated Cuéllar wondered. "Or simply because of their usual sense of insecurity?" He had no doubts about what to do next. "We must follow the tracks right away," he ordered, "in case they are running away."[42] The hunt was on.

The scouts found a large campsite that El Zurdo had clearly fled in great haste. Cooking pots and water barrels were lying overturned on the ground. The Indians had left behind meat and other foodstuffs, and even their bedding was scattered about the place.

Cuéllar could smell blood, metaphorically speaking.

The tracks were clear. The cavalry galloped on. They spied the Indians, moving fast along a jagged ridge above them. "Our commander knew only too well," Bernardo wrote, "that however hard he tried to hunt down the enemy, it would be useless. They were too far away. Even if he climbed the crags, the enemy were so fleet of foot that they would have scrambled to another ridge and then another."[43]

Cuéllar ordered the interpreter to shout to them, "Do not flee! We are only here to recover a couple of the hostages from you and then discuss the truce that you have asked for."

"We have no captives here. They have been taken elsewhere," came the reply. "We are many and we will defend the pass." With that, the Indians swore terrible insults and made lewd gestures. When Cuéllar ordered his men to attack, the Indians disappeared into the distant mountains. But one of the captives managed to escape.

"Their camp is on the Mimbres River, where I saw plenty of crops growing and a good herd of horses," the man explained. "But they knew they had to sue for peace on every front as soon as they heard about your expedition."[44]

The Apaches might want peace, but Cuéllar wanted war. Bernardo described how he ordered a forced march to a crossing point on the Casa Grandes River, still called Vado de Piedra, "Rocky Ford," twenty-two miles south of

Columbus, New Mexico, and then on to *Los Ojos de San Francisco*, "Saint Francis Springs," a group of fine pools of deep, sweet water, a mile or two south of the modern border. There, amid the lush vegetation, Cuéllar began preparing his army for battle. Messengers rode fast, carrying requests for provisions and reinforcements. Word was sent to El Paso, asking for an experienced tracker who knew the hills to the north. Bridles jangled, the sound of steel being whetted on the wet boulders grated through the air, and there was the clickety-click of riflemen cleaning their guns. For most of these soldiers this was the first time they would venture deep into Apache territory, up among the crags and parched valleys beyond modern Silver City, the bastions of the Indian heartland where sixty years later the great Geronimo himself would be born.

Cuéllar led this huge force across the modern border, gathering small groups of Ópata allies as it moved northeast. That afternoon, as the vanguard skirted the Florida hills south of modern Deming, scouts skirmished with Apaches, who fled toward the Mimbres Mountains. Five days later, the trackers found fresh signs of the enemy near some cornfields, the isolated patch of farmland you can still see south of I-10 just before it drops toward Las Cruces. The following day, a detachment of forty-odd Ópata scouts came upon an ill-prepared Apache encampment and slaughtered ten men, three boys, and fifteen women. They also took some women and children prisoner.

Reconnaissance parties found signs that most of the Apaches had recently climbed high into exceptionally harsh, precipitous terrain. Cuéllar stripped down his fighting force. He sent the main supply caravan under heavy guard to establish a base at a place he called *Ojo Caliente*, "Warm Spring." Aware that the horses might struggle among the crags and canyons, Cuéllar ordered most of his troops to march on foot, keeping only a small detachment of cavalry. The hardiest mules were shod with iron and loaded with enough food and ammunition for a month.

By now, Bernardo must have begun to wonder whether they were advancing into a trap.

The following day, a single scout led the fighting force into Provinger Canyon, below Cookes Peak, through "terrain that was very hard going for the pack animals."[45] Cuéllar had to put his Ópata allies to work, cutting down trees to improve the trail. On July 28, they entered a steep valley and the scouts returned with reports that the night before they had seen campfires. As night fell, Cuéllar led his men along a canyon running parallel to the main trail in an attempt to outflank the enemy, but in a sudden violent storm they found it impossible to pick their way through the rocky terrain in the wet and the dark.

The following day, the scouts reported the enemy was within reach. Cuéllar inspected his troops and their weapons. He gave each soldier fifteen extra bullets, powder, and flints. The Indian allies were armed with lances, pistols, and rifles. Forty men were left to guard the mules and the horses, so "their continual whinnying would not give us away."[46] Cuéllar sent a contingent of fifty Jumano Indians to occupy a height that the scouts reckoned would cut off any Apache retreat. Then, in the dead of night, a hundred volunteers and two hundred Indian allies crept silently toward the Apache camp.[47] Cuéllar ordered that absolute silence be maintained. The signal to attack would be a single rifle shot followed by the battle cry of the Indian allies.

The men moved quickly, but as dawn broke they were not yet in position. The scouts reported that all they could see were horses, so Cuéllar took a look himself, leading the men behind him so as not to split them up.

The Apaches had yet again given him the slip. Bernardo notes that "this greatly infuriated the commander," and "he sent 150 Indian allies to look for any enemy camp" they could find. If they did so, "half of them should remain hidden, while the others continued the search farther on."[48]

Almost as soon as they set out, the Indian allies "spotted an Apache camp" and "attacked with the typical impetuousness of a disorderly nation, hollering their battle cries." They "chased the enemy down off the heights, killing fourteen of them." But as they carried the pursuit onto the neighboring crag, a great host of Apaches "had more than enough time to arm themselves and come to the aid of their friends." They timed their retaliation to perfection, attacking "when most of our men had spread out to collect the horses and some useless old bits of leather that were lying around in the tepees." Suddenly, "our Indians realized that they could not contain the furious enemy charge and they appealed for urgent support."

"If we abandon this vantage point," Cuéllar declared, "the enemy will take it."

"But," Bernardo explained, there was nothing Cuéllar could do. "He had to rescue our allies." Moreover, Bernardo wrote, spitting scorn, "He could not even leave a company to guard the position, because these people do not have even the slightest experience of battle, and most of them were terrified by the endless raids they have suffered back home." Bernardo was not impressed by these volunteer soldiers.

The Apaches rained arrows onto the terrified troops from the cover of the trees. One went clean through the leg of a frightened soldier. Panic spread through the ranks. Cuéllar, Bernardo, and the other officers only just managed to rally their cowardly men. Then the riflemen opened fire, and it was the turn of the Apaches to run for their lives, flitting through the rocks and trees to reach the safety of higher ground. For the moment, the allies were safe, and Bernardo was in no doubt that Cuéllar's prompt action had saved them from oblivion. But the fighting continued.

Cuéllar ordered Bernardo to take two companies of volunteers to relieve the Jumanos who had taken up positions to cut off the Apache withdrawal. He led his men onto the crags above them, where he found them already retreating. "So on this occasion," Bernardo wrote, Captain Gálvez "had to do very little." The pride of a young officer entrusted with such a dangerous task in the heat of battle oozes from Bernardo's account, for all that he tried to hide it. He ordered his men to hold their positions and fire, but soon recognized the futility of such tactics. The Apaches simply disappeared into their surroundings.

Cuéllar's retreat was a *tour de force* of military command, and Bernardo explained it in excited detail. The soldiers moved slowly down the narrow valley, in formation, following three dry streambeds. The exhausted professional troops had the discipline and the marksmen to cover the whole army. First, one company would face the enemy and take aim, but hold their fire while the others fell back twenty paces. These would then halt, turn, and do the same for their comrades. Slowly, they reached a dangerously narrow and steep-sided gorge dominated by Apache archers. Cuéllar knew his men were too tired to take the high ground and skirt round this coffinlike pass. He ordered two lines of soldiers to face the heights on each side of the canyon, while the Jumanos covered the rearguard and the Ópata took the van. With guns bristling on all four fronts, the whole army shuffled into the gorge.

"Hold your fire," Cuéllar told his men.

The Apaches were fooled and came closer and closer. Still Cuéllar would not give the order. More and more Apaches approached, succumbing to their collective bravado, surrounding the invading army. With so many of the enemy in the marksmen's sights, finally the order came. The rifles cracked, gunshots and bullets ricocheting about the rocky walls of the claustrophobic canyon.

"We had the satisfaction to kill many of them," Bernardo wrote. At the final reckoning, they counted forty Apache dead.

Cuéllar's force emerged from the terrifying confines of the gorge and counted their own casualties. An Ópata ally was dead, a Norteño and three Jumanos were missing. Fifteen men were wounded, including the surgeon. Every officer knew they might all have been massacred that day. Bernardo de Gálvez had seen his first serious action in Apachería.

As the army withdrew toward El Paso, there was palpable relief. Bernardo described coming to "the banks of a little stream," lined by abundant fields all "planted with corn, squash, and beans." They stopped so the men could "pick the vegetables and feed the plants to their animals." Yet "for all they harvested, there was an infinite amount more" they had to leave behind.[49] There was a moment of rejoicing when one of the soldiers heard from across the river the shouts of his brother, who had been captured at Chihuahua, but had escaped.

Cuéllar was clearly angered by his Apache adversaries, who saw warfare as part of life and everyday life as part of their warfare. "How difficult it is to engage an enemy who bases victory on headlong flight," he complained.[50] But Bernardo was deeply impressed, and some years later he published a brilliant essay, *Observations and Reflections on Apache Warfare in New Spain*.[51]

"The Indian is generally of sound character because of his tough upbringing," he began. "The simplicity of the foods he eats," as well as "constantly going hunting and to war," made him "resilient" and "robust." Bernardo praised almost every aspect of the Apaches as a fighting force. "The skill, ability, and dexterity with which they carry out a raid is quite incredible. They camouflage their bodies with mud and their heads with grasses so that they look like bushes," he marveled. "They can creep up on our soldiers in total silence, yet at the same time they communicate by imitating the call of some nocturnal bird such as an owl or the howl of a coyote or a wolf." Then, suddenly, "they attack with such speed as is impossible to describe." Their weapon of choice was the bow and arrow, "by far the most terrible when they handle them. Indeed, I believe them to be better than rifles, for they have the same effect at short range, yet they can loose so many arrows that they can kill twenty men in the time it takes to reload."[52] "We Spaniards accuse them of cruelty," yet "I do not know what they must think of us?" Then he answered his own rhetorical question by explaining they "wage war against us out of hatred, a hatred born of such tyrannies they have suffered as are too shameful to mention."[53]

By contrast, Bernardo paints a picture of the Spanish troops as lumbering. They were not fit enough to campaign on foot, but needed their horses, which needed food, which required a whole mule train, which could only follow trails with plenty of water and left obvious tracks. "So it seems to me that for all that it would be impossible for we Spaniards to wage war as the Indians do, we could use tactics more like theirs, which are the best." Bernardo's method for achieving this was simplicity itself: "In the first place we should take more Indian allies on campaign, for like the Apaches they are fleet of foot, skillful, and sure shots with a bow and arrow." It is difficult to see how he could have been more candid.

At Chihuahua, Bernardo and Cuéllar received the alarming news of José de Gálvez's mental breakdown. Both of them rushed to join the escort then taking the inspector general to Mexico City.[54] The travails of that journey soon brought on another bout of Gálvez's lunacy, and Bernardo must have been dismayed as his uncle claimed, in quick succession, to be "the king of Prussia, then Charles XII of Sweden, Lieutenant Admiral of Spain, an immortal, and finally, to cap it all, the Eternal Father and even the Word of God on the Day of Judgment."[55]

Remarkably, José de Gálvez appeared so sane and stable by the time he reached Mexico City at the end of May 1770 that he was allowed to return to the heart of government, continuing to formulate policy for the northern frontier and bringing about the establishment of the Comandancia General of the Internal Provinces.[56] José de Gálvez never forgot northern New Spain, and many years later, when Charles III elevated him to the aristocracy, he took the title Marquis of Sonora, out of respect for the province that had sent him temporarily mad.

In Mexico City, Bernardo was appointed Commandant of the Nueva Vizcaya and Sonora Frontier, with 250 well-armed and well-provisioned troops at his command and orders to once again take the fight to the Apaches. He dallied in Chihuahua to watch a bullfight and let his men enjoy the fiesta, then the following day, presumably hungover from their revels, the army marched northeast and crossed the Rio Grande on the ancient Indian road later known as the Comanche Trail. They pursued a large Apache army through freezing rainstorms, which spoiled their provisions and dampened their spirits. Many men deserted. On November 1, 1770, Bernardo reached the Pecos River with the remaining 130 soldiers and Indian allies at a place he called Matias's Ford after his father, now Horsehead Crossing, ten miles north of Garvin, Texas.[57] By then, the company was in part surviving on unripe dates scavenged from the palm trees. That night there was plenty of talk in the ranks about returning to the comfort and safety of Chihuahua to restock.

But the following morning, Don Bernardo Vicente de Gálvez y Madrid showed himself a true leader and harangued his men: "Soldiers, our time has come. This is our last chance to show our mettle to the world. You have confronted cold and snow with joy. We have seen hunger thanks to rains sent from the heavens that have spoiled our supplies. I know not how many days or months before we face the enemy. But should we go to Chihuahua now, we will lose all trace of him, we will blush for shame at the time and money we will have wasted.

"I will go on alone, *yo solo*, even if none of you come with me. I will bring back a scalp to Chihuahua or I will die earning the king's bread that I have eaten. Over yonder is the road for home. Be gone, if your heart is base. But follow me if you yearn for glorious fight and no other reward than the grace of God!"[58] With that, brave Bernardo spurred on his horse and rode out alone into the swollen stream.

His men shouted with a single voice, "We will follow you to our deaths! We will eat our horses and then the very stones themselves!"

With cheers and whoops of joyous courage, the army crossed the Pecos. The scouts picked up the trail, and the men spent the night in breathless, silent vigil, their horses saddled, every man eager for the fray. They surrounded the enemy camp as dawn approached, and when the first light fell on the battlefield, Bernardo gave the proud and ancient battle shout of Castile: "Santiago!"

His men fell upon the panicked Apaches. Some threw themselves into the river and started swimming for their lives. Bernardo chased down the few who reached the other bank but let most of them drown in the fast-flowing water. He took a prize of 204 horses and mules and 36 men and women captives. Twenty-eight Apache men were killed without the loss of a single soldier. Three weeks later, the troops rode proudly into Chihuahua, bloody Indian scalps hanging from their saddlebags.[59]

Over the following months, the settlements of the northern frontier suffered wave after wave of raiding. In December, the annual caravan from New Mexico was attacked and all its horses and mules stolen. In April 1771, Bernardo won an impressive victory on the Puerco River, defeating an army of 250 Apaches with a force of barely 100 men. Such action did nothing to quieten the conflict. Later that year, he had to abandon the annual fiestas of Chihuahua and rode out alone to take charge of an operation to contain yet another raid. On the road, he was attacked by five Indians, but escaped with an arrow stuck in one arm and two serious wounds to his chest. He abandoned his convalescence to set out on one last campaign into Apachería but was thrown by his horse, badly hurting his ribs as he fell and causing an injury of which he complained for the rest of his life.

On September 22, 1771, at ten o'clock in the morning in the charming village of San Cristóbal, set among the cooling canals and market gardens of Xochimilco in the southern suburbs of Mexico City, the Marquis of Croix formally handed over the Viceroyalty of New Spain to the former Governor of Cuba Antonio María de Bucareli. A month later, José de Gálvez sought permission to return to Spain, but it is a measure of his miraculously rapid rehabilitation that he was ordered to remain in Mexico City to brief and support the new viceroy during the first months of his reign, and the two Andalusians struck up a cordial relationship.[60]

Bernardo returned to Mexico City in December 1771 and made preparations to return to Spain with his uncle José. Before he left, he handed over his command to Hugo O'Conor, another "Wild Goose," as the Irishmen who served in the Spanish military were known, a soldier who shared Bernardo's warrior spirit and deep respect for his Apache enemies. They gave him the nickname Red Chief because of his flaming hair and beard.[61] There can be little doubt that the irony was intentional and not lost on these bright, clever men. O'Conor would design a new defensive system for the northern border-lands based on a chain of presidios strung out like planets across a troubled heaven.

José and Bernardo de Gálvez took ship for Spain on February 18, 1772.[62] Both men realized the administration of the colonies should be their future, and Uncle José was no doubt already dreaming and scheming to make the government of the Americas the family business.

Bucareli proved something of a reluctant ruler. He wrote his only really close friend, the brilliant Irish-born army officer Alejandro O'Reilly, that he had "no desire to be a viceroy forever" and frankly admitted that he "had no idea what to make of the world" after his first experiences of Mexico City. "I need more time," he explained. Great "confusion reigns," he complained to O'Reilly, "between the old system and the new, which is only halfway to being estab-lished."[63] Moreover, "I am proceeding with great caution, so as not to coun-teract the innovations or undermine them without some understanding of their practical utility." Bucareli could not have identified more clearly for his contemporaries and modern readers the essential, interconnected problems of Bourbon authoritarianism. It is axiomatic that political change is not easy to effect on the ground and will often founder in the attempt. If major institu-tional changes are to succeed, then they must have some clear, practical benefit for all the parties involved in making those changes. Yet after long consulta-tion with Gálvez, the architect of change in New Spain, Bucareli candidly confessed to his friend that he could not see the point of the still half-baked reforms he was supposed to help bring to fruition. "God give me strength to unravel the chaos and confusion in these vast provinces," he prayed.[64]

CHAPTER 17

Junípero Serra,
Paradise Gained

Alta California

So we should not die of hunger, I ordered that at the end of each day's march, one of the mules should be slaughtered. We then made a hole in the ground, set a fire, and half fried, half roasted its flesh . . . We just shut our eyes and devoured it like famished lions. We ate twelve in all . . . We all smelled horribly of mule.

—GÁSPAR DE PORTOLÁ

TODAY, ESPECIALLY IN THE CONTEXT of Californian history, we most readily think of a "mission" as the physical architecture of church, cloister, and other buildings. But to Serra and the Franciscan padres, a "mission" was a concept, a spiritual campaign against the devil, a special operation against a spiritual enemy, an embassy from God that would reinforce the faith where the presence of the Church was faltering or introduce Christianity where the Church was altogether unknown. The word described a host of peaceful activities, from religious instruction to social indoctrination, which the padres believed would best strengthen the presence of Christianity and save the souls of the community to which they were missionaries. For most proselytizing pioneers in the New World, the physical presence of the settlements they established—the buildings and fields, the fences, walls, and irrigation systems—were the stage on which to play out their drama of indoctrination and conversion.

Throughout the history of Spanish colonization in the Americas, the purpose in founding so many missions was the conversion of Native Americans to Christianity so as to save their souls. It was believed that conversion went hand in glove with the "civilization" of the "savages." The Indians would come to love God as their toil in the fields and routine around the missions brought stability to their lives and put food in their stomachs. This policy was firmly rooted in a conviction that European society was innately superior because it was Christian. The friars' work was to replace the multiple cultures of the New World and their diverse economies and religions with the Old World ideal of hardworking peasant farmers tilling the soil, husbanding animals, marrying, raising children, and attending church.

On the basis of archeological evidence and the reports of a few passing sailors, scholars estimate that about 300,000 Native Americans were living in Alta California in 1769.[1] By the late 1820s, the best estimates suggest that number had reduced to 250,000.[2] It seems, then, that the arrival of Serra and Portolá did not herald any catastrophic collapse due to Old World disease, probably because the population had already been indirectly exposed to European contagion via neighboring tribes. However, experts in the field believe the proliferation of European animals and crops brought by missionaries and soldiers seriously disrupted traditional Indian ways of life, bringing about a fall in population.

By the early 1820s, the missions had flocks of 200,000 sheep and herds of 150,000 cattle and 20,000 horses. Similar numbers must have belonged to the presidios, while tens of thousands more must have strayed beyond the Spaniards' ken. The suggestion is that these ungulates became almost biblically pestilential, consuming everything before moving on, dispersing along the valleys of California in search of plants to graze. One groundbreaking study has the title *A Plague of Sheep*.[3] As the animals moved, they carried the seeds of European plants in their guts, slowly sowing them in nutritious dollops of manure until they began to overrun the indigenous vegetation. The theory postulates that as a result, ever more Indians migrated to the missions as the worlds of their ancestors disappeared, consumed by the multiple alien species. At the missions, they and their culture withered on the vine of an alien doctrine and a brutal regime of labor and early-morning prayer. However, about the only accurate sets of figures we have are for the population of the missions themselves, which reached a peak in the 1820s of around twenty thousand.[4] If there really were a quarter of a million Indians living in California at that time, clearly fewer than nine out of ten of them were attracted by European serfdom or were sufficiently deprived by environmental collapse to actually be counted as living in the missions.[5]

From the outset, in Alta California, Gálvez had wanted to dominate the harbors and havens of the Western Seaboard. He clearly understood the missions as staking a claim to territory, as much as Serra believed that through them God was staking a claim to the souls of the inhabitants. Missions and military posts had always been closely associated in the imperial imagination, but the isolation of Alta California meant that the cross and the sword were intimately entwined in what would prove a fractious and hostile marriage from which there could be no divorce.

Serra would personally found the first nine of the twenty-one missions eventually established in Alta California between 1769 and 1823. His description of the newly finished San Carlos at Carmel allows us to glimpse the physical surroundings in which the friars pursued their vocation. The main building was just over 150 feet long by 45 wide and was divided into six rooms, including a large store, an office, a parlor, and three cells, one of which was being used as a chapel until the church was finished. The sturdy structure was built of thick pine beams, half-rendered with gravel, covered with a mud daub, then whitewashed. The roof was made of pine and cottonwood timbers closely packed with gravel, covered with grass, and sealed with packed earth. "Ten doors with their locks, latches, and knockers had already been hung on their hinges," Serra was proud to report, "all made of pine, cottonwood, and some very fine and handsome wood that is a red color." They had furnished their new main mission house with water jars, bookshelves, folding chairs, two long benches, two tables, and a few traveling trunks or chests. As he explained, "What matters is that we have a place to live that we can lock up." A smaller building was intended to serve as a dormitory for women converts and had a couple of extra rooms attached, one of which was being used as a hen coop. A small barracks for guardsmen was ten yards or so in length. It had its own cooking area separate from the main kitchen hut, which served the religious community and any Indian visitors.[6]

The life of the neophytes was hard. A French naval officer who visited Monterey in 1786 described how "corporal punishment is inflicted on the Indians of both sexes who fail in their religious devotions, while plenty of sins that in Europe are considered the business of divine justice are here punished by being clapped in irons or locked in the stocks." Indians who ran away were hunted down by the soldiers and publicly whipped. A Russian critic claimed that runaway Indians still "bleeding from their wounds" were "bound with rawhide ties, tied to stakes and beaten with the strap." He may or may not have been exaggerating, for he goes on to describe how one man died after he was left out in the sun all day, sewn into the warm, blood-wet hide of a calf that had died that morning. Serra himself defended corporal punishment for the wayward, pointing out to a critical viceroy, "The padres have whipped their children, the Indians, throughout the conquest of these kingdom and so often that even the earliest saints did so."[7]

Gaspar de Portolá, Governor of California, took command of the military component of Serra's Santa Expedición, or "Holy Expedition," to establish missions and presidios at San Diego and Monterey. Fernando Rivera y Moncada would march an advance party overland to San Diego, followed by the main body of the expedition under Portolá. Captain Pedro Fages would travel with a contingent of Catalan Volunteers, who had been blooded in Sonora the previous year, aboard the *San Carlos*, captained by Vicente Vila. Juan Pérez, perhaps the most able seaman in the Pacific, would bring the *San Antonio*. The voyage to California was dangerous and difficult, for contrary prevailing winds meant pilots had to take the ships far out into the ocean in search of "changing more useful winds," then "go a long way north to get windward of their port of destination."[8] As if to illustrate the point, a third ship attached to the expedition was lost at sea on the way to San Diego.

Rivera mustered the advance party at a fine campsite that the Cochimí called Velicatá, 330 miles northwest of Loreto, once earmarked by the Jesuits as an excellent site for a mission. On Good Friday, March 24, 1769, at four o'clock in the afternoon, Rivera gave the order to load up the mules. Twenty-five soldiers, three muleteers, forty-two Baja Indian servants, all armed with bows and arrows, and Juan Crespí set out for their Promised Land.[9] The expedition cartographer, José Cañizares, described their journey through a "sterile world of thistles, thorns, and the odd palm tree," dominated by towering "boojum and saguaro cacti" and the endless sprawl of the "prickly pears." But by the beginning of April, they started to see "cottonwoods, cypresses, and alder tress," and in May they came across so "delightful and pleasant a campsite . . . with plenty of delicious well water and fecund ground ready to be planted" that Crespí thought it "the best of many good sites he had seen at which to found a mission."[10]

Pima Indians, however, already lived on the land. Rivera ended a hostile standoff near Ensenada by firing at the enemy archers. "The sound of a bullet was medicine enough," Cañizares reported, "to send the blighters packing."[11] But as they approached the modern international border, Rivera and Crespí had their first encounter with the Kumeyaay, who had inhabited the region around San Diego for twelve thousand years. Both sides were tentatively friendly, and the Spaniards visited an encampment of "sixty-two of them," by Cañizares's count. "They addressed us at great length, which left me none the wiser as I did not understand a word of it," he explained.[12]

The party finally reached the end of the rugged uplands on May 13 and saw the Tijuana River valley spread out below them with San Diego Bay in the distance. They followed the shore and turned inland to camp on the banks of the river. They were now within the modern United States. An Indian *cacique* approached and made a long speech. In an unsettling portent, one of his men cocked his bow and pointed his arrow at a trooper before withdrawing. That evening, the party could not "find firewood to make tortillas," so Rivera "allowed" the cooks "to burn his tent poles" instead, a chivalrous gesture he must have regretted within hours, for it poured with rain overnight. The next day, they saw two ships at anchor, their masts gently swaying with the swell.[13] The two parts of the expedition were reunited, and Crespí described how he and Brother Vizcaíno hugged each other. "It was a moment of great rejoicing and celebration for all of us," Crespí wrote, until "we found that their camp was more of a hospital, for almost all the soldiers and sailors from the two ships seemed to be dying of scurvy."[14]

Juan Pérez had arrived first with the *San Antonio* after a horrendous voyage that took fifty-five days, almost double the usual time it took to sail across the Atlantic to Europe. His men were weak and debilitated, but the *San Carlos* came into San Diego after a voyage of 110 days. Almost everything had gone wrong, and only Captain Vila's brilliance as a sailor and Fages's ability to maintain the morale of his troops had prevented disaster and mutiny. Fages and an experienced military engineer called Miguel Costansó were in no doubt that had they arrived any later, everyone who had sailed on the *San Carlos* would have "perished miserably."[15]

On May 1, Fages, Costansó, and twenty men had gone ashore in search of water. They waved white handkerchiefs at a band of Indians, who kept their distance. From time to time, the Indians "drove the end of their bows into the ground and danced around them at an indescribable speed," but then "ran off as soon as we approached." "Our boys could not catch them," Costansó reported, "because they were so weak after the long voyage that they had almost forgotten how to walk."[16]

Fages offered the Indians gifts of baubles and trinkets, and through gestures the Spaniards tried to explain they were thirsty. The Indians led them to a distant spinney that grew among the "sweet smells of rosemary, sage, and roses" that flourished among the "wild vines" on the banks of the San Diego River.[17] As they drank the cool, clear water, they smelled the fragrance of Paradise. Costansó enthused about the game and the birdlife, from buzzards to mockingbirds, cranes to hummingbirds, and crows to cardinals, with their pointed red plumes, not to mention the ducks and geese "of every shape and size." The sea, he crooned, was full of fish, including "sole and plaice that had the most delicate flavor despite their extraordinary size" and "clams and shellfish of every kind."[18]

They visited the "shady arbors and mud-plastered wigwams" where their hosts lived. "Every man, woman, and child came to greet them, thirty or forty families, in all." Costansó noticed their "curved wooden cudgels, in the shape of a saber, which they hurl spinning through the air, making a great noise," with which they could regularly hit a viper or other fast-moving prey from a great distance.[19]

By the time the Spaniards brought water to the ship, more men had died. Fages ordered the construction of a makeshift fort on the beach and set up the two cannons. They used the sails and awnings from the boats to make large tents to serve as hospitals for the sick. The expedition surgeon was suffering as much as his patients, but with his meager supply of medicines already used up, he made a valiant effort to gather herbs and plants from the undergrowth, claiming he knew their healing properties, then concocting his own potions to offer some hope of a cure.[20] By day, the sun burned down unrelentingly; by night, damp cold air came in off the sea. "Two or three of them died every day," Costansó reported.

The Catalans began to turn on their commander. A corporal accused Captain Fages of hoarding a consignment of brandy, chocolate, and vinegar, which the surgeon needed to tend to the sick, and of refusing to give the surgeon "some chickens so he could feed some of the men with scurvy." "Plenty of chickens were wandering about the camp," the corporal remembered, but "don Pedro insisted that they were all his," and in the end "he ate them all himself, one by one."[21]

Serra had stayed his departure from his Baja headquarters at Loreto until after Easter, then dallied at San Francisco Xavier to appoint Palóu as president of the Baja missions. "The very special love that this minister and I have had for one another for so long was reason enough to delay," Serra remembered. Palóu fussed over his friend, making sure he had "foodstuffs, clothing, and all sorts of other creature comforts for the journey."[22] But, Palóu wrote, "when I saw the open sore on his swollen leg, I could not hold back my tears."

At the beginning of April, as Portolá was making preparations for the departure of his party from Velicatá, Serra founded the mission there and was soon overjoyed when a dozen Indians who had almost no experience of the colonial world came to visit. "I saw with my own eyes," he exclaimed, "that they go about as naked as Adam did in Paradise before the Fall," and "we spent a long time with them, yet although they saw that we were wearing clothes, they showed no sign of being ashamed." In that instant, he must have felt that these "pagans" were indeed the innocent children of his dreams, model noble savages ripe for conversion, their souls in desperate need of salvation through baptism. "One by one, I put my hands on their heads as a sign of love, and I filled their cupped hands with dried figs, which they began to eat." Adam and Eve hid their shame from the Lord with fig leaves, so to give these innocents figs in a ritual that closely approximated the Eucharist and for them to eat the figs as though taking Communion was charged with symbolism for Serra. By way of return, the Indians gave them "some roast mescal and four largish fish," in another apparently divine reference, to Jesus's exhortation to the fishermen Peter and Andrew to proselytize by telling them that he would make them "fishers of men."[23]

As the expedition headed north, Serra's flesh swelled up so badly around the jagged weeping wound on his leg that he was forced to spend two days in bed, unable to say mass.

"Father President," Portolá addressed him gravely, "Your Reverence can see that you cannot go on. I will have you taken to the last mission so that you can recover and join us later."

Serra refused, replying, "Sir, do not speak to me of such things." Portolá had his men construct a stretcher, like a "gurney for a corpse," Palóu noted, so that the Indians could carry the chronically sick Franciscan. But Serra was so horrified that his stubborn persistence was going to cause hard work for his beloved neophytes that he turned to one of the muleteers and asked, "My son, you must have some treatment for the wound on my leg, surely?"

"What do I know? Do you think I am some sort of physician? I am a teamster," replied the startled man. "I have only ever dealt with the saddle sores of animals."

"Son, I am nothing but an animal, and my wound is a saddle sore. But it is so painful that I cannot sleep, so apply the same ointments to me as you would to a mule."

Everyone within earshot chuckled at such eccentricity. But the muleteer mixed herbs with tallow, fried them up, then applied a poultice to the wound. That night, Serra slept soundly. At dawn, the pain was gone, the swelling had gone down, and he sang Matins. Soon after, he sang Prime, and "Portolá and all his men were amazed."[24]

On May 21, the Feast of the Holy Trinity, the expedition "came across an old Indian gentleman, as naked as the others." They "feted him with food and he told them that many of his people lived nearby." Serra was excited by this news of potential converts, whom he described as "this copious crop of gentiles, all apparently ripe and ready for the reapers." Then, "as he was talking to us," the old man "squatted down, right there with us all gathered around, and did his business," even as he went on "chatting away." "Then, having unburdened himself, he stood up and calmly" announced that he wanted to become a Christian.[25]

By June, "the thorns and stones of Baja have come to an end," Serra reported ecstatically, "for here the hillsides are deep with soil and there are so many beautiful flowers" and "so many blooming roses that an apothecary could set up business here." They crossed a stunning valley where a natural spring gushed into a pond so deep that one of the Indian pearl divers could not touch the bottom. "There were enough vines thereabouts to rival Noah's vineyards," Serra enthused.[26] Finally, on July 1, they sighted San Diego Bay, and "their hearts filled with such joy that the soldiers fired off a long volley." A return volley from the ships spurred them on, and a little before noon, Crespí and Brother Parrón rushed out of camp to greet Serra.[27]

Portolá was horrified: "Without exception, every member of the seaborne expedition, soldier, sailor, and officer alike, is suffering from scurvy." They were "in such an unhappy and deplorable state that I was deeply moved," he wrote the viceroy. "Some were lying flat on their backs, others were half-paralyzed, others could barely stand. This terrible disease has claimed the lives of thirty-one men already." Scarcely a dozen men were up and about.[28] Portolá agreed that Juan Pérez should take the *San Antonio* to New Spain and appeal for help, despite the lamentable state of the crew. He made San Blas twenty days later.[29]

Portolá was determined to comply with his orders to secure the harbor at Monterey, but Vila was clear that he lacked enough able-bodied men to sail the *San Carlos* in support. So Portolá took what he admitted to the viceroy, with considerable understatement, was "a somewhat risky decision" and resolved to lead the overland expedition to Monterey himself with only the most chimerical promise of maritime support from the *San José*, which had sailed from San Blas on May 11 and, in point of fact, was never heard of again.[30] Rivera objected strongly. He knew from his long experience on Baja that they could not possibly carry enough food for such a long exploration. Portolá brushed such worries aside, grandly saying "he would eat whatever the soldiers ate, and that if there was not enough for them then nor would he eat."[31] Portolá also took Fages, Costansó, and some of the convalescent Catalans, telling the surgeon they "would surely recover during the march" thanks to "the change of scenery." Serra admitted that he could not make the journey with his festering leg, so he sent Brothers Crespí and Gómez and remained behind with Vizcaíno and Parrón to help the surgeon attend to the sick and to found the mission at San Diego. Portolá left eight more or less able-bodied soldiers to protect the missionaries, the camp, and the *San Carlos*.[32]

The expedition set out in marching formation on July 14, with Portolá and Fages riding at the head of the column of six Catalans and a large troop of Baja Indian sappers, carrying shovels, pickaxes, hatchets, and other tools of their rank, ready to open up the road ahead. Then came one hundred pack mules, carrying enough provisions to last six months, driven by their teamsters and guarded by a large number of soldiers. Rivera brought up the rear with the remainder of the cavalry, some Baja Indians, and a convoy of spare horses and mules.[33]

A fortnight out of San Diego, they reached the Santa Ana River, where they camped in "the most beautiful of meadows," according to Crespí. There, on the July 28, "at midday, they felt three great rumblings in the space of less than an hour." This first documented earthquake in Californian history shook Crespí into prayer. "The strongest tremor was the first, which lasted as long as it takes to say the Credo." The aftershocks he dismissed as taking "less than an Ave Maria," although "the ground shook a lot each time."[34]

As the Sierra Madre Mountains loomed into view above Santa Barbara, Rivera again challenged Portolá, emphasizing "the danger they were in" and pointing out that "Gálvez's orders were to send two ships ahead" of any land expedition. "Remember what happened to the Spaniards who first explored Florida," Rivera warned.[35] Portolá ignored him and commanded the expedition to turn west along the coast.[36]

In early September, about twenty miles north of modern Vandenberg Air Force Base, some friendly Indians brought the carcass of a huge if rather emaciated bear to the explorers' camp, so big that Crespí was deeply unsettled. But the soldiers were in a jocular mood and called the place Thin Bear Camp.[37] Today, the nearby lake is still called Oso Flaco Lake, "Thin Bear Lake." Perhaps the most surprising legacy of Portolá's march in search of Monterey is that many of the names the soldiers casually gave to places along the way are still in use today. The petroleum seeps near Los Angeles are called La Brea Tar Pits because *brea* means "pitch" in Spanish. Crespí complained that it was "so sticky that I could not wash it off my hands even with soap and hot water." Carpinteria, near Santa Barbara, is named for Indian carpenters the explorers found making a canoe. Forty-five miles farther along the coast, they shot a *gaviota*, a "seagull," at modern Gaviota. Twenty miles beyond that, Cañada Del Cojo was named after the local chief, who was lame, or *cojo*. And so it goes on. At Espada Creek, an Indian made off with a sword, an *espada*.[38]

The explorers were often accompanied by friendly Indians, and Costansó was especially impressed by the "lively, hardworking," and "good-looking" Chumash Indians from the islands and mainland shores along the Santa Barbara Channel, with their "domed houses up to twenty yards across, with a fireplace in the middle" and "a chimney hole, which accommodated up to three or four families." Crespí thought their pottery jars looked as if they had been turned on the wheel and praised their skillfully woven baskets decorated with coral and bone.[39] These are the first attempts by Europeans to document the society and customs of indigenous Californians. They commented on the Indians' long capes made of valuable otter skins, on the solid construction of their boats, their rowing skills, and their ability as hunters. But they were also intrigued by the way the women roasted seeds by shaking them with red-hot stones in special baskets and then milled them in enormous and beautifully worked mortars. Costansó reported the great sense of ceremony surrounding the funerals of important leaders and noted that while there seemed to be a general principle of monogamy, the chiefs were apparently allowed two wives. He also commented that *berdaches* seemed to be common, noting, "In all of their settlements they had no qualms about men who wore feminine jewelry and dressed and lived like women." Finally, he noted down a list of basic vocabulary, including the numbers from *pacà*, "one," to *kerxco*, "ten," and useful words such as *tomol*, "canoe"; *nucchù*, "head"; *huachajá*, "hand"; and, for some reason, *tocholò*, "armpit."[40]

The trail petered out high in the Santa Lucia mountains. The Baja sappers had to hack through tough bush to open a route over a high ridge. Some men who had left San Diego suffering from scurvy were still unwell; others had fallen sick along the way. Seventeen were now seriously incapacitated, placing a heavy burden on their comrades. Worse still, they had eaten over half of their rations.[41] A creeping desperation was abroad in the camp and an underlying tension among the officers. After three weeks, they dropped down slowly into a fine valley with a good river, which they followed to the sea, passing three or four large Indian settlements along the way.[42] On October 1, they looked out along the sweep of a great sandy bay from the mouth of the river.

Portolá surveyed the scene with increasing excitement. To identify Monterey, they were using both a sailing manual published thirty-five years earlier by an experienced Pacific captain and Sebastián Vizcaíno's original account of his voyage in 1602. Both sources placed their goal at 37°N. Costansó and Crespí brandished their sextants, sighted on the sun, and measured their position as 36°42" and 36°53", respectively.[43] They were almost exactly where they wanted to be. They began searching for a "good and unobstructed haven, protected from every wind," which was described as nestled in the lee of a pine-covered headland known as Pinos Point, at the southern end of a much larger bay that should have a long beach curving gently north toward a distant bulky promontory; and, just inland, there was supposed to be a "large salt lagoon."[44] They could see the two headlands and a long sandy shoreline and thought they must have found the bay described in the manual. In the early-evening light a nearby lagoon glittered like gold.

For three days, Rivera and his men explored the inlets around Pinos Point and scoured the shoreline as far as the lagoon. They saw the cliffs and beaches of a large and elongated cove that they thought might be Carmel Bay, but instead of "a river coursing with very good water," there was only a brook that barely babbled.[45] They found no sign of the perfect harbor, just a "small sandy bay."[46] Portolá called a formal council meeting and invited the Franciscans to attend.

Costansó offered his opinion: "We all thought it safe to assume that the *sierra* we have just crossed must be the Lucia Mountains, and we now believe that we are at the right latitude. It must be that Monterey is farther north and so we should explore the coast as far as 37½°. And I hope that thanks to such diligence we will find the port. If not, it is safe to say that it no longer exists."

Fages affirmed that he had "not the slightest doubt but that Monterey is behind us," but he saw sense in exploring farther north, just in case. The ever-capable Rivera was sure they were in the right place and that their manual must be wrong. He suggested they rest for a week, then pointed out that when the ships finally sailed for Monterey, the pilots would be looking for Pinos Point, so that might be a good place to establish camp?

The officers and the friars voted unanimously to continue the search.[47]

Their march took them through swamps. The rains came. They all suffered a dangerously debilitating attack of diarrhea. But to everyone's astonishment, far from "doing away with the whole expedition," as they feared, "the opposite happened and all those suffering from scurvy began to feel their symptoms getting better . . . Their pain relented, they began to move their arms and legs, finally they were all returned to perfect health." Obviously, whatever food they had scavenged or were given by friendly Indians must have been rich in vitamin C. But to them, it was a miraculous deliverance.

At Halloween, they climbed a hill and gazed across a great gulf to Drakes Bay, with the long promontory of Point Reyes in the distance and the Farallon Islands way off across the waves to the west.[48] The expedition descended into the little cove and valley of Linda Mar.[49]

On All Souls' Day, Portolá dispatched Sergeant Ortega, Rivera's right-hand man, to reconnoiter the coast with eight men. He moved through marshy ground, rounding the lagoons and inlets. He is almost certainly the first person in recorded history to have walked within the modern city limits of San Francisco. Ortega asked some Indians if they had sighted any ships, and he became convinced by their answers that the *San José* was waiting for them in a nearby anchorage. He rushed back to camp, firing his guns excitedly, but the senior officers "were unimpressed by this obviously mistaken translation of whatever gestures and gesticulations" the Indians had made.[50]

Portolá decided to persevere, hoping to reach Point Reyes. They climbed out of a "broad, lowland valley" onto a high ridge and saw "a great arm of the sea that ran between sixteen and twenty leagues inland" and "formed a well-protected harbor with two islands in the middle." They looked in wonder across the Golden Gate and the waters of the bay, with Alcatraz in the foreground, crowded by its flock of *alcatraces*, "pelicans." Crespí said, "To be frank, it is an enormous haven that could not only take all of His Majesty's fleets, but all the navies of Europe as well."[51]

The explorers were now largely dependent for food on the generosity of the Indians, so Portolá held his second official *junta*. No European had yet sailed through the Golden Gate into the greatest natural harbor in the world, but Spanish pilots had reported that slightly farther north was an estuary or lagoon that served as an excellent haven; they called it San Francisco.[52]

"I find," said Costansó, "that there is a quite remarkable fit between the lay of the coast before our eyes and the landmarks described by the pilots [in the manual]. So, I am in no doubt that we must have reached the Port of San Francisco, for all that pilots place it at 38°."

So that great body of water, the finest harbor in the world, was first called San Francisco Bay in error. All the officers agreed they must be at Drakes Bay, except for Rivera: "We should be very puzzled that we have not seen Monterey, although we have looked for it, nor are these headlands and the estuary of this great bay described in our manuals nor marked on our maps."

Rivera urged them to retrace their steps to Pinos Point and wait there for the ships.[53] With no means of crossing the Golden Gate, they turned back and, moving swiftly over the familiar terrain, were soon at Pinos Point. Rivera went high into the hills to see what he could see, but came back with the news that he had still not sighted Monterey. Costansó spoke for everyone when he wrote, "We had no idea what to make of it all. How can so famous a port, so renowned and so highly praised by reliable, intelligent, practical, and able navigators, not have been found despite such a diligent search? It is impossible that any such port ever existed here, for there is a range of very high hills," Big Sur, "that run steeply into the sea all along this stretch of coast. It would be no surprise to find that these old reports are wrong because their scientific instruments were defective."[54]

After a fortnight at Pinos Point, Portolá called his third *junta*. Rivera spoke his mind. He was angry; an experienced officer born in America, he had repeatedly warned his arrogant commander against such a foolish venture. He alone among the officers had recognized how wrong the sailing manuals were, he alone had understood the geography, for all that Costansó was the professional engineer.

"This is the third time I have been asked to sit in council and give my opinion," Rivera fumed. "The fact of the matter is that it is now up to our commander to ensure that we who have served him so faithfully and gladly are saved from total ruin. I warned him of the dangers. Every member of the expedition is well aware that I have done my job throughout . . . I fear the total lack of provisions may lead to mutiny among the men. There is a real danger they may desert; after all, two teamsters have already disappeared. They may turn to thievery or disobey their orders. So my view is that the commander should decide whether he is going to wait here for the ships, and all I ask is to be allowed to leave with the twenty men assigned to my command."

Rivera bluntly evoked the specter of mutiny among the men to justify his own request to be allowed to desert. Portolá, to his credit, accepted the logic of Rivera's argument and asked the *junta* to vote in favor of retreat.[55] They set up two large crosses on each side of Pinos Point, and at the foot of one of them they buried a bottle with a letter inside advising the ships' captains they were headed south. Then they struck camp.

Portolá recalled years later when describing his adventures to a friend: "So we should not die of hunger, I ordered that at the end of each day's march, one of the mules should be slaughtered. We then made a hole in the ground, set a fire, and half fried, half roasted its flesh. There was neither salt nor pepper to season the mule, so we just shut our eyes and devoured it like famished lions. We ate twelve in all, at once satisfying our hunger, satiating our appetites, and delighting our palates." By the end of the journey, he explained, "We all smelled horribly of mule."[56]

After forty days and forty nights they recognized the outcrops of La Joya in the distance. They had left three friars, a handful of Indians, and eight armed men to defend the ship at anchor, and the hospital tents full of extremely sick patients.[57] As they approached San Diego, they feared the worst, but three figures appeared in the distance and began moving along the shore toward them. Slowly, they began to make out the robes of three Franciscans. Serra and Parrón were sick, Brother Vizcaíno had a bandaged hand. But they were alive. "We all hugged one another warmly," Crespí remembered, "and then went off to dine most eagerly indeed on whatever the fathers might have to eat, and the joy of getting our hands on a tortilla or two was enough to make us forget all our tribulations."[58] Their joy was fleeting. Everyone listened with growing concern to Serra's account of what had happened at San Diego in their absence.

Serra had been outwardly full of optimism as he bade farewell to Crespí and Portolá when they set off for Monterey. But even his enthusiasm must have wavered as he looked out at a scene to rival many a painting of the Day of

Judgment. Only the vital green and plump pink silhouettes of trees and grapes against that endlessly soothing blue of the ocean and his fervent faith in the love of God could have kindled his spirits as he watched Portolá's party disappear north.

Nonetheless, the friars had set to work adorning the wigwam of wattle and daub that would be their makeshift chapel with a crucifix, devotional paintings, and a few pieces of liturgical silverware. Two days later, Serra celebrated a sung mass for a small assembly of soldiers, sailors, and Baja Indians who were well enough to attend.[59] Over the following weeks, they attended the sick, put up more "humble huts," as Palóu called them, and began to persuade the Kumeyaay to visit by offering them gifts of trinkets.[60] Now that most of the strangers had left, the Indians began to treat the men who remained behind as a resource to be exploited. They were especially interested in the Spaniards' textiles and pilfered clothing from time to time. One night, a sailor caught a little group who had paddled out to the *San Carlos* on their rafts and were cutting up one of its sails. Soon afterward, the Indians tried to make off with some ropes. Two soldiers were posted to the ship.[61]

On August 15, the Feast of the Assumption, Kumeyaay scouts watched with excitement as two soldiers and Brother Fernando Parrón rowed out to the *San Carlos* to say mass for the men aboard. Only four soldiers, two friars, an acolyte or two, the carpenter, and the blacksmith remained ashore.

Twenty armed Indians burst into the camp. They stole everything they could, taking clothing from the sick men's backs and blankets from their beds. The four soldiers rushed to don their leather coats, grabbed their shields, and loaded their guns. The blacksmith, Chacón, showed the greatest bravery in the fray. As Palóu said, "There can be no doubt but that the Holy Communion he had just received instilled such courage in his heart."

As the soldiers and tradesmen fought for their lives, Serra and Vizcaíno prayed. The two men watched aghast as a young Spanish altar boy from Guadalajara staggered into their hut, blood pouring from his mouth, an arrow through his gullet: "Absolution, Father, the Indians have murdered me," he gurgled.

"I gave him absolution," Serra reported to his superiors.

Brother Vizcaíno pulled back the straw matting that served as a door but was hit in the hand by an arrow. He may have been hoping to make a dash to the church for holy oil so they could give the dying boy Extreme Unction. Serra explained, "Within a quarter of an hour he was dead at my feet, drowned in his own blood. My hut was awash with blood, and the firing of arrows and the sound of the guns went on."

The fathers gazed down at the tragic cadaver at their feet and prayed to God that not another soul be lost in that needless fight.[62]

Portolá and his officers, concerned by the lack of food at San Diego, agreed that Rivera should march south with a detachment of two dozen men to secure supplies from Baja. This fine charade allowed Rivera to abandon the enterprise as he had wanted to do for so long, allowed Portolá to rid himself of a rancorous subordinate, and reduced the number of mouths to feed.[63] They now had enough provisions to last until the end of April, so Portolá determined that if no ship appeared by the Feast of Saint Joseph, March 19, the rest of the expedition would retreat overland to Baja. Serra and Crespí vowed to remain and prayed that "by the grace of God may we hang on until we have no strength left."[64]

As Saint Joseph's Day dawned, Portolá prepared the Holy Expedition for departure. But that evening, they saw the silhouette of a ship on the horizon against the glow of the setting sun. Juan Pérez had been determined to sail the *San Antonio* directly to Monterey in the belief that Portolá was still marooned there, but he had lost his anchor leaving the Santa Barbara Channel and so headed to San Diego to appropriate a replacement from the stricken *San Carlos*.[65] The Franciscans' prayers had been answered with a tangible miracle, such a wondrous coincidence as is the stuff of legends. Portolá told the viceroy, "I firmly believe that this has been the work of Saint Joseph himself."[66]

The return of the *San Antonio* with plenty of provisions and a handful of reinforcements made it practical to resume the settlement of Monterey, and within a month she had set sail with Serra aboard. Again, Portolá and Crespí set out along the overland route they had opened up the year before, filled with optimism. Without Rivera's harping voice of doom, they reveled in the pastoral beauty of the California springtime. The rivers ran fresh and clear, the flowers bloomed, the trees blossomed, and Crespí admired the friendly Indians living off the land, as Adam and Eve must have done before the Fall. As the expedition marched through Russell Valley, he wondered at the still virgin "pool, over a hundred yards long, very deep," and full of "fish and turtles," now the centerpiece of modern Westlake Village.[67]

Meanwhile, Serra endured six weeks of heavy storms that forced the *San Antonio* far to the south. She finally entered the broad bowl of Monterey Bay on May 31, Ascension Day, which for all the "discussion," Serra noted, "was unquestionably the same place where our Spanish forebears dropped anchor in 1602." He placed great store by this spiritual connection between landscape and history, and two days later, at Whitsun, when the Holy Ghost visited the Apostles, he celebrated high mass in a makeshift "chapel put up next to the very same oak tree, in the same little valley, by the same beach, where mass was said at the beginning of the last century" by the Carmelites who sailed with Sebastián Vizcaíno. Dressed in his long liturgical alb and a stole, Serra knelt before the altar and sang the hymn "Veni Creator Spiritus" before leading the men in procession to a large cross they had made, which was lying on the ground. "We all raised it up between us as I sang a blessing," he reported back to the College of San Fernando. After the mass was said, Portolá formally took possession of the country. The officers unfurled the royal standard, and Portolá tore grasses from the ground and threw them to the winds. He hurled stones onto the beach and shouted, "Long live the faith! Long live the king!" Serra blessed the land and the shore, facing each point of the compass in turn, and that night they held a great banquet on the beach.[68]

Portolá's work was done. He had been ordered to take possession of Monterey Bay, then hand over his command to Pedro Fages. On July 9, the first Governor of California sailed for New Spain, where he served as Governor of Puebla for eight years before returning to Spain, where he died in 1786.[69]

By contrast, the great personal mission that Serra had longed for all his life was just beginning. He started to interpret the realities of the world almost entirely in terms of providence, likening the discovery of two crates of lanterns and candles that had been shipped by mistake to a miraculous monstrance that María de Ágreda had brought from Spain during one of her nocturnal excursions. Serra was so elated because, as he explained to Gálvez with a playful twist to his words, the find allowed him to celebrate "Corpus Christi with such brilliance that it must have been enjoyed in Mexico City."[70]

Serra was obsessed with the outward expression of his spiritual leadership through religious ceremony. He felt the faith needed to be vigorously and incessantly enacted. It was a way of overcoming their isolation, reminding themselves they were still a part of the wider Christian communion. He complained to Palóu that "the lack of communication is one of our greatest hardships" and lamented that he was "starved of news" for "it was over a year since I have had a letter from a Christian land." He wrote his superiors at San Fernando, Gálvez, and also Viceroy Croix, asking for more missionaries and urging that a chain of missions be founded to establish a good line of communication all the way from San Francisco to San Diego.[71] Now that he was finally at work among pure "gentiles," the old man yearned for an umbilical cord to the mother Church: even his faith felt fragile on God's own frontier.

In May, the *San Antonio* arrived with ten new missionaries and a plethora of sumptuous liturgical gifts sent by the delighted viceroy, just in time for Corpus Christi to be celebrated with even greater pomp than the year before. Serra was ecstatic that "some newly converted little Christians served as altar boys" during the mass.[72] He turned his attention to relocating the temporary San Carlos Mission to its permanent site a good distance from Monterey in the Carmel Valley, a "truly delightful place with plenty of excellent, well-watered land that should yield bountiful crops."[73] He left a couple of young sailors, five soldiers, and forty Baja Indians to begin construction and set out to found San Antonio, twenty-five leagues to the south, up in the hills. When the party reached an ideal location beside a good stream, he had the mission bells hung from a nearby tree and then began to peal them with deafening vigor, shouting out, "Come, ye pagans, come to the faith of Jesus Christ!"

"Why tire yourself if there is not a single gentile anywhere nearby?" one of the new missionaries asked.

"Like María de Ágreda, my heart's desire is that this bell should be heard by all the world, or at least by every pagan in these mountains."

Serra never tired of trying to drown out the heathen silence all about him with noisy ritual. On this occasion, it worked. A single Salinan man turned up and watched the friars conduct mass, a moment of tentative Native American curiosity that they seized on as a portent of successful proselytizing to come. Within two years, Palóu reported proudly, 158 new Christians had been baptized at San Antonio. But the truly marvelous tale they told was of an ancient woman "who looked as if she must be over one hundred years old," who "asked to be baptized," explaining that "when she was young, her parents described how a man dressed in the same clothes as the friars had come to their lands, although he did not come on foot, but flew" through the air. The missionaries were skeptical at first, but then accepted this miracle as fact when all their converts confirmed this was a common myth among them. Most miraculous of all, this woman was called Águeda, clearly a bastardization of "Ágreda," the missionaries said.[74]

Fages briefly explored the southern shores of San Francisco Bay in the fall of 1770.[75] In the spring of 1772, he led a more extensive reconnaissance as far as the junction of the Sacramento and San Joaquin rivers, near modern Antioch. Crespí accompanied the expedition and drew the first map of the estuary system, adding the curious note that they had found a "large group of Indians who," quite unlike any other Native Californians, "were blond, white, and bearded" and were especially friendly. Interestingly, an Indian legend was documented in the late nineteenth century that a dozen or more of Sir Francis Drake's men had deserted him along that coast in 1579.[76]

The exploratory party was back at Monterey in early April 1772, but by the summer both mission and presidio were running out of food. The situation was so bad that Fages led most of his men into the hinterland to hunt bear and steal food from the Indians, while the missionaries survived on a little milk from their cows and vegetables from their plot. In August, news reached them that Juan Pérez had sailed his *San Antonio* a long way north, but had failed to locate Pinos Point and had been forced back to San Diego, where he unloaded his cargo. Fages left a handful of soldiers at Monterey and headed south to arrange the transport of necessary supplies. Serra went with him, accompanied by a young Rumsen Indian acolyte he had baptized as Juan Bautista, in honor of John the Baptist. On the way south, Serra founded San Luis Obispo, leaving one friar and four guards to feed themselves by trading beads with the Chumash Indians.

At San Diego, Serra announced his intention to establish another mission to the north, which Gálvez had personally commanded him to found in honor of San Buenaventura. Given the "lively multitude" of Indians living around Santa Barbara, Serra asked Fages to second fifteen soldiers, four sailors, and a muleteer to the mission. The governor refused to contemplate a new mission, let alone assign soldiers to the task. He was already seriously worried about security at San Gabriel, the original mission at Los Angeles. The previous fall, as the friars were surveying the site, they had been threatened by a large group of Indians. Although they became friendly when the defenseless Franciscans brandished a painting of Our Lady of the Sorrows, which Serra believed was a sign from God, Fages clearly thought they had a lucky escape and sent more soldiers to San Gabriel.

Serra was furious and began to write scathingly about Fages. He claimed the soldiers had been allowed to degenerate into an unruly mob of malcontents, at odds with themselves and the world. "They frequently drew their swords on one another" and behaved "utterly shamelessly toward the padres." They would ride out in the early morning in search of Indian encampments and "lassoed the women" with great "skill" to "feed their unstoppable lust." One of the friars reported that even at the mission itself he had witnessed "a trooper lewdly groping at an Indian woman . . . Not even the young lads who visited the mission escaped their beastliness." Serra blamed Fages for his failure as a leader of men.[77] His accusations clearly had some basis in fact, for Fages's own men turned on him, complaining to the viceroy about a continual lack of food and damning him for "treating them worse than slaves" when they labored on the construction of a mission and presidio and threatening to charge anyone who complained with treason.[78]

Fages responded to Serra's campaign of complaint by arranging a secret mail by which he sent his own criticism of the Franciscans to Viceroy Antonio María de Bucareli, while also obstructing all attempts by the friars to communicate with the outside world.[79] Serra was furious and called a council of the other missionaries then in San Diego. He made it clear that he was determined to go in person to Mexico City and lay the facts before Bucareli. On October 17, Serra, with his Rumsen acolyte Juan Bautista by his side, boarded the *San Antonio* and two weeks later disembarked at San Blas. That remarkably swift voyage was indicative of the ease with which a man might escape California, in marked contrast to the seemingly interminable tribulations of getting there.

At Guadalajara, both Serra and Juan Bautista were struck by a disease Palóu called *tabardillo*, possibly typhus. Both were given their last rites, but both recovered. Serra was struck down again at Querétaro, and a physician from the medical college insisted that he again take Communion for the last time. By chance, another doctor was passing, and curious to meet the founding father of Monterey, the doctor went to see Serra. There seemed little wrong with the patient. The doctor took Serra's pulse and exclaimed, "Are you giving Communion to this priest? If he needs his last rites, then you might as well give them to me as well. Get up, Father, you are perfectly well."[80]

Serra expressed little concern for his own life, of course, but he was upset that Juan Bautista might succumb, for he feared that the Rumsen would never trust the Franciscans again if the child did not come home alive.

Serra met Bucareli in late February or early March. The viceroy well knew of the bad blood between his visitor and Fages, but even so he must have been taken aback at Serra's direct and vehement approach.

"It is very important, indeed, that Pedro Fages be removed from his command at Monterey," Serra announced. "Otherwise, the soldiers will continue to desert and those who remain will suffer his terrible abuse. It would be a long business should I have to list for you the continual setbacks he has caused the mission program, let alone the problems he has caused me personally."[81]

Serra offered a detailed assessment of the number of troops he believed were needed as guards at each of the missions. He insisted the friars have absolute authority over the "organization, management, education, and punishment of all baptized Indians," to the exclusion of the military and civil authorities. The friars should also have the power to remove individual soldiers posted to the missions who behaved badly, especially those who were "sexually incontinent." Serra argued that the soldiers needed a pay raise and a proper store where they could buy supplies on credit, while the missions needed laborers to till the land, cowhands, and muleteers. He wanted Indian settlers from Baja sent north with livestock and equipment *and*, of especial importance, their womenfolk. "Until now the California Indians have found it very strange that they have only seen men without women," and they must understand that "Christians also get married."[82]

Bucareli listened attentively until the venerable old pioneer had finished, then asked for a written report detailing his copious complaints, demands, and recommendations. Bucareli presented Serra's report to the Junta de Guerra, the "Council of War," which addressed each point. Bucareli took responsibility for replacing Fages as diplomatically as possible, then the *junta* turned its attention to the major problem that Alta California was so remote. Serra had emphasized the extent to which a lack of experienced ship's captains and pilots threatened the fragile sea route, the only realistic way of supplying these new outposts of empire with food and hardware. The Junta agreed that California "should be afforded all possible support and assistance" and discussed Serra's insistence on the importance of opening up new overland routes to connect California with New Mexico and Sonora.[83]

Less than two years earlier, in May 1772, Juan Bautista de Anza had proposed an expedition to establish a route from his presidio at Tubac to Monterey. He had long been interested in exploring Arizona, California, and beyond, and he had recently been encouraged by Father Francisco Garcés, the maverick missionary at San Xavier del Bac, one of those classic romantic colonial figures who (like Lawrence of Arabia) was more at home traveling among the "natives" than living and working alongside Europeans. "Garcés seemed like an Indian; he would sit around with them, at night, with his legs crossed, and spend hours chatting with them. To sum up, God made him for the task," one churchman remembered.[84] Garcés had just spent two or three months exploring the Gila River and had enjoyed an extended sojourn among the Yuma, whose chief, Olleyquotequiebe, was especially convivial company and gave him detailed reports about the Europeans at San Diego and Monterey. Olleyquotequiebe explained that a great ocean lay just beyond "a large range of blue-colored mountains" in the west.

Costansó had already advised Bucareli to authorize Anza's expedition and suggested he should be accompanied by a couple of soldiers who had been to San Diego.[85] Now, Serra echoed that advice. The Junta agreed. The stage was set for an epic expedition.

CHAPTER 18

HARD ROAD TO PARADISE

ARIZONA & CALIFORNIA

In lands that have been little explored and have few major landmarks, it is
no great wonder that people get lost.

—JUAN BAUTISTA DE ANZA

JUAN BAUTISTA DE ANZA and Father Francisco Garcés planned to head
directly overland toward the confluence of the Gila and Colorado rivers as the
first stage in establishing a route to Alta California. But as they were mustering
the expedition at Tubac, in the fall of 1773, Apache raiders ran off 130 horses
that were grazing near the presidio. As a result, Anza set out on New Year's Day
1774 to travel through the settled valleys of northern Sonora, where he could
pick up replacement animals as he went.[1] He was also keen to meet a Cochimí
from Baja, Sebastián Tarabal, who had been part of Portolá's original overland
expedition to San Diego. Tarabal had appeared at the mission of El Altar, in
Sonora, during the Christmas festivities with a tragic but fascinating story.[2]

Having briefly settled at San Gabriel, the original mission at Los Angeles,
Tarabal and his family felt homesick and tried to go overland to Baja, managing
to cross the Sierra Nevada in winter, but then got lost in the vast sea of sand
known as the Algodones Dunes. Only Tarabal survived. He was rescued by
Olleyquotequiebe, the friendly Yuma chief, who sent him to El Altar. Tarabal
was terrified that he would be punished for absconding from San Gabriel, but
instead Anza welcomed him as a valuable guide.[3]

From El Altar, the expedition headed northwest to Sonoita, then followed
the river west, almost parallel with the modern border, to El Carrizal, where
they headed north into modern U.S. territory at Organ Pipe National Monument, just northeast of the spectacular volcanic peaks and cinder cones of
Pinacate. Garcés was worried when the mules and the cattle found crossing
a short stretch of sand hard going, for he, like Tarabal, knew the Algodones
Dunes lay ahead.

They found little water at Heart Tank and carried on to "six [natural] tanks filled with good rainwater" in the Cabeza Prieta hills, where they hunted the desert's bighorn sheep. Anza rode across rocky ground nearby that he guessed "must be hollow because the horses' hooves made a sound like a pumpkin." He reported that the Pápago habitually piled up the horns of dead sheep on that very spot and had urged the Spaniards to do the same "to stop the air escaping . . . and causing trouble for everyone."[4] The expedition continued north, stopping at watering holes in the arroyo that runs into the Gila River at Wellton. From there, Anza headed west into the Gila hills and dropped down to the verdant cool of the cottonwood groves along the riverbanks. The great bulk of Mount San Jacinto rose ahead of them in the far distance.

They were warmly welcomed by the Yumas, somewhere near where I-8 runs south of the Kofa Wildlife Refuge, and "at three in the afternoon we descended to the Gila River accompanied by more than two hundred men mounted on good mares, all of them pleased to see us, all hollering and grinning, punching the air and making other signs of friendship."[5] Olleyquotequiebe did not appear until sundown, when he rode in with a company of sixty men and apologized profusely for his late arrival.

"I see your men have their swords and their horses at the ready," he said to Anza. "So, I imagine you must have heard that some have opposed your expedition . . . Well, you can put them all at ease, sir, for it has come to nothing. Those involved were from upriver, and the moment they broadcast the idea, I threw them out of my territory. My people and I are overjoyed that you are traveling through our lands . . . , but you must let them get a good look at you and your men as they are wont to do, especially as most of them have never seen you before."

"Your men must come to meet me, as they wish, and I will indulge them as I would my own children and my friends," Anza replied. "Tell them to gather round."

When the Yumas had assembled, Anza asked them, "Is this man your chief?"

"Yes," came the resounding reply.

"In the name of our king, I hereby confirm him in that office so that he may govern you with greater authority; and so that the Spaniards respect your rights and laws, I am decorating him with this coin on which there is the portrait of His Majesty."

Anza then hung the coin from a red ribbon around Olleyquotequiebe's neck. He kissed it solemnly, and his people were filled with joy, or so Anza reported to Bucareli.[6]

Garcés knew from his travels that the Yumas had long been at war with the eastern Pápagos, but that they had recently formed an alliance with the well-armed Pimas from the Gila River. Olleyquotequiebe evidently needed the Spaniards to restore his military advantage.[7]

The Yumas helped the expedition cross the Gila River, carrying many loads of baggage and even manhandling Garcés himself across because he was such a nervous horseman that he refused to ride through the water. That night they camped beside the Yuma settlement of six hundred men, women, and children who lived on a "beautiful island" where the Gila River pays tribute to the Colorado.[8] Anza made the Indians stand in line and handed out gifts to each and every one. In the morning, the Yuma were treated to the spectacle of the expedition crossing the Colorado, presumably the strangest entertainment many had ever seen, especially after Anza had flares fired into the air, which "the Indians greatly enjoyed."[9]

On Thursday, February 10, the expedition lumbered downriver. Anza estimated that as many as five or six hundred Yuma and Sobaipuri helped to clear the trail and drive the animals to the edge of the territory controlled by the Quiquima, who lived toward the mouth of the river. Olleyquotequiebe accompanied the expedition a further twenty miles, to where the modern border follows the Colorado River, taking his leave near Paredones with tears in his eyes, apologizing that he had to go back, but explaining that he was now in enemy territory.

Two Cajuenche guides from the mountains led the expedition west toward the sand. They indicated where to dig wells, and Anza let the animals drink their fill. Then the expedition rode into the dunes and soon "lost the trail completely because the winds were blowing the sand around all over the place."[10] The mules flailed and foundered in the fine sand, and Anza realized it would be impossible to cajole them across the dunes.

Garcés thought he might be able to find a nearby settlement he had visited the year before near a watering hole beside a black hill. They searched until midnight, but failed to find it, "which was hardly surprising," Anza remarked sardonically, "for in lands that have been little explored and have few major landmarks, it is no great wonder that people get lost."

In the morning, the horses were sick "from eating some grasses that are plentiful in these parts and make them slobber lots of evil-smelling black saliva."[11] It was Ash Wednesday. Anza ordered the expedition to retreat toward the last serviceable watering hole, which the soldiers named *El Pozo de las Angustias*, "the Well of Anguish." But the mood began to change when they reached their next watering hole, which they called the *Aguaje de la Alegría*, the "Pool of Joy."[12]

Garcés volunteered to go downriver in search of information about how to reach San Diego. Anza seized the opportunity to get rid of the meddlesome maverick and let Garcés leave the main body of the expedition at Yuma. Thus unencumbered, Anza set out with two dozen men. Guided by a Cajuenche, they skirted the dunes to the south and reached Laguna Salada, just south of the border to the west of Mexicali. The salt lake was almost completely dry, but hundreds of fish were rotting in the mud. They turned north, through flat country with the crests of dunes to the right and the wall of the San Geronimo mountains to the left, and camped at a salty well. On March 6, they woke to find that their guide had absconded. Anza was briefly worried, but a search party soon found drinking water at a place he called Santo Tomás. Heading almost due north through the Colorado Desert, the search for water remained their priority. They finally found excellent wells in the Yuha Buttes, close to I-8, seven miles south of Plaster City.

Anza was excited because Sebastián Tarabal was sure that in the distance he could see the pass by which he had crossed the mountains. That afternoon, they reached extensive marshlands and good pastures around a saline spring set among some dunes, Harper's Well on San Felipe Creek, today the last perennial natural stream in the Colorado Desert, which drains into the Salton Sea.[13] Anza demonstrated his affection for his Cochimí guide by calling the place *San Sebastián el Peregrino*, "Saint Sebastian the Traveler." As they moved on, they surprised a group of Indians, who ran away. Anza sent Tarabal after them, and he came back with a lone woman. They gave her trinkets and tobacco and sent her back to her people. Two hours later, seven men turned up.

Tarabal and their leader had met before and recognized each other. These people reported that they had heard that "people like ourselves" were living three days' travel across the mountains. Anza's party turned toward Borrego Springs and followed Coyote Canyon as far as some fine springs with good water surrounded by trees and vines. Anza offered tobacco and glass beads to some Indians who impressed the Spaniards with their skill at hunting rabbits and hares using a sort of curved throwing stick.

Anza led his party out of the ravine up onto the nose of a ridge and camped at excellent springs on the edge of the highlands. They dropped down into the Cahuilla Valley, where the dusty town of Anza sprawls beside the Indian reservation, and spent a cold night in snow and sleet. In the early morning they dropped into the "wide and impressive" San Jacinto Valley, with the "large and attractive" expanse of Mystic Lake, where a vast flock of white geese were resting.[14] Finally, on March 22, they reached San Gabriel, a journey that they estimated at 268 leagues, or about 800 miles. The four padres welcomed them with "joy and happiness, the solemn ringing of the bells, and by singing a Te Deum," and a month later Anza rode into Monterey.[15]

Anza did not dally at Monterey, but immediately headed for home. He met Serra on the journey south and spent a night telling the old padre about the trials of forging an overland route to California, but by May 9, he was back at Yuma and a fortnight later the expedition reached Tucson.

Anza spent the following months raising a large expedition with the purpose of settling San Francisco, and in the fall of 1775, he led 240 friars, officers, soldiers, settlers—men, women, and children—140 mules, 500 horses, 30 mares, foals, and donkeys, and 355 head of livestock out of Tubac and down the Gila River.[16] At Agua Caliente, ten miles north of Dateland on I-8, they came across a group of Indians keen to make peace with their old enemy, the Yuma. But when Anza announced he would appoint a governor and a sheriff among them, an old Indian replied seriously, "The point of the law is to punish wrongdoing, but as we do no wrong, what is the point of your justice?"[17] Nonetheless, Anza invested a man called Carlos as Governor of the Coco Maricopas and handed out staffs of Spanish office to a number of other Indians.

The Yumas gave the expedition a clamorous reception, and a delighted Anza ordered a volley from the soldiers by way of return. With this gregarious, party atmosphere as a backdrop, Olleyquotequiebe displayed the kind of diplomatic good manners that Spaniards so appreciated by "asking after the health of His Majesty and his Excellency the Lord Viceroy."

"You are lucky to have seen them and to have heard them speak," he told Anza, "I would gladly take off my own ears and put on some Spanish ones so that I might understand what they have to say to me." Olleyquotequiebe pressed Anza for news of the padres and soldiers who were due to settle in his lands.

"I cannot manage all that you ask, but I am certain that, just as the king and the viceroy have sent me with all these troops and families to establish the true religion elsewhere, in due course you will be similarly rewarded," Anza replied.

"Then, if you have not settled my country by the time you return, I will go with you and petition the viceroy in person."

"I will gladly take you to Mexico City."[18]

That night, Anza presented Olleyquotequiebe with a gala set of Spanish clothes and explained that they were a personal gift from the viceroy. Alone in Anza's tent, he helped the Yuma chief dress in "a shirt, knickerbockers, a yellow bolero jacket decorated with brocade, and a braided blue cape," all topped off with a "black velvet *montera* cap" shining with "gemstones and plume."[19]

During these friendly exchanges, Olleyquotequiebe boasted to Anza about his success as a peacemaker among the surrounding tribes, but made an exception for the Kumeyaay "because he had heard that they had raided our settlements in California, stealing horses and murdering one of our people."[20] This was the first report Anza received about a terrifying raid on San Diego, carried out in the dead of night three weeks earlier. "We live in a vale of tears," Serra wrote to Viceroy Bucareli, reporting "the total destruction of San Diego and the murder of Father Luis Jaime at the hands of pagans and Christian converts from forty tribes. They burned down the church, the storehouse, the padres' quarters, and then the rest. They killed a carpenter and a blacksmith"— presumably brave Chacón—"and shot four soldiers through with arrows."[21]

Soon afterward, the newly appointed Governor Carlos arrived with an entourage of Coco Maricopas to sue for peace. He began by riding up and down in front of the Yuma, delivering a long and important speech. Olley-quotequiebe responded bluntly, "If you have come to seal our peace in good faith, then get down off your horse and speak to me on foot, as I am standing, and not prancing around in front of everyone."[22]

Carlos dismounted and sat on the ground. The people gathered round and the two men spoke briefly. Then one of the Yumas whom the Spaniards called Pablo el Feo, "Ugly Paul," a "great preacher, with a powerful voice, who they say is a shaman," delivered a long sermon denouncing conflict and exhorting all nations to be friends, brothers, and *queyé*, or "countrymen" in their language. "This man shouted loudly, with great fervor, becoming agitated, waving his arms around and making exaggerated gestures," according to Father Font, the singularly unsympathetic chronicler of the expedition.

Anza had grown up on the frontier, recognized the ceremony as significant, and realized the importance and honor of his own role as a witness to it. When Ugly Paul was finished, Anza stepped forward and encouraged Olleyquote-quiebe and Carlos to embrace. That night, at a great banquet in celebration, the "Yumas and Coco Maricopas stayed up very late around the fire, singing in their funereal fashion and banging their drums, all stretched out on the ground, half buried in the sand and piled up on top of one another like hogs, as is their custom," the friar observed scornfully.[23]

Anza personally located the best place to cross the swollen Colorado River, and the expedition then treated the Yumas to an even more spectacular piece of theater than they had enjoyed the year before, an iconic image of the Wild West worthy of Hollywood in its pomp. Men on foot, with the water up to their chests, led the strongest horses across, carrying the women and children, while a chain of ten men spread out downstream in case of mishap. Some of the animals missed their footing and had to swim, and there were a couple of scares when the men carrying the children slipped. Some baggage was swept away, while Father Font grumbled that the bundle in which he was carrying the holy oil and liturgical vessels was soaked. "I told the mule-teers to take good care of them and pleaded with Anza to do the same," the friar said, before adding, in a rare moment of self-awareness, "but they take no notice of me, which may be why it was the bundle they paid least attention."[24]

Font documented in detail an excellent example of his own insufferable nature. At the beginning of December, with the cold weather coming on, Anza decided to rest the expedition before heading into the Colorado Desert. In the evening, he broke open the hooch, *aguardiente*, either tequila or more probably grape spirit, and many of the company became so gloriously drunk that the cook failed to make supper. Font spent a sleepless night suffering from diar-rhea, and first thing in the morning, he celebrated a presumably poorly attended mass. In an evil temper, he remonstrated with Anza, "Sir, there seems to have been a deal of drunkenness last night."

"Some," Anza replied through his hangover.

"Why do you give them hooch, then?"

"I did not try to get them drunk."

"Well, that is a good thing. If that had been your intention, it would have been doubly sinful, for drunkenness is always a bad thing, just as it is a sin to get people drunk."[25]

Font was even more scandalized by the Indians, who "are so excessively licentious that I do not believe any other people in the world can rival them. They practically share their womenfolk in common, and they regale their guests by lending them women to sleep with." He was also horrified by some *berdaches*: "I saw some men who dressed like women and went about with the women whom Anza called queers . . . They were not normal men," and so Font "inferred that they were hermaphrodites." But "I later learned that they were sodomites, which means there will be plenty of work when the Holy Faith is established among them."[26]

Crossing the Colorado Desert was miserable. A harsh winter was setting in, and fifteen settlers were terribly sick and three of them were thought to be at death's door. Two mules died. In the bitter cold, Anza had to oversee the opening of the Yuha well by moonlight. To keep warm, they moved on, but had to head straight into a freezing north wind, which was a source of "endless hardship, especially for the women and children," and although it abated a little during the day, they could see dark clouds building in the hills, and in the early evening "it started blowing again ferociously with early signs of the snow and sleet" that lasted all night "and all day." The next evening it stopped snowing, but the landscape was blanketed white and glowed like dawn in the moonlight; "there was a frost so raw that we suffered a truly dreadful night." The next morning was clear and crisp, and in the bright early light Anza counted six more dead horses.[27] The animals continued to die by the wayside, and one night fifty head of cattle broke free and were found drowned, mired in the marshes of San Felipe Creek as they tried to satiate their thirst.

Anza managed to keep all his people alive, and most of the sick recovered despite the cold, which he explained that they had "attributed to the many watermelons they ate" before they entered the desert.[28] He thought that was cause for celebration and again broke open a barrel of hooch. A brazen widow began singing, then the onlookers clapped out the rhythm of a fandango and shouted ribald comments until the man she was traveling with lost his temper and hauled her away. Font wholeheartedly approved of the jealous companion and was outraged that Anza did not stop the party. In the morning, Font scolded his hungover flock during mass.[29]

A welcome wave of warmer weather came in, and they went into the mountains in low cloud and drizzle. Christmas Eve dawned with the disconcerting sight of several timid Indians appearing out of a morning mist so thick they could not see more than twelve yards. That afternoon, they reached Fig Tree Spring in Coyote Canyon. Anza again decided to allow his people a good dose of festive cheer and handed out a pint of liquor to each. Font complained bitterly and slunk away to sulk in his tent, slipping out from time to time because of his diarrhea. With the singing and dancing and the warm glow of the fire as a backdrop, an hour before midnight a pregnant settler gave birth to a boy, the first documented birth in modern California. He was baptized Salvador, "Savior," and there must have been a general feeling that he was indeed a herald of salvation after their freezing desert hell. Far away in Bethlehem, it was already Christmas Day.

Their journey became progressively easier as they made their way through the mountains and began the descent to San Gabriel, which they reached on January 4, 1776. It would be difficult to exaggerate Anza's triumph in leading such an assorted band of soldiers and settlers through demanding terrain and hostile weather, yet managing to arrive with more members of the expedition than he had set out with.

Fernando Rivera y Moncada was at San Gabriel, marching south to try to reestablish a sense of peace and security at San Diego following the murderous raid that Anza had heard about from Olleyquotequiebe. Rivera said it was rumored that as many as six hundred Indians had been in the assault, and he asked Anza to let him have a detachment of men to bolster his forces.

"I will not just second you my troops," Anza replied, "but I also offer to serve in person should that prove necessary."[30]

Meanwhile, Father Font thought San Gabriel the Promised Land and thoroughly enjoyed his dinner of excellent fatty mutton, rich milk, good cheese and butter, and delicious watercress. The following day, when he learned that Anza was going to San Diego, Font scolded him again: "It is very hard to always be the last one to find out what your plans are. You never include me in anything." He grumbled on and on long into the night, but Anza humored him so effectively that Font later wrote in his diary, "The commander changed completely and from then on he was much more friendly toward me," which only went to show that "with such gentlemen it is best to speak plainly." Anza makes no mention of the conversation in his own journal.[31]

San Diego was quiet by the time Anza arrived with Rivera, so he returned to San Gabriel to lead the expedition to Monterey. They arrived on March 10, 1776, and the Franciscans sang a solemn mass of thanksgiving. Font delivered a long sermon to the settlers in which he even allowed himself to praise Anza for getting them there.

Everyone was impatient to reach the Promised Land beside San Francisco Bay. Despite suffering crippling pains in his groins and side, Anza led a reconnaissance party, and on March 28, he and Font rode across modern Presidio Park, and at the water's edge the two men looked out across the Golden Gate. The troops raised a cross. Anza then led the way up the hill behind them, which was carpeted with wild violets. He knew at once he had found the perfect site for the presidio. From that height, he reported, "a gunnery could control the entrance to the harbor," while the surrounding land could support "a good-sized population."[32]

Anza continued to explore the Bay Area, passing the future site of Mission Dolores, measuring the height and width of El Palo Alto, the famous redwood for which the district is named, then making his way north along the far side of the bay. He turned east, skirting Suisun Bay, but as they tried to follow the San Joaquin River inland, they became bogged down and were forced to turn south. Somewhere near Tracy, Anza decided to head back to Monterey. They were the first Europeans in American history to document seeing the Central Valley.

Anza's job was done, and on April 14, he set out for Tubac, "my province," the place he thought of as home.[33]

Meanwhile, Francisco Garcés spent the winter exploring the Lower Colorado, happy to once again be at liberty among the Indians.[34] On Saint Valentine's Day, he set out upstream with Sebastián Tarabal. They struck up a firm friendship with the Mojave Indians, who told them that their young men occasionally made the arduous trip to the San Gabriel region.

With Mojave guides, Garcés and Tarabal reached San Gabriel on March 24, but Garcés soon set off on his travels again. By late April he was exploring northward along the Central Valley. He found a new route through the mountains and back to the Mojave, one that was completely unknown even to his Indian guides. An instinctive opportunist, Garcés used his influence to prevent his Mojave hosts from attacking some visiting Hualapai and so managed to persuade these terrified travelers to show him the way to the land of the Hopis.

The Hualapai led Garcés along a trail to Peach Springs, now part of Route 66. From there, they went northeast across the modern Hualapai Reservation on what is now Indian Road 18. This is truly harsh country, for mile after mile after mile. Finally, Garcés reached Supai, in its spectacular setting at the bottom of Havasu Canyon, within the Grand Canyon system, where even today mules are used to deliver mail to the post office. He called the canyon New Canfranc after a famous pass in the Pyrenees and described having to abandon his mule to descend a "wooden ladder" between "a very high crag on one side and a horrible abyss on the other."[35] He then followed the same Indian trail that Cárdenas had traveled, in 1540, when he first saw the Grand Canyon, and, on July 2, Garcés reached the great city-state Oraibi, the chief urban center of the Hopi.

The Hopis did not welcome him. "All day long, I was watched by the men, women, and children, but none would come near me," Garcés reported. Then the old Hualapai Indian who had guided him to the Hopi told him, "None of these people want you here and they are in an evil mood."

Garcés could hear plenty of discussion going on inside the houses, then "in the evening, I saw the men coming back from working in the fields, with their axes, hoes, and mattocks."[36]

Garcés was clearly terrified.

That night, against a sleepless backdrop of agitated Hopi leaders haranguing one another from the rooftops, Garcés describes the almost miraculous appearance of a Christian boy from Zuni who offered to take him to New Mexico in the morning. It is almost as though the frightened friar dreamed of this friendly savior in the darkness. In fact, the following day Garcés met with a group of Zuni travelers and explained that he had to return the way he had come but gave them letters for the authorities in New Mexico. He spent one last night at Oraibi and in the morning awoke to the sound of singing and dancing. "I saw Indians with feather headdresses and other ornaments, beating time, accompanied by pipers, followed by a great crowd of dancers."[37]

As the sun came up, a huge crowd came toward him. Four chiefs stepped forward. The tallest man spoke: "Why have you come here? Leave! Go home!"

Garcés babbled back in a mixture of Yuma, Hualapai, and Spanish, explaining how far he had come and where he had been and how he was trying to preach the word of Christ.

"No, no!" an old man shouted, twisting his face.

Garcés called for his mule and left.

It was July 4, 1776. On the far side of the continent, of course, another kind of American was defying European oppression with their own assertion of independence. John Dunlap was about to begin the most famous print run in American history.

On the West Coast, beside the Golden Gate, Lieutenant José Joaquín Moraga, who had been born at Guevavi, near Anza's home at Tubac in southern Arizona, was even then establishing the Presidio of San Francisco and waiting for the *San Carlos* to arrive with equipment and supplies. It is likely that on July 4 itself he found the two abundant springs above Fort Point that convinced him Anza had been right when he chose the hill covered in violets as the site for the presidio, although it was not formally established until September 17, the day on which the Church celebrates the Stigmata of Saint Francis.[38]

Anza was as good as his word to Olleyquotequiebe and took him to Mexico City to visit Viceroy Bucareli, who welcomed them at a public reception attended by an impressive array of dignitaries. Anza had dressed the Yuma chief in a "blue silk frock coat and breeches, with showy buttons, a bloodred jacket with gold brocade."[39] Bucareli reported back to José de Gálvez, now Secretary of the Indies, how pleased the Yumas were to be received with such love and warmth by the viceroy. Moved by Olleyquotequiebe's sincerity, Bucareli indicated his intention to hasten the arrangements for establishing missions and a presidio among the Yuma. Gálvez replied with a brief note to say that the king himself had asked that the Yumas be given as friendly treatment as possible. On February 13, 1777, Anza stood godfather to Olleyquotequiebe, who was baptized Salvador Carlos Antonio Palma in the Cathedral of Mexico City.[40]

CHAPTER 19

HALF A CONTINENT
IS SPANISH

LOUISIANA & ALASKA

The French flag has always flown over our public square, at the head of our militia, [and] been raised on our ships. It is under that banner that we wish to live and die.

—HIGH COUNCIL OF NEW ORLEANS

FROM ITS FOUNDATION, FRENCH LOUISIANA was a vast, vaguely defined territory that in European minds and on their maps encompassed almost the entire Mississippi watershed, from East Texas and Kansas to the Ohio River and Pittsburgh and north to the Great Lakes and Saskatchewan. But the capricious cartographic claims of Old World sovereigns and their covetous courtiers were roughly tempered by reality on the ground

An initial attempt to create a proprietary company on the English model, the Mississippi Company, founded in 1684, had quietly failed. But it was recast as the Company of the West when a maverick Scot called John Law persuaded the French Crown and thousands of private investors to pour twenty million livres, four million dollars, into his project for the commercial exploitation of Louisiana. The share price surged in a wild bout of speculation, followed by an equally precipitous collapse, known as the Mississippi Bubble. The company folded and Louisiana thenceforth cost the French Crown approximately two hundred thousand dollars a year.

In the 1720s, fewer than 2,000 French subjects were living in the Lower Mississippi Valley, including a few hundred German farmers who had settled a stretch of the river known as the Côte des Allemandes, 1,400 African slaves, and 150 indentured Indians, according to the official census.[1] Moreover, administrators in New Orleans complained time and again about the evil quality of the settlers arriving from France. "It is impossible to establish the colony with persons incapable of discipline," one report stated bluntly.[2] During the French and Indian War, one governor of Louisiana fumed bitterly about two dozen companies of reinforcements he had recently received. "One group has deserted, another succumbed to the horrors of the most extreme debaucheries of drink and licentiousness." These "vicious characters have done more damage here" and "are more dangerous to the colony than the enemy itself."[3] Such was the fetid reputation of Louisiana that despite the French Crown's offer of land grants there to an array of beggars, prostitutes, thieves, drunks, and murderers, most of them refused, and even condemned convicts resisted deportation. There were riots in the Paris prisons and fighting in the streets between press-gangs and their victims. Such settlers were in keeping with the chaotic character of a colony that had been fledged by the Canadian-born brothers Pierre and Jean-Baptiste Le Moyne, minor Gallic noblemen who made fortunes for themselves by enthusiastically embracing piracy, smuggling, and the embezzlement of naval supplies.[4]

Those unruly and beleaguered aliens were surrounded by thirty-five thousand Choctaws, Chickasaws, and Creeks, as well as a multitude of Indian tribes from the Illinois country and farther north.[5] In a sense, the French were simply a strange new tribe interloping on a changing landscape, and they had enormous respect for their Indian neighbors. Following one major summit, the French Governor of Louisiana had written home that the speeches of the Indian chiefs "have nothing barbarian about them." Indeed, "because of my office, I am in a better position than anybody to judge the soundness of their reason and the indispensable necessity of listening to them."[6] He clearly thought them better men than his own French settlers.

When France lost Canada to the British as a result of the French and Indian or Seven Years' War, Louisiana became an expensive and unnecessary burden on the French exchequer. During tense talks held in the utmost secrecy at Fontainebleau in the fall of 1762, in a deeply duplicitous move typical of the French approach to the Bourbon Family Pact, Louis XV formally offered Louisiana to his Spanish cousin Charles III, presenting this as a magnanimous act of gratitude. The Spanish first minister, Ricardo Wall, another Irishman, wondered whether Spain might find a way to gracefully withdraw, observing sardonically, "A great influence with the king has been the air of friendship with which the two courts will appear before the world as a result of so fine a deed."[7] Another cynical Spaniard stated they "sold it to him as a fine gift, but foisted upon him the government of new and unwilling subjects."[8]

In 1766, a senior naval officer from Seville, Antonio de Ulloa, was appointed as the first Spanish Governor of Louisiana. He had one of the most brilliant scientific minds of the age. He had discovered platinum; designed a canal route across central Spain; wrote a comprehensive report on the government, society, economy, and defense of Spanish America; was a member of the Royal Society in London; and spoke excellent French. But his only experience of government was as governor of a lawless mining town in Peru, which he described as "a theater of discord . . . animosity, anger, hate," and "unfettered rage." Ulloa had conspicuously failed to tame these "communities whose spirits burn in the violent flame of hatred," which he described as "souls in Purgatory."[9] It is a mystery why he was chosen to bring order to a place as potentially politically toxic as Louisiana.[10]

Ulloa disembarked at New Orleans on March 5, 1766, with only ninety soldiers, battered by the relentless rain and whipping wind of a violent thunderstorm, an appropriately ominous welcome. His official reception was as friendly as the weather. The local oligarchs, a cabal of largely illiterate gangsters who had formed the official French High Council, loathed him for his education, for his slight build, and his "sharp, weak voice," which "announced his disposition" in effeminate tones. These were tough frontiersmen, good at dealing day by day with the immediate practical realities of their isolated world almost completely unfettered by the French Crown. They knew Spain would try to police their local economy, largely based on smuggling, which amounted to a *de facto* ability to trade freely and largely untaxed across the Americas.

While the French governor, Charles Aubry, was sympathetic to Ulloa's plight, the three hundred geriatric, disabled, or alcoholic French veteran troops stationed at the colony under his command refused to recognize Spanish rule. Ulloa concluded that he was in no position to impose his authority at New Orleans and agreed to share the government with Aubry. "Nothing seemed more extraordinary than to see two different administrations, two flags, and two commanding officers in the same country," one of the oligarchs observed.[11]

Ulloa retreated from the hostile atmosphere at New Orleans to the mouth of the Mississippi to supervise the construction of a new fortification at La Balize, where he raised the Spanish flag to the sound of cannon fire on January 20, 1767.[12] He also ordered detachments of troops to build forts opposite the British positions at Manchac and Natchez (which became largely redundant when the British withdrew both garrisons the following year) and to establish a major stronghold near St. Louis that could control the confluence of the Missouri and the Mississippi rivers.[13]

Ulloa further infuriated the French oligarchs by celebrating his marriage to a Peruvian noblewoman at La Balize rather than throwing a sumptuous society party in New Orleans. Some of the most influential members of the High Council, the key institution of the hybrid administration, began to meet secretly in the garden of a wealthy widow who was engaged in a "scandalous liaison" with the French commissary, Nicolas Foucault. He was "openly living with her . . . even in his rooms in town," Ulloa complained, a middle-aged man perhaps horrified that his own young bride might be corrupted by such wanton licentiousness.[14]

The conspirators fomented discontent by spreading rumors that Ulloa was about to ban French wine and instead insist local merchants import rotgut from Catalonia. This was dangerous slander. Wine was enormously emblematic of social status in New Orleans, and it was said that during the French and Indian War supposedly penniless men had paid as much as eight hundred dollars for a barrel of Bordeaux claret.[15] A secret petition calling for the expulsion of the Spanish governor was signed by most of the leading townsmen. Then Ulloa learned that Foucault had told the German farmers the Spaniards would underpay them for their crops. Among his few French friends, Ulloa had come to trust Gilbert Antoine de St. Maxent, probably the richest man in New Orleans and by far the most civilized of the settlers. So the Spaniard asked him to distribute the outstanding funds to the Germans, a mere fifteen hundred dollars, and to reassure them in person that all was well. Foucault responded by sending a party of ruffians to intercept St. Maxent, and despite his social standing, he was bound and gagged and taken back to New Orleans. The still-unpaid Germans prepared to go to the capital to ask for their money, joined by hundreds of disaffected Acadians, refugees who had been forced by the British to leave their lands in Quebec and Maine and had headed south.[16]

Over five hundred German farmers and Acadians arrived in town, where the leading conspirators opened up their cellars, served up gallons of French wine, then handed out muskets to drunken shouts of "Long live the king, long live liberty in Louisiana!" and "Victory to the good wine of Bordeaux! Down with the stinking poison of Catalonia." Ulloa took refuge aboard ship with his pregnant wife and infant child.[17]

Aubry tried to bring the conspirators to their senses at a meeting of the High Council, for he realized that even at this advanced stage in their revolt they might still have negotiated a solution with mild-mannered Ulloa. Instead, the grandiloquent attorney general, technically a servant of the Spanish Crown, easily convinced his peers to vote for the expulsion of Ulloa. Had he been as good a lawyer as he was a rouser of rabbles, he would have realized that he was not simply exposing himself and his coconspirators to the charge of treason, but that he was also providing irrefutable evidence by asking them to record their vote in favor of rebellion. "The French flag has always flown over our public square, at the head of our militia," and "been raised on our ships.

It is under that banner that we wish to live and die," they announced.[18] At two o'clock in the afternoon of October 29, 1768, a notary served notice of their decision on the Spanish governor. Ulloa sailed for Cuba.

In Madrid, the Duke of Alba, the most senior aristocrat in the land, scion of the house of Álvarez de Toledo, cradle of the most ruthless soldiers in Spanish history, set the tone of Charles III's response:[19] "It seems to me that the most important thing is that the whole world and especially America must see that the king can put a stop to anything that undermines due respect for His Majesty."

Alba advocated the brutal repression of the colony with overwhelming force and the exemplary punishment of as many rebels as possible. The Secretary of the Indies concurred, "The crime committed by these people deserves the most severe and rigorous punishment." The Secretary of State, the Count of Aranda, warned that they would have to send such a force as "to prevent the possibility of any disgrace." Only the Secretary to the Treasury dissented, for it would fall to him to work out how to finance such an expedition.

This fury at the affront to Spanish honor went hand in glove with an almost all-consuming terror of the British. In London, the Colonial Secretary teased the Spanish Ambassador by suggesting Spain cede the problem province to England. But the Spaniard retorted that the Frenchmen of New Orleans had merely followed the terrible example of the English colonies, in which rebellion was brewing in response to the notorious Stamp Act.[20]

Some enthusiastic historians have even suggested that this French uprising in Louisiana somehow prefigured the Revolutionary War. The Bordeaux Rebellion and the Boston Tea Party, after all, both involved beverages and were essentially about American merchants taking direct action against unwelcome new taxation imposed without consent or consultation. But the obvious difference is that the oligarchs of New Orleans were nostalgic for the absolute rule of an absent monarch, while the Declaration of Independence was essentially a republican rejection of the status quo and a parliament and king who refused them representation. Moreover, in 1776, the delegates to the Continental Congress were well aware that they were pledging their lives, fortunes, and sacred honor to a greater cause, while the Frenchmen in Louisiana seem to have been too foolish to appreciate they were risking anything.

Charles III chose Alejandro O'Reilly, the Irish Wild Goose who was a close friend of Bucareli and an experienced army officer, to stamp royal authority on Louisiana. He had helped develop new defenses at Havana and restored order to the streets of Madrid following the riots of 1765. He landed at La Balize on July 20, 1769, with an armada of twenty-seven ships and an army of twenty-seven hundred experienced soldiers, five hundred more than the British force sent to attack Bunker Hill. Spain meant business.

Three leading conspirators came to make representation to him as envoys of the people and plead for leniency. As O'Reilly noted wryly, they really came to "reconnoiter my true forces and gage my intentions."[21] When the rebel Frenchmen saw his mighty armada, they were terrified.

The usually eloquent attorney general stuttered and stammered and groveled. "I have been chosen to assure Your Excellency of the submission of the colony. This colony has never had any intention of failing in the profound respect it professes for the great monarch." He rambled on, blaming Ulloa for the trouble, then finally explaining, "The Frenchman is docile and used to being governed with kindness. Your Excellency will find everyone submissive, and the colony implores justice of Your Excellency."

O'Reilly listened impassively and then replied, "It is not possible for men to judge things without first informing themselves of the facts."[22]

Even then, the stupid rebels failed to flee with their lives to British West Florida.

O'Reilly set his ships in a line along the riverfront at New Orleans and trained their fifty cannon on the city. The flagship fired a gun, the gangplanks lowered, and his rigorously disciplined soldiers occupied the main square in formation. The former French Governor Aubry and the "principal persons of the High Council and the town received our commander as he disembarked" to the thundering tattoo of the drums. "At that moment," an eyewitness reported, "the flagship fired its guns in salute." The sailors aboard all the ships "had lined up on the yardarms and the mastheads and shouted out five times, 'Viva el rey, long live the king!'" The artillerymen and the musketeers fired a deafening salvo and filled the air with acrid smoke.[23]

O'Reilly took formal possession of Louisiana. The Spanish flag was run up the flagpole and flown from the four gates of the city. While a Te Deum was sung in the cathedral, detachments of men secured the city's magazines. Three days later, O'Reilly quietly arrested nine leading rebels and "three of a lesser class," who could easily be coerced into testifying against their coconspirators, and put them on trial under Spanish law. They rested their defense on the notion that Ulloa had not formally taken possession of Louisiana under international law, and therefore they could not be guilty of treason against the Spanish Crown. Aubry proved to be a star witness for the prosecution, testifying that he had read out Louis XV's proclamations and had shared the government with Ulloa. "Bloody" O'Reilly, as he has forever been known since, declared all twelve defendants guilty. Six were jailed at Havana, six were shot by firing squad on October 25, 1769. Of the ringleaders, only the

French Crown official Nicolas Foucault was spared Spanish justice. He was remanded to Paris, where he was sentenced to imprisonment in the Bastille.[24]

With the political situation resolved, O'Reilly faced the problem of feeding the large force of troops he now had stationed at New Orleans. He turned to another Irish adventurer, Oliver Pollock, who had briefly settled in Pennsylvania before becoming a smuggler in the Caribbean. Pollock had almost certainly learned about O'Reilly's army in Havana and was shrewd enough to realize his troops would be difficult to feed. So he purchased "a cargo of flour" and landed at New Orleans, according to his own account, at a time when "there was no flour in the colony," for "the last had been sold at thirty dollars per barrel." "I offered O'Reilly my cargo," he explained, but "requested the General fix the price himself." They quickly agreed he would be paid fifteen dollars a barrel, and O'Reilly also granted Pollock the right to trade freely so long as he was resident in Louisiana.[25] The two men became firm friends, and within a few years Pollock became the richest, most influential merchant in New Orleans and a crucial supporter of the American Revolution.

New Orleans was a grid of perfectly straight streets, eleven blocks long and six deep. There were about eight hundred timber-frame houses with brick and mud in-fill known as *colombage*, most of them surrounded by a porch and raised eight feet off the ground. There was a "very handsome and commodious brick house" for the Capuchin monks, and a "prison and guardhouse" that was also a good strong building. The heart of the city was the wide plaza now called Jackson Square, open to the river, where a curious English traveler observed that "the church dedicated to Saint Louis" was "in so ruinous a condition that divine service has not been performed in it" for years and was instead celebrated in "one of the king's storehouses." A former barracks house that had stood along one side of the square had completely collapsed, and the city was defended by a flimsy stockade "with a trifling ditch" that largely seemed to be there to prevent slaves from getting in and out at night.[26]

O'Reilly began restructuring the administration of his province, replacing the High Council with a Spanish *cabildo*, a city council, which he allowed the leading Frenchmen of the colony to control. He secured funds to begin construction of a beautiful building for this powerful body, still today the architectural jewel of old New Orleans. He imposed licenses on shops, taverns, billiard parlors, and gambling dens, and he secured a voluntary contribution from the butchers, ensuring an income of two thousand pesos a year for the local government. He convened a great Indian Council at which he smoked a peace pipe with chiefs from almost all the tribes living within two hundred miles of New Orleans. He hung gold medals bearing an image of Charles III around the necks of the nine most important chiefs, drew his sword, and dubbed them on the shoulder as though knighting them. Afterward, following age-old Spanish practice, he had his troops perform a terrifyingly realistic mock battle to entertain his Indian guests while leaving them in no doubt as to his military might.[27]

In 1770, O'Reilly formally handed power to a civilian governor, Luis de Unzaga, a dashing figure, tall and handsome, with a great mane of dark hair and sparkling eyes.[28] Facing a colony in deep recession, Unzaga quickly adopted the kind of *laissez-faire* approach to illegal trade that had always been essential to the economy of Louisiana, thus winning the hearts of the French oligarchs while lining his own pocket. As one Frenchman put it, "He was thought to have been good for the finances of the colony . . . without neglecting his own."[29] Unzaga became a conspicuously gregarious member of society and married one of the most eligible heiresses in the colony, Elizabeth de St. Maxent, whose wealthy father, Gilbert, had been detained and tied up by the rebels on his way to pay off the Germans in 1768. At the same time, Unzaga worked hard to bring Louisiana into the Spanish commercial system, exporting tobacco, resin, pitch, and turpentine used in shipbuilding. But his only lasting success was to establish the lumber trade with Cuba, which remained lucrative into the nineteenth century.[30]

In the summer of 1772, with deft diplomacy, Unzaga dealt with a major political crisis among the Capuchins.

On July 19, a Spanish Capuchin, Father Cirilo, arrived at the head of a group of friars determined to adhere strictly to Saint Francis's rule of "austerity" and "the most extreme poverty." The leader of the long-established French friars, Father Dagobert, led a procession through the crowded main square to welcome the new brothers at the levee. To judge by his portrait in the *cabildo*, he was a truly formidable figure with his long beard and fiery dark eyes framed beneath bushy brows. Yet he was apprehensive, for his rule over his friars had always been in keeping with the moral laxity so characteristic of French Louisiana.

Within three weeks, Father Cirilo sent a scathing report to the Bishop of Havana in which the stern Spaniard refused to refer to the French friars as "Capuchins" because he thought them "unworthy of that holy name." They neglected confession, wore "shirts, breeches, stockings, and shoes" as though they were laymen, and every one of them had "a watch in his fob and a clock in his room." They ate food with silver cutlery and even had special little spoons for their coffee. Cirilo was appalled that young black and mixed-race women waited on the fathers at table and even lived in the convent courtyard. "One night, at four in the morning," he reported, "I managed to spot a white man sallying out of the chamber" of one unmarried girl who was "in a delicate situation." "For no reason and under no pretext whatsoever should these women be allowed to go into the friar's bedchambers," Cirilo told the bishop.[31] Father Cirilo deplored the way Dagobert allowed his three children by this "whore" to "eat at our table and from [his] own plate, and he shamelessly lets them call him *papá* . . . She is the absolute mistress of the whole place, and the friars are so fond of her that they compete to offer her the best plates of food before anyone else gets to taste it." Meanwhile, the consecrated wafers of the Eucharist were rotten with weevils, and the holy oil had turned rancid. Dagobert, Cirilo concluded, "is incapable of being trusted with the spiritual government of this colony."[32]

Unzaga wrote to the Secretary of the Indies, Julián de Arriaga, in support of Dagobert, commenting, "Enlightened prudence and a good deal of tolerance are needed here, for although this is a Spanish province, I cannot flatter His Majesty by saying the people have ceased to be French at heart." Cirilo's calumny, Unzaga suggested, was motivated by "ambition," and that "by sowing dissent among his brethren he had been so mean-spirited as to warrant his fall from the pedestal of probity." Unzaga gently extracted the price of that support by cajoling the oligarchs into investing in new churches and better housing for the clergy. New parishes were established. As money poured in, the Spanish Capuchins reached an accommodation with their errant French counterparts.[33]

Spanish Louisiana was temporarily at peace.

In January 1774, Junípero Serra returned to Alta California to live out the lengthy dotage of his already long life. He sailed aboard the *Santiago*, which was laden with food and provisions to relieve Monterey after many months of hunger and dearth.

The ship's captain, Juan Pérez, by then the most experienced Spanish pilot working Pacific waters, carried secret instructions from Viceroy Bucareli to continue north in a new voyage of exploration. In Madrid, José de Gálvez was still worried about rumors of Russian and English attempts to settle the northwest coast. Pérez's orders were to search for signs of any such incursions and to firmly stake Spanish claims to the land as far as he could by erecting crosses and burying documents asserting possession.[34]

Pérez set out from Monterey on June 18 with Estéban José Martínez Fernández y Martínez de la Sierra as his second-in-command, a proud and excitable man from Seville who, fifteen years later, would be one of the protagonists in a drunken argument at Nootka Sound that nearly led Britain and Spain to go to war. But that was all in the future when, on July 18, 1774, after many days sailing through rain and fog on increasingly fearsome swell, the lookout sighted the northern shores of the Queen Charlotte Islands, almost at the maritime frontier between British Columbia and Alaska, still disputed today by Canada and the United States.[35] The sailors saw columns of smoke rising above the pine forest, and the following day Haida Indians came out to the ships on an impressively large and beautifully decorated canoe to see what they might acquire by trade.

Father Crespí had accompanied the voyage and vividly described the scene as the Indians approached, seven men straining at the oars, while another, his body painted, danced and threw feathers into the water. "These natives are big and burly, with fine features, white and vermilion complexions, and their hair worn long. They wear otter and sealskin and pointy hats of closely woven grasses. They seemed peaceful and friendly to everyone." Esteban Martínez was struck by the number of metal bracelets worn by the women and he was revolted by the way they wore lip plugs made of painted shells. The Indian chief took a fancy to Martínez's red cap and traded it for a "beautiful" fur cloak, although Crespí remarked acerbically that some of the sailors regretted wearing the cloaks they had acquired, for "they ended up scratching the bites they were given by the little critters that these natives breed in their clothing."[36] The Haida were described by Europeans for the first time in history. We do not know what they thought of their visitors, but over the coming years they learned that European traders were often violent and unscrupulous. The Haida had a ferocious reputation among their neighbors, and they responded to European aggression in kind, assaulting passing ships with such élan that they gained great renown for their piracy.[37]

Pérez tried to sail farther north, and on July 21 he sighted Dall Island and recorded his latitude as 55°N. He was now in modern U.S. waters off Alaska, but he chose to err on the side of caution: "Having considered the inconstancy and confusion of the weather and the uncertainty of finding an anchorage farther north . . . I decided not to continue farther."[38] The *Santiago* headed for home, keeping clear of the rocky coast in thick fog. On August 7, the crew sighted Vancouver Island and carefully took soundings as they approached the rocky coast of the Hesquiat Peninsula, the southern reach of the entrance to Nootka Sound at a place now called Perez Rocks, where they found a temporary haven.[39] They met the local potentate, Chief Ma-kwee-na, and traded with him and his people. Again, Martínez seems to have been on the rough end of the exchanges. This time, someone went off with a set of his silver spoons, which the great British seafarer Captain James Cook bought four years later when he visited Nootka from a man "who wore them round his neck by way of ornament."[40] Pérez continued south, reaching Monterey by the end of August.

Pérez was chastised for his timidity in not exploring farther, and Bucareli was persuaded to launch another expedition the following year. The commander of this enterprise, sailing aboard the *Santiago* with Pérez as his pilot, went raving mad a few days out of port. The captain of a tiny schooner called the *Sonora* took command, leaving a young sailor from Lima, Juan Francisco de la Bodega y Quadra, in charge of the smaller vessel. Pérez seems to have infected the substitute commander and his officers aboard the flagship with his limited sense of adventure, and having made the first documented sighting of the Columbia River, they sailed the *Santiago* south to the safety of Monterey. But Bodega y Quadra took leave of his risk-averse superiors and urged the crew of the little *Sonora* onward, eventually landing the first Spaniards to walk on Alaskan soil near Mount Edgecumbe, before recording a maximum latitude of 58°30'N. He reported seeing no sign of the Northwest Passage, but otherwise gained little practical information for so much daring. However, his courage and initiative were good for his *reputación*, and many years later he was made a Knight of Santiago.

The *Sonora* and the *Santiago* were reunited at Monterey and headed south for home, but during that voyage, Pérez died of scurvy and was buried at sea on November 1.

CHAPTER 20

THE GOVERNORS

LOUISIANA & NEW MEXICO

I went with Bernardo de Gálvez. Although we hardly knew each other, I liked him very much, and as so often happens, the feeling was mutual. I much enjoyed the journey because he recounted all sorts of stories about himself, and in truth, his life is like a novel.

—FRANCISCO DE SAAVEDRA

ON HIS RETURN TO MADRID, JOSÉ DE GÁLVEZ began serving on the Council of the Indies and arranged for Bernardo to be appointed the youngest captain in the history of the Seville Infantry, one of the regiments that had served under O'Reilly at New Orleans.[1] In 1774, Bernardo enrolled at the Royal Military Academy at Avila, which had been newly founded under the directorship of O'Reilly "for the education of officers of outstanding ability, good conduct, and an aptitude for the art of war."[2] There, O'Reilly explained to a promising student called Francisco de Saavedra that he made them study mathematics and academic subjects as well military tactics and theory in order to break the grip "that ignorance has on power." Saavedra would be instrumental in designing the French naval policy that led to the great American victory at Yorktown.[3]

Saavedra and Bernardo were among the many graduates who served the following year on a massive expedition to seize control of Algiers on the North African coast, involving 50 fighting vessels, 250 merchant ships, and 20,000 men, under the overall command of O'Reilly. "I went with Bernardo de Gálvez," Saavedra remembered years later. "Although we hardly knew each other, I liked him very much, and as so often happens, the feeling was mutual. I much enjoyed the journey because he recounted all sorts of stories about himself, and in truth, his life is like a novel."[4]

This campaign was more of a horror story. O'Reilly landed his troops on a sandy beach, where they were immediately trapped under constant fire from enemy snipers and artillery positions on the dunes above. Bernardo was shot in the leg trying to take the high ground and valiantly remained on the field. Before sundown, O'Reilly was forced to order their retreat. His first major campaign had been an unmitigated disaster. Saavedra counted seven hundred corpses on the beach and helped evacuate more than two thousand wounded, "all crying out in great distress."[5] The Algerians claimed the Spanish losses were four times that number.[6] As one wounded aristocrat caustically commented, the "Moors must have found it difficult to believe we should have come such a long way in such warlike fashion simply to pay them a visit and spend a day by the seaside with them."[7] According to Saavedra, Bernardo composed an ironic song about the *débâcle* while convalescing at the attractive harbor town of El Puerto de Santa María near Cadiz, famous for its exquisite dry sherry and succulent shellfish.[8]

In January 1776, Bernardo met Saavedra in Seville. Full of excitement, Bernardo explained that his uncle José de Gálvez had just been appointed Secretary of the Indies. "He offered to introduce me to him," Saavedra recalled.[9]

As Secretary of the Indies, José de Gálvez brought a potent ethos of familial loyalty to an age when powerful men habitually relied on networks of friends and acquaintances who trusted one another and were dependent upon a strong sense that their individual success or failure was closely tied to a community of interest. He would appoint his elder brother Matias (Bernardo's father) first as Captain General and President of the Audiencia of Guatemala, then later as Viceroy of New Spain, where he would be succeeded, on his death, by Bernardo, who had already served as Governor of Louisiana and then Havana. In 1785, José was himself elevated to the aristocracy as Marquis of Sonora.

José de Gálvez was deeply concerned by the increasing encroachment into the Spanish Empire by Russian, French, and British explorers and merchants and the consequently growing threat of conflict across the continent. Fighting might potentially be triggered in many different theaters, but North America was of special concern. So, as José enthusiastically pursued the reform of government throughout Spanish America, he finally established the long-mooted Comandancia General that brought the Internal Provinces under the direct control of the crown, separating them from New Spain. Teodoro de Croix was appointed as overall captain general or commander in chief. Over the following years, in face of the insurmountable problems of imposing military control on such a broad spread of wild and largely unsettled terrain, the crown experimented with different arrangements of command until the Comandancia was brought under the authority of the Audiencia of Mexico in 1786.[10]

But, of course, as José de Gálvez took office as Secretary of the Indies, in 1776 he faced the most serious crisis in the history of European colonialism in the Americas.

The growing unrest in British North America and the Declaration of Independence asked a compelling question of England's Bourbon enemies: Should they support the rebels, and if so, how? For Louis XVI of France, the answer was as simple as the question itself, for the French had nothing to lose from an English victory and everything to gain in the unlikely event that the American Patriots should prevail. But in Madrid, the answer was fraught with complexity. Spanish hearts clearly reveled in the developing quarrel between an old enemy and the Thirteen Colonies, but as a basic ideological principle, Spanish statesmen objected to rebellion against a sovereign.

The Bourbons ruled as absolute monarchs, royal dictators by virtue of God's will. The king personally appointed and removed ministers who governed with his authority. The power of the English parliamentarians over their king was already anathema. American calls for free trade, independence, and democratic republican government were a horrifying rejection of royal authority, an assault on a divine order. This theoretical objection materialized in practical terms as the strikingly prescient fear that a Patriot victory would encourage discontented *criollos* across the Spanish Empire to likewise rebel for independence. "The Americas are already an important yet far-off part of the world," observed the Count of Aranda, who served as Charles III's Ambassador to France throughout the Revolutionary War, "which encourages an independent spirit." He was deeply concerned that many disgruntled Spanish *criollos* "would find succor for their patriotism in the example of the English Colonies and be inclined to emulate their" rebellion.[11]

Moreover, Charles's ministers in Madrid had long feared a resurgence of war with England in the New World, a war they were convinced Spain would lose. When thousands of British troops began disembarking in North America to confront the Continental Army, Spanish fear turned to terror. Before the Patriots astonished the world by defeating the British at Saratoga in 1777, only a handful of intellectual French fantasists and a few belligerent Bourbon fanatics actually believed the Americans might win. Spanish realists confronted the likely nightmare that either British troops would suffocate the rebellion, or, worse still, Parliament and Congress would accommodate each other. Then, King George's newly reunited subjects and their two huge armies would ally themselves with a passionately resurgent sense of bellicose British brotherhood and advance westward in all-conquering fury across Spanish America.[12] Charles III's first minister, the Count of Floridablanca, declaimed,

"We must prepare for war with England as though it were inevitable, but we must do everything we possibly can to prevent it." [13]

In Paris in 1777, however, Ambassador Aranda met Benjamin Franklin and Arthur Lee and was greatly impressed by the rebels' burgeoning self-confidence, for "without as yet being sure of their independence, they had turned up with the offer of a treaty." He began to realize that the Americans themselves might become a serious threat to Spanish America, and he warned Madrid that the Thirteen Colonies already had "two and half million inhabitants descended from Europeans . . . According to the rules of propagation, that number will double every twenty-five to thirty years, so that in fifty or sixty years there could be eight or ten million of them, more than in Europe herself, or even more given how attractive the laws of the new country will be." "Spain needs to secure the friendship of this new nation by means of a solemn treaty," he urged, for otherwise, should the rebels succeed, they would "establish a great American power with which Spain would have no ties, nor have laid the groundwork for establishing the borders between one and the other." He advised forging a formal alliance early "in order to securely define the limits of this powerful new neighbor." [14] A former Captain General of Havana concurred in a written opinion submitted to the Spanish cabinet. The Americans, he said, were "a fearsome force . . . now well used to armed conflict." But he added, ominously, that for all the assurances they might offer Spain when their backs were to the wall, they would soon ally themselves again with their English cousins. [15]

Early in 1777, the Council of State voted unanimously not to ally Spain to the rebel colonies. Soon afterward, Floridablanca made it clear to an increasingly agitated Aranda and the anxious French court that his administration would take whatever time might be necessary to decide what to do about the Americans. "The purpose of our every action or precautionary measure must be to take advantage of the immediate problems England faces in her colonies," he stated. "The most obvious benefit to Spain would be to throw the English out of Florida and the Gulf of Mexico." But he had also heard the warnings about an independent America, and he advocated direct diplomatic interference "in the drafting of any constitution" so as to try to ensure "the division of the American republic, the different states remain independent from one another, their interests so aligned, that we need not fear the emergence of a formidable new power on the borders of our America." [16]

When José de Gálvez took office in February 1776, he had agreed that it was "necessary to observe perfect neutrality" with respect to the American rebels, but quietly he began to bolster Spanish defenses in Cuba and Louisiana and issued instructions to extend the network of spies operating within the English colonies.[17] Spain already had an efficient system of espionage in the Caribbean and had established excellent sources in British West Florida, but elsewhere in North America the arrangements could be extremely homespun. For example, in 1769, a local fisherman who had been working the Florida coast near Cape Canaveral delivered a remarkable letter to the Bishop of Havana, sent by the Spanish priest, Father Camps, of a mysterious new plantation-colony, called New Smyrna, south of St. Augustine, in which he pleaded for supplies of holy oil and consecrated hosts so he could celebrate mass.[†]

Bucareli and the bishop realized that Camps might prove a useful source of information about East Florida, and Cuban fishermen were instructed to remain in constant contact with New Smyrna. The Spaniards were delighted to discover, two years later, that Camps was confessor to the Catholic wife of the British Governor at St. Augustine, but they were deeply perturbed when she told him Britain would soon declare war on Spain.[18] Britain had no intention of declaring war, so it is plausible that her apparently compliant treachery in the confessional may have been a calculated act of misinformation, undertaken in cooperation with her husband.

[†]The history of the unusual Florida settlement of New Smyrna began with a love story worthy of the Arabian Nights, a romance that unfolded in the Ottoman provincial capital of Smyrna, today the bustling Turkish city of Izmir on the Anatolian coast. There, the British Consul, a rough and roguish Scotsman called Andrew Turnbull, courted and finally married Maria Gracia Dura Bin, the beautiful daughter of a local Greek merchant and the first Greek woman to settle in North America, according to her tombstone in Charleston (findagrave .com/cgi-bin/fg.cgi?page=gr&GRid=12776013). On retiring from government service, Turnbull established a prosperous medical practice in London, but he could not resist the urge to roam and a life in the sunshine.

He secured a grant to establish a colony for Greek settlers on an enormous tract of land south of St. Augustine and convinced five or six hundred Orthodox Christian Greeks to join him, including "two hundred wild tribesmen from the mountains of the Peloponnesus." Determined to recruit more settlers, he advertised on the Spanish island of Menorca, then under British control, and eight or nine hundred Catholics joined his expedition. Finally, about fourteen hundred colonists crossed the Atlantic on eight ships to establish their homes on Turnbull's plantation of ten thousand acres, which he called New Smyrna in honor of his wife (Doggett, *Dr. Andrew Turnbull*; Griffin, *Mullet on the Beach*).

Once in Florida, Father Camps, the priest of the Catholic Menorcans, struggled to obtain holy oil, consecrated water, wafers, and other elements essential to the sacraments and celebrating mass. When a Cuban fisherman made a clandestine landing off the New Smyrna coast, Camps wrote his letter to the Bishop of Havana, asking for supplies.

Two months after learning of the Declaration of Independence, José de Gálvez advised the Council of Castile that the time had come to "enter into a tacit and clandestine understanding with the American colonists so as to encourage them to stout resistance and fill them with hope."[19] He clearly believed that war with England was inevitable and knew he would need a governor in New Orleans who was both an energetic soldier and a man he could trust personally and absolutely. O'Reilly had already advised appointing Bernardo as military commander because "he was familiar with French ways and spoke the language" and "he has gained a knowledge of the Indians, which will be useful."[20] So on September 19, 1776, in a supremely pragmatic act of nepotism, José de Gálvez named his nephew Governor of Louisiana and told him to discreetly support the American Patriots.[21]

Meanwhile, in early August 1776, Captain George Gibson of Philadelphia had arrived in New Orleans with a bundle of letters from General Charles Lee asking Governor Unzaga for "muskets, blankets, and medicines, especially quinine."[22] Gibson had made a daring descent of the Ohio and Mississippi rivers with fifteen men drawn from his own company of hardy backwoodsmen known as Gibson's Lambs, traveling through territory controlled by hostile Indians and British Loyalists, even slipping past the English stronghold at Natchez under the cover of darkness. At New Orleans, Gibson sought out Oliver Pollock, whom he had known in Pennsylvania.[23] Pollock found quarters for the Americans and then badgered Unzaga into agreeing to a secret rendezvous at which Gibson delivered his mail and explained in person that he was also empowered by Lee and the Virginia Safety Committee to ask for Spanish support in a proposed attack on a number of British possessions in West Florida. Should the rebels succeed in capturing Pensacola, Gibson asked, "would his Catholic Majesty receive possession of the same from the Americans?"[24]

Unzaga gave Gibson the impression that he would urge Madrid to support the idea and wrote in encouraging tones to Lee, but Unzaga inevitably explained that he could do nothing without permission from the king.[25] Unzaga also knew there were British spies in New Orleans and that open support for the rebels might lead to war, but he was clearly sympathetic to the Patriots. Gibson had also explained that the Americans were short of gunpowder, and Unzaga knew well enough that an army that could not fire its guns could swiftly lose a war.[26] So he agreed to "grant a *bateau* load of Powder," twelve thousand pounds in total, but in a piece of theater designed to confuse British spies, Unzaga had Gibson arrested and imprisoned. Gibson signed a promissory note for 1,850 Spanish silver dollars to be drawn on the Colony of Virginia, and Unzaga "privately delivered" the powder to Pollock "out of the King's store." Pollock sent almost a hundred barrels, three-quarters of it, upriver with an escort of forty or more Americans, while Gibson was officially repatriated by sea to Philadelphia, along with the rest of the powder and a letter from Pollock tendering "my hearty Services . . . to the Country to which I owe everything but my birth."[27] Pollock proved to be an astonishingly staunch Patriot for a man who had barely lived two years in the American colonies. Years later, he invoked the thrill of rebellion, remembering how "my soul panted for the success of American arms."[28] Some enthusiastic biographers have suggested that he accidently invented the dollar sign as a result of poor penmanship in a letter to Jefferson, although it had long been used to mark slaves in the Spanish Empire.[29]

On Christmas Eve 1776, Gálvez wrote Unzaga vindicating his decision, advised him that further consignments of "weapons, munitions, clothes, and quinine that the English colonists have requested" would soon be delivered to New Orleans, and ordered the governor to pursue the "the most ingenious and secret way of supplying these things" to the Americans "by appearing to sell them to private merchants." Gálvez also ordered the Captain General of Havana to ship whatever "surplus gunpowder and muskets might be available" to Louisiana.[30]

Meanwhile, barges carrying the bulk of the powder made the slow journey up the Mississippi, and the party was forced to winter near the junction with the Arkansas River. Finally, on May 2, 1777, they landed their cargo in Pennsylvania, "to my very great satisfaction," Pollock remembered, for it was "a very signal and seasonal supply."[31] He did not exaggerate. Without it, both Wheeling and Fort Pitt would almost certainly have been captured by the British, and that would probably have changed the course of the war in the west.[32]

Bernardo de Gálvez disembarked at New Orleans on December 2, 1776, and formally took over the governorship from Unzaga on New Year's Day. An admiring French colonist remembered years later that Bernardo had "arrived with self-confidence, bonhomie, tact, frankness, and a sense of justice and kindliness."[33] Powerful, intelligent, worldly, well connected, good company, and just turned thirty, Bernardo was heartachingly eligible in almost every way.

All he lacked was a fortune, and his eager eye soon fell on Unzaga's dazzling sister-in-law, Félicitas de St. Maxent. An old Louisiana hand described Creole women as "well shaped and of agreeable figure, lively, alert and agile" before adding that they were "seldom deformed, good mothers, devoted to their husbands and their children" and "rarely unfaithful."[34] The great Prussian naturalist Alexander von Humboldt described Félicitas as "of outstanding beauty and beloved by all" in a letter to Miguel de Costansó, the military engineer who had opened up Alta California alongside Portolá, Serra, and Anza.[35] She also had a brilliant mind and marvelous cosmopolitan chutzpah.

Following Bernardo's tragic death ten years later, at the height of his political power serving as Viceroy of New Spain, Félicitas gathered up their four children and sailed for Europe. She settled into a large and luxurious house in the heart of Madrid, where she was patroness of the most celebrated literary and political salon at court. But in the increasingly paranoid atmosphere in the aftermath of the French Revolution, the liberal spirit of intellectual inquiry she had encouraged seemed like Enlightenment extremism. She was banished to Valladolid along with her French cook, her Parisian hairdresser, her coachman, and her Haitian slave.[36] Bernardo's ambition lent luster to her many attractions, for she was the daughter of Gilbert Antoine de St. Maxent. One of the few oligarchs who had supported Ulloa, he was a founder of St. Louis and was now the richest merchant and landowner in Louisiana. Through that marriage, Bernardo gained the goodwill of New Orleans society and allied himself to the power and influence of his father-in-law.[37]

When Bernardo first saw her, presumably at a New Year's Eve ball, Félicitas was a nineteen-year-old widow with an infant daughter. There was clearly as much passion about their union as there was convenience, for when Bernardo fell so gravely sick the following fall that he was given the last rites, he told his father confessor "that he was formally engaged to Félicitas, and given his current plight, he wanted to marry her, so that should God take his life, he might die knowing he had been true to his word," the priest later recalled.[38] This was a bold move. As an army officer and senior government official Bernardo needed royal assent before he could marry. But urgency was the better part of valor, and they celebrated the wedding in secret on November 2. The most obvious explanation for this hurry is that they had already begun an affair, which placed an enormous obligation on Bernardo to make an honest woman of Félicitas before he might die. However, the marriage proved so miraculous a cure that nine and a half months later their first child, Matilde, was born into a world on the brink of war.[39]

In the late spring of 1777, as Bernardo was falling in love with Félicitas, a merchant arrived from Havana with a secret cargo of guns, powder, bayonets, medicine, and serge cloth for uniforms and carrying a secret letter explaining that all these goods were for the Americans, but because they belonged to the king, they must be transferred with the utmost secrecy. Instead, the ham-fisted officials at Havana had provided real documentation for the consignment, and within hours rumors of royal aid for the American rebels were being repeated throughout New Orleans.

Bernardo took matters into his own hands by publicly acknowledging that the goods were indeed crown property but insisting that the guns were for his own men, the powder was to replace some that had spoiled, and that the medicines were for the royal hospital. The cloth, he said, had been eaten by moths.[40] The British were furious, but at least Bernardo could plausibly deny his involvement in supplying the Americans. The whole consignment was then hurriedly shipped upriver on Pollock's "deeply loaded" boats, each propelled by two dozen oarsmen. By the end of the year, the Irish American calculated he had organized the clandestine transport of supplies to the value of $74,087.[41]

That summer, the American commander at Fort Pitt, George Morgan, wrote Bernardo, clearly more in hope than expectation, asking him to provide logistical support for a revolutionary assault on Mobile and Pensacola. Morgan also asked that the Americans be allowed to trade freely at New Orleans.

"Although it would please me greatly, I cannot do it," Bernardo replied. "But you may rest assured that I will offer what assistance as I can, although it must appear that I am ignorant of it all. The trade you want can be established however you desire, and those who carry it on will be given my protection."[42]

The following winter, the Continental Congress commissioned a near-bankrupt drunkard called James Willing as a navy captain and ordered him to collect the provisions piling up at New Orleans and bring them to Fort Pitt. Willing had just spent three years at Natchez, squandering his inheritance, failing as a merchant, and running up colossal debts, so his support for the revolution was as self-interested as it was fervent. He also convinced Congress to instruct him to "make prize of all British property on the river," much of it owned by his creditors, and then "apply to the [Spanish] governor of this province for the liberty to make sale of them" at New Orleans.[43]

Willing interpreted his instructions broadly, and with a band of thirty men he set off aboard an armed boat called the *Rattletrap*. When they got to Kaskaskia, Willing took the opportunity to steal furs and brandy from some leading French settlers he referred to as "damn rogues," presumably men whose acumen he blamed for his failure as a trader.[44] At Natchez, he seized property and slaves from a prominent British plantation owner, which convinced the rest of the population to swear an oath to be neutral in the Revolutionary War. But as he approached Manchac, his brutal diplomacy descended into piracy and hooliganism. The rampage was almost certainly fueled by the toxic cocktail of too much hard liquor and the empowerment of this failed and humiliated man. Farm animals were slaughtered, wine butts burst, buildings burned, and, by one report, a young woman was deliberately poisoned.[45]

But Willing's men also proved effective at capturing a number of armed ships, which might otherwise have secured the river for the British. Downstream, panicked Loyalists fled for protection with their slaves and their chattels to Spanish Louisiana. Willing was "perfectly and intimately acquainted with all the gentlemen upon the river at whose houses he had often been entertained in the most hospitable manner and frequently indulged his propensity of getting drunk," one victim complained, yet he happily "robbed" the man's house "of everything that could be carried away" and told his men "to drive down my negroes and if opposed to shoot 'em down."[46]

Some of the refugees who escaped Willing's rampage broadcast their sense of "duty to proclaim to all the world" the great "succor [Bernardo] had the goodness to offer us."[47] But even as he showed exemplary charity to these civilians, he allowed Willing and his men to sell their spoils by public auction. This led to fervent protests and a lengthy exchange between Bernardo and the captain of a British gunship. Variously cordial, legalistic, tetchy, and obsessive, the Englishman won enough of the argument to oblige Bernardo to negotiate with Pollock and Willing for the release of all the property taken on the lower part of the river that was under Spanish control.

In the following weeks, British gunships caused more trouble. Bernardo de Gálvez began to realize that New Orleans was vulnerable and wrote to Havana for help. His nervous frustration was evident in an increasingly unfriendly attitude to Willing. Even Pollock lost patience with the young American and wrote to Congress complaining that "the small party you sent under Willing without any order or subordinations has thrown the whole river into confusion and created enemies and expense." Pollock could not wait to be rid of him, but Willing would not leave. "What his next pretense for tarrying here will be, God knows."[48] Pollock finally got him aboard a sloop bound for Philadelphia and sent him home with a "box of the best Havana cigars" for the members of Congress. The boat, Willing, and the cigars were captured at sea by the British and taken to New York.[49]

Henry Hamilton, the English Governor of Detroit, was known as the Hair Buyer for his generosity in paying Indians for American scalps. George Washington thought him a "constant source of trouble," and he clearly represented a serious threat on the western flank. So Fort Pitt, on the site of modern Pittsburgh, became the focus of a new aggressive strategy intended to gain control of Detroit. Washington assured everyone that "the enterprise could not have been committed to better hands" than those of the charismatic George Rogers Clark.[50]

Clark was an upper-class Virginian who had been taught classics and French at school alongside James Madison and John Tayler of Caroline. An early, eloquent, almost visionary exponent of the promise of the Ohio country, Clark had a keen mind with an inquisitive bent and was fascinated by natural phenomena. Most of all, he cut quite the figure of a swashbuckling maverick heartthrob, with his "black, penetrating, sparking eyes" and flame-colored hair, his love of fine horses, his knowledge of Indians, and his empathy with the wilderness.[51]

Congress realized the enormous value of securing a supply route up the Mississippi River and understood that the Illinois Country south of the Spanish settlement at St. Louis was strategically crucial. The Commerce Committee let it be known with some pleasure that "Bernardo de Gálvez is much disposed to favor the interests of the United States."[52] So, when George Rogers Clark arrived at Williamsburg after a long season fighting Indians, Thomas Jefferson ordered him to capture Illinois.[53]

On July 4, 1778, dressed only in "hunting shirt and breechcloth," Clark led his band of 120 rough-and-ready frontiersmen in a surprise attack on Kaskaskia, every one of them "naked of foot and limb," but with "powder horn, gun, and knapsack on his shoulder." The American invaders took the village without a shot being fired.[54] Clark quickly won over the French inhabitants of the region, who swore an oath of allegiance as soon as they learned that France had formally allied herself to the United States.[55] He then set about establishing peace with the diverse and apprehensive Indian tribes along the length of the Mississippi, as far as the Great Lakes. He achieved this Herculean task through a mixture of steadfast bravery when a contingent of chiefs tried to take him hostage and his remarkable clemency following that treachery.[56]

Clark reported that at St. Louis "a friendly correspondence immediately commenced between the Spanish officers and ourselves," which "added much to the general tranquility and happiness."[57] "An intimacy had commenced between don Leyba, [the Spanish] Lieutenant-Governor of Western Illinois, and myself. He omitted nothing in his power to prove his attachment to the Americans with such openness as left no room for a doubt; as I was never before in company of any Spanish gentlemen I was much surprised . . . for instead of finding that reserve thought peculiar to that nation, I here saw . . . freedom almost to excess."[58]

A titillating but unsubstantiated tradition in the Clark family is that during this visit he also commenced some sort of intimacy with Leyba's beautiful sister.[59] The notion seems to be borne out by a letter sent to Clark by a close friend some years later that reported that Leyba's widow had died, but that "Mademoiselle Terese is still a maid, & & &," and concluding, "If I could find the opportunity of sending you something good to toast your sweetheart I would." According to Clark's niece, as an old man he had told her that had he "been properly treated" by his country, "I would have an elegant aunt," Teresa, "whom I would have loved very much. I have often seen him shed tears when he would make the above remark." Neither Congress nor Virginia paid off the debts Clark had incurred during the war, and he said he did not believe it honorable to marry "a lady educated as she was and accustomed to all the luxuries of wealth."[60]

Whatever the realities of such a romance, Clark's alliance with the Spaniards allowed him to supply his troops and hold the Illinois Country for the United States. He had neither money nor credit on his own account, while the bills and notes he was authorized to issue in the name of Virginia were only accepted because Oliver Pollock honored them at New Orleans. Yet Pollock himself only remained solvent because Bernardo advanced him secret loans out of the Spanish treasury.[61]

At Detroit, Henry Hamilton, the Hair Buyer, convinced himself that the Spanish were "feeble," the French "fickle," and that swift action could defeat the "enterprising and brave" rebels because they were short of "resources."[62] He led an army of almost 250 Indians, Frenchmen, volunteers, and militiamen toward Illinois.

In his overconfidence, Hamilton dallied on the Wabash River following the easy capture of Vincennes, Indiana, and so allowed Clark time to launch "one of the most heroic and dramatic undertakings of the whole Revolution." In desperately cold conditions, he cajoled his starving, rag-and-bobtail army of 127 men into crossing miles of frozen floodwaters. Then, half-hidden, he got them to march up and down flying their banners, waving their flags, and pounding their drums for all they were worth, all just in sight and earshot of the town. Clark confessed his surprise to Leyba that this subterfuge convinced the Hair Buyer that he was surrounded by so large an army that it persuaded Hamilton to surrender both town and fort without a fight.[63]

As acting Governor of Louisiana, Bernardo was responsible for nearly a million square miles of notionally Spanish territory, an area almost as large as New Spain. But while the viceroy in Mexico ruled about five and a half million inhabitants, in Louisiana there were barely five thousand colonists and slaves. There were also thousands of uncounted and largely independent Indians. As he took office, Bernardo's overriding concern was the seemingly impossible task of organizing an effective defense of his frontier province when the inevitable war with Britain came.

Bernardo was both acting governor and military commander, Colonel of the Louisiana Regiment, the only professional military force in the province, made up of four hundred assorted infantrymen and a dozen officers, "most of them old and ready for retirement."[64] That summer, José de Gálvez instructed that other high-flying member of the family, his brother Matías de Gálvez, Bernardo's father, then serving as king's lieutenant on the Canary Islands, to begin recruiting a second battalion for Louisiana from among his local population of *isleños*. He was entreated to enlist men who were at least five and half feet tall, "tough," but "not disabled, nor crippled, nor sick, nor disfigured, nor men of dishonorable background" such as "Gypsies, hangmen, butchers, and convicts."[65] This cataract of supposedly negative qualities eloquently indicates the kind of characters who were typically enlisted for military service. The reasons for this were simple, as the Cabildo of the Canaries demonstrated by passing a resolution protesting that the loss of useful and productive laborers would be damaging to the islands and advocating instead that Matías enlist beggars and layabouts.[66]

He ignored the *cabildo* and initiated a rigorous program of recruitment. Seven hundred men and their families took ship for Louisiana, although some were delayed in Cuba when war finally broke out, some deserted, and others died of disease. By July 1779, 153 bachelors and 329 married recruits along with their 1,000 wives and children landed at New Orleans. But the cost of living meant that the official salary of a single *real* per day was not enough to feed a family. So while Bernardo assigned the bachelors to the existing battalion, he arranged for the family men to become civilian farmers.[67]

Long before his father's successful recruitment program in the Canaries bore such meager fruit, Bernardo had realized that any formal expansion of the army would be bogged down by bureaucracy. Within months of taking charge, he ordered a census, which established that almost two thousand inhabitants were capable of bearing arms. Bernardo had campaigned on the northern frontier of New Spain and knew the value of organizing soldier-settlers into militias. A small battalion of infantry militiamen was already based in New Orleans, and a tiny artillery unit had been established by O'Reilly, but Bernardo now created seventeen new companies across the colony. He also well understood the political value of attaching prestige to military service, so, in addition, he founded the New Orleans Rifles, a mounted unit made up of the richest, most influential men in Louisiana. They even paid for their own flashy uniforms. Bernardo spoke of arming them with pistols and carbines. But they merely carried sabers, suggesting the extent to which he may have expected them to actually do any fighting. He then imposed a strong sense of social class on the Illinois Country by founding a cavalry regiment for the rough but ready "elite" of St. Louis. For the same reasons of fomenting pride in the corporate identity of the colony and a sense of social elevation through military service, he also created two companies of *negros*, or "blacks," and *pardos*, or "coloreds," men of Indian, African, and European mixed race.[68]

Unzaga's remarkable success in bolstering the Louisiana economy had been largely a consequence of turning a blind eye to illegal trade with the fast-growing population of English settlers on the other side of the Mississippi.[69] Bernardo's second-in-command, Martín de Navarro, who went on to run the civil administration of the colony in the 1780s, commented that "the English made the most of being able to navigate freely on the Mississippi" and quickly "established a trade that was worth many millions of *reales* a year . . . That is how the province survived and became richer by the day." Indeed, "its current condition is due solely to English contraband." So "when Bernardo de Gálvez arrived, Louisiana was thriving on those profits brought by alien hands in such clandestine fashion."[70] But José de Gálvez had appointed Bernardo to prepare Louisiana for the coming war, and that involved stopping the English smuggling.[71]

Bernardo understood how difficult and dangerous it would be to stamp out so secret and lucrative a commerce while maintaining the cooperation of the colonists. Navarro lamented that "it hurt so zealous a governor" to accept he must turn a blind eye to "so miserable a business!"

Bernardo was merely biding his time. He so charmed the British merchants in New Orleans with his Andalusian affability that they praised his "generosity and humanity" and claimed he was "treating them with the greatest indulgence."[72] He seized his moment when an English boat captured a ship taking Louisiana tar to Havana, sending the Frenchmen and Spaniards into paroxysms of outrage.[73] On the night of April 17, 1777, by the light of a waxing moon, a detachment of soldiers impounded thirteen English boats that had shown "the extreme audacity to put out gangplanks" along the sovereign Spanish banks from Manchac to La Balize.[74] This unprecedented action led to ugly confrontation with the Welsh captain of a well-armed British frigate, who tried to bully Bernardo into releasing the impounded boats. With eighteen cannon trained on New Orleans, Bernardo went aboard the frigate and, brimming with bravado, faced down the Welshman, who sailed away in a storm cloud of his own bombastic threats.[75]

The governor had fired the opening salvo in his war on English contraband. He cloaked his iron fist in a velvet glove. He began licensing French merchants so that the French commissioners at New Orleans reported that "Gálvez is a natural friend of every Frenchman" and "he has withdrawn the customs guards from the harbor."[76] He allowed New Orleans merchants to trade with Cuba and Yucatán and slashed the import duty from 5 percent to 2 percent. Most historians accept that within months Bernardo had virtually stamped out all illegal English trade with Louisiana.[77] "And what happened then?" Navarro asked. Well, "the settlers no longer enjoyed the affluence that is a consequence of trade."[78]

The army and militia were obviously central to the defense of Louisiana in the coming war with England, yet Bernardo was under no illusions that he could "repulse even the slightest push by the enemy without having our Indian neighbors on our side."[79] He was so impressed by the way the French and the English attracted the Indians with gifts in the traditional way and then established a thriving trade in all sorts of luxuries and novelties "that they used to know nothing about and now think of as essential" that he had recommended adopting the approach in northern New Spain. He observed that many Louisiana Native Americans were dependent on alcohol, but he refused to compromise his sense of morality by recommending such an obviously degenerate form of corruption that it was prohibited by the Laws of the Indies. However, most government administrators in Madrid must have been astonished when he enthused about easing the prohibition on selling them firearms. The Indians of Louisiana, he explained, "have forgotten how to make and use their bows and arrows," which meant they were at the mercy of the Europeans who supplied them with guns and ammunition.[80] Moreover, control of the supply of weapons was not the only advantage: José de Gálvez perhaps explained to the flabbergasted officials that on the frontier a mounted Indian warrior at full gallop could fire two dozen arrows accurately in the time it took a musketeer to reload; it might be better that they have guns.

Toward the end of 1777 there were signs that Spanish overtures to their Native American neighbors were beginning to pay off. First, an emissary of the Biloni nation sought Bernardo's permission before attacking a group of Atakapas, which led to a summit meeting at Pointe Coupée involving representatives of a dozen or more tribes. Soon afterward, a delegation of Choctaws asked to be allowed to fly the Spanish flag, but Bernardo refused because some of their villages were in British territory. The Governor of Louisiana was beginning to command respect and authority, although even he did not fully understand why or how.[81]

*   *   *

In August 1776, at the royal summer retreat of San Ildefonso, just outside Madrid, a military officer, Francisco Bouligny, who had served under O'Reilly, had presented José de Gálvez with a depressing account of economic conditions in Louisiana and an ambitious plan to improve the situation by promoting immigration. Gálvez was sufficiently impressed to send Bouligny back to New Orleans as lieutenant governor, while settlers were recruited from the Malaga hill country near the Gálvez hometown of Macharaviaya. But within months of Bouligny's return the following year, for completely unknown reasons, Bernardo de Gálvez developed a violent dislike for his new right-hand man.[82] Such a reaction was so out of character that we have to assume Bernardo had a compelling reason to loathe him.

When the main group of sixty settlers arrived in the summer of 1778, Bernardo was only too glad to allow Bouligny to set off with them to establish New Iberia, over a hundred miles away on the prairies around Bayou Teche. The grand houses lining Main Street today are fulsome evidence of the eventual success of the place, but it was hard work, and the first settlement was flooded during April rains. When Spain finally declared war on England, Bouligny left New Iberia to serve with uncommon courage and distinction during the campaigns in West Florida. After the war was over, he married into a Creole family and continued to serve as a soldier-administrator in New Orleans. His descendants are prominent members of Louisiana society to this day, and the Bouligny Tavern is one of the best gastropubs in New Orleans.[83]

In 1778, Bernardo reported to José that a group of "English and American refugees escaping the revolution . . . came across" some good "high land near the confluence of the Amit River and Bayou Manchac," which was "good for growing crops," and there "they founded a tiny village they called Galbez-town [sic]." Bernardo had protested about the name, but they insisted, "Please do not change the name. We have found refuge here during your governorship, and we want the name to serve as a vote of thanks and a record of when the place was founded."[84]

Bernardo was delighted because the settlement was both sustainable and would provide an early warning of an English or Indian invasion. He decided to settle some of the Canary Islanders there and left Lieutenant Francisco Collell behind to oversee construction of a new settlement and to hire a couple of black slaves (from Bernardo's father-in-law) to clear the ground. By June, they had built forty-two cabins, and the surrounding forest was denuded of trees. Soon, Galveztown had thirty-two city blocks amid tree-lined streets.[85] By January 1779, new settlers began to arrive, and in the spring the first weddings were celebrated.

The warmer weather was accompanied by disease. Over the summer, tens of adults and countless children died. Bernardo sent a physician to assess the crisis, who requested medicines and bedding to set up a hospital. For some reason, he was slow to diagnose the symptoms, but in time he realized that the highly contagious fever and skin pustules were symptoms of smallpox. By the time the epidemic abated the following winter, over 150 people were dead, a third of the population.[86]

The late eighteenth century saw the extreme geographical limits of Spanish reach in North America. Two events from that period reveal the fragility of that frontier in the face of Indian and European hostility. The story will turn to the Nootka Crisis, which marked the beginning of the end of the empire in the north, but first we must revisit New Mexico and encounter Juan Bautista de Anza for the last time.

Following the reoccupation of the Rio Grande valley by Diego de Vargas in the 1690s, the Spanish and Mexican Indian colonists slowly reestablished the Kingdom of New Mexico. A new presidio and administrative town were built at a strategic location on the Rio Grande in 1706 and named after the then viceroy, the Duke of Alburquerque, eventually losing an "R" from its original spelling. The missions slowly began to flourish, and by midcentury fourteen thousand Pueblos were counted as Christians.

Many Pueblos still resisted the new order, especially the Hopis, who were fiercely jealous of their traditional beliefs. According to Hopi tradition, "twenty summers" after the Pueblo Revolt, some elders at Awatovi who had been happy as Christians welcomed the missionaries again and began to rebuild their church. Emboldened, many turncoats showed outright "disrespect of the old ways and lawless people caused violence in the streets. There was fighting in the plaza . . . hooligans threatened the old [people] and pursued the young girls."

The Awatovi *kikmongwi* visited each of the Hopi villages in turn. Ensconced smoking in the kiva, he explained to one chief after another that "evil is in my village . . . The Castilian sorcerers are among us again, causing the people to turn against one another." Then he explained what he wanted: "I want you to send your warriors to bring Awatovi to an end." He preferred to destroy his own pueblo and people than see them turn Christian. Chief after chief replied that for Hopi to make war on Hopi "would be an evil thing," until finally, the *kikmongwi* of Oraibi and the *kalatakmongwi* of Walpi agreed.

The Hopi warriors set a cordon around Awatovi and struck at dawn. They hauled the ladders out of the kivas, trapping the men inside, and threw bundles of burning wood into the sacred chambers. "They found strings of chili peppers . . . and threw them into the kivas, causing stinging fumes to mix with the smoke. At first there were screaming and coughing, but soon there was only silence." Then they set fire to the town. As the terrified people tried to flee, they were mercilessly slaughtered. In one last twist in this twisted tale, the victors squabbled over the women who had been taken captive, so they murdered them as well.[87]

The governors of Spanish New Mexico took little further interest in the Hopi for another eighty years, but the Plains Indians remained a serious threat to the kingdom. Often supplied with guns and ammunition by French merchants who traded illegally at Santa Fe, they frequently plundered Spanish settlements and the Pueblo Indians, which led to massive reductions in the populations of the northeastern pueblos such as Pecos and Galisteo.[88]

"Red Chief" Hugo O'Conor's strategy to dominate the frontier with a line of presidios stretching from California to Texas had failed: four hundred soldiers could never control thousands of miles of deserts, mountains, brush, and woodland, even when supported by large militias, such as the four companies based at El Paso. In the summer of 1778, Teodoro de Croix, now serving as Commandant of the Internal Provinces, convened his most experienced frontier commanders in a council of war to instigate a new policy toward the Apaches. Instead of the toxic to and fro of violent Indian raiding and brutal military retaliation, Croix concluded that the Spanish authorities should adapt the French concept of "peace by purchase," which had been so successful, and try to foment trade with the enemy and reward Indian allies with gifts.

The great Apache fighter and California trailblazer Juan Bautista de Anza was one of the commanders at Chihuahua. There, he was sworn in as Governor of New Mexico by Croix, appointed to the office by Charles III, who thought him capable of containing and perhaps winning, once and for all, a guerrilla war that seemed as old as the hills and canyons in which it was fought. Anza was one of the architects of the new policy of peace by purchase, but he was a hardened frontier warrior who knew that velvet gloves needed iron fists. In New Mexico, he faced the most daunting task of all, to tame the Comanches. Before he could begin to tread softly, Anza knew he must let such a relentless enemy feel the full force of a mighty big stick.

Anza arrived at Santa Fe in December 1778, determined to defeat the great Comanche war leader whom the Spaniards called Cuerno Verde, or "Green Horn." He had acquired almost legendary status when, a decade earlier, a ferocious warrior led an almost suicidal assault on Ojo Caliente wearing a sumptuous headdress decorated with enormous green horns. He had been wounded during the attack, and the New Mexicans had been much impressed by the number of Comanches who willingly lost their lives to recover their stricken chief. It is now believed that this foolhardy assailant died of his injuries and his son inherited the horned headdress and his father's *reputación*. Called Tabivo Narityante, "Handsome and Brave," by the Comanches, it is said that Cuerno Verde developed an insatiable appetite for revenge.[89]

Anza and Narityante were heads and tails of the same coin, as the Spanish say. Both had their mettle toughened on the brutal frontier between the European and Native American worlds where they were born. Both men had lost a father to an Apache enemy, fathers who bequeathed them legacies of honor and reputation. The Fates led these two men to fight for the futures of their peoples.

On Sunday, August 15, 1779, Anza led six hundred soldiers, militiamen, and Pueblo warriors out of Santa Fe and headed north. Five days later, skirting the San Juan Mountains northwest of Taos, he was joined by two hundred Ute and Apache allies. They crossed the Poncha Pass and then struck east along the trail now asphalted as Route 24, heading for modern Colorado Springs.[90] At half past ten on Tuesday morning, one of the scouts appeared at a gallop. They had seen a considerable number of enemy combatants ten or fifteen miles ahead. Anza rode ahead to gauge the situation and saw that the Comanches must have only just begun to pitch camp, erecting the pole frames of their tepees, when their own scouts had seen the massive force bearing down on them.

As they hurried to gather their belongings, Anza gave the order to attack with the troops he had available. Eighteen brave Comanches were slain as they fought a desperate rearguard action to cover the retreat of their comrades. Anza estimated almost a thousand fighting men must have escaped with their families, but he was evidently surprised that the skirmish had been so one-sided and noted in his official journal that the enemy had made none of their usual preparations for battle. When he interrogated his prisoners, he learned that Cuerno Verde himself was away raiding in New Mexico with a detachment of his best warriors. Anza had inadvertently taken the Comanches completely by surprise in their own territory, but in doing so, he had revealed his position. Cuerno Verde would be ready for him.

Anza turned his invading army south. Scouts soon reported that Cuerno Verde was advancing to meet them. Anza ordered his troops to prepare an ambush from the dense cover of vegetation where the trail crossed a narrow gully. With the sun setting in the west, Cuerno Verde rode into the trap. Anza attacked, personally leading his central column of troops directly toward the enemy, the sun behind him, we must assume. At first Cuerno Verde stood firm, but when he saw two columns outflanking him left and right, he gave the order for a lightning retreat. Suddenly, the Comanches were gone.

Anza's lieutenants advised a tactical withdrawal, fearful of the Comanche fame for attacking by night. But their general gently scolded them for cowardice, or so he later reported, and ordered that "for sake of our military honor we must wait in that place until dawn."

Brave and foolhardy like his father, Cuerno Verde returned the next day with fifty men, his horned headdress a fine silhouette against the morning sun. Again, Anza tried to outflank him. Again, Cuerno Verde chose to retreat. But this time, the New Mexicans managed to isolate the Comanche chief in the gully along with his son, four war captains, and a medicine man. Trapped under intense musket fire, they dismounted and took cover behind their horses. Outnumbered, outgunned, outwitted, they fought to their deaths, and when the day was done, Anza gazed down at the corpse of Tabivo Narity- ante, Cuerno Verde, removed the legendary headdress, and sent it to Teodoro de Croix. Anza finally achieved a peace agreement with the Comanches in 1786, the year he also secured peace with the Navajos.

With Cuerno Verde dead, Anza turned his attention to the Hopi. He knew they remained hostile from Father Garcés's reports of his journey to Oraibi during Anza's second expedition to California. He also had journals written by the missionary at Zuni who had recently attempted to preach to these "obsti- nate" people. But Anza also knew that three years of drought and famine had rendered the Hopi vulnerable to the new policy of peace by purchase. Some had sold their children into slavery for food, so Anza sent a friar to offer them succor in exchange for their souls. He also required them to move to the Rio Grande valley, to the bosom of the colonial kingdom. Many emaciated men and women refused, preferring death on their own terms to the spiritual Purga- tory of Christianity, but some agreed to relocate, including the whole popula- tion of Walpi. In the end, about two hundred Hopis went to live along the Rio Grande, where smallpox struck in 1780, brought across the plains from Texas and Louisiana by Apache raiders.[91] The vast majority of the Hopis had remained indomitable, in an archipelago of independent pueblos that still held out against the European invaders.

Anza's successes were, ironically enough, the roots of his downfall. His defeat of Cuerno Verde and the cowing of the Comanches gave the kingdom a new sense of security. When Anza tried to impose a series of reforms designed to make the New Mexicans take greater responsibility for their own defense, they saw little advantage in complying. Instead, they leveled the usual accusa- tions of cronyism and corruption at their governor and complained directly to Croix. In 1787, Anza was appointed Governor of Sonora, and that summer he left Santa Fe for the last time. Already in poor health, he was further weakened by the arduous journey to Arizpe. One of the most remarkable characters in the Spanish history of the Southwest lived out the final year of his life at home in Sonora, slowly dying in his bed in the land that had made him. Death came for the governor on December 19, 1788.

CHAPTER 2 I

"BERNARDO DE GÁLVEZ, SPANISH HERO OF THE AMERICAN REVOLUTION"

THE DEEP SOUTH[1]

Yo solo, I alone, have risked my life, boys, so as not to expose a single soldier in my army, and so the navy might see there is less danger than is claimed.

—BERNARDO DE GÁLVEZ

ON APRIL 1 2, 1 7 7 9, Charles III signed a treaty committing Spain to a "defensive and offensive alliance with France against England" at his suburban garden-palace at Aranjuez, outside Madrid. Ten weeks later, the Spanish Ambassador to the Court of Saint James formally declared war, demanding the return of Gibraltar and Menorca in Europe, that the British abandon Central America, and, most important of all for Bernardo de Gálvez, should cede control of the Gulf of Mexico from Mobile and Pensacola to the Bahama Channel.[2]

At New Orleans, Bernardo convened his Junta de Guerra. He spread out a map of the Mississippi and underlined the gravity of the situation. The town was vulnerable on many fronts: by land, across the lakes, the bayous, the estuary, and the river herself. Almost all his officers favored strengthening their defenses in preparation for a siege and then appealing to Havana for help.[3] In August, Bernardo received official confirmation that Spain and England were finally at war. He was promoted to the rank of *Gobernador en Propiedad*, "Governor Permanent" of Louisiana, with orders to attack British West Florida.

He was worried that Madrid had made no formal alliance with the Americans. He was under orders to treat them with scrupulous neutrality when he had expected to work closely with his American allies.[4] Suddenly, Spanish

Louisiana must face the British alone, with an army of less than a thousand men, mostly inexperienced militiamen and a few old soldiers, many of them sick. His spies had intercepted a dispatch in which the Governor of British West Florida had written to his superiors, "Thank God that we are all firm and relishing the opportunity to strike a blow against the Dons of New Orleans."[5] Britain was preparing to invade Louisiana, and Bernardo would struggle even to defend his capital. As he pondered his predicament, a violent hurricane hit New Orleans, and "in less than three hours all the boats on the river were lost, many houses collapsed, and for twenty leagues round about the settlements were ruined. Our provisions were spoiled, the trees were uprooted, the men were dismayed, the women and children were scattered about the countryside, and the whole world was flooded. It was so terrible that neither pen nor pencil can explain the devastation."[6]

Bernardo was as much Apache in the field as he was Andalusian at a *soirée*. He craved action, the more dashing or daring the better, and he had orders to go on the offensive. He told his Junta de Guerra that once the enemy mustered in a single force, they would be invincible. The Spaniards must take out British positions while the enemy were still dispersed.[7] He sent orders to Francisco Collell, at Galveztown, to make ready for conflict, despite the smallpox epidemic. On August 30, 1779, Collell, this almost completely forgotten hero of the Revolutionary War, captured seven British boats on the Mississippi and took 125 men prisoner. It was the first Spanish military action of the conflict on North American soil.

Meanwhile, at New Orleans, Bernardo addressed a large crowd of colonists, exhorting them to prepare for war: "Spain has recognized American independence," he lied, "so it is to be feared the English will open hostilities." He announced his appointment as Governor Permanent but explained, "Before I can assume that office, I must swear before the *cabildo* to defend the province and sacrifice every last drop of my blood for the king. But how can I secure this colony with the few troops we have? I cannot accept unless I have the support of the inhabitants of this province in fulfilling my obligations and each man doing his part for the honor of Spanish arms!"[8]

To rapturous applause and loud cheers, Bernardo was carried on the shoulders of the crowd to the *cabildo* building, where he was invested as Governor Permanent of Louisiana in the presence of his people. That night, they lit lamps and fires all over their ruined town. Among flickering shadows, almost every man could be heard promising to give his life for the king.

On August 27, with Oliver Pollock beside him, Bernardo led 667 under-requipped veterans, raw recruits, militiamen, slaves, freemen, and even a handful of American volunteers on a ninety-mile march through swamps and forest, gathering over six hundred Indians and settlers as he went. Their long march upriver was miserable, but Bernardo established a remarkable rapport with his men. "He was not just affable, which comes so naturally to him," his right-hand man, Martín de Navarro, wrote to Madrid, but "he was always the first to make ready his bivouac in the open air," and his men eagerly "followed his example, taking great pride in their lack of tents." And "if a shortage of bread meant he had to eat rice, all of them tucked in as though it were the greatest delicacy."[9]

On September 7, Bernardo's men attacked the British post at Manchac. His father-in-law, Gilbert de St. Maxent, was the first man to breach the stockade, squeezing through a loophole. Inside, he found a subaltern and two dozen men, who offered little resistance. In the confusion, one of the Englishmen was killed and five escaped into the fog. Bernardo had seen his first action in the Revolutionary War, but the British had stolen a march on him by withdrawing the bulk of their troops to Baton Rouge to consolidate their defenses.

By now, disease was sweeping through the ranks of Bernardo's irregulars. He left the bulk of his army at Manchac, pressing on to Baton Rouge with only two hundred professional soldiers. The English had built up great defensive earthworks that were impregnable to such a small force, so he ordered his sappers to dig trenches with the utmost stealth and improvise a redoubt for his guns, while the bulk of his troops distracted the enemy by cutting down trees and digging ditches on the other side of the fort.

On September 21, at a quarter to six in the morning, as a veil of thick mist began to lift, Bernardo's brilliant gunner, Julián Álvarez, began firing his cannons with devastating precision. By three in the afternoon, he had blown apart so much of the fort that the garrison commander, Lieutenant Colonel Alexander Dickinson, sued for peace. Bernardo insisted the surrender include the garrison of Fort Panchac at Natchez, which was naturally well defended and might well have withstood the most sustained attack the Spaniards could mount.[10] That night, Bernardo's Indian allies slaughtered fifty women and children attached to the Baton Rouge garrison who had sought refuge in the woods.[11] Twenty-four hours later, Dickinson formally surrendered; the British handed over their flags to Bernardo and gave up their weapons to his proud soldiers. A small party then set out upstream for Natchez accompanied by a British officer with orders for the commander there to surrender and a letter from Pollock to the settlers urging them "towards the glorious cause of Liberty" and telling them that "Spain has declared the independency of the United States."[12] Pollock may or may not have known this was a lie.

"And that is the history of our campaign," Bernardo reported to Madrid. "Then, His Majesty's men had to go home because there was nothing else to conquer." Leaving garrisons to control the "430 leagues of the best and most fertile lands along the Mississippi" that he had taken for Spain,[13] he returned to New Orleans with his prisoners of war and treated them so well that the *London Magazine* published extracts from Dickinson's glowing report to General Campbell at Pensacola: "In justice to Don Bernardo . . . I must say that the officers and soldiers who are prisoners of war at this place are treated with the greatest generosity and attention, not only by the officers, but even the Spanish soldiers seem to take pleasure in being civil and kind." Bernardo allowed many of the officers to go to Pensacola and even England, on the condition that they should not again take up arms against Spain.[14] Generous to his enemies, Bernardo was fulsome in his praise of his own men, especially the militia and the black and mixed-race companies "who were always in the front line, exchanging fire with the enemy," and whom he decorated with silver medals of twice the usual size.[15] Many of his officers were rewarded with promotion, while Bernardo himself was given the rank of field marshal, confirming his overall command of operations in the Gulf of Mexico.[16]

The Spaniards inflicted one minor defeat after another on the British. At Galveztown they took four ships headed for Pensacola. At the pass between Pontchartrain and Maurepas, fourteen Creole militiamen captured an English ship manned by fifty-six professional soldiers.[17] In May 1780, an army of three hundred British regulars and nine hundred Indian allies assaulted St. Louis, but as the *Gazeta de Madrid* reported, "for all their stubborn obstinacy, they were unexpectedly repelled" by Leyba and his men after a "very lively firefight."[18]

Thanks to guile, pluck, Spanish discipline, and hard work, not to mention a hefty dose of British apathy and incompetence, Spain and America were winning the war in the west. From his headquarters in Morristown, George Washington wrote Charles III's special envoy to Congress, Juan de Miralles, "I am happy in the opportunity of congratulating you on the important success" scored by "the arms of his Catholic Majesty," which will "promote the common cause" and "probably have a beneficial influence on the affairs of the southern States."[19]

Far away, near Waxhaw Creek on the Carolinas border, in the spring of 1780, three hundred British cavalry slaughtered a detachment of Patriots. Andrew Jackson and his brother helped their mother as best they could to tend to the wounded and bury the dead. That summer his eldest brother died of heat exhaustion on the battlefield, and the thirteen-year-old Andrew went to serve as an errand boy to Colonel Davie and saw action at Hanging Rock. Over the following winter a ghastly civil war erupted around Waxhaw, and "men hunted one another like beasts of prey."[20] He saw his cousin chased down and killed by British soldiers, who then took Andrew and his brother Robert captive. When the spirited lads refused to clean the commander's muddy boots, the Englishman slashed at their heads with his sword, inflicting terrible wounds. The two brothers were sent to Camden jail, where Robert died of smallpox. The following fall, Andrew's mother left him at Waxhaw and went to Charleston to nurse the Patriot wounded, where she caught cholera and died. A troubled young man destined to be the American nemesis of the Spanish Empire east of the Mississippi, Andrew Jackson had already lost everyone. He was only fifteen.

Bernardo de Gálvez returned to New Orleans and began to marshal his forces for a major campaign to capture Mobile and Pensacola. George Washington was so "impressed" by Spanish plans to attack Florida that he suggested to his French allies that they propose a joint operation with the Spanish. But those plans were almost foiled by Bernardo's own side, for he ran into the jealous rivalry of Diego Navarro, Governor-General of Cuba. Despite clear instructions from José de Gálvez that "the king has decided that his primary military objective in the Americas is to expel the English from the Mexican Gulf and the Mississippi," Navarro first objected to Bernardo's proposal, then offered an alternative scheme, before he finally refused to send Bernardo enough troops to carry out his plan.[21]

Bernardo lost patience. He sent Colonel Esteban Miró to Havana to negotiate with Navarro and gathered 1,350 men at New Orleans, including 24 slaves, 26 Americans, and an ambitious young lieutenant, Manuel de Zéspedes, the future governor of Spanish Florida.[22] On January 14, 1780, they took ship aboard a fifty-foot *saetía* galley, two frigates, two brigs (one of which was baptized the *Galveztown*), three barges, and a small galliot, carrying a total of fifty-seven cannon between them.

That summer, the *Madrid Mercury* published, with fulsome patriotic pride, "the Diary that I, Bernardo de Gálvez, kept of the Expedition against *Mobila*." Once again we have the pleasure of being able to read his own account of a thrilling military campaign.[23]

Bernardo's little fleet was buffeted by wind and hail as it sailed east along the Gulf Coast, and then, as they regrouped near the entrance to Mobile Bay, they were battered by a terrible tempest that blew for seven days. Most of the ships ran aground and took a desperate beating from the heaving seas. Aboard the *Galveztown*, Bernardo reported, they were shipping nine inches of water an hour. With some of the ships safely over the sandbar and into the sound, while the rest remained exposed on the Gulf shore, "the storm grew so violent as to make it impossible to help one another." When the wind relented slightly, St. Maxent again showed his extraordinary courage by rescuing troops and sailors from some of the ships that were beginning to break up and ferrying them across the sandbar into the sound. But the following day "dawned with a powerful southwester that brought rain, thunder, and lightning." When the storm calmed, Bernardo took stock of the disaster. He counted eight hundred shipwrecked men, "most of them half-naked, who had only been able to save themselves." They had lost most of their ammunition and artillery; they had little food.

"Yet, I believed in the strength and character of my men," the *Mercury* reported Bernardo as writing, "and that in the midst of so terrifying a calamity they would remain steadfast in their desire to face the enemy. So, seeing as Misfortune had deprived us of the means to besiege the place, I ordered the men to make scaling ladders from the broken timbers of the ships scattered along the coast so that we might continue on to Mobile and set about storming the fortress."[24]

At that moment, a tiny sloop appeared on the horizon, bringing news that Miró had forced Navarro into sending five ships and almost six hundred soldiers to support the operation.[25] Such was the elation among Bernardo's forces that when three of those reinforcement vessels ran aground, "it had no other effect on the men than to make them happy, for they had become so hardened to overcoming such difficulties."[26]

Bernardo landed his reinvigorated army at the mouth of the Dog River and, over the following days, advanced slowly on Mobile. On March 1, Bernardo reconnoitered the fortress and saw for himself that it was in a "ruinous state."[27]

He wrote the British commander, Captain Durnford, with great delicacy, that "if I did not have almost two thousand men at my command and you little more than a hundred, I would not suggest you surrender," but then explained, "You shall suffer all the extremes of war should pointless resistance anger my troops, who are already chafing at certain misfortunes they have suffered." Durnford read Bernardo's letter, then gave Bernardo's messenger a hearty lunch "and continued until near five o'clock drinking a cheerful glass to the health of our king."

Both commanders and their officers clearly knew that the vital question was whether the British could hold out long enough for relief to arrive from Pensacola. Durnford was certain that he had hid his parlous position from Bernardo's messenger and sent him back with a curt response. When Durnford told his men he had informed the Spaniards that "were I to give up this fort on your demand, I should be regarded as a traitor to my king and country," they "all joined in three cheers." He then sent Bernardo a present of a dozen bottles of wine. Bernardo reciprocated with a case of Bordeaux claret, Spanish wine, lemons, oranges, sweets and pastries, and a box of Cuban cigars. It was a delightfully generous way of letting the Englishman know the besieging forces were well provisioned.[28]

For a week, the Spaniards were busy constructing their batteries, digging trenches, and putting up defenses, all under occasional fire from the fort. Then, at ten o'clock on the morning of March 12, Bernardo gave the order to begin the relentless bombardment of the English enemy. The walls and watch-towers crumbled. By sundown, Durnford knew the fight was over and ordered the white flag run up its staff.

Bernardo's Indian scouts told him that the British Governor of Pensacola, John Campbell, was bearing down on them from the north with a large force. So, Bernardo offered the British a surrender with the full honors of war to expedite the capitulation. When he discovered how few men Durnford had under his command, Bernardo regretted those generous terms he had so easily granted.[29]

Across Europe, in Scotland, London, Amsterdam, Paris, and Madrid, the press reported the fall of Mobile. On June 6, the articles of capitulation and Bernardo's covering letter were read to a session of the Continental Congress.[30] On July 4, the *Avignon Mail* lauded "this brave and able general, barely thirty-three years old, who so early showed the energy and courage that herald the most able soldiers."[31]

There was general rejoicing at this initial success. But in Madrid, José de Gálvez was furious that Navarro's recalcitrance had prevented Bernardo from pressing home the advantage. With Navarro's support, the Spanish troops should have been able to occupy Pensacola before Campbell had time to return. José excoriated Navarro, accusing him of delaying the expedition against Pensacola with "groundless excuses" and reminding him that "in war he who is most vigorous and pays least attention to the inevitable dangers wins the day . . . The ships of our Royal Navy are meant to attack and pursue our enemies for the glory and security of our nation," he fumed, implying Navarro was a coward and little short of a traitor.[32]

Bernardo himself asked acerbically, "Has the characteristic military virtue of our nation deserted us? Have we so little constancy that a single setback is enough to stop us? At any moment peace may surprise us and all others shall rejoice, but will we soldiers whom the king will have found useless in war be able to wear with pride our rusty swords that we did not unsheathe when the moment demanded it of us?"[33]

Navarro was cowed into supplying four thousand men, fifteen warships, and fifty transport vessels, but the authorities in Havana continued to be aggressively obstructive. Finally, thirty-odd ships sailed out of Havana, but as Bernardo confided to his uncle's special envoy in Cuba, "he did not dare to ask for more men lest it delay their departure" further still.[34]

Aboard his flagship, Bernardo felt the thrill of impending action. He had fought a long, hard political battle as well as shown great daring on the Mississippi and at Mobile to prepare for this moment. He knew the narrow pass into Pensacola Bay was protected by the big guns of Fort Barrancas on the mainland, and a small battery and blockhouse located on Sigüenza Point, the tip of the long, narrow Santa Rosa Island. On March 4, 1781, at nine o'clock in the morning, with the ships sailing swiftly on the open sea, he gathered his officers and announced that their first objective was to secure control of Sigüenza Point so the whole fleet could anchor safely in the sound, protected behind the barrier island. They sighted land at dawn on March 9, and that night there was hard work for the sailors assigned to the launches as they landed fourteen hundred men onto the Gulf shore at modern Casino Beach.[35]

The first contingent of grenadiers and light infantry reached Sigüenza Point by daybreak and were surprised to find the battery consisted of a few half-constructed fortifications and three abandoned cannons. In the early morning half-light, the Spaniards watched undetected as launches from two enemy frigates anchored in the bay approached and seven unsuspecting Englishmen came ashore. Bernardo's soldiers broke cover to take them prisoner, and "Fort Barrancas and the two frigates opened up some lively fire on our troops," Bernardo recorded. He ordered his gunners to set up two cannons on the bayside and fired on the frigates, forcing them to withdraw. To his considerable annoyance, he watched as a British brig captured a schooner that had most of his personal baggage aboard, including twenty thousand dollars in coin, his dining silver, and, worse still, his wine. But most important, Bernardo had the chance to see the range of the guns at Barrancas.[36]

Bernardo knew it was imperative to reach a safe anchorage before a storm scattered the ships and marooned his army on Santa Rosa. But that would require crossing the treacherous sandbar at the entrance to the bay, and as one otherwise well-disposed American biographer so acerbically put it, "The loss of the *Volante* and the grounding of several other vessels at Mobile had not won Gálvez the reputation of being an expert authority on entering ports."[37] The navy commandant, José Calvo, sent four men to take soundings, then, at three o'clock in the morning, he ordered the bulky flagship *San Ramón* to lead the fleet into the bay, "more out of a sense of obligation to the king and my own honor than because it was a reasonable decision to take," he confessed.[38] Bernardo came aboard, as he admitted, to "play his role in these maneuvers and put himself at risk." Calvo simply sent him back ashore, pointing out that he would be more useful in command of the artillery.[39] As the *San Ramón* entered the narrows, the English gunners at Fort Barrancas began to bombard the channel. Suddenly, her keel hit the sand and she lurched to one side. For twenty minutes, she was a sitting target. When she finally refloated, Calvo turned her about and sailed for the safety of the open sea.[40]

That afternoon, Bernardo went aboard the flagship and suggested to the naval officers that they sail the smaller vessels in ahead of the *San Ramón*, "so as to avoid holding up the other boats," he explained in his official published account, "should she ground on the sandbar a second time."[41] The future Venezuelan revolutionary hero Francisco de Miranda was then serving as an officer under Bernardo. A charismatic diarist, he described how Bernardo "gave thanks to all aboard the ship for trying to put his plan into action," then announced that "he now realized it was not possible without running the obvious risk of losing the flagship," but, he assured his audience, he knew "that the frigates could make it."[42]

This was a diplomatic disaster. With this superficially sensible suggestion, Bernardo trampled roughshod over Calvo's obligation as the senior navy officer to ensure the security of his flagship, which was integral to the protection of the rest of the fleet, while also insulting the man's personal honor, not to mention the reputation of the whole navy. "Calvo's officers rallied so vehemently to his defense that they seriously considered abandoning the whole campaign and leaving the troops behind on their sandy island," Miranda explained.[43]

For the next six days the feud between army and navy smoldered dangerously while the remainder of their supplies and munitions were ferried ashore and ships were sent to support a contingent of nine hundred soldiers who were approaching overland from Mobile. The weather began to deteriorate, and it became more difficult for the launches to come ashore. Bernardo became nervous and again urged the naval officers to bring the fleet into the bay.

Calvo responded with unconscionable insolence, "Your Lordship is neither ignorant of the arts of war, nor the norms of military prudence, which teach us to flee from extreme danger. What is the point of sacrificing the king's subjects for no reason as though they were sheep?"[44]

Bernardo flew into a rage. He ordered one of his engineers to go aboard the *San Ramón*, taking Calvo the gift a thirty-two-inch-caliber cannonball fired from Barrancas. Bernardo was making a practical point, for he had studied basic ballistics at Avila, and he had experienced, well-trained artillery officers to hand. During the brief skirmish for control of Santa Rosa Island and the bombardment of the *San Ramón*, they had seen that almost every cannonball fired from Barrancas had cleared the channel, landing on the beach at Sigüenza Point. But instead of discreetly arguing the matter, Bernardo instructed his unfortunate messenger to loudly ask Calvo "to show the honor and courage to follow him." For "he"—Bernardo—"was going to lead the way fearlessly aboard the *Galveztown*." He told his man to deliver this ugly message in full earshot of the entire crew.

"Our general is an impudent upstart and a traitor to his king and country," Calvo fumed. "He has just insulted me and the whole Royal Navy. Let the coward be foisted on his own petard!"[45]

Bernardo boarded his little *Galveztown* and ordered the crew to fly an admiral's pennant to indicate that his tiny flotilla was now an independent fleet. Then he sailed his brig headlong into the narrows with a gallant galliot and a handful of brave launches following in his wake. His whole army gathered on the beach at Sigüenza Point to watch, despite the ceaseless, thundering barrage of fire from Fort Barrancas. The boats sailed so close to the shore they could hear the soldiers cheering them on as the cannonballs whistled about them, tearing into the sails and the rigging. On they ran through the little sea-lane between friend and foe until they rounded the cape and entered the calm waters of the sound. Bernardo's men broke out into long and loud applause that resounded across the bay, and there was a great shout of "Long live the general!"[46]

Bernardo ordered the fifteen guns aboard the *Galveztown* loaded with powder and fired them in salute to Fort Barrancas.[47] Then he addressed his men: "*Yo solo*, I alone, have risked my life, boys, so as not to expose a single soldier in my army, and so the navy might see there is less danger than is claimed."

With the relief and excitement of his success, he harangued the soldiers long and hard, roundly criticizing the navy and the officers in Havana. "I have been forced to lead by example, yet not one of the navy ships has followed," he bellowed. "They have responded with insults, telling me that if the enemy cannonballs do not kill me, then the king will have my head!"

His crowd erupted with emotion, shouting their congratulations a thousand times as he embraced his officers and thanked the artillery commander for his covering fire. "Long live the king! Long live the king! Long live the king!"[48]

The following afternoon, Calvo watched impassively from the bridge of the *San Ramón* as Bernardo boarded a little gig and guided the remainder of the fleet across the sandbar. Isolated and alone, the humiliated naval commander sailed for Havana, his reputation shredded by collective hubris.

Bernardo de Gálvez had won the most important victory of his most famous campaign. He had defeated Calvo and gained control of the navy. There was still work to be done, but the Spanish Fates were closing in on British Pensacola. Now, it was only a matter of time before Governor Campbell would have to surrender.

In January the following year, Charles III, far from beheading this swashbuckling hero, made Bernardo the Count of Gálvez and awarded him a coat of arms showing his valiant figure aboard the *Galveztown*, his sword drawn, blue pennant flying, underneath the motto *Yo solo*—"I alone."[49]

On the morning of March 22, Bernardo's most trusted lieutenant, José de Ezpeleta, emerged from the forest onto the beach opposite Santa Rosa at the head of nine hundred reinforcements, firing their guns to announce their arrival. He had marched his men round behind Barrancas to the north without being detected, and they were now pitching camp on a headland where the shore turns sharply north before swinging east again to Pensacola.

Bernardo crossed the bay with a detachment of five hundred grenadiers and musketeers to provide extra protection for Ezpeleta's exhausted troops.[50] The following afternoon, sixteen ships from Havana carrying fourteen hundred soldiers sailed through the channel and into the bay while the English gunners at Barrancas sent a barrage of 107 cannonballs whizzing noisily and harmlessly over their heads.

Over the following days, Bernardo moved the entire army round the bay to a place called O'Neil's Field on the east bank of Bayou Chico, only a mile and a half from the settlement of Pensacola defended by Fort George. He accompanied the main body of men, who were ferried the five miles or so around the coast, while Ezpeleta led a few hundred men overland on "an extremely arduous march" to flush out any British forces or their Indian allies and so secure the rear. Again and again, they suffered lethal Indian raids, and one night, "in the dark, thick forest, two detachments of Spanish troops each thought the other was the enemy and opened fire, killing some and wounding others."[51] The British set up three field cannon and launched a surprise attack, during which the Indians scalped a handful of Bernardo's own Indian allies before Ezpeleta rallied the troops and Bernardo sent the light infantry to force the enemy to withdraw to Fort George.[52]

Bernardo began scouting out Fort George and decided to launch his assault from a shoulder of forested land to the northwest of a fortification known as Queen Anne's Redoubt. He began moving the army up the bank of the bayou, ready to occupy the high ground. British deserters were trickling into camp almost daily, and one of them, a captain of Maryland Loyalists, told Bernardo that Campbell had quarreled with his Choctaw allies, who had withdrawn some distance from the fort. That offered a degree of reassurance, although within days another deserter reported that three hundred Creek warriors had turned up, offering to fight for the British. Bernardo began making his own overtures to the key Native American nations, asking for their support or urging them to remain neutral.[53]

As the Spanish army was preparing to advance and dig in, the naval forces redeemed their wounded honor by capturing all the British vessels still in the bay with barely a shot fired or even a scuffle, except for the battle frigate *Mentor*, which was set on fire by her captain and crew before they abandoned ship.[54]

Bernardo continued to gain ground with painstaking patience, ordering his men to dig in a new camp a few hundred yards to the northeast. The day was suspiciously quiet until, at four o'clock in the afternoon, "various detachments of Indians came ahead and began firing at the Spanish light infantry," who were there to defend the maneuver. British regulars followed with two field cannons. Bernardo himself advanced into the midst of the fray to see if he could outflank the enemy and cut them off. Standing on the front line, a single "shot hit a finger of his left hand and then made a furrow in his abdomen," and he had to retire to his tent so the surgeons could patch him up. Ezpeleta took command and ordered the Spanish gunners to fire relentlessly at the attacking troops. By nightfall, the skirmish was over.[55]

Six days later, lookouts spotted fourteen ships approaching across the waters of the Gulf. For two hours, Bernardo and his men waited, fearing they must be a British fleet, until finally receiving word from Santa Rosa that the ships were Spanish. Miró's diplomacy and Bernardo's now-towering reputation for bravado and military brio had persuaded the authorities in Havana to support the assault on Pensacola.

Bernardo now had over 5,500 men under his command, supported by 1,500 marines and 725 French naval personnel. With the odds decisively in his favor, he prepared to gain Fort George by slow attrition. Under constant bombardment, Ezpeleta oversaw the construction of two redoubts, but during one violent sortie the British succeeded in forcing the Spaniards to abandon one of the positions with considerable loss of life. They pursued their fleeing victims with "bayonets fixed, killing and wounding all those they found in the connecting trench," Miranda recalled.

But the decisive moment in the battle came soon after dawn on May 8, 1781. "We heard a huge explosion, which greatly alarmed us." Bernardo and

Ezpeleta "immediately went to the trench where the noise had been heard," and "we saw a great column of smoke rising to the clouds and soon realized the explosion had been inside the fort and its whole battery was now in flames."[56] A grenade from one of the Spanish mortars had hit the powder magazine with devastating results. The explosion instantly destroyed Queen Anne's Redoubt and killed eighty men. The Spanish infantry quickly took possession of the position and began firing guns and mortars at the next line of defense, known as Prince of Wales Redoubt. Six hours later, Campbell hoisted the white flag. Bernardo had won West Florida for Spain.[57]

Spain soon sent word to the Americans through French intermediaries that Bernardo was ready to engage in a joint campaign against St. Augustine. George Washington replied, "It gives me great pleasure to find so good a disposition in Don Bernardo de Galvez to concert his operations in such a manner," but apologized that the "present political situation" meant that such an alliance would be impossible. As at Mobile, Bernardo had offered Campbell generous terms because he was keen to turn his attention to an assault on British Jamaica and needed to avoid protracted negotiations. But while he insisted that the defeated combatants should not take part in any future action against Spain, he allowed Campbell to transport many of his men to New York.

In Philadelphia, the Americans were furious. "I cannot . . . perswade [sic] myself that Governor Gálvez who . . . hath manifested the most Friendly Sentiments & attachment for us would admit of terms so . . . detrimental to these States," a perplexed and incredulous Samuel Huntington wrote Washington. A Marylander asserted, with bitter irony, that "the Success of the Spaniards . . . will be more prejudicial to our Operations, than their failure would have been."[58] Washington was himself annoyed, but he understood that Bernardo was not to blame and wrote magnanimously, "I am obliged by the extract of General Galvez's letter to the Count de Grasse, explaining at large the necessity he was under of granting the terms of capitulation to the garrison of Pensacola, which the commandant required. I have no doubt, from General Galvez's well known attachment to the cause of America, that he would have refused the articles, which have been deemed exceptionable, had there not been very powerful reasons to induce his acceptance of them."[59]

The significance of Bernardo's military successes to the outcome of the American Revolution has long been intuited by a few and ignored by the many. A leading Spanish military historian has described his "military campaigns" as of the "first magnitude" and clearly demonstrates that the war was going badly for the Patriots until Manchac and Baton Rouge. But while Bernardo's victories made a significant contribution to the American resurgence, the extent of that contribution should not be unduly exaggerated. Clearly our proud Spanish historian is giving in to patriotic hyperbole when he writes that "in all justice" Bernardo "ought to rank alongside Washington and other American heroes as one of the main protagonists of independence."[60]

Nonetheless, underlying his sentiments is a good deal of truth. In 1783, Congress resolved to hang his portrait in the Capitol, but that good intention was soon forgotten. However, Bernardo's contribution to American history is now being recognized. The Order of the Granaderos de Galvez was founded at San Antonio, Texas, in 1975 to promote his memory, and the following year Congress "authorized the erection of a statue of Bernardo de Galvez on public ground in the District of Columbia," a gift from the government of Spain that stands today in Galvez Park where the E Street Expressway emerges into the open air. In 2014, Congress resolved, "Whereas . . . honorary citizenship is and should remain an extraordinary honor not lightly conferred, Bernardo de Gaalvez [sic] is proclaimed posthumously to be an honorary citizen," only the eighth foreigner in U.S. history to be so feted.[61] His portrait was finally hung in the Capitol, also in 2014. ¡Olé!

In 1781, as the Americans defeated the British at Yorktown, Madrid was rocked by major indigenous uprisings in Peru and Colombia that heralded the long struggle toward independence in all her American colonies and the disintegration of the Spanish Empire around the globe. Spain urgently needed to negotiate peace and to establish her borders with the fledgling United States, and when the British chose to cut their losses in southern North America and ceded East Florida to Spain, the St. Marys River was firmly established as the frontier.

Bernardo de Gálvez personally recommended Manuel de Zéspedes y Velasco as Governor of Florida. Bernardo had seen the diplomacy with which Zéspedes had handled the informal royal visit to Havana of the Prince of Wales, the future William IV, then serving as a midshipman in the fleet of Admiral Hood. On June 27, 1784, Zéspedes disembarked at St. Augustine and was welcomed ashore by his outgoing British counterpart, Patrick Tonyn, who took him to see the governor's residence. During the previous period of Spanish rule, before the British took over, this little palace was famous for the elegance of its neoclassical patios and reception rooms and the beauty of its extensive gardens. There had been orchards of Chinese oranges and Seville oranges, peaches, cherries, figs, pomegranates, grapefruits, and an arbor shaded by vines.

But the British had felled the trees and ripped out much of the woodwork to use as kindling. The roof leaked, the place smelled of mildew, and it was home

Francisco de Goya y Lucientes, *Charles III in Hunting Dress*, 1786. "A giant among Bourbon midgets" — for all that, Goya's famous portrait makes him look more like a "gamekeeper than a monarch." MADRID: MUSEO DEL PRADO

Anonymous, *José de Gálvez y Gallardo*. José de Gálvez was born to humble parents in a mountain hamlet but rose to be Inspector General of New Spain and then Secretary of the Indies despite suffering a mental breakdown in northern Mexico, possibly induced by consuming peyote. MEXICO CITY: MUSEO NACIONAL DE HISTORIA. COURTESY OF AGE FOTOSTOCK/ALAMY STOCK PHOTO

FOLLOWING PAGE: José de Páez, *The Destruction of the Saint Sabá Mission in the Province of Texas and the Martyrdom of the Priests, Fray Alonso Giraldo de Terreros and Fray José de Santiesteban*, c. 1758. One of the earliest documented raids by Comanches set back the Spanish occupation of Texas by many decades. MEXICO CITY: MUSEO NACIONAL DE ARTE. COURTESY OF THE ARTCHIVES/ALAMY STOCK PHOTO

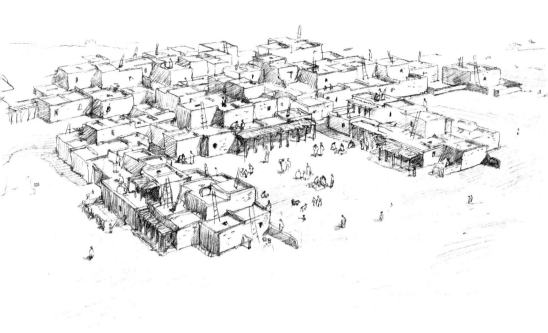

THIS PAGE: Richard Schlecht, *Quarai Pueblo*, 1620. The Spaniards gave the Native Americans of New Mexico the name Pueblos because their towns looked so much like the traditional pueblos, or villages, of Andalusia. PHOTO COURTESY OF THE ARTIST AND THE NATIONAL PARK SERVICE

Taos Pueblo, North Block. The great Pueblo Revolt of 1680 was planned from the ceremonial kiva in Taos by the Pueblo patriot Po'pay. PHOTO BY THE AUTHOR

José Germán de Alfaro, *Count Bernardo de Gálvez*, 1785. Admirer and adversary of Apaches, Spanish hero of American Independence, and scion of the extraordinarily successful Gálvez family. MEXICO CITY: MUSEO NACIONAL DE HISTORIA. COURTESY OF THE PICTURE ART COLLECTION/ ALAMY STOCK PHOTO AND U.S. SENATE COMMISSION ON ART

J. F. W. Des Barres, *A Chart of the Bay and Harbour of Pensacola in the Province of West Florida, [London]*, 1780. Bernardo de Gálvez's finest hour was the successful assault on British-held Pensacola in 1781, during which he sailed his tiny ship the *Galveztown* past the guns of Fort Barrancas. COURTESY OF THE LIBRARY OF CONGRESS, GEOGRAPHY AND MAP DIVISION

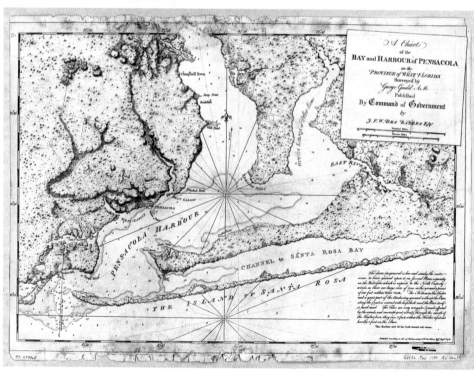

José Mosqueda, *Junípero Serra*, 19th century. Serra was a determined Franciscan from Mallorca who founded the famous California missions. "The padres have whipped their children, the Indians, throughout the conquest of these kingdoms," he said in justification of his own rigor. His canonization in 2015 proved extremely controversial. COURTESY OF SANTA BÁRBARA MISSION ARCHIVE-LIBRARY

FACING PAGE, TOP: Ramón Murillo, *Cavalryman of the Internal Provinces Frontier*, 1804. The huge sweep of northern New Spain where the Spanish and Native American worlds collided was a troubled frontier where soldiers and largely Apache raiders were continually at war. COURTESY OF THE MINISTERIO DE CULTURA Y DEPORTE

BOTTOM LEFT: Anonymous, *Juan Bautista de Anza*, 19th century. Anza was the most effective military leader in northern New Spain; he forged an overland route from Sonora to California and went on to be Governor of New Mexico. COURTESY OF PALACE OF THE GOVERNORS PHOTO ARCHIVES (NMHM/DCA), 50828

BOTTOM RIGHT: Anonymous, *Pedro Fages, Governor of Alta California*, 1780. Governor Fages was popular neither with his men nor the missionaries, but he opened the overland route from San Diego to Monterey. On the return journey, his expedition ran out of food so he ordered them to eat their mules. By the time the reached San Diego, he reported, "we all smelled horribly of mule." COURTESY OF SANTA CLARITA HISTORICAL SOCIETY

THIS PAGE: Ramón Murillo, *Hussars of Texas in Action of War*, 1804. SEVILLE: ARCHIVO GENERAL DE INDIAS, MAPAS Y PLANOS, UNIFORMES, 57. COURTESY OF THE MINISTERIO DE CULTURA Y DEPORTE

Francisco de Goya y Lucientes, *The Family of Charles IV*, 1800. Madrid was rife with rumor that the Universal Minister, Godoy (on the right), rose to power because he was the lover of Queen María Luisa. The royal couple and their favorite were referred to as the Holy Trinity. MADRID: MUSEO DEL PRADO

LEFT: De Agostini, *Portrait of Antonio Lopez de Santa Anna* (1795–1876). Antonio de Padua María Severino López de Santa Anna y Pérez de Lebrón had as many facets to his personality as he had names: a brutal and effective soldier, a mercurial politician, a breeder of fighting cocks, that rarest of creatures —a liberal strongman; he was President of Mexico on eleven separate occasions. MEXICO CITY: MUSEO NACIONAL DE HISTORIA. COURTESY OF WORLD HISTORY ARCHIVE / ALAMY STOCK PHOTO

RIGHT: Ralph Eleaser Whiteside Earl, *Andrew Jackson*, 1835. Governor Callava lectured Jackson about the courtesies of international diplomacy and gave him a textbook on the subject to study at home. The calculated insult of an educated metropolitan European aimed at Jackson's sensibilities about his backwoods character, the man might as well have called the American a "cracker" to his face. WASHINGTON, D.C.: SMITHSONIAN AMERICAN ART MUSEUM

only to the myriad critters that scurried and scampered for cover as Zéspedes contemplated his new home. After twenty years of vandalism and neglect, the palace was almost a ruin. The majestic bulk of the Castillo de San Marcos, by contrast, was in excellent condition. The massive walls of the star-shaped fortress were ringed by a broad moat. A narrow bridge led through the solid gate into a vestibule, and beyond was the capacious central courtyard surrounded by magazines, stores, offices, and barracks. There was a deep well and flushing latrines, washed out twice a day by the high tide. Zéspedes was impressed.

Zéspedes must have greatly enjoyed the official handover on July 12, when the Spanish flag was run up the flagpole and Father Camps, the priest of the Menorcans who had settled at New Smyrna, celebrated a Te Deum. Zéspedes cut a grand and bonhomous figure with impeccable manners, who excelled as a generous host. The American general Nathanael Greene, who visited him at St. Augustine with the new U.S. Indian agent for the south, Benjamin Hawkins, described the "truly elegant" French dinner they were served with an unabashed sense of gluttony. "I believe in my soul," he assured his incredulous wife, that "from one hundred and fifty to two hundred dishes of different kinds [were] served up in seven courses," all washed down with a "variety of Spanish and . . . French wines." This endless feast "lasted five hours and as I was obliged to taste most of the dishes," after which, he confessed, "I was not unlike a stuffed pig."[62]

The wealthiest English citizens welcomed the incoming Spanish officers with a round of fabulous parties, beginning with a gala ball on July 14. As violins and flutes played, the Irish officers of the Spanish Hibernia Regiment went to work translating and interpreting for the two sides. But as the warm, humid night progressed, news arrived that a gang of ruffians had kidnapped eight black slaves from the kitchens of a prominent British resident.

As outgoing governor, Patrick Tonyn briefed Zéspedes and his officers about this desperate bunch of *banditti*, as Tonyn called them. Most had either been expelled or deserted from the Continental Army, and under the leadership of an outlaw from South Carolina called Daniel McGirt, who owned a plantation on the St. Johns River, they had become highwaymen and livestock rustlers. Tonyn urged his Spanish counterpart to show them no mercy.[63]

However, it was far from clear to Zéspedes whether McGirt or Tonyn was the more troublesome bandit. Zéspedes proclaimed an amnesty, and soon afterward five of McGirt's men turned themselves in. Zéspedes listened to what they had to say, then allowed them to emigrate. Meanwhile, Tonyn pursued his own vendetta against the remaining ruffians, launching a brutal attack in which he murdered one man and made off, with "the fastest horse . . . in the province, all their saddles, bridles, and clothes, even their hats and shoes."[64] Zéspedes posted a guard at McGirt's farm for the gangster's own protection, but the following year, Zéspedes had him arrested along with his leading henchmen. They were expelled from Florida, and following McGirt's pathetic attempt to establish a Loyalist British enclave in Appalachia, he was sent to South Carolina, where he died soon afterward.[65]

During his first fourteen months in office, Zéspedes had to deal with the continued presence of the unruly Tonyn, who was responsible for evacuating thousands of often troublesome British subjects, many of them Loyalists who had lost everything in the war. They gathered at St. Marys, where there were constant brawls between Tories and Patriots, hooligans on both sides still enjoying the spirit of the war. In one incident, a British ship's captain attacked a counterpart from Philadelphia with his telescope and threw him down his gangplank. Zéspedes concluded the Englishman must be insane, but Tonyn excused him on the grounds that he was merely protecting the rights of a British sailor who had deserted from the Philadelphia ship. Finally, in November 1785, Tonyn left East Florida, never to return, having completed the awful task of removing into exile almost ten thousand individuals who had already suffered terribly as a result of supporting the wrong side during the Revolutionary War.

Zéspedes turned his friendly nature to the vigorous pursuit of good relations with the Indian population, which Bernardo had taught him would be essential to the survival of Spanish Florida.[66] He instigated two major conferences attended by the chiefs and military leaders of the Seminoles and Lower Creeks. The formal exchanges took place in the main plaza of St. Augustine, with the Creeks wearing linen shirts, their heads shaved into a triangle of hair at the back of the head, each with a plumage of gorgeous feathers held in place by a headband. Before all the Spanish officers and priests, Zéspedes displayed a portrait of Charles III and promised peace in the name of the king. The Indian elders agreed to do their best to keep the youngbloods in check and asked that the trading posts on the St. Johns and St. Marks rivers be maintained.

Zéspedes permitted the existing Indian-trading business of Panton, Leslie & Company to continue its operations, which had as a silent partner the powerful Upper Creek chief known as "Mad Dog" McGillivray, the son of an Indian mother and a Scottish father. Thus, the affable Spaniard established friendly relations with his indigenous neighbors, which were formally sealed by officials from both sides interlocking forearms, smoking pipes, and drinking Spanish *aguardiente*, literally "firewater."[67]

To establish some sort of defensive frontier in the north, Zéspedes offered Spanish protection to twenty-two former British Loyalist families who settled along the St. Marys River, forming a human bulwark against the Americans. When war broke out between the Creeks and the new State of Georgia, he had to station troops at Amelia Island and sent a gunboat to patrol the river to deter Indian or American assault.

Amid so much discord, most of the Spanish and English officer classes had largely maintained friendly relations and clearly enjoyed one another's company, in no small part thanks to Zéspedes's affable largesse. But his laid-back approach came with its own troubles. Nathanael Greene wrote his wife that the Spanish governor's "daughters are not handsome, [for] their complexion is rather tawny," before giving his true feelings away by describing their "sweet languishing Eyes." Indeed, he said, they "look as if they could love with great violence. They sang and played the Harpsichord and did everything to please . . . the softer emotions." "Hawkins," Green reported, deflecting his own sentiments, "professed himself smitten."[68]

One of Zéspedes's own officers serving in the Hibernia Regiment was so violently smitten that he persuaded the elder daughter, Dominga, to marry him in secret. Such a clandestine liaison with an officer of lowly rank was a terrible slur on Zéspedes's honor and a public insult to his authority and he immediately had both of them locked up. But after he had spoken to Dominga at length and then interviewed the Irishman, this naturally tenderhearted man concluded that they were indeed in love and that honor could be most effectively be preserved by giving his approval for the match.

While Zéspedes had shown himself capable of negotiating with Indians, he found it impossible to even begin to tame the American frontiersmen. In a report to the Spanish Crown, he described them as "a species of white rene-gade, known as *crackers*," who "are nomadic like Arabs and can be distin-guished from savages only by their complexions, their language, and the depraved superiority of their cunning and bad faith." He explained that they had largely supported the British during the war and many of them had taken refuge in Indian territory, forming close bonds with the Indians who had also mostly supported the Loyalists. As many as six hundred frontiersmen had become "naturalized citizens of Creek society" and had taken squaws and started families. They lived like Indians, hunting and tracking game, sleeping in makeshift shelters, always "beyond the reach of all civilized law."

Zéspedes explained in succinct detail the essential process of American expansion as it happened on the ground. These "crackers" opened up Indian territory by encroaching on Indian lands, which allowed the government of Georgia to unjustly claim the territory where they were squatting was part of the state. When the restless crackers moved on, they were followed by a "second class of cracker," Zéspedes went on, "less antisocial," but "likewise enemies of all civil control and lacking the rudiments of religious morality." As they drifted away, "a third type of settler" arrived who, for all that they "sought grants of legal title to the land" demonstrated little obedience to their new nation, for "everywhere on the frontier, the authority of the government is weak and held in low esteem." Finally, they would sell up cheaply to more law-abiding folk who began to farm and build communities. "Far from opposing these land grabs," Zéspedes complained, "the southern states of America encourage them."[69] He estimated that a hundred families "from the best caste of crackers" were squatting along the St. Marys and St. Johns rivers.

This growing population of American squatters was problematic because they were developing commercial ties with American merchants and encouraging them to trade with Indian communities far up the St. Marys. Zéspedes had learned of one ship that had even come all the way from Halifax, Nova Scotia. He was deeply concerned, for he knew that the troops available to him in Spanish Florida would struggle to contain these wild backwoodsmen with almost no knowledge of the law. His province depended on American de jure respect for the Peace of Paris and he well understood that the real problem was not so much the "crackers," but the many politicians in the United States who had far more respect for military might than they did the Law of Nations.

PART IV

Sunset and Perdition

THE EBB TIDE

BERNARDO DE GÁLVEZ completed his total triumph over his rivals at Havana when he was appointed Captain General of Cuba in 1784. Having enjoyed that sweetest of victories, the following year, on the death of his father, he became Viceroy of New Spain, where he earned the adoration of the king's colonial subjects by keeping Mexico City fed during a terrible famine. But in 1786 this formidable servant of the crown, "so tough that since childhood he had seemed like Hercules," felt too ill to attend mass, and a month later he was "very sick" indeed, according to the Captain of Halberdiers. There were dark rumors that Bernardo had been poisoned because his powerful enemies had whispered to the king that he was scheming to rebel against the crown and proclaim himself ruler of New Spain.[1]

In October, his doctors advised him to receive the Holy Sacrament. His barber shaved him while still lying in his sickbed. He rose falteringly to dress in full military uniform. Surrounded by his closest advisers and the most senior political figures in the city, he waited with great dignity in the viceregal palace. A long procession of priests and friars paraded the consecrated host beneath an ornate canopy from the cathedral across the main square, through clouds of sweet-smelling incense, in an absolute silence broken only by the sharp chime of the bells rung to announce the mysterious presence of the Eucharist. Bernardo was too weak to kneel before his God and had to be supported as he listened to the prayers and took Communion. Mexico City wept.[2]

With the specter of death ever present, Bernardo wrote Uncle José to explain he could no longer run the government and resigned his powers in favor of his counselors and the Audiencia. Days later, he dictated his will and asked to be buried in the parish church of San Fernando, opposite the sepulcher of his father. He fought on for another fortnight, but finally, at a quarter past four in the morning of November 30, "he expired on a deathbed soaked with the tears of his friends," who had sat vigil with him unto the last. The following day, his cadaver was displayed in the palace ballroom, which was hung with crimson damask silk. The halberdiers stood guard by torchlight while "countless people came to see him, all moved by respect and the deepest sorrow." "The whole Kingdom of New Spain has been left overflowing with tears and pierced by the quickest of pain," the Archbishop of Mexico wrote Charles III, invoking Saint Theresa of Avila's evocation of divine love.[3]

Six days later, Félicitas de St. Maxent gave birth to their daughter María Guadalupe, named for the miraculous Madonna of Mexico.[4]

In May of the following year, Bernardo was given such a splendid official funeral "that my pen cannot do it justice," the great Mexican statesman and historian Carlos María de Bustamante wrote two generations later. The cortege was accompanied through the dark, nighttime streets by armed troops and a band playing a mournful dirge; the people "shed many tears." A large number of *intendentes* who had only recently been sent from Spain by José de Gálvez as part of his last great restructuring of the colonial administration attended this magnificent send-off. It must have been clear to each of them that Bernardo had set an exemplary standard in the conduct of royal office. He would be an impossible act to follow.[5]

Days later, Félicitas took ship for Spain, but by the time she reached Madrid, "Uncle José" had already died, on July 17, 1787. Bustamante wrote that José had supposedly succumbed to apoplexy but added, "That could just mean he was poisoned or even garroted," before referring to salacious gossip that he had died soon after a heated quarrel with the king in which he had defended Bernardo's memory from the outrageous accusations of sedition.[6] One popular verse also hinted darkly:

A pretty dirty business,
Was the death of Gálvez, they say,
And he has no power now,
His nation feels no sorrow,
Malaga, alone, laments a son . . .

Like salt dissolved in water,
Or fleeting sparks from the forge,
The Gálvez are all now no more.[7]

This was the end of an extraordinary era of imperial consolidation for Bourbon Spain, especially in North America. Symbolically enough, the monarch who had reigned over that ascendency, Charles III, had been out of sorts for days when, on the evening of December 6, 1788, he took to his bed with a bad cough and running a high fever. A week later, with considerable trepidation, physicians of the royal household advised him to receive Extreme

Unction. "They think it a great burden," Charles remarked, "but thank God! For I have been readying myself for this moment for a fortnight . . . I have acted my role as the king, but now the play is finished." He joked with the French Ambassador about the dangers of being ministered to by doctors, then turned to his first minister, the Count of Floridablanca, asking, "What? Did you think I would go on forever?" Then Charles took leave of his family: "My children, why are you upset? I have to die. Carlos, my son, I leave you in charge of our Christian faith, of my subjects, and especially the poor." At twenty to one in the morning, one of the most effective absolute monarchs in world history died at the age of seventy-two.[8] For his colonial subjects, he had, perhaps, been too effective at imposing his government.

A few weeks before the king's death, a prominent political philosopher, Gaspar de Jovellanos, delivered a resounding eulogy of his sovereign's long reign to the prestigious Royal Society of Economists: "Yes, ye Spaniards, the greatest blessing of the many Charles III has lavished upon ye has been to sow those shining seeds that have enlightened ye all and opened up the path to reason." For intellectuals, Charles had overseen a government that fostered the Enlightenment in Spain and across the empire. "Oh, good Charles," Jovellanos effused, "to thee we owe our glory and our gratitude, for without thy protection, thy generosity, and without thy fervent love of thy subjects, these precious seeds should have perished."[9] Jovellanos spoke for a generation that felt immensely proud to have opened up Spain, or at least the educated echelons of Madrid society, to the modernizing ideals then gripping much of Europe and America. Charles's reign represented a long period of reform that had allowed men such as the Gálvez to flourish. But Jovellanos also sounded a warning, urging Charles's first minister, the Count of Floridablanca, to remain "vigilant." "The holy language of truth" may be "heard in our gatherings, be read in our writings, and be imprinted in our hearts," but it was now time to ensure it should "flood across our every horizon" and into the wider world.[10]

Charles III's son and successor, Charles IV, proved to be a weak ruler at a time of great crisis for the Bourbon dynasty, for Spain, and for the Spanish Empire. The traditional histories that paint him as a near nincompoop wholly dominated by his ambitious and clever queen, María Luisa of Parma, and their unscrupulous favorite greatly exaggerate the reality. But they nonetheless emphatically capture the spirit of court and kingdom during a much-troubled age. He retained Floridablanca as his leading minister, but the early years of the reign were dominated by the rippling tremors of the French Revolution and the spirit of rebellion that seemed to have gripped the globe since the Americans' War of Independence. There were also sporadic outbreaks of rioting across Spain following a series of failed harvests. Charles IV had little love for his deposed French cousin, Louis XVI, but he felt keenly the wounds and the threat to the Bourbon dynasty and to the very institution of monarchy itself. He and his ministers were terrified that revolution would uproot their own royalty as well. They were determined to stifle any seditious sentiment and introduced a comprehensive system of censorship in an attempt to cut off Spaniards from dangerous foreign influences. Intellectuals were aggressively discouraged from speaking their minds or even thinking. Some were even imprisoned, while Gaspar de Jovellanos was rusticated to the remote north to write a report on coal mining. Troops were stationed along the borders, the seas were turned into a moat and the Pyrenees ramparts against revolution, but they also became the walls of a prison.

Floridablanca took a hard line against Revolutionary France, but the French Ambassador quietly and successfully campaigned against him until Charles replaced him. As his new first minister, Charles chose the Count of Aranda because he had built up strong personal relationships with a number of influential French Enlightenment figures while Ambassador to Versailles during the protracted machinations surrounding Spanish assistance to the American Patriots. But when Louis XVI was imprisoned in the summer of 1792, and France was gripped by the Reign of Terror, Aranda also fell from grace. Against this troubled backdrop and faced with a pressing need to radically change a foreign policy that had for so long been based on a series of family alliances with France, Charles IV appointed a young army officer called Manuel Godoy as his "Universal Minister," an almost all-powerful royal favorite in the mold of the early seventeenth-century Habsburg *validos* or *privados*, the Duke of Lerma and the Count-Duke of Olivares.

Godoy had arrived in Madrid as an impoverished soldier from the minor nobility, with a reputation for grace and gaiety. Given that background, his political rise was astonishing, and to the consternation of the royal courtiers, he appeared to owe everything to an extraordinary personal hold over the queen. It will never be possible to explain with any certainty why the royal couple selected him to rule their realms for them. He had limitless charisma, worked hard for long hours, and, perhaps most important, had a capacity to explain in simple terms the complexities of government to these "two politically bewildered monarchs who relied on their minister to see them through the surrounding turmoil," as one eminent historian has characterized the Spanish sovereigns.[11] In short, it seems they liked and trusted him. Years later, writing his memoirs in exile, Godoy candidly recognized that he was wholly the creation of Charles and María Luisa and owed them everything. They had raised him to the rank of captain general, bestowed regal powers upon him, secured him great wealth, and honored him with a dukedom. Thus, they secured his total loyalty, and in 1797 he became one of the family when he married Charles's first cousin María Teresa de Borbón. Nonetheless, the whole court and foreign diplomatic corps were convinced he was the lover of the queen, and after he became Universal Minister, Godoy, king, and queen were commonly referred to as the Holy Trinity.[12]

The gossips related that Godoy had charmed María Luisa with songs of love. The influential English clergyman Joseph Blanco White claimed Godoy's elder brother had been her lover first, but that she fell for young Manuel when he acted as go-between. "The voluptuous and love-sick princess," it was said, "was able to bring tremendous pressure on him" and "to resist would mean disgrace."[13] In reality, Godoy seems to have first caught the eye of both king and queen when he was thrown from his horse while riding in their escort. Soon afterward, he began to play chess with Charles, who then appointed him as a Gentleman of the Bedchamber, even as the gossips gleefully announced that that the queen was pregnant by Godoy and not the king.

There is no concrete evidence of any sexual relationship between this dashing twenty-one-year-old guardsman and María Luisa, who had just turned thirty-seven on her husband's accession to the throne. As the English society hostess Lady Holland wrote, "It is impossible with truth to ascertain what are the ties between him and the queen."[14] With the hindsight of our own enlightened age, we should perhaps also ask whether this vigorous sexual predator might not have also seduced the king? Or both?

The many portraits by Francisco de Goya y Lucientes perhaps offer the most appealing and insightful commentaries on that turbulent epoch. Goya may be best known today for the ghastly "black paintings," produced in the insanity of his dotage, and his series of etchings *The Horrors of War*, but the loosened brushwork in his representations of the leading figures of his age, of royalty, aristocrats, the Duke of Wellington, and Joseph Bonaparte is filled with gay irony and a lively sardonic spirit. They are psychological X-rays that plumb the inner reality of the sitter. Yet, despite his repeatedly revealing and depicting some "cruel and uncomfortable truth" to be found in the darkest recesses of his subject's soul, almost all the most powerful people in Spain were eager to have Goya paint their portrait. "From the king down," he boasted in 1791, "everyone knows me!"[15] In 1800, he painted *The Family of Charles IV*, a formal group portrait that shows the Bourbon dynasty on the eve of disaster. For almost a hundred years unkind commentators endlessly repeated some variation of the observation that the sitters looked like a "baker and his wife after they won the lottery."[16] Notwithstanding, Godoy lauded

Goya as the living incumbent in a long tradition of great Spanish painters inspired by Titian and his patrons Charles V and Philip II and epitomized by the great seventeenth-century artist-diplomat Diego Velázquez.[17]

In *The Family of Charles IV*, Goya took inspiration from Velázquez's most famous work, *Las Meninas*, showing himself at the easel, in the background, on the extreme left of the canvas. Immediately in front of him, the heir to the throne, Ferdinand, Prince of Asturias, shines in a bright blue suit and the sash of the Order of Charles III, which had been created by his grandfather in excited commemoration of the birth of Charles IV's first son in 1771, following five barren years of marriage. The child died in infancy, but the order was closely associated with the dynasty. The colors blue and white are a reference to the traditional attributes of the Madonna of the Immaculate Conception, to whom Charles III had prayed fervently in the hopes his son would sire an heir. Queen María Luisa is center stage, tall, haughty, yet Goya conveys the sense that she had been a great beauty in her youth, while laying bare the reality of having given birth to fourteen children. She is separated from the handsome, blond Godoy by the portly majesty of the king and the little Duke of Cadiz, thought by some to be the lover's child.[18] In a painting that is entirely about a dynasty, it is indeed extraordinary to find Godoy, the royal favorite, so prominently portrayed as part of the family.

Salacious scandal and the sovereign's seeming indifference to his shameful cuckolding perfectly symbolized for the Spanish establishment the moral malaise at the heart of the monarchy. They hated their queen as much as they pitied their pathetic king. Worse still, the government was in the hands of an inexperienced upstart who was universally loathed and almost friendless apart from his royal benefactors. Godoy governed in peculiar isolation from his peers, and according to Lady Holland, he was so susceptible "to the power of beauty, that those who have favors to solicit, entrust their cause to the prettiest female in their family, who pleads *tête-à-tête* in the cabinet allotted and fitted up for the purpose of such secret audiences."[19]

The pressure on Bourbon Spain to go to war with Revolutionary France in defense of the dynasty was intense. But while Godoy's absurdly elevated military rank may have belied his ignorance of battle, he had served as a junior officer, and he knew that the Spanish army was obviously in no condition to win battles against the French revolutionary troops. He tried to avoid conflict. But when King Louis XVI was executed in January 1793, the whole Spanish nation united in righteous, outraged Catholic anger and clamored for the fight. Then on March 7, France declared war on Spain.

Godoy had the good sense to seek an alliance with Britain, but then infuriated his new ally by failing to provide the necessary naval support. The exasperated British Ambassador complained of his "utter unfitness to conduct the affairs of a great country at a crisis like the present."[20] Godoy proudly lamented, "The Fates condemned me to sail the ship of state, all alone and by myself, during the toughest epoch in the annals of European history."[21]

Spaniards were baying for blood, but despite the energetic support of the people, the dithering government and the incompetence of its military officers lost them the war. With French troops advancing toward Madrid, Godoy panicked and sued for peace. The price of that peace was hugely symbolic, for France requested and acquired Hispaniola, the island where Columbus had begun the colonization of the Americas in 1492. Charles IV thought it a cheap price to pay in the face of dynastic Armageddon and gratefully granted Godoy the title the Prince of Peace.

Instead of peace, however, Spain was almost permanently at war throughout Charles's reign: first with France, then Britain, then Britain again, then France again, until, finally, Arthur Wellesley, the great Irish-born British general who was rewarded for his service with the title Duke of Wellington, rid Spain of French occupation as a prelude to delivering his *coup de grâce* to Napoleon Bonaparte at Waterloo. Rarely, in history, has peninsular Spain been the victim of invasion, for it is protected by the sea and the mountains, but all the ghastly horror of the Napoleonic Wars was visited the length and breadth of the Iberian Peninsula. Known in England and America as the Peninsular War and to Spaniards as the War of Independence, that brutal conflict changed the history of Spain, the Spanish Empire, and the world.

CHAPTER 22

APOGEE & DISASTER

CANADA & SPAIN

Gardem España—God damn Spain!

—CAPTAIN JAMES COLNETT

IN 1774, FOLLOWING THEIR FIRST VOYAGE to the northern reaches of the Pacific coast, the great mariner Juan Pérez had reported that his second-in-command, Esteban Martínez, was a hopelessly incompetent navigator. Yet over the following decade, Martínez established himself as the most experienced sailor on the supply route to Alta California. During that time, more and more foreign traffickers began sailing to the Northwest to trade otter pelts, which fetched a high price in Europe, trespassing on territory and commerce claimed exclusively by Spain. So, in 1788, Martínez was given command of two ships and sent to gauge the extent of foreign incursions. Pérez's warnings appeared prescient when Martínez completely lost the respect of his men during a heated argument with one of the pilots over their location. When the expedition returned, most of the junior officers alleged their commander had falsified navigational data, and the pilot accused him of "total insanity due to drunkenness. Only a man full of liquor could have committed such excess." [1] Worse still, they said, when Martínez encountered a handful of Russian trading posts, he abandoned himself to an orgy of alcoholic bonhomie and spent weeks ashore at Dutch Harbor, Unalaska, with a merchant called Potap Zaikov, swilling wine, brandy, and vodka, and feasting on fresh meat, cheese, ham, and chocolate.

While his men maligned him, Martínez filed a report replete with the intelligence he had gleaned during his revels with Zaikov. The Russians, he warned, were preparing to establish a permanent outpost at Nootka Sound to steal a march on British merchantmen sailing out of Canton. Martínez advised that Spain should occupy the harbor the next spring to head off so many rivals. He may have been a drunken *bon vivant*, but he had unquestionably carried out his orders to discover the extent of the trespass on the Northwest coast.

The following year, Martínez ignored a royal warrant ordering him to return to his wife in Seville and assumed command of two ships sent to Nootka Sound with instructions to establish a small fortress and a barracks for the most northerly garrison in the empire. He was given strict orders to firmly inform any foreigners he encountered that Nootka was Spanish, and while he was to make reasonable attempts to avoid conflict, he was permitted to use all force necessary in the assertion of that claim.

Trouble was inevitable on the Northwest coast in 1789 as ships from around the globe raced to gain a foothold on what many believed to be virgin territory. Martínez knew the Russians were already ensconced farther up the coast, but that summer assorted Americans, Englishmen, Scotsmen, Portuguese, Filipinos, Chinese artisans and laborers, Hindu Indian deckhands, as well Spaniards took up temporary residence as neighbors of the Native American Chief Ma-kwee-na and his people at Friendly Bay on Nootka Sound. Through a mixture of guile and force, Martínez gained a firm grip on this global *mélange* in the name of King Charles III of Spain, who, although Martínez did not know it, was already dead.

As Martínez approached the entrance to Nootka Sound, he intercepted an American fur-trading vessel commanded by Robert Gray. He explained that he had wintered there with his colleague John Kendrick, who had established a little outpost called Fort Washington in a nearby cove. Gray also told Martínez that a suspicious vessel called the *Ifigenia* had recently arrived, flying a Portuguese flag and notionally under a Portuguese captain, although it was clearly commanded by a Scotsman called Douglas. "It will make me a good prize," Martínez boasted, and presented Gray and his men with a generous quantity of wine, brandy, hams, and sugar.[2]

The following day, Martínez, Douglas, and Kendrick dined in an atmosphere of delightfully duplicitous diplomatic courtesy aboard the Spanish flagship. They then attended a long ceremony of welcome organized by Chief Ma-kwee-na, who greeted Martínez warmly, remembering him from their previous meeting, in 1774. The Spaniard asked about some silver spoons that had been stolen from him, and the chief told him the thief had been dead for a long time. The next day Kendrick made a speech in the local language in praise of Martínez, and Douglas offered a return luncheon for the Spaniard and the American. That night, they all enjoyed a naming ceremony for one of Ma-kwee-na's children.

Martínez was keen to keep on friendly terms with the Americans. Spain and the Patriots had been allies in the Revolutionary War, and Kendrick had even taken part in the famous Boston Tea Party. But more important, Martínez quickly came to an agreeable arrangement with them over the fur trade, and while he declared in his official reports that he had conducted only a modest amount of business with the Americans, it seems likely that he was quietly selling them large numbers of pelts for personal profit. They all became firm friends throughout that long and dangerous summer, at the end of which Kendrick's son John asked to convert to Catholicism and join the Spanish navy.

Overnight, Martínez carefully studied Douglas's paperwork. The Scot and his associates were part of an illegal operation run by an unscrupulous naval officer, John Meares, on behalf of a shady consortium of investors organized to defraud the British East India Company. But they had shown astonishing stupidity by failing to study these Portuguese documents, in which, among other things, the Governor of Macao instructed Douglas to impound any Spanish "vessel which may attack you" and to "bring the ship . . . to Macao."[3] Martínez read these instructions with interest, and in the morning, he imprisoned Douglas and seized the ship.

Ma-kwee-na smelled trouble and moved his people miles up the coast, but Martínez soon freed Douglas to sail away because he and his men were a pointless drain on supplies. Within a week, a second British boat with a bogus Portuguese identity sailed into Nootka. She was a maneuverable schooner that could be manned by a handful of men, the ideal vessel to reconnoiter the coast in search of the ever-elusive Northwest Passage and to do a little trading for furs along the way. Martínez arrested her captain and confiscated the ship and put it to good use.

Over that summer, two more British ships anchored in Friendly Bay, both linked to Meares. However, by then the shady consortium had sold out to a group of London merchants, who had set the whole business on a sound footing under English law. The first ship to arrive was captained by Thomas Hudson. With his natural flare for a good time, Martínez threw a splendid feast for his guest, then invited him to attend an elaborate ceremony during which Martínez took formal possession of the land in the name of King Charles III. The highest-ranking officers of every nationality present were obliged to sign a document recording the act, and a copy was buried in a jar at the foot of a large cross. There were loud shouts of "Long live the king!" The king who was already dead. After an enjoyable week at Nootka, Hudson sailed away, a useful witness to the Spanish claim to possession.

The last Englishman to hove into view on the Nootka horizon that summer was Captain James Colnett, a Royal Navy officer moonlighting for the London merchants. When Martínez came aboard Colnett's ship, the

Englishman claimed that he was sailing in the service of King George III and that he had come to take possession of the land for Britain and establish a trading post. The Spaniard explained that he had already done these things for Spain, then persuaded the gullible Colnett to bring his ship into port despite being warned that Martínez had already impounded two of the company ships.

In port, the two men stayed up drinking while Martínez declined Colnett's incessant requests to be allowed to establish a trading post at Nootka. The following day, the bad-tempered, hungover Englishman repeatedly tried to evade surrendering his paperwork to the Spanish officials, but eventually he went aboard the flagship, where he found Martínez enjoying the end of a long lunch with the Americans and one of the priests. The Spaniard again asked the Englishman for his papers.

"My orders are directed to me alone," Colnett asserted.

"It is imperative that you show me the documents and an inventory of your cargo, so I can comply with my orders," Martínez insisted.

"I have no other papers than my passport." Colnett stalled, brandishing a document that he refused to show to the Spaniard. He raised his voice. "Will you lend me a launch to weigh anchor and set sail?"

"I am not minded to do so until you show me your passport and other papers."

Martínez opened a copy of the Laws of the Indies and explained that he was required to impound any vessel without legal authority to be there. Colnett waved his license from the South Sea Company and lied, "This is my grant and license from the King of England."

"Remember, sir, that you are talking to a ranking officer of His Catholic Majesty, while you are not here in any official capacity and are not entitled to call yourself a representative of the English king."

"I am acquainted with the Maritime Law of Nations. You will soon find out you have been wrong to detain me!" Colnett responded, stamping his feet and smashing the palm of his hand down on the table and grabbing for his sword. "I am leaving, and if you do not like it, you can open fire." He then shouted out the notorious phrase that Martínez rendered as "Gardem España" in his official report: "God damn Spain!"[4]

That was fighting talk. Martínez lost his temper and had Colnett arrested at gunpoint. Only the intervention of the Americans prevented him from putting the stubborn Englishman in the stocks. Martínez impounded Colnett's ship and discovered the wherewithal to start a colony tightly packed into her hold, including fifty Chinese carpenters and other tradesmen, who claimed to have been tricked aboard in Canton with a promise of passage to Bengal.

The following morning, everyone at Nootka was rudely woken by the sound of cannon fire from the American ships and Fort Washington. It was July 4. The Spanish guns answered with great gusto. Colnett's humiliation was complete.

At the end of July, the long-awaited relief ship *Aranzazú* arrived in Nootka from Mexico with most of her provisions spoiled, the distressing news that Charles III was dead, and orders from the viceroy to abandon Nootka. The pigs ate the rotten food, the friars mourned the monarch, and Martínez showed his mettle by sending urgent word to Mexico that he would hold out at Nootka until the end of October, should the viceroy wish to change his order. Sadly for Martínez and his hopes for Spanish Nootka, news of so much foreign traffic on the distant Northwest coast reached Mexico as the viceroy was preparing to hand over his office to his replacement. The resulting delay meant that before word of arrangements for a further relief expedition reached Martínez, he had buried his cannon and equipment, fixed carved wooden signs to a tree proclaiming Spanish possession, and sailed for San Blas.

However fleetingly, Nootka had been the final extension of the Spanish Empire in North America. Like so much colonial territory, it had been won and held by a brilliant if troubled individual with only limited support from the crown. But it had been too far from Mexico City and Madrid to be governed by the newly centralizing and authoritarian Bourbon state, a tenuous and distant outpost of an empire that had overreached itself.

In Madrid, every government minister and royal official was spellbound by the proletarian nightmare unfolding in France. The new Bourbon monarch, Charles IV, was terrified he would suffer the same fate as his cousins. In London, the youngest British Prime Minister in history, William Pitt, was worried. He owed his almost adolescent elevation to the patronage of George III, but only months earlier the increasingly eccentric king had stopped his carriage in Windsor Great Park and struck up an earnest conversation with a venerable oak tree that he had mistaken for Frederick the Great of Prussia. The following year, Pitt faced a potentially bruising election campaign in a country still suffering the biting economic effects and emotional traumas of the American Revolution. He cast a glance toward rebellious France, realized how damaging it would be to the Bourbon Family Pact, and turned his greedy gaze on the Spanish Empire. Pitt was already fomenting unrest in Spanish America and talking to men such as Francisco de Miranda, the Liberator of Venezuela. Latin America was ripe for commercial exploitation, succulent fruit that would help to heal British imperial pride.

Rumors that Spaniards had detained British ships on the Northwest coast began to reach London over Christmas and the New Year. William Pitt the Younger now had a *cause célèbre*, not to mention a *casus belli*. As the sober Council of State in Madrid explained to Charles IV, "Nootka was a charade that chance provided the British to disguise their hostile and ambitious designs," which they "conceived as soon as the French Revolution offered a favorable opportunity to take on the divided House of Bourbon."[5]

Despite divisions within Pitt's cabinet and their almost total ignorance of what had happened, the British Prime Minister fired off a claim against Spain for damages and demanded the restitution of the property seized and an apology for the insult against the British flag.[6] The Spanish Council of State was alarmed by such a bizarrely disproportionate and presumably hasty response from "Mad" George III's ministers. The Count of Floridablanca drafted a polite but firm reply, reasserting Spanish claims to Nootka. Also, as quietly as possible, he began putting the navy on a war footing and reinforcing military garrisons in the Americas. The British seemed excessively agitated by reports of these Spanish activities.

In April 1790, John Meares landed in Britain with a dossier of reports and accounts from the men who had supposedly suffered at Spanish hands. He was invited to tell his tale to the cabinet. A range of influential and powerful people, including Pitt, had a vested interest in molding Meares's story to suit their own ends. He did not disappoint them, and the ministers hardened their stance. Within a fortnight, presumably with the help of propagandists linked to the government, Meares published an incendiary *Memorial*, filled with tales of heinous outrages committed by Esteban Martínez and a spurious claim to have built his own British outpost at Nootka before the Spaniards arrived. Most inflammatory of all, Meares announced that British ships had been impounded and their crews imprisoned, without any mention of their Portuguese flags and paperwork. The government distributed his diatribe as widely as possible, and Meares's employers published further fictions designed to stoke public anger. The abolition of slavery was then one of the most heated issues in British politics, and these documents railed against the "remorseless butchers" of Spain who had "murdered millions of the natives of that continent" and "ten million . . . of their wretched descendants are, with broken heart supplicating heaven to relieve them from their rigorous bondage" and "to send to their deliverance some compassionate nation."[7]

Pitt and his propagandists knew their audience all too well. The Anglo-Saxon peoples enjoy nothing more perhaps than a pandemic of righteous rage to justify a raucous outbreak of the hooligan spirit. In the summer of 1790, the ever-drunken British plebeians and their notoriously dipsomaniac consuls eagerly worked themselves into a fury of nationalistic umbrage. By the time several respected sailors had rubbished Meares's version of events, a mood of pure belligerence was abroad in the land. The die was cast.

Future U.S. Chief Justice John Rutledge was in London and heard Pitt address the House of Commons on May 6. He wrote Thomas Jefferson that he had dined with some members of Parliament afterward and was amazed that "they were all for war, talked much of *Old England*," and "laughed at the idea of drubbing the Dons." Indeed, he explained a few days later, "owing to a strange infatuation, there is not a man in this nation who does not seem to think he will be enriched by a Spanish war . . . In my life, I do not remember to have been among such insolent bullies."

Buoyed by the jingoistic euphoria, the public and parliamentary debate escalated from calls for restitution and punishment for the insults at Nootka into exhortations that Spain be forced to abandon the ancient principle of Possession by First Discovery, which was painted as an absurd popish anachronism in the Age of Enlightenment. Despite the manifest hypocrisy of Britain putting forward such an argument, the idea that occupation and settlement, rather than the passing presence of some explorer, should determine sovereignty had sufficient practical logic that it quickly gained traction. Spain, in other words, should allow British subjects the quiet enjoyment of any empty land in the Americas. The political climate forced Pitt to reflect these new demands in his dealings with Madrid. The fleet was prepared, men were pressed, and war became a possibility.[8]

The Spanish Council of State met in October and advised the king that any concessions to these demands would anyway soon lead to "the very war which we desire to avoid, but," moreover, they would make that war "more costly ruinous, and ineffective, in recovering domains ceded or usurped as a result of the very concessions made to elude the present evil."[9] Rutledge thought that "were the Spaniards to act with vigor, they might ruin England." Had the king listened to his council, that assessment might well have been proved correct.[10] But with a prescience born of long experience and a measured mind, Rutledge added a caveat: "The Spaniards generally make war in a very peaceable manner." They "wait to see how their enemies will begin." The French response, he concluded, would be decisive.[11]

After a bitter debate, the revolutionary French National Assembly ruled that it must approve any declaration of war by the king, further castrating royal power. Charles IV was fearful for his cousins and told his ministers not to press the matter. Spain must stand alone. But Floridablanca was old and accustomed to the comforting promise of French support, and he had the ear of the king. On October 28, Floridablanca signed the Nootka Convention, by which Spain made reparation for Martínez's supposed excesses and more humiliatingly still agreed that British subjects might fish along the whole Pacific coast, ceded them the right to trade with Native Americans, and permitted them to settle so long as they were more than ten leagues distant from the nearest place occupied by Spain.[12] Overawed by British intimidation, Charles IV offered what appears to have been abject capitulation.

Britain could never have won the war so long as Spain avoided full-scale confrontation between the fleets on the high seas. But Charles and Floridablanca gave in because of the French Revolution, which had robbed Spain of an old if unreliable ally, and more important, because they were terrified that the rebellion would spread across the Pyrenees. Those fears were well founded, for Charles would lose his throne to Revolutionary France. Next to this tangible threat to monarchy and dynasty that haunted the king and his ministers day and night, a handful of foreign settlers in the distant north of an enormous empire must have seemed so remote as to be beyond the realms of their imaginations.

Martínez's settlement and assertion of Spanish authority over Nootka was the last act of imperial expansion of any significance made by Spain in North America. It was the high tide of empire. But the Spanish Crown failed to provide the new settlement with support because it was simply one colony too far. So, it is perhaps fair to say the tide of empire turned at the moment Martínez weighed anchor on October 28, 1789, and sailed out of Nootka Sound for the last time. By the time Floridablanca signed the Nootka Convention a year later, the ebb tide was in full flow. The Spanish Empire had been a long time in the making; her decline would be nasty, brutish, and short.

In 1795, Godoy began to abandon Spanish claims and pretensions in the Lower Mississippi Basin. First, he conceded the United States' claim that the northern limit of West Florida ran along the thirty-first parallel and so surrendered the Ohio valley and Natchez. He also opened the Mississippi River to American shipping, and then in December, he offered to give Louisiana to France in exchange for Haiti. The French declined the deal, but forced the Prince of Peace, Godoy, to declare war on Britain the following year. Royal Navy ships under the command of Lord Nelson blockaded Cadiz and almost completely severed Spanish trade with the New World. As a result, the Spanish American colonies had to open their ports to foreign shipping, especially United States' merchantmen, which fast developed into such a convenient and lucrative commercial relationship that Madrid was never again able to force her colonies to conduct all their trade through the metropolitan monopoly.

With Spain so hopelessly weakened by war and the loss of trade, the ascendant Napoleon Bonaparte tried to force Charles IV to give up Louisiana and Florida. The king could not be persuaded over Florida, but he agreed to "trade" Louisiana to France in exchange for a throne for Queen María Luisa's brother. Napoleon never kept his side of that bargain, but in October 1802 Charles gave official instructions to the Spanish administration in New Orleans to hand over the province. The French officials never arrived because, barely six months later, Napoleon notoriously "flipped" Louisiana, selling it to Thomas Jefferson for fifteen million dollars. That obvious affront to Spanish pride was fast followed by the notorious cataclysm off Cape Trafalgar, near the entrance to the Mediterranean. On October 21, 1805, the British Royal Navy destroyed the combined fleets of France and Spain, sinking twenty-two Spanish ships, effectively ending forever Spanish pretensions to be a global maritime power and so severing the Spanish head from the body of her empire.

With the disasters of war on every horizon, Godoy raised the art of corruption to a disturbingly sublime level, dispensing patrimony and privilege to family and followers. He even made his own father president of the Council of Finance. His opponents turned to the heir to the throne, Ferdinand, Prince of Asturias, an unhappy youth who loathed his mother's favorite with the full force of some deep desire for Oedipal vengeance by proxy. Godoy knew the end of his life as favorite in Madrid must be nigh, so he begged Napoleon to conquer Portugal and appoint him as ruler of its southern region, the Algarve.

When French troops began marching into Spain, the Spanish opposition hatched a plot to oust the king and his favorite and replace them with young Prince Ferdinand. They mobilized a mob of hirelings, disgruntled soldiers, and disaffected toughs, which gathered outside the gates of the royal garden palace at Aranjuez, just south of Madrid, in the early spring of 1808. The king addressed the rabble, assuring them that the French soldiers were not invading Spain, but were preparing for a combined assault on Portugal. The protesters retired to the local taverns, and all seemed calm as the royal household prepared for bed.

Godoy retired to his nearby mansion, where he entertained a mysterious female visitor. Soon after she left, he heard a shot ring out. At this signal Ferdinand was to place a burning candle in his window to alert a bugler to sound the call to riot. After a long evening of drinking, the protesters were in euphorically raucous mood. As soon as Godoy sensed the commotion outside, he rushed to his roof to see what was happening. The mob stormed his house, tearing down paintings and smashing other works of art. This was the age of rococo, that fabulously vulgar moment in European aesthetic history inspired by Versailles and the fallen French Bourbons, an age of impossibly ornate

glass and multifaceted mirrors, of fantastical chandeliers and gilded curli-
cues, of a thousand tasteless statuettes, vases, and other exuberant and price-
less ceramic *objets d'art*. The mob smashed the lot in a glorious, crashing
cacophony of orgiastic vandalism. In the confusion, a distracted footman
failed to notice Godoy hiding inside a bedroom used by one of the maidser-
vants and locked the door. The former royal favorite hid himself there for a
day and a half, avoiding detection by rolling himself up inside a carpet when
a posse of servants broke down the door. In the end, he gave himself up and
was forced into exile in France.[13]

The following day, Charles IV abdicated in favor of Ferdinand VII. A few
days later, the new king entered Madrid amid a joyous crowd. But with the
city under the control of French troops, Napoleon pressured Ferdinand and
his parents to travel to the border to meet him. They crossed into France,
where the French ruler forced both Charles IV and Ferdinand VII to renounce
the throne of Spain in favor of his own brother Joseph Bonaparte.

When the news reached Madrid, an angry crowd gathered outside the
royal palace to prevent the last remaining members of the royal family from
being removed to France. On May 2, fighting broke out, and the patriotic
mob of Madrid *majos* forced the French soldiers stationed inside the city to
withdraw. A vast force of thirty-five thousand French troops immediately
retook the capital with great brutality. The following day, May 3, two hundred
Spaniards were summarily executed by firing squad.

Perhaps no artist has ever better captured the spirit of such a turbulent
moment than Goya in his *Second of May 1808* and *Third of May 1808*. The
first overflows with drama as the crowd of *majos* attacks the French cavalry.
At the heart of the image, our eye is drawn to the intense stare of a man
raising his dagger as he drags a bloodied French hussar from his saddle. This
same figure reappears in the *Third of May*, center stage again, but now dishev-
eled, in only his breeches and an incandescent white shirt lit bright by a
shining lantern. The same expression of violence catches our attention, but
now it is overlaid with terror. Goya paints him with his hands outstretched,
evoking so many images of Christ's crucifixion. Close beside him, the tonsured
head of a Franciscan friar bows in prayer, revealing the face of the man
behind him, grim with fear. One of three shadowy figures in the background
shields his eyes from his own fate. Another turns away from the faceless line
of eight French infantrymen who are pulling the triggers of their guns.
Four or five bleeding cadavers slump over one another on the ground. Goya
depicted the intense intimacy of that most infamous massacre beneath a brilliantly dark night sky with the royal palace and the Madrid skyline glowing
in the distance.[14]

Across the kingdom, Spaniards began mobilizing in the name of Ferdinand VII to resist the occupation. At first, locally organized armies and militias scored unexpected victories over the French troops, but the patriot cause was fatally fragmented by deep political differences and geographical distance. The disparate forces they put in the field were no match for the French cavalry. As the war unfolded, many Spanish patriots took to the hills and resorted to small-scale strikes on the enemy that they called *guerrilla*, or "little warfare."

In one notable skirmish, as French troops began their final assault on the little walled town of Ejea de los Caballeros, near Saragossa, the townsfolk retired to the rooftops. Then, as some brave soul flung open the gates of the town and the enemy soldiers charged in, the patriots let loose thirty-two fighting bulls into the streets. As the Frenchmen tried to climb to safety up the sides of the houses, the locals hurled down at them every missile they could find, until when "the last Frenchman was dead, the entertainment was over." That day, "the bulls' horns were more victorious and more glorious than Napoleon's armies at Marengo, Jena, and Austerlitz," an excited journalist reported.[15]

For the next six years, Spain was devastated by a horrific war fought on her own soil to a constant tattoo of atrocity and depravity. As news of the French invasion crossed the Atlantic, rebellions broke out throughout the American colonies. In Mexico, the revolutionary parish priest Miguel Hidalgo issued his famous Grito de Dolores, a popular declaration of independence described in greater detail below; Buenos Aires effectively became independent in May 1810, although the official declaration did not come until 1816. Rebellions also erupted in Peru and Colombia. Chaos reigned across the Spanish Empire, as the remains of Ferdinand VII's administration took refuge at Cadiz, which sits on a tiny and almost impregnable peninsula poking out hopefully into the Atlantic in the deep south of Spain. There, within the walls of their isolated stronghold, the great intellectual Jovellanos led the convention of the strikingly liberal Cortes of Cadiz and set about instigating a series of radically modernizing reforms.

A number of deputies even made the journey from the American colonies. One deputy made the prolonged journey from Santa Fe to advocate founding a separate episcopal see for New Mexico, which the Cortes quickly approved in principle.[16] Miguel Ramos Arizpe from Saltillo in the Sierra Madre, who would become famous as the Father of Mexican Federalism, ended up representing California, Puerto Rico, and even Caracas. His main aim was to counteract the seemingly unstoppable expansion of the United States through the creation of a giant new Comandancia Oriental, an *intendencia* stretching from the Chihuahua highlands to the distant frontier between Texas and

Louisiana. But Arizpe also railed against the fundamental problem that Spaniards saw the Americas and their inhabitants as inferior. "I cannot comprehend that six secretariats are being established to govern the eleven million men who live in [Spain], while there is a single secretariat for all the Americas with fifteen million." [17] He attacked the myopic chauvinism on which such an imbalance was founded and the deep-seated racism that classified the king's Indian, black, and mixed-race subjects as *castas*, in a complex hierarchy of racial and social castes that were thought inferior to Europeans. [18]

The Cortes eventually promulgated its famously liberal Constitution of Cadiz in 1812, which has ever since been both an enlightened touchstone to Spanish political thinking and a millstone around its neck. But for all that lasting influence, the Cortes was essentially engaged in intellectual fiddling while Spain metaphorically and often literally burned. Half the kingdom was still in French hands, while the Cadiz government had only the flimsiest influence over the other half. Spain needed a fighting force, not a constitution, and one irate guerrilla general is said to have ordered a firing squad to execute a copy of the document. [19]

The tenacity of the Spanish guerrillas kept the war alive, weakening French morale with a ceaseless barrage of little blows. But the war was eventually won on the battlefield by the Duke of Wellington, whose contempt for his Spanish allies is legendary. "I have never known the Spaniards do anything, much less do anything well," he complained, following the headlong flight of General Cuesta's men from the battlefield at Talavera. [20] By the beginning of 1813, morale among the French troops had been gravely damaged by a long hard winter during which they cowered under the constant threat of attack from the guerrillas and disheartening reports of Napoleon's disastrous campaign in Russia, during which he lost as many as half a million men.

The Duke of Wellington began his campaign to rid Spain of the French with notable successes, but then suffered a series of setbacks that forced him to withdraw to Portugal to regroup. In the spring of 1813, he stormed across the Spanish plain with a vast army of 120,000 British, Spanish, and Portuguese troops. Outflanking the French troops along the great Iberian rivers, the Duero and the Tagus, he finally routed Joseph Bonaparte at Vitoria, in the Basque country. The fighting continued in and around the Pyrenees, but by the end of the year Wellington had carried the war across the border and into France herself. Following the Battle of Waterloo, in modern Belgium, in 1815, Napoleon was deposed, exiled on the island of Saint Helena.

CHAPTER 23

Mexican Independence

New Spain & México

Friends and countrymen, henceforth for us there will be neither king nor
tribute. For three centuries, we have carried that shameful burden, that
terrible stain of tyranny and servitude . . . The moment of emancipation
has come, the bells of liberty have rung . . . I ask you to do your duty . . .
Long live the Virgin of Guadalupe! Long live América!

—FATHER MIGUEL HIDALGO, THE GRITO DE DOLORES

THE ORIGINS OF MEXICAN INDEPENDENCE are rooted in its people's
sense of pride in their American roots, which had been expressed two centuries earlier by Garcilaso de la Vega in his *Florida* and Gaspar de Villagrá in
The History of New Mexico. When they had recast the European obsession
with Ancient Rome and Greece in terms of Inca and Aztec history, they
reflected a growing sense that Creole identity was distinct from that of their
Spanish neighbors. A century later, the Franciscan commentator Agustín de
Vetancurt was brimming with just such pride when he wrote in his *Treatise
on Mexico City* that the "beauty of the city is in her inhabitants," especially
"the twenty thousand womenfolk of every social station, the poorest of whom
had her pearls and her jewelry." Even "the humblest of officials sport their
ruffs and black capes and go about by carriage or on horseback . . . with no
distinction between the rich nobleman or great landowner and the tradesmen.
That may seem like social anarchy, but it is the brio of this land and it inspires
great self-confidence in even a humble heart." [1]

During the Enlightenment of the eighteenth century, Europeans became
fascinated with ancient and even prehistoric history. Magpie collectors amassed
eclectic assortments of coins, statues, stone inscriptions, and old bones, to be
displayed alongside the feathers of exotic birds and artifacts brought from
remote corners of the globe. In New Spain, antiquaries among the Creole elite

began to accumulate and revere objects associated with the pre-Columbian history of their land. They began to explore the Aztec past and invoked that American antiquarianism as a banner of resistance to their economic and political subjugation to distant Madrid.[2]

What is more, while the elites theorized about their pre-Columbian past as an antidote to European ethnic chauvinism, a more popular sense of Mexican identity flourished around the famous image of the Our Lady of Guadalupe, the dark-skinned *mestiza* Madonna who had appeared to the Indian Juan Diego, in 1531, on a hill long associated with the Aztec goddess Tonantzin. Vetancurt had trumpeted that "Mexico could boast of being the most devout and most charitable city in all of Christendom," but by the late eighteenth century religion in Latin America was almost as dangerously heterodox in character as the "the people were diverse in color, habits, temperaments, and language."[3]

In a land where Indians, Africans, and Europeans, not to mention the descendants of Jews, Moors, and no doubt a few Asians, had been mixing and remixing their genetic and cultural diversity for so many generations, even Catholicism was becoming a source of rebelliousness.

Many other economic and political forces gave crucial momentum to Mexican Independence, but the ever-present and highly nuanced set of issues surrounding race and ethnicity, so characteristic of New Spain and Spanish America in general, were the fertile soil in which the seeds of rebellion took root.

The whole population of New Spain was markedly distinct from their cousins across the sea in Europe, and nowhere is that more obvious than in a striking and to modern eyes shocking new artistic genre that appeared in Mexico City in the eighteenth century. Leading artists and their studios began to produce series of works known as *casta*, or "caste," paintings, which depicted the many different racial mixes among Indian, African, and European to be seen in the streets, shops, taverns, and homes of New Spain. The new fashion flourished. Many series were commissioned by Spanish royal officials as a means of representing the ethnic reality of the New World to their masters in Madrid. Even King Charles III is known to have possessed a set.[4]

Well over a hundred separate series have been identified in recent years, and with only a few exceptions they conform to a basic program of sixteen different images, each showing a man and a woman of different racial backgrounds and their usually female offspring, along with a caption that provides the epithet commonly used to describe them. Some show their subjects engaged in types of behavior associated with their ethnicity, often in an overtly jocular manner reflecting popular prejudices, such as the frequent representation of *mulata* women violently assaulting their menfolk. That humor can also be read as reflecting deep-seated ideological prejudices about ethnicity within the Spanish and *criollo* elite.[5]

Muslim, Jew, and Christian, Arab, Moor, Basque, and Caucasian, had long shared the Iberian Peninsula, while from the fifteenth century the native *isleños* of the Canary Islands and the "Egyptians," the *gitanos*, or Gypsies, had become a familiar sight in Spain. These different groups largely lived separate, parallel lives. Their interactions were mostly cordial, often friendly, and sometimes they intermarried; but they were also distant, sometimes violent neighbors.

Since the time of the Catholic Monarchs, those relationships were characterized by a Christian intolerance, notoriously epitomized by the Inquisition. Nonetheless, Moriscos were still permitted a considerable degree of autonomy in the management of their affairs throughout the sixteenth century. So, the Spanish colonial officials who came to the New World were familiar with the idea of formal ethnic separation. As a result, they established a República de Indios, an "Indian Republic," or form of self-government that preserved some of the administrative systems that had been in place before the conquest. This gave the indigenous people of New Spain considerable autonomy in their government and society, and many Mexica aristocratic families retained their noble status within the system, albeit always under the overarching sovereignty of the Spanish Crown and often the tutelage of an *encomendero*.

Considerable moral pressure came from religious figures such as Bartolomé de las Casas to protect Indian communities from Spanish and African interference, and periodic attempts were made to exclude non-Indians, even their Spanish or *criollo* masters, from living within Indian villages. Even in Mexico City, the central blocks known as the *traza*, the "plan" or "planned sector," were reserved for European houses. Indians had to have their homes in the suburbs and were only permitted to enter the *traza* for work. As part of that segregation, priests were required to record Indian baptisms separately from those of Spaniards and *criollos*. But Mother Nature took her course, and the touchstone of sexual attraction engendered perhaps the richest genetic alchemy that Europeans, Americans, and Africans had ever known. Names of new categories, or *castas*, emerged into widespread use to describe the myriad permutations of ancestry seen in the homes, streets, and byways of New Spain. Henceforth, until Mexican Independence, the baptism of children of pure Spanish blood, pure Indian blood, and the mixed *castas* were recorded in different ledgers.[6]

During the sixteenth century, Spaniards had become obsessed with the concept of *limpieza de sangre*, or "clean blood," a bloodline free of Jewish or

Muslim ancestry. It became a prerequisite for obtaining any significant official post that a man prove all four grandparents had been Old Christians. In the New World, as one English observer explained, that obsession became "a kind of science among" the Spaniards, who applied to the "several different *castas* . . . all their proper denominations," for "it is accounted most creditable to mend the breed by ascending or growing whiter." White men, in other words, should attempt to whiten the colonial stock by siring children by *casta* women.[7]

Miguel Cabrera, the leading artist working in Mexico during the second half of the eighteenth century, produced an especially fine set of *casta* paintings in the early 1760s. In the first work in the series, *Spaniard and Indian: Mestiza*, he shows the Spaniard from behind, revealing little more than his fashionable French hat, coat, and wig, and a glimpse of his pale cheek as he turns toward his stunning Amerindian consort. She is the glorious centerpiece of the painting, a paragon of beauty with lively eyes and a coy smile, jet-black hair adorned with a radiant red flower, all set off by a brilliant white head scarf and her pearl choker and earrings and her fine lace dress of white silk and her gorgeously embroidered Indian shawl. Yet preempting the European craze for Orientalism by almost a century, her ruddy dark complexion and exotic garb would have alerted a European gaze to her ethnicity, while in the painting her little *mestiza* daughter, equally richly attired, gazes lovingly upward at her parents with her half-European eyes.

The sumptuous dress of the subjects is typical of *casta* painting, a deliberate display of colonial wealth and therefore Creole worth. The representation of humble social classes of great racial and ethnic diversity dressed in expensive clothes that most Europeans could never afford was a bold assertion of colonial pride in both the economic riches and also the ethnic and cultural wealth of the Americas.

In another work in this series by Cabrera, *Spaniard and African: Mulato*, a black woman sits in almost majestic profile wearing a black shawl over a gloriously embroidered dress of Manila silk; her Spanish husband, with his wide-brimmed hat, the mark of the hidalgo, holds their daughter, similarly splendidly dressed in blue silk. In an early piece by José de Ibarra, painted in 1725, *Black and Indian: Lobo*, an opulently attired African in a long gold-trimmed blue cape worn over a luxuriously brocaded frock coat holds a whip in his right hand, while his Indian wife looks over her shoulder toward him, and their pensive daughter gazes out at the viewer. The offspring of African and Indian parents were referred to as either *lobos*, "wolves," or as *zambos*, which English acquired as "sambo," a term once used to describe mixed-race people of predominantly African ancestry.

The offspring of a Spanish and *mestizo* union benefited from being known as *castizos*, meaning "pure" or "firmly rooted," while those of Spanish and *mulata* blood were tainted as *Moriscos*, the technical term for Christians of known Muslim descent who were supposedly but unsuccessfully expelled from Spain in 1609. In ever-more-bizarre turns in the taxonomy, the progeny of a *mestizo* and an Indian were known as coyotes, while the children of *lobos* or *mulato* and Indians or Africans became known as *chinos* because the word *china* meant "servant" in the Andean language Quechua. *Cambujo*, Spanish for a horse with a reddish-black coat, was used to cover a whole range of other mixes, while a *cambujo*'s children by a *china* were known as *jenízaros*, or "janissaries," after the famous legionnaires of the Ottoman Empire. Perhaps not surprisingly, the terminology becomes ever more uncertain, and the phrase *tente en el aire*, "up in the air," covered a multitude of unions between people of already mixed ancestry, while *no te entiendo*, "I don't understand you," should be self-explanatory.[8]

These paintings offer a highly structured system of classification. Reality was more nuanced. Racial identity can be remarkably fluid in a truly diverse world. Social standing, *reputación*, manners, and dress, what contemporaries referred to as *calidad*, or "qualities," could all help someone to shift their identity, even to the extent that individuals once classified as *castas* sometimes managed to *become* Spanish Creoles.[9] Over the centuries, people paid to have a more beneficial *casta* status ascribed to their children or even to themselves, asked favors of priests or officials, or resorted to bribing witnesses to testify in favor of their reclassification by those empowered to do so.[10] Nonetheless, a strong correlation between race and socioeconomic condition has always been one of the foundation stones of any colonial system. That discrimination made for a deeply fractured society in which the privileged "Spanish" were always terrified that the resentment and hatred felt by *casta*, Indian, and African might boil over into violent rebellion.

The situation was complicated in New Spain by another crucial fissure in the social structure. Political power was reserved for Spaniards born in Spain, the *peninsulares* or, more pejoratively, the *gachupines*. Even the richest and most prominent *criollos* were excluded from the most important offices within the administration. In that context, it is striking that the *casta* paintings do not distinguish between *criollos* and Spaniards, but simply refer to both as Spanish. That may reflect the aspirations of many *criollos* to suppress that hated distinction while maintaining the rest of the system. But it is similarly striking that with their healthy, youthful appearance, their diet of succulent foodstuffs, their expensive clothes, their trades, shops, and comfortable houses, these subjects are clearly an artistic celebration of the inhabitants of Mexico in all their diversity. These works portray the core, the heart, of Mexican society; they speak to the essence of what it was to be American, that essential tension between deeply rooted and largely conflicting European and Amerindian identities.

Under the Habsburg monarchy, the reach of the crown was short and its touch relatively light, the empire was expanding, trade was growing, and the *criollos* had plenty of opportunities. But with the Bourbons' energetic pursuit of reform, heralded by the arrival of José de Gálvez, many wealthy *criollos* were forced onto the horns of a terrible dilemma. On the one horn, they resented their second-class status and the power of the *gachupines*, but on the other, their economic and mercantile interests were inextricably intertwined with those of that exclusive political elite.

That tension became more problematic as the numbers and wealth of the *criollos* increased toward the end of the eighteenth century. Some began to complain loudly, even directing their grievances at the king. Some published gushing eulogies of the New World for readers at home and in Spain.[11] The Declaration of Independence in the United States and the Patriot victory in the Revolutionary War gave further inspiration to the already-potent sense of a Creole identity then developing among Latin Americans. *Criollos* were fiercely proud that New Spain was the fulcrum of trade between Asia, America, and Europe and that their wealth had built Mexico City, famed across the globe for its beauty. They loved their homelands and their continent.

As Spain spun out of control in the Napoleonic Charybdis, Indians and *castas* became more unsettled, and more and more *criollos* began to doubt the ability of Spain to impose her authority. Matters began to come to a head in 1804, when Charles IV forced the Church to sell off its key assets in New Spain and lend the money to the crown at a fixed rate of interest. Because the Church was the main local lender, as it called in its loans and sold off property, there was an economic earthquake.[12] The following year, Mexican merchants were cut off from Spain by the destruction of her navy at Trafalgar.

With the Spanish Empire in turmoil, at Querétaro in the Bajío region to the north of Mexico, a group of *criollos* began plotting to seize power. They drew intellectual inspiration from a clever and educated churchman called Miguel Hidalgo, who had been rusticated to the small town of Dolores because of his flamboyant love of gambling and dancing and his outrageous homilies in praise of fornication.[13]

A panicked messenger rode his sweating horse into Dolores in the early hours of September 16, 1810, and roused Father Hidalgo. The postmaster at Querétaro had betrayed the plotters; the moment had come to call the peasantry to rise up. The rebel priest pealed the church bells with such vigorous urgency that their cacophonous ring has become forever celebrated as the *Grito de Dolores*, the "Shout of Dolores," as felicitous a coincidence as historical nomenclature could hope for given that *dolores* means "pain" or "sorrow" and *grito* can equally be translated as "cry" or "scream." As for the protagonist, his name *hidalgo* is a perfect metaphor for the nobility of the *criollos* whose *grito* began to break the chains of colonialism.

Bleary-eyed parishioners congregated at the little church, uncertain of what their errant priest might be up to. No one wrote down his sermon, but plenty of versions have been published:

> Friends and countrymen, henceforth for us there will be neither king nor tribute. For three centuries, we have carried that shameful burden, that terrible stain of tyranny and servitude, which we must learn to wash away through our endeavors. The moment of emancipation has come, the bells of liberty have rung, and if you understand her value, then you will help me defend her from the claws of the tyrants. I ask you to do your duty, for the cause is holy and God will protect us. Long live the Virgin of Guadalupe! Long live América![14]

Hidalgo then raised as his banner an image of the Madonna of Guadalupe, and with his friend and coconspirator Captain Ignacio Allende by his side and an Indian drummer to beat a tattoo, he led his poorly armed, largely untrained, but enthusiastic parishioners on the most exciting adventure of their lives.[15]

The colonial authorities were far from certain of the loyalty of the standing Army of New Spain, which numbered ten thousand trained troops and twenty thousand militiamen.[16] As peasants and tough miners from the silver camps surrounding Dolores joined the cause, the rabble numbered forty thousand.[17] They murdered royalist and Spanish soldiers and wealthy and powerful *criollos* and looted their homes and businesses, slaughtering their women and children, leaving the naked cadavers strewn among the corn. Then the rebels turned their murderous violence on one another as they fought over the booty they had taken.[18] Hidalgo's rebellion was out of control. Wealthy *criollos* were appalled, and many who had supported greater autonomy from Spain abandoned their dreams of home rule as they woke up to the reality of a revolution that depended on an Indian peasant class long brutalized by colonial violence. As the uprising began to resemble a civil war, the rebels would largely be contained in key geographic areas around the Bajío and parts of Guerrero and Jalisco. The war for Mexican Independence would ebb and flow for over a decade before its resolution. Over that time, Spain, crippled by war and internal political conflict, proved unable to send more than about nine thousand troops to assist the preservation of her most prized viceroyalty.[19]

On February 21, 1794, Antonio de Padua María Severino López de Santa Anna was born at Xalapa, a prosperous little town in the steamy hill country above Veracruz that dominated the main road to Mexico City and is famous for its gorgeous displays of flowers and its fiery capsicums. Santa Anna remains a deeply controversial figure today, but sometimes hero, sometimes villain, he dominated the first four decades of Mexican Independence, as colorful, as fecund, and as spicy as Xalapa's *jalapeño* horticulture. "From my earliest years, I was drawn to a glorious career in the army, which I felt to be my true vocation," Santa Anna remembered years later.[20] As a soldier with a powerful political and military base in Veracruz, he became a hero of Mexican Independence, the kingmaker in the volatile politics of his nascent nation, and eventually her president, before finally falling headlong into perdition when the United States annexed half his country following the Mexican-American War. History has remembered Santa Anna as a villain, one of "the most cunning, most ambitious, most designing and most dangerous statesmen I have seen," wrote the Scottish wife of a Spanish Ambassador to Mexico.[21]

Two months before the Grito de Dolores, the sixteen-year-old Antonio López de Santa Anna persuaded his parents to allow him to enlist as an army cadet. He saw action almost immediately as one of many raw recruits involved in Colonel Joaquín de Arredondo's bloody suppression of Indian uprisings in the Oriente, south of the Rio Grande, and in the Sierra Gorda. Santa Anna seems to have relished combat from the outset and was mentioned in dispatches after only three engagements.

Meanwhile, there was fighting talk among Americans in Louisiana who coveted the good cotton-growing lands across the border.[22] The Spanish Ambassador in Washington, Luis de Onís, had long been protesting about the designs of Southern American adventurers on Texas. Following the Grito of Dolores, he added a new refrain of complaint about the freedom accorded to the insurgents within the United States, to which the ears of Secretary of State James Monroe were equally deaf.[23] With the War of 1812 looming, the United States could not afford to provoke Spain, but President James Madison allowed Mexican insurgent Gutiérrez de Lara free rein to recruit 130 Americans under Augustus Magee for an invasion of Texas. On August 8, 1812, as some of the first skirmishing between British, Native American, and American troops took place at Maguaga, Michigan, Gutiérrez's Republican Army of the North crossed the border and quickly captured Nacogdoches and Trinidad de Salcedo. Apaches, Tonkawas, and some rebel Tejanos joined the incursion, and San Antonio fell in April the following year.

News of the filibuster reached Colonel Arredondo in January 1813, and by the end of May he had established his headquarters at Laredo. After the Gutiérrez's force gained the upper hand in initial skirmishing against local militiamen, he became overconfident. He executed some of his Spanish prisoners and told Magee that after the revolution Texas would become a part of the new Mexican republic, which caused most of the American volunteers to desert him and soon led the Tejanos to remove him in favor of José Álvarez de Toledo, a Cuban chancer favored by the Governor of Louisiana.

Colonel Arredondo marched on San Antonio, and the two opposing armies met in wooded country near the Medina River. The royalist forces were well ensconced in a "V" formation, and the rebels came under heavy fire as soon as they attacked. Their Indian allies fled, certain no booty was to be gained, and many of the Tejanos soon followed. Only the small contingent of Americans and the insurgent cavalry advanced fully into the fray. Arredondo's men kept their discipline and fell back, holding their lines, their artillery keeping up a constant barrage. As Arredondo's forces gained the upper hand, he ordered the band to play while his men slaughtered the retreating insurgents.[24] Arredondo noted with satisfaction that he had lost only fifty-five men while "the battlefield was covered with about a thousand dead, the greater part Americans." He put his prisoners and the wounded to death "as just punishment." He reported proudly, albeit with no little exaggeration, that he had the satisfaction of "engaging thirty-two hundred enemy . . . with only sixteen hundred brave, intrepid, and invincible soldiers." Santa Anna was among the many men Arredondo named in a long list of commendations for bravery that day.[25] The young *jalapeño* had felt the heat of Americans in battle for the first time and discovered he had a taste for their fire.

In 1812, the Cortes of Cadiz legislated for ballots across New Spain to choose the electors who would then appoint provincial delegates to be sent as their representatives in Spain. In Mexico City, when the mob learned that not a single *peninsular* had been elected, there were rowdy scenes on the streets as the *criollos* celebrated. Interestingly, in that resounding victory for the *criollo* party and in the dependence of the colonial regime on *criollo* military support to hold the revolution in check, we can see the balance of power shifting decisively away from the Spain and the *peninsulares*.

Wellington's victories over Napoleon allowed Ferdinand VII to return to Spain in 1814 and impose a quasi-absolute monarchy. The Army of New Spain responded with the vigorous suppression of the rebels, but it was unable to snuff them out completely. When news reached the Americas in 1820 that a liberal revolution in Spain had forced the king to reinstate the Constitution of 1812, the Spanish commander of the garrison at Veracruz announced to the assembled Spanish merchants of the town, "Gentlemen, you have made me proclaim and swear to the Constitution; now expect independence, for that is going to be the result of all this."[26] It was the prescient remark of a man who had understood the political and social tensions of New Spain. The imposition of the liberal constitution undermined the status quo and the key institutions such as the army and the Church that had held the conservative coalition of *criollos* and *peninsulares* together.

Colonel Agustín de Iturbide had been one of the leading army officers most steadfastly loyal to the colonial administration, described by one American observer as "the most cruel and bloodthirsty persecutor of the Patriots," a "bold and unscrupulous" man "distinguished for his immorality in a society not remarkable for strict morals."[27] As the conservative *criollos* contemplated the destructive effects of the liberal constitution on the bases of their power and wealth, Iturbide seized the moment and defected to the rebel side. During intense negotiations with the tough and resourceful African-Mexican insurgent Vicente Guerrero, to the south of Mexico City at the town of Iguala, Iturbide hit upon a brilliant compromise that conceded enough to almost every political position in that many-faceted conflict. Mexico, he suggested, should become independent, and the social and racial hierarchy would be abolished, which had been the core demands of the rebels; but Catholicism would be the official religion and the army would retain, even increase, its power by being charged with guaranteeing these three cornerstones of Independence, Catholicism, and Equality, which became known as the *Trigarante*, or "Three Guarantees." Iturbide himself would be made commander in chief of a new Army of the Three Guarantees. But, crucially, Iturbide secured agreement that the new nation would be a kingdom and that Ferdinand VII of Spain would be offered the crown; and Iturbide included a clause that allowed for Mexico to elect an emperor should neither Ferdinand nor any other suitable European prince agree to take the throne. Having secured broad agreement to these proposals, they were formally announced as the Plan of Iguala on February 24, 1821.

As a loyal soldier, Santa Anna had been a staunch supporter of the status quo throughout the War of Independence and proved himself indefatigable in hunting down insurgents and especially relentless in his search for the rebel leader Guadalupe Victoria. Santa Anna delayed for over a fortnight before he finally decided to change sides and support the Plan of Iguala, by which time almost every other *criollo* in the army had already done so. Soon afterward, he came across Victoria, who seemed physically broken after months on the run. Displaying his supreme understanding of politics, Santa Anna offered his erstwhile prey command of the forces in Veracruz, winning the heart of almost every Indian and *casta* in the province, demonstrating that common touch so frequent in men raised between the mess and the barracks, but he also had magical ability to charm the most powerful and influential of men.

The Mexican War of Independence had barely touched New Mexico, California, and the future Arizona Territory, remote regions where settlers and colonists had a strong sense of their isolation. In a world that was wholly dependent upon colonial institutions, they felt a strong sense of imperial identity. So across the north, royal officials were at first opposed to the Plan of Iguala, and populations loyal to Spain delayed declaring independence.

Finally, on July 19, the citizens of San Antonio swore allegiance to Mexico as a member of the clergy held a crucifix aloft. That morning, 2,516 non-Indian Tejanos became Mexicans. That afternoon, a young man filled with hope and ambition rode into Nacogdoches. Stephen Austin had to come to assert his rights to a grant issued to his father by the Spanish government, allowing him to bring three hundred Anglo-American settlers into Texas. On August 12, he recorded in his diary how "at daylight, three men . . . brought the glorious news of the independence of Mexico," which the people "hailed with acclamations of *viva la Independencia* and every other demonstration of joy."[28] That afternoon, at San Antonio, he was given a warm welcome by the governor, and a few days later Austin formally presented his plans for the colony.[29] He spent the following months surveying huge tracts of land before he settled on the rich bottomlands between the Colorado and Brazos rivers. By December, the first of his settlers were beginning to arrive.[30]

In early September 1821, members of the garrison at Tucson took part in another short ceremony to swear their fealty to the new kingdom of Mexico. Soon the thousand colonists in modern Arizona were no longer Spaniards. Five days later, the eight thousand inhabitants of El Paso, then part of New Mexico, pledged their loyalty. Three days after that, on September 11, the people of Santa Fe joined them. Some thirty thousand "Spaniards" and ten thousand Pueblos followed suit.

In November, an intrepid trader from Missouri called William Becknell led a small party of adventurers down off the Plains and into Santa Fe. He must have half expected to be arrested as an interloper and a smuggler, but was instead welcomed by the governor, who encouraged his company to settle in New Mexico and establish a permanent trading link with the United States. Becknell had opened the famous Santa Fe Trail.[31]

On January 6, 1822, Epiphany, the important liturgical Feast of the Magi, the Three Kings, a great party at Santa Fe began in the early morning with the church bells pealing wildly, including a spectacular dance by the Indians from Tesuque Pueblo, and ended with a gala ball that continued into the small hours. In the following days, forty electors from fourteen different municipalities across New Mexico chose a *diputación* of seven representatives who would elect a deputy to send to the National Congress. It was the first province to do so in the newly independent nation, and the electors' actions were wholly unauthorized by the Iturbide government.[32]

Rumors of revolution reached Monterey, California, around Christmastime, but the thirty-two hundred Spaniards and *criollos* waited before they accepted the reality of Independence.[33] Finally, an American ship brought certain news in July 1822, and then an envoy of the new government arrived at the end of September. Following two days of speeches and banqueting, in front of the citizens and the troops in full dress uniform, the Spanish flag was lowered in complete silence. The venerable white-haired governor would not allow Spain be insulted by watching the soldiers lower the flag to the ground. He stepped forward with his symbolically weary Spanish pride and caught up the flag in his arms before it fell onto the newly Mexican soil and then bowed his ancient head and stood motionless while the last Spanish banner to fly over New Spain was struck from its halyards. Then this ancient official of imperial Spain turned to the Mexican government envoy, stoically opened his toothless mouth, and curtly explained the silence of the onlookers: "They do not cheer because they are not used to independence."

But when the flag of Mexico was hoisted aloft, the Californian populace finally took up the cry of "Long live independence!"[34]

CHAPTER 24

NEMESIS, ANDREW JACKSON

FLORIDA

I have before me the message of the President of the U States of the 25th of March last, and its contents led me to believe that nothing of a hostile character would be attempted.

—JOSÉ MASOT, GOVERNOR OF WEST FLORIDA

WHILE MEXICAN INDEPENDENCE brought an end to the Viceroyalty of New Spain, Andrew Jackson would prove to be the Spanish nemesis in the east. He is remembered as both a vicious and unscrupulous villain called Sharp Knife by his Indian adversaries and a quintessential American frontier hero, a colossus among Patriots. These two interpretations are not mutually exclusive. He was clearly ruled by an unhealthy combination of passions, especially hatred and anger, well-seasoned with hubris and rancor, all easily roused because of a generous dose of gullibility. He was, perhaps, even more unlikable than his great heroic British contemporary the Duke of Wellington. Such men are needed in wartime, and as this book has demonstrated again and again, such men are needed to carve out empires; they are the forces of nature who mold men's lives.

In May 1805, the former Vice President of the United States Aaron Burr arrived in Nashville, a fugitive from Yankee moral opprobrium. Ten months earlier, he had assassinated his own political career by shooting Alexander Hamilton in a duel. Jackson offered Burr a friendly welcome at his large log cabin by the Cumberland River, where the Hermitage stands today. Burr talked grandly of forcing the Spaniards out of both Floridas, and aware that his host had recently been elected Commander of the Tennessee Militia, Burr convinced Jackson to commit militiamen to his cause.

The following year Jackson told his men to ready themselves. But Burr's ambition went well beyond an expropriation of land for the United States, and he was later tried for treason, accused of planning to annex for himself a great swath of the South with Mexican assistance. He was eventually acquitted, but Jackson was furious, for the whole business had made him look a fool. The filibuster of Florida had become a point of pride for this natural conquistador.[1]

At the outbreak of the War of 1812, an internal conflict was already brewing among the Muskogee Indians, long known to English-speaking settlers as Creeks because they lived along the rivers and streams of Alabama and Georgia. The Creek War erupted, in 1813, with a skirmish at Burnt Corn. The trouble was rooted in an existential dispute between conservative "Red Sticks," determined to maintain their traditions, and the kind of "progressive" Indians who had been drawn into the world of European Americans by men such as Benjamin Hawkins, the U.S. Indian agent who had been so taken with Governor Zéspedes's flirtatious daughters at St. Augustine. Hawkins had spent the intervening years living among the Muskogees, becoming sufficiently integrated to unsettle many of his Anglo neighbors, while working hard to educate his hosts in European ways. He encouraged Indians to own slaves and grow cotton, and he helped them establish a sort of police force to operate outside the traditional system of clan-based justice centered on restitution and revenge.[2]

On March 27, 1814, Jackson's army of militiamen and "progressive" Muskogee allies slaughtered almost a thousand nativist Red Stick warriors at Horseshoe Bend on the Tallapoosa River. It should have been the decisive battle of the Creek War, for the Seminoles and Creeks in southern Florida were ready to sue for peace. But in the aftermath of victory, Jackson forced both the losing side and the Indians who had fought with him to sign away "22 million acres of the cream of Creek country." That thoroughly dishonorable treatment of his allies was controversial, and Hawkins complained to Washington. Keeping the tradition of dishonesty alive, Jackson's supporters subsequently removed that correspondence from the archives.[3] Nonetheless, it was a successful strategy for Jackson because it goaded the Florida Indians to resume the fight, and the continuing conflict allowed him to urge the government in Washington to allow him to cross the border into Spanish territory to take the fight to the enemy. He had found an excuse to invade Florida, and he had every intention of annexing the territory for the United States. President Madison may or may not have deliberately delayed the dispatch of a reply forbidding the invasion; but his apparent silence was all the encouragement Jackson needed.

At the outbreak of the War of 1812, as a bulwark against a likely American incursion into Spanish Florida, Spain had armed many Seminoles and runaway

African-American slaves who lived peacefully among them. In 1814, Spain opened up the Gulf Coast to the British, who began to arm the Red Sticks and handed out red coats.[4] Many more American slaves also fled south through the conflict zone to take up arms alongside them and fight for their freedom. Following a failed assault on the American Fort Bowyer at Mobile, British forces retreated to Pensacola, where relations with the Spanish governor became ever more tense. In early November, Jackson contrived to let the British intercept his letter to Washington in which he claimed to have a force of seven thousand men ready to attack Pensacola and suggested he had permission to "give up the Town to 24 hours pillage." The "inhabitants were thrown into the greatest consternation & alarm," by this ruse, according to a prominent Scottish merchant who was most worried about his own wares.[5]

Jackson attacked Pensacola on the morning of November 7, 1814. His army of almost three thousand men easily overwhelmed a hundred British officers and enlisted men, their few Indian allies, and the Spanish garrison, which surrendered almost immediately. A Scottish merchant vividly described how as he was evacuating his family to a ship and loading valuable goods into a canoe, "the Americans entered the East end of the Town . . . firing volleys of musquetry close to the warf." The owner of the canoe absconded with the merchandise while the Scotsman hastened to the ship. "All the negroes . . . ours along with them fled to the other side of the Bay to save their lives." The bombardment had cost the merchant's firm money in fugitive slaves. The British then withdrew to Fort Barrancas and blew it apart, to the horror of the inhabitants and the fury of Jackson, for the destruction rendered Pensacola impossible to defend. Yet, "instead of the Massacre & pillage . . . Jackson & his army . . . obtained a lasting name for their humanity & good order," the Scot proclaimed, "not a single excess was committed." Although, he later reported to his brother, that for all that Jackson was "very friendly to me," he had nonetheless requisitioned one of the Scot's prize stallions.[6]

Jackson then rushed his army to the defense of New Orleans, where he inflicted a glorious defeat on the British in the final battle of the War of 1812. But that is another story. Meanwhile, a new wave of violence between settlers and Indians swept along the new border between Indian and American territory as squatters rushed in behind the surveyors and the soldiers protecting them.

A tiny rogue contingent of British Royal Marines remained near Apalachicola, claiming to represent Creek interests, while thousands of Nativist refugees were making new homes in Florida, and a group of escaped slaves ensconced themselves at place the Americans called Negro Fort. American slave owners were especially horrified by this independent community. The slave owners lamented that their "southern property will not be worth holding unless most energetic steps are taken" and urged all "vigor beyond the law" "to repress the insidious attempts of . . . the British" to foster "an establishment so pernicious to the Southern States."[7] Spanish officials were clearly powerless to intervene, but the radical *London Examiner* suggested that they had little interest in doing so. "There may be some truth in the supposition," it claimed, that Spain was secretly negotiating with America so as "to put some money in her pocket by the sale of Florida."[8]

Jackson informed the Governor of Pensacola that if the Spanish did not do something about Negro Fort, he would. The Spaniard agreed, but tried to buy time by explaining the necessity of conferring with Havana. But Jackson was ready for war.

On July 10, 1816, two American ships under the command of Jared Loomis, laden with cannon and provisions, anchored off the mouth of the Apalachicola River and waited. When a messenger arrived from upstream with news that U.S. Colonel Duncan Clinch was advancing on Negro Fort from Georgia, Loomis weighed anchor. The ships entered the slow and languid river, gently moving upstream through the hot, stifling air, amid the Spanish moss hanging from the dark trees. They must have seen alligators basking on the banks and vultures perched motionless above them. It was eerily quiet.[9]

At first, Clinch insisted on locating the cannon much too close to Negro Fort, but then confessed he knew next to nothing about artillery. Loomis lost his temper and announced the navy would manage the bombardment alone. Before dawn, on July 27, the ships slid silently under the bluffs below the maroon stronghold and began testing the range while the men heated up a stock of cannonballs. After four shots, Loomis had the fort in his sights, the British Union Flag flying above it beside the Red Ensign of the Royal Navy, the former slaves flaunting their freedom. The fifth cannonball was rammed into the barrel white-hot. The gunner fired. He scored a direct hit on the powder magazine inside Negro Fort.

"The explosion was awful, and the scene horrible beyond description," Clinch wrote soon afterward. "Our first care . . . was to rescue the unfortunate beings that survived. The war yells of the Indians, the cries and lamentations of the wounded, compelled the soldier to pause in the midst of victory, to drop a tear for the sufferings of his fellow beings."[10]

Almost three hundred men, women, and children, almost all of them black, were killed. Negro Fort was all but annihilated. It is said that the explosion was heard a hundred and fifty miles away at Pensacola, where Governor Zúñiga guessed that the Americans must be waging war within Spanish sovereign territory. There was nothing he could do.

The total destruction of Negro Fort emboldened American frontiersmen to launch raids across the border to kill Indians and kidnap free blacks for sale in the Georgia slave market. The royal marine who had established Negro Fort in the first place returned and began a smuggling operation along the Apalachicola River in cahoots with a spirited seventy-year-old merchant, another Scotsman, Alexander Arbuthnot, whom Jackson later murdered for that spirit of mercantile adventure. Pirates and chancers occupied Amelia Island opposite St. Augustine in full view of Fort San Marcos. The Spanish Ambassador to the United States, Luis de Onís, complained to Madrid that it was "incomprehensible that Havana cannot send a frigate with two hundred men to retake Amelia Island." [11]

Spanish control over the Floridas had clearly become a jurisdictional fiction. All across Latin America, rebellion and revolution were calling time; the sun was finally setting on the Spanish Empire.

On December 14, 1816, James Monroe, newly elected president, wrote Andrew Jackson prophesying that "the advantage of the late treaties with the Indians is incalculable" because, "in extending our settlements, along the Mississippi, and towards the Mobile," they meant that "as soon as our population gains a decided preponderance in those regions, Florida, will hardly be considered by Spain, as part of her dominions." Monroe assured Jackson that his "victory at New Orleans, for which we owe so much to you . . . and the honorable peace . . . have checked the opposition." [12] Monroe clearly sensed that Florida would inevitably become American sooner rather than later and knew that Jackson was the perfect rough-and-ready messiah to fulfill that destiny. But it was a deeply risky sentiment for the new president to express in pen and ink, especially to so combustible a hothead.

In January 1817, on a damp and foul London morning, John Quincy Adams, one of the commissioners who had negotiated the Treaty of Ghent, bringing the War of 1812 to an end, visited the British Foreign Secretary and expressed his concern that Spain might have offered Florida to Britain. Lord Castlereagh assured him, "As to that, I can set you at ease at once."

"Such rumors have . . . been positively and very circumstantially asserted in your own public journals," Adams insisted.

"Yes, but our public journals are *so* addicted to lying. No, if it is supposed that we have any trickish policy of thrusting ourselves in there between you and Spain, we are very much misunderstood." But Castlereagh then delivered a significant caveat: "If we should find you hereafter pursuing a system of encroachment upon your neighbors, what we might do defensively is another consideration."

"I do not precisely understand what your Lordship intends by this advice," Adams claimed disingenuously enough.

"Great Britain has done everything for Spain. We have saved her, we have delivered her. We have restored her Government to her," Castlereagh replied, invoking Wellington's victory over France in the Peninsular War. Castlereagh insisted that while Britain had indeed tried to mediate between Spain and her American colonies, that had always been in a spirit of total neutrality, with no ulterior motive of increasing British territory.

Andrew Jackson would have been disoriented by such courteous double-speak in the comfortably dilapidated surroundings of old Whitehall and would no doubt have been furious that a distant British government should issue so clear a warning to the United States. Adams merely took note, assured Castlereagh that "the policy of the American Government towards Spain has hitherto been precisely the same . . . impartial neutrality," and moved on to a broader discussion about the revolutions taking place across Latin America.[13]

Hellish violence overran the Florida borderlands between Indian, American, and Spanish territories. White squatters murdered peaceful Indians and stole their livestock. American soldiers burned a place called Fowltown to the ground, and the Georgia militia butchered an entire village of allied Creeks at Chehaw. Indian reprisals included the brutal murders of defenseless women and children, the wholesale massacre of forty-odd soldiers and civilians aboard a supply convoy on the Apalachicola, and a sickening report about the scalping of infants and babies' brains being bashed out on the gunwales of a riverboat.[14]

Caught in the eye of such chaos, President Monroe sent troops to Amelia Island, which they secured without firing a shot in anger. Ambassador Onís protested, but the Spanish Foreign Minister, José García de León y Pizarro, was already resigned to the surrender of Florida to the United States, for all that his king, Ferdinand VII, was determined to obstruct him.[15]

Jackson, still champing at the bit, now sought permission to assault any Spanish stronghold that might be harboring Indian fugitives. When Monroe failed to respond, Jackson simply announced that he had received a letter from a Tennessee congressman authorizing an invasion of Florida, which, Jackson said, he could not show anyone because he had already burned it. He prepared his expedition as fast as he could, before orders could arrive to detain him. On March 12, 1817, he led the Georgia militia, "nine hundred bayonets strong, and some . . . friendly Creeks" across the international border and into Spanish Florida. They had suffered "bad roads, high waters, & constant rain, with the dreary prospects of great scarcity of provisions," he wrote home as they endured freezing temperatures during the march south.[16] Jackson was hurrying these men to rendezvous with a supply ship from New Orleans at the old Negro Fort, now rechristened Fort Gadsden in honor of Jackson's aide-de-camp. "The Spanish Government is bound by treaty to keep her Indians at peace with us," he assured his superiors. "They have acknowledged their incompetency to do this, and are consequently bound, by the law of nations, to yield us all facilities to reduce them." He had already written to the Spanish Governor of Pensacola, warning him that Jackson would interpret any interference in his intervention as an act of war.[17]

Jackson's army reinforced the old Negro Fort, then set out east toward a series of Seminole settlements on Lake Miccosukee. When they reached Talla-hassee, they found the place already deserted. It was April Fools' Day. But then a battered contingent of Tennessee Volunteers appeared, and even though they were depleted in numbers and demoralized in spirit by an outbreak of measles and the many other privations of their march south, their arrival soon raised Jackson's spirits. Shortly afterward, sixteen hundred Creek allies joined him. Jackson was elated; he now had enough men under his command for a full-scale assault on the main Seminole settlement of Miccosukee, which had taken in thousands of Red Stick refugees. During the initial approach, a detachment of Americans mistook their Creek allies for the enemy and opened fire. In the confusion, the occupants of the settlement escaped. When Jackson entered the town, he found "more than fifty fresh scalps of all ages from the Infant to the aged matron" "suspended" from "a red pole in the center of the Council houses."[18]

A few days later, Jackson led his men to Fort San Marcos at the mouth of the Apalachicola River. He flew a white flag and the Spanish commanding officer corresponded, inviting the American officers to come and go as they pleased. When enough of them had congregated inside the fort, Jackson wrote the Spaniard that "the Wife of Chenubbe, a noted chief, now a prisoner in my camp, informs me that the Hostile Indians & Negroes obtained their supply of ammunition from St. Marks. To prevent the recurrence of so gross a violation of neutrality . . . I deem it expedient to garrison that fortress with American Troops."[19] The Spaniard could do nothing, other than negotiate the release of his garrison and their removal to Pensacola. Andrew Jackson personally hauled up the Stars and Stripes in place of the Spanish banner. He had won the fort without a fight, but he was even more delighted to discover that Arbuthnot, the Scotsman Jackson loathed for trading with Red Sticks, Seminoles, and maroon communities had been visiting San Marcos. He imme-diately clapped the venerable old adventurer in irons.

With San Marcos under his control, Jackson marched west to take the war to the Suwannee River, where the Seminole leader "King Bowlegs" had allowed a large community of runaway American slaves to settle under his friendly tutelage. In the first skirmish of this new campaign, the Tennessee Volunteers killed an Indian who had been chopping down a tree to get at some honey and wounded two women and a child who were with him. The Creek allies saw their first serious action, coming up against a determined band of Red Sticks, who held the Creeks at bay for some time, before escaping into the forest. The allies took a hundred women and children prisoner and ran off a few hundred head of cattle, which Jackson then requisitioned to feed his hungry army. He urged his men to move quickly, but they could not outpace the Red Stick messengers carrying their warning to Bowlegs and his African vassals, so by the time Jackson's three columns of regulars, Tennesseans, and Creeks reached the Suwannee, their prey had again vanished.

Jackson had harried the Red Sticks, the Seminoles, and the maroon slaves, and he had occupied San Marcos. But he had defeated no one and he was annoyed. Suddenly, one night, with the men gathered around their camp-fires, three figures approached out of the gloom, mistakenly believing that Bowlegs was still in charge. As they came into the light, the Americans were astonished to see one of them wearing a British military uniform, a man called Ambrister who worked with Arbuthnot. Jackson had Ambrister arrested and remanded to San Marcos, then hastily convened a court-martial and put both men on trial. The officers he appointed as jury appealed for leniency toward Ambrister, but Jackson overruled them, declaring, "The volume of testimony justifying their condemnation presents scenes of wickedness, corruption, and barbarity at which the heart sickens." They must have been "authorized Agents of Great Britain," he concluded.[20] Although Jackson and his court had no jurisdiction and by his own admission the two should have been treated as prisoners of war, he had Ambrister shot by firing squad and then hanged the venerable Scot Arbuthnot from a yardarm.

A senior American officer had murdered two British nationals on Spanish soil. Even Andrew Jackson must have feared that he had overplayed the hand that he had anyway dealt to himself. He surely realized that should he return to the United States at this juncture, not only would the administration probably punish him, possibly hang him, but he might well have lost the support of the hawks who wanted him to annex Florida. Like the great Cortés, he had "burned his boats" and it was all or nothing now.

"It has been stated," Jackson wrote to the leading war hawk, Secretary of War John C. Calhoun, "that the Indians at war with the U States have free

AMÉRICA

access into Pensacola; That they are kept advised from that quarter of all our movement; that they are supplied from thence with ammunition . . . & that they are now collecting in large bodies to the amount of 4 or 500 warriors in that city."[21] Jackson brazenly failed to explain the source of these fictions. He had decided to take Pensacola.

As the American army advanced, the Spanish Governor of West Florida, José Masot, did his best to deter them. First, he denied every charge of helping Indians raid into U.S. territory. Then he protested, ordering Jackson to vacate West Florida and warning him, "If you will proceed contrary to my expectations I will repulse you force to force."[22] Jackson responded with an interminable tirade, accusing Spain of every kind of collaboration with the Indians before concluding, "If the peaceable surrender be refused, I shall enter Pensacola by violence and assume the Government."[23]

The Spanish garrison withdrew to Fort Barrancas, allowing Jackson to occupy the town of Pensacola on May 23. He then tried to persuade Masot to surrender by offering more reasonable terms, but the Spaniard replied, "I have before me the message of the President of the U States of the 25th of March last, and its contents led me to believe that nothing of a hostile character would be attempted."[24] Jackson wrote back, "I applaud your feeling as a Soldier in wishing to defend your Post," before telling him, "The sacrifice of a few brave men is an act of wantonness."[25]

Masot forced Jackson to besiege Barrancas. The Spaniards fired the first shots in anger at the positions where the Americans had dug in their nine-pound cannon and a battery of howitzers. Jackson returned the fire, but his guns failed to find the range. In the dark of night, the American artillerymen moved their weapons closer and in the morning began bombarding the fort. Under sustained fire that lasted well into the afternoon, Masot lost his nerve and capitulated, on the condition that the victors respect Spanish property and allow the garrison to withdraw to Havana. Jackson assured Calhoun that this surrender amounted "to a complete cession to the u states of that portion of the Floridas" and praised the "officers and soldiers" for their "determination" and that "patriotic feeling" "at the Close of a campaign which has terminated so honorably and happily."[26]

News of this supremely arrogant, self-evidently illegal, unsanctioned, but stunningly successful annexation of Spanish West Florida caused a sensation in Washington. There was plenty of popular approval, which would give many congressmen pause for thought when they returned in the fall for the second session. But for the administration, Jackson's antics were a serious problem. First and foremost, he had openly defied the military authority of Congress and the president. It was almost as though he had challenged the government to a duel. Then, there was real concern about a possible international response, especially from Britain. Moreover, the illegal annexation meant that were America to hold on to West Florida, the threat of its recovery for the crown of Spain would hang over the territory forever.

Such naked aggression also disrupted the difficult negotiations then being conducted by John Quincy Adams and Ambassador Onís to establish the international frontier between all Spanish territory and the United States. Adams knew that Onís and his foreign minister were inclined to give up the Floridas as part of that deal, but that they faced opposition in Spain. Now that Jackson had charged in like a fighting bull let loose on a Spanish street, Spain could not possibly sanction the secession. On July 8, Onís told Adams that he had received "new instructions from Spain which would have enabled him to conclude a treaty . . . if it had not been for this unfortunate incident." Nonetheless, Adams was the only member of the cabinet who supported Jackson's antics, even repeating the stream of fictions about Spanish support for Indian raids, which even Jackson was still only convincing himself must be true.[27] For Adams's present purpose, Jackson's campaign had shone a timely spotlight on the weakness of the Spanish position in Florida. In essence, the argument was that Spain was obliged to keep her Indians in order, and if she failed, the United States had a perfect right to do so. Adams was prepared to overlook the American failure to control her squatters, militia, and even soldiers, whose behavior repeatedly provoked the Red Sticks and Seminoles. Both Onís and Adams could plainly see that they were discussing territory over which Spain clearly had only the most limited *de facto* control.

In the fall, Congress embarked on the then-longest debate in its history, over what had become known as the Seminole War. In the New Year, Speaker Henry Clay made an impassioned speech to a packed House of Representatives in which he excoriated Jackson for his "open, undisguised, and unauthorized hostility" and for acting outside "the pale of the Constitution." "There was . . . no justification for the occupation of Pensacola and the attack on Barrancas," he pronounced. "Recall . . . the free nations which have gone before us. Where are they now and how have they lost their liberties?" he asked rhetorically, then answered by invoking the classical figures of Alexander the Great, Julius Caesar, and Napoleon, notorious military tyrants who had robbed Greece, Rome, and France of their republican freedoms. "The patriotic arm even of Brutus could not preserve the liberties of his country," Clay commented, provocatively praising the murder of Caesar. "We are fighting a great moral battle for the benefit . . . of all mankind . . . Let us assert our constitutional powers and vindicate the instrument from military violation."[28]

Clay, the most powerful war hawk of 1812, had nailed Jackson as a tyrant in the making, all but accusing him of treason and publicly describing him as deeply un-American. When Jackson read the transcript, he was incandescent with rage. He had thought Clay a supporter and an ally.[29] He told friends he would challenge Clay to a duel; he threatened extreme violence on the Senate committee investigating the Seminole War; he promised to cut off the ears of its chairman.[30] Then, after months of such absurd brouhaha, events overtook the politicians. Even as Congress concluded that it was not prepared to condemn Jackson, Adams and Onís struck an accord by which Spain would cede Florida to the United States.

The argument was over, but this tale has two final, delicious twists. First, Congress massively reduced the size of the army, ostensibly as a budgetary necessity in a time of economic hardship, but for many congressmen it was an effective strategy to turn General Andrew Jackson into a civilian. They had made redundant their most dangerous soldier. Jackson had the last laugh, most obviously when he was elected president, in 1828, but more immediately when Monroe—desperate to get one of the loosest yet most effective cannons in American history as far away from Washington as possible—appointed him Governor of Florida and sent him to Pensacola.

Governor Andrew Jackson had a long wait while the indolent bureaucracy transferred Florida to the United States with the lentitude of a Southern after-noon. His active and suspicious imagination spent the time pondering the multiple criminal goings-on that he concluded must be the cause of the delay. With the potent fuel of paranoia and indignation combusting in the crucible of his bizarre brain, he instructed an agent to sound out the outgoing Spanish governor, José Callava. In a remarkably succinct exposition of Jackson's under-standing of human nature, he asked this spy to find out whether Callava was "a coward full of duplicity, or a candid, honorable man?"[31]

As the administrative process ground toward its conclusion, Jackson waited outside Pensacola. Whether out of petulance or ignorance of proper proce-dure, he failed to formally present his credentials to the Spanish authorities, which no doubt slowed the process further, and that only made him angrier still.

Governor Callava eventually became so fed up with his opposite number that he deliberately held up the handover by a further two days, blaming the plodding incompetence of American officers auditing the arsenal. He then gave Jackson a long lecture about the basic courtesies of international diplo-macy, as well as a textbook on the subject to study at home. It was the calcu-lated insult of an educated metropolitan European aimed at the American's contorted sensibilities about his backwoods character, and Jackson felt the cut all the way to the bone. The man might as well have called him a "cracker" to his face, except, of course, that would have been too crude. But, unusually, Jackson briefly contained his anger.

Jackson finally entered Pensacola on July 27, 1821. Once in charge, he turned his attention to revenge. He saw an opportunity in championing a wealthy widow in her dispute, which had been running since 1806, with the executors of her husband's will. Most of the documents needed to decide the case belonged to the Spanish government, according to the terms of the treaty. Jackson decided to requisition the paperwork and erected his hackles into a shining coxcomb of fury. Callava later described how "at four in the afternoon . . . I was dining at the table of Colonel George M. Brooke," the commander of the American garrison at Pensacola. A large company of Spanish and American officers and a few of their wives were in the middle of their sumptuous repast when one of Callava's men "presented himself . . . with an officer of the United States, telling me that he was a prisoner." He explained that he was effectively being held hostage until Callava surrendered the relevant documents.

Callava sent a message to Jackson, asking him to solicit the papers "in writing for such as he might find it proper to claim . . . under the treaty, or other particular circumstances." After more to-and-fro, an American soldier appeared, shouting, "'Colonel Callava, to the dungeon!' An occurrence so strange and abusive in the presence of those who surrounded me at table" that it "could not but raise a blush in my face." It also brought on a convenient attack of indigestion, and Callava tried to make a discreet retreat to his home. He was again accosted by Jackson's men as he was leaving. "Brooke's wife was very much grieved."

After further shenanigans, Callava retired to his bed, but an hour later Jackson's agents "entered my apartment" and "surrounded my bed with soldiers with drawn bayonets in their hands." They "demanded the papers" and threatened "to use arms against my person." An officer came in "and ordered me to dress myself," and "they took me to a private house where they presented me to Don Andrew Jackson." "The house was filled with people of all ages and classes," noted the Spaniard.

Jackson had an audience. What he expected might happen next is far from clear, but he now personally tried to make Callava give up the documents. Callava insisted on responding in writing. When he finished penning his refusal, "Jackson took the paper from before me and with much violence and furious gestures spoke for some time." The Spaniard claimed not to understand a word of this tirade. Jackson then read him "the order for committing me and my steward to prison."

"Do you not shudder and are you not struck with horror at insulting me?" the astonished Spaniard asked.

"You can protest before God himself," Jackson replied.

With Callava and his steward locked up, American troops ransacked his residence.[32]

Colonel Brooke and the other American officers were deeply embarrassed, and by the time this extraordinary charade had been played out, they had become sufficiently merry to move their party to the jailhouse, where they spent the rest of the night "feasting and drinking and derisively mocking Andrew Jackson."[33] By his own standards, Jackson had humiliated the haughty European who had tried to teach him about diplomacy. By the standards of the rest of the world, he had proved himself an uncivilized hooligan. But for many in Washington, he was their hooligan and he had won Florida for the United States, albeit by ignoring the law and the consensus on morality. Andrew Jackson had approached Spanish Florida with the unprincipled greed of the worst kind of frontier squatter and won. It is intriguing to speculate just how much he would have relished riding alongside his sixteenth-century Spanish predecessors: Cortés, Coronado or Oñate, Narváez or Soto, or even Menéndez de Avilés?

The following morning, Callava was released. It was August 23, 1821. The following day, the Viceroy of New Spain, another Wild Goose, Juan O'Donojú, recognized the independence of Mexico by the Treaty of Córdoba. Spain, however, refused to ratify the treaty and denied the viceroy's powers to grant independence. But in reality, the Spanish Empire in North America had ceased to exist, with the exception of the fortress of San Juan de Ulúa, near Veracruz, where the garrison continued to fly the Spanish flag until 1825.

CHAPTER 25

The Alamo & San Jacinto

Texas

Remember the Alamo!

—TEXAN BATTLE CRY

As soon as he took up his post in Washington, the first Mexican Ambassador to the United States offered his government a grim appraisal of American attitudes to his hopeful new nation:

> The arrogance of these Republicans does not allow them to see us as equals, but as their inferiors. I judge their vanity such that they believe their Capital will be that of all the Americas. They have a visceral love of our money, but not of us, nor are they capable of any kind of alliance or contract that does not favor them, without any understanding of reciprocity. In time, they shall be our sworn enemies, and that is how we should treat them from now on . . . In every session of Congress and the sessions of the states they speak of nothing but the reform of the army and the militias, doubtless for no other reason than the covetous gaze they direct at Texas.[1]

Mexico had inherited the Spanish claim to about 850,000 square miles of land that now forms part of the United States, delineated by John Quincy Adams and Luis de Onís as lying west of the Sabine River, then north to the Red River, following it westward before turning north and continuing along the Arkansas River as far as the forty-second parallel, the modern boundary between California and Oregon, which marked the northern limit, touching the Pacific coast at the mouth of the Winchuck River.

Independence gave new life to the politics of these northern frontier provinces. Local landowners and merchants gained immediate access to powerful offices and representation at the Cortes. At a local level, elected councils were established to run municipal affairs, even in the Indian pueblos. But only about forty-five thousand *criollos* and *castas* lived in those lands, about one person for every nineteen square miles, roughly the population density of icebound Greenland.[2] The Native American population of the area at that time is unknown, but it must have been well over half a million.

The politics of Mexico in the early decades following independence developed in complex and angry ways. Stephen Austin was witness to the incipient chaos. He set out for Mexico City early in 1822, determined to have his land grant ratified by the new government. Adopting the disguise of an impoverished hobo to cross the notoriously bandit-ridden badlands to Monterrey, by the end of April he gazed down on the majestic Valley of Mexico, with her plumed volcanoes and bustling capital, the greatest city in the Americas. "It is truly a large and splendid place," Austin wrote home to his family, "larger than New York and more splendidly built." He assured his business partner that he believed the Mexican Congress to be "in good order," if "rather slow" in its deliberations, and that "the most perfect harmony prevails." In fact, he had arrived at another tumultuous turn in Mexican history. "Much sensation . . . broke out on the night of May 18," with "the firing of musketry and cannon in the air." The guns, he noted with sanguine alarm, "were loaded with balls."

In a bid to secure the title of emperor, Agustín de Iturbide had resigned as president and ordered his loyal troops onto the streets. To the symphony of gunfire, they proclaimed, "Long live Agustín I, Emperor of Mexico." Austin wrote of the events to his younger brother with palpable excitement: the night air rang with "loud shouts from the soldiers and citizens." The following morning, with a mob baying from the galleries of the Mexican Congress, the frightened delegates elected Iturbide to Montezuma's historic throne.

On the day of Iturbide's inauguration, there was "a constant scene of rejoicing, the army paraded and the church-bells have kept a constant roar since daylight." Austin was a foreigner in what was soon to become his native land, and he reported home with trepidation, "There are dark clouds hanging over this part of the country, many are dissatisfied and disappointed at the election."[3]

Austin's land grant was of negligible importance alongside such momentous events, and he became disillusioned by the lack of official interest in his affairs. The apparent futility of his mission tainted his opinion of Mexico City, which he now described as "at least one century behind many other places in point of intelligence and improvement in the arts . . . The population is very much mixed and the great proportion of them are most miserably poor and wretched, beggars are numerous . . . robberies and assassinations are frequent." Austin clearly went in fear of his life, and with his nascent prejudice fueled by personal paranoia his assessments descended into priggish chauvinism: "The people are bigoted and superstitious to an extreme."[4]

But Austin was well educated and resourceful. He turned his attention to learning Spanish and hired an influential lobbyist. Moreover, he was a Mason at a time when Freemasonry was a crucial factor in Mexican politics. Thus, he almost miraculously managed to have Iturbide sign his land grant and get it ratified by Congress. The only foreign *empresario* to emerge from the crisis with a contract to settle Texas, Austin had also established a formidable network of allies in the capital. He left Mexico City on April 18, 1823, with his own particular vision of what it was to be Mexican: "They are a strange people," he wrote home, marveling at "the power which appearances have on them, even when they know they are deceived . . . *Dios castiga el escándalo más que el crimen*, is their motto, God punishes the exposure more than the crime."[5]

Austin returned to a colony that had been ravaged by drought and failed harvests. His people had been reduced to eating starving deer and mustangs. They had made enemies of the neighboring Native American tribes, especially the Karankawa, descendants of the same Indians whom those very first Europeans to walk the shores of Texas, Esteban Dorantes, Andrés Dorantes, Cabeza de Vaca, and Alonso del Castillo, claimed had enslaved them. When Austin mobilized his militia to expel the Karankawa from his colony, they disappeared into the bush, leaving a cooking pot behind containing the bones of two men. They had almost certainly been engaged in an ancient funeral rite, but the Americans were horrified and immediately called the place Cannibal Creek. The incident heralded an endlessly troublesome relationship. Austin mostly managed to maintain an uneasy peace despite his colonists' enthusiasm for violent reprisals against these hunter-gatherers and the frequent dissatisfaction of his unruly settlers, who seemed to be endlessly jealous of one another's land, yet stubbornly reluctant to pay for their own. He dealt with all this with remarkable pragmatism.

By contrast, Haden Edwards, the *empresario* of an adjacent American colony at Nacogdoches, approached his governorship with such despotic avarice and blunt stupidity that he was stripped of his grant by the Mexican government. In response, he and his cronies took up arms in rebellion and declared themselves the independent Republic of Fredonia. Austin was appalled at such inflammatory antics and rallied his own colonists to the cause of Mexican law and order, mustering the militia in readiness to support the Mexican army when it arrived to suppress the roustabouts. After a brief skirmish at Nacogdoches, Edwards and his rabble fled over the Sabine River and disappeared into Louisiana. Austin had distanced himself and his colonists from American filibusters in dramatic and determined fashion, but the sad escapade set a-rattling the sabers of many a newspaper editor in the United States and many a political firebrand in Mexico.

Iturbide reigned as emperor just long enough to serve as a herald of the many years of political instability to come. His nemesis was Mexico's natural king-maker, Santa Anna.

Santa Anna had gate-crashed the Mexican War of Independence as a ruthless and effective military commander almost at the eleventh hour, but he was in time to share in the glory of victory and claimed to have brokered the peace between the Spanish ambassador and Iturbide. As a result, he was appointed Commander General of Veracruz, the province where he was born, and so gained control of the main roads from the coast to the capital. He established a regional power base, learned to strong-arm the local bigwigs while making many friends, and amassed vast estates, at which he escaped the hurly-burly of national politics for the pleasures of family life, had a good few amorous adventures, and bred prize roosters and fought them.

On December 2, 1822, Santa Anna launched his revolt against Iturbide. "I decided to devote myself to reestablishing law and justice across the nation," he wrote in his memoirs.[6] He denounced the emperor in favor of a republican and federalist government. There is a potential confusion here, for in Mexico, unlike the United States, the ideal of federalism was all about ensuring the maximum independence of the states within a union. Very much the local *caudillo*, or "leader," he was also that rarest of political creatures, a liberal strongman. But Mexicans were slower to respond to his call for revolt than he and his allies had hoped, and he was forced to spend the winter besieged at Veracruz. Then the political tide turned with the coming of spring, and within weeks Iturbide had been expelled from Mexico. When he inadvisably returned a few months later, he was executed. Cometh the hour, cometh the scapegoat. Santa Anna continued to force the issue of republican federalism until Guadalupe Victoria was installed as president in 1824.

The first constitution of the United States of Mexico was drafted in 1824 in this atmosphere of liberal optimism and regional fervor. It granted sweeping autonomy to the new states and gave them control of the federal government in Mexico City, a complete reversal of the Bourbon system. While this suited the vast majority of populous and relatively wealthy states in central and southern Mexico, it made governing the large and distant provinces of the northern frontier more difficult.

Early attempts to absorb California and New Mexico into two vast new provinces incorporating Sonora and Sinaloa and Chihuahua and Durango quickly foundered. Instead, California and New Mexico were established as territories that were supposed to be administered by the federal government. Yet the frontier regions had only the most limited representation in a legislature packed with delegates who took little interest in the northern provinces, which they felt had nothing to do with them. In the absence of strong leadership from the central government, officials in California and New Mexico tried to govern as best they could, but they were forced to rely on Spanish legislation that originated with the liberal Cortes of Cadiz. The consequences were chaotic.

Although some Tejanos advocated establishing their own state, the non-Indian population of Texas was clearly too small and its location on the frontier with the United States too sensitive. After considerable wrangling, Coahuila and Texas emerged from the political soup as a single state. The new state legislature in Saltillo abolished the Texas *diputación* and *jefe político* and ordered the removal of the documents recording land grants across Texas to the new state capital. When the Town Council of San Antonio accepted the arrangement, a mob of armed citizens gathered in front of the Alamo and had to be calmed down by a priest.[7]

By 1833, Tadeo Ortiz, a tireless advocate for populating Texas with colonists from almost anywhere except the United States, including the Canary Islands, Ireland, Switzerland, and Germany, concluded that the union with Coahuila had been "a sin against Texas," an "anomaly and a contradiction," a direct result of "favoritism," "intrigue," and "negligence." He was certain that "from this epoch dates the misery of the people" and all "the troubles in Texas." As a consequence, the "prestige and power of the name of Mexico were in decline" in the region. Corrupt land commissioners were granting huge tracts of land to Americans of "low morality . . . from the southern states" who were, notwithstanding, "accustomed to a prompt administration of justice," which was not being provided them by the Mexican state. And so, "considering themselves neglected" in that respect, they had "appropriated the sovereign right of trying and sentencing criminals . . . in conformity with the principles of English jurisprudence." This dangerous situation needed rectifying fast, otherwise the loss of Texas to the United States, Ortiz asserted, would be "inevitable."[8]

In 1827, General Manuel de Mier y Terán arrived in Texas with orders to survey the entire province and gauge the political mood of the American colonists. He set out with a team of able assistants, including José María

Sánchez, who wrote a perceptive account of their journey that makes it clear just how distant Texas was both geographically and psychologically from Mexico City. Mier y Terán had begun the journey traveling in a heavy coach, which he soon abandoned on the banks of the Trinity River.[9] In late April, his party reached San Felipe de Austin, on the *Brazos de Díos*, the river of "God's Embrace."

They were struck by the way the houses were "not arranged symmetrically into streets, but were all higgledy-piggledy without any sense of order," like almost any village in New England or, indeed, England. Sánchez also noted that only one in ten of the inhabitants were Mexicans. There were "two miserable little shops, one selling nothing but whiskey and rum, sugar and coffee," and the other a general store. To Sánchez, the Americans were "lazy sinners" who lived on "salted meat, corn bread, and coffee and whey," spiced up with "strong liquor." They were "hard on their slaves" and "left them to do most of the work."[10] Mier y Terán concurred that the Americans were "poor laborers," but thought this largely because they all seemed to be "fugitive convicts, their faces branded to mark them as thieves and scoundrels" as was the custom of their country. They were insolent and arrogant: "Most of them think that Mexico is full of nothing but ignorant Blacks and Indians," and "they have told me to my face that as an educated man I must be French or Spanish."[11] Amid such companions, Austin stood out for his "political finesse," which the Mexicans thought "evident in everything he does." He "has lulled the authorities to sleep while he works away assiduously in his own interests," Sánchez warned, and "I reckon this colony will spark the flames of the rebellion by which we lose Texas."[12]

As these educated Mexicans voiced to each other the fears of men who felt like isolated foreigners in their native land, the heavens provided the dramatic backdrop of a classic Texas storm: "The rain fell with such fury that it seemed as though the sky were falling on our heads. The woods burned with the awful flashes of the lightning, and all we could hear was the constant waxing and waning of the thunder." All night they suffered, and in the morning they "gave thanks to Our Lord to have survived such a storm unscathed."[13]

It was an ill omen.

Without attempting to unravel the tangle of Mexican politics, it is important to note that Santa Anna was a hugely popular governor of Veracruz because he navigated the destructive factionalism of the two different branches of Freemasonry that at the time dominated Mexican politics, remaining resolutely aloof from these partisan squabbles. He was also deeply committed to the foundation of schools and promoting education, strengthened the militias and the police force, waged war on rural banditry, ordered the prompt payment of the judiciary, backed irrigation projects and the maintenance of city streets, and personally demanded the construction of a cemetery in Xalapa.[14]

In September 1828, Santa Anna attempted to preempt the presidential election result by demanding that his friend and ally the mixed-race General Vicente Guerrero be made president. Guerrero would almost undoubtedly have won a popular vote, but the constitution stipulated that the presidency be elected by representatives of the state legislatures, and his opponent, Manuel Gómez Pedraza, would clearly win that vote easily. Santa Anna led eight hundred loyal troops up the mountain road to the capital. Again, the popular uprising was slow to materialize, and he was forced to find refuge in Oaxaca, where he was extremely lucky to hold out against the government troops besieging him. Then, finally, the spirit of resistance spread, and further rebellions forced Gómez Pedraza to flee. Once again, Santa Anna went from outlaw to hero almost overnight.

Since the expulsion of Spanish troops from San Juan de Ulúa, in 1825, Mexico had coveted Cuba, which it saw as a potential springboard for Spanish invasion and an obstacle to Mexican shipping in the Gulf and the Caribbean. There had been minor maritime contretemps ever since, but as Santa Anna basked in glory at Veracruz on August 1, 1829 he learned that an army of thirty-five hundred Spanish soldiers had disembarked 250 miles to the north at Tampico. The threat had become reality.

Santa Anna ordered his cavalry to set off overland, and a week later his infantry regiments sailed to rendezvous with them on an improvised flotilla he put together by requisitioning every ship in the Veracruz harbor. As soon as he reached Tampico, he led a daring night raid on the occupied town. A less hasty assailant would have had time to learn that the main body of the Spanish army had already moved north. The Spaniards returned, trapping him in the town, and Santa Anna had to take refuge with the French consul.

Once more, Fortune favored Santa Anna. The Spanish army had been badly hit by disease, and the officers' morale was further damaged by the evident lack of local support for their invasion. They failed to press home their short-lived advantage, allowing Mier y Terán time to arrive with reinforcements. Santa Anna, impetuous as ever, delivered the *coup de grâce*, attacking the enemy in the midst of the violence of a hurricane, an audacious act of bellicose valor that was lauded by Mier y Terán as "masterful." The Spaniards surrendered. Two nights later, Mexico City "awoke in the early hours to the sound of cannon fire and the pealing of the church bells."

Fireworks flashed and whizzed, and excited news sellers ran hither and thither, shouting "Spanish Surrender!" while strangers embraced in the streets. Publicans uncorked their bottles and shared a toast with whoever was passing.[15] Spain did not finally recognize Mexican Independence until 1836.

In the wake of Santa Anna's historic victory over the Spanish, the vice president gathered a group of reactionary traditionalists to take up arms against Guerrero and offered the presidency to Santa Anna. He turned it down and instead mobilized his troops to loyally defend republicanism, federalism, and his friends. He had badly misjudged the national mood, for the winds of change were very much in the reactionaries' sails. Luck was again his champion, for his men had gauged the situation better than he. They deserted him in such large numbers that he was unable to engage the reactionaries in combat. He prudently resigned his commands and retired to his estates to plan in private the republican-federalist fightback and enjoy a homestead recently blessed by the arrival of his beloved daughter Guadalupe. What else could he have called her?

The new administration under the leadership of Anastasio Bustamente cautiously advanced its conservative agenda until it made the ludicrously foolhardy decision to have Guerrero executed. "Everywhere, a cry of indignation resounded at so shameful and cruel an act . . . a detestable deed not easily forgotten," Santa Anna raged. "Heroic Veracruz was the first place to call publicly for the removal of the minster responsible," he boasted in his memoirs.[16]

Guerrero had been Guadalupe's godfather.

The British Vice-Consul in Veracruz reported at the time, "Santa Anna's troops are in high spirits and little doubt can be entertained of the result being favorable to them."[17] The rebellious spirit was so strong that it was barely dented when Santa Anna suffered the first serious defeat of his military career on March 3, 1832, at Tolome, in which he lost almost five hundred men. The setback brought out his wily pragmatism, and he called for a reinstatement of the legal president-elect, Gómez Pedraza, the man Santa Anna had himself ousted from power, as a way of lending his rebellion constitutional legitimacy. His troops destroyed the detachment of reactionary forces attempting to block his march to Mexico City, but he failed to pin down the main body of enemy troops, despite pursuing them for weeks. Santa Anna agreed to a truce. The terms of peace were conciliatory and allowed for the return of Gómez Pedraza to see out the final months of his term of office before the next elections.

On April 1, 1833, Santa Anna was elected President of Mexico. He immediately retired to his estates in Veracruz, leaving his vice president to lead the government, telling him, "The reins of government should be in the hands of a citizen like you, not in those of a poor soldier like me."[18]

Santa Anna was largely an absentee president, but he did meet with Stephen Austin, who had traveled to the capital in November 1833 to petition for a separate State of Texas. Austin was convinced that "if our application fails . . . the consequence will no doubt be war."[19] In receiving the anxious *empresario* Santa Anna was flanked by three generals, a gifted politician called Manuel Lorenzo de Zavala, who had a keen interest in Texas, and a senator from Coahuila implacably opposed to any division of his state.

The part-time president was in a congenial mood and playfully threw out the suggestion that Texas might become a territory administered by the federal government, a rather obvious ruse by which he succeeded in uniting Austin, Zavala, and the senator in their opposition. Santa Anna then pushed them to thrash out a compromise by which the government offered a series of concessions that might in theory help prepare Texans for statehood in the future.[20] Most important, almost certainly as a result of Zavala's advice, Santa Anna agreed to rescind a highly contentious law introduced by the reactionary government in 1830 that had suspended all further immigration from the United States into Texas.

Austin was persuaded that war was not inevitable, but he still felt it prudent to claim in his reports back to San Felipe that he had personally persuaded Santa Anna to "hang up" the idea of making Texas a territory. Santa Anna had offered up a useful fiction; Austin made his own victory out of it. He professed to be satisfied that many of his key demands had been met.[21]

Santa Anna's absenteeism weakened the office of president, which allowed Congress to become so dangerously radical that one leading liberal or military figure after another proclaimed against it, and political resistance descended into armed rebellion. "The political character of this country," Stephen Austin lamented, "seems to partake of its geological features: all is volcanic."[22]

Once more, Santa Anna stepped in to restore order, but under a government with a markedly more reactionary agenda, which, in 1836, introduced a new and aggressively centralizing constitution, which it called the *Siete Leyes*, "Seven Laws"—a needlessly provocative nod toward the Castilian legal code, the *Siete Partidas*, established by Alfonso the Wise in the thirteenth century, celebrated in Spain almost as the Magna Carta is in the United States and Britain. The Liberals quickly dubbed it the Seven Plagues. It lasted only five years, but during that time it provoked revolts across the country, in Alta California, in New Mexico, and most notoriously in Texas.[23]

*   *   *

The root causes of Texan independence have been copiously studied and examined from almost every angle. Its proximity to the United States and the massive influx of American immigrants, most of whom had never been to deepest Mexico and were resistant to becoming Mexicans, left most Texans alienated by geography as much as culture.

Yet some of the most ardent advocates of independence must have been instinctively wary of Texas joining the United States, for many residents were fugitives from justice, debt, or simply their responsibilities. Not least among them was the young hero-villain of Texas legend William Barret Travis, a murderer and an outlaw who had abandoned a family and a law practice in Alabama, fleeing the consequences of a life that had gone terribly wrong. But largely the noisy bravado of such men was even more politically dysfunctional and impotent than the Mexican state they so enjoyed abhorring. The calm and measured minds of men such as Stephen Austin held sway in Texas, ambitious and visionary *empresarios* who were building their own empires, glorious American Edens that flourished along the banks of great rivers such as the Brazos or the Trinity in what seemed like a Promised Land far from the reach of central government. So long as they feared the potency of Washington more than the impotency of Mexico, Texans had good reason to remain part of the Mexican union.

Stephen Austin was arrested at San Luis Potosí on January 3, 1834, as he returned to Texas, and remanded to Mexico City, where he was thrown into the dungeons of the Inquisition. "I do not know of what I am accused," he complained, and asked, "What system of jurisprudence is this of confining those accused without permitting them to manifest their innocence?" By the time he was discharged six months later, he had lost all patience with Mexico and Mexicans.[24] The new reactionary government had lost the confidence of the most influential man in Texas.

The touchstone to rebellion in Texas was the abolition of slavery. Successive Mexican governments had been curbing slavery little by little since independence, but on September 15, 1829, President Guerrero issued a decree abolishing slavery across the whole of Mexico. Texans were aghast, but Austin reassured the colonists that the federalist Constitution of 1824 allowed Texas an exemption from implementing the new proscription, while Texan ingenuity devised further loopholes to circumvent an outright ban on the continuing import of slaves.[25] The introduction of the reactionary Constitution of 1836, the *Siete Leyes*, however, removed the grounds for exemption.

A terrible fear of slave insurrection, the ever-present nightmare of the slave owner, gripped Anglo-Texans. Stephen Austin was at times troubled by "Negro

Slavery," which he referred to in a letter to his cousin Mary in 1831 as "that curse of curses and worst of reproaches on civilized man."[26] But his life's endeavor unquestionably depended upon it, and he made his views as of August 1835 clear enough when he wrote Mary from New Orleans, "Texas must be a slave country. It is no longer a matter of doubt." In his eagerness to rehearse a set of arguments designed to encourage the authorities in the United States to support massive levels of American immigration into Texas, he warned, "A population of fanatical abolitionists in Texas"—Mexicans in other words—"would have a very pernicious and dangerous influence on the overgrown slave population of [Louisiana]." Texas without slavery would be a tempting haven for Louisiana's blacks and a hotbed for rebellion. He urged "a great immigration of good and efficient families," American families, so that "Texas should be . . . fully Americanized," which, he added, without a hint of irony, would promote the "cause of philanthropy and liberty." While that might necessarily be temporarily "under the Mexican flag," he asked whether, just as "a gentle breeze shakes off a ripe peach, can it be supposed that the violent political convulsions of Mexico will not shake off Texas so soon as it is ripe enough to fall?"[27]

In October 1835, most American settlers in Texas and many Mexicans rebelled, occupying San Antonio de Béxar.

Santa Anna had no patience for the Texans. By December he was at San Luis Potosí, mustering a formidable army of 6,111 soldiers and 2,500 camp followers. He marched them over the Rio Grande and the Nueces, through the winter rain, and reached San Antonio on February 23. He had lost four hundred men, but despite lumbering across hundreds of miles of territory for six weeks with this enormous train of people and animals, he took the Texans completely by surprise. They barely had time to evacuate the town and barricade themselves inside the fortified buildings of the Franciscan convent known as *el Álamo*, "the Cottonwood."

Santa Anna considered besieging the Alamo, but he was keen to give his raw recruits a taste for battle and impatient to engage the main body of rebel Texan troops then camped on the Trinity River under the command of Sam Houston. The Mexicans began preparing for an all-out assault.

Santa Anna sent a senior officer to offer Colonel William Barret Travis honorable terms should he surrender, but Travis refused to consider capitulation. Instead, he made a rousing speech to his men and fired his cannon at the enemy. Over the next week, more divisions of Mexicans arrived. At four o'clock on the morning of March 6, Santa Anna gave the dread order of *"Degüello!"*—literally "Slit throats!" It was to be what the conquistadors had called a "war of blood and fire." No quarter would be given. It was not.

The notorious Battle of the Alamo lasted ninety minutes, the length of a soccer match. The story of the ensuing slaughter has been retold often and with much variety, but in that telling the legendry heroism of the losers has usually obscured the crude reality. Four Mexican divisions assaulted the mission, far too large a space for 183 men to defend. More and more Texans were mown down from their positions along the walls, but their comrades stayed where they were and only began to fall back when they saw Travis himself go down, fighting like a man possessed. They retreated to positions in the old mission buildings, and the last survivors sought refuge within the church.

Texas mythology has long celebrated Davy Crockett as one of the great heroes of this battle, his body found surrounded by sixteen dead Mexicans, one of them with Crockett's hunting knife buried in his heart. Then, as Walt Disney further popularized the legend with a television series about Crockett's career, a mysterious manuscript turned up in Mexico. Purportedly the diary of a young officer called José Enrique de la Peña, it recorded a very different story.

According to Peña, seven Texans "survived the general carnage" and surrendered. "Among them was a large and comely man of even countenance . . . who, resigned to his fate, displayed an honorable nobility. He was David Crockett, famous in North America for his uncommon adventures." One of the Mexican officers urged Santa Anna to spare the man's life, but the president was indignant at the suggestion and ordered his execution. All seven men were hacked to death by a group of officers. "Surpassing the soldiers in cruelty, they stepped forward, their swords drawn, and fell upon these defenseless men like tigers upon their prey."[28]

Any challenge to a national myth does damage to a people's collective sense of identity, and some devotees were deeply outraged by the suggestion that Crockett had not died a hero, but had meekly surrendered to save his life, only to be savagely executed as reward for his cowardice. Their howls of protest aimed to prove that the document was a forgery. However, it has since been demonstrated beyond any doubt that the manuscript is real, both by scientifically testing the paper and the ink and with reference to other documents associated with Peña.[29] The matter of authenticity, then, is settled. But that does not mean the story told by Peña is true, for it is also clear from reading his work that he, too, was a blowhard, determined to discredit Santa Anna. So the story of the brutal murder of a popular American suited Peña's purposes all too well. He tells us that he himself "turned away horrified in order not to see such a barbarous act." By his own admission, he did not witness these murders at all. So, the death of Davy Crockett remains a mystery as susceptible to mythologizing as anyone may wish it to be.

Time was of the essence for the Mexicans. Santa Anna received word from his advance party that "the filibuster Houston and his gang are waiting on the other side of the [Colorado] ... preparing for battle."[30] Houston had eight hundred men in the field, but more were trickling in from the United States every day. Santa Anna organized his soldiers into three divisions, more maneuverable and easier to feed during their advance across Texas. He led the main body of troops along the most direct route, and during the march, he received word that General José de Urrea had taken almost five hundred men prisoner at Goliad. As prisoners, they were a troublesome encumbrance. So, in the most controversial act of the conflict, Santa Anna ordered them all shot. He defended this notorious order by citing a government decree that ordered the execution of all armed foreign filibusters, but even his own officers were reluctant to carry it out and were traumatized by doing so.[31] Peña excoriated his general for this "crime." He claimed that the Texans had surrendered on the condition their lives would be spared. "There were few who approved of the carnage at Goliad," and "the army in general raised its voice to condemn it."[32]

Santa Anna and the main body of men were the first division to reach San Felipe de Austin. He decided to pursue Houston, who was said to be at Gross's Pass, but the Brazos River was too high to get the army across. Santa Anna set out with a detachment of five hundred men in search of a better crossing point. As he reconnoitered the river, he learned that the rebel government was at Harrisburg, barely ten miles hence. "There was not a moment to lose," he remembered, "so I set off at once with six companies of grenadiers and chasseurs and a small cannon. That night we crossed the plain and reached the settlement. A rifle shot disturbed the dogs and the bureaucrats who were scurrying off to the safety of a steamboat."[33] The Mexicans found the little town smoldering, set alight by the Texan politicians as they fled to the safety of Galveston Island. Santa Anna turned his attention back to Houston, who was still ensconced at Gross's Pass.

Houston ordered his troops to take up positions in thick woods where the San Jacinto River flows into Buffalo Bayou above Galveston Bay. Both generals knew there could be no escape; the Texans were trapped between Santa Anna and the river. But Houston must also have realized that this would almost certainly be his only opportunity to confront Santa Anna in the field with superior numbers. If Texas was ever to be independent, then this was the moment to fight.

The Mexican army was tired and hungry, so Santa Anna allowed them to eat and rest. General Cos arrived the following morning with four hundred raw recruits. They, too, needed time to rest, but the Mexicans now outnumbered the rebels. Houston knew he must act. To his delight and astonishment, according to Peña's account at least, a slave appeared and told him that the Mexicans had eaten their lunch and then all gone to sleep.[34] Amazingly, this intelligence was essentially true. Santa Anna set the example for this bizarre behavior. He had been up all night, keeping the sentries vigilant, and decided to take a nap while the men gathered their strength for action. But the officer he instructed to keep the army alert preferred to enjoy a long shave and a change of clothes to pestering soldiers to keep watch.

Houston's men were able to creep up to within yards of the Mexican camp before they were detected, and with the famous cry of "Remember the Alamo!" they opened fire. "At two o'clock in the afternoon on April 21, 1836," Santa Anna recalled with remarkable frankness, "I had gone to sleep in the shade of an oak tree, waiting for the heat of the day to pass, when the filibusters surprised my army with admirable skill. Imagine my surprise when I opened my eyes and saw that I was surrounded by men aiming their rifles at me."[35] He suppressed part of his story, however, for in the confusion of battle, an orderly brought him a horse. Santa Anna fled the field, hoping to rally the rump of the army.

A posse of Texans gave chase as he rode the poor horse so hard that it collapsed. He just had time to hide among some pine trees before his pursuers caught up with him. That night, he waded the river at Thompson's Pass and took shelter in an abandoned farmhouse, where he exchanged his sodden uniform for some dry and rustic clothing he came across. In the morning, he continued his escape. But at midday, two Texan scouts stopped him and asked, "Have you seen General Santa Anna?"

"He went that way," the general replied.[36]

They had no idea who he was, but took him prisoner anyway, only realizing the true value of their prize when they marched him into Houston's camp and the Mexican prisoners of war shouted out, "¡El Presidente!"

Peña claimed that six hundred Mexican "victims were immolated by the criminal and unforgivable negligence" of their president, while Houston lost only two men.[37] Stories abound about the disastrous adherence of wartime leaders to deeply ingrained cultural practices, from the devout Jew Mattathias of the Old Testament, who would not fight on the Sabbath, to the Aztec insistence that taking captives was the only point of going to war. But there is indeed something truly absurd about the stereotypes involved in this story of a band of English-speaking pirates managing to steal an entire state because a bunch of Mexicans were taking a *siesta*.

To put the Texan War of Independence into perspective, during the conflict Santa Anna had six thousand men in the field, mostly raw recruits armed with old weapons in poor condition, and if Peña is to be believed, many did not even have adequate footwear. Houston's forces at San Jacinto were less than 1,000, and the total number of Texan volunteers under arms during the conflict was about 3,700. By contrast, the British and French armies at the famous Battle of Waterloo, of 1815, each numbered almost 70,000, while there were an estimated 140,000 casualties during the First Carlist War of 1833 to 1839, a civil conflict that is today almost unheard of outside Spain.[38]

Santa Anna was at pains to point out that Houston "was generous and humane in his conduct," but had been wounded during the battle and soon sought medical attention in New Orleans.[39] Over the following days, the Mexican *caudillo* had to negotiate with less gentlemanly captors.

Santa Anna insisted that he had ceased to be President of the Republic from the moment of his capture and anyway Congress had already appointed a caretaker to the office; any concessions the Texans might extract from him would have no value. They would, he said, have to be ratified by his Congress anyway. Finally, on May 14, at a town called Velasco, now part of Freeport, Santa Anna signed a treaty by which all Mexican troops would withdraw beyond the Rio Grande. He also entered into a clandestine private agreement to make efforts to have the independence of Texas recognized by the Mexican government.

These halfhearted concessions did not secure his release, and his jailors almost surrendered him to a mob of volunteers from New Orleans. Instead, the Texan politicians saved him, but chained him up at Orazimba, where passing drunks and other rowdies entertained themselves by firing shots into his cell to make him jump, as though he were a dancing bear to be baited or a bull to be fought. Santa Anna responded by telling his captors that he was fearless in the face of death, although deeply saddened by the thought of never seeing his family again.

Stephen Austin, however, had recently returned from Washington. He had more respect for the President of Mexico and thought he could be put to good use. Austin suggested that Santa Anna write to President Andrew Jackson.[40] Jackson responded with an invitation to the White House, and in November 1836, Santa Anna set out with an escort to travel the breadth of the United States, ascending the Ohio by paddle steamer. At Louisville, Kentucky, Northern abolitionists welcomed him as a hero.

Jackson and Santa Anna shook hands at the White House on January 19, 1837, at a formal reception attended by plenty of foreign dignitaries, which delighted the Mexican.[41] Two days later, he returned for informal talks that lasted six hours. Jackson wore an old robe and puffed away on a long-stem pipe. They had a lot in common, these patriotic old soldiers with a love of their country estates and disdain for politicians. They instinctively liked each other. Santa Anna opened the negotiation by asking Jackson how much the United States was willing to pay for Texas. It was a wily move, for Santa Anna knew better than anyone that the territory was all but lost to Mexico.

Jackson did not bite, but pointed out that any deal would have to involve the Texans, and he could not meet with them without acknowledging their independence from Mexico. That said, Jackson offered $3.5 million for everything north of 38° and east of the Rio Grande, before adding, "But before we promise anything, General Santa Anna must say he will use his influence."[42]

Santa Anna played what chess masters call a Russian game and invoked the Mexican Congress: "They alone can decide this matter."[43] The United States sent Santa Anna back to Veracruz in style, aboard a naval corvette called the *Pioneer*, which greatly pleased him.

Soon afterward, Jackson met with Texan diehard William H. Wharton, who pressed the cause of the new nation of Texas. The U.S. president broached the idea of a purchase, but Wharton was scandalized. As far as the Texans were concerned, they had won their independence on the battlefield. It was an affront to suggest their sovereign country could be put up for sale by Mexico!

Jackson was trapped. He could not recognize Texas as an independent nation without offending Mexico, nor could he acquire the territory for the United States without insulting radicals such as Wharton. He was rescued by the U.S. Congress, which passed a series of resolutions paving the way for the United States to recognize the Republic of Texas. Jackson nominated Alcée La Branche of Louisiana as the U.S. Chargé d'Affaires to Texas and summoned Wharton to the White House. A group of men waited to learn if Congress would confirm the assignment before it adjourned. At midnight on the last day of Andrew Jackson's presidency, word reached them that the Senate had approved the appointment.

Old Hickory poured wine for his guests. They raised the glasses. "Texas!" said the president. How long, each man must have wondered, would Texas remain independent?

CHAPTER 26

THE MEXICAN-AMERICAN WAR

MÉXICO

My feeling of shame as an American was far stronger than theirs could be as Mexicans . . . for it was a thing for every right-minded American to be ashamed of and I was ashamed of it, most cordially and intensely ashamed.

—NICHOLAS TRIST

SANTA ANNA RETURNED TO MEXICO in a state of national disgrace so relative that he was given a hero's welcome by the people of Veracruz. Within two years, he was again in the saddle, literally, charging toward the fire of enemy cannon to expel another seaborne invasion of Mexico at the conclusion of an absurd conflict appropriately known as the Pastry War of 1838. The hostilities erupted when France attempted to extort the vast sum of six hundred thousand pesos from Mexico as compensation for damages caused to French businesses during one of the many upheavals that followed independence, including eighty thousand pesos for the owner of a pastry shop who had been bankrupted when rioters ate all his wares.[1] When Mexico refused to pay, the French navy appeared off Veracruz and began landing troops under cover of fog and darkness in the small hours of a December morning.

Santa Anna sprang from his bed, rallied his men, and led the advance, bayonets fixed, forcing a French retreat. But during the skirmishing, his horse was shot from under him. The animal died instantly. Santa Anna fell to the ground unconscious, his left leg smashed to smithereens.[2] "I came to and knew at once my sorry state," he later wrote. "I prayed fervently that God might cut short my days so I should die a glorious death."[3]

The limb turned quickly gangrenous; the surgeons huddled round. They amputated below the knee. A week went by, Santa Anna's life hung in the balance. But two months later, he had recovered sufficiently for Guadalupe Victoria to plead with his recuperating old comrade to take the helm of the nation at yet another time of revolutionary crisis. In March 1839, Santa Anna was rapturously reinaugurated as President of Mexico. Further upheavals followed, but at the start of the new decade, he established the most stable government since independence. However, the numerous enlightened and pragmatic measures taken in this period have been eclipsed in popular memory by the bizarre business of the burial of his amputated leg.

Antonio López de Santa Anna had undergone an almost-miraculous resurrection; rising from his sickbed, lifted from unimaginable depths of personal despair, he had been elevated to new celestial heights, in which he even embraced the business of government. But in a strange quirk of psychological trickery, his close encounter with the Angel of Death sired in him a morbid fascination with the demise of his left leg.

The remaining stump, it must be said, gave him constant pain and often oozed blood. He learned to walk and ride on finely crafted wooden substitutes but became obsessively guilty at outliving his amputated member. This strange passion reached its eccentric zenith in 1842, when he ordered his leg disinterred from its humble grave at his favorite estate near Veracruz in order that it be given a grand funeral with full military honors on September 27, the twenty-first anniversary of the glorious entry of the Army of the Three Guarantees into Mexico City, which had secured independence for the new nation.

The newspaper the *Diario del Gobierno* described how the government and municipal officials attended a Te Deum that "resounded about the vaults of the beautiful basilica" before listening to rousing speeches under an awning set up among the shade trees of the Alameda park. The crowd of dignitaries and military officers then set off toward the Cemetery of Santa Paula, forming two long files, slowly processing ahead of an outsize and "brilliantly decorated funeral urn within which was a small casket containing the leg of His Excellency the President, which was injured at Veracruz. The rearguard was made up of two infantry regiments and a cavalry detachment, each with its band of musicians and gunners." They were accompanied by a large contingent of schoolchildren. When the cavalcade reached the cemetery, some of the leading dignitaries carefully placed the urn on the top of a "high podium—or column—which was decorated with symbols and attributes of the Republic." The ceremony concluded with an artillery salute, and that afternoon there was a bullfight in town, a play in the theater, and musicians performing on the promenade, and later there were "fireworks in the main square."[4]

The ceremony is a fine example of that all-but-intangible moment when splendidly playful baroque excess blunders headlong into the abyss of kitsch perdition. The funeral of Santa Anna's leg was soon ridiculed in the streets and then in the newspapers. Slowly but surely, he and his government began to fall from grace.

Meanwhile, Texas festered, infecting parts of Coahuila and Neuvo León, where a handful of hopefuls declared independence as the Republic of the Rio Grande. That daydream ended on October 23, 1840, when the rebels abandoned their Texan allies on the battlefield at Ojo de Agua. The treachery was, it seems, prearranged, and the Mexican military was so confident of victory that bills were posted inviting the population of nearby Saltillo to watch "the defeat of these Texans who have dared to enter the motherland."[5] There was great excitement and the whole town turned up, as though to a bullfight. As city officials directed spectators to their seats, the Mexican troops took up their positions. Hawkers cried their wares and stalls sold fruit, drinks, and enchiladas.

A dust cloud was spied in the distance to the south and a clarion sounded long and shrill. The Texans were coming. The crowd shouted its encouragement as the infantry jumped into their trenches. The cavalry spread out, ready to charge. Then the big guns began to fire—*boom, boom, boom*—shelling the oncoming enemy. This was the signal for the rebels to turn coat. Thus betrayed and under intense bombardment, the Texans took cover in some ruined farm buildings. Cheered on by their delirious fans, detachment after detachment of Mexican soldiers charged. Accounts differ, but it seems the Texans finally broke ranks and, pursued by the Mexican cavalry, fled for the safety of a nearby gorge. They all, it was said, made it home to Texas alive.[6]

In the following years, Mexican forces made significant incursions into Texas and repeatedly occupied San Antonio, but never tried to hold any ground. The Texan militias retaliated. During one fateful raid across the Rio Grande, 250 Texan men were captured and imprisoned on a ranch near Saltillo. Most of them made a daring escape in the dead of night, overpowering their guards and heading for the border with a fine haul of guns and ammunition. But here the sporting veneer of this frontier banditry was brought up abruptly short. Mexican troops recaptured 176 of the fugitives, and Santa Anna ordered that they be decimated, quite literally in the Ancient Roman sense of the punishment: 169 white beans and 17 black beans were placed in a bag, and the blindfolded prisoners drew lots. The 17 souls who drew the black *frijoles* were attended to by a priest and shot at sunset.[7]

Tension mounted as the Texan and American governments contemplated annexation. Foolishly if not unreasonably, Mexico warned Washington that it would consider any debate of the matter by Congress "equivalent to a declaration of war."[8]

That warning was a red rag to an eager bull. President John Tyler harangued Congress in his annual message, implying it was an attempt to interfere in American democracy. "Texas," he declaimed, "is separated from the United States by a mere geographical line . . . It is homogenous in its population, commerce, language, and political institutions." Moreover, "most of her inhabitants have been citizens of the United States." He urged Mexico to abandon her pretentions to recover the lost nation: "These United States threw off their colonial dependence and established independent governments, and Great Britain, after having wasted her energies in the attempt to subdue them for a lesser period than Mexico has attempted to subjugate Texas, had the wisdom and justice to acknowledge their independence." So "the Executive has not hesitated to express to the Government of Mexico how deeply it deprecated a continuance of the war." The whole tenor of Tyler's message was that Texas was rightfully part of the United States, without actually stating as much. He even invoked "the Creator of the Universe," who gave "man the earth for his resting place," not the "general calamity" of "war." "Wars," he said menacingly, "may sometimes be necessary, but all nations have a common interest in bringing them speedily to a close."[9]

Only the objections of Northern abolitionists and Texan ambivalence toward annexation checked the determination of the Southern slave states to bring Texas into the Union. But as the British Foreign Minister, Lord Aberdeen, pointed out to the Mexican Ambassador when he tried to solicit British support for the recovery of Texas, nothing was more likely to entrench attitudes in Texas than Mexican insistence on recovering the independent nation. "And what can Mexico expect from her determination?" Aberdeen asked. "Not only will she never recover Texas, but the consequent war with the United States will probably lead to the loss of other provinces, especially California."[10]

Indeed, the United States so coveted California and was so paranoid that Britain or France might steal a march there that Commodore Thomas ap Catesby Jones, commander of the American fleet in the Pacific, had already occupied Monterey in 1842. He hoisted the Stars and Stripes, before the United States apologized and ordered him to abandon Mexican soil the following day, offering the implausible excuse he had believed the two countries to be at war.

"For Mexicans, Texas had become a question of *amour propre*," a matter of national *reputación*.[11] The American consul in Tampico described the "stubborn and malignant feeling in the mind of every Mexican against the United States."[12] For the United States, it was a matter of time before "manifest destiny" became reality. In 1845, that time seemed to have arrived.

The U.S. Senate finally voted in favor of annexation, and President James Polk came to office having narrowly won an election largely fought over Texas. Finally, with resounding symbolism, on July 4, the government in Austin passed a bill in favor of joining the United States. General Zachary Taylor began amassing troops at Corpus Christi Bay, and in March 1846 he moved to occupy the left bank of the Rio Grande. A detachment of Mexican troops moved into Matamoros, across the river. On April 24, General Arista notified Taylor that he considered hostilities to have commenced.

The first shots of the Mexican-American War were fired when a detachment of one hundred American scouts rode into an ambush. All of them were captured, killed, or wounded. Arista then led his troops across the Rio Grande and forced Taylor to engage him at Palo Alto. The Mexicans suffered heavy casualties, but quickly regrouped, only to be hit hard again at the Resaca de Guerrero, "Warrior's Wash." In Washington, Polk ordered the mobilization of thirty thousand men.

Taylor advanced over the Rio Grande into modern Mexico and marched on Monterrey, which capitulated after lively skirmishing. But his swift victory came at a high price, for he had to allow the main body of Mexican troops in the north to withdraw, ready to fight another day. That day soon came.

Santa Anna had fallen from grace in 1844 and been sent into exile on Cuba. Now, "with the declaration of war," he boasted, "the good Mexican people remembered my record of service and there was a popular call for my return."[13] Cometh the conflict, cometh Santa Anna. He amassed a large force of raggle-taggle soldiers, convicts emptied from jails, vagrants, and Indian peasants who spoke no Spanish and had no interest in the war.[14]

While the American soldiers enjoyed "much horse racing," according to one young German from Illinois, "and the drill ground was used for ball games," Santa Anna moved his men north in a brutal forced march.[15] They were tired, hungry, and bitterly cold. One man described how they set fire to every palm tree in the valley to keep warm. As the tops began to burn, "horrible waves" rolled across an "ocean of flame" that hung "in midair," lighting up the "starving and exhausted troops, who looked like an army of made up of the dead."[16] Santa Anna advanced these sorry men into a narrow gorge called La Angostura, just south of Saltillo. The Americans were waiting, "occupying a line of remarkable strength," as Taylor reported in dispatches. "The road at this point becomes a narrow defile," with "a succession of deep and impassable gullies" on the right flank and "rugged ridges" to the left, which as good as "paralyze[d] the artillery and cavalry of the enemy."[17] Nonetheless, Santa Anna urged his men into battle.

The Battle of Buena Vista raged for two days. Henry Clay Jr., son of the great Whig senator who had lost the 1844 presidential election, was badly wounded trying to defend an artillery position. Shot through the leg and bleeding profusely, he handed his pistols to one of his men. They were his father's dueling pistols, made in London in the 1790s. "Take them back to my father," Clay said, "and tell him I have done all I can with them!" [18] Clay then drew his sword and died bravely facing the Mexican bayonet charge, while his men escaped with the big guns and the pistols. [19] Jefferson Davis, Taylor's son-in-law, "though severely wounded, remained in the saddle until the close of the action," and "his Mississippi riflemen were highly conspicuous for their gallantry and steadiness." [20] In the thick of the fray, Taylor told Captain Bragg to put double shot into his guns, giving the famous order "Give them a little more grape, Captain Bragg," which Taylor later used as his campaign slogan when he ran for president. [21]

Again, Santa Anna had his horse shot from under him, and the stump of his amputated leg began to bleed. Groups of men and detachments of troops fought one another all over the precipitous ground around the ravine. Finally, when the fighting was finished, the Mexicans held the field and Taylor was forced to withdraw. But even Santa Anna knew he could not ask his broken army to continue the campaign. He, too, retreated. Both commanders claimed victory. It might be more realistic to conclude that both armies had been defeated.

The war was won and lost in the heart of Mexico. General Winfield Scott landed his men on the Mexican coast without challenge and secured the capitulation of Veracruz with relative ease. He then marched his army up the road to Mexico City and won a spectacular victory over Santa Anna at the narrow pass of Cerro Gordo, largely thanks to the brilliant scouting work of Robert E. Lee. Santa Anna himself only managed a narrow escape with the U.S. cavalry in close pursuit. They captured his carriage, various documents, some money, and one of his wooden legs, which the men then used as a bat in a game of baseball hastily improvised to celebrate the victory, or so it was said years later. [22]

Lee was again the hero as the American forces approached Mexico City from the south, when he found a route through a huge lava flow known as El Pedregal that the Mexicans had failed to defend because it was universally believed to be impassable. Scott met fierce resistance from the notorious San Patricio Battalion, largely made up of Catholic Irishmen who had deserted the American ranks. They knew they were guilty of treason and would be hanged if they surrendered, so they fought to the death. As General Scott approached the capital, Mexican guns savaged the first wave of assailants, but when the Americans stormed the Castle of Chapultepec, located on high ground, Santa Anna took the momentous decision to abandon Mexico City. The war was all but over.

Governor-General Manuel Armijo of New Mexico had grown splendidly corpulent, engorged, he claimed, on a life of fraud and embezzlement: "I have been stealing all my life," he told a former governor, "and I have the money in my pocket to prove it."[23] He was by turns charming and ruthless, an unfamiliar and terrifyingly mercurial figure for the many American traders who were forced to deal with him. "Few men have done more to jeopard [sic] the interests of American traders," the famous Plains merchant Josiah Gregg complained, nor "to bring the American character itself into contempt."[24]

But Armijo had prospered in an environment in which most people struggled to survive. In early July 1846, he learned an American army was already marching across the Great Plains and convened a council of the most powerful men in the province to discuss how best to respond. The six *caciques* who met at the Palace of the Governors all understood as well as Armijo that the situation was far more complicated than a simple war between two nations. For many of them, the commercial ties between New Mexico and the United States were closer and more lucrative than the historical and political connections with Old Mexico to the south. Even at that critical juncture, Armijo himself was waiting for his brother to return from Missouri as part of a large trading caravan that was crossing the plains only a week or two ahead of the American troops. Armijo had even personally assured a group of Missouri merchants that should war break out with the United States, the people of New Mexico would refuse to fight. Moreover, these *caciques* of New Mexico knew there was little chance of either money or men from Mexico. They were on their own.

During the summer, thousands of farmers and frontiersmen from across New Mexico armed themselves and came to Santa Fe, ready to defend their young country despite very real worries about leaving wives and families at the mercy of Indian raids. They found a champion in Colonel Diego Archuleta, a seemingly fine upstanding man, both able politician and proud soldier. He exhorted Governor Armijo to defend New Mexico against the Americans, and in the interests of satisfying honor and protecting *reputación* the governor appeared to acquiesce. On August 8, Armijo issued a general proclamation to his "Fellow Countrymen," telling them, "At last the moment has arrived when your nation requires her children to commit themselves completely, to make the ultimate sacrifice . . . The eagle which made us equal calls upon you today . . . to maintain the independence of our nation by your noble efforts and heroic patriotism."[25]

Four days later, the familiar figure of James Magoffin, a veteran merchant of the Plains trade and a former citizen of Chihuahua, rode into town with Captain Philip St. George Cooke. They went straight to the Palace of the Governors with a clear message from Colonel Stephen Kearny, commander and founding officer of the U.S. Army of the West, who was bearing down on Santa Fe with a force of about five hundred Mormons and twelve hundred volunteers from Missouri. He offered the peaceful occupation of all land east of the Rio Grande, which, he said, his government claimed as part of Texas.

Armijo protested profusely in front of Archuleta and a handful of his other officers, but dispatched a masterly ambiguous response to Kearny's offer. On the one hand he threatened battle, on the other he offered to negotiate.[26] Cooke left Magoffin to continue his negotiations with Armijo in secret and to get the message to Kearny. Magoffin could see as well as anyone that Armijo had little interest in making an honorable stand in the interests of Mexican *reputación*, so he gave him the extra incentive of a large bribe. Armijo began making plans to escape with his loot.

Meanwhile, Kearny had been making solid progress across the Plains and had sent messengers on ahead to assure the New Mexicans that he wanted a peaceful occupation and that they would all become Americans and be treated as U.S. citizens. The main body of the army began to make contact with the inhabitants, first a pretty young maiden who shook hands with some of them and asked for a smoke, then an American rancher who drove a few fine "beeves" into camp and treated the troops to dinner. Soon afterward, a patrol brought in some Mexicans, who reported that at least six hundred men, women, and children had congregated at the nearby village of Las Vegas to welcome the Americans. Kearny met with the *alcalde*, who thanked Kearny for his professions of peace, but nevertheless explained to the American colonel that he was a loyal Mexican.

The following day, July 3, as the army took peaceful possession of Las Vegas, a messenger arrived with Kearny's promotion to brigadier general. Filled with pride, he climbed onto a flat roof, and, flanked by Mexican officials and American officers, he addressed the throng below: "I have come among you by the orders of my government to take possession of your country . . . as friends, not as enemies, as protectors, not conquerors. We come for your benefit, not for your injury." Then, the *alcalde* and two of his officers took the oath of allegiance to the United States.[27] Kearny repeated the same ceremony at Tecolate and San Miguel. But as he proceeded, he received reports that Armijo was massing forces in Apache Canyon just beyond the ruins of Old Pecos Pueblo.

The patriotic New Mexican militiamen who had been gathering all summer at Santa Fe had indeed occupied the canyon. On August 16, Armijo led his professional dragoons to join them, but when he saw the field of battle, any patriotic resolve he may have felt deserted him along with any courage. Within weeks, the citizens of New Mexico formally denounced him for stating clearly to their leaders of the militia "that he would not risk facing battle with men so lacking in military training and that he would use his own regular troops as he thought best." Armijo consulted the dragoon officers, who offered to take the fight to the enemy, and the men cheered, "¡Viva, viva, viva!" But then, giving neither warning nor explanation, Armijo ordered his dragoons to spike their cannon and retreat. He then fled, abandoning Santa Fe and his wife, taking command of a little caravan carrying money and trade goods worth twenty thousand pesos or more.[28]

That evening, one of the American soldiers reported, "a large, fat fellow, mounted on a mule, came towards us . . . and congratulat[ed] the general. He said, with a roar of laughter, 'Armijo and his troops have gone to hell and the canyon is all clear!'" Without a soldier to lead them, even the bravest New Mexican militiamen had gone away.[29] Three days later, Kearny was invested as Military Governor of New Mexico and addressed the population of Santa Fe in the central plaza, assuring them he had come in peace: "I am your governor; henceforward, look to me for protection."[30]

In September, Kearny set out for California, but for all his professions of a creed of peace and love toward the New Mexicans, he left others to deal with the more squalid aspects of occupation. One traveler, a member of the Royal Geographical Society in London, recalled how "every house was a gin or whisky shop continually disgorging reeling, drunken . . . [American] volunteers" who "filled the streets, brawling and boasting, but never fighting."

Meanwhile, "Mexicans wrapped in sarape scowled upon them as they passed . . . and Pueblo Indians and priests jostled the rude crowds of brawlers at every stop." Everywhere, he noted "the most bitter feeling and determined hostility . . . against the Americans."[31]

Before the end of the year, Kearny's subordinates found a use for their raucous soldiers when they had to suppress a major uprising led by Archuleta and a former Alcalde of Taos Pueblo. As the Mexican patriots advanced on Santa Fe, the drunken gunners blasted them with cannon fire. Afterward, their commanders began hanging enemy officers by the score until the secretary of war stepped in to point out that treason was an absurd charge to level at Mexican citizens who were evidently enemy combatants.[32]

President Polk had been resolute in his determination to annex Alta California to the United States and had secretly encouraged Americans living there to rebel. In 1845, under the pretext of surveying the route of the Pacific

Railroad, Captain John Frémont led a large contingent of experienced frontiersmen and scientists on an expedition across the northern reaches of New
Mexico, including modern Colorado and Utah, and into California. He arrived
in Monterey in January 1846 to find tensions running high in a complex web
of distrust and enmity between American settlers and the local administration, between Mexican officials and the Californio settlers, and even among
the Californios themselves.

The Mexican commander at first granted Frémont permission to rest his
men along the San Joaquin River, but then ordered them to leave when they
began harassing ranchers and settlers at San José and elsewhere. Frémont
responded by hoisting an American flag, then slipped away overnight, heading
north into Oregon, where he waited. He soon received orders to head south in
preparation for the outbreak of war with Mexico. He set up camp near Sutter's
Fort in Sacramento County and began persuading nervous American settlers
in the region that they could declare themselves independent of Mexico and
the Californios.

On June 10, 1846, a handful of Americans ran off a herd of horses belonging
to Mexican forces that were then mustering at Santa Clara. The Americans
then rode on to Sonoma, where they woke up General Mariano Guadalupe
Vallejo, who was asleep in his bed, and forced him to offer them brandy and
sign articles of capitulation. They took him prisoner and locked him up along
with other leading members of the Sonoma community.

The drunken Americans then devised their famous flag with a bear and
star and flew it above the Mexican fort, declaring the independence of the
Bear Flag Republic of California. Frémont forced a local woman, Rosalía
Vallejo de Lesse, to write to the commander of a Californio force that was
already marching to retake the town, warning him that if he brought his men
any nearer, the rebels would lock all the men, women, and children in their
houses and burn them to the ground. "Those hated men inspired me with
such a large dose of hate against their race that though twenty-eight years
have elapsed since that time, I have not yet forgotten," she later testified.[33]

On July 2, 1846, Commodore John D. Sloat, commander of the Pacific
Squadron, sailed into the harbor at Monterey. Five days later he raised an
American flag, invited the Californios to surrender, then sent a detachment
of troops to occupy San Francisco Bay. The Bear Flag insurgents rallied to his
command, and Frémont sailed to San Diego.

The Californios regrouped and marched south to Los Angeles, but they
were unable to resist the Americans. Most took refuge in the hills, while their
military commanders fled south to Sonora and Baja, allowing Commodore
Robert F. Stockton to enter Los Angeles on August 13 and proclaim himself

Governor of California. However, the Californio resistance proved remarkably resolute in the face of terrible odds. They took back Santa Barbara and San Diego, before forcing an American surrender at Los Angeles itself. But it was a brief albeit heroic ascendency, for Stockton and Frémont massed their men and quickly recovered San Diego.

Stephen Kearny's march across the Great Plains to Santa Fe had been hard, but his traverse of the Colorado Desert was infernal. It "was intensely hot and the sand deep," one soldier wrote in his field notes, and "many animals were left on the road to die of thirst." They "gave way by the score . . . a feast day for the wolves, which followed in packs, making the air resound with their howls as they battled for the carcasses."[34] Finally, climbing high into the cooling fog of the Laguna Mountains, almost on the same trail that Juan Bautista de Anza had opened almost a century before, they reached the famous Warner Ranch and ate mutton and drank beer and were happy. There, an English settler told Kearny that Stockton had taken San Diego.

One fine December morning, as 1846 drew to a close, Kearny's party gazed from their Pisgah onto the Promised Land of California. Thirty miles out of San Diego, with his forces dangerously strung out along the trail, Kearny engaged a contingent of Californios at the Battle of San Pasqual, which was hard fought with the loss of eighteen American lives. For some still unknown reason, the Californios withdrew despite having the upper hand, allowing Kearny to continue to San Diego, where he found Stockton styling himself Governor of California. The now combined American forces, numbering well over a thousand men, marched north toward Los Angeles.

The final battle of the war was a tame affair, fought over two days along the San Gabriel River. Only three men were killed, but with the numbers of U.S. troops growing daily and the Mormon and New York battalions on the way, the Californios finally accepted their fate. On January 13, 1847, they signed the Treaty of Cahuenga, which guaranteed them the same rights as U.S. citizens and suspended the war in California until such time as Mexico and the United States should again be at peace.

That peace came in 1848, when Mexico offered her hopelessly ignominious capitulation. By the Treaty of Guadalupe Hidalgo, the United States forced Mexico to cede all of Alta California and New Mexico, along with the extensive lands to the north that now comprise the states of Washington, Oregon, Colorado, Utah, and Arizona. About eighty-five Mexican citizens were given the choice of moving to Mexico and remaining Mexican or becoming U.S. citizens.[35] On February 2, as the peace negotiations reached their conclusion, one of the Mexican negotiators said to his American counterpart, Nicholas

Trist: "This must be a very proud moment for you, sir, but it is quite humiliating for us."

The Mexican was wrong, for Trist later told his family, "Could those Mexicans have seen into my heart at that moment, they would have known that my feeling of shame as an American was far stronger than theirs could be as Mexicans." He believed the annexation of half their nation "was a thing for every right-minded American to be ashamed of and I was ashamed of it, most cordially and intensely ashamed."[36]

Five years later, in 1853, President Franklin Pierce appointed James Gadsden as ambassador to Mexico, with instructions to try to acquire as much land as he could along the southern border of the United States. By the Gadsden Treaty of 1854, President Santa Anna notoriously sold 29,640 square miles of his country, which today form the southern reaches of New Mexico and Arizona, to the United States for $10 million.

Puerto Rico, 1898

Now, we must close forever the story of our golden legend, which began with Christopher Columbus in 1492. After four hundred years, we are coming home from the Indies.

—MIGUEL MOYA OJANGUREN

THE FINAL SCENE IN THIS DRAMA of a Spanish Empire that became American returns to the troubled waters where it began with thuggery and rape in the Caribbean and the settlement of Puerto Rico by pigs and goats. The annexation of Puerto Rico by the United States, in 1898, is no more than an epilogue, a last minor codicil to be executed in the long will and testament of Spanish imperialism. Indeed, there was almost no fighting during the invasion of Puerto Rico, very much a minor sideshow in the Spanish-American War, for all that the island was likened in strategic importance in the Caribbean to Malta in the Mediterranean by the great American naval tactician Alfred Thayer Mahan.[1]

Over the course of the nineteenth century, Spain had charged headlong into political perdition, a once brave and noble bovine mortally wounded by perfidious France and run ragged by the heretics of Albion. The Spanish Crown had been crucified by the collapse of the Bourbon Pact, killed by Napoleonic invasion, and barely resurrected by the Peninsular War, a conflict largely fought by foreigners on Spanish soil.

Meanwhile a chorus of colonial subjects declared independence from the wounded motherland: in the River Plate, the Argentine, in Florida and Louisiana, and in those twin jewels of empire, the viceroyalties of Mexico and Peru. In thirteen luckless years between 1811 and 1824, Spain lost a continent. Without an empire to exploit nor a stable government at home, Spaniards were a people bereft, in search of a *raison d'être*. They plunged their country into a suicidal vortex of revolution, liberal extremism, and royalist restoration, of bloodletting and mutual hatred, of intestine shock to rival even the youthful excess of Mexico.

The radical president of the short-lived First Spanish Republic described his nation as "an enormous cadaver stretching from the Pyrenees to the sea at Cadiz . . . , an immense corpse in the laboratory of history."[2] The brilliant Basque novelist Pío Baroja summed up the sense of desperation: "There have been thirteen constitutions here since the Cortes of Cadiz. There have been revolutions, counterrevolutions, wars, and proclamations. Yet all were founded on naught but fine words and eloquence and naught has come of them. The only thing that has not been tried is something sensible and measured, free of stubborn rhetoric, and rooted in hard work!"[3]

As the nineteenth century drew to a close, all that remained of the mighty Spanish Habsburg hegemon, the empire "upon which the sun had never set," were Puerto Rico, the Philippines, and "the richest colony in the whole world," the ineffable isle, Cuba.[4] We "Spaniards would sooner see the island sunk in the ocean than occupied by a foreign power," a government minister announced in midcentury.[5]

But the growing Cuban economy owed nothing to irksome Spanish bureaucracy and everything to American investment in the sugar industry. Wealthy Cubans had developed close ties to the United States, and many *criollos* hoped their island might join the Union. Others longed for independence, and an armed revolt eventually erupted in the 1860s in the poor and mountainous region of the Oriente. That led to a long *guerrilla* insurgency, which ended in stalemate when Spain made important concessions to the rebels that included agreeing to a trade deal with the United States and abolishing slavery. But the spirit of independence smoldered on in Cuba and burned brightly among the many exiled rebels living in America, notably the national hero José Martí, who worked tirelessly for his cause.

By contrast with their "Cuban brothers," few Puerto Ricans were interested in independence or rebellion. But in New York, a group calling themselves the Club Boriquen, honoring the pre-Columbian indigenous name for their island, allied themselves with the Cuban Revolutionary Party when they learned that rebellion had again been proclaimed in the Oriente.[6] In April 1895, Martí landed on Cuba, and by the time he was killed in early skirmishing, he had already set ablaze a full-scale war for the island's independence.

In America, lobbyists for the Cuban rebels did their job, and the yellow press reveled in the vilification of a Catholic and European colonial power. A renowned correspondent, Harding Davis, described the execution of a twenty-year-old insurgent with "a handsome, gentle face . . . and great wistful eyes. He was shockingly young for such a sacrifice. As the officer gave the command, he straightened himself . . . held up his head, and fixed his eyes on the morning light . . . a picture of pathetic helplessness, but of such courage and dignity . . . The men fired . . . the Cuban's head snapped back . . . his body fell slowly, he sank in the wet grass and did not move again."

Spanish officers, it was reported in New York, forced young girls fleeing the conflict to undress and then searched them in cabins aboard an American ship. William Randolph Hearst ensured that a journalist working for the *New York Journal* rescued from prison one beautiful and virtuous maiden who had courageously resisted the lecherous advances of her jailor. "Blood on the roadsides, blood on the fields, blood on the doorsteps, blood, blood, blood! The old, the young, the weak, the crippled—all are butchered without mercy," the *New York World* reported. But such human drama merely spiced yet another kind of "atrocity": "No man's property is safe . . . millions and millions of dollars' worth of American sugar cane, buildings and machinery have already been lost."[7]

President William McKinley had little appetite for involving America in a war for Cuba, but the hysteria of the press and the violence of public opinion forced him to send the USS *Maine* to Havana to protect American interests. Why she exploded, killing 2 officers and 268 American crewmen, remains a matter of debate. It was quite probably an accident. McKinley tried to diffuse the atmosphere by sending a team of navy specialists to investigate, but as they had every reason to blame anyone except the navy, they concluded that the *Maine* had been mined. With the U.S. Congress baying for Spanish blood, America sent an ultimatum to Madrid. On April 21, 1898, war was declared.

Like a great Pacific wave, the war broke ten days later in the Philippines, where the year before the Spanish authorities had quelled an incipient nationalist uprising by paying off the revolutionary leaders. Theodore Roosevelt, almost in his last act before he resigned as Assistant Secretary of the Navy to lead his private regiment of Rough Riders in the coming war, sent Admiral Dewey to stake an American claim to the crumbling Spanish Empire in Asia. Dewey resupplied at Hong Kong, and when war was declared, he destroyed the temporary Spanish fleet then docked at Manila in the Battle of Cavite, following a daring midnight entry through the heavily mined entrance to the bay. In August, Spain formally surrendered in the Philippines.

Admiral Pascual Cervera, the Spanish commander of the Cuban fleet, advised Madrid that he would be unable to defeat the United States at sea. Privately, he thought any kind of war against the United States a hopeless cause, for "we are in decline" and "utterly penniless," while "they are very rich!"[8] But the clamor of Iberian jingoism drowned him out. A series of charity bullfights were organized in Madrid, with profits going to support the war effort, and the headline of *El Imparcial* screamed, "Spain Will Not Be Cowed!" Those "Yankees jangling their moneybags will never frighten the

Spanish people," for "war frightens *them* much more than it does *us*," the editor in Madrid announced, wielding his pen in honor of those who would have to draw their swords abroad. For although "the United States is materially stronger than Spain," he had to admit, a "fighting bull is more powerful still than a man," and the Americans have already seen "how a bull can be fought and mastered." Yet the editor knew his readers were aware that in bullfighting sometimes the matador is gored and occasionally he dies. For all its patriotic bombast, this editorial betrays a fatalistic sense of inevitability, concluding that "if Spain must fall, then she shall fall fearlessly and with honor, the last chivalrous nation" on earth, the land that gave birth to the greatest tragicomic hero of all time, Don Quixote.[9]

This eternal will to self-immolation on the altar of *pundonor*, of *honra*, of *reputación*, that beautiful breast that suckles the heartbreaking and deadly nobility of Spain, was satirized at the time by one of the most iconic anti-establishment intellectuals in Madrid, José Martínez Ruiz, usually known by his nickname Azorín. Filled with a profoundly pithy pathos, his dialogue between a Patriot and a Pragmatist bares naked that essential spirit, by turns the glory and the nemesis of every conquistador we have met on these pages:

Patriot: Let's save our honor! Long live the honorable mother country! We need to go to war!
Pragmatist: War would be a great misfortune. We don't have the money and we don't have the ships. How are you going to fight such a powerful nation?
Patriot: We will all die gloriously.
Pragmatist: Folly!
Patriot: Cowardice!
Pragmatist: Reason!
Patriot: Honor![10]

As war was looming, on March 1, 1898, the Spanish Captain General of Puerto Rico, Manuel Macías, ordered the release from prison of a high school teacher and former army officer called Ángel Rivero, who had spent a fortnight locked up for breaking army regulations by becoming involved in politics. Years later, Rivero founded the North Pole Soda Company and invented the legendary *portoriqueña* drink Kola Champagne.

Macías appointed him captain of the Twelfth Artillery Regiment and told him, "If war comes, which it will, you sir, a good *portoriqueño*, will have the honor of defending . . . the Castillo of San Cristóbal," the massive fortress named after Saint Christopher in honor, of course, of Columbus, the first European to visit Puerto Rico, in 1493.[11]

On May 10, Rivero saw the American ship *Yale* drifting toward the coast and asked permission to fire on her. His commanders dithered while she withdrew, and when it was too late, they ordered him to fire anyway. "The missile fell well short . . . the *Yale* speeded up her retreat and took up a position on the horizon," Rivero recalled proudly. "It was the first shot fired during the Spanish-American War in Puerto Rico." Two days later, he was woken at five in the morning by "formidable cannon fire. I rushed up to the battery, where my men showed signs of being very surprised." But their weapons were primed and they were soon returning fire. "A hail of missiles flew above our heads, a real storm of hot iron, which went on for three hours . . . , hours that seemed like centuries." A six-inch shell struck one of the cannons, and the "gunner fell to the ground, his skull smashed open." Others were rushed to the infirmary. Then, "at that moment it dawned on a beautiful May day in the tropics," and the American ships sailed away in search of Admiral Cervera's Spanish squadron.[12]

On July 17, following an intense siege, the Spanish army formally surrendered at Santiago de Cuba. General William Rufus Shafter was delighted, greatly enjoyed the company of Spanish officers, and described the Spanish troops in his dispatches as "orderly, tractable, and generally the best-behaved men I have known." This was in marked contrast to the Cuban rebel forces, whom Roosevelt thought "nearly useless" and whom Shafter refused permission to bear arms in Santiago for fear of their ill discipline.[13]

Before the end of the month, General Nelson Miles had sailed out of nearby Guantánamo, heading for Puerto Rico. He launched a surprise attack on the superb natural harbor at Guánica with its little town on the southwest coast of the island. A small detachment of U.S. marines quickly put to flight the twelve militiamen who had no enthusiasm for defending the dilapidated fort armed only with ancient sawn-off Remington rifles.

With a bridgehead established, Miles disembarked his men and marched them toward the nearby coastal town of Ponce. The following day, July 26, the French Ambassador in Washington, acting as a go-between, met President McKinley with a formal inquiry from the government in Madrid about possible terms on which the war might be ended. The next day, General Wilson reached Puerto Rico with a large contingent of reinforcements and threatened to bombard Ponce from the sea.

The British, Dutch, and German consuls began to negotiate the surrender of the city. They exchanged a series of frantic telegrams with General Macías, who was unable to decide whether to order a retreat or try to hold the position.

The citizens themselves began urging the Spaniards to leave, terrified their wooden town would be burned to ashes. Finally, Macías succumbed to pressure and ordered the Spanish garrison to withdraw to the hills. Ponce had fallen.

By the end of July, the Americans had landed fifteen thousand men on Puerto Rico. In another tactically masterly move, Miles ordered his forces to move on the capital, San Juan, in four columns. There was fierce skirmishing as the U.S. troops advanced. Again, Rivero gives us an intimate glimpse of battle, quoting from a letter written by a young infantryman who took cover with his commander with bullets flying on all sides.

"I heard him moan and his head fell and my heart beat fast," the youth reported. "I asked him, 'Are you hurt, sir?'

"'Yes,' he replied.

"I asked him where and he started to laugh. 'In my . . . well, I can't sit down!'"[14]

His captain had been hit in the backside.

Under persistent fire, the Spanish defensive forces began to fall back. But just as the Americans prepared their crucial assault on the garrison town of Aibonito, which controlled the main road through the mountains, on August 12 the War Department sent a telegram announcing that Spain had signed a peace protocol and ordering an immediate end to hostilities.

At midday on October 18, Captain Rivero left the artillery barracks, sparkling in his Spanish military dress uniform, and walked down to the Plaza Alfonso XII, the main square of San Juan, named after the recently deceased Spanish king. There, standing beside his new friend Lieutenant Colonel Rockwell of the U.S. Army, Rivero waited. "At last the city clock struck the hour of twelve and the crowds . . . watched . . . almost breathless . . . eyes fixed upon the flagpole. At the sound of the first gun," the *New York Times* reported, American troops "hoisted the Stars and Stripes while the band played the Star-Spangled-Banner" and "the crowds cheered."[15] Captain Rivero kept his emotions to himself.

A few weeks later, Lieutenant Colonel Rockwell asked his friend, "Captain, your services would be invaluable to my government. May I recommend that Washington keep you in our employ?"

"Colonel," Rivero replied, "the insignia I wear on my collar are Spanish. How would you respond should I suggest such a thing?"

"Forgive me, I have managed to be rude in my eagerness to help you. But you must surely accept if we pay you? How much does the Spanish Government pay?"

"Nothing, I am a supernumerary without a salary."

"Nobody should work without pay. I can take care of that!"

"Thank you, but military honor forbids such a thing!"[16]

The Treaty of Paris was signed on December 10, 1898. Spain conceded every-thing: Cuba, the Philippines, little Guam, and Puerto Rico. "One cannot imagine what it is to treat with the Americans when one is defeated," a French diplomat observed. "They have the blood of Indians in their veins."[17]

Miguel Moya Ojanguren was editor in chief of the bestselling Madrid news-paper *El Liberal* and the most influential journalist of his generation, a brilliant orator, and serving Deputy to the Cortes for both Cuba and Puerto Rico.[18] A fortnight earlier, in anticipation of the final humiliation of Imperial Spain, he had published a leading article that expressed the lament of a humbled and grieving nation under the headline "Evil Day": "Now, we must close forever the story of our golden legend, which began with Christopher Columbus in 1492. After four hundred years, we are coming home from the Indies."[19]

Abbreviations

AE	Paris, Archives du Ministère des Affaires Etrangères
AGI	Seville, Archivo General de Indias
AGN	Mexico City, Archivo General de la Nación
AGS	Simancas, Archivo General de Simancas
AHN	Madrid, Archivo Histórico Nacional
BNE	Madrid, Biblioteca Nacional de España
BNM	Mexico City, Biblioteca Nacional de México
BNP	Paris, Bibliothèque Nationale de France
CDI	Pacheco, Joaquín Francisco, and Francisco de Cárdenas (eds.), *Colección de documentos inéditos relativos al descubrimiento, conquista y colonización de las posesiones españolas en América . . .* 42 vols. (Madrid: 1864–84).

BIBLIOGRAPHY

PRIMARY SOURCES (ONLINE ARCHIVES)

AMERICAN STATE PAPERS: memory.loc.gov/ammem/amlaw/lwsp.html
Foreign Relations, Military Affairs, and Miscellaneous

CALENDAR OF STATE PAPERS: british-history.ac.uk/cal-state-papers/venice
Venetian

DIGITAL AUSTIN PAPERS: digitalaustinpapers.org/document?id=APB4609.xml
Stephen F. Austin to Samuel Williams, Mexico City, November 26, 1833

PAPAL ENCYCLICALS ONLINE: papalencyclicals.net

PRIMARY SOURCES (UNPUBLISHED)

ARCHIVO GENERAL DE INDIAS, SEVILLE
In the late eighteenth century, Charles III ordered that all Spanish government papers relating to the overseas empire be conserved at the Archivo General de Indias, in Seville, which was located in the old Casa Lonja, the magnificent Merchants' Exchange building. Much of the material is now available on the Ministerio de Cultura y Deporte's PARES website: pares.mcu.es. The following groups of *legajos*, or "bundles," are cited in the notes. Where the note refers to a secondhand citation from a scholarly work, the reference may be to the old numbering system. It is anyway often easier to find the document by searching with keywords rather than through the online structure of the website.

Contaduría 286
Contratación 135A, 4675, and 5788
Cuba 81, 112, 174, 184A, 184C, 191, 192, 573, 1054, 1146, 1227, and 2370
Escribanía 178
Estado 34, 86A, and 86B
Guadalajara 1, 5, 31, 51, 88, 252, 273, 275, 390, 416, 511, 516, 517, and 590
Indiferente 415, 418, 450, 739, 744, 1578, and 1713
Justicia 970 and 1000
México 22B, 24, 25, 28, 68, 203, 204, 1242, 1365, 1366, 1370, 1509, 1513, 1701, 1702, 2453, and 2477
MP-Escudos 273A and 1781

MP-México 5
Panamá 234
Pasajeros, L.3 and E.4070
Patronato 1, 5, 19, 20, 21, 22, 52, 60, 65, 180, 181, 184, and 254
Santo Domingo 1220, 1221, 1598, 2082, 2082B, 2083, 2453, 2542, 2543, 2547, 2554, 2586, 2596, 2661, and 2662

ARCHIVO GENERAL DE SIMANCAS, VALLADOLID
SGU Leg. 6612
SGU Leg. 6912
SGU Leg. 6913

ARCHIVO HISTÓRICO NACIONAL, MADRID
Estado 2845, 2883, 3884, 4168, and 4224
Ordenes Militares-Expedientillos N.1081
Ordenes Militares-Santiago Exp. 5925
Sección Jesuitas Leg. 22

ARCHIVO DE PROTOCOLOS DE MONTILLA, CORDOVA
Registro de Escrituras de Juan Martínez de Córdoba, 1570

BIBLIOTECA COLOMBINA, SEVILLE
Fernández de Oviedo y Valdés, Gonzalo: "Manuscript fragment of *Historia General*," 57-5-43

BIBLIOTECA NACIONAL DE ESPAÑA, MADRID
Ultramar 14: "Relación de la campaña que hizo don Bernardo de Gálvez contra los ingleses, en la Luisiana, September 1799"

BIBLIOTECA NACIONAL DE MÉXICO, MEXICO CITY
Archivo Franciscano 41/929.10, f.14v & f.15, "Gálvez to Pineda," Alamos, July 15 and July 23, 1769

ARCHIVO GENERAL DE LA NACIÓN, MEXICO CITY
Californias, vols. 66 and 72
Civil, vol. 1988
Correspondencia de Virreyes, Croix, vol. 14
Patronato Misiones 25, Exp. 36
Provincias Internas, vols. 97 and 98

ARCHIVO PÚBLICO DE MÉXICO
Misiones, vol. 25

ARCHIVO FRANCISCO DE MIRANDA, ACADEMIA NACIONAL DE LA HISTORIA DE VENEZUELA, CARACAS
Diario de lo mas particular ocurrido desde el día de nuestra salida del puerto de La Habana: Viajes, vol. 3, *España, América*

ARCHIVO GENERAL DEL GOBIERNO DE GUATEMALA
A1.60, Exp. 45, 364, Leg. 5365

UNIVERSITY OF CALIFORNIA, BERKELEY, BANCROFT LIBRARY
M-M 1714 "Melchior Pérez's Petition," 1551

VATICAN ARCHIVES, VATICAN CITY/UNIVERSITY OF ARIZONA, TUCSON
Vatican Archives (Marcellino da Civezza) 202:35 and Microfilm at U of A: Francisco Antonio
Barbastro, "Apuntes del Padre Fr. Francisco Antonio Barbastro . . . 1768–1781," Baviácora,
September 10, 1788

BRITISH LIBRARY, LONDON
Spanish Papers (Wellesley, Seville): LR 21 A 17: Anon. "Corrida de Toros, en obsequio a los
Franceses," [1808]
Add Mss 36,339
Add Mss 31,219, Codex Aubin, f.46v

PUBLIC RECORD OFFICE, KEW
SP 94/164 Bristol to Egremont, Escorial, November 2, 1761
America and West Indies, Floridas 1702–1782, N° 533
CO 5/561, Young to Tonyn, July 30, 1784
FO 72/26, St. Helens to Grenville, April 10, 1793

UNIVERSITY OF GLASGOW
Sp Coll Ms Hunter 242 (U.3.15), *History of Tlaxcala*

BIBLIOTHÈQUE NATIONALE DE FRANCE, PARIS
Fonds Français, 10,766
AE: CP, Espagne, 532

PRIMARY SOURCES (PRINTED)

Adams, Eleanor B., "Fray Silvestre Vélez de Escalante: Letter to the Missionaries of New
    Mexico," *New Mexico Historical Review* 40:4 (1965), 319–35.
Adams, John Quincy, *Memoirs of John Quincy Adams, Comprising Portions of His Diary
    from 1795–1848*, vol. 3, ed. Charles Francis Adams (Philadelphia: 1874).
Alegre, Francisco Javier, *Historia de la Compañía de Jesús en Nueva-España*, vol. 3 (Mexico
    City: 1842).
Alv Ixtlilxochitl, Fernando de, *Obras históricas de don Fernando de Alva Ixtlilxochitl*, ed.
    Alfredo Chavero, 2 vols. (Mexico City: 1891), 1:402–3.
Álvarez Chanca, Diego, "Carta del doctor Álvarez Chanca al Cabildo de Sevilla," in *Cartas
    de particulares a Colón y relaciones coetáneas*, ed. Juan Gil and Consuelo Valera (Madrid:
    1984), 152–76.
Anon., *Mémoire sur la Louisiane* (Paris: 1813).
Anza, Juan Bautista de, "Diary of 1779 Comanche Campaign": http://96.71.175.153/AnzaWeb/
    anza79.html.

Archivo Documental Español, vol. 5, *Negociaciones con Francia (1563)* (Madrid: 1952).

Austin, Stephen F., "Journal of Stephen F. Austin on His First Trip to Texas, 1821," *Quarterly of the Texas State Historical Association* 7:4 (1904), 286–307.

——, "The 'Prison Journal' of Stephen F. Austin," *Quarterly of the Texas State Historical Association* 2:3 (1899), 183–210.

Baegert, Juan Jacobo, *Noticias de península americana de California* (Mexico City: 1942).

Baker, Maury, and Margaret Bissler Haas, "Bernardo de Gálvez's Combat Diary for the Battle of Pensacola, 1781," *Florida Historical Quarterly* 56:2 (1977), 176–79.

Bassett, John S. (ed.), *Correspondence of Andrew Jackson*, vol. 2 (Washington, DC: 1927).

Beals, Herbert K. (ed. and trans.), *Juan Pérez on the Northwest Coast: Six Documentos of His Expedition in 1774* (Portland, OR: 1989).

Benavides, Alonso de, *Memorial que fray Juan de Santander de la Orden de san Francisco . . . presenta a la Magestad Catolica del Rey don Felipe Quarto* (Madrid: 1630).

Bernáldez, Andrés, *Historia de los reyes católicos d. Fernando y Doña Isabel*, 2 vols. (Seville: 1870).

Bigs [Bigges], Capt. Walter, "A Summarie and True Discourse of Sir Frauncis Drake's West Indian Voayge," in *Sir Francis Drake's West Indian Voyage, 1585–86*, ed. Mary F. Keeler (London: 1981), 205–7.

Blanco White, Joseph (pseudonym: don Leucadio Doblado), *Letters from Spain* (London: 1822).

Bolton, Herbert E. (ed.), *Kino's Historical Memoir of Pimería Alta*, 2 vols. (Cleveland: 1919).

Boneu Companys, Fernando (ed.), *Documentos secretos de la expedición de Portolá a California. Juntas de Guerra* (Lérida: 1973).

Boyd, Julian P., et al. (eds.), *The Papers of Thomas Jefferson*, vol. 16 (Princeton: 1961).

Burnett, Edmund C. (ed.), *Letters of Members of the Continental Congress* (Washington, DC: 1923).

Calderón de la Barca, Fanny, *Life in Mexico: The Letters of Fanny Calderón de la Barca*, ed. Howard T. Fisher and Marion Hall Fisher (New York: 1966).

Calderón Quijano, José Antonio (ed.), *Documentos para la historia del Estado de Colima* (Mexico City: 1972).

——(ed.), *Los virreyes de Nueva España en el reinado de Carlos III*, 3 vols. (Seville: 1967).

Cañizares, José [Bernabéu Albert, Salvador], "'Por tierra nada conocida': El diario inédito de José de Cañizares a la Alta California," *Anuario de Estudios Americanos* 60:1 (2003), 235–76.

Cano Sánchez, Angela, and Elena Mampei González, *Crónicas del descubrimiento de la Alta California* (Barcelona: 1984).

Cantillo, Alejandro de (ed.), "Tratado de alianza defensiva y ofensiva celebrado entre las coronas de España y Francia contra la de Inglaterra," in *Tratados de paz y de comercio desde el año de 1700 hasta el día* (Madrid: 1843).

Castelar, Emilio, *Discursos Parlamentarios y Politicos en La Restauracion*, 4 vols. (Madrid: 1877).

Céliz, Fray Francisco, *Diary of the Alarcón Expedition into Texas, 1718–1719* (Los Angeles: 1935).

Champigny, Chevalier de, "Memoir on the Present State of Louisiana," in *Historical Memoirs of Louisiana, from the First Settlement of the Colony to the Departure of Governor O'Reilly in 1770*, ed. B. F. French, 5 vols. (New York: 1853).

Clayton, Lawrence A., *The Hispanic Experience in North America: Sources for Study in the United States* (Columbus: 1992).

Clayton, Lawrence A., Vernon James Knight, and Edward C. Moore (eds.), *The De Soto Chronicles*, 2 vols. (Tuscaloosa: 1995).

Columbus, Christopher [Cristóbal Colón], "Diario del primer viaje," in *Cristóbal Colón: Textos y documentos completos*, ed. Consuelo Valera (Madrid: 1982), 15–138.

———, *Letters from America: Columbus's First Accounts of the 1492 Voyage*, ed. and trans. B. W. Ife (London: 1992).

———, "Memorial a A. Torres (1494)," in *Cristóbal Colón: Textos y documentos completos*, ed. Consuelo Valera (Madrid: 1982), 147–62.

A Compilation of Messages and Papers of the Presidents, vol. 4 (New York: 1897).

Convention Between His Britannick Majesty and the King of Spain. Signed at the Escurial, the 28th of October, 1790 (London: 1790).

Cook, James, *A Voyage to the Pacific Ocean*, 3 vols. (London: 1784).

Corona Núñez, José, and Francisco Paso y Troncoso (eds.), *Relaciones geográficas de la Diócesis de Michoacán, 1579–1580* (Guadalajara: 1958).

Costansó, Miguel de, *Diario histórico de los viages de mar, y tierra hechos al norte de la California* ([Mexico City: 1770]).

Courlander, Harold (ed.), *The Fourth World of the Hopis: The Epic Story of the Hopi Indians as Preserved in Their Legends and Traditions* (Albuquerque: 1971).

Courrier d'Avignon, July 4, 1780.

Covarrubias, Sebastián de, *Tesoro de la lengua castellana o española* (Madrid: 1611).

Craddock, Jerry R., "Antonio de Otermín's Attempted Reconquest of New Mexico, Winter 1681–1682," 37–39 and appendix: escholarship.org/uc/item/41d6w72g.

———, "Fray Marcos de Niza, *Relación* (1539), Edition and Commentary," *Romance Philology* 53:1 (1999), 69–118.

Craddock, Jerry R., and John H. R. Polt, "The Trial of the Indians of Acoma, 1598–1599": escholarship.org/uc/item/14v3j7sj.

Craddock, Jerry R., David J. Weber, and John H. R. Polt, "Zaldívar and the Cattle of Cíbola. Vicente de Zaldívar's Report of His Expedition to the Buffalo Plains in 1598": escholarship.org/uc/item/6hz1x4s4.

Craddock, Jerry R., John H. R. Polt, and Barbara De Marco, "Oñate's Report to the Viceroy March 2, 1599": escholarship.org/uc/item/8s9oh6b6#page-1.

Crespí, Fray Juan [ed. Geo Butler Griffin], "Diario que yo Fray Juan Crespi . . . formó del viaje de la fragata de su Magestad nombrada Santiago," *Publications of the Historical Society of Southern California* 2:1 (1891), 143–213.

———, "An Unpublished Diary of Fray Juan Crespi, O. F. M (San Diego to Monterey, April 17 to November 11, 1770)," *The Americas* 3:1 (1946), 102–14; 3:2 (1946), 234–43; 3:3 (1947), 368–81.

Cuevas, Mariano (ed.), *Documentos inéditos del siglo XVI para la historia de México* (Mexico City: 1914).

Cuneo, Michele da, "Relación de Miguel de Cuneo," in *Cartas de particulares a Colón y relaciones coetáneas*, ed. Juan Gil and Consuelo Valera (Madrid: 1984), 235–60.

———, "La Relazione," in *Repertorium Columbianum*, vol. 12, *Italian Reports on America, 1493–1522: Accounts by Contemporary Observers*, ed. Geoffrey Symcox, T. J. Cachey, and John C. Lucas (Turnhout: 2002).

Dávila Padilla, Fray Augustín, *Historia de la fundación y discurso de la provincia de Santiago de México de la orden de predicadores*, 2nd ed. (Brussels: 1625).

De Marco, Barbara, and Jerry R. Craddock, "Diego Pérez de Luján: Relación de la expedición de Antonio de Espejo a Nuevo México, 1582–1583": escholarship.org/uc/item/5313v23h.

———, "Documents Concerning the Suspension of Juan de Oñate's Expedition to New Mexico": escholarship.org/uc/item/6pjo700h.

———, "Lope de Ulloa y Lemos's Inspection of Juan de Oñate's Equipment and Personnel Destined for the Conquest of México": escholarship.org/uc/item/3nt8h54n.

———, "Relación de Hernán Gallegos sobre la expedición del padre fray Agustín Rodríguez y el capitán Francisco Sánchez Chamuscado a Nuevo México, 1581–1582": escholarship .org/uc/item/4sv5h1gz.

De Marco, Barbara, Jerry R. Craddock, and John H. R. Polt, "Juan de Oñate Defends Himself Against the Charges for Which He Was Convicted in 1614": escholarship.org/uc/item /0p76r2wj.

Diario del Gobierno de la República Méxicana 2654:24 (September 28, 1842).

Díaz del Castillo, Bernal, *La verdadera de la conquista de la Nueva España*, ed. Genaro García, 2 vols. (Mexico City: 1904).

Diccionario de Autoridades (Madrid: 1734).

Documentos para la Historia de México, Cuarta Série, vol. 2 (Mexico City: 1856).

Documentos para servir a la historia del Nuevo México, 1538–1778 (Madrid: 1962).

Dorantes de Carranza, Baltasar, *Sumaria relación de las cosas de la Nueva España* (Mexico City: 1987 [c. 1600]).

Dumont de Montigny, Jean-François-Benjamin, *The Memoir of Lieutenant Dumont, 1715–1747*, ed. and trans. Gordon M. Sayre and Carla Zecher (Chapel Hill, NC: 2012).

Dürer, Albrecht, *Albrecht Dürer: Diary of His Journey to the Netherlands, 1520–1521*, ed. J. A. Goris and G. Marlier (London: 1970).

El Imparcial, March 15, 1898.

El Liberal, November 28, 1898.

Elvas, Gentleman of, *Relaçao verdadeira dos trabalhos que o governador D. Fernando de Souto e certos fidalgos portugueses passaram no descobrimento da província da Florida. Agora novamente feita por um fidalgo de Elvas* [1557].

Emory, W. H., *Notes of a Military Reconnaissance from Fort Leavenworth to San Diego, California* (Washington, DC: 1848).

Enciso Contreras, José (ed.), *Epistolario de Zacatecas, 1549–1599* (Zacatecas: 1996).

Escalante, Fray Silvestre Vélez de, "Carta del Padre Fray Silvestre de Escalante, escrita en 2 e abril de 1778 años," in *Documentos para servir a la historia del Nuevo México, 1538–1778* (Madrid: 1962), 305–24.

Espinosa, Fray Isidro Félix de, *Crónica de los colegios de propaganda fide de la Nueva España*, ed. Lino G. Canedo (Washington, DC: 1964).

The Examiner, August 2, 1818.

Farmar, Robert, *Journal of the Siege of Pensacola* (1781).

Fernández de Navarrete, Martín, *Colección de viajes y descubrimientos que hicieron por mar los españoles*, 5 vols. (Madrid: 1825–37).

Fernández de Oviedo y Valdés, Gonzalo, *Historia general*, ed. Pérez de Tudela, 5 vols. (Madrid: 1959).

Flint, Richard, *Great Cruelties Have Been Reported: The 1544 Investigation of the Coronado Expedition* (Dallas: 2002).

Flint, Richard, and Shirley Cushing Flint (eds.), *Documents of the Coronado Expedition, 1539–1542* (Dallas: 2005).

Font, Fray Pedro, *Anza's Expedition of 1775–1776: Diary of Pedro Font*, ed. Frederick J. Teggart (Berkeley: 1913).

French, B. F. (ed.), "Memoir of Robert Cavelier de la Salle," in *Historical Collections of Louisiana*, Part One (New York: 1846).

Gaceta de México 2:23 (December 5, 1786).

Gálvez, Bernardo de, "Diario de Bernardo de Galvez y Gallardo," in *Noticias y reflexiones sobre la guerra que se tiene con los apaches en la provincia de Nueva España*, ed. Felipe Teixidor in Anales del Museo Nacional de Arqueología, Historia y Etnografía, series (época) 4, vol. 3 (Mexico City: 1925), appendix 2.

———, "Diario que yo D. Bernardo de Galvez Brigadier de los Reales Exercitos . . . , y encargado de la expedcion contra Panzacola y la Mobila formo . . . en ella," *Mercurio histórico y político*, June 1780, 198–220.

———, *Diario de las operaciones de la expedición contra la plaza de Panzacola concluida por las armas de S.M. católica* (Tallahassee: 1966 [1781]).

———, *Noticias y reflexiones sobre la guerra que se tiene con los apaches en la provincia de Nueva España*, ed. Felipe Teixidor, in *Anales del Museo Nacional de Arqueología, Historia y Etnografía*, series (época) 4, vol. 3 (Mexico City: 1925).

Gálvez, José de, *Informe sobre las rebeliones populares de 1767*, ed. Felipe Castro Gutiérrez (Mexico City: 1990).

Garcés, Francisco, *Diario de exploraciones en Arizona y California en los años de 1775 y 1776*, ed. John Galvin (Mexico City: 1968).

García, Genaro (ed.), *Documentos inéditos ó muy raros para la historia de México*, 36 vols. (Mexico City: 1905–11).

García Icazbalceta, Joaquín, *Colección de documentos para la historia de México*, 2 vols. (Mexico City: 1980).

Garcilaso de la Vega, Inca, *Comentarios reales de los Incas* (Lisbon: 1609).

———, *La Florida del Inca* (Lisbon: 1605).

Gayangos, Pascual de, *Cartas y relaciones de Hernán Cortés al Emperador Carlos V* (Paris: 1866).

Gazeta de Madrid, February 1781.

Gil, Juan, and Consuelo Valera (eds.), *Cartas de particulares a Colón y relaciones coetáneas* (Madrid: 1984).

Godoy, Manuel, *Memorias*, ed. Emilio la Parra and Elisabel Larriba (Alicante: 2008).

Goodwin, R. T. C., and Jerry R. Craddock, "Information Concerning Baltazar Dorantes de Carranza, November 5, 1573": escholarship.org/uc/item/27t9v1n5.

Gregg, Josiah, *Commerce of the Prairies* (Norman, OK: 1954 [1834]).

Hackett, Charles W. (ed.), *Historical Documents Relating to New Mexico, Nueva Vizcaya, and Approaches Thereto, 1773, Collected by Adolph F. A. Bandelier and Fanny R. Bandelier*, 3 vols. (Washington, DC: 1923).

——— (ed.), *Pichardo's Treatise on the Limits of Louisiana and Texas*, 5 vols. (Austin: 1946 [c. 1808–12]).

Hakluyt, Richard (ed.), *Voyages, Navigations, Trafiques, and Discoveries of the English Nation . . .* , 3 vols. (London: 1600).

Hatcher, Mattie Austin, "Joaquín de Arredondo's Report of the Battle of Medina, August 18, 1813. Translation," *Quarterly of the Texas State Historical Association* 11:3 (1908).

Herrera y Tordesillas, Antonio de, *Historia general de los hechos de los castellanos*, 4 vols. (Madrid: 1601–15).

Hidalgo, Miguel de, "Discurso de Miguel de Hidalgo" [1810]: biblioteca.tv/artman2/publish /1810_115/Discurso_de_Miguel_Hidalgo_al_Pueblo_de_Dolores_pa_604.shtml.

Hoffman, Fritz L., "The Mezquía Diary of the Alarcon Expedition into Texas, 1718," *Southwestern Historical Quarterly* 41:4 (1938), 312–23.

Imhoff, Brian (ed.), *The Diary of Juan Domínguez de Mendoza's Expedition into Texas, 1683–1684* (Dallas: 2002).

Innerarity, John, "Letters of John Innerarity: The Seizure of Pensacola by Andrew Jackson, November 7, 1814," *Florida Historical Society Quarterly* 9:3 (1931), 127–34.

James, James A. (ed.), *George Rogers Clark Papers 1771–1781: Collections of the Illinois State Historical Library*, vols. 8–9, *Virginia Series*, vols. 3–4 (Springfield, IL: 1912).

Journals of the Continental Congress, vol. 17 (Washington, DC: 1910).

Jovellanos, Gaspar Melchor de, "Elogio a Carlos III," in *Obras en prosa*, ed. José Caso González (Madrid: 1978).

Juan, Jorge, and Antonio de Ulloa, *Noticias secretas de América*, ed. Rufino Blanco-Fombona, 2 vols. (Madrid: 1918).

Keeler, Mary F. (ed.), *Sir Francis Drake's West Indian Voyage, 1585–1586* (London: 1981).

Kino, Eusebio Francisco, *Las misiones de Sonora y Arizona*, ed. Francisco Fernández del Castillo (Mexico City: 1989).

——, *Vida del P. Francisco J. Saeta, S. J: sangre misionera en Sonora*, ed. Ernest J. Burrus (Mexico City: 1961).

Lafora, Nicolás de, *The Frontiers of New Spain*, ed. Lawrence Kinnaird (Berkeley: 1958).

——, *Relación del viaje que hizo a los Presidios Internos situados en la frontera de la América Septentrional*, ed. Vito Alessio Robles (Mexico City: 1939).

Lanning, John Tate, "Cortes and His First Official Remission of Treasure to Charles V," *Revista de Historia de América* 2 (1938), 5–29.

Las Casas, Bartolomé de, *Historia de las Indias*, ed. Agustín Millares Carlo, 3 vols. (Mexico City and Buenos Aires: 1951).

Lexington Herald Leader, January 5, 2017.

London Magazine, April 1780.

López de Santa Anna, Antonio, *Mi historia militar y política* (Mexico City: 2016 [1905]).

Manning, William R. (ed.), *Diplomatic Correspondence of the United States. Inter-American Affairs, 1831–1860*, vol. 8 (Washington, DC: 1937).

Martínez, Bartolomé, "Relación de Bartolomé Martínez," in *The Spanish Jesuit Mission in Virginia, 1570–1572*, ed. Clifford M. Lews and Albert J. Loomie (Chapel Hill, NC: 1953), 148–65.

Martínez, José Luis (ed.), *Documentos Cortesianos*, 4 vols. (Mexico City: 1990).

Martínez Martínez, María del Carmen, "Cartas de Alonso del Castillo Maldonado desde México," in *Estudios sobre América, siglos XVI–XIX*, ed. Antonio Gutiérrez Escudero and María Luisa Laviana Cuetos (Seville: 2005), 89–106.

Martyr d'Anghiera, Peter [Peter, Martyr of Anghiera], *De Orbe Novo: The Eight Decades of Peter Martyr d'Anghera*, ed. and trans. Francis Augustus MacNutt, 2 vols. (New York and London: 1912).

——, *The Discovery of the New World in the Writings of Peter Martyr of Anghiera*, ed. Ernesto Lunardi et al., trans. Felix Azzola and Luciano F. Farina (Rome: 1992).

Mercado, Tomás, *Suma de tratos y contratos* (Madrid: 1587).

Mercurio histórico y político, June 1780.

Mier y Terán, Manuel de, *Texas by Terán: The Diary Kept by General Manuel de Mier y Terán on His 1828 Inspection of Texas*, ed. Jack Jackson and trans. John Wheat (Austin: 2000).

Morales Padrón, Francisco (ed.), *Diario de don Francisco de Saavedra* (Seville: 2004).

Morgado, Alonso de, *Historia de Sevilla: en la qual se contienen sus antiguedades* (Seville: 1587).

Moser, Harold D., David R. Hoth, and George H. Hoemann (eds.), *The Papers of Andrew Jackson*, vol. 4, 1816–1820 (Knoxville: 1994).

Mota y Escobar, Alonso de la, *Descripción geográfica de los reynos de Nueva Galicia, Nueva Vizcaya y Nuevo León.* Colección de Obras Facsimilares no. 1 ([Jalisco]: 1966 [1605]).

Mota y Padilla, Matías de la, *Historia de la conquista de la Nueva Galicia*, ed. José Ireneo Gutiérrez (Guadalajara: 1920 [1742]).

———, *Historia de la conquista de la provincia de la Nueva-Galicia* (Mexico City: 1870 [1742]).

Navarro, Martín de, "Reflexiones políticas luisiana," in *Documentos históricos de la Florida y la Luisiana, siglos XVI al XVII*, ed. Manuel Serrano y Sanz (Madrid: 1912).

Naylor, Thomas H., and Charles W. Polzer, *Pedro de Rivera and the Military Regulations for Northern New Spain, 1724–1729* (Tucson: 1988).

New York Times, October 19, 1898.

Núñez Cabeza de Vaca, Álvar, *La relación de dio Álvar Núñez* (Zamora: 1542).

Obregón, Baltasar, *Historia de los descubrimientos de la Nueva España*, ed. Eva María Bravo (Seville: 1997 [1584]).

O'Callaghan, E. B., et al. (eds.), *Documents Relative to the Colonial History of the State of New York*, 15 vols. (Albany: 1853–87).

O'Neil, Charles E., "The Louisiana Manifesto of 1768," *Political Science Reviewer* 19 (1990), 247–89.

Oré, Luis Gerónimo de, "Relación de Luis Gerónimo de Oré," in *The Spanish Jesuit Mission in Virginia, 1570–1572*, ed. Clifford M. Lews and Albert J. Loomie (Chapel Hill, NC: 1953), 170–92.

Otte, Enrique (ed.), *Cartas Privadas de Emigrantes a Indias, 1540–1616* (Seville: 1993).

Pacheco, Joaquín Francisco, and Francisco de Cárdenas (eds.), *Colección de documentos inéditos relativos al descubrimiento, conquista y colonización de las posesiones españolas en América . . .* 42 vols. (Madrid: 1864–84).

Palóu, Francisco, *Junípero Serra y las misiones de California. Relación histórica de la vida y apostólicas tareas del venerable fray Junípero Serra*, ed. José Luis Anta Félez (Madrid: 2002).

———, *The Life of Friar Juniper*, in *The Little Flowers of St. Francis of Assisi*, trans. W. Heywood (London: 1906).

———, *Noticias de la Nueva California*, 2 vols. (San Francisco: 1874).

Papers of the Continental Congress, 1774–1789.

Paso y Troncoso, Francisco del, *Epistolario de Nueva España*, 16 vols. (Mexico City: 1939–42).

Pedraza, Luis de, *Historia de Sevilla*, ed. F. Morales Padrón (Seville: [1979?] [1530s]).

Peña, José Enrique de la, *With Santa Anna in Texas: A Narrative of the Revolution*, ed. and trans. Carmen Perry (Austin: 1997 [1975]).

Pérez de Ribas, Andrés, *Historia de los triunfos de nuestra Santa Fé entre gentes las más bárbaras, y fieras de nuestro orbe* (Madrid: 1645).

Pérez de Villagrá, Gaspar, *Historia de la Nueva México, 1610*, ed. and trans. Miguel Encinias, Alfred Rodríguez, and Joseph P. Sánchez (Albuquerque: 1992).

———, *Historia de la Nueva México*, ed. Felipe I. Echenique March (Mexico City: 1993).

——, *Historia de la Nueva Mexico*, ed. Manuel M. Martín Rodríguez (Alcalá de Henares: 2010 [1610]).

——, *History of New Mexico*, ed. Gilberto Espinosa (Los Angeles: 1933).

Pérouse, Jean F. G. de la, "A Visit to Monterey in 1786: And a Description of the Indians of California," *California Historical Society Quarterly* 15:3 (1936), 216–23.

——, *Voyage de La Pérouse autour du monde, pendant les années 1785, 1786, 1787 et 1788*, 3 vols. (Paris: 1832).

Pino, Pedro Bautista, *The Exposition of the Province of New Mexico, 1812*, ed. and trans. Marc Simmons and Adrian Bustamante (Santa Fe: 1995).

Pittman, Capt. Phillip, *The Present State of European Settlements on the Mississippi*, ed. Frank H. Hodder (Cleveland: 1906).

Poinsett, Joel R., *Notes on Mexico Made in the Autumn of 1822* (New York: 1969).

Polo, Marco, *Travels*, ed. and trans. Ronald Latham (Harmondsworth: 1974 [c. 1298]).

Pontalba, Joseph Xavier de, "Memoir on Louisiana, Paris, September 15, 1801," in *A History of Louisiana*, ed. Alcée Fortier, 4 vols. (New York: 1904).

Portolá, Gaspar de, *Diary of Gaspar de Portolá During the California Expedition of 1769–1770*, ed. Donald Eugene Smith and Frederick J. Teggart (Berkeley: 1909).

Priestley, Herbert Ingram, *The Luna Papers, 1559–1561*, 2 vols. (Deland, FL: 1928).

Prieto, Guillermo, *Memorias de mis tiempos* (Mexico City: 1906).

Ramusio, Giovanni Battista, *Terzo volume delle navigationi et fiaggi* (Venice: 1556).

Recopilación de leyes de los reynos de Las Indias (Madrid: 1681).

Records of the House of Representatives, 34th Congress, 3rd Session, RG 233, National Archives, August 29, 1856.

Reid, Jennifer (ed.), *Religion, Postcolonialism, and Globalization: A Sourcebook* (New York: 2015).

Rivera, Pedro de, *Diario y derrotero de lo caminado, visto, y obcervado en el discurso de la visita general de Precidios, situados en las Provincias Ynternas de Nueva España* (Guatemala: 1736).

Rodríguez de Montalvo, Garci, *Las sergas de Esplandián* (Seville: 1510).

Rowland, Dunbar, and Patricia Galloway (eds.), *Mississippi Provincial Archives, French Dominion, 1749–1763*, 5 vols. (Baton Rouge: 1984).

Rubí, Marquis of, "Dictámenes que de orden del Exmo. Sor. Marqués de Croix . . . Expone el Mariscal de Campo Marqués de Rubí en orden a la mejor situación de los presidios . . . ," in *La frontera norte y la experiencia colonial*, ed. María del Carmen Velázquez (Mexico City: 1982), 27–89.

Ruxton, George F., *Adventures in Mexico and the Rocky Mountains* (London: 1847).

Saavedra, Francisco de, *Los decenios: autobiografía de un sevillano de la Ilustración* (Seville: 1995).

——, *Diario de don Francisco de Saavedra*, ed. Francisco Morales Padrón (Seville: 2004).

Seco Serrano, Carlos (ed.), *Cartas de Sor María de Jesús de Ágreda y de Felipe IV*, Epistolario España, vol. 4, Biblioteca de Autores Españoles, 2 vols. (Madrid: 1958).

Sempere-Martínez, Juan A. (ed.), and Damian Bacich (trans.), "Documents Concerning the Revolt of the Indians of the Province of New Mexico in 1680," 61–62: escholarship.org/uc/item/5xvot5bq.

Serra, Junípero, *Writings of Junípero Serra*, ed. Antonine Tibesar, 4 vols. (Washington, DC: 1955).

Serrano y Sanz, Manuel (ed.), *Documentos históricos de la Florida y la Luisiana, siglos XVI al XVII* (Madrid: 1912).

Servies, James A. (ed.), *The Log of HMS Mentor, 1780–1781: A New Account of the British Navy at Pensacola* (Pensacola: 1982).

Shafer, Philip K., Heather McMichael, and Jerry R. Craddock, "Analysis and Edition of 'Deposition of Several Tigua, Tano and Piro Indians Before Antonio de Otermín, Governor of New Mexico, Concerning a Suspected Revolt Against the Spanish' El Paso, July 19–August 1, 1683," 63ff: escholarship.org/uc/item/1n65q9fp.

Sigüenza, Fray José de, *Fundación del Monasterio de el Escorial por Felipe II*, ed. Miguel Sánchez y Pinillos (Madrid: 1881).

Smith, Buckingham (ed. and trans.), *Letter of Hernando de Soto and Memoir of Hernando de Escalante Fontaneda* (Washington, DC: 1854).

Smith, Paul (ed.), *Letters of Delegates to Congress, 1774–1789*, 26 vols. (Washington, DC: 1976–2000).

Solís de Merás, Gonzalo, *Pedro Menéndez de Avilés y la conquista de la Florida (1565). Memorial que hizo el Doc. Solís de Merás de todas la jornadas y sucesos del Adelantado Pedro de Menéndez*, ed. J. M. Gómez-Tabanera (Oviedo: 1990).

Stanger, Frank M., and Alan K. Brown, *Who Discovered the Golden Gate? The Explorer's Own Accounts* (San Mateo: 1969).

Symcox, Geoffrey, T. J. Cachey, and John C. Lucas (eds.), *Repertorium Columbianum*, vol. 12, *Italian Reports on America, 1493–1522: Accounts by Contemporary Observers* (Turnhout: 2002).

Tello, Antonio, *Crónica miscelánea* (Guadalajara: 1891).

Tió, Aurelio, *Nuevas fuentes para la historia de Puerto Rico* (San Germán: 1961).

Tonti, Henri de, *Dernières découvertes dans l'Amérique septentrionale de M. de la Salle La Salle* (Paris: 1697).

Torre y del Cerro, José de la, *El Inca Garcilaso de la Vega (Nueva Documentación)* (Seville: 2012 [1935]).

Turkanoff, Vasali, *Statement of My Captivity Among the Californians* (Los Angeles: 1953).

Valera, Consuelo (ed.), *Cristóbal Colón: Textos y documentos completos* (Madrid: 1982).

Vargas, Diego de, *To the Royal Crown Restored: The Journals of Don Diego de Vargas, New Mexico, 1692–94*, ed. John L. Kessell, Rick Hendricks, and Meredith D. Dodge (Albuquerque: 1995).

Varner, John Grier, and Jeanette Johnson Varner (ed. and trans.), *The Florida of the Inca* (Austin: 1951).

Vassall, Elizabeth, *The Spanish Journal of Lady Elizabeth Holland* (London: 1910).

Vega y Carpio, Félix Lope de, *El arte nuevo de hacer comedias* (Madrid: 1609).

Vespucci, Amerigo, *The Letters of Amerigo Vespucci and Other Documents Illustrative of His Career*, ed. Clements R. Markham (London: [1894]).

Vetancurt, Fray Agustín de, *Tratado de la ciudad de México* (Mexico City: 1982 [1698]).

Villiers du Terrage, Marc de, *Les dernières années de la Louisiane française* (Paris: 1905).

Viniegra, Juan Manuel, "Apuntamiento instructivo de la expedición que el illustrisimo señor Don Joseph de Galvez visitador general de Nueva España hizo . . . ," in *Crónicas del descubrimiento de la Alta California*, ed. Angela Cano Sánchez and Elena Mampei González (Barcelona: 1984).

Vitoria, Francisco de, *Political Writings*, ed. Anthony Pagden and Jeremy Lawrance (Cambridge: 1991).

Vizcaíno, Sebastián [ed. Geo B. Griffin], "Letter of Sebastián Vizcaíno to the King of Spain, Announcing His Return from the Exploration of the Coast of the Californias, as Far as the Forty-Second Degree of North Latitude—Dated 23d May, 1603," *Publications of the Historical Society of Southern California* 2:1 (1891), 68–73.

Voth, Henry R., *The Traditions of the Hopi*, Field Columbian Museum, pub. 96, vol. 8 (Chicago: 1903).

Whitaker, Arthur Preston, "Antonio de Ulloa," *Hispanic American Historical Review*, 15 (1935).

Wolff, Hans (ed.), *América: Early Maps of the New World* (Munich: 1992).

SECONDARY SOURCES

Achúe Zapata, José Enrique, "Some News About Don Garci López de Cárdenas," in *The Latest Word from 1540: People, Places, and Portrayals of the Coronado Expedition*, ed. Richard Flint and Shirley Cushing Flint (Albuquerque: 2011), 39–72.

Adorno, Rolena, "The Negotiation of Fear in Cabeza de Vaca's Naufragios," *Representations* 33 (1991), 163–99.

Adorno, Rolena, and Charles Patrick Pautz, *Alvar Núñez Cabeza de Vaca: His Account, His Life, and the Expedition of Pánfilo Narváez*, 3 vols. (Lincoln, NE, and London: 1999).

Aiton, Arthur S., *Antonio de Mendoza, First Viceroy of New Spain* (New York: 1967).

Alamán, Lucas, *Historia de Méjico desde los primeros movimientos que prepararon su independencia en el año de 1808, hasta la época presente*, 5 vols. (Mexico City: 1942 [1849–52]).

Alegría, Ricardo E., *Juan Garrido: El conquistador negro en las Antillas, Florida, México y California* (San Juan: 1990).

Alessio Robles, Vito, *Acapulco, Saltillo, y Monterrey en la historia y en la leyenda* (Mexico City: 1978).

———, *Coahuila y Texas: Desde la consumación de la independencia hasta el tratado de paz de Guadalupe Hidalgo*, 2 vols. (Mexico City: 1945).

Alexander, William D., *Papers of the Hawaiian Historical Society*, no. 1, *The Relations Between the Hawaiian Islands and Spanish America in Early Times* (1992).

Altman, Ida, *The War for Mexico's West: Indians and Spaniards in New Galicia, 1524–1550* (Albuquerque: 2010).

Anderson, Fred, *Crucible of War: The Seven Years' War and the Fate of Empire in British North America, 1754–1766* (New York and London: 2000).

Andrés Martín, Juan Ramón de, "La reacción realista ante las conspiraciones insurgentes en las fronteras y costas de Texas (1813–1816). Primeros antecedentes de la invasión de Javier Mina en 1817," *Signos Históricos* 18 (2007), 8–35.

Antolín Espino, María del Populo, "El virrey marqués de Cruillas," in *Los virreyes de Nueva España en el reinado de Carlos III*, vol. 1, ed. José Antonio Calderón Quijano (Seville: 1967).

Archer, Christon I., "Soldados en la escena continental: los expedicionarios españoles y la guerra de la Nueva España, 1810–1825," in *Fuerzas militares en Iberoamérica, siglos XVIII y XIX*, ed. Juan Ortiz Escamilla (Mexico City: 2005), 139–55.

Archibald, Robert, "Indian Labor at the California Missions: Slavery or Salvation?" *Journal of San Diego History* 24:2 (1978), 172–82.

Ashburn, Percy M., *The Ranks of Death: A Medical History of the Conquest of America* (New York: 1947).

Atkinson, A. T., *Papers of the Hawaiian Historical Society*, no. 4, *Early Voyagers of the Pacific Ocean* (1893).

Bacarisse, Charles A., "The Union of Coahuila and Texas," *Southwestern Historical Quarterly* 61:3 (1958), 341–49.

Bakewell, P. J., *Silver Mining and Society in Colonial Mexico: Zacatecas, 1546–1700* (Cambridge: 1971).

Baltasar, Juan Antonio, *Apostólicos Afanes de la Compañía de Jesús en la América Septentrional* (Barcelona: 1754).

Barker, Eugene C., *The Life of Stephen Austin: Founder of Texas* (Dallas: 1925).

Baroja, Pío, *Opiniones y paradojas*, ed. Miguel Sánchez-Ostiz (Madrid: 2000).

Barr, Juliana, *Peace Came in the Form of a Woman: Indians and Spaniards in the Texas Borderlands* (Chapel Hill, NC: 2007).

Bauer, Jack, *The Mexican War, 1846–1848* (New York: 1974).

Beer, William, "The Capture of Fort Charlotte," *Publications of the Louisiana Historical Society* 1:3 (1896), 31–34.

——, "The Surrender of Fort Charlotte, Mobile, 1780," *American Historical Review* 1:4 (1896), 696–99.

Beerman, Eric, "La bella criolla Felicitas de Saint Maxent, viuda de Bernardo de Gálvez, en España," in *Norteamérica a finales del siglo XVIII: España y los Estados Unidos* (Madrid: 2008), 281–96.

——, "The Death of an Old Conquistador: New Light on Juan de Oñate," *New Mexico Historical Review* 54:4 (1979), 305–19.

——, "Governor Bernardo de Gálvez's New Orleans Belle: Felicitas de St. Maxent," *Revista Española de Estudios Norteamericanos* 7 (1994), 39–43.

Bernabéu Albert, Salvador, "El 'Virrey de California' Gaspar de Portolá y la problemática de la primera gobernación californiana (1767–1769)," *Revista de Indias* 52:195/196 (1992), 271–95.

Bernabéu Albert, Salvador, and Daniel García de la Fuente, "Un Comanche en las Cortes de Cádiz: Los informed y trabajos de Ramos Arizpe," *Revista Historia de la Educación Latinoamericana* 16:23 (2014), 217–30.

Berner, Brad K. (ed.), *The Spanish-American War: A Documentary History with Commentaries* (Madison: 2014).

Beverley, Robert, *History and Present State of Virginia*, ed. Louis B. Wright (Chapel Hill, NC: 1947 [1705]).

Bishop, Morris, *The Odyssey of Cabeza de Vaca* (New York and London: 1933).

Black, Jeremy, *British Foreign Policy in an Age of Revolutions, 1783–1793* (Cambridge: 2000).

Blakeslee, Donald J., Richard Flint, and Jack T. Huges, "Una Barranca Grande, Recent Archaeological Evidence and a Discussion of Its Place in the Coronado Route," in *The Coronado Expedition to Tierra Nueva: The 1540–1542 Route Across the Southwest*, ed. Richard Flint and Shirley Cushing Flint (Boulder: 1997), 309–20.

Bobb, Bernard E., *The Viceregency of Antonio María Bucareli in New Spain, 1771–1779* (Austin: 1962).

Bolton, Herbert E., *Anza's California Expeditions* (Berkeley: 1930).

——, *Athanase de Mézières and the Louisiana-Texas Frontier, 1768–1780*, 2 vols. (Cleveland: 1914).

——, *Coronado: Knight of Pueblos and Plains* (Albuquerque: 1949).

———, *Rim of Christendom: A Biography of Eusebio Francisco Kino, Pacific Coast Pioneer* (New York: 1936).

Boneu Companys, Fernando, *Gaspar de Portolá: Explorer and Founder of California*, trans. Alan K. Brown (Lérida: 1983).

Borah, Woodrow, "Hernán Cortés y sus intereses marítimos en el Pacífico. El Perú y la Baja California," *Estudios de Historia Novohispana* 4:4 (1971), 2–28.

Boyd, Mark F., "Events at Prospect Bluff on the Apalachicola River, 1808–1818," *Florida Historical Quarterly* 16:2 (1937), 55–96.

Boyle, Susan C., *Los Capitalistas: Hispano Merchants and the Santa Fé Trail* (Albuquerque: 1997).

Bradburn, Douglas, and John C. Coombs, *Early Modern Virginia: Reconsidering the Old Dominion* (Charlottesville: 2011).

Brain, Geoffrey, introduction to *Final Report of the United States de Soto Expedition Commission*, ed. John R. Swanton (Washington, DC: 1985 [1939]).

Brasher, Nugent, "The Chichilticale Camp of Francisco Vázquez de Coronado," *New Mexico Historical Review* 82:4 (2007), 433–68.

Broom, Brian, "Mississippi's River Monsters," *Clarion-Ledger* (Jackson, MS), June 6, 2015.

Brown, Alan K., "The Various Journals of Juan Crespi," *The Americas* 21:4 (1965), 375–98.

Broyles, Bill, et al., *Last Water on the Devil's Highway: A Cultural and Natural History of Tinajas Altas* (Tucson: 2012).

Buckley, Eleanor Claire, "The Aguayo Expedition into Texas and Louisiana, 1719–1722," *Quarterly of the Texas State Historical Association* 15:1 (1911), 1–65.

Burgoyne, Bruce E., *Waldeck Soldiers of the American Revolutionary War* (Westminster: 1991).

Burrus, Ernest J., *Kino and Manje: Explorers of Sonora and Arizona* (Rome: 1971).

——— (ed. and trans.), *Kino's Plan for the Development of Pimería Alta, Arizona and Upper California. A Report to the Mexican Viceroy* (Tucson: 1961).

Bustamante, Carlos María de, *Suplemento a la historia de los tres siglos de Mexico, durante el gobierno español escrita por el padre Anre´s Cavo*, vol. 3 (Mexico City: 1838).

Calleja Leal, Guillermo, "Bernardo Gálvez y la intervención decisiva de la corona de España en la guerra de la independencia de los Estados Unidos de Norteamérica," *Revista de Historia Militar* 96 (2004), 147–218.

Callender, Charles, and Lee M. Kochems, "The North American Berdache," *Current Anthropology* 24:4 (1983), 443–70.

Campbell, Thomas J., "Eusebio Kino, 1644–1711," *Catholic Historical Review* 5:4 (1920), 353–76.

Cano Sánchez, Angela, and Elena Mampei González (eds.), *Crónicas del descubrimiento de la Alta California* (Barcelona: 1984).

Cantrell, Gregg, *Stephen F. Austin: Empresario of Texas* (Austin: 2016).

Carr, Raymond, *Spain, 1808–1975*, 2nd ed. (Oxford: 1982 [1966]).

Carrera, Magali M., *Imagining Identity in New Spain: Race, Lineage, and the Colonial Body in Portraiture and Casta Paintings* (Austin: 2003).

Carstens, Kenneth, and Nancy Carstens (eds.), *The Life of George Rogers Clark, 1751–1818: Triumphs and Tragedies* (Westport, CT: 2004).

Carstens, Nancy, "The Making of a Myth: George Rogers Clark and Teresa de Leyba," in *The Life of George Rogers Clark, 1751–1818: Triumphs and Tragedies*, ed. Kenneth Carstens and Nancy Carstens (Westport, CT: 2004), 60–79.

Castillo, Francisco Andújar, "El reformismo militar de Carlos III: mito y realidad," *Cuadrenos de Historia Moderna* 41 (2016), 337–54.

Castillo Gómez, Antonio, and Verónica Sierra Blas, *Cinco siglos de cartas: historia y prácticas epistolares en las épocas moderna y contemporánea* (Huelva: 2014).

Caughey, John, "Bernardo de Galvez and the English Smugglers on the Mississippi, 1777," *Hispanic American Historical Review* 12:1 (1932), 46–58.

———, "Willing's Expedition Down the Mississippi, 1778," *Louisiana Historical Quarterly* 15 (1932), 5–36.

Cervantes, Miguel de, *Don Quijote* (Madrid: 1605 and 1615).

Chandler, R. E., "Eyewitness History: O'Reilly's Arrival in Louisiana," *Louisiana History: Journal of the Louisiana Historical Association* 20:3 (1979), 317–24.

Chapman, Charles E., *A History of California: The Spanish Period* (New York: 1925).

Chávez, Angélico, "Nuestra Señora del Rosario: La Conquistadora," *New Mexico Historical Review* 23:2 (1948), 94–128.

———, *Our Lady of Conquest* (Santa Fe: 2010).

———, "Pohé-Yemo's Representative and the Pueblo Revolt of 1680," *New Mexico Historical Review* 42:2 (1967), 85–126.

Chávez, Thomas E., *Spain and the Independence of the United States: An Intrinsic Gift* (Albuquerque: 2002).

Chesnel, P., *Histoire du Cavelier de la Salle: exploration et conquête du Bassin du Mississippi* (Paris: 1901).

Chevalier, François, *Land and Society in Colonial Mexico: The Great Hacienda*, trans. Alvin Eustis (Berkeley and Los Angeles: 1970).

Chipman, Donald E., *Moctezuma's Children: Aztec Royalty Under Spanish Rule, 1520–1700* (Austin: 2005).

———, "The Oñate-Moctezuma-Zaldívar Families of Northern New Spain," *New Mexico Historical Review* 52:4 (1977), 297–310.

Chipman, Donald E., and Harriett Denise Joseph, *Spanish Texas, 1519–1821*, rev. ed. (Austin: 2010).

Christelow, Allan, "Contraband Trade Between Jamaica and the Spanish Main, and the Three Port Act of 1766," *Hispanic American Historical Review* 22:2 (1942), 309–43.

———, "French Interest in the Spanish Empire During the Ministry of the Duc de Choiseul, 1759–1771," *Hispanic American Historical Review* 21:4 (1941), 515–37.

Connell, Evan S., "A Masterpiece of Loathing," *Harper's*, September 2003, 41–53.

Cook, Noble D., *Born to Die: Disease and New World Conquest, 1492–1650* (Cambridge: 1998).

Cook, Sherburne F., "Historical Demography," in *The Handbook of North American Indians*, vol. 8, *California*, ed. Robert F. Heizer (Washington, DC: 1978), 91–98.

———, *The Population of the California Indians, 1769–1970* (Berkeley: 1976).

Cook, Warren L., *Flood Tide of Empire: Spain and the Pacific Northwest, 1543–1819* (New Haven: 1973).

Cortés, Hernán, *Cartas de relación*, ed. Ángel Delgado Gómez (Madrid: 1993).

Costello, Julia G., and David Hornbeck, "Alta California: An Overview," in *Colombian Consequences*, vol. 1, *Archeological and Historical Perspectives on the Spanish Borderlands West*, ed. David Hurst Thomas (Washington, DC: 1989), 303–31.

Covey, Cyclone, *Cabeza de Vaca's Adventures in the Unkown Interior of America* (Albuquerque: 1998).

Covington, James W., "Drake Destroys St. Augustine: 1586," *Florida Historical Quarterly* 44: 1–2 (1965), 81–93.

Craddock, Jerry R., and Barbara De Marco, "Ytinerario de la expeción de Juan de Oñate a Nuevo México 1597–1599": escholarship.org/uc/item/1f92f9b1.

Cuevas, Father Mariano, *Historia de la Nación Mexicana* (Mexico City: 1952).

Cummins, Light Townsend, "The Gálvez Family and Spanish Participation in the Independence of the United States of America," *Revista Complutense de Historia de América* 32 (2006), 179–96.

———, *Spanish Observers of the American Revolution, 1775–1783* (Baton Rouge and London: 1991).

D'Auvergne, Edmund, *Godoy, the Queen's Favorite* (Boston: 1913).

Danvilla y Collado, Manuel, *El reinado de Carlos III*, vol. 3 (Madrid: 1893).

Davies, Roy, "The Word 'Dollar' and the Dollar Sign": projects.exeter.ac.uk/RDavies/arian/dollar.html.

De Marco, Barbara, "Voices from the Archives I: Testimony of the Pueblo Indians on the 1680 Pueblo Revolt," *Romance Philology* 53 (1999), 375–448.

Díaz-Trechuelo Spínola, María Lourdes, María Luisa Rodríguez Baena, and Concepción Parajón Parody, "Don Antonio María Bucareli y Ursúa (1771–1779)," in *Los virreyes de Nueva España en el reinado de Carlos III*, vol. 1., ed. José Antonio Calderón Quijano (Seville: 1967), 383–658.

Din, Gilbert C., *The Canary Islanders of Louisiana* (Baton Rouge: 1988).

———, "Lieutenant Colonel Francisco Bouligny and the Malagueño Settlement at New Iberia, 1779," *Louisiana History* 17:2 (1976), 187–202.

———, "Protecting the 'Barrera': Spain's Defenses in Louisiana, 1763–1779," *Louisiana History: The Journal of the Louisiana Historical Association* 19:2 (1978), 183–211.

Dobyns, Henry, *Their Number Become Thinned: Native American Population Dynamics in Eastern North America* (Knoxville: 1983).

Dockstader, Frederick J., *The Kachina and the White Man: The Influences of White Culture on the Hopi Kachina Cult* (Albuquerque: 1985 [1954]).

Doggett, Carita, *Dr. Andrew Turnbull and the New Smyrna Colony of Florida* (Jacksonville: 1919).

Doherty, Herbert J., "Andrew Jackson vs the Spanish Governor: Pensacola 1821," *Florida Historical Quarterly* 34:2 (1955), 142–58.

Douglas, Alfred (Lord), *Two Loves* (London: 1894).

Douglass, William A., "On the Naming of Arizona," *Names* 27 (1979), 217–34.

Dowling, Lee, "*La Florida del Inca*: Garcilaso's Literary Sources," in *The Hernando de Soto Expedition: History, Historiography, and "Discovery" in the Southeast*, ed. Patricia Galloway (Lincoln, NE, and London: 2005), 98–154.

Duffen, William A., and William K. Hartmann, "The 76 Ranch Ruin and the Location of Chichilticale," in *The Coronado Expedition to Tierra Nueva: The 1540–1542 Route Across the Southwest*, ed. Richard Flint and Shirley Cushing Flint (Boulder: 1997), 158–75.

Dunn, William E., "The Apache Mission on the San Sabá River: Its Founding and Failure," *Southwestern Historical Quarterly* 17:4 (1914), 379–414.

Durand, José, "La biblioteca del Inca," *Nueva Revista de Filología Hispánica* 2:3 (1948), 239–64.

Dye, David H., "Reconstruction of the de Soto Expedition Route in Arkansas: The Missis-sippi Alluvial Plain," in *The Expedition of Hernando de Soto West of the Mississippi, 1541–1543. Proceedings of the de Soto Symposia 1988 and 1990*, ed. Gloria A. Young and Michael P. Hoffman (Fayetteville: 1993), 36–57.

Early, Ann M., "Finding the Middle Passage: The Spanish Journey from the Swamplands to Caddo County," in *The Expedition of Hernando de Soto West of the Mississippi, 1541–1543. Proceedings of the de Soto Symposia 1988 and 1990*, ed. Gloria A. Young and Michael P. Hoffman (Fayetteville: 1993).

Elliott, John H., *Empires of the Atlantic World: Britain and Spain in America, 1492–1830* (New Haven: 2006).

———, *The Old World and The New, 1492–1650* (Cambridge: 1970).

Enciso Contreras, José, and Ana Hilda Reyes Veyna, *Juanes de Tolosa, descubridor de las minas de Zacatecas. Información de méritos y servicios* (Zacatecas: 2002).

Engelhardt, Zephyrin, *The Missions and Missionaries of California*, 2 vols. (Santa Barbara: 1929).

Esdaile, Charles J., *Spain in the Liberal Age: From Constitution to Civil War, 1812–1939* (Oxford: 2000).

Espinosa, J. Manuel, "The Origin of the Penitentes of New Mexico: Separating Fact from Fiction," *Catholic Historical Review* 79 (1992), 454–77.

Ewen, Charles R., and John H. Hann, *Hernando de Soto Among the Apalachee: The Arche-ology of the First Winter Encampment* (Gainesville: 1998).

Fabie, Antonio María, *Viajes por España de Jorge de Einghen, del Baron León de Rosmithal de Blatna, de Francisco Guicciardini, y de Andrés Navajero* (Madrid: 1879).

Feherenbach, T. R., *Lone Star: A History of Texas and the Texans* (Boston: 2000 [1968]).

Ferrer del Río, Antonio, *Historia del reinado de Carlos III en España* (Madrid: 1856).

Finch, Boyd, "William Claude Jones: The Charming Rogue Who Named Arizona," *Journal of Arizona History* 31:4 (1990), 405–24.

Flint, Richard, *No Settlement, No Conquest: A History of the Coronado Entrada* (Albu-querque: 2008).

Flint, Richard, and Shirley Cushing Flint (eds.), *The Coronado Expedition to Tierra Nueva: The 1540–1542 Route Across the Southwest* (Boulder: 1997).

———, (eds.) *The Latest Word from 1540: People, Places, and Portrayals of the Coronado Expedition* (Albuquerque: 2011).

Fogelson, Raymond D., "Who Were the Aní-Kutáni? An Excursion into Cherokee Historical Thought," *Ethnohistory* 31:4 (1984), 255–63.

Folsom, Bradley, "Joaquín de Arredondo in Texas and Northeastern New Spain, 1811–1821," PhD dissertation, University of North Texas (2014).

Forbes, Jack D., "Melchior Díaz and the Discovery of Alta California," *Pacific Historical Review* 27:4 (1958), 351–57.

Forbes, James G., *Sketches, Historical and Topographical of the Floridas* (New York: 1821).

Fortier, Alcée, *A History of Louisiana*, 4 vols. (New York: 1904).

Foster, William C., *Historic Native Peoples of Texas* (Austin: 2008).

Fowler, Will, *Santa Anna of Mexico* (Lincoln, NE, and London: 2009).

Fowler, William M. Jr., *Empires at War: The French and Indian War and the Struggle for North America, 1754–1763* (New York: 2005).

Frederick, Julia C., "Luis de Unzaga and the Bourbon Reform in Spanish Louisiana, 1770–1776," PhD thesis, Louisiana State University (2000).

Fuentes Mares, José, *Santa Anna: aurora y ocaso de un comediante* (Mexico City: 1967).

Fuson, Robert H., *Ponce de León and the Spanish Discovery of Puerto Rico and Florida* (Blacksburg, VA: 2000).

Galindo y de Vera, León, *Historia, vicisitudes y política tradicional de España respecto de sus posesiones en las costas de África* (Madrid: 1884).

Galloway, Patricia (ed.), *The Hernando de Soto Expedition: History, Historiography, and "Discovery" in the Southeast* (Lincoln, NE, and London: 2005).

Gannon, Michael V., *The Cross in the Sand: The Early Catholic Church in Florida, 1513–1870* (Gainesville: 1965).

Garate, Donald T., *Juan Bautista de Anza: Basque Explorer in the New World, 1693–1740* (Reno and Las Vegas: 2003).

———, "Who Named Arizona? The Basque Connection," *Journal of Arizona History* 40:1 (1999), 53–82.

García Icazbalceta, Joaquín, *Don Fray Juan de Zumarrága. Primer obispo y arzobispo de México*, ed. Rafael Aguayo Spencer and Antonio Castro Leal, 4 vols. (Mexico City: 1944).

García Sáiz, María Concepción, "La imagen del mestizaje," in *El mestizaje americano*, exhibition catalog, Museo de América, Madrid, October–December 1985.

Gatschet, Albert S., *The Karankawa Indians, the Coast People of Texas*, with notes by Alice W. Oliver and Charles A. Hammond, Archaeological and Ethnological Papers of the Peabody Museum 1:2 (Cambridge, MA: 1891).

Gayarré, Charles, *Histoire de la Louisiane*, 2 vols. (New Orleans: 1847).

———, *History of Louisiana*, 2 vols. (New York: 1854).

Gerhard, Peter, "Pearl Diving in Lower California," *Pacific Historical Review* 25:3 (1956), 239–49.

Gil, Juan, "Álvar Núñez, el chamán blanco," *Boletín de la Real Academia Española* 3 (1993), 69–72.

Gillespie, Jeanne L., "The Codex of Tlaxcala: Indigenous Petitions and the Discourse of Heterarchy," *Hipertexto* 13 (2011), 59–74.

Gilman, Carolyn, "Why Did George Rogers Clark Attack Illinois?" *Ohio Valley History* 12:4 (2012), 3–18.

Giraud, Marcel, *Histoire de la Louisiane française*, 2 vols. (Paris: 1953).

Gómez Canedo, Lino, *Primeras exploraciones y poblamiento de Texas (1686–1694)* (Monterrey: 1968).

Gómez Imaz, Manuel, *Servicios patrioticos de la Suprema Junta en 1808 y relaciones hasta ahora inéditas* (Seville: 1908).

Gómez Ruiz, Manuel, and Vicente Alonso Juanola, *El ejército de los Borbones*, 7 vols. (Madrid: 1989–2006).

González, Javier Roberto, "Mal Hado-Malfado. Reminiscencias del *Palmerín de Olivia* en los *Naufragios* de Álvar Núñez Cabeza de Vaca," *Káñina* 23:2 (1999), 55–66.

González Cabrera Bueno, José, *Navegación especulativa y práctica* (Manila: 1734).

González Gómez, César, "March, Conquest, and Play Ball: The Game in the Mexican-American War, 1846–1848," *Base Ball* 5:2 (2011), 1–20.

González Rodríguez, Luis, "Hernán Cortés, la Mar del Sur y el descubrimiento de Baja California," *Anuario de Estudios Americanos* 42:1 (1985), 573–644.

González de la Vara, Martín, "La política del federalismo en Nuevo México (1821–1836)," *Historia Mexicana* 36:1 (1986), 81–111.

Goodwin, R. T. C., "Álvar Núñez Cabeza de Vaca and the Textual Travels of an American Miracle," *Journal of Iberian and Latin American Studies* 14:1 (2008), 1–12.

——, *Crossing the Continent, 1527–1540: The Story of the First African-American Explorer of the American South* (New York: 2008).

——, "'De lo que sucedió a los demás que entraron en las Indias': Álvar Núñez Cabeza de Vaca and the Other Survivors of Pánfilo Narváez's Expedition," *Bulletin of Spanish Studies* 84:2 (2007), 147–73.

——, *Spain: The Centre of the World, 1519–1682* (London and New York: 2015).

——, "'Yo quisiera esto más claro, e más larga claridad en ello.' Reconstrucion: Historiographical Misrepresentations of Africans and Native Americans, and the Law," *Bulletin of Spanish Studies* 92:2 (2015), 179–206.

Gough, Barry M., *Gunboat Frontier: British Maritime Authority and Northwest Coast Indians, 1846–1890* (Vancouver: 1984).

Gracy, David B., "'Just as I Have Written It:' A Study of the Authenticity of the Manuscript of José Enrique de la Peña's Account of the Texas Campaign," *Southwestern Historical Quarterly* 105:2 (2001), 254–91.

Grafton, Anthony, *New Worlds, Ancient Texts: The Power of Tradition and the Shock of Discovery* (Cambridge, MA: 1992).

Graullera Sanz, Vicente, *La esclavitude en Valencia en los siglos XVI y XVII* (Valencia: 1978).

Gray, David H., "Canada's Unresolved Maritime Boundaries," *Geomatica* 48:2 (1994), 131–44.

Grayson, Peter W., "The Release of Stephen F. Austin from Prison," *Quarterly of the Texas State Historical Association* 14:2 (1910), 155–63.

Greenburg, Amy S., *A Wicked War: Polk, Clay, Lincoln, and the 1846 US Invasion of Mexico* (New York: 2012).

Greene, Meg, *The Transcontinental Treaty, 1819: A Primary Source Examination of the Treaty Between the United States and Spain over the American West* (New York: 2006).

Griffin, Patricia C., *Mullet on the Beach: The Minorcans of Florida, 1768–1788* (Jacksonville: 1990).

Grivas, Ted, "General Stephen Watts Kearny and the Army of the West," MA thesis, University of Southern California (1953).

Guedea, Virginia, "The Old Colonialism Ends, the New Colonialism Begins," in *The Oxford History of Mexico*, ed. Michael C. Meyer and William H. Beezley (Oxford: 2000), 277–300.

Guerrero Acosta, José Manuel, "De las trincheras de Gibraltar a las arenas de Pensacola: el ejército español en la independencia de los Estados Unidos," *Coming to the Americas*, 28th Congress of the International Commission of Military History, Norfolk (2003).

Guillén Robles, F., *Historia de Málaga y su provincia* (Málaga: 1873).

Gutiérrez Escudero, Antonio, and María Luisa Laviana Cuetos (eds.), *Estudios sobre América, siglos XVI-XIX. La Asociación Española de Americanistas en su vegésimo aniversario* (Seville: 2005).

Hackel, Steven W., *Children of Coyote, Missionaries of Saint Francis: Indian-Spanish Relations in Colonial California, 1769–1850* (Chapel Hill, NC: 2005).

——, *Junipero Serra: California's Founding Father* (New York: 2013).

Hackett, Charles, and Charmion Clair Shelby, *Revolt of the Pueblo Indians of New Mexico and Otermin's Attempted Reconquest, 1680–1682*, 2 vols. (Albuquerque: 1942).

Hadley, Diana, Thomas H. Naylor, and Mardish K. Schuetz-Miller (eds.), *The Presidio and Militia on the Northern Frontier of New Spain: A Documentary History*, vol 2., pt. 2, *The Central Corridor and the Texas Corridor, 1700–1765* (Tucson: 1997).

Hall, Gwendolyn Midlo, *Africans in Colonial Louisiana: The Development of Afro-Creole Culture in the Eighteenth Century* (Baton Rouge: 1992).

Hämäläinen, Pekka, *The Comanche Empire* (New Haven: 2009).

Hamill, Hugh M., *The Hidalgo Revolt: Prelude to Mexican Independence* (Gainesville: 1966).

Hammond, George, "Oñate and the Founding of New Mexico," *New Mexico Historical Review*, 1:4 (NM: 1926).

Hammond, George P., and Agapito Rey (eds.), *Don Juan de Oñate: Colonizer of New Mexico, 1595–1628*, 2 vols., Coronado Cuarto Centennial Publications, 1540–1940, vols. 5 and 6 (Albuquerque: 1953).

Hanna, Warren L., "Legend of the Nicasios: The Men Drake Left Behind at Hova Albion," *California History* 58:2 (1979), 154–65.

Hartmann, William K., "Pathfinder for Coronado: Reevaluating the Mysterious Journey of Marcos de Niza," in *The Coronado Expedition to Tierra Nueva: The 1540–1542 Route Across the Southwest*, ed. Richard Flint and Shirley Cushing Flint (Boulder: 1997), 61–83.

Harvey, John P., *Muslims in Spain, 1500–1614* (Chicago: 2005).

Hass, Lisbeth, "Contested Eden: California Before the Gold Rush," *California History* 76:2–3 (1997), 331–55.

Heidler, David S., and Jeanne T. Heidler, *Old Hickory's War: Andrew Jackson and the Quest for Empire* (Baton Rouge: 2003 [1996]).

Henderson, Alice Corbin, *Brothers of Light: Penitentes of the Southwest* (New York: 1937).

Henige, David, "Primary Source by Primary Source? On the Role of Epidemics in New World Depopulation," *Ethnohistory* 33:3 (1986), 293–312.

Hernández Sánchez-Barba, Marino, "Bernardo de Gálvez, militar y político en la Florida occidental (Un bicentenario y una reparación histórica)," *Arbor* 109:452 (1981), 41–54.

Herodotus, *The Histories*, Bk. 4, ed. Robert B. Strassler, trans. Andrea L. Purvis (New York: 2007).

Herrera, Carlos, "Infidelity and the Presidio Captain: Adultery and Honor in the Lives of María Rosa Tato y Anza and José Antonio Vildósola, Sonora, New Spain, 1769–1783," *Journal of the History of Sexuality* 15:2 (2006), 204–27.

Herrera Navarro, Jerónimo (ed.), *Rodríguez de Campomanes, epistolario (1778–1802)*, 2 vols. (Madrid: 2004).

———, *Juan Bautista de Anza: The King's Governor in New Mexico* (Norman, OK: 2015).

Hess, Dan, "The Bankrupt Irishman Who Created the Dollar Sign by Accident," *Atlas Obscura*, November 23, 2015.

Heusinger, Edward W., *Early Explorations and Mission Establishments in Texas* (San Antonio: 1936).

Higuera, Ernesto, *Hidalgo: reseña biográfica con una iconografía del iniciador de nuestra independencia* (Mexico City: 1955).

Hilt, Douglas, *The Troubled Trinity: Godoy and the Spanish Monarchs* (Tuscaloosa: 1987).

Hodge, Frederick W., George P. Hammond, and Agapito Rey (eds. and trans.), *Fray Alonso de Benavides' Revised Memorial of 1634*, Coronado Cuarto Centennial Publications, 1540–1940, vol. 4 (Albuquerque: 1945).

Hoffman, Paul E., *Florida's Frontiers* (Bloomington: 2002).

——, *Luisiana* (Madrid: 1992).

——, "Narváez and Cabeza de Vaca in Florida," in *The Forgotten Centuries: Indians and Europeans in the American South, 1521-1704*, ed. Charles Hudson and Carmen Chaves Tesser (Athens, GA: 1994), 50-73.

——, *A New Andalucia and a Way to the Orient: The American Southeast During the Sixteenth Century* (Baton Rouge: 1990).

——, *Spain and the Roanoke Voyages* (Raleigh: 1987).

Holmes, Jack, *Honor and Fidelity: The Louisiana Infantry Regiment and the Louisiana Militia Companies, 1766-1821* (Birmingham, AL: 1965).

Hopkins, James F., and Mary W. M. Hargreaves, *The Papers of Henry Clay*, vol. 2 (Lexington, KY: 1961).

Hordes, Stanley M., *To the End of the Earth: A History of the Crypto-Jews of New Mexico* (New York: 2005).

Horowitz, David L, *Ethnic Groups in Conflict* (Los Angeles: 1983).

Howard, David, *Conquistador in Chains: Cabeza de Vaca and the Indians of the Americas* (Tuscaloosa: 1997).

Hudson, Charles, *The Juan Pardo Expeditions: Exploration of the Carolinas and Tennessee, 1566-1568* (Washington, DC: 1990).

Hughes, Anne E., "The Beginnings of Spanish Settlement in the El Paso District," in *University of California Publications in History* (Berkeley: 1914).

Ife, B. W., *Reading and Fiction in Golden-Age Spain: A Platonic Critique and Some Picaresque Replies* (Cambridge: 1985).

Ife, B. W., and R. T. C. Goodwin, "'Many Expert Narrators': History and Fiction in the Spanish Chronicles of the New World," in *Remapping the Rise of the Novel*, ed. Jenny Mander (Oxford: 2007).

Ives, Ronald L., "The Last Journey of Melchior Díaz," *Journal of Geography* 59 (1960), 61-66.

Ivey, James E., "'The Greatest Misfortune of All': Famine in the Province of New Mexico, 1667-1672," *Journal of the Southwest* 36:1 (1994), 76-100.

Jackson, Hal, *Following the Royal Road: A Guide to the Historic Camino Real de Tierra Adentro* (Albuquerque: 2006).

Jackson, Robert H., *Indian Population Decline: The Missions of Northwestern New Spain, 1687-1840* (Albuquerque: 1994).

James, James A., "Oliver Pollock, Financier of the Revolution in the West," *Mississippi Valley Historical Review* 16:1 (1929), 67-80.

——, *Oliver Pollock: The Life and Times of an Unknown Patriot* (New York: 1937).

Jiménez, Alfredo, *El Gran Norte de México: Una frontera imperial en la Nueva España (1540-1820)* (Madrid: 2006).

John, Elizabeth A. H., "Bernardo de Gálvez on the Apache Frontier: A Cautionary Note for Gringo Historians," *Journal of Arizona History* 29:4 (1988), 427-30.

Jones, Oakah L., *Los Paisanos: Spanish Settlers on the Northern Frontier of New Spain* (Norman, OK: 1996).

Kagan, Richard, *Lawsuits and Litigants in Castile, 1500-1800* (Chapel Hill, NC: 1981).

Kagan, Richard L., and Geoffrey Parker (eds.), *Spain, Europe and the Atlantic World: Essays in Honour of John Elliot* (Cambridge: 1995).

Kamen, Henry, *Philip V of Spain: The King Who Reigned Twice* (New Haven: 2001).

———, *Spain, 1469–1714: A Society in Conflict* (London: 1983).

Katzew, Ilona, *Casta Painting: Images of Race in Eighteenth-Century Mexico* (New Haven: 2004).

Kealhofer, Lisa, "The Evidence for Demographic Collapse in California," in *Bioarchaeology of Native American Adaptation in the Spanish Borderlands*, ed. Brenda J. Baker and Lisa Kealhofer (Gainesville: 1996).

Keleher, William A., *Turmoil in New Mexico* (Santa Fe: 2007 [1952]).

Kelly, Edith Louise, and Mattie Austin Hatcher, "Tadeo Ortiz de Ayala and the Colonization of Texas, 1822–1833: IV," *Southwestern Historical Quarterly* 32:4 (1929), 311–43.

Kelsey, Harry, "The California Armada of Juan Rodríguez Cabrillo," *Southern California Quarterly* 61:4 (1979), 313–36.

Kendrick, T. D., *Mary of Ágreda: The Life and Legend of a Spanish Nun* (London: 1967).

Kenmotsu, Nancy Adele, James E. Bruseth, and James E. Corbin, "Moscoso and the Route in Texas: A Reconstruction," in *The Expedition of Hernando de Soto West of the Mississippi, 1541–1543. Proceedings of the de Soto Symposia 1988 and 1990*, ed. Gloria A. Young and Michael P. Hoffman (Fayetteville: 1993), 106–31.

Kessell, John L., "Anza, Indian Fighter: The Spring Campaign of 1766," *Journal of Arizona History* 9:3 (1968), 155–63.

———, "Esteban Clemente: Precursor of the Pueblo Revolt," *El Palacio* 86:4 (1980–81), 16–17.

———, *Mission of Sorrows: Jesuit Guevaví and the Pimas, 1691–1767* (Tucson: 1970).

———, *Spain in the Southwest: A Narrative History of Colonial New Mexico, Arizona, Texas, and California* (Norman, OK: 2002).

Kinnaird, Lawrence, *Spain in the Mississippi Valley, 1765–1794*, 3 parts (Washington, DC: 1949).

———, "The Western Fringe of Revolution," *Western Historical Quarterly* 7:3 (1976), 253–70.

Knaut, Andrew L., *The Pueblo Revolt of 1680: Conquest and Resistance in Seventeenth-Century New Mexico* (Norman, OK: 1995).

Knight, Alan, *Mexico: The Colonial Era* (Cambridge: 2002).

Koskenniemi, Martti, "Empire and International Law: The Real Spanish Contribution," *University of Toronto Law Journal* 61:1 (2011), 1–36.

Ladd, Edmund J., "Zuni on the Day the Men in Metal Arrived," in *The Coronado Expedition to Tierra Nueva: The 1540–1542 Route Across the Southwest*, ed. Richard Flint and Shirley Cushing Flint (Boulder: 1997), 225–33.

Lafaye, Jacques, *Quetzalcoatl and Guadalupe: The Formation of Mexican National Consciousness, 1531–1813* (Chicago: 1976).

Lárraga, Maribel, "La mística de la feminidad en la obra de Juan Villagutierre Sotomayor: historia de la conquista pérdida y restauración del reyno y provincia de la Nueva México en la América Septentrional (1698)," PhD thesis, University of New Mexico (1999).

Laughton, J. K., "Jenkins' Ear," *English Historical Review* 4:16 (1889), 741–49.

Lawson, Edward W., "What Became of the Man Who Cut Off Jenkins' Ear?" *Florida Historical Quarterly* 37:1 (1958), 33–42.

Lee, Kun Jong, "Pauline Typology in Cabeza de Vaca's *Naufragios*," *Early American Literature* 34:3 (1999), 241–62.

Lejarza, Fray Fidel de, "Escenas de martirio en el río San Sabá," *Archivo Ibero-Americano* 12 (1943), 441–95.

León, Alonso de, *Historia de Nuevo León con noticias sobre Coahuila, Tejas, Nuevo México* (Mexico City: 1909).

León-Portilla, Miguel, *Hernán Cortés y la Mar del Sur* (Madrid: 2005).

Leonard, Irving, *Books of the Brave* (Cambridge, MA: 1949).

Lewis, James A., "Cracker: Florida Style," *Florida Historical Quarterly* 63:2 (1984), 184–204.

Lews, Clifford M., and Albert J. Loomie, *The Spanish Jesuit Mission in Virginia, 1570–1572* (Chapel Hill, NC: 1953).

Licht, Fred, "Goya's Portrait of the Royal Family," *Art Bulletin* 49:2 (1967), 127–28.

Lockey, Joseph B., "Florida Banditti, 1783," *Florida Historical Quarterly* 24:2 (1945), 87–107.

Long, Edward, *The History of Jamaica or General Survey of the Modern State of the Island*, 2 vols. (London: 1774).

López de Gómara, Francisco, *Conquista de México*, ed. José Luis de Rojas (Madrid: 2001).

———, *Historia general de las Indias* (Saragossa: 1552).

López-Herrera Sánchez, Juan, *La insula inefable* (Madrid: 2017).

Luxenberg, Alisa, "Further Light on the Critical Reception of Goya's 'Family of Charles IV' as Caricature," *Artibus et Historiae* 23:46 (2002), 179–82.

Lynch, John, *Bourbon Spain: 1700–1808* (Cambridge, MA: 1989).

Lyon, Eugene, *The Enterprise of Florida: Pedro Menéndez de Avilés and Spanish Conquest of 1565–1568* (Gainesville: 1976 [1974]).

Macaulay, Neill, "The Army of New Spain and the Mexican Delegation to the Spanish Cortes," in *Mexico and the Spanish Cortes, 1810–1822: Eight Essays*, ed. Nettie Lee Benson (Austin: 1966).

Madariaga, Salvador de, *El auge y ocaso del imperio español en América* (Madrid: 1986 [1939]).

Mahan, Alfred T., *Lessons of the War with Spain, and Other Articles* (Boston: 1899).

Mann, Kristin D., *The Power of Song: Music and Dance in the Mission Communities of Northern New Spain, 1590–1810* (Stanford: 2010).

Mansfield, Edward D., *The Mexican War: A History of Its Origin* (New York: 1849).

Maravall, José, *Antiguos y modernos* (Madrid: 1966).

Margry, Pierre, *Découverte et établissements des Français dans l'ouest et dans le sud de L'Amérique septentrionale, 1614–1754*, 5 vols. (Paris: 1879).

Marín Tello, María Isabel, "El castigo ejemplar a los indígenas en la época de José de Gálvez en el virreinato de Nueva España," *Cuadernos de la historia* 31 (2009), 27–43.

Márquez Padorno, Margarita, *Miguel Moya Ojanguren (1856–1920): talento, voluntad y reforma en la prensa española* (Madrid: 2015).

Martín Rodríguez, Manuel, "'Aqui fue Troya nobles caualleros': ecos de la tradición clásica y otros intertextos en la *Historia de la Nueva Mexico*, de Gaspar Pérez de Villagrá," *Silva* 4 (2005), 139–208.

———, *Gaspar de Villagrá: legista, soldado y poeta* (León: 2009).

Martínez, María Elena, *Genaological Fictions: Limpieza de Sangre, Religion, and Gender in Colonial Mexico* (Stanford: 2008).

Mathes, Michael, "Asesinato y descubrimiento: el motín de Fortún Ximénez y la incorporación de California al Imperio Español," *Meyibó* 1 (1990), 31–49.

———, "The Expedition of Juan Rodríguez Cabrillo, 1542–1543: An Historiographical Reexamination," *Southern California Quarterly* 76:3 (1994), 247–53.

Matter, Robert Allen, "Missions in the Defense of Spanish Florida, 1566–1710," *Florida Historical Quarterly* 54:1 (1975), 18–38.

Maughan, Scott Jarvis, "Francisco Garcés and New Spain's Northwestern Frontier, 1768–1781," PhD dissertation, University of Utah (1968).

Maura, Juan, *El gran burlador de América: Álvar Núñez Cabeza de Vaca* (Valencia: 2008).

——, "Los 'Naufragios' de Alvar Núñez Cabeza de Vaca: o el arte de la automitificación," PhD thesis, University of New Mexico (1987).

McAlister, L. N., "Pensacola During the Second Spanish Period," *Florida Historical Quarterly* 37:3–4 (1959), 281–327.

——, *Spain and Portugal in the New World, 1492–1700* (Minneapolis: 1989).

McCarty, Kieran, "Bernardo de Galvez on the Apache Frontier: The Education of a Future Viceroy," *Journal of the Southwest* 36:2 (1994), 103–30.

McConnell, Michael N., *Army and Empire: British Soldiers on the American Frontier, 1758–1775* (Omaha: 2004).

McDonald, Dedra S., "Intimacy and Empire: Indian-African Interaction in Spanish Colonial Mexico, 1500–1800," *American Indian Quarterly* 22:1–2 (1998), 134–56.

McMichael, Francis A., *Atlantic Loyalties: Americans in Spanish West Florida, 1785–1810* (Athens, GA: 2008).

Meighan, Clement W., "Indians and California Missions," *Southern California Quarterly* 69:3 (1987), 187–201.

Melville, Elinor G., *A Plague of Sheep: Environmental Consequences of the Conquest of Mexico* (Cambridge: 1998).

Memoria del VI Simposio de Historia y Antropología (Hermosillo: 1981).

Mena Marqués, Manuela B., "Reflections on Goya's Portaits," in *Goya: The Portraits,* exhibition catalog, ed. Xavier Bray, National Gallery, London, October 2015 to January 2016.

Meyer, Michael C., and William H. Beezley (eds.), *The Oxford History of Mexico* (Oxford: 2000).

Milanich, Jerald T., and Susan Milbrath (eds.), *First Encounters: Spanish Explorations in the Caribbean and the United States, 1492–1570* (Gainesville: 1989).

Millett, Nathaniel, "Britain's Occupation of Pensacola and America's Response: An Episode of the War of 1812 in the Southeastern Borderlands," *Florida Historical Quarterly* 84:2 (2005), 229–55.

——, *The Maroons of Prospect Bluff and Their Quest for Freedom in the Atlantic World* (Gainesville: 2013).

Mitchell, Chuck, transcript from comments, Florida Archaeological Council, Jacksonville Forum (1989).

Mitchem, Jeffrey M., "Artifacts of Exploration: Archaeological Evidence from Florida," in *First Encounters: Spanish Explorations in the Caribbean and the United States, 1492–1570,* ed. Jerald T. Milanich and Susan Milbrath (Gainesville: 1989), 99–109.

Molina Martínez, Miguel, "La participación canaria en la formación y reclutamiento del batallón de Luisiana," in *IV Coloquio de historia canario-americana (1980),* ed. Francisco Morales Padrón, 2 vols. (Salamanca: 1982), 133–244.

Moncada, Maya, *El ingeniero Miguel Constanzó: un militar ilustrado en la Nueva España del siglo XVIII* (Mexico City: 1994).

Montané Martí, Julio César, and Carlos Lazcano Sahagún, *El descubrimiento de California: las expediciones de Becerra y Grijalva a la Mar del Sur* (Ensenada: 2004).

Montero de Pedro, José, *Españoles en Nueva Orleans y Luisiana* (Madrid: 1979).

Moore, John P., "Antonio de Ulloa: A Profile of the First Spanish Governor of Louisiana," *Louisiana History: The Journal of the Louisiana Historical Association* 8:3 (1967), 189–218.

——, *Revolt in Louisiana: The Spanish Occupation, 1766–1770* (Baton Rouge: 1976).

Morales Folguera, José Miguel, *Arquitectura y urbanismo hispanoamericano en Luisiana y Florida Occidental* (Málaga: 1987).

Morales Padrón, Francisco (ed.), *IV Coloquio de historia canario-americana (1980)*, 2 vols. (Salamanca: 1982).

——, *Historia de Sevilla: la ciudad del quinientos* (Seville: 1989).

Morineau, Michel, *Incroyables gazettes et fabuleux métaux: les retours des trésors américains d'après les gazettes hollandaises (XVIᵉ–XVIIIᵉ siècles)* (London and New York: 1985).

Morison, Samuel E., *Admiral of the Ocean Sea: A Life of Christopher Columbus* (Boston: 1942).

——, *The European Discovery of America: The Northern Voyages, 1500–1700* (New York: 1971).

Morris, John M., "The Policy of the British Cabinet in the Nootka Crisis," *English Historical Review* 70:277 (1955), 562–80.

Morte Acín, Ana, *Misticismo y conspiración: Sor María de Ágreda en el reinado de Felipe IV* (Saragossa: 2010).

Muhlstein, Anka, *La Salle: Explorer of the North American Frontier*, trans. Willard Wood (New York: 2013).

Munro-Fraser, J. P., *History of Marin County, California* (San Francisco: 1880).

Murga Sanz, Vicente, *Juan Ponce de León: fundador y primer gobernador del pueblo puertorriqueño; descubridor de la Florida y del Estrecho de Bahamas* (Barcelona: 1971 [1959]).

Narrett, David E., *Adventurism and Empire: The Struggle for Mastery in the Louisiana Florida Borderlands* (Chapel Hill, NC: 2015).

Navagero, Andrea, "Viajes por España" and "Cartas," in *Viajes por España de Jorge de Einghen, del Baron León de Rosmithal de Blatna, de Francisco Guicciardini, y de Andrés Navajero*, ed. and trans. Antonio María Fabie (Madrid: 1879).

Navarro García, Luis, *Don José de Gálvez y la Comandancia General de la Pronvicias Internas del norte de Nueva España* (Seville: 1964).

——, "El Virrey Marqués de Croix (1766–1771)," in *Los virreyes de Nueva España en el reinado de Carlos III*, 3 vols., ed. José Antonio Calderón Quijano, vol. 2 (Seville: 1967), 159–381.

——, "The North of New Spain as a Political Problem in the Eighteenth Century," in *New Spain's Far Northern Frontier: Essays on Spain in the American West, 1540–1811*, ed. David J. Weber (Dallas: 1979), 201–15.

——, *La política americana de José de Gálvez* (Málaga: 1998).

——, *Las reformas borbónicas en América: el plan de intendencias y su aplicación* (Seville: 1995).

Nequatewa, Edmund, *Truth of a Hopi* (Flagstaff: 1967).

New Mexico Union (Santa Fe), April 17, 1873.

Nugent, Walter, *Habits of Empire: A History of American Expansion* (New York: 2008).

Nunemaker, J. Horace, "The Bouligny Affair in Louisiana," *Hispanic American Historical Review* 25:3 (1945), 338–63.

Odom, Wesley S., *The Longest Siege of the American Revolution: Pensacola* ([Pensacola]: 2009).

Ogg, Frederic Austin, *The Old Northwest: A Chronicle of the Ohio Valley and Beyond*, vol. 19 (New Haven: 1921).

Olivera, Ruth R., and Liliane Crété, *Life in Mexico Under Santa Anna, 1822–1855* (Norman, OK: 1991).

Orellano Norris, Lola, "General Alonso de León's Expedition Diaries into Texas (1686–1690): A Linguistic Analysis of the Spanish Manuscripts with Semi-Paleographic Transcriptions and English Translations," PhD thesis, Texas A&M University (2010).

——, *Alonso de León's Expedition into Texas, 1686–1690* (College Station, TX: 2017).

Ortiz Escamilla, Juan, *Fuerzas militares en Iberoamérica, siglos XVIII y XIX* (Mexico City: 2005).

Otte, Enrique, *Cartas privadas de emigrantes a Indias, 1540–1616* (Seville: 1988).

Padgett, James A. (ed.), "Bernardo de Gálvez's Siege of Pensacola in 1781 (as Related in Robert Farmar's Journal)," *Louisiana Historical Quarterly* 26 (1943), 311–29.

Palmer, Frederick, *Clark of the Ohio: A Life of George Rogers Clark* (New York: 1930).

Paniagua Pérez, Jesús, "El proyecto fracasado del último obispo del norte de la Nueva España. Hacia la creación de la diócesis de Nuevo México," *Anuario de Estudios Americanos* 70:1 (2013), 99–127.

Paoli Bolio, Franciso José, "Miguel Ramos Arizpe y sus argumentos independentistas en las Cortes de Cádiz," in *Las Cortes de Cádiz, la Constitución de 1812 y las independencias nacionales en América*, ed. Antonio Colomer Viadel (Valencia: 2012), 327–37.

Parker, Geoffrey, *The Grand Strategy of Philip II* (New Haven and London: 1998).

Parmentier, Richard J., "The Mythological Triangle: Poseyemu, Montezuma, and Jesus in the Pueblos," in *The Handbook of American Indians*, vol. 9, *The Southwest*, ed. Alfonso Ortiz (Washington, DC: 1979), 609–23.

Parry, J. H., *The Audiencia of New Galicia in the Sixteenth Century: A Study in Colonial Government* (Cambridge: 1968).

Pearce, Edward, *Pitt the Elder: Man of War* (London: 2010).

Pearson, Charles E., and Paul E., Hoffman, *The Last Voyage of El Nuevo Constante: The Wreck and Recovery of an Eighteenth-Century Spanish Ship off the Louisiana Coast* (Baton Rouge: 1995).

Peña, Salvador Ignacio de la, "Convite Evangélico á compasión y Socorro de la Viña del Señor," University of Arizona Library, Tucson, microfilm 71.

Pennington, Campbell W., *The Material Culture: The Pima Bajo of Central Sonora, Mexico* (Salt Lake City: 1980).

Penyak, Lee M., "Safe Harbors and Compulsory Custody: Casas de Depósito in Mexico, 1750–1865," *Hispanic American Historical Review* 79:1 (1999), 83–99.

Perea, Fray Esteban de, *Verdadera relación de la grandiosa conversión qué ha habido en el Nuevo México* (Seville: 1632).

Pérez, Joseph, *La revolución de las comunidades de Castilla (1520–1521)* (Madrid: 1977 [1970]).

Perrupato, Sebastián, "Antiguos y modernos en la universidad española de la segunda mitad del siglo XVIII. Avances de secularización en el plan de reforma universitario elaborado por Gregorio Mayans y Siscar (1767)," *Historia y sociedad* 27 (2014), 165–88.

Phares, Ross, *Cavalier in the Wilderness* (Baton Rouge: 1952).

Polk, Dora, *The Island of California: A History of the Myth* (Lincoln, NE: 1991).

Pollock, Oliver, *To the Honourable the Legislature of Virginia* (1811).

Porras Barrenechea, Raúl, *El Inca Garcilaso en Montilla (1561–1614)* (Lima: 1955).

Porras Muñoz, Guillermo, "Acta de matrimonio de Bernardo de Gálvez y Felicitas Saint Maxent," *Boletín del Archivo General de la Nación* (Mexico) 16:2 (1945), 277–81.

——, *Bernardo de Gálvez* (Madrid: 1952).

——, "Diego de Ibarra y la Nueva España," *Estudios de Historia Novohispana* 2:2 (1968), 1–28.

——, "Hace doscientos años: 'México llorosa . . . ,'" *Estudios de Historia Novohispana* 10:10 (1991), 309–24.

——, "Martín López, carpintero de Ribera," *Revista de Indias* 31–32 (1948), 307–29.

Powell, P. W., and María L. Powell, *War and Peace on the North Mexican Frontier: A Documentary Record*, vol. 1 (Madrid: 1971).

Pradeau, Alberto Francisco, "Cerro de las bolas y planchas de plata. Maravilla del siglo XVIII," in *Memoria del VI Simposio de Historia y Antropología* (Hermosillo: 1981), 106–61.

——, *La expulsión de los Jesuítas de las provincias de Sonora, Ostimuri y Sinaloa en 1767* (Mexico City: 1959).

Priestley, Herbert Ingram, *José de Gálvez: Visitor-General of New Spain (1765–1771)* (Berkeley: 1916).

——, *Tristán de Luna. Conquistador of the Old South: A Study of Spanish Imperial Strategy* (Glendale, CA: 1936).

Puig-Samper, Miguel Ángel, "Humboldt, un prusiano en la corte del rey Carlos IV," *Revista de Indias* 59:216 (1999), 329–40.

Quinn, David Beers, *The Roanoke Voyages, 1584–1590*, 2 vols. (London: 1955).

Quintero Saravia, Gonzalo M., "Bernardo de Gálvez y América a finales del siglo XVIII," PhD thesis, Universidad Complutense de Madrid (2015).

——, *Bernardo de Gálvez: Spanish Hero of the American Revolution* (Chapel Hill, NC: 2018).

Ramos, Raúl A., *Beyond the Alamo: Forging Mexican Ethnicity in San Antonio, 1821–1861* (Chapel Hill, NC: 2008).

Ratchford, Fannie E., "Three 'First' Texas Poems," *Southwest Review* 12:2 (1927), 132–42.

Ratcliffe, Sam D., "'Escenas de Martirio': Notes on 'The Destruction of Mission San Sabá,'" *Southwestern Historical Quarterly* 94:4 (1991), 507–34.

Reff, Daniel T., "Contextualizing Missionary Discourse: The Benavides 'Memorials' of 1630 and 1634," *Journal of Anthropological Research* 50:1 (1994), 51–67.

Reilly, Stephen E., "A Marriage of Expedience: The Calusa Indians and Their Relations with Pedro Menéndez de Avilés in Southwest Florida," *Florida Historical Quarterly* 59:4 (1981), 395–421.

Remini, Robert V., *Andrew Jackson*, 3 vols. (New York: 1977–84).

Ricklis, Robert A., *The Karankawa Indians of Texas: An Ecological Study of Cultural Tradition and Change* (Austin: 1996).

Río, Ignacio del, "Autoritarismo y locura en el noroeste novohispano. Implicaciones políticas del enloquecimiento del visitador general José de Gálvez," *Estudios de Historia Novohispana* 22:22 (2000), 111–37.

Rivarola, José Luis, "El taller del Inca Garcilaso. Sobre las anotaciones manuscritas en la *Historia General* . . . ," *Revista de Filología Española* 75:1 (1995), 57–84.

Rivero, Ángel, *Crónica de la guerra hispanoamericana en Puerto Rico* (Madrid: 1922).

Robertson, James A. (ed.), *Louisiana Under the Rule of Spain, France, and the United States, 1785–1807*, 2 vols. (Cleveland: 1911).

Rodríguez, Jimena, "Mareantes y mareados: El estrecho de Anián y las *Naos* a California," *Romance Notes* 55: Special Issue (2015), 133–45.

Rodríguez Casado, Vicente, *Primeros años de dominación española en la Luisiana* (Madrid: 1942).

Rodríguez O., Jaime E., and Kathryn Vincent (eds.), *Myths, Misdeeds, and Misunderstandings: The Roots of Conflict in U.S.-Mexican Relations* (Wilmington, DE: 1997).

Rodríguez-Sala, María Louisa, *Exploraciones en Baja y Alta California, 1769–1775* (Zapopan: 2002).

Rogel, Juan, "Relación de Juan Rogel, 1607–1611," in *The Spanish Jesuit Mission in Virginia, 1570–1572*, ed. Clifford M. Lews and Albert J. Loomie (Chapel Hill, NC: 1953), 115–22.

Romero de Terreros, Juan M., "The Destruction of the San Sabá Apache Mission: A Discussion of the Casualties," *The Americas* 60:4 (2004), 617–27.

Romero de Terreros, Manuel, "La misión franciscana de San Sabás en la provincia de Texas. Año de 1758," *Anales del Instituto de Investigaciones Estéticas* 9:36 (1967), 51–58.

Rountree, Helen C., *Pocahontas, Powhatan, Openchancanough: Three Indian Lives Changed by Jamestown* (Charlottesville and London: 2008).

Rowse, A. L., *The Elizabethans and America* (New York: 1959).

Ruidíaz y Caravia, Eugenio, *Conquista y colonización de la Florida por Pedro Menéndez de Avilés* (Madrid: 1989 [1893]).

——, *La Florida: su conquista y colonización por Pedro Menéndez de Avilés*, 2 vols. (Madrid: 1893).

Ruiz Islas, Alfredo, "Hernán Cortés y la Isla California," *Iberoamericana* 7:27 (2007), 39–58.

Ruiz Medrano, Ethelia, *Reshaping New Spain: Government and Private Interests in the Colonial Bureaucracy, 1535–1550* (Boulder: 2006).

Russell, Philip L., *The History of Mexico: From the Pre-Conquest to Present* (New York and London: 2010).

Sacks, Benjamin, "The Creation of the Territory of Arizona," *Arizona and the West* 5:1 (1963), 29–62.

Sáinz Sastre, María Antonia, *La Florida en el siglo XVI: exploración y colonización* (Madrid: 2012).

Sale, Kirkpatrick, *The Conquest of Paradise: Christopher Columbus and the Columbian Legacy* (New York: 1990).

Salinas de la Torre, Gabriel (ed.), *Testmonios de Zacatecas* (Mexico City: 1946).

Sampson, Alexander, "Informaciones de servicio/Probanzas de meritos y servicios: Administering a New World. Self-Fashioning, Novelistic Discourse and the Truth of History," paper read to Association for Spanish and Portuguese Historical Studies, Albuquerque, April 4–7, 2013.

Sanchez, Jane C., "Spanish–Indian Relations During the Otermín Administration," *New Mexico Historical Review* 58:2 (1983), 133–51.

Sánchez, José María, *Viaje a Texas* (Mexico City: 1926).

Sánchez, Joseph P., *Spanish Bluecoats: The Catalonian Volunteers in Northwestern New Spain, 1767–1810* (Albuquerque: 1990).

Sánchez, Joseph P., Robert L. Spude, and Art Gómez, *New Mexico: A History* (Norman, OK: 2013).

Sando, Joe S., *Pueblo Nations: Eight Centuries of Pueblo Indian History* (Santa Fe: 1992).

——, *Pueblo Profiles: Cultural Identity Through Centuries of Change* (Santa Fe: 1998).

——, "The Pueblo Revolt," in *Po'pay: Leader of the First American Revolution*, ed. Joe S. Sando and Herman Agoyo (Santa Fe: 2005), 5–53.

Sando, Joe S., and Herman Agoyo, *Po'pay: Leader of the first American Revolution* (Santa Fe: 2005).

Sandweiss, Martha A., Rick Stewart, and Ben W. Huseman, *Eyewitness to War: Prints and Daguerreotypes of the Mexican War, 1846–1848* (Fort Worth: 1989).

Santibáñez, Enrique (ed.), *La diplomacia mexicana* (Mexico City: 1910).

Sauer, Carl O., "The Road to Cíbola," *Ibero-Americana* 3 (1932), 1–50.

——, *Seventeenth Century North America* (Berkeley: 1980).

Schaedel, Richard P., "The Karankawa of the Texas Gulf Coast," *Southwestern Journal of Anthropology* 5:2 (1949), 117–37.

Schambach, Frank F., "The End of the Trail: Reconstruction of the Route of Hernando de Soto's Army Through Southwest Arkansas and East Texas," in *The Expedition of Hernando de Soto West of the Mississippi, 1541–1543. Proceedings of the de Soto Symposia 1988 and 1990*, ed. Gloria A. Young and Michael P. Hoffman (Fayetteville: 1993), 78–102.

Schmitt, Eberhard, and Friedrich Karl von Hutten, *Das Gold de Neuen Welt: Die Papiere des Welser-Konquistadors und Gneralkapitäns von Venezuela Philipp von Hutten, 1534–1541* (Hildburghausen: 1996).

Scholes, France V., *Church and State in New Mexico, 1610–1650* (Albuquerque: 1937).

——, *Troublous Times in New Mexico, 1659–1670* (Albuquerque: 1942).

Schroeder, Albert H., and Dan S. Matson, *A Colony on the Move: Gaspar Castaño de Sosa's Journal, 1590–1591* ([Salt Lake City?]: 1965).

Schwartz, Seymour I., *The Mismapping of America* (Rochester: 2003).

Schwarz, Ted, *Forgotten Battlefield of the First Texas Revolution: The Battle of Medina, August 18, 1813* (Austin: 1985).

Selig, Robert A., *The Washington-Rochambeau Revolutionary Route in the State of Delaware, 1781–1783* (Dover, DE: 2003).

Sesmero Ruiz, Julián, *Los Gálvez de Macharaviaya* (Málaga: 1987).

Shaffer, Ellen, "Father Eusebio Francisco Kino and the Comet of 1680–1681," *Historical Society of Southern California Quarterly* 34:1 (1952), 57–70.

Shelby, Charmion Clair, "St. Denis's Declaration Concerning Texas in 1717," *Southwestern Historical Quarterly* 26:3 (1923), 165–83.

Shepherd, William R., "The Cession of Louisiana to Spain," *Political Science Quarterly* 19:3 (1904), 439–59.

Simmons, Marc, "New Mexico's Smallpox Epidemic of 1780–1781," *New Mexico Historical Review* 41:4 (1966), 319–26.

——, "The Tlascalans in the Spanish Borderlands," *New Mexico Historical Review* 39:2 (1964), 101–10.

Smith, Joseph, *The Spanish-American War: Conflict in the Caribbean and the Pacific, 1895–1902* (London: 1994).

Snow, Dean R., and K. M. Lanphear, "European Contact and Indian Depopulation in the Northeast: The Timing of the First Epidemics," *Ethnohistory* 35:1 (1988), 15–33.

Soniat du Fossat, Guy, *Synopsis of the History of Louisiana*, trans. Charles T. Soniat (New Orleans: 1903 [1791]).

Sotto, Serafín María de, Count of Clonard, *Historia orgánica de las armas de infantería y caballería españolas desde la creación del Ejercito permanente hasta el día*, 16 vols. (Madrid: 1851–59).

Spiess, Lincoln B., "Benavides and Church Music in New Mexico in the Early 17th Century," *Journal of the American Musicological Society* 17:2 (1964), 144–56.

———, "Church Music in Seventeenth-Century New Mexico," *New Mexico Historical Review* 40 (1965), 5–21.

Starkey, David J., E. S. van Eyck van Heslinga, and J. A. de Moor (eds.), *Pirates and Privateers: New Perspectives on the War on Trade in the Eighteenth and Nineteenth Centuries* (Exeter: 1997).

Stein, Stanley J., and Barbara H. Stein, *Apogee of Empire: Spain and New Spain in the Age of Charles III, 1759–1789* (Baltimore and London: 2003).

———, *Silver, Trade, and War: Spain and America in the Making of Early Modern Europe* (Baltimore and London: 2000).

Stewart-Shaheed, K. Denea, "Seductive Imperial Narratives and Conquest Subjectivities: An Alternative Paradigm for Reading Contemporary Empire," PhD thesis, University of Houston (2006).

Sugden, John, "The Southern Indians in the War of 1812: The Closing Phase," *Florida Historical Quarterly* 60:30 (1982), 273–312.

Swanton, John R. (ed.), *Final Report of the United States de Soto Expedition* (Washington, DC: 1985 [1939]).

Tanner, Helen H. (ed.), *General Greene's Visit to Saint Augustine in 1785* (Ann Arbor: 1964).

———, *Zéspedes in East Florida, 1784–1790* (Jacksonville: 1989 [1963]).

Taylor, Matthew S., "Cabeza de Vaca and the Introduction of Disease to Texas," *Southwestern Historical Quarterly* 111:4 (2008), 418–27.

Taylor, Mendell L., "The Western Services of Stephen Watts Kearny, 1815–1848," PhD thesis, University of Oklahoma (1944).

Tays, George, "The Passing of Spanish California, September 29, 1822," *California Historical Society Quarterly* 15:2 (1936), 139–42.

Thackeray, Francis, *A History of the Right Honorable William Pitt, Earl of Chatham*, 2 vols. (London: 1827).

Thibodeau, Alyson M., John T. Chesley, and Joaquin Ruiz, "Lead Isotope Analysis as a New Method for Identifying Material Culture Belonging to the Vázquez de Coronado Expedition," *Journal of Archaeological Science* 39:1 (2012), 58–66.

Thomas, David Hurst, *Colombian Consequences*, vol. 1, *Archeological and Historical Perspectives on the Spanish Borderlands West* (Washington, DC: 1989).

Thomas, Hugh, *The Conquest of Mexico* (London and New York: 1993).

———, *Goya: The Third of May 1808* (London: 1972).

———, *Who's Who of the Conquistadors* (London: 2000).

Tomlinson, Janis A., *Goya in the Twilight of Enlightenment* (New Haven: 1992).

Torget, Andrew, "Cotton Empire: Slavery and the Texas Borderlands," PhD dissertation, University of Virginia (2009).

Toro, Alfonso, *La familia Carvajal: estudio histórico sobre los judios y la Inquisición de la Nueva España en el siglo XVI* (Mexico City: 1944).

Townsend, Camilla, "Mutual Appraisals: The Shifting Paradigms of the English, Spanish, and Powhatans in Tsenacomoco, 1560–1622," in *Early Modern Virginia: Reconsidering the Old Dominion*, ed. Douglas Bradburn and John C. Coombs (Charlottesville: 2011), 57–89.

Turner, Sam, "Discovery of Florida Reconsidered," *Florida Historical Quarterly* 92:1 (2013), 1–31.

Tyler, Daniel, "Gringo Views of Governor Manuel Armijo," *New Mexico Historical Review* 45:1 (1970).

Undereiner, George J., "Fray Marcos de Niza and His Journey to Cibola," *The Americas* 3:4 (1946–47), 415–86.

Usner, Daniel H. Jr., *American Indians in the Lower Mississippi Valley: Social and Economic Histories* (Lincoln, NE: 1992).

——, *Indians, Settlers, and Slaves: The Lower Mississippi Valley Before 1783* (Chapel Hill, NC: 1992).

Van Valen, Gary, "Anglo Perceptions of a Cofradía: The Penitentes of New Mexico," *Secolas Annals* 27 (1996), 49–57.

Varela Marcos, Jesús, "Los prolegómenos de la visita de José de Gálvez a la Nueva España (1766). Don Francisco de Armona y la instrucción secreta del Marqués de Esquilache," *Revista de Indias* 46 (1986), 453–71.

Vargas Ugarte, Rubén, "The First Jesuit Mission in Florida," *United States Catholic Historical Society: Historical Records and Studies*, vol. 25 (New York: 1935), 59–148.

——, "Nota sobre Garcilaso," *Mercurio Peruano* 20:137–38 (1930), 106–7.

Varjabedian, Craig, and Michael Wallis, *En Divina Luz* (Albuquerque: 1994).

Vázquez, Josefina Z., "The Colonization and Loss of Texas: A Mexican Perspective," in *Myths, Misdeeds, and Misunderstandings: The Roots of Conflict in U.S.-Mexican Relations*, ed. Jaime E. Rodríguez O. and Kathryn Vincent (Wilmington, DE: 1997), 47–78.

——, "El origen de la guerra con Estados Unidos," *Historia Mexicana* 4:2 (1997), 285–309.

Velasco Ceballos, Rómulo (ed.), *La administración de D. Frey Antonio María de Buareli y Ursúa, cuadragésimo sexto virrey de México*, 2 vols. (Mexico City: 1936).

Velázquez, María del Carmen, "La Comandancia General de las Provincias Internas," *Historia Mexicana* 27:2 (1977), 163–76.

——, *La frontera norte y la experiencia colonial*, ed. María del Carmen Velázquez (Mexico City: 1982).

Vilches, Elvira, *New World Gold: Cultural Anxiety and Monetary Disorder in Early Modern Spain* (Chicago: 2010).

Wagner, Henry R., *Apocryphal Voyages to the Northwest Coast of America* (Worcester: 1931).

Washington, George, *The Writings of George Washington*, ed. Jared Sparks, 12 vols. (Boston: 1840).

Waters, Frank, *The Book of the Hopi* (New York: 1977 [1963]).

Weaver, Richard A., "The 1776 Route of Father Francisco Garcés into the San Bernardino Valley, California: A Reevaluation of the Evidence and Its Implications," *Journal of California and Great Basin Anthropology* 4:1 (1982), 142–47.

Weber, David J., *Foreigners in Their Native Land: Historical Roots of the Mexican Americans* (Albuquerque: 2003 [1970]).

——, *The Mexican Frontier, 1821–1846: The American Southwest Under Mexico* (Albuquerque: 1982).

——, *The Spanish Frontier in North America* (New Haven: 1992).

Weddle, Robert S., *San Juan Bautista: Gateway to Spanish Texas* (Austin: 1991 [1968]).

——, "The San Sabá Mission: Approach to the Great Plains," *Great Plains Journal* 4:2 (1965), 29–38.

——, *Wilderness Manhunt: The Spanish Search for La Salle* (College Station, TX: 1999 [1973]).

——, *The Wreck of the* Belle, *the Ruin of La Salle* (College Station, TX: 2001).

Weddle, Robert S., Donald E. Chipman, and Carol A. Lipscomb, "The Misplacement of Mission San Francisco de los Tejas in Eastern Texas and Its Actual Location at San Pedro de los Nabedaches," *Southwestern Historical Quarterly* 120:1 (2016), 75–84.

West, Elizabeth Howard, "The Indian Policy of Bernardo de Gálvez," in *The Proceedings of the Mississippi Valley Historical Association for the Year 1914-1915*, vol. 3, ed. Milo M. Quaife (Cedar Rapids: 1916), 95–101.

White, Richard S., "The Painting: *The Destruction of Mission San Sabá*; Document of Service to the King," PhD dissertation, Texas Tech University, 2000.

Wiget, Andrew O., "Truth and the Hopi: An Historiographic Study of Documented Oral Tradition Concerning the Coming of the Spanish," *Ethnohistory* 29:3 (1982), 181–99.

Wilcox, Michael V., *The Pueblo Revolt and the Mythology of Conquest: An Indigenous Archeology of Contact* (Berkeley: 2009).

Wilkinson, James, *Memoirs of My Own Times*, 2 vols. (Philadelphia: 1816).

Williams, Harold D., "Bernardo de Galvez and the Western Patriots," *Revista de Historia de América* 65–66 (1968), 53–70.

Wilson, James, and John Fiske (eds.), *Appleton's Cyclopaedia of American Biography*, 7 vols. (New York: 1886–1900).

Wood, Raymund F., "The Discovery of the Golden Gate: Legend and Reality," *Southern California Quarterly* 58:2 (1976), 205–25.

———, "Francisco Garcés, Explorer of Southern California," *Southern California Quarterly* 51:3 (1969), 185–209.

Woodbury, George, and Edna Woodbury, *Prehistoric Skeletal Remains from the Texas Coast* (Gila Pueblo, AZ: 1935).

Woolley, John, and Gerhard Peters (eds.), American Presidency Project: presidency.ucsb.edu.

Wright, Harold Bell, *Long Ago Told (Huh-Kew Ah-Kah): Legends of the Papago Indians* (New York and London: 1929).

Wright, Irene A. (ed. and trans.), *Further English Voyages to Spanish America, 1583-1594* (London: 1951).

Wright, Richard, "Negro Companions of the Spanish Conquistadors," *American Anthropologist* 4:2 (1902), 217–28.

Yela Utrilla, Juan R., *España ante la independencia de los Estados Unidos* (Madrid: 1988 [1922]).

Young, Gloria A., and Michael P. Hoffman (eds.), *The Expedition of Hernando de Soto West of the Mississippi, 1541-1543: Proceedings of the de Soto Symposia 1988 and 1990* (Fayetteville: 1993).

Zerecero, Anastasio, *Memorias para la historia de las revoluciones en México* (Mexico City: 1975).

Zubillaga, Félix, *La Florida: la misión jesuítica (1566-1572) y la coloniziación española* (Rome: 1940).

EXHIBITION CATALOGS

Castas Mexicanas, Museo de Monterrey, Mexico, San Antonio Museum of Art, TX, Museo Franz Mayer, Mexico City, 1989–90.

Goya: 250 aniversario, ed. Juan J. Luna and Margarita Moreno de las Heras, Museo Nacional del Prado, Madrid, March to June 1996.

Goya: The Portraits, ed. Xavier Bray, National Gallery, London, October 2015 to January 2016.

El hilo de la memoria: trescientos años de presencia española en los actuales Estados Unidos, ed. Falia González Día and Pilar Lazaro de la Escosura, Archivo General de Indias, Seville, June to October 2008.

El mestizaje americano, Museo de América, Madrid, October–December 1985.

Notes

INTRODUCTION

1. Reid, Jennifer (ed.), *Religion, Postcolonialism, and Globalization: A Sourcebook* (New York: 2015), 16ff; Papal Encyclicals Online: papalencyclicals.net/Alex06/alex06inter.htm.

2. AGI: Patronato 1, N.6, R.2.

3. Kagan, Richard, *Lawsuits and Litigants in Castile, 1500–1800* (Chapel Hill, NC: 1981).

4. *Recopilación de leyes de los reynos de Las Indias* (Madrid: 1681), law 20.

5. Las Casas, Bartolomé de, *Historia de las Indias*, ed. Agustín Millares Carlo, 3 vols. (Mexico City and Buenos Aires: 1951), 3:113.

PROLOGUE

1. Las Casas, *Historia*, 1:352.

2. Álvarez Chanca, Diego, "Carta del doctor Álvarez Chanca al Cabildo de Sevilla," in *Cartas de particulares a Colón y relaciones coetáneas*, ed. Juan Gil and Consuelo Valera (Madrid: 1984), 152–76, 158.

3. Columbus, Christopher [Cristóbal Colón], "Diario del primer viaje," in *Cristóbal Colón: Textos y documentos completos*, ed. Consuelo Valera (Madrid: 1982), 15–138, 51, November 4; and see Columbus, Christopher [Cristóbal Colón], *Letters from America: Columbus's First Accounts of the 1492 Voyage*, ed. and trans. B. W. Ife (London: 1992).

4. Vespucci, Amerigo, *The Letters of Amerigo Vespucci and Other Documents Illustrative of His Career*, ed. Clements R. Markham (London: [1894]), 34 and 47.

5. Cuneo, Michele da, "La Relazione," in *Repertorium Columbianum*, vol. 12, *Italian Reports on America, 1493–1522: Accounts by Contemporary Observers*, ed. Geoffrey Symcox, T. J. Cachey, and John C. Lucas (Turnhout: 2002), 177; "Relación de Miguel de Cuneo," in *Cartas de particulares a Colón y relaciones coetáneas*, ed. Juan Gil and Consuelo Valera (Madrid: 1984), 235–60, 241. For route and name Ayay, see Martyr d'Anghiera, Peter [Peter, Martyr of Anghiera], *The Discovery of the New World in the Writings of Peter Martyr of Anghiera*, ed. Ernesto Lunardi et al., trans. Felix Azzola and Luciano F. Farina (Rome: 1992), 234–35.

6. Martyr, *Discovery*, 234–35.

7. Cuneo, "Relazione," 177.

8. Ibid., 177–78.

9. Vespucci, *Letters*, 46.

10. Columbus [Colón], "Diario," 77, 79, and 101, December 9, 13, and 25.

11. Álvarez Chanca, "Carta," 166.

12. Cuneo, "Relazione," 178.

13. Álvarez Chanca, "Carta," 170.

14. Las Casas, *Historia*, 1:358–59.

15. Fernández de Oviedo y Valdés, Gonzalo, *Historia general*, ed. Pérez de Tudela, 5 vols. (Madrid: 1959), 1:48–49.

16. Columbus, Christopher [Cristóbal Colón], "Memorial a A. Torres (1494)," in *Cristóbal Colón: Textos y documentos completos*, ed. Consuelo Valera (Madrid: 1982), 147–62, 154.

17. Las Casas, *Historia*, 1:348.

18. Ibid., 1:408–9.

19. Bernáldez, Andrés, *Historia de los reyes católicos d. Fernando y Doña Isabel*, 2 vols. (Seville: 1870), 78.

INTRODUCTION TO PART ONE

1. Lanning, John Tate, "Cortes and His First Official Remission of Treasure to Charles V," *Revista de Historia de América* 2 (1938), 5–29; AGI: Contratación 4675; Gayangos, Pascual de, *Cartas y relaciones de Hernán Cortés al Emperador Carlos V* (Paris: 1866), 28–34.

2. Dürer, Albrecht, *Albrecht Dürer: Diary of His Journey to the Netherlands, 1520–1521*, ed. J. A. Goris and G. Marlier (London: 1970), 37.

3. Pérez, Joseph, *La revolución de las comunidades de Castilla (1520–1521)* (Madrid: 1977 [1970]), 148–50, 150 n.135.

CHAPTER ONE

1. AGI: México 203 n.19, Información de Juan González Ponce de León, 1532; Tió, Aurelio, *Nuevas fuentes para la historia de Puerto Rico* (San Germán: 1961), 30ff.

2. AGI: México 204 n.3, Información a pedimento de Juan Garrido de Color Negro, 1538; Alegría, Ricardo E., *Juan Garrido: El conquistador negro en las Antillas, Florida, México y California* (San Juan: 1990), 125ff.

3. Tió, *Nuevas fuentes*, 84.

4. Las Casas, *Historia*, 2:230.

5. Ibid., 2:262–63.

6. Ibid., 2:355–56.

7. AGI: Indiferente 418, L.1, ff.164r–164v.

8. Murga Sanz, Vicente, *Juan Ponce de León: fundador y primer gobernador del pueblo puertorriqueño; descubridor de la Florida y del Estrecho de Bahamas* (Barcelona: 1971 [1959]), 34.

9. For what follows, see Tió, *Nuevas fuentes*, 33ff.

10. Ibid., 86.

11. Fernández de Oviedo, *Historia*, 2:91; Fuson, Robert H., *Ponce de León and the Spanish Discovery of Puerto Rico and Florida* (Blacksburg, VA: 2000), 74.

12. Tió, *Nuevas fuentes*, 51.

13. CDI: 34:336ff.

14. Las Casas, *Historia*, 2:367–68.

15. Murga Sanz, *Ponce de León*, 51–52.

16. Ibid., 63.

17. Tió, *Nuevas fuentes*, 51; Fernández de Oviedo, *Historia*, 2:95.

18. Tió, *Nuevas fuentes*, 51–52.

19. CDI: 32:275–80.

20. Fernández de Oviedo, *Historia*, 2:95–96.

21. Ibid., 2:100–101.

22. Tió, *Nuevas fuentes*, 53–54.

23. Ibid., 251; AGI: Justicia, Leg. 1000, R2, f.3r; Graullera Sanz, Vicente, *La esclavitude en Valencia en los siglos XVI y XVII* (Valencia: 1978), 119.

24. AGI: Indiferente 418, L.3, ff.158r–159r.

25. Martyr d'Anghiera, Peter [Peter, Martyr of Anghiera], *De Orbe Novo: The Eight Decades of Peter Martyr d'Anghera*, ed. and trans. Francis Augustus MacNutt, 2 vols. (New York and London: 1912), 1:274, Decade 2, Bk. 10.

26. Murga Sanz, *Ponce de León*, 100 n.5 refs AGI: Indiferente 418 L.3, f.139v.

27. Turner, Sam, "Discovery of Florida Reconsidered," *Florida Historical Quarterly* 92:1 (2013), 1–31, 8.

28. Ibid., 12–20.

29. Fernández de Navarrete, Martín, *Colección de los viajes y descubrimientos que hicieron por mar los españoles*, 5 vols. (Madrid: 1825–37), Doc. 36, instrucción a Juan de Solís, November 24, 1514, 3:136–37; the quotation is from Herrera y Tordesillas, Antonio de, *Historia general de los hechos de los castellanos*, 4 vols. (Madrid: 1601), Dec. 1, Bk. 9, 247.

30. Herrera y Tordesillas, *Historia*, 247.

31. Turner, "Discovery," 23 n.49 refs Tío, *Nuevas fuentes*, Doc. 8, 435–61.

32. Ibid. 24 identifies the victim as probably Pedro Bello.

33. Herrera y Tordesillas, *Historia*, 248.

34. Tió, *Nuevas fuentes*, 37–38 and 59–60; Fernández de Oviedo, *Historia*, 2:101.

CHAPTER TWO

1. Díaz del Castillo, Bernal, *La verdadera de la conquista de la Nueva España*, ed. Genaro García, 2 vols. (Mexico City: 1904), 1:266.

2. López de Gómara, Francisco, *Conquista de México*, ed. José Luis de Rojas (Madrid: 2001), 90–91.

3. Díaz del Castillo, *Verdadera conquista*, 1:150.

4. Thomas, Hugh, *The Conquest of Mexico* (London and New York: 1993), 397.

5. Tió, *Nuevas fuentes*, 63, 79–82, and 106.

6. Porras Muñoz, Guillermo, "Martín López, carpintero de Ribera," *Revista de Indias* 31–32 (1948), 307–29, appendix 8 refs AGI: Escribanía 178.

7. Thomas, *Conquest*, 423.

8. Tió, *Nuevas fuentes*, 108.

9. AGI: Pasajeros, L.3, E.4070.

CHAPTER THREE

1. Hoffman, Paul, *A New Andalucia and a Way to the Orient: The American Southeast During the Sixteenth Century* (Baton Rouge: 1990), 11.

2. Fogelson, Raymond D., "Who Were the Aní-Kutání? An Excursion into Cherokee Historical Thought," *Ethnohistory* 31:4 (1984), 255–63.

3. Martyr, *De Orbe Novo*, Dec. 7, Bk. 2. I have loosely followed the MacNutt translation.

4. Ibid., Dec. 7, Bks. 2–4; Hoffman comprehensively explains how this idea that a large swath of the eastern United States was a "New Andalusia" in his *New Andalucia*.

5. Fernández de Oviedo, *Historia*, 4:323–24.

6. Hoffman, *New Andalucia*, 51–57.

7. Ibid., 61–62.

8. Ibid., 67 and 71.

9. For what follows, except where indicated, I have followed Fernández de Oviedo, *Historia*, 4:326ff.

10. Pedraza, Luis de, *Historia de Sevilla*, ed. F. Morales Padrón (Seville: [1979?] [1530s]), 96.

11. Mercado, Tomás, *Suma de tratos y contratos* (Madrid: 1587), Ch. 1.

12. Pedraza, *Historia*, Bk. 2, Ch. 8, 108–9.

13. Ibid., Bk. 1, Ch. 5, 43–45.

14. Navagero, Andrea, "Viajes por España" and "Cartas," in *Viajes por España de Jorge de Einghen, del Baron León de Rosmithal de Blatna, de Francisco Guicciardini, y de Andrés Navajero*, ed. and trans. Antonio María Fabie (Madrid: 1879), 266.

15. Morgado, Alonso de, *Historia de Sevilla: en la qual se contienen sus antiguedades* (Seville: 1587), 56.

16. Morales Padrón, Francisco, *Historia de Sevilla: La ciudad del quinientos* (Seville: 1989), 168–71.

17. Díaz del Castillo, *Verdadera conquista*, Ch. 205, 247; Las Casas, *Historia*, Bk. 3, Ch. 25.

18. Adorno, Rolena, and Charles Patrick Pautz, *Alvar Núñez Cabeza de Vaca: His Account, His Life, and the Expedition of Pánfilo Narváez*, 3 vols. (Lincoln, NE: 1999), 2:422ff; Martínez Martínez, María del Carmen, "Cartas de Alonso del Castillo Maldonado desde México," in *Estudios sobre América, siglos XVI–XIX* (Seville: 2005), 89–106; also see Castillo Gómez, Antonio, and Verónica Sierra Blas, *Cinco siglos de cartas: historia y prácticas epistolares en las épocas moderna y contemporánea* (Huelva: 2014), 197ff.

19. Maura, Juan, *El gran burlador de América: Álvar Núñez Cabeza de Vaca* (Valencia: 2008), 14; Adorno and Pautz, *Alvar Núñez*, 2:422ff; Martínez Martínez, "Cartas," 89–106; also see Castillo Gómez and Sierra Blas, *Cinco siglos de cartas*, 197ff.

20. I have cited Cabeza de Vaca's famous account, *La relación que dió Álvar Núñez Cabeza de Vaca*, first published at Zamora in 1542, from Adorno and Pautz, *Alvar Núñez*, 2:274; Harvey, John P., *Muslims in Spain, 1500–1614* (Chicago: 2005), 371.

21. Núñez, *Relación*, ff.5v–6r, 32–34; Fernández de Oviedo, *Historia*, Ch. 1.

22. historiadelnuevomundo.com/index.php/2011/01/el-requerimiento.

23. CDI: 1:450–55.

24. Núñez, *Relación*, f.6v, 36.

25. Ibid., f.7r, 38.

26. Ibid., f.7v, 40.

27. Ibid., f.7v, 40.

28. Ibid., f.8r, 42.

29. Ibid., f.8v, 44.

30. Fernández de Oviedo, *Historia*, 4:278ff, preface.

31. Núñez, *Relación*, f.10r, 50.

32. Fernández de Oviedo, *Historia*, Ch. 1.

33. Henige, David, "Primary Source by Primary Source? On the Role of Epidemics in New World Depopulation," *Ethnohistory* 33:3 (1986), 293–312, 300 asserts diarrhea or dysentery; Ashburn, Percy M., *The Ranks of Death: A Medical History of the Conquest of America* (New York: 1947), 160 suggests dysentery because typhoid would have been described as a fever; Dobyns, Henry, *Their Number Become Thinned: Native American Population Dynamics in Eastern North America* (Knoxville: 1983), 262 suggests typhoid as the most likely Old World pathogen; as do Snow, Dean R., and K. M. Lanphear, "European Contact and Indian Depopulation in the Northeast: The Timing of the First Epidemics," *Ethnohistory* 35:1 (1988), 15–33, 17; and Covey, Cyclone, *Cabeza de Vaca's Adventures in the Unknown Interior of America* (Albuquerque: 1998), 60; for overview, see Taylor, Matthew S., "Cabeza de Vaca and the Introduction of Disease to Texas," *Southwestern Historical Quarterly* 111:4 (2008), 418–27.

34. Mitchem, Jeffrey M., "Artifacts of Exploration: Archaeological Evidence from Florida," in *First Encounters: Spanish Explorations in the Caribbean and the United States, 1492–1570*, ed. Jerald T. Milanich and Susan Milbrath (Gainesville: 1989), 99–109, 103; Hoffman, Paul E., "Narváez and Cabeza de Vaca in Florida," in *The Forgotten Centuries: Indians and Europeans in the American South, 1521-1704*, ed. Charles Hudson and Carmen Chaves Tesser (Athens, GA: 1994), 50–73, 63.

35. Núñez, *Relación*, ff.19v–20r.

CHAPTER FOUR

1. "Tercera Carta," see Cortés, Hernán, *Cartas de relación*, ed. Ángel Delgado Gómez (Madrid: 1993), 430–41, 445, and 447; Martínez, José Luis (ed.), *Documentos Cortesianos*, 4 vols. (Mexico City: 1990), Doc. 21, Cortés to Charles V, May 15, 1522, 1:230–31; León-Portilla, Miguel, *Hernán Cortés y la Mar del Sur* (Madrid: 2005), 43.

2. Rodríguez, Jimena, "Mareantes y mareados: El estrecho de Anián y las *Naos* a California," *Romance Notes* 55: Special Issue (2015), 133–45, 135; Wagner, Henry R., *Apocryphal Voyages to the Northwest Coast of America* (Worcester: 1931), 6; Polo, Marco, *Travels*, ed. and trans. Ronald Latham (Harmondsworth: 1974), Bk. 3, Chs. 5 and 6, or Ch. 129, and other variants.

3. Martínez, *Documentos*, Doc. 30, instructions of Charles V to Cortés, June 26, 1523, 1:271.

4. Fernández de Oviedo, *Historia*, 4:284.

5. Leonard, Irving, *Books of the Brave* (Cambridge, MA: 1949), 36ff; Herodotus, *The Histories*, Bk. 4, ed. Robert B. Strassler, trans. Andrea L. Purvis (New York: 2007), 110–17 and 327–28.

6. Cortés, *Cartas*, "Cuarta Carta," 473–74 and see n.56.

7. Fernández de Oviedo, *Historia*, 4:284.

8. Leonard, *Books*, 38–40.

9. Rodríguez de Montalvo, Garci, *Las sergas de Esplandián* (Seville: 1510). The following is my own rendering of chapters 157 to 178, heavily abridged and adapted, but retaining the atmosphere and language of Rodríguez's original: californax.com/calx1/do42_calxElNombreCalifornia/0043_BCalx-LasSergasHoja4.htm.

10. Cortés, *Cartas*, "Quinta Carta," 527–28.

11. Alv Ixtlilxochitl, Fernando de, *Obras históricas de don Fernando de Alva Ixtlilxochitl,* ed. Alfredo Chavero, 2 vols. (Mexico City: 1891), 1:402–3.

12. Ife, B. W., and R. T. C. Goodwin, "'Many Expert Narrators': History and Fiction in the Spanish Chronicles of the New World," in *Remapping the Rise of the Novel,* ed. Jenny Mander (Oxford: 2007), 59–74.

13. Díaz del Castillo, *Verdadera conquista,* Ch. 177.

14. Martínez, *Documentos,* Doc. 56, award of lands to Isabel Montezuma, June 27, 1526, 1:377ff; Chipman, Donald E., *Moctezuma's Children: Aztec Royalty Under Spanish Rule, 1520–1700* (Austin: 2005), 48–51.

15. Díaz del Castillo, *Verdadera conquista,* Ch. 181; Herrera y Tordesillas, *Historia,* Dec. 3, Bk. 8, 2:253.

16. Martínez, *Documentos,* Doc. 53, letter from Cortés to Audiencia of Santo Domingo, May 23, 1526, 1:362ff.

17. Ibid., Doc. 49, royal warrant issued by Charles V, November 24, 1525, 1:346.

18. Ibid.

19. Fernández de Navarrete, *Colección,* Doc. 36, report of the voyage made by Saavedra, 5:466, and Doc. 37, report made in Madrid by Vicente de Nápoles, 5:476.

20. Alexander, William D., *Papers of the Hawaiian Historical Society,* no. 1, *The Relations Between the Hawaiian Islands and Spanish America in Early Times* (1992), 2.3.

21. Atkinson, A. T., *Papers of the Hawaiian Historical Society,* no. 4, *Early Voyagers of the Pacific Ocean* (1893), 2.

22. Parry, J. H., *The Audiencia of New Galicia in the Sixteenth Century: A Study in Colonial Government* (Cambridge: 1968), 14ff.

23. Martínez, *Documentos,* Doc. 165, contract between Queen and Cortés, October 27, 1529, 3:78–85.

24. Borah, Woodrow, "Hernán Cortés y sus intereses marítimos en el Pacífico. El Perú y la Baja California," *Estudios de Historia Novohispana* 4:4 (1971), 2–28, 5.

25. Martínez, *Documentos,* Doc. 214, instructions to Hurtado de Mendoza, May 1532, 4:300–304.

26. León-Portilla, *Hernán Cortés,* 94–99; Díaz del Castillo, *Verdadera conquista,* Ch. 200.

27. Montané Martí, Julio César, and Carlos Lazcano Sahagún, *El descubrimiento de California: las expediciones de Becerra y Grijalva a la Mar del Sur* (Ensenada: 2004), esp. 43ff; for merman, see CDI: 14:128ff and AGI: Patronato 20, N.5, R.7.

28. Díaz del Castillo, *Verdadera conquista,* Ch. 200.

29. AGI: Patronato 180, R.52, published in Martínez, *Documentos,* 4:51–59, report of Grijalva and his pilot; Montané Martí, Julio Cesar, and Carlos Lazcano Sahagún, *El descubrimiento de California: las expediciones de Becerra y Grijalva a la Mar del Sur* (Ensenada: 2004), 49ff; and Mathes, Michael, "Asesinato y descubrimiento: el motín de Fortún Ximénez y la incorporación de California al Imperio Español," *Meyibó* 1 (1990), 31–49.

30. Díaz, *Verdadera conquista,* Ch. 200; Montané Martí and Lazcano Sahagún, *Descubrimiento,* 57; Paso y Troncoso, Francisco del, *Epistolario de Nueva España,* 16 vols. (Mexico City: 1939–42), 14:188–92; Martínez, *Documentos,* Doc. 243, 4:97–103, 100–1, royal instructions in respect to the South Sea and Guzmán, 1534.

31. Montané Martí and Lazcano Sahagún, *Descubrimiento,* 58; García Icazbalceta, Joaquín, *Colección de documentos para la historia de Mexico,* 2 vols. (Mexico: 1980), 2:30–34; González Rodríguez, Luis, "Hernán Cortés, la Mar del Sur y el descubrimiento de Baja California,"

Anuario de Estudios Americanos 42:1 (1985), 573–644, 622; Martínez, *Documentos*, Doc. 243, 4:97–103, 101 royal instructions in respect to the South Sea and Guzmán, 1534.

32. Díaz del Castillo, *Verdadera conquista*, Ch. 200.

33. Alegría, *Juan Garrido*, 87–89.

34. Ibid., 99–101.

35. Martínez, *Documentos*, Doc. 248, 4:136–41, request to desist from entry by Guzmán, February 24, 1535.

36. Herrera y Tordesillas, *Historia*, Dec. 5, Bk. 8, Ch. 9.

37. Martínez, *Documentos*, Doc. 254, 4:150–52, letter from Guzmán to the king, June 8, 1535.

38. Ibid., Doc. 255, 4:153–61, depositions about the marquis's new land, December 10, 1535.

39. Ibid.

40. Ibid., Doc. 253, letter from Cortés to Oñate, May 14, 1535, 4:148–49.

41. Díaz del Castillo, *Verdadera conquista*, Ch. 200.

42. López de Gómara, Francisco, *Historia general de las Indias* (Saragossa: 1552), Ch. 198.

43. Díaz del Castillo, *Verdadera conquista*, Ch. 200; Ruiz Islas, Alfredo, "Hernán Cortés y la Isla California," *Iberoamericana* 7:27 (2007), 39–58, 56; Polk, Dora, *The Island of California: A History of the Myth* (Lincoln, NE: 1991), 121ff.

CHAPTER FIVE

1. Altman, Ida, *The War for Mexico's West: Indians and Spaniards in New Galicia, 1524–1550* (Albuquerque: 2010), 104–5; AGI: Guadalajara 5, R.6, N.13; Calderón Quijano, José Antonio (ed.), "Visita de Lebrón de Quiñones, 1554," in *Documentos para la historia del Estado de Colima* (Mexico City: 1972), f.31r; AGI: Patronato 20, N.5, R.14; also see Goodwin, R. T. C., "'De lo que sucedió a los demás que entraron en las Indias': Álvar Núñez Cabeza de Vaca and the Other Survivors of Pánfilo Narváez's Expedition," *Bulletin of Spanish Studies* 84:2 (2007), 147–73, 154–57; and AGI: Patronato 65, N.1, R.4, "Información de Antonio de Aguayo," March 19, 1557.

2. Mota y Padilla, Matías de la, *Historia de la conquista de Nueva Galicia*, 80 locates the reunion on the Río Yaquimí, the Mayo River; Sauer, Carl O., "The Road to Cíbola," *Ibero-Americana* 3 (1932), 1–50, 20 n.18 refs Archivo Público de México; *Misiones*, vol. 25, places them much farther south at a place called Los Ojuelos, near Ocoroni, which may or may not be correct but fits better with the distances given in the various sources.

3. Fernández de Oviedo, Cabeza de Vaca, and Herrera de Tordesillas (probably following Cabeza de Vaca's *Naufragios*) report that Cabeza de Vaca and Esteban led this scouting party that first made contact with the Spanish slavers. In *Historia*, Mota y Padilla used a source that may still be in the Municipal Archive in Guadalajara that led him to believe that this was Andrés Dorantes. Maura, Juan, "Los 'Naufragios' de Alvar Núñez Cabeza de Vaca: o el arte de la automitificación," PhD thesis, University of New Mexico (1987), 170ff offers good reason not to reject that suggestion; also see my core argument in *Crossing the Continent, 1527–1540: The Story of the First African-American Explorer of the American South* (New York: 2008), esp. Chs. 9, 10, and 16; and my "'De lo que sucedió.'" Quotation is from Mota y Padilla, *Historia*, 181.

4. Mota y Padilla, *Historia*, 181.

5. Núñez, *Relación*, f.59r–60r; Fernández de Oviedo, *Historia*, Ch. 6.

6. Herrera y Tordesillas, *Historia*, Dec. 6, Bk. 1, Ch. 7, 3:11; Maura, *Burlador*, 93 n.24.

7. Goodwin, R. T. C., "Álvar Núñez Cabeza de Vaca and the Textual Travels of an American Miracle," *Journal of Iberian and Latin American Studies* 14:1 (2008), 1–12; Gil, Juan, "Álvar Núñez, el chamán blanco," *Boletín de la Real Academia Española* 3 (1993), 69–72; Schmitt, Eberhard, and Friedrich Karl von Hutten, *Das Gold de Neuen Welt: Die Papiere des Welser-Konquistadors und Gneralkapitäns von Venezuela Philipp von Hutten, 1534–1541* (Hildburghausen: 1996).

8. Aiton, Arthur S., *Antonio de Mendoza, First Viceroy of New Spain* (New York: 1967), 4–9.

9. The quotation is abridged from the text at papalencyclicals.net/Paulo3/p3subli.htm.

10. Koskenniemi, Martti, "Empire and International Law: The Real Spanish Contribution," *University of Toronto Law Journal* 61:1 (2011), 1–36, 11–12.

11. Vitoria, Francisco de, *Political Writings*, ed. Anthony Pagden and Jeremy Lawrance (Cambridge: 1991), 251.

12. Ibid., 287–90.

13. Ibid., 278.

14. Gatschet, Albert S., *The Karankawa Indians, the Coast People of Texas*, with notes by Alice W. Oliver and Charles A. Hammond, Archaeological and Ethnological Papers of the Peabody Museum 1:2 (Cambridge, MA: 1891), 120–21; Ricklis, Robert A., *The Karankawa Indians of Texas: An Ecological Study of Cultural Tradition and Change* (Austin: 1996), 9–10; Woodbury, George, and Edna Woodbury, *Prehistoric Skeletal Remains from the Texas Coast* (Gila Pueblo, AZ: 1935); also see Schaedel, Richard P., "The Karankawa of the Texas Gulf Coast," *Southwestern Journal of Anthropology* 5:2 (1949), 117–37.

15. Fernández de Oviedo, *Historia*, Bk. 16, Ch. 7, 4:315; González, Javier Roberto, "Mal Hado-Malfado. Reminiscencias del *Palmerín de Olivia* en los *Naufragios* de Álvar Núñez Cabeza de Vaca," *Káñina* 23:2 (1999), 55–66.

16. Núñez, *Relación*, f.26r, 114; see Covarrubias, Sebastián de, *Tesoro de la lengua castellana o española* (Madrid: 1611) for my translation of *soplar* as "whisper."

17. Lee, Kun Jong, "Pauline Typology in Cabeza de Vaca's *Naufragios*," *Early American Literature* 34:3 (1999), 241–62, 244.

18. Adorno and Pautz, *Álvar Núñez*, 2:283–85.

19. Núñez, *Relación*, f.27v, 120.

20. Fernández de Oviedo, *Historia*, Bk. 16, Ch. 4, 4:301.

21. Núñez, *Relación*, f.43v–44r, 188–90, f.24v, 108, and f.48r, 202; see for example Callender, Charles, and Lee M. Kochems, "The North American Berdache," *Current Anthropology* 24:4 (1983), 443–70.

22. Stewart-Shaheed, K. Denea, "Seductive Imperial Narratives and Conquest Subjectivities: An Alternative Paradigm for Reading Contemporary Empire," PhD thesis, University of Houston (2006), 106–7; and see Maura, *Burlador*, 138ff responding to Adorno and Pautz, *Alvar Núñez*, 2:271ff.

23. Fernández de Oviedo, *Historia*, Bk. 16, Ch. 4, 4:304.

24. Douglas, Alfred (Lord), *Two Loves* (London: 1894).

25. Fernández de Oviedo, *Historia*, Bk. 16, Ch. 4, 4:305.

26. Núñez, *Relación*, f.36v, 156, and f.40v, 172.

27. Ibid., ff.37v–38r, 160–62.

28. Ibid., f.38r, 162.

29. Ibid., ff.39r–v, 166–68.

30. Adorno, Rolena, "The Negotiation of Fear in Cabeza de Vaca's Naufragios," *Representations* 33 (1991), 163–99; Goodwin, R. T. C., " 'Yo quisiera esto más claro, e más larga claridad en ello.' Reconstrucion: Historiographical Misrepresentations of Africans and Native Americans, and the Law," *Bulletin of Spanish Studies* 92:2 (2015), 179–206.

31. Fernández de Oviedo, *Historia*, Bk. 16, Ch. 4, 4:307.

32. Ibid., 4:306.

33. Núñez, *Relación*, ff.51v–52r, 216–18.

34. Ibid., f.55v, 232.

35. Fernández de Oviedo, *Historia*, Bk. 16, Ch. 4, 4:305.

36. Núñez, *Relación*, ff.57r–v, 238–40.

CHAPTER SIX

1. Ruiz Medrano, Ethelia, *Reshaping New Spain: Government and Private Interests in the Colonial Bureaucracy, 1535–1550* (Boulder: 2006), 116ff.

2. Flint, Richard, and Shirley Cushing Flint (eds.), *Documents of the Coronado Expedition, 1539–1542* (Dallas: 2005), "Coronado to King," December 15, 1538, Doc. 1, 21.

3. Cuevas, Mariano (ed.), *Documentos inéditos del siglo XVI para la historia de México* (Mexico City: 1914), "Carta de Zumárraga," April 4, 1537, 83–84.

4. García Icazbalceta, Joaquín, *Don Fray Juan de Zumarrága. Primer obispo y arzobispo de México*, ed. Rafael Aguayo Spencer and Antonio Castro Leal, 4 vols. (Mexico City: 1944), 3:91–93.

5. CDI: 15:375; Goodwin, R. T. C, and Jerry R. Craddock, "Information Concerning Baltazar Dorantes de Carranza, November 5, 1573," f.14r: escholarship.org/uc/item/27t9v1n5; Flint and Flint, *Documents*, Doc. 3, 45ff; Ramusio, Giovanni Battista, *Terzo volume delle navigationi et fiaggi* (Venice: 1556), ff.355r–v; Ruiz Medrano, *Reshaping*, table 2.3.

6. Flint and Flint, *Documents*, Doc. 3, 49; Goodwin, " 'De lo que sucedió,' " 160ff.

7. Obregón, Baltasar, *Historia de los descubrimientos de Nueva España*, ed. Eva María Bravo (Seville: 1997 [1584]), 49.

8. Craddock, Jerry R., "Fray Marcos de Niza, *Relación* (1539), Edition and Commentary," *Romance Philology* 53:1 (1999), 69–118; Flint and Flint, *Documents*, Doc. 6; AGI: Patronato 20, N.5, R.10, blocks 1 and 2.

9. Craddock, "Fray Marcos," f.3v, 84–85.

10. Flint and Flint, *Documents*, Doc. 2, "Coronado to Mendoza," March 8, 1539, 35. The letter is only known from a version published by Ramusio in his *Terzo volume*. We know that the date must be wrong. Moreover, it is impossible to know how much material Ramusio interpolated into his version. See, for example: Undereiner, George J., "Fray Marcos de Niza and His Journey to Cibola," *The Americas* 3:4 (1946–47), 415–86, 423–24.

11. Craddock, "Fray Marcos," f.4r, 85.

12. The biblical image is used by Wright, Richard, "Negro Companions of the Spanish Conquistadors," *American Anthropologist* 4:2 (1902), 217–28, 225.

13. Craddock, "Fray Marcos," ff.7r–7v, 91–93.

14. Hartmann, William K., "Pathfinder for Coronado: Reevaluating the Mysterious Journey of Marcos de Niza," in *The Coronado Expedition to Tierra Nueva: The 1540–1542 Route Across the Southwest*, ed. Richard Flint and Shirley Cushing Flint (Boulder: 1997), 61–83.

15. CDI: 4:211ff.

16. Flint and Flint, *Documents*, Doc. 8, "Testimony of Witnesses," Havana, November 1539, 103; AGI: Patronato 21, N.2, R.4, ff.66r–70v.

17. Flint, Richard, *Great Cruelties Have Been Reported: The 1544 Investigation of the Coronado Expedition* (Dallas: 2002), 253–54; Brasher, Nugent, "The Chichilticale Camp of Francisco Vázquez de Coronado," *New Mexico Historical Review* 82:4 (2007), 433–68; and see chichilticale.com, Duffen, William A., and William K. Hartmann, "The 76 Ranch Ruin and the Location of Chichilticale," in *The Coronado Expedition to Tierra Nueva: The 1540–1542 Route Across the Southwest*, ed. Richard Flint and Shirley Cushing Flint (Boulder: 1997), 158–75.

18. Flint and Flint, *Documents*, Doc. 17, "Viceroy to King," April 17, 1540, 233ff.

19. Flint, Richard, *No Settlement, No Conquest: A History of the Coronado Entrada* (Albuquerque: 2008), 2.

20. Flint and Flint, *Documents*, Doc. 12, "Muster Roll," 135ff; AGI: Patronato 60, N.5, R.4, "Méritos de Zaldívar," 1566.

21. Ibid., Doc. 32, "Melchior Pérez's Petition," 1551, 533ff; University of California, Berkeley, Bancroft Library, M–M 1714.

22. British Library, London: Add Mss 31,219, Codex Aubin, f.46v; Flint, *No Settlement*, 58ff; and see Flint and Flint, *Documents*, Doc. 13, "Indians Participating in the Expedition," 1576, 164ff; University of Glasgow: Sp Coll Ms Hunter 242 (U.3.15), *History of Tlaxcala*, f.317v; and see Gillespie, Jeanne L., "The Codex of Tlaxcala: Indigenous Petitions and the Discourse of Heterarchy," *Hipertexto* 13 (2011), 59–74, 66 and fig. 3.

23. Flint and Flint, *Documents*, Doc. 33, "Escobar's Service," 554ff, 570, and Doc. 30, "Jaramillo's Narrative," 1560s, 508ff, 513; AGI: México 204, N.14, f.4v, and AGI: Patronato 20, N.5, R.8, f.1v; Pennington, Campbell W., *The Material Culture: The Pima Bajo of Central Sonora, Mexico* (Salt Lake City: 1980), 217 identifies the *yerba de flecha* as a species of euphorbiaceae, the *Sebastiana appendiculatum*; Flint and Flint, *Documents*, Doc. 28, "Castañeda de Nájera's Narrative," 1560s, New York Public Library, Rich Collection, n.63, 378ff, f.27v, 444.

24. Bolton, Herbert E., *Coronado: Knight of Pueblos and Plains* (Albuquerque: 1949).

25. Almost all the primary sources along with the almost exhaustively comprehensive analysis have been published by Richard Flint and Shirley Cushing Flint, whose scholarly dedication, determination, insight, and interpretation are both inspirational and exemplary.

26. Flint and Flint, *Documents*, "Castañeda," f.30r, 445.

27. Ibid., Doc. 19, "Coronado to Mendoza," July 1540, 252ff.

28. Ibid., "Castañeda," f.31r, 446.

29. Achúe Zapata, José Enrique, "Some News About Don Garci López de Cárdenas," in *The Latest Word from 1540: People, Places, and Portrayals of the Coronado Expedition*, ed. Richard Flint and Shirley Cushing Flint (Albuquerque: 2011), 39–72.

30. Ladd, Edmund J., "Zuni on the Day the Men in Metal Arrived," in *The Coronado Expedition to Tierra Nueva: The 1540–1542 Route Across the Southwest*, ed. Richard Flint and Shirley Cushing Flint (Boulder: 1997), 225–33.

31. Flint and Flint, *Documents*, Doc. 22, "Traslado de las nuevas," 289ff; AGI: Patronato, 20, N.5, R.8.

32. Flint, *Great Cruelties*, "Troyano," 54v–55r, 179–80, and "Ledesma," 84v–85r, 244–45.

33. Flint and Flint, *Documents*, "Coronado to Mendoza," ff.361r and 362r, 267 and 268.

34. Ibid., "Coronado to Mendoza," f.363r, 270.

35. Ibid., "Castañeda," ff.11v–12r, 439.

36. AGI: Patronato Misiones 25, Exp. 36; only Jerry Craddock could have produced a photograph of this document with so little trouble; also see Sauer, "Road," 32 n.37.

37. Dockstader, Frederick J., *The Kachina and the White Man: The Influences of White Culture on the Hopi Kachina Cult* (Albuquerque: 1985 [1954]), 9ff.

38. McDonald, Dedra S., "Intimacy and Empire: Indian-African Interaction in Spanish Colonial Mexico, 1500–1800," *American Indian Quarterly* 22:1–2 (1998), 134–56; Dockstader, *Kachina*.

39. Flint and Flint, *Documents*, Doc. 15, "Narrative of Alarcón's Voyage," 185ff; Ramusio, *Terzo volume*, ff.363r–370v; Hakluyt, Richard (ed.), *Voyages, Navigations, Trafiques, and Discoveries of the English Nation . . .* , 3 vols. (London: 1600), 3:425–49; also see Herrera y Tordesillas, *Historia*, Dec. 6, Chs. 13–15, 208ff.

40. Flint and Flint, *Documents*, "Castañeda," f.34r, 447.

41. Ibid., "Castañeda," ff.36v–37r, 448.

42. Tello, Antonio, *Crónica miscelanea* (Guadalajara: 1891), Bk. 2, 409–11; also see Forbes, Jack D., "Melchior Díaz and the Discovery of Alta California," *Pacific Historical Review* 27:4 (1958), 351–57; and Ives, Ronald L., "The Last Journey of Melchior Díaz," *Journal of Geography* 59 (1960), 61–66.

43. Flint and Flint, *Documents*, Doc. 29, "Relación del Suceso," 1540s, 504–5; AGI: Patronato 20, N.5, R.8, f.2v.

44. Flint and Flint, *Documents*, "Alvarado," 307, f.1r.

45. Ibid., "Castañeda," 478, f.117v.

46. Ibid., "Castañeda," 491, ff.150r–152r.

47. Ibid., Doc. 29, "Relación del Suceso," 505, f.3v.

48. Ibid.

49. Flint, *Great Cruelties*, 181.

50. Flint and Flint, *Documents*, Doc. 28, "Castañeda," 454, ff.53v–54r.

51. Early, Ann M., "Finding the Middle Passage: The Spanish Journey from the Swamplands to Caddo County," in *The Expedition of Hernando de Soto West of the Mississippi, 1541–1543: Proceedings of the de Soto Symposia 1988 and 1990*, ed. Gloria A. Young and Michael P. Hoffman (Fayetteville: 1993), 68–77; Broom, Brian, "Mississippi's River Monsters," *Clarion-Ledger* (Jackson, MS), June 6, 2015.

52. Flint and Flint, *Documents*, "Castañeda," 454, f.55r.

53. Flint, *No Settlement*, 143.

54. Flint and Flint, *Documents*, "Castañeda," 456, ff.59v–61r.

55. Flint, *Great Cruelties*, 374.

56. Ibid., 184–85.

57. Flint, *No Settlement*, 153; Flint, *Great Cruelties*, 308; Flint and Flint, *Documents*, "Castañeda," 458.

58. Flint and Flint, *Documents*, Doc. 26, "Coronado to King," 1541, 317ff; AGI: Patronato 184, R.34.

59. Flint and Flint, Doc. 26, "Coronado to King," 323, f.1r, and Doc. 30, "Jaramillo's Narrative," 1560s, 521; AGI: Patronato 20, N.5, R.8, f.2v.

60. Ibid., Doc. 30, "Jaramillo's Narrative," 522.

61. Ibid., "Castañeda," 464, f.82r.

62. Ibid., "Castañeda," 465, ff.82r–82v.

63. Blakeslee, Donald J., Richard Flint, and Jack T. Huges, "Una Barranca Grande, Recent Archaeological Evidence and a Discussion of Its Place in the Coronado Route," in *The*

Coronado Expedition to Tierra Nueva: The 1540–1542 Route Across the Southwest, ed. Richard Flint and Shirley Cushing Flint (Boulder: 1997), 309–20; Thibodeau, Alyson M., John T. Chesley, and Joaquin Ruiz, "Lead Isotope Analysis as a New Method for Identifying Material Culture Belonging to the Vázquez de Coronado Expedition," *Journal of Archaeological Science* 39:1 (2012), 58–66; and see images of objects found at seymourharlan.com/My_Homepage_Files/Page50.html.

64. Flint and Flint, *Documents*, Doc. 26, "Coronado to King," 324–25.

65. Ibid., Doc. 30, "Jaramillo's Narrative," 522–23.

66. Flint, *No Settlement*, 160–61; Flint, *Great Cruelties*, 159 and 335.

67. Flint and Flint, *Documents*, "Castañeda," 483, f.129v.

68. Ibid., Doc. 30, "Jaramillo's Narrative," 523–24.

69. Bakewell, P. J., *Silver Mining and Society in Colonial Mexico: Zacatecas, 1546–1700* (Cambridge: 1971), 6.

70. "Nueva Galicia a su majestad . . . XX de diciembre de 1549" in Enciso Contreras, José (ed.), *Epistolario de Zacatecas, 1549–1599* (Zacatecas: 1996), 28–33, 32.

71. Kelsey, Harry, "The California Armada of Juan Rodríguez Cabrillo," *Southern California Quarterly* 61:4 (1979), 313–36; Mathes, Michael, "The Expedition of Juan Rodríguez Cabrillo, 1542–1543: An Historiographical Reexamination," *Southern California Quarterly* 76:3 (1994), 247–53; Herrera y Tordesillas, *Historia*, vol. 3, Dec. 7, Bk. 5, Chs. 3 and 4.

CHAPTER SEVEN

1. AGI: Indiferente 415, L.1, ff.41r–45r.

2. Fernández de Oviedo, *Historia*, 3:351.

3. Elvas, Gentleman of, *Relaçao verdadeira dos trabalhos que o governador D. Fernando de Souto e certos fidalgos portugueses passaram no descobrimento da província da Florida. Agora novamente feita por um fidalgo de Elvas* [1557].

4. In addition to Juan Maura's brilliant modern biography of Cabeza de Vaca much cited above, for this period see Howard, David, *Conquistador in Chains: Cabeza de Vaca and the Indians of the Americas* (Tuscaloosa: 1997); or Bishop, Morris, *The Odyssey of Cabeza de Vaca* (New York and London: 1933).

5. Clayton, Lawrence A., Vernon James Knight, and Edward C. Moore (eds.), *The De Soto Chronicles*, 2 vols. (Tuscaloosa: 1995).

6. Fernández de Oviedo, *Historia*, 2:156 and 3:351.

7. AGI: Patronato 19, R.13, "Relación: Luys Hernández de Viedma."

8. Varner, John Grier, and Jeanette Johnson Varner (ed. and trans.), *The Florida of the Inca* (Austin: 1951), introduction.

9. Garcilaso de la Vega, Inca, *Comentarios reales de los Incas* (Lisbon: 1609), Bk. 1, Ch. 15.

10. AGI: Panamá 234, L.3, ff.265v–266v, "Título de tesorero."

11. Porras Barrenechea, Raúl, *El Inca Garcilaso en Montilla (1561–1614)* (Lima: 1955), 265–66.

12. Garcilaso de la Vega, *Comentarios reales*, Bk. 5, Ch. 29.

13. Porras Barrenechea, *Inca*, 265–66.

14. Garcilaso de la Vega, *Comentarios reales*, Bk. 4, Chs. 3, 9, and 23.

15. López de Gómara, *Historia*, Ch. 181.

16. Garcilaso de la Vega, *Comentarios reales*, Bk. 5, Ch. 23.

17. Porras Barrenechea, *Inca*, 17 refs Libro Tercero de Bautismos de la Parroquia de Santiago de Montilla, ff. 199 and 205.

18. Torre y del Cerro, José de la, *El Inca Garcilaso de la Vega (Nueva Documentación)* (Seville: 2012 [1935]), Docs. 123–28, 182ff; Porras Barrenechea, *Inca*, 44–45 refs Archivo de Protocolos de Montilla, Registro de Escrituras de Juan Martínez de Córdoba, 1570, ff.513r–513v.

19. Vargas Ugarte, Rubén, "Nota sobre Garcilaso," *Mercurio Peruano*, 20:137–38 (1930), 106–7.

20. It is the edition published at Saragossa in 1554; see Rivarola, José Luis, "El taller del Inca Garcilaso. Sobre las anotaciones manuscritas en la *Historia General*...," *Revista de Filología Española* 75:1 (1995), 57–84; Porras Barrenechea, *Inca*, 225.

21. Torre y del Cerro, *El Inca Garcilaso*, Docs. 8, 14, and 129; Vargas Ugarte, "Nota," 106–7.

22. Dowling, Lee, "*La Florida del Inca*: Garcilaso's Literary Sources," in *The Hernando de Soto Expedition: History, Historiography, and "Discovery" in the Southeast*, ed. Patricia Galloway (Lincoln, NE, and London: 2005), 98–154.

23. Durand, José, "La biblioteca del Inca," *Nueva Revista de Filología Hispánica* 2:3 (1948), 239–64; Porras Barrenechea, *Inca*, 266.

24. Leonard, *Books*.

25. Garcilaso de la Vega, Inca, *La Florida del Inca* (Lisbon: 1605), Bk. 2, Chs. 26 and 27.

26. Dowling, "Sources," 106.

27. Cervantes, Miguel de, *Don Quijote* (Madrid: 1605 and 1615), Pt. 2, Ch. 3.

28. Ife, B. W., *Reading and Fiction in Golden-Age Spain: A Platonic Critique and Some Picaresque Replies* (Cambridge: 1985), 10.

29. Garcilaso de la Vega, *Florida*, Bk. 2, Pt. 1, Ch. 1.

30. floridahistory.com/inset444.html.

31. Ibid.

32. Garcilaso de la Vega, *Florida*, Bk. 2, Pt. 1, Ch. 1.

33. Ibid., Ch. 3.

34. Ibid., Ch. 6.

35. Ibid., Chs. 7 and 8.

36. Ibid., Ch. 11.

37. floridahistory.com/inset444.html.

38. Garcilaso de la Vega, *Florida*, Bk. 1, Ch. 13.

39. Ibid., Bk. 2, Pt. 1, Ch. 13.

40. Biblioteca Colombina, Seville: 57-5-43.

41. I have been less free with Garcilaso's speech than he was with Vitachuco's original words, if he ever existed. Nonetheless, I have taken much liberty.

42. Garcilaso de la Vega, *Florida*, Bk. 2, Pt. 2., Ch. 1.

43. Ewen, Charles R., and John H. Hann, *Hernando de Soto Among the Apalachee: The Archeology of the First Winter Encampment* (Gainesville: 1998); for quotations: 28 refs Mitchell, Chuck, transcript from comments, Florida Archaeological Council, Jacksonville Forum (1989).

44. Garcilaso de la Vega, *Florida*, Bk. 2, Pt. 2, Ch. 25.

45. Ibid., Bk. 3, Ch. 9.

46. Ibid., Bk. 3, Chs. 9–11.

47. Fernández de Oviedo, *Historia*, 2:169.

48. Brain, Geoffrey, introduction to *Final Report of the United States de Soto Expedition Commission*, ed. John R. Swanton (Washington, DC: 1985 [1939]), xi–lxxii; Dye, David H., "Reconstruction of the de Soto Expedition Route in Arkansas: The Mississippi Alluvial Plain," in Young and Hoffman, *Proceedings*, 36–57, 37–38.

49. Fernández de Oviedo, *Historia*, 2:178.

50. Dye, "Reconstruction," 48.

51. Garcilaso de la Vega, *Florida*, Bk. 4, Ch. 11.

52. AGI: Patronato 19, R.3, "Relación de Viedma," image 16.

53. Garcilaso de la Vega, *Florida*, Bk. 4, Ch. 13.

54. Ibid., Bk. 5, Pt. 1, Ch. 1.

55. AGI: Patronato 19, R.3, "Relación de Viedma," image 17.

56. Flint and Flint, *Documents*, "Castañeda," 467–68, f.90r.

57. Garcilaso de la Vega, *Florida*, Bk. 5, Pt. 1, Ch. 7.

58. Schambach, Frank F., "The End of the Trail: Reconstruction of the Route of Hernando de Soto's Army Through Southwest Arkansas and East Texas," in Young and Hoffman, *Proceedings*, 78–102, 88ff.

59. AGI: Patronato 19, R.3, image 18.

60. Kenmotsu, Nancy Adele, James E. Bruseth, and James E. Corbin, "Moscoso and the Route in Texas: A Reconstruction," in Young and Hoffman, *Proceedings*, 106–31.

61. AGI: Indiferente 737, N.59, "Relación que trajo Luis Hernández de Biedma," f.64r.

62. Elvas, *Relaçao*.

INTRODUCTION TO PART TWO

1. Vizcaíno, Sebastián [ed. Geo B. Griffin], "Letter of Sebastián Vizcaíno to the King of Spain, Announcing His Return from the Exploration of the Coast of the Californias, as Far as the Forty-Second Degree of North Latitude—Dated 23d May, 1603," *Publications of the Historical Society of Southern California* 2:1 (1891), 68–73.

CHAPTER EIGHT

1. Priestley, Herbert Ingram, *Tristán de Luna. Conquistador of the Old South: A Study of Spanish Imperial Strategy* (Glendale, CA: 1936); CDI: 13:280ff, Luna to King, September 24, 1559.

2. Priestley, *Luna*, 140.

3. Priestley, Herbert Ingram, *The Luna Papers, 1559–1561*, 2 vols. (Deland, FL: 1928).

4. Dávila Padilla, Fray Augustín, *Historia de la fundación y discurso de la provincia de Santiago de Mexico de la orden de predicadores*, 2nd ed. (Brussels: 1625), 226.

5. *Archivo Documental Español*, vol. 5, *Negociaciones con Francia (1563)* (Madrid: 1952), Doc. 616, "Chantonnay y Francés de Alava to Felipe II," 18–19, Doc. 629, "Perrenot a Felipe II," 51–52, and Doc. 778, "Perrenot to Philip II," 460–61; Lyon, Eugene, *The Enterprise of Florida: Pedro Menéndez de Avilés and Spanish Conquest of 1565–1568* (Gainesville: 1976 [1974]), 36 n.40 refs AGI: Patronato 254, R.38; and also see Ruidíaz y Caravia, Eugenio, *La Florida: su conquista y colonización por Pedro Menéndez de Avilés*, 2 vols. (Madrid: 1893), appendix 3, pt. 3, "Memorial," 443.

6. Lyon, *Enterprise*, 37ff.

7. Solís de Merás, Gonzalo, *Pedro Menéndez de Avilés y la conquista de la Florida (1565). Memorial que hizo el Doc. Solís de Merás de todas la jornadas y sucesos del Adelantado Pedro de Menéndez*, ed. J. M. Gómez-Tabanera (Oviedo: 1990), 4–29.

8. Lyon, *Enterprise*, 26 n.15 refs AGI: Justicia 970 and Contratación 135-A.

9. See my sections on the Comuneros, law, and institutions in Goodwin, R. T. C., *Spain: The Centre of the World, 1519–1682* (London and New York: 2015).

10. Ruidíaz y Caravia, Eugenio, *Conquista y colonización de La Florida por Pedro Menéndez de Avilés* (Madrid: 1989 [1893]), appendix 3, 444.

11. Solís de Merás, *Pedro Menéndez*, 63–64.

12. Ibid., 67.

13. Ruidíaz y Caravia, *Conquista*, appendix 1, no. 20, "Menéndez to the King," October 15, 1565, 312.

14. AGI: Patronato 52, N.3, R.3, "Méritos y servicios de Diego López" 1569, f.21, image 4.

15. Solís de Merás, *Pedro Menéndez*, Ch. 14.

16. CDI: 5:532ff, 536; Smith, Buckingham (ed. and trans.), *Letter of Hernando de Soto and Memoir of Hernando de Escalante Fontaneda* (Washington, DC: 1854).

17. Solís de Merás, *Pedro Menéndez*, Ch. 14.

18. Ibid.

19. Ibid.; also see Reilly, Stephen E., "A Marriage of Expedience: The Calusa Indians and Their Relations with Pedro Menéndez de Avilés in Southwest Florida," *Florida Historical Quarterly* 59:4 (1981), 395–421.

20. Ibid.

21. Hoffman, *New Andalucia*, 247–48.

22. Ibid.

23. Hudson, Charles, *The Juan Pardo Expeditions: Exploration of the Carolinas and Tennessee, 1566–1568* (Washington, DC: 1990).

24. Hoffman, *New Andalucia*, 242–44.

25. Ibid., 243; Ruidíaz y Caravia, *Conquista*, appendix 2, no. 8, 462–63.

26. Vargas Ugarte, Rubén, "The First Jesuit Mission in Florida," *United States Catholic Historical Society: Historical Records and Studies*, vol. 25 (New York: 1935), 59–148, 61–63, and 68ff, Docs. 1–6, and see Doc. 16.

27. Beverley, Robert, *History and Present State of Virginia*, ed. Louis B. Wright (Chapel Hill, NC: 1947 [1705]), 61.

28. Martínez, Bartolomé, "Relación de Bartolomé Martínez," in *The Spanish Jesuit Mission in Virginia, 1570–1572*, ed. Clifford M. Lews and Albert J. Loomie (Chapel Hill, NC: 1953), 148–65, 148ff; AGI: Contaduría 286, N.1, September 1561; published on encyclopediavirginia.org; Townsend, Camilla, "Mutual Appraisals: The Shifting Paradigms of the English, Spanish, and Powhatans in Tsenacomoco, 1560–1622," in *Early Modern Virginia: Reconsidering the Old Dominion*, ed. Douglas Bradburn and John C. Coombs (Charlottesville: 2011), 57–89, see 57ff.

29. Zubillaga, Félix, *La Florida: la misión jesuítica (1566–1572) y la coloniziación española* (Rome: 1940), 394 n.9; Ruidíaz y Caravia, appendix 1, Doc. 16, 297–300.

30. Martínez, "Relación," 151.

31. Rountree, Helen C., *Pocahontas, Powhatan, Openchancanough: Three Indian Lives Changed by Jamestown* (Charlottesville and London: 2008), 16ff.

32. Oré, Luis Gerónimo de, "Relación de Luis Gerónimo de Oré," in Lews and Loomie, *Spanish Jesuit*, 170–92, 172.

33. Rogel, Juan, "Relación de Juan Rogel, 1607–1611," in Lews and Loomie, *Spanish Jesuit*, 115–22, 115–17; Martínez, "Relacíon," 150–52.

34. Covington, James W., "Drake Destroys St. Augustine: 1586," *Florida Historical Quarterly* 44:1–2 (1965), 81–93, 81–82; and see Rowse, A. L., *The Elizabethans and America* (New York: 1959), 10–11.

35. Quinn, David Beers, *The Roanoke Voyages, 1584–1590*, 2 vols. (London: 1955), Doc. 47, "*The Primrose* Journal of Drake's Voyage. Florida and Virginia," 1:303–13; and see Wright, Irene A. (ed. and trans.), *Further English Voyages to Spanish America, 1583–1594* (London: 1951), Doc. 32, "Pedro Menédez to House of Trade, Saint Augustine, June 17, 1586," 163–64, and Doc. 33, "Royal Officials at Florida, to Crown, Saint Augustine, June 17, 1586," 164–65.

36. Quinn, *Roanoke*, 1:304.

37. Bigs [Bigges], Capt. Walter, "A Summarie and True Discourse of Sir Frauncis Drake's West Indian Voayge," in *Sir Francis Drake's West Indian Voyage, 1585–86*, ed. Mary F. Keeler (London: 1981), 205–7.

38. Hoffman, Paul E., *Spain and the Roanoke Voyages* (Raleigh: 1987).

39. Hoffman, Paul E., *Florida's Frontiers* (Bloomington: 2002), 73ff.

CHAPTER NINE

1. Mota y Padilla, *Historia* (1920), 180.

2. AGI: México 68, R.12, N.29, "Carta del licenciado Lorenzo de Tejada," March 11, 1545.

3. Dorantes de Carranza, Baltasar, *Sumaria relación de las cosas de la Nueva España* (Mexico City: 1987 [c. 1600]), 268 says he was called Barbalonga because he had a "very long beard," *la barba muy larga*; Enciso Contreras, José, and Ana Hilda Reyes Veyna, *Juanes de Tolosa, descubridor de las minas de Zacatecas. Información de méritos y servicios* (Zacatecas: 2002); AGI: Patronato, R.5, Leg. 80; Mota y Escobar, Alonso de la, *Descripción geográfica de los reynos de Nueva Galicia, Nueva Vizcaya y Nuevo León*. Colección de Obras Facsimilares no. 1 ([Jalisco]: 1966 [1605]), 64.

4. *Libro de Cabildo de Zacatecas* in Salinas de la Torre, Gabriel (ed.), *Testmonios de Zacatecas* (Mexico City: 1946), 109ff; AGI: Guadalajara 31.

5. Otte, Enrique, *Cartas privadas de emigrantes a Indias, 1540–1616* (Seville: 1988), 212.

6. AGI: Patronato 181, quoted in Powell, P. W., and María L. Powell, *War and Peace on the North Mexican Frontier: A Documentary Record*, vol. 1 (Madrid: 1971), 215–16.

7. Mota y Escobar, *Descripción geográfica*, 67.

8. Chevalier, François, *Land and Society in Colonial Mexico: The Great Hacienda*, trans. Alvin Eustis (Berkeley and Los Angeles: 1970), 148–54; AGI: Patronato 21, N.4, R.2; Sampson, Alexander, "Informaciones de servicio/Probanzas de meritos y servicios: Administering a New World. Self-Fashioning, Novelistic Discourse and the Truth of History," paper read to Association for Spanish and Portuguese Historical Studies, Albuquerque, April 4–7, 2013; Bakewell, *Silver Mining*, 11; Porras Muñoz, Guillermo, "Diego de Ibarra y la Nueva España," *Estudios de Historia Novohispana* 2:2 (1968), 1–28, 5.

9. Chipman, Donald E., "The Oñate-Moctezuma-Zaldívar Families of Northern New Spain," *New Mexico Historical Review* 52:4 (1977), 297–310, 304 n.15 refs AHN: Ordenes Militares-Santiago, Exp. 5925.

10. Chipman, "Families," 298–99.

11. Mota y Padilla, *Historia*, 195–97; Chipman, "Families," 305; Chipman, *Moctezuma's Children*, 106.

12. Mota y Escobar, *Descripción geográfica*, 87–88.

13. Obregón, *Historia de los descubrimientos*, 181.

14. Ibid., 178–79.

15. "Testimonio dado en Méjico sobre el descubrimiento de doscientas leguas adelante . . . que pidió Fr. Agustin Rodriguez . . . ," CDI: 15:80ff, 89; NB: this was at AGI: Patronato 22, R.5 but is now missing.

16. AGI: Patronato 22, R.4, ff.71r–100v; De Marco, Barbara, and Jerry R. Craddock, "Relación de Hernán Gallegos sobre la expedición del padre fray Agustín Rodríguez y el capitán Francisco Sánchez Chamuscado a Nuevo México, 1581–1582": escholarship.org/uc/item/4sv5h1gz; CDI: 15:82–86.

17. AGI: Patronato 22, R.4, ff.104r–148v; De Marco, Barbara, and Jerry R. Craddock, "Diego Pérez de Luján: Relación de la expedición de Antonio de Espejo a Nuevo México, 1582–1583": escholarship.org/uc/item/5313v23h.

18. Toro, Alfonso, *La familia Carvajal: estudio histórico sobre los judios y la Inquisición de la Nueva España en el siglo XVI* (Mexico City: 1944); Hordes, Stanley M., *To the End of the Earth: A History of the Crypto-Jews of New Mexico* (New York: 2005); Schroeder, Albert H., and Dan S. Matson, *A Colony on the Move: Gaspar Castaño de Sosa's Journal, 1590–1591* ([Salt Lake City?]: 1965); and see Carvajal contract: AGI: Indiferente 416, "Orden del rey a la Casa de Contratación," Toledo, June 14 1579, fol. 7v.

19. Hackett, Charles Wilson (ed.), *Historical Documents Relating to New Mexico, Nueva Vizcaya, and Approaches Thereto, 1773, Collected by Adolph F. A. Bandelier and Fanny R. Bandelier*, 3 vols. (Washington, DC: 1923), 1:218ff, "Carta de Velasco a SM," January 30, 1595, and 224ff, "Petición al virrey . . . y capitulaciones . . . con Don Juan de Oñate," September 21, 1595; AGI; Indiferente 744; Craddock, Jerry R., and Barbara De Marco, 2015: escholarship.org/uc/item/0w8064q7.

20. Archivo General de la Nación, Mexico City: Civil, vol. 1988, ff.226r–230v, 228r.

21. AGI: MP-Estampas 1; Patronato 22, R. 13, fols. 1019–21.

22. For Philip's gout, see *Calendar of State Papers, Venetian*, 9:416; in November 1596, Philip suspended all payments from his treasury; Parker, Geoffrey, *The Grand Strategy of Philip II* (New Haven and London: 1998), 279; AGI: México 1064, ff.96r–v; and De Marco, Barbara, and Jerry R. Craddock, "Documents Concerning the Suspension of Juan de Oñate's Expedition to New Mexico": escholarship.org/uc/item/6pjo700h.

23. AGI: México 1064; De Marco and Craddock, "Documents Concerning the Suspension of Juan de Oñate's Expedition to New Mexico"; and AGI: Patronato 22, R.4, ff.354r–422r and 307r–374r; De Marco and Craddock, "Lope de Ulloa y Lemos's Inspection of Juan de Oñate's Equipment and Personnel Destined for the Conquest of México": escholarship.org/uc/item/3nt8h54n.

24. AGI: México 25, 22-B, f.22v, "Traslado de la visita de don Lope de Ulloa y Lemos"; De Marco and Craddock, "Lope de Ulloa y Lemos's Inspection."

25. Ibid.

26. Martín Rodríguez, Manuel, "'Aqui fue Troya nobles caualleros': ecos de la tradición clásica y otros intertextos en la *Historia de la Nueva Mexico*, de Gaspar Pérez de Villagrá," *Silva* 4 (2005), 139–208, 151.

27. Pérez de Villagrá, Gaspar, *Historia de la Nueva Mexico*, ed. Manuel M. Martín Rodríguez (Alcalá de Henares: 2010 [1610]); the translations of Villagrá's *Historia* are all mine. I have

worked from Martín Rodríguez's edition, the parallel text and translation edited by Miguel Encinias, Alfred Rodríguez, and Joseph P. Sánchez, *Historia de la Nueva México, 1610* (Albuquerque: 1992), and the prose translation by Gilberto Espinosa, *History of New Mexico* (Los Angeles: 1933).

28. Martín Rodríguez, *Historia*, 42, f.IIIv; Pérez de Villagrá, *Historia*, front matter.

29. Pérez de Villagrá, *Historia*, front matter.

30. Hackett, *Historical Documents*, 1:380–88.

31. Adapted from lines 65–70.

32. Lines 85ff.

33. Lines 146, 147, 158, 188, 191, 201.

34. f.6v, 74–75, lines 9ff.

35. ff.8r–v, 77, lines 97ff.

36. Pérez de Villagrá, Gaspar, *Historia de la Nueva México*, ed. Felipe I. Echenique March (Mexico City: 1993), 90; Martín Rodríguez, "Aquí fue Troya," 156–57; and Pérez de Villagrá, *Historia*, n.136.

37. Pérez de Villagrá, *Historia*, canto 10, lines 272ff.

38. AGI: Guadalajara 1, 12r.

39. Douay-Rheims: Exodus 12:38: "And a mixed multitude without number went up also with them, sheep and herds and beasts of diverse kinds, exceeding many."

40. AGI: Patronato 22, R.13, "Ytinerario" f.1153r; see Craddock, Jerry R., and Barbara De Marco, "Ytinerario de la expeción de Juan de Oñate a Nuevo México 1597–1599": escholarship.org/uc/item/1f92f9b1.

41. For wearing of finery, see Hammond, George P., and Agapito Rey (eds.), *Don Juan de Oñate: Colonizer of New Mexico, 1595–1628*, 2 vols., Coronado Cuarto Centennial Publications, 1540–1940, vols. 5 and 6 (Albuquerque: 1953), 6:611.

42. Pérez de Villagrá, *Historia*, canto 14; see Encinias et al., *Historia*, 131 n.6.

43. AGI: Patronato 22, R.13, f.1154r.

44. AGI: Patronato 22, R.13, "Ytinerario" f.1153r; see Craddock and De Marco, "Ytinerario"; and see Pérez de Villagrá, *Historia*, canto 15.

45. CDI: 16:102ff.

46. Ibid.

47. Sigüenza, Fray José de, *Fundación del Monasterio de el Escorial por Felipe II*, ed. Miguel Sánchez y Pinillos (Madrid: 1881), 210.

48. AGI: Patronato 22, R.13, "Ytinerario," f.1224r.

49. AGI: México 28, 17-B, ff.12v–13r; De Marco, Barbara, Jerry R. Craddock, and John H. R. Polt, "Juan de Oñate Defends Himself Against the Charges for Which He Was Convicted in 1614": escholarship.org/uc/item/0p76r2wj.

50. Craddock, Jerry R., David J. Weber, and John H. R. Polt, "Zaldívar and the Cattle of Cíbola. Vicente de Zaldívar's Report of His Expedition to the Buffalo Plains in 1598": escholarship.org/uc/item/6hz1x4s4; AGI: Patronato 22, R.13, 1019r–1021r, ff.1195r–1196v, ff.1243v–1245v.

51. Ibid., f.1030r.

52. Ibid.

53. "Ytinerario," October 6; and see AGI: Patronato 22, R.13/17 for this and background to the following.

54. AGI: Patronato 22, R.13/17.

55. Ibid.

56. AGI: México 28, 17-B, ff.3v and 12v; Craddock, Jerry R., John H. R. Polt, and Barbara De Marco, "Oñate's Report to the Viceroy March 2, 1599": escholarship.org/uc/item/8s9oh6b6 #page-1; AGI: Patronato 22.

57. AGI: Patronato 22, R.13/17.

58. Ibid.

59. Martín Rodríguez, Manuel, *Gaspar de Villagrá: legista, soldado y poeta* (León: 2009), 111.

60. AGI: Guadalajara 1, ff.1r–2r; De Marco et al., "Juan de Oñate Defends Himself."

61. Pérez de Villagrá, *Historia*, cantos 21 and 22.

62. The following abbreviation of Villagrá's representation of the debates among the Acomas draws on two episodes: the first, in canto 18, is set in the build up to Oñate's first arrival at Acoma, the second, in canto 21, is the buildup to the murder of Zaldívar.

63. AGI: Patronato 22, R.13, 1036r–1085f; see Craddock, Jerry R., and John H. R. Polt, "The Trial of the Indians of Acoma, 1598–1599": escholarship.org/uc/item/14v3j7sj.

64. AGI: Patronato 22, R.13.

65. Ibid., R.13/10, Zaldívar's testmony, 31v–32r, and Villagrá's testimony, 40v.

66. AGI: México 28, 17-B, ff.1r–2r; De Marco et al., "Juan de Oñate Defends Himself"; Velasco says 600, Alonso Sánchez, 800.

67. AGI: Guadalajara 1, f.6v/2v; De Marco et al., "Juan de Oñate Defends Himself."

68. All this condensed from canto 1, lines 1–49.

69. AGI: México 24, N.22 and AGI: Patronato 22, R.13 ff.1143r–1150v and 1228r–1233v; see Craddock et al., "Oñate's Report to the Viceroy."

70. Hammond, George, "Oñate and Founding of New Mexico," *New Mexico Historical Review*, 1:4 (NM: 1926), 463.

71. Martín Rodríguez, *Gaspar de Villagrá*, see 147 and appendix 2.

72. Ibid., 143–45.

73. Ibid., 152–53.

74. Ibid., 154ff.

75. AGI: Guadalajara 1, 9r/5r; De Marco, et al., "Juan de Oñate Defends Himself."

76. Simmons, Marc, "The Tlascalans in the Spanish Borderlands," *New Mexico Historical Review* 39:2 (1964), 101–10.

77. Martín Rodríguez, *Gaspar de Villagrá*, 273ff refs AGI: Indiferente 450, L.A6 and AGI: Contratación 5788, L.2, ff.207v–08v and 573, N.15, R.1/14; Oñate appointed Knight of Santiago, AHN: OM-Expedientillos, N.1081; Eric Beerman, "The Death of an Old Conquistador: New Light on Juan de Oñate," *New Mexico Historical Review* 54:4 (1979), 305–19.

CHAPTER TEN

1. Wiget, Andrew O., "Truth and the Hopi: An Historiographic Study of Documented Oral Tradition Concerning the Coming of the Spanish," *Ethnohistory* 29:3 (1982), 181–99, 185.

2. Nequatewa, Edmund, *Truth of a Hopi* (Flagstaff: 1967), 42ff.

3. Voth, Henry R., *The Traditions of the Hopi*, Field Columbian Museum, pub. 96, vol. 8 (Chicago: 1903), 268ff.

4. Wiget, "Truth," 192.

5. Waters, Frank, *The Book of the Hopi* (New York: 1977 [1963]), 23–24.

6. Wiget, "Truth," 186.

7. Nequatewa, *Truth*, 45.

8. "Petition of Fray Juan de Prada, September 26, 1638," in Hackett, *Historical Documents*, 3:107.

9. Benavides, Alonso de, *Memorial que fray Juan de Santander de la Orden de san Francisco ... presenta a la Magestad Catolica del Rey don Felipe Quarto* (Madrid: 1630), title page, 4.

10. Ibid., 15ff.

11. Reff, Daniel T., "Contextualizing Missionary Discourse: The Benavides 'Memorials' of 1630 and 1634," *Journal of Anthropological Research* 50:1 (1994), 51–67, 60.

12. Hodge, Frederick W., George P. Hammond, and Agapito Rey (eds. and trans.), *Fray Alonso de Benavides' Revised Memorial of 1634*, Coronado Cuarto Centennial Publications, 1540–1940, vol. 4 (Albuquerque: 1945), appendix 4, 109ff.

13. Ibid., appendix 4, 114, 120, and 121.

14. Chávez, Angélico, "Nuestra Señora del Rosario: La Conquistadora," *New Mexico Historical Review* 23:2 (1948), 94–128, 124; and see Chávez, Angélico, *Our Lady of Conquest* (Santa Fe: 2010).

15. Spiess, Lincoln B., "Church Music in Seventeenth-Century New Mexico," *New Mexico Historical Review* 40 (1965), 5–21.

16. Pérez de Ribas, Andrés, *Historia de los triunfos de nuestra Santa Fé entre gentes las más bárbaras, y fieras de nuestro orbe* (Madrid: 1645), Bk. 2, Ch. 36.

17. Mann, Kristin D., *The Power of Song: Music and Dance in the Mission Communities of Northern New Spain, 1590–1810* (Stanford: 2010), 85.

18. Spiess, Lincoln B., "Benavides and Church Music in New Mexico in the Early 17th Century," *Journal of the American Musicological Society* 17:2 (1964), 144–56.

19. Perea, Fray Esteban de, *Verdadera relación de la grandiosa conversión qué ha habido en el Nuevo México* (Seville: 1632), f.579v.

20. Mann, *Power*, 86.

21. Benavides, *Memorial*, 22.

22. Espinosa, J. Manuel, "The Origin of the Penitentes of New Mexico: Separating Fact from Fiction," *Catholic Historical Review* 79: (1992), 454–77; Henderson, Alice Corbin, *Brothers of Light: Penitentes of the Southwest* (New York: 1937); Van Valen, Gary, "Anglo Perceptions of a Cofradía: The Penitentes of New Mexico," *Secolas Annals* 27 (1996), 49–57; Varjabedian, Craig, and Michael Wallis, *En Divina Luz* (Albuquerque: 1994); Price, Roland, and Harry Revier (dirs.), *Lash of the Penitentes*, YouTube: youtube.com/watch?v=ddzoWM 6AXNo.

23. Benavides, *Memorial*, 24.

24. Morte Acín, Ana, *Misticismo y conspiración: Sor María de Ágreda en el reinado de Felipe IV* (Saragossa: 2010), 182.

25. Benavides, *Memorial*, 80; and see Kendrick, T. D., *Mary of Ágreda: The Life and Legend of a Spanish Nun* (London: 1967), 32ff.

26. Morte Acín, *Misticismo*, 183.

27. Hodge et al., *Fray Alonso*, 7.

28. Kendrick, *Mary of Ágreda*, 36.

29. Morte Acín, *Misticismo*, 371.

30. Seco Serrano, Carlos (ed.), *Cartas de Sor María de Jesús de Ágreda y de Felipe IV*, Epistolario España, vol. 4, Biblioteca de Autores Españoles, 2 vols. (Madrid: 1958), 207–9, "María to Philip," February 18, and "Philip to María," February 26, 1650.

31. Lárraga, Maribel, "La mística de la feminidad en la obra de Juan Villagutierre Soto-mayor: historia de la conquista pérdida y restauración del reyno y provincia de la Nueva México en la América Septentrional (1698)," PhD thesis, University of New Mexico (1999), 137ff.

32. Scholes, France V., *Church and State in New Mexico, 1610–1650* (Albuquerque: 1937), 19ff and 69ff.

33. Ibid., 117–20.

34. Ibid., 143–44 n.6.

35. Ibid., 146 n.17.

36. Ibid., 139.

37. Ibid., 155–67.

38. Scholes, France V., *Troublous Times in New Mexico, 1659–1670* (Albuquerque: 1942), 1–5.

39. Ibid., 6 ns.4 and 5.

40. Ibid., 19–20.

41. Ibid., 22.

42. Adams, Eleanor B., "Fray Silvestre Vélez de Escalante: Letter to the Missionaries of New Mexico," *New Mexico Historical Review* 40:4 (1965), 319–35.

43. Scholes, *Troublous Times*, 89.

44. Nequatewa, *Truth*, 43–44.

45. Ibid., 44.

46. Scholes, *Troublous Times*, 47.

47. Adapted from ibid., 61.

48. Scholes, *Troublous Times*, 137.

49. Ibid., 203.

50. The dialogue is adapted from ibid., 207–8.

51. Ivey, James E., "'The Greatest Misfortune of All': Famine in the Province of New Mexico, 1667–1672," *Journal of the Southwest* 36:1 (1994), 76–100.

52. Hackett, *Historical Documents*, 3:271ff.

53. Ivey, "Famine," 88–91.

CHAPTER ELEVEN

1. Sempere-Martínez, Juan A. (ed.), and Damian Bacich (trans.), "Documents Concerning the Revolt of the Indians of the Province of New Mexico in 1680," 61–62: escholarship.org/uc/item/5xvot5bq.

2. Kessell, John L., "Esteban Clemente: Precursor of the Pueblo Revolt," *El Palacio* 86:4 (1980–81), 16–17.

3. Hackett, Charles, and Charmion Clair Shelby, *Revolt of the Pueblo Indians of New Mexico and Otermin's Attempted Reconquest, 1680–1682*, 2 vols. (Albuquerque: 1942), 2:299–300; also see testimony of Pedro Naranjo in De Marco, Barbara, "Voices from the Archives I: Testimony of the Pueblo Indians on the 1680 Pueblo Revolt," *Romance Philology* 53 (1999), 375ff, 417.

4. Wilcox, Michael V., *The Pueblo Revolt and the Mythology of Conquest: An Indigenous Archeology of Contact* (Berkeley: 2009), 155; Horowitz, David L, *Ethnic Groups in Conflict* (Los Angeles: 1983), 3–55.

5. Knaut, Andrew L., *The Pueblo Revolt of 1680: Conquest and Resistance in Seventeenth-Century New Mexico* (Norman, OK: 1995), 164ff.

6. De Marco, "Voices," 375–448, 394, 404, and 417–18.

7. Chavez, Angelico, "Pohé-Yemo's Representative and the Pueblo Revolt of 1680," *New Mexico Historical Review* 42:2 (1967), 85–126, see n.36 on 120–22.

8. De Marco, "Voices," 39.

9. Ibid., 20.

10. Goodwin, *Crossing the Continent*, 368–69; Dockstader, *Kachina*, 11.

11. Parmentier, Richard J., "The Mythological Triangle: Poseyemu, Montezuma, and Jesus in the Pueblos," in *The Handbook of American Indians*, vol. 9, *The Southwest*, ed. Alfonso Ortiz (Washington, DC: 1979), 619ff.

12. Sando, Joe S., *Pueblo Nations: Eight Centuries of Pueblo Indian History* (Santa Fe: 1992), 67.

13. De Marco, "Voices," 393.

14. Sempere-Martínez, "Documents," 22ff.

15. Ibid., 54.

16. Ibid., 23ff.

17. Craddock, Jerry R., "Antonio de Otermín's Attempted Reconquest of New Mexico, Winter 1681-1682," 37–39 and appendix: escholarship.org/uc/item/41d6w72g; Hackett and Shelby, *Revolt of the Pueblo*, 1:liii.

18. Sempere-Martínez, "Documents," 27–30.

19. Ibid., 31–33.

20. The exchange is based on the reported speech in Sempere-Martínez, "Documents," 37.

21. De Marco, "Voices," 406.

22. Sempere-Martínez, "Documents," 39.

23. Ibid.

24. Ibid., 48.

25. Ibid.

26. Sando, Joe S., "The Pueblo Revolt," in *Po'pay: Leader of the First American Revolution*, ed. Joe S. Sando and Herman Agoyo (Santa Fe: 2005), 5–53, 39–40.

27. Sando, Joe S., *Pueblo Profiles: Cultural Identity Through Centuries of Change* (Santa Fe: 1998), 23.

28. De Marco, "Voices," 393 and 405.

29. Escalante, Fray Silvestre Vélez de, "Carta del Padre Fray Silvestre de Escalante, escrita en 2 e abril de 1778 años," in *Documentos para servir a la historia del Nuevo México, 1538–1778* (Madrid: 1962), 305–24, 311ff.

30. Sanchez, Jane C., "Spanish–Indian Relations During the Otermín Administration," *New Mexico Historical Review* 58:2 (1983), 133–51.

31. Sempere-Martínez, "Documents," 66.

32. Ibid., 201.

33. Ibid., 247; also see Hughes, Anne E., "The Beginnings of Spanish Settlement in the El Paso District," in *University of California Publications in History* (Berkeley: 1914), 295–392.

34. Chávez, "Nuestra Señora," 114–15.

35. Vargas, Diego de, *To the Royal Crown Restored: The Journals of Don Diego de Vargas, New Mexico, 1692–94*, ed. John L. Kessell, Rick Hendricks, and Meredith D. Dodge (Albuquerque: 1995), 3–21.

36. Shafer, Philip K., Heather McMichael, and Jerry R. Craddock, "Analysis and Edition of 'Deposition of Several Tigua, Tano and Piro Indians Before Antonio de Otermín, Governor of New Mexico, Concerning a Suspected Revolt Against the Spanish' El Paso, July 19–August 1, 1683," 63ff: escholarship.org/uc/item/1n65q9fp; and see Sanchez, "Spanish–Indian Relations," 143ff.

CHAPTER TWELVE

1. Imhoff, Brian (ed.), *The Diary of Juan Domínguez de Mendoza's Expedition into Texas, 1683–1684* (Dallas: 2002).

2. Muhlstein, Anka, *La Salle: Explorer of the North American Frontier*, trans. Willard Wood (New York: 2013), 175ff.

3. Chesnel, P., *Histoire de Cavelier de la Salle: exploration et conquête du Bassin du Mississippi* (Paris: 1901), 5ff.

4. Tonti, Henri de, *Dernières découvertes dans l'Amérique septentrionale de M. de la Salle La Salle* (Paris: 1697), 197.

5. Margry, Pierre, *Découverte et établissements des Français dans l'ouest et dans le sud de L'Amérique septentrionale, 1614–1754*, 5 vols. (Paris: 1879), 2:359ff; and see French, B. F. (ed.), "Memoir of Robert Cavelier de la Salle," in *Historical Collections of Louisiana*, Part One (New York: 1846), 20ff.

6. Margry, *Découverte*, 2:354ff.

7. Weddle, Robert S., *Wilderness Manhunt: The Spanish Search for La Salle* (College Station, TX: 1999 [1973]), 24.

8. Orellano Norris, Lola, "General Alonso de León's Expedition Diaries into Texas (1686–1690): A Linguistic Analysis of the Spanish Manuscripts with Semi-Paleographic Transcriptions and English Translations," PhD thesis, Texas A&M University (2010), 26–27; Orellano Norris, Lola, *Alonso de León's Expeditions into Texas, 1686–1690* (College Station, TX: 2017).

9. Ibid.

10. Weddle, *Wilderness*, 99.

11. Simmons, "Tlascalans in the Spanish Borderlands," 101–10.

12. Orellano Norris, "General," 81–82.

13. Ibid., 82.

14. Ibid., 262 n.97 puts the argument beyond doubt.

15. Ibid., 20r, 88ff.

16. Adapted from quotation in Weddle, *Wilderness*, 147.

17. In seventeenth-century Spanish, an "X" could sound either like an *aitch*, as in the guttural sound in the name Juan, or it could sound like an aspirated *ess-cee-aitch*, which is why you still sometimes see Sherry spelled Xerex on bottles. "B"s and "V"s are interchangeable and the final "E" would have been short, which spells "Schevlay," near as damn it to Chevilly. Gómez Canedo, Lino, *Primeras exploraciones y poblamiento de Texas (1686–1694)* (Monterrey: 1968), "Carta de Fray Damían Mazanet a Sigüenza y Góngora (1609)," 9.

18. Ibid., "Mazanet to Sigüenza y Góngora," 7.

19. Orellano Norris, "General"; AGI: México 616, ff.37v–50r, 42r, 105.

20. AGI: México, 39v, 100.

21. Ibid., 41r, 103.

22. AGI: México, 37v–50r, 44r, 109–10.

23. Gómez Canedo, *Primeras*, "Mazanet to Sigñuenza y Góngora," 13.

24. Orellano Norris, "General"; AGI: México 616, ff.37v–50r, 46v, 115.

25. IAGI: México 46r, 114.

26. Ratchford, Fannie E., "Three 'First' Texas Poems," *Southwest Review* 12:2 (1927), 132–42; León, Alonso de, *Historia de Nuevo León con noticias sobre Coahuila, Tejas, Nuevo México* (Mexico City: 1909), 336–37; Weddle, *Wilderness*, 187–88.

27. Orellano Norris, "General"; AGI: México 616, ff.37v–50r, 49v, 122.

28. For this abbreviation of the La Salle story, I have followed Weddle, Robert S., *The Wreck of the Belle, the Ruin of La Salle* (College Station, TX: 2001).

29. Gómez Canedo, *Primeras*, "Mazanet to Galve," 159.

30. Weddle, Robert S., Donald E. Chipman, and Carol A. Lipscomb, "The Misplacement of Mission San Francisco de los Tejas in Eastern Texas and Its Actual Location at San Pedro de los Nabedaches," *Southwestern Historical Quarterly* 120:1 (2016), 75–84.

31. Chipman, Donald E., and Harriett Denise Joseph, *Spanish Texas, 1519–1821*, rev. ed. (Austin: 2010), 97.

CHAPTER THIRTEEN

1. Shaffer, Ellen, "Father Eusebio Francisco Kino and the Comet of 1680–1681," *Historical Society of Southern California Quarterly* 34:1 (1952), 57–70.

2. Alegre, Francisco Javier, *Historia de la Compañía de Jesús en Nueva-España*, vol. 3 (Mexico City: 1842), 156; cervantesvirtual.com/portales/expulsion_jesuitas/obra-visor/historia -de-la-compania-de-jesus-en-nuevaespana-tomo-iii—0/html/07d90391-ee7f-4e9f-8271 -25d2d4ffc63d_10.html; Campbell, Thomas J., "Eusebio Kino, 1644–1711," *Catholic Historical Review* 5:4 (1920), 353–76, 374; Bolton, Herbert E. (ed.), *Kino's Historical Memoir of Pimería Alta*, 2 vols. (Cleveland: 1919), 1:32–33.

3. Bolton, *Kino*, 43ff.

4. Adapted from quotation in Burrus, Ernest J., *Kino and Manje: Explorers of Sonora and Arizona* (Rome: 1971), 44–45.

5. Ibid., 300 and 311.

6. Ibid., 295.

7. Ibid., 300 and 311.

8. Kino, Eusebio Francisco, *Las misiones de Sonora y Arizona*, ed. Francisco Fernández del Castillo (Mexico City: 1989), 29.

9. Kino, Eusebio Francisco, *Vida del P. Francisco J. Saeta, S. J: sangre misionera en Sonora*, ed. Ernest J. Burrus (Mexico City: 1961), 160ff.

10. Burrus, Ernest J. (ed. and trans.), *Kino's Plan for the Development of Pimería Alta, Arizona and Upper California: A Report to the Mexican Viceroy* (Tucson: 1961).

11. Adapted from quotation in Burrus, *Kino and Manje*, 95.

12. Burrus, *Kino and Manje*, 102–3 and 360–61; Kino, *Misiones*, 56 and 62.

13. Burrus, *Kino and Manje*, 365.

14. Ibid., 365.

15. Ibid., 341.

16. Kino, *Misiones*, 58.

17. Burrus, *Kino and Manje*, 343–45.

18. Ibid., 371–72.

19. The quotations are adapted from Bolton, Herbert E., *Rim of Christendom: A Biography of Eusebio Francisco Kino, Pacific Coast Pioneer* (New York: 1936), 373.

20. Kino, *Misiones*, 62–63.

21. Ibid., 76.

22. Burrus, *Kino and Manje*, 561ff; Kino, *Misiones*, 65.

23. Bolton, *Rim*, 410.

24. Burrus, *Kino and Manje*, 388ff.

25. Wright, Harold Bell, *Long Ago Told (Huh-Kew Ah-Kah): Legends of the Papago Indians* (New York and London: Appleton, 1929), 65ff.

26. Burrus, *Kino and Manje*, 413.

27. Broyles, Bill, et al., *Last Water on the Devil's Highway: A Cultural and Natural History of Tinajas Altas* (Tucson: 2012).

28. Burrus, *Kino and Manje*, 415.

29. Ibid., 395ff.

30. Ibid., 243 n.83.

31. Kino, *Misiones*, 68ff.

32. Ibid., 70ff.

33. Bolton, *Rim*, 437 and 456ff.

34. Ibid., 585.

CHAPTER FOURTEEN

1. Gayarré, Charles, *History of Louisiana*, 2 vols. (New York: 1854), 60–61 and 69–70.

2. Kamen, Henry, *Spain, 1469–1714: A Society in Conflict* (London: 1983), 257.

3. Kamen, Henry, *Philip V of Spain: The King Who Reigned Twice* (New Haven: 2001), 10.

4. Webber, David J., *The Spanish Frontier in North America* (New Haven: 1992), 142ff; Matter, Robert Allen, "Missions in the Defense of Spanish Florida, 1566–1710," *Florida Historical Quarterly* 54:1 (1975), 18–38, 32ff.

5. Webber, *Spanish Frontier*, 159.

6. Adapted from quotation in Kamen, *Philip*, 72.

7. Webber, *Spanish Frontier*, 160.

8. Gayarré, *History*, 166–67 for quotation; and for a colorful account, see Phares, Ross, *Cavalier in the Wilderness* (Baton Rouge: 1952).

9. Hackett, Charles W. (ed.), *Pichardo's Treatise on the Limits of Louisiana and Texas*, 5 vols. (Austin: 1946 [c. 1808–12]), 4:305ff.

10. Gayarré, *History*, 168–69 for quotations; Weddle, Robert S., *San Juan Bautista: Gateway to Spanish Texas* (Austin: 1991 [1968]), 101ff.

11. Espinosa, Fray Isidro Félix de, *Crónica de los colegios de propaganda fide de la Nueva España*, ed. Lino G. Canedo (Washington, DC: 1964), 780.

12. texasbeyondhistory.net/adaes.

13. Adapted from quotations in Weddle, *Juan Bautista*, 128–29.

14. Weddle, *Juan Bautista*, 135.

15. Adapted from Shelby, Charmion Clair, "St. Denis's Declaration Concerning Texas in 1717," *Southwestern Historical Quarterly* 26:3 (1923), 165–83.

16. Weddle, *Juan Bautista*, 140.

17. Hoffman, Fritz L., "The Mezquía Diary of the Alarcon Expedition into Texas, 1718," *Southwestern Historical Quarterly* 41:4 (1938), 312–23, 317.

18. Heusinger, Edward W., *Early Explorations and Mission Establishments in Texas* (San Antonio: 1936), 76–77.

19. Weddle, *Juan Bautista*, 152.

20. Céliz, Fray Francisco, *Diary of the Alarcón Expedition into Texas, 1718–1719* (Los Angeles: 1935), 77.

21. Chipman and Joseph, *Spanish Texas*, 118; Buckley, Eleanor Claire, "The Aguayo Expedition into Texas and Louisiana, 1719–1722," *Quarterly of the Texas State Historical Association* 15:1 (1911), 1–65, 11.

22. en.wikipedia.org/wiki/Nacogdoches,_Texas; and en.wikipedia.org/wiki/Pilgrim %27s_Pride.

23. Jones, Oakah L., *Los Paisanos: Spanish Settlers on the Northern Frontier of New Spain* (Norman, OK: 1996), 29.

24. Buckley, "Aguayo," 29ff.

25. "Rear Admiral Charles Stewart to the Duke of Newcastle," October 12, 1731, in Laughton, J. K., "Jenkins' Ear," *English Historical Review* 4:16 (1889), 741–49, 742.

26. Lawson, Edward W., "What Became of the Man Who Cut Off Jenkins' Ear?" *Florida Historical Quarterly* 37:1 (1958), 33–42.

27. Ibid., 34.

28. Pearce, Edward, *Pitt the Elder: Man of War* (London: 2010), 59.

29. Chipman and Joseph, *Spanish Texas*, 157–60.

30. Dunn, William E., "The Apache Mission on the San Sabá River: Its Founding and Failure," *Southwestern Historical Quarterly* 17:4 (1914), 379–414.

31. Ibid.," 393.

32. Bolton, Herbert E., *Athanase de Mézières and the Louisiana-Texas Frontier, 1768–1780*, 2 vols. (Cleveland: 1914), 2:207.

33. Dunn, "Apache Mission," 399.

34. Ibid., 401.

35. Romero de Terreros, Juan M., "The Destruction of the San Sabá Apache Mission: A Discussion of the Casualties," *The Americas* 60:4 (2004), 617–27.

36. Lejarza, Fray Fidel de, "Escenas de martirio en el río San Sabá," *Archivo Ibero-Americano* 12 (1943), 441–95; White, Richard S., "The Painting: *The Destruction of Mission San Sabá*: Document of Service to the King," PhD dissertation, Texas Tech University (2000), appendix A; Romero de Terreros, "Destruction," 625–27.

37. Ratcliffe, Sam D., "'Escenas de Martirio': Notes on 'The Destruction of Mission San Sabá,'" *Southwestern Historical Quarterly* 94:4 (1991), 507–34, 519; White, "Painting," 85ff; Romero de Terreros, Manuel, "La misión franciscana de San Sabás en la provincia de Texas. Año de 1758," *Anales del Instituto de Investigaciones Estétics* 9:36 (1967), 51–58.

38. See Molina's account in Hadley, Diana, Thomas H. Naylor, and Mardish K. Schuetz-Miller (eds.), *The Presidio and Militia on the Northern Frontier of New Spain: A Documentary History*, vol 2., pt. 2, *The Central Corridor and the Texas Corridor, 1700–1765* (Tucson: 1997), 521ff.

39. Adapted from quotations in Barr, Juliana, *Peace Came in the Form of a Woman: Indians and Spaniards in the Texas Borderlands* (Chapel Hill, NC: 2007), 87.

40. Hadley et al., *Presidio and Militia*, 520.

41. l. 24, ll. 1–7, ll. 38–39; ll. 326, ll. 330–31, ll. 335–335, ll. 339–41, ll. 382–85, l. 400, ll. 402–4, ll. 436; l. 577.

42. Weddle, Robert S., "The San Sabá Mission: Approach to the Great Plains," *Great Plains Journal* 4:2 (1965), 29–38, 32–34.

INTRODUCTION TO PART THREE

1. Anderson, Fred, *Crucible of War: The Seven Years' War and the Fate of Empire in British North America, 1754–1766* (New York and London: 2000), 52–65.

2. Fowler, William M. Jr., *Empires at War: The French and Indian War and the Struggle for North America, 1754–1763* (New York: 2005), 1.

3. Thackeray, Francis, *A History of the Right Honorable William Pitt, Earl of Chatham*, 2 vols. (London: 1827), 1:388 and 415–16.

4. Lynch, John, *Bourbon Spain: 1700–1808* (Cambridge, MA: 1989), 2.

5. Stein, Stanley J., and Barbara H. Stein, *Apogee of Empire: Spain and New Spain in the Age of Charles III, 1759–1789* (Baltimore and London: 2003), 3ff.

6. Ferrer del Río, Antonio, *Historia del reinado de Carlos III en España* (Madrid: 1856), Bk. 1, Ch. 1, n.158: cervantesvirtual.com/obra-visor/historia-del-reinado-de-carlos-iii-en -espana—o/html.

7. Thackeray, *Pitt*, 1:461ff.

8. Elliott, John H., *Empires of the Atlantic World: Britain and Spain in America, 1492–1830* (New Haven: 2006), 307–8.

9. Castillo, Francisco Andújar, "El reformismo militar de Carlos III: mito y realidad," *Cuadrenos de Historia Moderna* 41 (2016), 337–54; Maravall, José, *Antiguos y modernos* (Madrid: 1966); and Perrupato, Sebastián, "Antiguos y modernos en la universidad española de la segunda mitad del siglo XVIII. Avances de secularización en el plan de reforma universitario elaborado por Gregorio Mayans y Siscar (1767)," *Historia y sociedad* 27 (2014), 165–88.

10. Christelow, Allan, "French Interest in the Spanish Empire During the Ministry of the Duc de Choiseul, 1759–1771," *Hispanic American Historical Review* 21:4 (1941), 515–37, 532 n.66 refs BNP: fonds français 10,766, ff.156–157.

11. Adapted from quotation in Christelow, "French Interest," 522 n.26 refs AE: CP, Espagne, 532, ff.281–88.

12. Stein and Stein, *Apogee*, 13 n.34 refs BNP: fonds français 10,767, f.123, and see 13 n.31 for fears about New Spain; and Christelow, Allan, "Contraband Trade Between Jamaica and the Spanish Main, and the Three Port Act of 1766," *Hispanic American Historical Review* 22:2 (1942), 309–43, 313 n.8, which refs British Library, London: Add Mss 36,339 ff.303–32.

13. Porras Muñoz, Guillermo, *Bernardo de Gálvez* (Madrid: 1952), 5.

14. Priestley, Herbert Ingram, *José de Gálvez: Visitor-General of New Spain (1765–1771)* (Berkeley: 1916), vii–ix; Sesmero Ruiz, Julián, *Los Gálvez de Macharaviaya* (Málaga: 1987).

15. Priestley, *Gálvez*, 4 n.3 refs Francisco Carrasco, Marqués de la Corona, to Viergol, March 13, 1776; AHN: Leg. 3211.

16. AGI: Estado 86A, N.2; and see Navarro García, Luis, *La política americana de José de Gálvez* (Málaga: 1998).

17. Palóu, Francisco, *Junípero Serra y las misiones de California. Relación histórica de la vida y apostólicas tareas del venerable fray Junípero Serra*, ed. José Luis Anta Félez (Madrid: 2002), 39.

18. Hackel, Steven W., *Junipero Serra: California's Founding Father* (New York: 2013), 14–15; *The Americas*, 43:2 (1986), 223 for ref: Llabrés i Martorell, Pere, "Fray Junípero Serra i Ferrer: frie de Mallorca i del sur temps," *Comunicacio: Revista d'Estudis Teologics de Malorca* (1985), 3–17; and Schwartz, Stephen, "The Cult of Junipero Serra," SFGATE (*San Francisco Chronicle*), April 28, 1996: https://www.sfgate.com/news/article/The-Cult-of-Junipero-Serra-On-the-island-of-2984863.php.

19. The quotations are adapted from Palou, Francisco, *The Life of Friar Juniper*, in *The Little Flowers of St. Francis of Assisi*, trans. W. Heywood (London: 1906), 215–17 and 199–202; sacred-texts.com/chr/lff/lff000.htm.

20. Serra, Junípero, *Writings of Junípero Serra*, ed. Antonine Tibesar, 4 vols. (Washington, DC: 1955), 1:2–4.

21. Ibid., 1:10.

22. Palóu, *Relación*, 50.

23. Ibid., 53–55.

24. Hackel, *Serra*, 84–136.

CHAPTER FIFTEEN

1. Naylor, Thomas H., and Charles W. Polzer, *Pedro de Rivera and the Military Regulations for Northern New Spain, 1724–1729* (Tucson: 1988), 183; Garate, Donald T., *Juan Bautista de Anza: Basque Explorer of the New World, 1693–1740* (Reno: 2003), 157ff and n. 5.

2. Pradeau, Alberto Francisco, "Cerro de las bolas y planchas de plata. Maravilla del siglo XVIII," in *Memoria del VI Simposio de Historia y Antropología* (Hermosillo: 1981), 106–61, 117.

3. Ibid., 128.

4. Garate, Donald T., "Who Named Arizona? The Basque Connection," *Journal of Arizona History* 40:1 (1999), 53–82; Douglass, William A., "On the Naming of Arizona," *Names* 27 (1979), 217–34.

5. Pradeau, "Cerro de las bolas," 130.

6. Garate, *Juan Bautista*, 26 refs AHN: Estado, Leg. 2845 (1), f.37v, "Apunte instructivo de la expedición que el ilustrísimo don José de Gálvez . . . hizo . . . or Juan Manuel de Viniegra" (1773), 199.

7. Baltasar, Juan Antonio, *Apostólicos Afanes de la Compañía de Jesús en la América Septentrional* (Barcelona: 1754), Bk. 3, Ch. 12, 433–34. Garate, *Juan Bautista*, 205–7 n.126 refs AGI: Guadalajara, Leg. 88, Juan Bautista de Belauzarán al Vierrey, f.564, and then in ns. 128 and 129 Garate suggests that the apparently slightly garbled phrase "le despojaron el casco de su cabellera" may mean they removed his helmet and notes that some scholars argue that Apaches did not yet scalp victims at this point in history. However, Baltasar's only other use of the word *cabellera* in the same work is clearly in the context of scalping (Bk. 2, Ch. 15, 321).

8. Kessell, John L., "Anza, Indian Fighter: The Spring Campaign of 1766," *Journal of Arizona History* 9:3 (1968), 155–63, 155–56; Herrera, Carlos R., *Juan Bautista de Anza: The King's Governor in New Mexico* (Norman, OK: 2015), 31–44; quote is from Peña, Salvador Ignacio de la, "Convite Evangélico á compasión y Socorro de la Viña del Señor," University of Arizona Library, Tucson, microfilm 71.

9. I have adapted the quotations from Kessell, "Anza, Indian Fighter," 155–63, quotations 158–63, 157 refs *Documentos para la Historia de México*, Cuarta Série, vol. 2 (Mexico City: 1856), 109–12.

10. Lafora, Nicolás de, *The Frontiers of New Spain*, ed. Lawrence Kinnaird (Berkeley: 1958), 8 refs AGI: Guadalajara, 103-4-15 [273].

11. Lafora, Nicolás de, *Relación del viaje que hizo a los Presidios Internos situados en la frontera de la América Septentrional*, ed. Vito Alessio Robles (Mexico City: 1939), 66–70, 68.

12. Lafora, *Frontiers*, 12 n.9 refs AGI: Guadalajara, 103-4-15 (273), Rubí to Cruillas, July 27, 1766; Lafora, *Relación*, 72–75.

13. Ibid., 87–89, 89.

14. Ibid., 93–94.

15. Ibid., 104–5.

16. Ibid., 102–3.

17. Kessell, John L., *Mission of Sorrows: Jesuit Guevaví and the Pimas, 1691–1767* (Tucson: 1970), 174ff, 175 ns. 61 and 62 ref AGI: Guadalajara 511, "Extractto de la Rebistta de Ynspeccion, executtada de Orden del Rey, por mi el Mariscal de Campo de sus [exercitos], [Marqués] de Rubi," Tubac, December 21, 1766, and signed at San Miguel, February 21, 1767.

18. Rubí, Marquis of, "Dictámenes que de orden del Exmo. Sor. Marqués de Croix . . . Expone el Mariscal de Campo Marqués de Rubí en orden a la mejor situación de los presidios . . .," in *La frontera norte y la experiencia colonial*, ed. María del Carmen Velázquez (Mexico City: 1982), 27–89, 33–34.

19. Herrera, Carlos, "Infidelity and the Presidio Captain: Adultery and Honor in the Lives of María Rosa Tato y Anza and José Antonio Vildósola, Sonora, New Spain, 1769–1783," *Journal of the History of Sexuality* 15:2 (2006), 204–27.

20. Vega y Carpio, Félix Lope de, *El arte nuevo de hacer comedias* (Madrid: 1609), lines 327–28.

21. Penyak, Lee M., "Safe Harbors and Compulsory Custody: Casas de Depósito in Mexico, 1750–1865," *Hispanic American Historical Review* 79:1 (1999), 83–99.

22. Quotation adapted from Herrera, "Infidelity," 216 n.43 refs AGI: Guadalajara, 517, "Tato y Anza to Vildósola," January 24, 1780.

23. The quotation is adapted from the translation in Herrera, "Infidelity," n.62 refs AGI: Guadalajara 275, "Croix to Gálvez," Chihuahua, October 23, 1778, and AGI: Guadalajara 517, "Extracto, Croix," Arispe, April 23, 1780.

CHAPTER SIXTEEN

1. Lynch, *Bourbon Spain*, 317 n.59 refs Bristol to Egremont, Escorial, November 2, 1761, PRO, SP 94/164. The shipment was worth 16 million pesos (Morineau, Michel, *Incroyables gazettes et fabuleux métaux: les retours des trésors américains d'après les gazettes hollandaises [XVIᵉ–XVIIIᵉ siècles]* [London and New York: 1985], 401–2).

2. AGI: Estado 86B, N.100, ff.1r, 2v, and 3v.

3. Varela Marcos, Jesús, "Los prolegómenos de la visita de José de Gálvez a la Nueva España (1766). Don Francisco de Armona y la instrucción secreta del Marqués de Esquilache," *Revista de Indias* 46 (1986), 453–71; Antolín Espino, María del Populo, "El virrey marqués de Cruillas," in *Los virreyes de Nueva España en el reinado de Carlos III*, vol. 1, ed. José Antonio Calderón Quijano (Seville: 1967), 1:1–157; 83–94, 115, and 132ff; Priestley, *José de Gálvez*, 135ff, esp. 149 and 151–52.

4. Antolín Espino, "Virrey," 99–100, 100 n.1 refs AGI: México 2453, "Villalba to Arriaga," July 31, 1765, and 143–44; 144 n.41 refs AGI: México 1701.

5. Antolín Espino, "Virrey," 141–42, 141 n.39 refs AGI: México 1702.

6. Rivera, Pedro de, *Diario y derrotero de lo caminado, visto, y obcervado en el discurso de la visita general de Precidios, situados en las Provincias Ynternas de Nueva España* (Guatemala: 1736), paragraph XI, Leg. 950; and Navarro García, Luis, "The North of New Spain as a Political Problem in the Eighteenth Century," in *New Spain's Far Northern Frontier: Essays on Spain in the American West, 1540–1811*, ed. David J. Weber (Dallas: 1979), 201–15, 207.

7. Navarro García, Luis, *Don José de Gálvez y la Comandancia General de la Pronvicias Internas del norte de Nueva España* (Seville: 1964), 146 n.43 refs AGI: Guadalajara 416, "Pineda to Cruillas," March 20, 1766.

8. Navarro García, Luis, *Las reformas borbónicas en América: el plan de intendencias y su aplicación* (Seville: 1995), appendix; AGI: Indiferente 1713, "Informe y Plan de Intendencias . . . Nueva España," §9.

9. Navarro García, *Gálvez*, 156 n.72 refs AGI: Indiferente 1713, México 2477, and Guadalajara 252 and 390 and 158ff.

10. Navarro García, *Gálvez*, 145 n.40 refs AGI: Guadalajara 416, 154 n.65 refs AGI: Guadalajara 416, "Gálvez to Arriaga," Mexico June 17, 1766, and 155 n.69 refs AGI: México.

11. Lynch, *Bourbon Spain*, 281ff; and see "Consulta del consejo extraordinario" April 30, 1767, in Danvilla y Collado, Manuel, *El reinado de Carlos III* vol. 3 (Madrid: 1893), 3:628–33.

12. Pradeau, Alberto Francisco, *La expulsión de los Jesuítas de las provincias de Sonora, Ostimuri y Sinaloa en 1767* (Mexico City: 1959), 25 refs Cuevas, Father Mariano, *Historia de la Nación Mexicana* (Mexico City: 1952), 1:542.

13. Pradeau, *Expulsión*, 49–50.

14. Ibid., 63 and 65.

15. Bernabéu Albert, Salvador, "El 'Virrey de California' Gaspar de Portolá y la problemática de la primera gobernación californiana (1767–1769)," *Revista de Indias* 52:195–96 (1992), 271–95.

16. Palóu, *Noticias*, vol. 1, ch. 2.

17. Bernabéu, "Portolá," 277 n.13; Baegert, Juan Jacobo, *Noticias de península americana de California* (Mexico City: 1942), 216.

18. Bernabéu, "Portolá," 288 n.46 refs AGN: Californias, vol. 72, ff.16–20r, f.17r, "Portolá to Croix," Loreto, December 28, 1767.

19. Bernabéu, "Portolá," 290 n.50 refs AGN: Californias, vol. 72, ff.29r–29v, "Portolá to Croix," Loreto, February 3, 1768.

20. Baegert, *Noticias*, 217–19.

21. Bernabéu, "Portolá," 283–85 ns. 31–37 ref AGN: Californias, vol. 72, ff.16–27v, "Letters from Portolá to Croix," Loreto, December 28, 1767, February 3 and 18, and March 22.

22. Bernabéu, "Portolá," 293.

23. Gálvez, José de, *Informe sobre las rebeliones populares de 1767*, ed. Felipe Castro Gutiérrez (Mexico City: 1990), 38–39, and see 39 n.20.

24. Navarro García, Luis, "El Virrey Marqués de Croix (1766–1771)," in *Los virreyes de Nueva España en el reinado de Carlos III*, ed. José Antonio Calderón Quijano, vol. 2 (Seville: 1967), 159–381, 283–84, 284 n.11 refs AGI: México 1365, "Gálvez to Croix," Potosí, July 24, 1767.

25. Navarro García, "Croix," 278–79 n.6 refs AGI: México 1366, "Gálvez to Croix," San Luis de Potosí, July 26, 1767.

26. Navarro García, "Croix," 281–82, 282 n.8 refs AGI: México 1365, "Urbina to Gálvez," Potosí, July 16, 1767.

27. Navarro García, "Croix," 286 n.19 refs AGI: México 1365, "Gálvez to Croix," Potosí, August 9, 1767.

28. Priestley, *Gálvez*, 228, did the sums.

29. Gálvez, *Informe*, 77; Priestley, *Gálvez*, 229.

30. AGI: Estado 34, N.36, "Informaciones de las expediciones y providencias de la visita de Real Hacienda," August 27, 1773, image 6/76; Gálvez, *Informe*, 61; AGI: México 1365, "Gálvez to Croix," Potosí, October 8, 1767; Herrera Navarro, Jerónimo (ed.), *Rodríguez de Campomanes, epistolario (1778-1802)*, 2 vols. (Madrid: 2004), 2:641-42, no. 633, "Gálvez to Campomanes, February 26, 1768"; Río, Ignacio del, "Autoritarismo y locura en el noroeste novohispano. Implicaciones políticas del, enloquecimiento del visitador general José de Gálvez," *Estudios de Historia Novohispana* 22:22 (2000), 111-37, 120 n.21 refs AGI: Guadalajara 416, f.1060, "Manifiesto de la conducta observada por don Eusebio Ventura Beleña," 1772.

31. Engelhardt, Zephyrin, *The Missions and Missionaries of California*, 2 vols. (Santa Barbara: 1929), 331ff; Palóu, *Life*, ch. 12.

32. Navarro García, *Gálvez*, 162.

33. Costansó, Miguel de, *Diario histórico de los viages de mar, y tierra hechos al norte de la California* ([Mexico City: 1770]), 9-10.

34. Gerhard, Peter, "Pearl Diving in Lower California," *Pacific Historical Review* 25:3 (1956), 239-49, 248 n.42 refs AGI: Guadalajara 416.

35. Navarro García, *Gálvez*, 189 n.138 refs AGI: Guadalajara 416, "Cuéllar a Gálvez," April 28, 1769, and "Gálvez to Cuéllar," May 17, 1769.

36. Marín Tello, María Isabel, "El castigo ejemplar a los indígenas en la época de José de Gálvez en el virreinato de Nueva España," *Cuadernos de la historia* 31 (2009), 27-43.

37. Río, "Autoritarismo," 120 n.22 refs BNM: Archivo Franciscano 41/929.10, f.14v and f.15, "Gálvez to Pineda," Alamos, July 15 and July 23, 1769.

38. Viniegra, Juan Manuel, "Apuntamiento instructivo de la expedición que el illustrisimo señor Don Joseph de Galvez visitador general de Nueva España hizo . . . ," in *Crónicas del descubrimiento de la Alta California*, ed. Angela Cano Sánchez and Elena Mampei González (Barcelona: 1984), 261ff, 273-74; Río, "Autoritarismo," 122 n.26 notes another copy at AHN: Estado, Leg. 2845 (1), f.37v, and 122 n.27 refs "Manifiesto . . . Beleña," f.1066v.

39. Covarrubias, *Tesoro* (Madrid: 1611); *Diccionario de Autoridades* (Madrid: 1734).

40. Viniegra, "Apuntamiento," 274.

41. Except where indicated, this follows Bernardo's official journal of the expedition, AGN: Provincias Internas 98, expediente 1, 593ff, "Diario que lleva el Comandante Militar don Lope de Cuellar." I am very much indebted to Jerry Craddock and the marvelous Cibola Project at Berkeley, CA, for locating a copy for me. McCarty, Kieran, "Bernardo de Galvez on the Apache Frontier: The Education of a Future Viceroy," *Journal of the Southwest* 36:2 (1994), 103-30 offers an excellent summary and analysis of this document.

42. (597r).

43. (597v).

44. (598r-v).

45. (602r).

46. (603v).

47. Gálvez writes "Cholome," another name for the Jumanos who originated around La Junta de los Ríos.

48. (604r).

49. (611r).

50. (615v).

51. Gálvez, Bernardo de, *Noticias y reflexiones sobre la guerra que se tiene con los apaches en la provincia de Nueva España*, ed. Felipe Teixidor, in *Anales del Museo Nacional de Arqueología, Historia y Etnografía*, series (época) 4, vol. 3 (Mexico City: 1925); John, Elizabeth A. H., "Bernardo de Gálvez on the Apache Frontier: A Cautionary Note for Gringo Historians," *Journal of Arizona History* 29:4 (1988), 427–30.

52. Gálvez, *Noticias*, 542.

53. Ibid., 539–41.

54. Navarro García, *Gálvez*, 190–93.

55. Viniegra, "Apuntamiento," 276.

56. Navarro García, *Gálvez*, 191ff.

57. The coordinates are 31°14' N, 102°29' W; a quick comparison of the images on Google Maps and Apple Maps gives a reasonable idea of how the river would have swelled when in flood. Bearing in mind that the river system was then dammed at no point, the water would have been fast moving as well.

58. Gálvez, Bernardo de, "Diario que forma de los acaecimientos que han ocurrido en la campaña que hizo don Bernarndo de Galvez y Gallardo," AGN: Provincias Internas, vol. 97, in Gálvez, *Noticias*, appendix 3.

59. Gálvez, Bernardo de, "Diario Bernardo de Galvez y Gallardo," in Gálvez, *Noticias*, appendix 2.

60. Díaz-Trechuelo Spínola, María Lourdes, María Luisa Rodríguez Baena, and Concepción Parajón Parody, "Don Antonio María Bucareli y Ursúa (1771–1779)," in *Los virreyes de Nueva España en el reinado de Carlos III*, vol. 1, ed. José Antonio Calderón Quijano (Seville: 1967), 383–658, 392–93 n.16 refs AGI: México 1242, "O'Reilly to Bucareli," Madrid May 17, 1771.

61. Navarro García, *Gálvez*, 194–96.

62. Navarro García, "Croix," 377–80.

63. Bobb, Bernard E., *The Viceregency of Antonio María Bucareli in New Spain, 1771–1779* (Austin: 1962), 31 n.56 refs AGI: México 1242, "Bucareli to O'Reilly," December 27, 1771; n.57 refs AGI: México 1509 and 1370, "Bucareli to Arriaga," Mexico, February 22, 1771; and 32 ns. 58–60 ref AGI: México 1242, "Bucarelí to O'Reilly," Havana, August 12, 1771.

64. Díaz-Trechuelo et al., "Bucareli," 391 n.11 refs AGI: México 1242, "Bucarelí to O'Reilly," Havana, August 12, 1771, and 397 with 396 n.23 refs AGI: México 1242, "Bucarelí to O'Reilly," Mexico, October 27, 1771.

CHAPTER SEVENTEEN

1. Cook, Sherburne F., *The Population of the California Indians, 1769–1970* (Berkeley: 1976); Jackson, Robert H., *Indian Population Decline: The Missions of Northwestern New Spain, 1687–1840* (Albuquerque: 1994), 7, writes: "Most recent research supports many of Cook's early conclusions."

2. Kealhofer, Lisa, "The Evidence for Demographic Collapse in California," in *Bioarchaeology of Native American Adaptation in the Spanish Borderlands*, ed. Brenda J. Baker and Lisa Kealhofer (Gainesville: 1996), 56–92; Cook, Sherburne F., "Historical Demography," in *The Handbook of North American Indians*, vol. 8, *California*, ed. Robert F. Heizer (Washington, DC: 1978), 91–98.

3. For an overview of these ideas, see Hackel, Steven W., *Children of Coyote, Missionaries of Saint Francis: Indian-Spanish Relations in Colonial California, 1769–1850* (Chapel Hill, NC: 2005), 65ff; and Melville, Elinor G., *A Plague of Sheep: Environmental Consequences of the Conquest of Mexico* (Cambridge: 1998).

4. Costello, Julia G., and David Hornbeck, "Alta California: An Overview," in *Colombian Consequences*, vol. 1, *Archeological and Historical Perspectives on the Spanish Borderlands West*, ed. David Hurst Thomas (Washington, DC: 1989), 303–31; Meighan, Clement W., "Indians and California Missions," *Southern California Quarterly* 69:3 (1987), 187–201, see 188 n.2.

5. Hackel, *Children*, 15ff; Hackel, *Serra*, 165; Kealhofer, "Evidence," 59ff.

6. Serra, *Writings*, 1:254–56.

7. Archibald, Robert, "Indian Labor at the California Missions: Slavery or Salvation?" *Journal of San Diego History* 24:2 (1978), 172–82; Pérouse, Jean F. G. de la, *Voyage de La Pérouse autour du monde, pendant les années 1785, 1786, 1787 et 1788*, 3 vols. (Paris: 1832), 2:125; there an English translation of his sojourn in California in Pérouse, Jean F. G. de la, "A Visit to Monterey in 1786: And a Description of the Indians of California," *California Historical Society Quarterly* 15:3 (1936), 216–23, 219; Archibald, "Indian Labor," n.12 quotes Turkanoff, Vasali, *Statement of My Captivity Among the Californians* (Los Angeles: 1953), 14; Serra, *Writings*, 3:412.

8. Costansó, *Diario*, 17.

9. Palóu, *Relación*, 93–94.

10. Crespí, "Diario," 54; Cañizares, "Diario," 254, 257–60.

11. Cañizares, "Diario," 270–72.

12. Ibid., 274.

13. Ibid., 275–76.

14. Crespí, "Diario," 250.

15. Boneu Companys, Fernando (ed.), *Documentos secretos de la expedición de Portolá a California. Juntas de Guerra* (Lérida: 1973), 123–26 refs AHN: Secc. Jesuitas, Leg 22, "Fages and Costansó to Gálvez," San Diego, July 4, 1769.

16. Costansó, *Diario*, 19–20.

17. Ibid., 20–21.

18. Ibid., 23.

19. Ibid., 21.

20. Ibid., 24–25.

21. Serra, *Writings*, 1:403.

22. Ibid., "Journal," 1:42; Palóu, *Relación*, 94–95.

23. Serra, *Writings*, "Journal," 1:62; Matthew 4:19.

24. Palóu, *Relación*, 101.

25. Serra, *Writings*, "Journal," 66 and 89.

26. Ibid., 84–90.

27. Palóu, *Relación*, 101; Serra, *Writings*, "Serra to Palóu, San Diego, July 3, 1769," 142–44.

28. Boneu Companys, *Documentos*, 120–21 refs AGN: Méjico, "Portola to Croix," San Diego, July 4, 1769.

29. Boneu Companys, *Documentos*, "Portolá to Croix," 120–21 and 18; Costansó, *Diario*, 27.

30. Portolá, Gaspar de, *Diary of Gaspar de Portolá During the California Expedition of 1769–1770*, ed. Donald Eugene Smith and Frederick J. Teggart (Berkeley: 1909), 48.

31. Boneu Companys, *Documentos*, "Tercera Junta," 53-63.

32. Ibid., "Portolá to Croix," 120-21; Costansó, *Diario*, 29.

33. Costansó, *Diario*, 30.

34. Crespí, "Diario," 316-19.

35. Boneu Companys, *Documentos*, "Tercera Junta," 53-63, 59-60.

36. Portolá, *Diary*, 24.

37. Crespí, "Diario," 466-70.

38. Sánchez, Joseph P., *Spanish Bluecoats: The Catalonian Volunteers in Northwestern New Spain, 1767-1810* (Albuquerque: 1990), 46-47; Crespí, "Diario," 698.

39. Costansó, *Diario*, 33; Crespí, "Diario," 264-66 and 336-38.

40. Costansó, *Diario*, 35-40.

41. Ibid., 42.

42. Portolá, *Diary*, 60-64.

43. Costansó, *Diario*, 41; I assume Costansó took one sighting; Crespí definitely took the other: Crespí, "Diario," 538.

44. González Cabrera Bueno, José, *Navegación especulativa y práctica* (Manila: 1734), 303; Vizcaíno, Sebastián [ed. Geo B. Griffin], "Letter of Sebastián Vizcaíno to the King of Spain, Announcing His Return from the Exploration of the Coast of the Californias, as Far as the Forty-Second Degree of North Latitude—Dated 23d May, 1603," *Publications of the Historical Society of Southern California* 2:1 (1891), 68-73.

45. González Cabrera Bueno, *Navegación*, 303; Boneu Companys, *Documentos*, 24 and "Primera Junta," 27-33, 32.

46. Boneu Companys, *Documentos*, "Primera Junta," 27-33, 29.

47. Ibid., 29-33.

48. Costansó, *Diario*, 42-43; Portolá, *Diary*, 64-68.

49. Crespí, "Diario," 590.

50. Costansó, *Diario*, 44.

51. Portolá, *Diary*, 68; Crespí, "Diario," 596-98 and 608 n.106.

52. González Cabrera Bueno, *Navegación*, 302; Wood, Raymund F., "The Discovery of the Golden Gate: Legend and Reality," *Southern California Quarterly* 58:2 (1976), 205-25.

53. Boneu Companys, *Documentos*, "Segunda Junta," 42-46.

54. Ibid., 48-49 n.36 refs Costansó, Miguel de, "Diario de la Expedición infructosa por tierra," Museo Naval Madrid: Virreinato de México, T. I., no. 22.

55. Ibid., "Tercera Junta," 53-63.

56. Chapman, Charles E., *A History of California: The Spanish Period* (New York: 1925), 226.

57. Costansó, *Diario*, 46.

58. Crespí, "Diario," 670.

59. Palóu, *Relación*, 107-8.

60. Ibid., 108.

61. Ibid.

62. Serra, *Writings*, 1:150; Palóu, *Relación*, 110; Crespí, "Diario," 672.

63. Boneu Companys, *Documentos*, "Cuarta Junta," 73-80.

64. Serra, *Writings*, 1:160.

65. Palóu, *Relación*, 119; Boneu Companys, *Documentos*, "Portolá a Croix," San Diego, April 17, 1770, 135-37.

66. Boneu Companys *Documentos*, 103 n.130 refs "Portolá to Croix," April 17, 1770, 135-37.

67. Crespí, "Diario," 680ff and 692.

68. Serra, *Writings*, 1:168; Boneu Companys, *Documentos*, 108 and "Testimonio de la toma de posesión de Monterrey," June 3, 1770, 149–50.

69. Boneu Companys, Fernando, *Gaspar de Portolá: Explorer and Founder of California*, trans. Alan K. Brown (Lérida: 1983), 349–50, 368.

70. Serra, *Writings*, 1:182–84.

71. Ibid., 1:158 and 162–94; Engelhardt, *Missions and Missionaries*, 2:105.

72. Palóu, *Relación*, 126; Serra, *Writings*, 1:198.

73. Serra, *Writings*, 1:170.

74. Palóu, *Relación*, 140–42.

75. Rodríguez-Sala, María Louisa, *Exploraciones en Baja y Alta California, 1769–1775* (Zapopan: 2002), 87ff and 231ff, 88 n.76 refs AGN: Correspondencia de Virreyes, Croix, vol. 14, ff.414–18, AGN: Californias, vol. 66, Exp. 67, ff.150–53, and AGI: Guadalajara 516, "Salida que hizo el Teniente de Voluntarios."

76. Munro-Fraser, J. P., *History of Marin County, California* (San Francisco: 1880), 96–97; Hanna, Warren L., "Legend of the Nicasios: The Men Drake Left Behind at Hova Albion," *California History* 58:2 (1979), 154–65.

77. Serra, *Writings*, 1:359–63.

78. Velasco Ceballos, Rómulo (ed.), *La administración de D. Frey Antonio María de Buareli y Ursúa, cuadragésimo sexto virrey de México*, 2 vols. (Mexico City: 1936), 1:278–81; Serra, *Writings*, 1:404–5.

79. Serra, *Writings*, 1:264–84.

80. Palóu, *Relación*, 163–65.

81. Serra, *Writings*, 1:298–300.

82. Ibid., 1:302ff.

83. Velasco Ceballos, *Administración*, 1:128ff.

84. Font, Fray Pedro, *Anza's Expedition of 1775–1776: Diary of Pedro Font*, ed. Frederick J. Teggart (Berkeley: 1913), 128.

85. Díaz-Trechuelo Spínola et al., "Antonio María Bucareli y Ursúa," 1:479ff; quotation on 480: *"una gran cordillera de color azul."*

CHAPTER EIGHTEEN

1. Anza, *Diarios*, 99.

2. Bolton, Herbert E., *Anza's California Expeditions* (Berkeley: 1930), 81.

3. Maughan, Scott Jarvis, "Francisco Garcés and New Spain's Northwestern Frontier, 1768–1781," PhD dissertation, University of Utah (1968), 105 n.46 refs "Apuntes del Padre Fr. Francisco Antonio Barbastro . . . 1768–1781," Baviácora, September 10, 1788: Marcellino da Civezza, Vatican Archives, 202:35 (microfilm at University of Arizona, Tucson); Serra, *Writings*, 2:42 offers a slightly different account.

4. Anza, *Diarios*, 115ff; Bolton, *Anza's Expeditions*, 2:316ff.

5. Anza, *Diarios*, 123.

6. Ibid., 124–26.

7. Garcés, Francisco, *Diario de exploraciones en Arizona y California en los años de 1775 y 1776*, ed. John Galvin (Mexico City: 1968), at end of long entry for February 6.

8. Ibid., February 8 and 9, 127.

9. Anza, *Diarios*, 128.

10. Ibid., 139.

11. Ibid., 141 and 144.

12. Garcés, *Diario*, February 17.

13. Bolton, *Anza's Expeditions*, 81.

14. Anza, *Diarios*, 163 and 164.

15. Ibid., 167.

16. Font, *Diary*, 59–61.

17. Garcés, *Diario*, 21.

18. Anza, *Diarios*, 228ff.

19. Ibid., 230; Font, *Diary*, 100.

20. Anza, *Diarios*, 228.

21. Serra, *Writings*, 2:400.

22. Font, *Diary*, 96.

23. Ibid., 97.

24. Anza, *Diarios*, 231–32; Font, *Diary*, 99–100.

25. Font, *Diary*, 111–12.

26. Ibid., 117–18.

27. Anza, *Diarios*, 240–41.

28. Ibid., 242.

29. Font, *Diary*, 139.

30. Anza, *Diarios*, 257.

31. Font, *Diary*, 164ff and 169–70.

32. Velasco Ceballos, *Administración*, 2:216–20, "Bucareli to Gálvez," Mexico, August 27, 1776, 218.

33. Anza, *Diarios*, 312.

34. Wood, Raymund F., "Francisco Garcés, Explorer of Southern California," *Southern California Quarterly* 51:3 (1969), 185–209; for his route across the *sierra*, see Weaver, Richard A., "The 1776 Route of Father Francisco Garcés into the San Bernardino Valley, California: A Reevaluation of the Evidence and Its Implications," *Journal of California and Great Basin Anthropology* 4:1 (1982), 142–47.

35. Garcés, *Diario*, 68.

36. Ibid., 72.

37. Ibid., 76.

38. Bolton, *Anza's Expeditions*, 3:407ff.

39. Velasco Ceballos, *Administración*, 2:216–20, 220, "Bucareli to Gálvez," Mexico, August 27, 1776.

40. Bolton, *Anza's Expeditions*, 5:363ff, "Bucareli to Gálvez," Mexico City, October 27, 1776; 5:395ff, "Bucareli to Gálvez," Mexico City, November 26, 1776; 5:398ff, "Gálvez to Bucareli," Madrid, December 24, 1766; and 5:402ff.

CHAPTER NINETEEN

1. Usner, Daniel H. Jr., *Indians, Settlers, and Slaves: The Lower Mississippi Valley Before 1783* (Chapel Hill, NC: 1992), 46ff, 48–49 table 2.

2. Hall, Gwendolyn Midlo, *Africans in Colonial Louisiana: The Development of Afro-Creole Culture in the Eighteenth Century* (Baton Rouge: 1992), 7 n.11 refs Service Historique

de l'Armée, Chateau de Vincennes, France: Ser. A1 2592, f.95, "Etat de la Louisiane au mois de juin 1720."

3. Adapted from the translation in Rowland, Dunbar, and Patricia Galloway (eds.), *Mississippil Provincial Archives, French Dominion, 1749–1763*, 5 vols. (Baton Rouge: 1984), 5:185ff, "Kerlérec to Moras, New Orleans, October 20, 1757."

4. Giraud, Marcel, *Histoire de la Louisiane française*, 2 vols. (Paris: 1953), 1:104ff; Dumont de Montigny, Jean-François-Benjamin, *The Memoir of Lieutenant Dumont, 1715–1747*, ed. and trans. Gordon M. Sayre and Carla Zecher (Chapel Hill, NC: 2012), 31–32; MPA 3:337–38.

5. Usner, Daniel H. Jr., *American Indians in the Lower Mississippi Valley: Social and Economic Histories* (Lincoln, NE: 1992), 34ff, 36 table 1.

6. Rowland and Galloway, *Mississippi Archives*, 5:167ff, 71, "Kerlérec to de Machault, New Orleans, April 1, 1756."

7. Shepherd, William R., "The Cession of Louisiana to Spain," *Political Science Quarterly* 19:3 (1904), 439–59, 455 n.1 refs AHN: Estado 3889, "Wall to Grimaldi, November 13, 1762." Shepherd does not give the Spanish. I have adapted his translation.

8. Ferrer del Río, *Historia*, 1:377.

9. Juan, Jorge, and Antonio de Ulloa, *Noticias secretas de América*, ed. Rufino Blanco-Fombona, 2 vols. (Madrid: 1918), 2:93–94.

10. Moore, John P., "Antonio de Ulloa: A Profile of the First Spanish Governor of Louisiana," *Louisiana History: The Journal of the Louisiana Historical Association* 8:3 (1967), 189–218. Ulloa's governorship and its context is fully examined in Moore, John P., *Revolt in Louisiana: The Spanish Occupation, 1766–1770* (Baton Rouge: 1976).

11. Champigny, Chevalier de, "Memoir on the Present State of Louisiana," in *Historical Memoirs of Louisiana, from the First Settlement of the Colony to the Departure of Governor O'Reilly in 1770*, ed. B. F. French, 5 vols. (New York: 1853), 5:159.

12. Whitaker, Arthur Preston, "Antonio de Ulloa," *Hispanic American Historical Review*, 15 (1935), 155–94.

13. Din, Gilbert C., "Protecting the 'Barrera': Spain's Defenses in Louisiana, 1763–1779," *Louisiana History: The Journal of the Louisiana Historical Association* 19:2 (1978), 183–211, 188–89.

14. Gayarré, Charles, *Histoire de la Louisiane*, 2 vols. (New Orleans: 1847), 2:243. NB: This is the translation into French of Ulloa's Spanish original, which is at AGI: Santo Domingo 2453, "Noticia de los acaecimientos de la Luisiana."

15. Rodríguez Casado, Vicente, *Primeros años de dominación española en la Luisiana* (Madrid: 1942), 145–46, 145 n.11 refs AGI: Santo Domingo 2542, "October 26, 1768."

16. Gayarré, *Histoire*, 244ff; Rodríguez Casado, *Primeros años*, 154–55.

17. Rodríguez Casado, *Primeros años*, 146, 164, and 170; Moore, *Revolt*, 161; Villiers du Terrage, Marc de, *Les dernières années de la Louisiane française* (Paris: 1905), 260 and 263.

18. O'Neil, Charles E., "The Louisiana Manifesto of 1768," *Political Science Reviewer* 19 (1990), 247–89, 254 refs AGI: Cuba 1054, and quotes on 267.

19. All the quotations from this cabinet meeting are adapted from Gayarré, *History*, 2:248ff.

20. Moore, *Revolt*, 188 n.7 refs AHN: Estado 3883, "Masserano to Grimaldi, February 24, 1769."

21. Caughey, John, "Bernardo de Gálvez and the English Smugglers on the Mississippi, 1777," *Hispanic American Historical Review* 12:1 (1932), 46–58, 223 n.45 refs AGI: Santo Domingo 1220, "O'Reilly to Munian, August 31, 1769."

22. Chandler, R. E., "Eyewitness History: O'Reilly's Arrival in Louisiana," *Louisiana History: Journal of the Louisiana Historical Association* 20:3 (1979), 317–24.

23. Quotations adapted from Chandler, "Eyewitness," 322; Caughey, "Bernardo de Gálvez", 22.

24. Caughey, "Bernardo de Gálvez," 25 n.50 refs AGI: Santo Domingo 2543, "Rodríguez, October 29, 1769," and Cuba 81, "Testimonio sacado por . . . Rodríguez"; Gayarré, *History*, 316–41; Moore, *Revolt*, 185–215.

25. Wilkinson, James, *Memoirs of My Own Times*, 2 vols. (Philadelphia: 1816), 2:appendix 1, "Deposition of Oliver Pollock, Washington, June 8, 1808."

26. Pittman, Capt. Phillip, *The Present State of European Settlements on the Mississippi*, ed. Frank H. Hodder (Cleveland: 1906), 42ff.

27. Caughey, "Bernardo de Gálvez," 36ff n.20 refs AGI: Santo Domingo 1221, "O'Reilly to Arriaga, October 17, 1769."

28. Frederick, Julia C., "Luis de Unzaga and the Bourbon Reform in Spanish Louisiana, 1770–1776," PhD thesis, Louisiana State University (2000), 203.

29. Villiers du Terrage, *Dernières années*, 352 quotes the anon., *Mémoire sur la Louisiane* (Paris: 1813).

30. Frederick, "Luis de Unzaga"; Montero de Pedro, José, *Españoles en Nueva Orleans y Luisiana* (Madrid: 1979), 31–34.

31. The quotations are adapted from the English translations in Gayarré, *History*, 3:56ff.

32. Ibid., 3:72ff.

33. Ibid., 3:95ff; Frederick, "Luis de Unzaga," 222–23.

34. Cook, Warren L., *Flood Tide of Empire: Spain and the Pacific Northwest, 1543–1819* (New Haven: 1973), 54ff.

35. Gray, David H., "Canada's Unresolved Maritime Boundaries," *Geomatica* 48:2 (1994), 133ff.

36. For Crespí quotations, see Crespí, Fray Juan [ed. Geo. Butler Griffin], "Journal of Fray Juan Crespi Kept During the Same Voyage—Dated 5th October, 1774," *Publications of the Historical Society of Southern California* 2:1 (1891), 143–213, 152–54, and 159; for Martínez, see Beals, Herbert K. (ed. and trans.), *Juan Pérez on the Northwest Coast: Six Documentos of His Expedition in 1774* (Portland, OR: 1989), 101.

37. Gough, Barry M., *Gunboat Frontier: British Maritime Authority and Northwest Coast Indians, 1846–1890* (Vancouver: 1984), 95ff.

38. Adapted from translation of Pérez's logbook in Beals, *Juan Pérez*, 81.

39. Beals, *Juan Pérez*, 145.

40. Cook, *Flood Tide*, 65; Cook, James, *A Voyage to the Pacific Ocean*, 3 vols. (London: 1784), 2:282.

CHAPTER TWENTY

1. Sotto, Serafín María de, Count of Clonard, *História orgánica de las armas de infantería y caballería españolas desde la creación del Ejercito permanente hasta el día*, 16 vols. (Madrid:

1851–59), 9:376 and 400–401; Quintero Saravia, Gonzalo M., "Bernardo de Gálvez y América a finales del siglo XVIII," PhD thesis, Universidad Complutense de Madrid (2015), 249ff.

   2. For his service in France, see Wilson, James, and John Fiske (eds.), *Appleton's Cyclopaedia of American Biography*, 7 vols. (New York: 1886–1900), 2:584–85; Quintero Saravia, Gonzalo M., *Bernardo de Gálvez: Spanish Hero of the American Revolution* (Chapel Hill, NC: 2018), 249; Quintero Saravia, "Bernardo," 250–52, 251 n.1363 refs "Real Orden, January 31, 1774."

   3. The quotations are in Saavedra, Francisco de, *Los decenios: autobiografía de un sevillano de la Ilustración* (Seville: 1995), 73; for his influence on Yorktown, see Morales Padrón, Francisco (ed.), *Diario de don Francisco de Saavedra* (Seville: 2004), 203ff; and see Quintero Saravia, "Bernardo," 256 and 273ff; Gómez Imaz, Manuel, *Servicios patrioticos de la Suprema Junta en 1808 y relaciones hasta ahora inéditas* (Seville: 1908), 207–10.

   4. Saavedra, *Decenios*, 80–81.

   5. Ibid., 91 and 93.

   6. Quintero Saravia, "Bernardo," 268 n.1454 refs AGI: Santo Domingo 2586, 11, ff.927r–928v; Galindo y de Vera, León, *Historia, viscisitudes y política tradicional de España respecto de sus posesiones en las costas de África* (Madrid: 1884), 324.

   7. Ferrer del Río, *Historia*, 3:117–25, quotation on 124.

   8. Saavedra, *Decenios*, 97.

   9. Ibid., 99.

   10. Velázquez, María del Carmen, "La Comandancia General de las Provincias Internas," *Historia Mexicana* 27:2 (1977), 163–76.

   11. Yela Utrilla, Juan R., *España ante la independencia de los Estados Unidos* (Madrid: 1988 [1922]), 89–91 n.1 refs AHN: Estado 4168, "Aranda to Grimaldi, Faonainebleau, November 9, 1776."

   12. The correspondence between Grimaldi in Madrid and Aranda in Paris is described and discussed by Yela Utrilla, *España*, esp. 1:41ff.

   13. Quintero Saravia, "Bernardo," 364.

   14. Yela Utrilla, *España*, 2:39ff refs AHN: Estado 3884, "Aranda to Grimaldi, January 13, 1777," and 1:89–91 n.1 refs AHN: Estado 4168, "Aranda to Grimaldi, Fontainebleau, November 9, 1776."

   15. Yela Utrilla, *España*, 2:54ff refs AHN: Estado 3884, "Marquis of Castejón, February 3, 1777."

   16. Yela Utrilla, *España*, 2:53ff refs AHN: Estado 3884, "Gálvez, February 2, 1777," and 1:183ff; Chávez, Thomas E., *Spain and the Independence of the United States: An Intrinsic Gift* (Albuquerque: 2002), 75 n.16 refs AHN: Estado 3884, f.69, Exp. 6, "Floridablanca to Aranda, January 13, 1777."

   17. Cummins, Light Townsend, *Spanish Observers of the American Revolution, 1775–1783* (Baton Rouge and London: 1991), 35 n.25 refs AGI: Cuba 1227, "Gálvez to Torre," February 28, 1776"; Yela Utrilla, *España*, 68–69 n.4 refs AGI: Cuba 1227, "Gálvez to Havana, February 28, 1776."

   18. Cummins, *Spanish Observers*, 9–11, 19–21.

   19. Caughey, "Bernardo de Galvez," 67 n.2e refs AGI: Santo Domingo; Yela Utrilla, *España*, 1:78 n.3 AS., E., 1.1736, "Diectamen de Gálvez, September 27, 1776."

   20. Quintero Saravia, "Bernardo," 277 n.1493 refs AGI: Santo Domingo 2586, "Nombramiento de Bernardo de Gálvez, May 7, 1776."

   21. Cummins, Light Townsend, "The Gálvez Family and Spanish Participation in the Independence of the United States of America," *Revista Complutense de Historia de América* 32 (2006), 179–96, 183ff.

22. Quoted in Caughey, "Bernardo de Galvez," 86 n.5 refs AGI: Santo Domingo 2596.

23. James, James A., *Oliver Pollock: The Life and Times of an Unknown Patriot* (New York: 1937), appendix 1, 347ff, "Events in the public career of Oliver Pollock 1776–1782, as related by himself, Philadelphia, September 18, 1782."

24. Chávez, *Spain*, 30 fig. 1 reproduces the note Gibson wrote to confirm the offer, AGI: Santo Domingo 2586.

25. Chávez, *Spain*, 29–30 n.36 refs AGI: Santo Domingo 2596, "Unzaga to Gálvez, September 30, 1776."

26. O'Callaghan, E. B., et al. (eds.), *Documents Relative to the Colonial History of the State of New York*, 15 vols. (Albany: 1853–87), 8:509.

27. James, *Pollock*, 70.

28. Pollock, Oliver, *To the Honourable the Legislature of Virginia* (1811); James, James A., "Oliver Pollock, Financier of the Revolution in the West," *Mississippi Valley Historical Review* 16:1 (1929), 67–80, 68.

29. Hess, Dan, "The Bankrupt Irishman Who Created the Dollar Sign by Accident," *Atlas Obscura*, November 23, 2015; Davies, Roy, "The Word 'Dollar' and the Dollar Sign": projects.exeter.ac.uk/RDavies/arian/dollar.html.

30. Adapted from quotation in Selig, Robert A., *The Washington-Rochambeau Revolutionary Route in the State of Delaware, 1781–1783* (Dover, DE: 2003), 31 n.67 refs AHN: Estado 4224; Cummins, "Gálvez Family," 183 n.21 refs another copy at AGI: Santo Domingo 2596.

31. AGI: Cuba 573; James, *Pollock*, appendix 1, 347; Wilkinson, *Memoirs*, 2:appendix 1, "Deposition of Oliver Pollock, Washington, June 8, 1808."

32. Chávez, *Spain*, 31.

33. Adapted from Pontalba, Joseph Xavier de, "Memoir on Louisiana, Paris, September 15, 1801," in *A History of Louisiana*, ed. Alcée Fortier, 4 vols. (New York: 1904), 2:203ff, 206.

34. Soniat du Fossat, Guy, *Synopsis of the History of Louisiana*, trans. Charles T. Soniat (New Orleans: 1903 [1791]), 29.

35. Adapted from quotation in Beerman, Eric, "Governor Bernardo de Gálvez's New Orleans Belle: Felicitas de St. Maxent," *Revista Española de Estudios Norteamericanos* 7 (1994), 39–43; Puig-Samper, Miguel Ángel, "Humboldt, un prusiano en la corte del rey Carlos IV," *Revista de Indias* 59:216 (1999), 329–40, 335 n.27 refs Moncada, Maya, *El ingeniero Miguel Constanzó: un militar ilustrado en la Nueva España del siglo XVIII* (Mexico City: 1994), 332ff.

36. Beerman, Eric, "La bella criolla Felicitas de Saint Maxent, viuda de Bernardo de Gálvez, en España," in *Norteamérica a finales del siglo XVIII: España y los Estados Unidos* (Madrid: 2008), 281–96.

37. Hernández Sánchez-Barba, Marino, "Bernardo de Gálvez, militar y político en la Florida occidental (Un bicentenario y una reparación histórica)," *Arbor* 109:452 (1981), 41–54, 47ff.

38. Porras Muñoz, Guillermo, "Acta de matrimonio de Bernardo de Gálvez y Felicitas Saint Maxent," *Boletín del Archivo General de la Nación* (Mexico) 16:2 (1945), 277–81.

39. Beerman, "Bella criolla," 294.

40. Caughey, "Bernardo de Galvez," 88–90, ns. 18–20 ref various documents within AGI: Santo Domingo 1598.

41. James, *Pollock*, 80–81.

42. Adapted from English translation in Caughey, "Bernardo de Galvez," 91 n.24 refs AGI: Santo Domingo 2596, "Bernardo to Morgan, August 9, 1777."

43. Caughey, John W., "Willing's Expedition Down the Mississippi, 1778," *Louisiana Historical Quarterly* 15 (1932), 5–36; Caughey, "Bernardo de Galvez," 102ff, quotation on 105 n.11 refs AGI: Cuba 2370, "Willing to Pollock, May 30, 1778."

44. James, James A. (ed.), *George Rogers Clark Papers 1771–1781: Collections of the Illinois State Historical Library*, vols. 8–9, *Virginia Series*, vols. 3–4 (Springfield, IL: 1912), 3:67–68, "Willing to Clark, September 1, 1778."

45. Caughey, "Bernardo de Galvez," 109 n.24 refs AGI: Cuba 191, "Francis Farrell, June 20, 1778."

46. Quoted in James, *Pollock*, 119–20.

47. Quoted in Caughey,"Bernardo de Galvez," 111–12 ns. 32 and 33 ref AGI: Santo Domingo 2596.

48. Adapted from the quotation in Caughey, "Bernardo de Galvez," 129 n.81 refs AGI: Cuba 2370, "Pollock to Congress, July 6, 1778," and *Papers of the Continental Congress, 1774–1789*, "Papers of Oliver Pollock," 87–89, "Pollock to Congress, August 11, 1778": fold3.com/image/185100.

49. *Papers of the Continental Congress*, "Papers of Oliver Pollock," 87–89, "Pollock to Congress, October 8, 1778": fold3.com/image/185104; also quoted in Caughey, "Bernardo de Galvez," 132.

50. Washington, George, *The Writings of George Washington*, ed. Jared Sparks, 12 vols. (Boston: 1840), 7:343–45, "Washington to Brodhead, New Windsor, December 29. 1780"; Williams, Harold D., "Bernardo de Galvez and the Western Patriots," *Revista de Historia de América* 65–66 (1968), 53–70, 60 n.18 refs Ogg, Frederic Austin, *The Old Northwest: A Chronicle of the Ohio Valley and Beyond*, vol. 19 (New Haven: 1921), 45–47.

51. James, *Pollock*, 3ff.

52. Williams, "Western Patriots," 58 n.15 refs Burnett, Edmund C. (ed.), *Letters of Members of the Continental Congress* (Washington, DC: 1923), 2:380.

53. Gilman, Carolyn, "Why Did George Rogers Clark Attack Illinois?" *Ohio Valley History* 12:4 (2012), 3–18.

54. Kinnaird, Lawrence, "The Western Fringe of Revolution," *Western Historical Quarterly* 7:3 (1976), 253–70, 262 (no ref.) quotes in translation from Leyba to Gálvez, July 11, 1778.

55. Ibid., 262.

56. James, *Life*, 109–30.

57. James, *George Rogers Clark Papers*, 3:234.

58. Ibid., 3:129.

59. Palmer, Frederick, *Clark of the Ohio: A Life of George Rogers Clark* (New York: 1930), 291ff.

60. Carstens, Nancy, "The Making of a Myth: George Rogers Clark and Teresa de Leyba," in *The Life of George Rogers Clark, 1751–1818: Triumphs and Tragedies*, ed. Kenneth Carstens and Nancy Carstens (Westport, CT: 2004), 60–79.

61. Kinnaird, "Western Fringe," 263ff.

62. James, *Life*, 131.

63. Ibid., 137–45, quotation on 137; for Captain Vigo, the spy, see James, *George Rogers Clark Papers*, 3:140; Kinnaird, "Western Fringe," 265 (no ref.) quotes Clark to Leyba, March 1, 1778.

64. Quintero Saravia, "Bernardo," 294 n.1585 refs AGI: Cuba 184A, "Bernardo to José Gálvez, June 12, 1778," and AGI: Santo Domingo 2596, "Bernardo to José de Gálvez," June 9, 1778."

65. Din, Gilbert C., *The Canary Islanders of Louisiana* (Baton Rouge: 1988), 15–16, and see n.1 refs AGI: Santo Domingo 2661, "Royal Order, August 15, 1777"; Quintero Saravia, "Bernardo," 337 n.1825 refs AGI: Santo Domingo 2661, "José to Matías de Gálvez, August 4, 1777"; quotation is from Molina Martínez, Miguel, "La participación canaria en la formación y reclutamiento del batallón de Luisiana," in *IV Coloquio de historia canario-americana (1980)*, ed. Francisco Morales Padrón, 2 vols. (Salamanca: 1982), 1:138 n.10 refs AGI: Santo Domingo 2661, "José to Matías de Gálvez, August 4, 1777."

66. Molina Martínez, "Participación canaria," 1:137 n.7 refs AGI: Santo Domingo 2661, "Resolución del Cabildo, September 10, 1777," downloaded at: coloquioscanariasamerica .casadecolon.com/index.php/CHCA/article/view/7288/6202.

67. Molina Martínez, "Participación canaria," 157 ns. 32 and 33 ref AGI: Santo Domingo 2662, "Miró to José de Gálvez, July 7, 1779."

68. Quintero Saravia, "Bernardo," 297ff ns. 16–18 ref Gómez Ruiz, Manuel, and Vicente Alonso Juanola, *El ejército de los Borbones*, 7 vols. (Madrid: 1989–2006), 3:131; and Holmes, Jack, *Honor and Fidelity: The Louisiana Infantry Regiment and the Louisiana Militia Companies, 1766–1821* (Birmingham, AL: 1965).

69. Hoffman, Paul E., *Luisiana* (Madrid: 1992), 133.

70. Navarro, Martín de, "Reflexiones políticas luisiana," in *Documentos históricos de la Florida y la Luisiana, siglos XVI al XVII*, ed. Manuel Serrano y Sanz (Madrid: 1912), no. 15, 361ff, see 365ff. There is an English translation in Robertson, James A. (ed.), *Louisiana Under the Rule of Spain, France, and the United States, 1785–1807*, 2 vols. (Cleveland: 1911), 235ff.

71. Caughey, "Bernardo de Galvez," 46–58, 51 n.24 refs AGI: Cuba 174, "José de Gálvez to Bernardo, November 25, 1776."

72. Quintero Saravia, "Bernardo," 304 n.1646 refs AGI: Cuba 188-C, "British Merchants to Lloyd, April 26, 1777."

73. Caughey, "Bernardo de Galvez," 52–53 n.27 refs AGI: Santo Domingo 2596, "Bernardo de Gálvez to José, May 12, 1777."

74. Navarro, "Reflexiones," 361ff, see 365ff. There is an English translation in Robertson, *Louisiana Under the Rule*, 235ff.

75. Din, "Protecting the 'Barrera,'" 203 n.70 refs AGI: Cuba 1146, "Bernardo de Gálvez to Torre, May 6, 1777."

76. The quotation in Villiers du Terrage, *Les Dernières années*, 355.

77. Quintero Saravia, "Bernardo," 306.

78. Navarro, "Reflexiones," 235ff.

79. Quintero Saravia, "Bernardo," 308–9 n.1665 refs AGI: Santo Domingo 2547, "Bernardo to José de Gálvez, October 24, 1778."

80. Adapted from quotations in West, Elizabeth Howard, "The Indian Policy of Bernardo de Gálvez," in *The Proceedings of the Mississippi Valley Historical Association for the Year 1914–1915*, vol. 3, ed. Milo M. Quaife (Cedar Rapids: 1916), 95–101, 100–101.

81. Quintero Saravia, "Bernardo," 316–18.

82. Nunemaker, J. Horace, "The Bouligny Affair in Louisiana," *Hispanic American Historical Review* 25:3 (1945), 338–63.

83. Din, Gilbert, "Lieutenant Colonel Francisco Bouligny and the Malagueño Settlement at New Iberia, 1779," *Louisiana History* 17:2 (1976), 187–202.

84. Din, *Canary Islanders*, 28ff; Quintero Saravia, "Bernardo," 340 n.1839 refs AGI: Santo Domingo 2547, "Bernardo to José de Gálvez, no. 233, January 19, 1779"; an English translation

in Kinnaird, Lawrence, *Spain in the Mississippi Valley, 1765–1794*, 3 parts (Washington, DC: 1949), 1:326ff.

85. Din, *Canary Islanders*, 31; Morales Folguera, José Miguel, *Arquitectura y urbanismo hispanoamericano en Luisiana y Florida Occidental* (Málaga: 1987), 302–3; Kinnaird, *Spain in the Mississippi*, 323–25 n.267 refs AGI: Cuba 2351, "Collel to Gálvez, January 15, 1779."

86. Kinnaird, *Spain in the Mississippi*, 340–42 n.282 refs AGI: Cuba 235, "Collell to Gálvez, June 15, 1779"; Din, *Canary Islanders*, 32–35 ns. 4–12 ref AGI: Cuba 2351, various letters from Collell to Gálvez from April 1, 1779, and 569, "Libro Maestro de Galveztown, 1779."

87. Courlander, Harold (ed.), *The Fourth World of the Hopis: The Epic Story of the Hopi Indians as Preserved in Their Legends and Traditions* (Albuquerque: 1971), 177ff.

88. Sánchez, Joseph P., Robert L. Spude, and Art Gómez, *New Mexico: A History* (Norman, OK: 2013), 60ff.

89. Hämäläinen, Pekka, *The Comanche Empire* (New Haven: 2009); Pino, Pedro Bautista, *The Exposition of the Province of New Mexico, 1812*, ed. and trans. Marc Simmons and Adrian Bustamante (Santa Fe: 1995), 39.

90. Anza's campaign diary is online: 96.71.175.153/AnzaWeb/default.html.

91. Simmons, Marc, "New Mexico's Smallpox Epidemic of 1780–1781," *New Mexico Historical Review* 41:4 (1966), 319–26.

CHAPTER TWENTY-ONE

1. Quintero Saravia, *Bernardo*.

2. Cantillo, Alejandro de (ed.), "Tratado de alianza defensiva y ofensiva celebrado entre las coronas de España y Francia contra la de Inglaterra," in *Tratados de paz y de comercio desde el año de 1700 hasta el día* (Madrid: 1843), 552ff, esp. Article 7.

3. Caughey, "Bernardo de Galvez," 150–51 n.7 refs AGI: Cuba 112, "Junta de Guerra, July 13, 1779."

4. Quintero Saravia, "Bernardo," 377 n.2029 refs AGI: Santo Domingo 2082, "Navarro, June 29, 1779."

5. Caughey, "Bernardo de Galvez," 149–50 n.5 refs AGI: Santo Domingo 2082, copy of "Johnstone to Horn."

6. Serrano y Sanz, Manuel (ed.), *Documentos históricos de la Florida y la Luisiana, siglos XVI al XVII* (Madrid: 1912), 344: palmm.digital.flvc.org/islandora/object/fsu%3A86832#page /344/mode/2up.

7. The official account of the campaign in the Mississippi is in Serrano y Sanz, *Documentos*, 343ff. "Relación de la campaña que hizo don Bernardo de Gálvez contra los ingleses, en la Luisiana, September 1799," note reads BNE: manuscript that was Biblioteca de Ultramar 14.

8. Serrano y Sanz, *Documentos*, 346.

9. Quintero Saravia, "Bernardo," 393–94 ns. 2084 and 2086 ref AGS: SGU, Leg. 6912.2, "Navarro to José de Gálvez, September 20, 1779."

10. James, *Pollock*, 199.

11. Burgoyne, Bruce E., *Waldeck Soldiers of the American Revolutionary War* (Westminster: 1991), xxii; see Odom, Wesley S., *The Longest Siege of the American Revolution: Pensacola* ([Pensacola]: 2009), 43 n.9.

12. Caughey, "Bernardo de Galvez," 158 n.36 refs AGI: Cuba, 192, "Pollock to Natchez, September 8 1779."

13. Quintero Saravia, "Bernardo," 391 n.2072 refs AGI: Santo Domingo 2082B, "Extracto de lo acaecido en la expedición hecha por Bernardo de Gálvez, November 11, 1779."

14. Anon., "American Affairs," *London Magazine*, April 1780, 189ff.

15. Quintero Saravia, "Bernardo," 395–96 n.2093 refs AGS: SGU, Leg. 6612.2, "Bernardo to José de Gálvez, October 16, 1779."

16. Quintero Saravia, "Bernardo," 397.

17. Caughey, "Bernardo de Galvez," 161.

18. Quintero Saravia, "Bernardo," 389 n.390 refs *Gazeta de Madrid* (February 1781).

19. Washington, *Writings*, 6:476ff.

20. Remini, Robert V., *Andrew Jackson and the Course of American Empire, 1767–1821*, vol. 1 (New York: 1977), 19.

21. Calleja Leal, Guillermo, "Bernardo Gálvez y la intervención decisiva de la corona de España en la guerra de la independencia de los Estados Unidos de Norteamérica," *Revista de Historia Militar* 96 (2004), 147–218, 170 n.43 refs Guerrero Acosta, José Manuel, "De las trincheras de Gibraltar a las arenas de Pensacola: el ejército español en la independencia de los Estados Unidos," *Coming to the Americas*, 28th Congress of the Intenrational Commission of Military History, Norfolk (2003), 202.

22. Tanner, Helen H., *Zéspedes in East Florida, 1784–1790* (Jacksonville: 1989 [1963]), 12.

23. Gálvez, Bernardo de, "Diario que yo D. Bernardo de Galvez Brigadier de los Reales Exercitos . . . , y encargado de la expedcion contra Panzacola y la Mobila formo . . . en ella," *Mercurio histórico y político*, June 1780, 198–220: hemerotecadigital.bne.es/issue.vm?id=00122 11294&search=&lang=en.

24. Gálvez, "Diario que yo . . . ," 203, 205, and 206.

25. Quintero Saravia, "Bernardo," 403 n.2122 refs AGI: Santo Domingo 2543, "Diario de Miró."

26. Gálvez, "Diario que yo . . . ," 208.

27. Quintero Saravia, "Bernardo," 411 n.2160 refs McConnell, Michael N., *Army and Empire: British Soldiers on the American Frontier, 1758–1775* (Omaha: 2004), 50 and 90.

28. Quintero Saravia, "Bernardo," 413; *Mercurio*, 215.

29. Beer, William, "The Surrender of Fort Charlotte, Mobile, 1780," *American Historical Review* 1:4 (1896), 696–99, 697 refs Public Record Office: America and West Indies, Floridas 1702–1782, no. 533; also see Beer, William, "The Capture of Fort Charlotte," *Publications of the Louisiana Historical Society*, 1:3 (1896), 31–34.

30. *Journals of the Continental Congress*, vol. 17 (Washington, DC: 1910), 490.

31. *Courrier d'Avignon*, July 4, 1780, 214.

32. Quintero Saravia, "Bernardo," 423–24 ns. 228 and 229 ref AGI: Santo Domingo 2082, "Gálvez to Navarro, Aranjuez, April 20, 1780."

33. Quoted at length by Quintero Saravia, "Bernardo," 462–65; Caughey, "Bernardo de Galvez," 197 n.36 refs AGI: Santo Domingo 2082, November 30, 1780.

34. Saavedra, Francisco de, *Diario de don Francisco de Saavedra*, ed. Francisco Morales Padrón (Seville: 2004), 140.

35. Gálvez, Bernardo de, *Diario de las operaciones de la expedición contra la plaza de Panzacola concluida por las armas de S.M. católica* (Tallahassee: 1996 [1781]), 3–4; Farmar, Robert, *Journal of the Siege of Pensacola* (1781); Odom, *Longest Siege*, 21—this last has an excellent set of maps, a useful timeline, and various illustrations showing uniforms, flags, and the like used by both sides during the campaign.

36. Gálvez, *Diario de las operaciones*, 4; Baker, Maury, and Margaret Bissler Haas, "Bernardo de Gálvez's Combat Diary for the Battle of Pensacola, 1781," *Florida Historical Quarterly* 56:2 (1977), 176–79, 179—this is an English translation of the "Diario Gral de la Operacion executa . . . Bernardo de Galvez," in the Archivo General del Gobierno de Guatemala: A1.60, Exp. 45, 364, Leg. 5365; Odom, *Longest Siege*, 13 n.23 refs Servies, James A. (ed.), *The Log of HMS* Mentor, *1780–1781: A New Account of the British Navy at Pensacola* (Pensacola: 1982), 22.

37. Caughey, "Bernardo de Galvez," 202.

38. Quintero Saravia, "Bernardo," 471 n.2421 refs AGI: Santo Domingo 2083, included within Navarro to Gálvez, Havana, April 6, 1781.

39. Gálvez, *Diario de las operaciones*, 4.

40. Padgett, James A. (ed.), "Bernardo de Gálvez's Siege of Pensacola in 1781 (as Related in Robert Farmar's Journal)," *Louisiana Historical Quarterly* 26 (1943), 311–29.

41. Gálvez, *Diario de las operaciones*, 5.

42. Quintero Saravia, "Bernardo," 471 n.2422 refs Miranda, Francisco de, *Diario de lo mas particular ocurrido desde el dia de nuestra salida del puerto de La Habana*, Archivo Francisco Miranda: *Viajes*, vol. 3, *España, América*, ff.70ff.

43. Miranda, ibid.

44. Quintero Saravia, "Bernardo," 472–73.

45. Ibid., 474.

46. Gálvez, *Diario de las operaciones*, 8.

47. Caughey, "Bernardo de Galvez," 203 n.12 refs AGI: Indiferente 1578, Saavedra to Gálvez, April 7, 1781.

48. Quintero Saravia, "Bernardo," 475–76 n.2435 refs Galvez, *Diario de las operaciones* (second manuscript).

49. AGI: MP-Escudos 273A, 1781.

50. Baker and Haas, "Combat Diary," 181; Gálvez, *Diario de las operaciones*, 12.

51. Gálvez, *Diario de las operaciones*, 15.

52. Odom, *Longest Siege*, 70–71.

53. Gálvez, *Diario de las operaciones*, 20.

54. Ibid., 19–20.

55. Ibid., 21–22.

56. Quintero Saravia, "Bernardo," 527ff.

57. McAlister, L. N., "Pensacola During the Second Spanish Period," *Florida Historical Quarterly* 37:3–4 (1959), 281–327.

58. Narrett, David E., *Adventurism and Empire: The Struggle for Mastery in the Louisiana Florida Borderlands* (Chapel Hill, NC: 2015), 103 n.53 refs Smith, Paul (ed.), *Letters of Delegates to Congress, 1774–1789*, 26 vols. (Washington, DC: 1976–2000), 17:440–41 and 17:367.

59. Washington, *Writings*, 8:175ff.

60. Calleja Leal, "Bernardo," 215.

61. H. R. 12042—94th Congress (1975–76); H. J. Res. 105—113th Congress (2013–14), Public Law no. 113–229 (December 16, 2014).

62. Tanner, *Zéspedes*, see introduction to second edition, xv–xvi; and Tanner, Helen H. (ed.), *General Greene's Visit to Saint Augustine in 1785* (Ann Arbor: 1964).

63. Tanner, *Zéspedes*, 37 and 43.

64. Lockey, Joseph B., "Florida Banditti, 1783," *Florida Historical Quarterly* 24:2 (1945), 87–107, 91 n.8 refs Public Records Office: CO 5/561, "Young to Tonyn," July 30, 1784.

65. Lockey, "Florida Banditti," 95–96.

66. Lewis, James A., "Cracker: Florida Style," *Florida Historical Quarterly* 63:2 (1984), 184–204, 188.

67. Tanner, *Zéspedes*, 56–59.

68. Tanner, *Zéspedes*, see introduction to second edition, xv–xvi; and Tanner, *General Greene's Visit.*

69. Lewis, "Cracker," 187ff n.7 refs AGI: Santo Domingo 2554, "Las Casas to Campo de Alange," August 14, 1790, ff.529r–540r; I have adapted Lewis's translations.

INTRODUCTION TO PART FOUR

1. Bustamante, Carlos María de, *Suplemento a la historia de los tres siglos de Mexico, durante el gobierno español escrita por el padre Anre's Cavo*, vol. 3 (Mexico City: 1838), 66ff: archive.org/stream/cihm_34491#page/n92/mode/1up.

2. Porras Muñoz, Guillermo, "Hace doscientos años: 'México llorosa . . . ,'" *Estudios de Historia Novohispana* 10:10 (1991), 309–24, 309–10.

3. Ibid., 310–15; quotations on 315 n.18 ref *Gaceta de México* 2:23 (December 5, 1786), 251–55, and 321 n.27 refs AGI: México 1513, "Núñez de Haro to the King, Mexico, November 30, 1786."

4. Ibid., 309–24; Bustamante, *Suplemento*, 66ff.

5. Bustamante, *Suplemento*, 71.

6. Ibid., 75; Priestley, *Gálvez*, 10–11.

7. Priestley, *Gálvez*, 12 refs Guillen Robles, F., *Historia de Málaga y su provincia* (Málaga: 1873), 601.

8. Ferrer del Río, *Historia*, 4:286ff.

9. Jovellanos, Gaspar Melchor de, "Elogio a Carlos III," in *Obras en prosa*, ed. José Caso González (Madrid: 1978), 174–92, 191.

10. Ibid., 36–37.

11. Lynch, *Bourbon Spain*, 387.

12. Hilt, Douglas, *The Troubled Trinity: Godoy and the Spanish Monarchs* (Tuscaloosa: 1987), 33.

13. Blanco White, Joseph (pseudonym: don Leucadio Doblado), *Letters from Spain* (London: 1822), 333; D'Auvergne, Edmund, *Godoy, the Queen's Favorite* (Boston: 1913), 35, quoted by Hilt, *Troubled Trinity*, 25.

14. Vassall, Elizabeth, *The Spanish Journal of Lady Elizabeth Holland* (London: 1910), 118.

15. Mena Marqués, Manuela B., "Reflections on Goya's Portaits," in *Goya: The Portraits*, exhibition catalog, ed. Xavier Bray, National Gallery, London, October 2015 to January 2016, 15 and 16.

16. Luxenberg, Alisa, "Further Light on the Critical Reception of Goya's 'Family of Charles IV' as Caricature," *Artibus et Historiae* 23:46 (2002), 179–82; Licht, Fred, "Goya's Portrait of the Royal Family," *Art Bulletin* 49:2 (1967), 127–28.

17. Tomlinson, Janis A., *Goya in the Twilight of Enlightenment* (New Haven: 1992), 96ff.

18. Identification of sitters in *Goya: 250 aniversario*, exhibition catalog, eds. Luna, Juan J. and Margarita Moreno de las Heras, Museo Nacional del Prado, Madrid, March to June 1996, cat. 110; Connell, Evan S., "A Masterpiece of Loathing," *Harper's*, September 2003, 41–53.

19. Vassall, *Spanish Journal*, 118.

20. Lynch, *Bourbon Spain*, 390 n.39 refs Public Records Office: FO 72/26 "St. Helens to Grenville, April 10, 1793."

21. Godoy, Manuel, *Memorias*, ed. Emilio la Parra and Elisabel Larriba (Alicante: 2008), 137.

CHAPTER TWENTY-TWO

1. Quoted in Cook, *Flood Tide*, 124.

2. Ibid., 147.

3. Ibid., 152.

4. Ibid., 171ff.

5. Ibid., 233.

6. Morris, John M., "The Policy of the British Cabinet in the Nootka Crisis," *English Historical Review* 70:277 (1955), 562–80, 563–64.

7. Cook, *Flood Tide*, 218.

8. Black, Jeremy, *British Foreign Policy in an Age of Revolutions, 1783–1793* (Cambridge: 2000), 236ff.

9. Cook, *Flood Tide*, 233.

10. Black, *British*, 254.

11. Boyd, Julian P., et al. (eds.), *The Papers of Thomas Jefferson*, vol. 16 (Princeton: 1961), Rutledge to Jefferson, May 6 and May 12, 1790, 413ff and 426ff.

12. *Convention Between His Britannick Majesty and the King of Spain. Signed at the Escurial, the 28th of October, 1790* (London: 1790).

13. Hilt, *Godoy*, 240ff.

14. *Goya: 250 aniversario*, cat. 142; Thomas, Hugh, *Goya: The Third of May 1808* (London: 1972).

15. Anon., "Corrida de Toros, en obsequio a los Franceses," [1808], British Library, London, Spanish Papers (Wellesley, Seville): LR 21 A 17.

16. Paniagua Pérez, Jesús, "El proyecto fracasado del último obispo del norte de la Nueva España. Hacia la creación de la diócesis de Nuevo México," *Anuario de Estudios Americanos* 70:1 (2013), 99–127.

17. Paoli Bolio, Francisco José, "Miguel Ramos Arizpe y sus argumentos independentistas en las Cortes de Cadiz," in *Las Cortes de Cadiz, la Constitución de 1812 y las independencias nacionales en América*, ed. Antonio Colomer Viadel (Valencia: 2012), 327–37.

18. Bernabéu Albert, Salvador, and Daniel García de la Fuente, "Un Comanche en las Cortes de Cadiz: Los informed y trabajos de Ramos Arizpe," *Revista Historia de la Educación Latinoamericana* 16:23 (2014), 217–30.

19. Esdaile, Charles J., *Spain in the Liberal Age: From Constitution to Civil War, 1812–1939* (Oxford: 2000), 33.

20. Carr, Raymond, *Spain, 1808–1875*, 2nd ed. (Oxford: 1982 [1966]), 106.

CHAPTER TWENTY-THREE

1. Vetancurt, Fray Agustín de, *Tratado de la ciudad de México* (Mexico City: 1982 [1698]), 3.

2. Knight, Alan, *Mexico: The Colonial Era* (Cambridge: 2002), 287.

3. Vetancurt, *Tratado*, 4; García Sáiz, María Concepción, "La imagen del mestizaje," in *El mestizaje americano*, exhibition catalog, Museo de América, Madrid, October–December 1985, 45–55, 48.

4. García Sáiz, "Imagen del mestizaje," 45–55, 54.

5. Katzew, Ilona, *Casta Painting: Images of Race in Eighteenth-Century Mexico* (New Haven: 2004), 111ff.

6. Martínez, María Elena, *Genaological Fictions: Limpieza de Sangre, Religion, and Gender in Colonial Mexico* (Stanford: 2008), 142ff.

7. Long, Edward, *The History of Jamaica or General Survey of the Modern State of the Island*, 2 vols. (London: 1774), 2:260–61; quoted by Katzew, *Casta Painting*, 51.

8. *Castas Mexicanas*, exhibition catalog, Museo de Monterrey, Mexico, San Antonio Art Museum of Art, TX, Museo Franz Mayer, Mexico City, 1989–90 ([n.p.] 1989), 24–29.

9. Carrera, Magali M., *Imagining Identity in New Spain: Race, Lineage, and the Colonial Body in Portraiture and Casta Paintings* (Austin: 2003).

10. McMichael, Francis A., *Atlantic Loyalties: Americans in Spanish West Florida, 1785–1810* (Athens, GA: 2008), 40.

11. Lafaye, Jacques, *Quetzalcoatl and Guadalupe: The Formation of Mexican National Consciousness, 1531–1813* (Chicago: 1976), 7ff.

12. Guedea, Virginia, "The Old Colonialism Ends, the New Colonialism Begins," in *The Oxford History of Mexico*, ed. Michael C. Meyer and William H. Beezley (Oxford: 2000), 277–300, 282ff.

13. Hamill, Hugh M., *The Hidalgo Revolt: Prelude to Mexican Independence* (Gainesville: 1966), 53ff; Meyer and Beezley, *Oxford History of Mexico*, 274ff.

14. Hidalgo, Miguel de, "Discurso de Miguel de Hidalgo" [1810]: biblioteca.tv/artman2/publish/1810_115/Discurso_de_Miguel_Hidalgo_al_Pueblo_de_Dolores_pa_604.shtml.

15. Alamán, Lucas, *Historia de Méjico desde los primeros movimientos que prepararon su independencia en el año de 1808, hasta la época presente*, 5 vols. (Mexico City: 1942 [1849–52]), 1:273ff.

16. Macaulay, Neill, "The Army of New Spain and the Mexican Delegation to the Spanish Cortes," in *Mexico and the Spanish Cortes, 1810–1822: Eight Essays*, ed. Nettie Lee Benson (Austin: 1966).

17. Zerecero, Anastasio, *Memorias para la historia de las revoluciones en México* (Mexico City: 1975), 37.

18. Higuera, Ernesto, *Hidalgo: reseña biográfica con una iconografía del iniciador de nuestra independencia* (Mexico City: 1955), 80ff; Alamán, Lucas, *Historia de Méjico*, 5 vols. (Mexico City: 1942 [1849]), 1:370ff.

19. Archer, Christon I., "Soldados en la escena continental: los expedicionarios españoles y la guerra de la Nueva España, 1810–1825," in *Fuerzas militares en Iberoamérica, siglos XVIII y XIX*, ed. Juan Ortiz Escamilla (Mexico City: 2005), 139–55.

20. López de Santa Anna, Antonio, *Mi historia militar y política* (Mexico City: 2016 [1905]), 9.

21. Calderón de la Barca, Fanny, *Life in Mexico: The Letters of Fanny Calderón de la Barca*, ed. Howard T. Fisher and Marion Hall Fisher (New York: 1966), 65.

22. Folsom, Bradley, "Joaquín de Arredondo in Texas and Northeastern New Spain, 1811–1821," PhD dissertation, University of North Texas (2014), 86; Torget, Andrew, "Cotton Empire: Slavery and the Texas Borderlands," PhD dissertation, University of Virginia (2009).

23. Andrés Martín, Juan Ramón de, "La reacción realista ante las conspiraciones insurgentes en las fronteras y costas de Texas (1813–1816). Primeros antecedentes de la invasión de Javier Mina en 1817," *Signos Históricos* 18 (2007), 8–35, 11–12.

24. Folsom, "Arredondo," 103ff; Schwarz, Ted, *Forgotten Battlefield of the First Texas Revolution: The Battle of Medina, August 18, 1813* (Austin: 1985), 89ff.

25. Hatcher, Mattie Austin, "Joaquín de Arredondo's Report of the Battle of Medina, August 18, 1813. Translation," *Quarterly of the Texas State Historical Association* 11:3 (1908), 225ff.

26. Alamán, Lucas, *Historia de Méjico*, 5:16.

27. Poinsett, Joel R., *Notes on Mexico Made in the Autumn of 1822* (New York: 1969), 68–69.

28. Austin, Stephen F., "Journal of Stephen F. Austin on His First Trip to Texas, 1821," *Quarterly of the Texas State Historical Association* 7:4 (1904), 286–307, 296.

29. Barker, Eugene C., *The Life of Stephen Austin: Founder of Texas* (Dallas: 1925), 35.

30. Feherenbach, T. R., *Lone Star: A History of Texas and the Texans* (Boston: 2000 [1968]), 136ff.

31. Boyle, Susan C., *Los Capitalistas: Hispano Merchants and the Santa Fé Trail* (Albuquerque: 1997), 17.

32. González de la Vara, Martín, "La política del federalismo en Nuevo México (1821–1836)," *Historia Mexicana* 36:1 (1986), 81–111, 83.

33. Weber, David J., *The Mexican Frontier, 1821–1846: The American Southwest Under Mexico* (Albuquerque: 1982), 1–7.

34. Tays, George, "The Passing of Spanish California, September 29, 1822," *California Historical Society Quarterly* 15:2 (1936), 139–42.

CHAPTER TWENTY-FOUR

1. Heidler, David S., and Jeanne T. Heidler, *Old Hickory's War: Andrew Jackson and the Quest for Empire* (Baton Rouge, 2003 [1996]), 1–5.

2. Ibid., 9.

3. Ibid., 26.

4. Sugden, John, "The Southern Indians in the War of 1812: The Closing Phase," *Florida Historical Quarterly* 60:30 (1982), 273–312.

5. Innerarity, John, "Letters of John Innerarity: The Seizure of Pensacola by Andrew Jackson, November 7, 1814," *Florida Historical Society Quarterly* 9:3 (1931), 127–34, 127ff; and see Millett, Nathaniel, "Britain's Occupation of Pensacola and America's Response: An Episode of the War of 1812 in the Southeastern Borderlands," *Florida Historical Quarterly* 84:2 (2005), 229–55.

6. Innerarity, "Letters," 128ff.

7. Millet, Nathaniel, *The Maroons of Prospect Bluff and Their Quest for Freedom in the Atlantic World* (Gainesville: 2013), 215.

8. *The Examiner*, August 2 (1818), 481–82.

9. Boyd, Mark F., "Events at Prospect Bluff on the Apalachicola River, 1808–1818," *Florida Historical Quarterly* 16:2 (1937), 55–96, 77–81.

10. Forbes, James G., *Sketches, Historical and Topographical of the Floridas* (New York: 1821), 203.

11. Nugent, Walter, *Habits of Empire: A History of American Expansion* (New York: 2008), 125 n.53.

12. Bassett, John S. (ed.), *Correspondence of Andrew Jackson*, vol. 2 (Washington, DC: 1927), 266.

13. Adams, John Quincy, *Memoirs of John Quincy Adams, Comprising Portions of His Diary from 1795–1848*, vol. 3, ed. Charles Francis Adams (Philadelphia: 1874), 289ff.

14. Heidler and Heidler, *Old Hickory*, 160 and 107.

15. Greene, Meg, *The Transcontinental Treaty, 1819: A Primary Source Examination of the Treaty Between the United States and Spain over the American West* (New York: 2006), 36.

16. Moser, Harold D., David R. Hoth, and George H. Hoemann (eds.), *The Papers of Andrew Jackson*, vol. 4, 1816–1820 (Knoxville: 1994), 183ff.

17. American State Papers: Military . . . 1:698–99, "Jackson to Calhoun," March 25, 1818.

18. Heidler and Heidler, *Old Hickory*, 142ff; Moser, *Papers*, 186–87, "Jackson to Caso y Luengo," April 6, 1818.

19. Moser, *Papers*, 186–87, "Jackson to Caso y Luengo," April 6, 1818.

20. Ibid., 197–200, "Jackson to Calhoun," May 5, 1818.

21. Ibid.

22. Ibid., 203–6, "Masot to Jackson," May 18 and May 22, 1818.

23. Ibid., 206–10, "Jackson to Masot," May 23, 1818.

24. Bassett, *Correspondence*, 372, "Masot to Jackson," May 24, 1818.

25. Moser, *Papers*, 210–11, "Jackson to Masot," May 25, 1818.

26. Bassett, *Correspondence*, 2:376ff, "Jackson to Calhoun," June 2, 1818.

27. Adams, *Memoirs*, 4:105ff.

28. Hopkins, James F., and Mary W. M. Hargreaves, *The Papers of Henry Clay*, vol. 2 (Lexington, KY: 1961), 636–62.

29. Bassett, *Correspondence*, 2:409, "Jackson to Preston," February 2, 1819.

30. Heidler and Heidler, *Old Hickory*, 218.

31. Doherty, Herbert J., "Andrew Jackson vs The Spanish Governor: Pensacola 1821," *Florida Historical Quarterly* 34:2 (1955), 142–58, 145.

32. American State Papers: Foreign Relations: 4:768–71.

33. Doherty, "Jackson," 153; American State Papers: Miscellaneous: 2:828–31.

CHAPTER TWENTY-FIVE

1. Santibáñez, Enrique (ed.), *La diplomacia mexicana* (Mexico City: 1910), 1:103.

2. en.wikipedia.org/wiki/List_of_countries_and_territories_by_population_density.

3. Digital Austin Papers, 2.1:517ff, Stephen Austin to James Austin, Mexico, May 22, 1822; and 504ff, Stephen Austin to Hawkins, c. May 1, 1822.

4. Ibid., 2.1:530ff, Stephen Austin to James Austin, Mexico, July 8, 1822.

5. Ibid., 3:103; quoted in Cantrell, Gregg, *Stephen F. Austin: Empresario of Texas* (Austin: 2016), 130.

6. López de Santa Anna, *Mi historia*, 20.

7. Bacarisse, Charles A., "The Union of Coahuila and Texas," *Southwestern Historical Quarterly* 61:3 (1958), 341–49, 349.

8. Adapted from English translation in Kelly, Edith Louise, and Mattie Austin Hatcher, "Tadeo Ortiz de Ayala and the Colonization of Texas, 1822–1833: IV," *Southwestern Historical Quarterly* 32:4 (1929), 311–43.

9. Mier y Terán, Manuel de, *Texas by Terán: The Diary Kept by General Manuel de Mier y Terán on His 1828 Inspection of Texas*, ed. Jack Jackson, trans. John Wheat (Austin: 2000), 3ff; Sánchez, José María, *Viaje a Texas* (Mexico City: 1926).

10. Sánchez, *Viaje*, 73.

11. Quotations adapted from the translation in Mier y Terán, *Texas by Terán*, 98–99.

12. Sánchez, *Viaje*, 4.

13. Ibid., 75–76.

14. Fowler, Will, *Santa Anna of Mexico* (Lincoln, NE, and London: 2009), 96ff.

15. Prieto, Guillermo, *Memorias de mis tiempos* (Mexico City: 1906), 37–38.

16. López de Santa Anna, *Mi historia*, 31–33.

17. Quoted in Fowler, *Santa Anna*, 137.

18. Adapted from quotation in Fowler, *Santa Anna*, 144.

19. Quoted in Weber, *Mexican Frontier*, 246.

20. Alessio Robles, Vito, *Coahuila y Texas: Desde la consumación de la independencia hasta el tratado de paz de Guadalupe Hidalgo*, 2 vols. (Mexico City: 1945), 1:474ff.

21. Digital Austin Papers, Austin to Williams, Mexico City, November 26, 1833.

22. Quoted in Weber, *Mexican Frontier*, 31.

23. Weber, *Mexican Frontier*, 3.

24. Austin, Stephen F., "The 'Prison Journal' of Stephen F. Austin," *Quarterly of the Texas State Historical Association* 2:3 (1899), 183–210, 209–10; Grayson, Peter W., "The Release of Stephen F. Austin from Prison," *Quarterly of the Texas State Historical Association* 14:2 (1910), 155–63.

25. Ramos, Raúl A., *Beyond the Alamo: Forging Mexican Ethnicity in San Antonio, 1821–1861* (Chapel Hill, NC: 2008), 114ff; Alessio Robles, *Coahuila*, 1:230ff; and see Vázquez, Josefina Z., "The Colonization and Loss of Texas: A Mexican Perspective," in *Myths, Misdeeds, and Misunderstandings: The Roots of Conflict in U.S.-Mexican Relations*, eds. Rodríguez O., Jaime E., and Kathryn Vincent (Wilmington, DE: 1997), 47–78, 57ff.

26. Austin to Mary Austin Holley, December 29, 1831: digitalaustinpapers.org/document ?id=APB4302.

27. Austin to Mary Austin Holley, August 21, 1835: digitalaustinpapers.org/document ?id=APB4851.

28. Adapted from the translation in Peña, José Enrique de la, *With Santa Anna in Texas: A Narrative of the Revolution*, ed. and trans. Carmen Perry (Austin: 1997 [1975]), 53.

29. Gracy, David B., "'Just as I Have Written It:' A Study of the Authenticity of the Manuscript of José Enrique de la Peña's Account of the Texas Campaign," *Southwestern Historical Quarterly* 105:2 (2001), 254–91.

30. López Santa Anna, *Mi historia*, 41.

31. Ibid.

32. Peña, *With Santa Anna*, 91.

33. López Santa Anna, *Mi historia*, 42.

34. Peña, *With Santa Anna*, 131.

35. López Santa Anna, *Mi historia*, 43–44.

36. Quoted in Alessio Robles, *Coahuila*, 2:161.
37. Peña, *With Santa Anna*, 132.
38. The figures are all from various Wikipedia pages and necrometrics.com/wars19c .htm.
39. López Santa Anna, *Mi historia*, 44.
40. *A Compilation of Messages and Papers of the Presidents*, vol. 4 (New York: 1897), 1493ff.
41. López Santa Anna, *Mi historia*, 46.
42. Remini, *Jackson*, 363.
43. López Santa Anna, *Mi historia*, 46.

CHAPTER TWENTY-SIX

1. Fuentes Mares, José, *Santa Anna: aurora y ocaso de un comediante* (Mexico City: 1967), 157.
2. García, Genaro (ed.), *Documentos inéditos ó muy raros para la historia de México*, 36 vols. (Mexico City: 1905–11), 34:64ff.
3. López Santa Anna, *Mi historia*, 53.
4. *Diario del Gobierno de la República Méxicana* 2654:24 (September 28, 1842), 235.
5. Alessio Robles, Vito, *Acapulco, Saltillo, y Monterrey en la historia y en la leyenda* (Mexico City: 1978), 224.
6. Olivera, Ruth R., and Liliane Crété, *Life in Mexico Under Santa Anna, 1822–1855* (Norman, OK: 1991), 166.
7. Alessio Robles, *Coahuila*, 277ff.
8. Manning, William R. (ed.), *Diplomatic Correspondence of the United States. Inter-American Affairs, 1831–1860*, vol. 8 (Washington, DC : 1937), Doc. 3506, 555ff.
9. Abbreviated from Woolley, John, and Gerhard Peters (eds.), American Presidency Project, John Tyler, Third Annual Message, December 5, 1843: presidency.ucsb.edu/ws/index .php?pid=29647.
10. Alessio Robles, *Coahuila*, 300.
11. Ibid., 322.
12. Bauer, Jack, *The Mexican War, 1846–1848* (New York: 1974), 17.
13. López Santa Anna, *Mi historia*, 61.
14. Alessio Robles, *Coahuila*, 338.
15. González Gómez, César, "March, Conquest, and Play Ball: The Game in the Mexican-American War, 1846–1848," *Base Ball* 5:2 (2011), 1–20, 15.
16. Quoted in Alessio Robles, *Coahuila*, 355.
17. Quoted in Mansfield, Edward D., *The Mexican War: A History of Its Origin* (New York: 1849), 126–27.
18. Eblen, Tom, "Henry Clay's Pistols Recall Era When Politicians Settled Grudges with Bullets, Not Tweets," *Lexington Herald Leader*, January 5, 2017.
19. Greenburg, Amy S., *A Wicked War: Polk, Clay, Lincoln, and the 1846 US Invasion of Mexico* (New York: 2012), 162ff.
20. Mansfied, *Mexican War*, 139.
21. Sandweiss, Martha A., Rick Stewart, and Ben W. Huseman, *Eyewitness to War: Prints and Daguerreotypes of the Mexican War, 1846–1848* (Fort Worth: 1989), 26.
22. Gónzalez Gómez, "March," 17.

23. Adapted from quotation in Tyler, Daniel, "Gringo Views of Governor Manuel Armijo," *New Mexico Historical Review* 45:1 (1970), 23–46.

24. Gregg, Josiah, *Commerce of the Prairies* (Norman, OK: 1954 [1834]), 159.

25. Keleher, William A., *Turmoil in New Mexico* (Santa Fe: 2007 [1952]), 9–10.

26. Taylor, Mendell L., "The Western Services of Stephen Watts Kearny, 1815–1848," PhD thesis, University of Oklahoma (1944), 136 n.24 refs Emory, W. H., *Notes of a Military Reconnaissance from Fort Leavenworth to San Diego, California* (Washington, DC: 1848), House Executive Document, no. 41, 30th Congress, 1st Session, 25.

27. Quoted in Taylor, "Western Services," 139 n.33 refs Emory, *Notes*, 27–28.

28. Adapted from translation in Weber, David J., *Foreigners in Their Native Land: Historical Roots of the Mexican Americans* (Albuquerque: 2003 [1970]), 122–24.

29. Grivas, Ted, "General Stephen Watts Kearny and the Army of the West," MA thesis, University of Southern California (1953), 29 n.3 refs Emory, *Notes*, 53.

30. Taylor, "Western Services," 147.

31. Ruxton, George F., *Adventures in Mexico and the Rocky Mountains* (London: 1847), 189 and 197.

32. Sánchez et al., *New Mexico*, 110.

33. Hass, Lisbeth, "Contested Eden: California Before the Gold Rush," *California History* 76:2–3 (1997), 331–55, 340–41.

34. Grivas, "General Kearny," 67–68 ns. 1 and 4 ref Emory, *Notes*, 161 and 163.

35. Russell, Philip L. *The History of Mexico: From the Pre-Conquest to Present* (New York and London: 2010).

36. Vázquez, Josefina Zoraida, "El origen de la guerra con Estados Unidos," *Historia Mexicana* 4:2 (1997), 285–309, 306.

EPILOGUE

1. Mahan, Alfred T., *Lessons of the War with Spain, and Other Articles* (Boston: 1899), 28–30.

2. Castelar, Emilio, *Discursos Parlamentarios y Politicos en La Restauracion*, 4 vols. (Madrid: 1877), 2:219; and Carr, *Spain*, 350.

3. Baroja, Pío, *Opiniones y paradojas*, ed. Miguel Sánchez-Ostiz (Madrid: 2000).

4. López-Herrera Sánchez, Juan, *La insula inefable* (Madrid: 2017).

5. Adapted from translation in Carr, *Spain*, 379.

6. Berner, Brad K. (ed.), *The Spanish-American War: A Documentary History with Commentaries* (Madison: 2014), 24–25.

7. Ibid., 10–16.

8. Adapted from translation in ibid., 30; and see Carr, *Spain*, 387.

9. *El Imparcial*, March 15, 1898.

10. Abbreviated from translation in Berner, *Spanish-American*, 32–33.

11. Rivero, Ángel, *Crónica de la guerra hispanoamericana en Puerto Rico* (Madrid: 1922), 1–4.

12. Ibid., 66.

13. Smith, Joseph, *The Spanish-American War: Conflict in the Caribbean and the Pacific, 1895–1902* (London: 1994), 161.

14. Rivero, *Crónica*, 197.

15. *New York Times*, October 19, 1898.

16. Rivero, *Crónica*, 4.

17. Smith, *Spanish-American*, 193.

18. Márquez Padorno, Margarita, *Miguel Moya Ojanguren (1856–1920): talento, voluntad y reforma en la prensa española* (Madrid: 2015).

19. *El Liberal*, November 28, 1898.

INDEX

Abara *(cacique)*, 80
Aberdeen, George Hamilton
  Gordon, Earl of, 400
abolition of slavery, 390, 400,
  410
Abram y Salom, Joanna, 224
Acadians, 288
*The Account Given by Álvar
  Núñez* (Cabeza de Vaca),
  61
Account of the Sacrileges
  (Arroyo), 211
Acoma (town), 84, 141–42, 147
Acoma Indians, 141, 143–52
Adams, John Quincy, 239,
  372–73, 377–78, 381
Aeneid (Virgil), 131, 143
Africans, 43, 57, 58, 73
Ágreda, María de, 161–63, 185,
  189, 199–200, 225, 269–70
Agua Caliente, 278
Aguada, 27, 29
Aguaje de la Alegría ("Pool of
  Joy"), 276
aguardiente, 280, 332
Aguas de la Luna ("Waters of
  the Moon"), 200
Aguayo, Marquis San Miguel
  de, 208
Agüeybana, 29–30
Aguilar, Captain, 153
Agustin I. *See* Iturbide,
  Agustín de
Aimable (ship), 187–88
Ais Indians, 119–20
Alaminos, Antón de, 31–34
Alamo, 207, 391
Álamos, 243–44
Alarcón, Hernando de, 80–83,
  200
Alarcón, Martín de, 206–7
Alaska, 1, 195, 236, 294–95
Alba, Duke of, 289
Alburquerque (Albuquerque),
  231
Alcaraz, Diego de, 60

Alcatraz, 265
alcohol, 280, 310, 332
Alexander VI, 3–4
Alfonso X, the Wise, 389
Alfonso XIII, xxii
Algodones Dunes, 274
Algonquian Indians, 123
Allende, Ignacio, 362
Alta California
  and Anza's expedition, 274
  and Bourbon reforms, 9
  and Díaz's expeditions, 83
  and Gálvez's expeditions,
    237, 238
  and Kino's missionary
    efforts, 192
  and Kino's missionary
    expeditions, 195
  and maritime supply routes,
    344
  and the Mexican-American
    War, 405–7
  and Santa Anna's "Seven
    Laws," 389
  and Serra's missionary
    efforts, 254–56, 273, 293
  and Treaty of Guadalupe
    Hidalgo, 407
  and Vizcaíno's expeditions,
    109
Alvarado, Hernando de, 84, 89
Alvarado, Pedro de, 36
Álvarez, Julián, 319
Amadis of Gaul (Montalvo),
  36, 53
Amazons, 12, 23, 39, 53
Ambrister, Robert C., 375
Amelia Island, 333, 372, 373
American Duties Act, 237
American Revolution
  and Bernardo de Gálvez,
    223, 321–30, 332
  and Bordeaux Rebellion, 289
  and Charles IV's reign,
    339–40
  refugees of, 311

and Spanish *criollos*, 298
and trade in New Orleans,
  291, 304–5
Analco, 155
Anaya, Cristóbal de, 178
Anicatixe, 41
Antelope Mesa, 83
Antilles, 11, 12
Anza the Elder, Juan Bautista,
  221, 227–30, 233
Anza the Younger, Juan
  Bautista de
  Arizona and California
    expeditions, 274–78,
    278–82, 284
  background, 226, 229
  and Bourbon reforms, 221
  and Comanche resistance to
    Spanish rule, 313–15
  and expulsion of Jesuits
    from New Spain, 240
  and Rubí's expeditions, 232
  and Serra's missionary
    efforts, 273
  and Spanish concept of
    honor, 233–34
Apache Canyon, 404–5
Apache Indians
  and Anza's expedition, 226,
    227–34, 274
  and Bernardo Gálvez, 251–53
  and Cuéllar's expedition,
    243–44, 246–50
  and cultural diversity among
    Native Americans, 171
  and hostage exchanges, 245
  hostilities with Spanish
    explorers, 129, 140–41
  and imperial competition in
    Texas, 209, 211
  and Kino's missionary
    expeditions, 194, 196, 198
  and Mexican independence,
    364
  and New Mexico
    expeditions, 154

A Note on the Author

Dr. Robert Goodwin is an honorary research fellow at University College London. His two trade books, *Crossing the Continent, 1527–1540: The Story of the First African-American Explorer of the American South* and *Spain: The Centre of the World, 1519–1682*, were published to critical acclaim. He appears on Spanish radio and TV and writes for Spanish newspapers. He lives between London and Seville, where he regularly conducts archival research.